The Critical Response to Samuel Beckett

**Recent Titles in
Critical Responses in Arts and Letters**

The Critical Response to Mark Twain's
Huckleberry Finn
Laurie Champion, editor

The Critical Response to Nathaniel Hawthorne's
The Scarlet Letter
Gary Scharnhorst, editor

The Critical Response to Tom Wolfe
Doug Shomette, editor

The Critical Response to Ann Beattie
Jaye Berman Montresor, editor

The Critical Response to Eugene O'Neill
John H. Houchin, editor

The Critical Response to Bram Stoker
Carol A. Senf, editor

The Critical Response to John Cheever
Francis J. Bosha, editor

The Critical Response to Ann Radcliffe
Deborah D. Rogers, editor

The Critical Response to Joan Didion
Sharon Felton, editor

The Critical Response to Tillie Olsen
Kay Hoyle Nelson and Nancy Huse, editors

The Critical Response to George Eliot
Karen L. Pangallo, editor

The Critical Response to Eudora Welty's
Fiction
Laurie Champion, editor

The Critical Response to Dashiell Hammett
Christopher Metress, editor

The Critical Response to H. G. Wells
William J. Scheick, editor

The Critical Response to Raymond Chandler
J. K. Van Dover, editor

The Critical Response to Herman Melville's
Moby Dick
Kevin J. Hayes, editor

The Critical Response to Kurt Vonnegut
Leonard Mustazza, editor

The Critical Response to Richard Wright
Robert J. Butler, editor

The Critical Response to Jack London
Susan N. Nuernberg, editor

The Critical Response to Saul Bellow
Gerhard Bach, editor

The Critical Response to William Styron
Daniel W. Ross, editor

The Critical Response to Katherine Mansfield
Jan Pilditch, editor

The Critical Response to Anaïs Nin
Philip K. Jason, editor

The Critical Response to Tennessee Williams
George W. Crandell, editor

The Critical Response to Andy Warhol
Alan R. Pratt, editor

The Critical Response to Thomas Carlyle's
Major Works
D. J. Trela and Rodger L. Tarr, editors

The Critical Response to John Milton's *Paradise Lost*
Timothy C. Miller, editor

The Critical Response to Erskine Caldwell
Robert L. McDonald, editor

The Critical Response to Gloria Naylor
Sharon Felton and Michelle C. Loris, editors

PATCHOGUE-MEDFORD LIBRARY

The Critical Response to Samuel Beckett

Edited by
CATHLEEN CULOTTA ANDONIAN

Critical Responses in Arts and Letters, Number 30
Cameron Northouse, *Series Adviser*

GREENWOOD PRESS
Westport, Connecticut • London

848.
914
Beckett
CRI

Library of Congress Cataloging-in-Publication Data

The critical response to Samuel Beckett / edited by Cathleen Culotta Andonian.
    p. cm.—(Critical responses in arts and letters, ISSN 1057–0993 ; no. 30)
   Includes bibliographical references and index.
   ISBN 0–313–28910–7 (alk. paper)
   1. Beckett, Samuel, 1906–   —Criticism and interpretation.
I. Andonian, Cathleen Culotta. II. Series.
PR6003.E282Z6234   1998
848′.91409—dc21   97–44888

British Library Cataloguing in Publication Data is available.

Copyright © 1998 by Cathleen Culotta Andonian

All rights reserved. No portion of this book may be reproduced by any process or technique, without the express written consent of the publisher.

Library of Congress Catalog Card Number: 97–44888
ISBN: 0–313–28910–7
ISSN: 1057–0993

First published in 1998

Greenwood Press, 88 Post Road West, Westport, CT 06881
An imprint of Greenwood Publishing Group, Inc.

Printed in the United States of America

The paper used in this book complies with the Permanent Paper Standard issued by the National Information Standards Organization (Z39.48–1984).

10 9 8 7 6 5 4 3 2 1

Copyright Acknowledgments

The editor and publisher gratefully acknowledge permission for use of the following material:

Bonamy Dobrée, "Symbolism To-day," *The Spectator* (18 April 1931): 641-42. Taken from *The Spectator*.

Arthur Calder-Marshall, "Dubliners," *The Spectator* 152 (1 June 1934): 863. Taken from *The Spectator*.

Clas Zilliacus, "Samuel Beckett and His *Whoroscope*." Reprinted by permission of the editors of *Moderna Språk (Journal of the Modern Language Association of Sweden), vol.* 67, no. 1 (1973): 4-6.

Vivian Mercier, "Savage Humor," *Commonweal* 66, no. 7 (17 May 1957): 188, 190. Copyright © Commonweal Foundation.

Kate O'Brien, "Fiction," *The Spectator* (25 March 1938): 546. Taken from *The Spectator*.

B. S. Johnson, "A Master Stylist," *The Spectator* (13 December 1963): 800. First published in *The Spectator*.

A. J. Leventhal, "Nought into Zero," *The Irish Times* (24 December 1953): 6. Reproduced, with permission, from *The Irish Times*.

John Coleman, "Under the Jar," *The Spectator* 204 (8 April 1960): 516. First published in *The Spectator*.

Charles I. Glicksberg, "Samuel Beckett's World of Fiction," *The Arizona Quarterly* 18, no. 1 (Spring 1962): 32-47. Copyright belongs to Arizona Board of Regents.

Brian Wicker, "Samuel Beckett and the Death of the God-Narrator," *The Journal of Narrative Technique* 4, no. 1 (Jan. 1974): 62-74.

Enoch Brater, "Not Going Places," *The New Republic* 172, no. 10 (8 March 1975): 25-26. Reprinted by permission of *THE NEW REPUBLIC* © 1975, The New Republic, Inc.

Brian T. Fitch, "*L'Innommable* and the Hermeneutic Paradigm," *The Chicago Review* 33, no. 3 (Fall 1975): 100-106. © *Chicago Review*. All rights reserved.

Roch C. Smith, "Naming the M/inotaur: Beckett's Trilogy and the Failure of Narrative," *Modern Fiction Studies* 29, no. 1 (Spring 1983): 73-80.

Morton Gurewitch, "Beckett and the Comedy of Decomposition," *The Chicago Review* 33, no. 2 (1982): 93-99. Reprinted by permission of *Chicago Review*.

Robert Sandarg, "Ashes to Ashes, Dust to Dust," *Journal of Beckett Studies* 1, nos. 1-2 (Spring 1992): 55-65. Reprinted by permission of the editors of *The Journal of Beckett Studies*.

Anthony Hartley, "Theatre," *The Spectator* (12 August 1955): 222. First published in *The Spectator*.

Harold Clurman, "Theatre," *The Nation* 182 (5 May 1956): 387-90. This article is reprinted from *The Nation* magazine. © The Nation Company, Inc.

Vivian Mercier, "The Uneventful Event," *The Irish Times* (18 February 1956): 6. Reprinted with permission from *The Irish Times*.

Ramona Cormier and Janis L. Pallister, "*En attendant Godot*: Tragedy or Comedy?" We wish to thank *L'Esprit Créateur* for their permission to reprint "*En attendant Godot*: Tragedy or Comedy?" which appeared in the Fall 1971 issue, vol. 11, no. 3, pp. 44-45.

Copyright Acknowledgments

Jeffrey Nealon, "Samuel Beckett and the Postmodern: Language Games, *Play*, and *Waiting for Godot.*" *Modern Drama* 31, no. 4 (Dec. 1988): 520-28. Published with the permission of *Modern Drama*.

Vivian Mercier, "How to Read *Endgame*," *The Griffin* 8 (June 1959): 10-14.

Harold Clurman, "Theatre," *The Nation* 230 (16 February 1980): 187-88. This article is reprinted from *The Nation Magazine*. © The Nation Company, Inc.

Per Nykrog, "In the Ruins of the Past: Reading Beckett Intertextually," *Comparative Literature 36,* no. 4 (Fall 1984): 289-311.

Tom F. Driver, "Rebuke to Nihilism," *The Christian Century* 77 (2 March 1960): 256–57. Copyright 1960, Christian Century Foundation. Reprinted by permission from the March 2, 1960 issue of *The Christian Century*.

James Knowlson, "*Krapp's Last Tape*: The Evolution of a Play, 1958-75," *The Journal of Beckett Studies,* no. 1 (Winter 1976): 50-65. Reprinted by permission of the editors of *The Journal of Beckett Studies*.

Frank Kermode, "Beckett Country," *The New York Review of Books* 2 (19 March 1964): 9-11. Reprinted with permission from *The New York Review of Books*. Copyright © 1964 Nyrew, Inc.

H. Porter Abbott, "Farewell to Incompetence: Beckett's *How It Is* and 'Imagination Dead Imagine,'" *Contemporary Literature* 11, no. 1 (Winter 1970): 36-47.

Leo Bersani and Ulysse Dutoit, "Beckett's Sociability," *The Raritan* 12, no. 1 (Summer 1992): 1-19. Published by permission of *Raritan Quarterly*.

Patrick Starnes, "Samuel Beckett: An Interview," *The Antigonish Review* 10 (1972): 49-53. Reprinted from *The Antigonish Review*.

Jay A. Levy, "Conversations with Samuel Beckett," *The American Scholar* 61, no. 1 (Winter 1992): 124-32.

Roy Walker, "It's Tragic, Mysterious and Wildly Funny: That's What You Get When the B.B.C. Asks Samuel Beckett to Write a Play," *Tribune* (London), 18 January 1957, p. 8. From *Tribune,* Jan. 18, 1957.

Julia Strachey, "Beckett Country," *The Spectator* (20 September 1957): 373. Taken from *The Spectator*.

Germaine Baril, "From Characters to Discrete Events: The Evolving Concept of Dramatis Personae in Beckett's Radio Plays," *The Review of Contemporary Fiction* 7, no. 2 (Summer 1987): 112-19. © 1987 by *The Review of Contemporary Fiction*. Reprinted with permission.

William F. Van Wert, "'To Be Is to Be Perceived' . . . Time and Point of View in Beckett's *Film*," *Literature/Film Quarterly* 8, no. 2 (April 1980): 133-40. First published in *Literature/Film Quarterly*, 8, no. 2 (1980) © Salisbury State University, Salisbury, MD 21801.

Iain Hamilton, "Godot Arrives," *Time* 94 (31 October 1969): 55. First published in *The Illustrated London News*, November 1, 1969.

"Kyrie Eleison Without God." *Time* 94 (31 October 1969): 55. © 1969 Time Inc. Reprinted by permission.

Harold Clurman, "Theatre," *The Nation* 193 (7 October 1961): 234-35. This article is reprinted from *The Nation Magazine*. © The Nation Company, Inc.

Richard Gilman, "The Stage: Beckett's *Happy Days*," *The Commonweal* 75, no. 3 (13 October 1961): 69-70. Copyright © Commonweal Foundation.

Renée Riese Hubert, "The Paradox of Silence: Samuel Beckett's Plays," *Mundus Artium* 2 (Summer 1969): 82-90. Article was originally published in *Mundus Artium* Vol. 2, Summer 1969.

Barbara Bray, "The New Beckett," *The Observer* (16 June 1963): 29. © *The Observer*.

A. J. Leventhal, "Samuel Beckett: about him and about," *Hermathena* 114 (Winter 1972): 5-22. First published *Hermathena*. A Trinity College Dublin Review.

Rosangela Barone, "On the Route of a Walking Shadow: Samuel Beckett's *Come and Go*," *Etudes Irlandaises* 10 (December 1985): 117-28. By kind permission of the author and *Etudes Irlandaises*.

Jay Carr, "Bare Bones: As a lady slips her moorings, Beckett sounds a hopeful note," *The Detroit News* (19 April 1981): 1F, 6F. Reprinted with permission of *The Detroit News*, a Gannett newspaper, copyright 1981.

Copyright Acknowledgments

S. E. Gontarski, "Review: The World Première of *Ohio Impromptu,* Directed by Alan Schneider at Columbus, Ohio," *Journal of Beckett Studies,* no. 8 (Autumn 1982): 133-36. Reprinted by permission of the editors of *Journal of Beckett Studies.*

Alec Reid, "Impact and Parable in Beckett: A First Encounter with *Not I,*" *Hermathena* 141 (Winter 1986): 12-21. I am grateful for permission to publish this article, which first appeared in *Hermathena.*

Mary Catanzaro, "Recontextualizing the Self: The Voice as Subject in Beckett's *Not I,* " *The South Central Review* 7, no. 1 (Spring 1990): 36-49. Originally appeared in *The South Central Review (SCMLA).*

Mary Ann Caws, " A Rereading of the Traces," *L'Esprit Créateur* 11, no. 3 (Fall 1971): 14-20. Copyright © 1971 by *L'Esprit Créateur.* Reprinted by permission of the publisher.

Michael Parsons, "Samuel Beckett: 'Imagination Dead Imagine.'" This review was first published in *The New Left Review* 38 (July-August 1966): 91-92.

John J. Mood, "'Silence Within': A Study of the *Residua* of Samuel Beckett," *Studies in Short Fiction* 7 (1970): 385-401. Copyright 1970 by Newberry College.

Raymond Federman, "The Impossibility of Saying the Same Old Thing the Same Old Way—Samuel Beckett's Fiction Since *Comment c'est,*" *L'Esprit Créateur* 11, no. 3 (Fall 1971): 21-43. Copyright © 1971 by *L'Esprit Créateur.* Reprinted by permission of the publisher.

David Porush, "Beckett's Deconstruction of the Machine in *The Lost Ones,*" *L'Esprit Créateur* 26, no. 4 (Winter 1986): 87-98.

Cathleen Culotta-Andonian, "Conceptions of Inner Landscapes: The Beckettian Narrator of the Sixties and Seventies," *Symposium* 36, no. 1 (Spring 1982): 3-13. Reprinted with permission of the Helen Dwight Reid Educational Foundation. Published by Heldref Publicaations, 1319 18th Street, N.W., Washington, D. C. 20036-1802. Copyright 1982.

J. E. Dearlove, "The Weaving of Penelope's Tapestry: Genre in the Works of Samuel Beckett," *Journal of Beckett Studies* 11-12 (1989): 123-29. Reprinted by permission of the editors of *Journal of Beckett Studies.*

Tseng Li-Ling, "Samuel Beckett's *For to End Yet Again:* A Conflict between 'Syntax of Energy' and 'Syntax of Weakness,'" *Twentieth Century Literature* (Spring 1992): 101-23.

Nicoletta Pireddu, "Sublime Supplements: Beckett and the 'Fizzling Out' of Meaning," *Studies in Short Fiction* 29 (1992): 303-14. Copyright 1992 by Newberry College.

Martin Esslin, "Who's Afraid of Samuel Beckett?" *Theatre History Studies* 10 (1990): 173-82. Originally published in *Theatre History Studies* 10 (1990).

Mel Gussow, "An Intimate Look at Beckett the Man," *The New York Times* (Sunday, December 31, 1989): 3H, 28H. © 1989 by The New York Times Co. Reprinted by permission.

William A. Henry III, "Giving Birth 'Astride of a Grave,' Samuel Beckett 1906-1989," *Time* 136, no. 2 (8 January 1990): 69. Copyright 1990 Time Inc. Reprinted by permission.

Every reasonable effort has been made to trace the owners of copyright materials in this book, but in some instances this has proven impossible. The editor and publisher will be glad to receive information leading to more complete acknowledgments in subsequent printings of the book, and in the meantime extend their apologies for any omissions.

Contents

Series Foreword by Cameron Northouse   xvii

Acknowledgments   xix

Introduction   1

1. Early Prose and Poetry

Symbolism To-day
Bonamy Dobrée   13

Dubliners
Arthur Calder-Marshall   14

Samuel Beckett and His *Whoroscope*
Clas Zilliacus   15

Savage Humor
Vivian Mercier   17

2. The Novel: *Murphy, Watt,* and The Trilogy

Fiction
Kate O'Brien   21

A Master Stylist
B. S. Johnson   22

Nought into Zero
A. J. Leventhal   23

Under the Jar
John Coleman   26

Samuel Beckett's World of Fiction
Charles I. Glicksberg   27

Samuel Beckett and the Death of the God-Narrator
Brian Wicker   39

Not Going Places
Enoch Brater   51

L'Innommable and the Hermeneutic Paradigm
Brian T. Fitch   54

Naming the M/inotaur: Beckett's Trilogy and the Failure
of Narrative
Roch C. Smith   62

Beckett and the Comedy of Decomposition
Morton Gurewitch   70

Ashes to Ashes, Dust to Dust
Robert Sandarg   79

3. Early Theatrical Works

Theatre (Review of *Waiting for Godot*)
Anthony Hartley   91

Theatre (Review of *Waiting for Godot*)
Harold Clurman   93

The Uneventful Event
Vivian Mercier   95

En attendant Godot: Tragedy or Comedy?
Ramona Cormier and Janis L. Pallister   96

Contents

Samuel Beckett and the Postmodern: Language Games,
Play, and *Waiting for Godot*
Jeffrey Nealon — 106

How to Read *Endgame*
Vivian Mercier — 114

Theatre (Review of *Endgame*)
Harold Clurman — 118

In the Ruins of the Past: Reading Beckett Intertextually
Per Nykrog — 120

Rebuke to Nihilism
Tom F. Driver — 143

Krapp's Last Tape: The Evolution of a Play, 1958-75
James Knowlson — 146

4. Return to Prose: *How It Is*

Beckett Country
Frank Kermode — 161

Farewell to Incompetence: Beckett's *How It Is* and
Imagination Dead Imagine
H. Porter Abbott — 166

Beckett's Sociability
Leo Bersani and Ulysse Dutoit — 176

5. Interviews and Personal Reminiscences

Samuel Beckett: An Interview
Patrick Starnes — 191

Conversations with Samuel Beckett
Jay A. Levy — 195

6. Radio and Film

It's Tragic, Mysterious and Wildly Funny: That's What You
Get When the B.B.C. Asks Samuel Beckett to Write a Play
Roy Walker — 207

Beckett Country
Julia Strachey — 209

From Characters to Discrete Events: The Evolving Concept
of Dramatis Personae in Beckett's Radio Plays
Germaine Baril — 211

"To Be Is to Be Perceived" . . . Time and
Point of View in Beckett's *Film*
William F. Van Wert — 219

7. Beckett is Awarded the Nobel Prize

Godot Arrives
Iain Hamilton — 227

Nobel Prize: Kyrie Eleison Without God — 229

8. Late Theatrical Works

Theatre (Review of *Happy Days*)
Harold Clurman — 233

The Stage: Beckett's *Happy Days*
Richard Gilman — 235

The Parodox of Silence: Samuel Beckett's Plays
Renée Riese Hubert — 237

The New Beckett
Barbara Bray — 245

Samuel Beckett: about him and about
A. J. Leventhal — 247

Contents

On the Route of a Walking Shadow: Samuel Beckett's
Come and Go
Rosangela Barone   262

Bare Bones: As a lady slips her moorings, Beckett
sounds a hopeful note
Jay Carr   273

Review: The World Première of *Ohio Impromptu*,
Directed by Alan Schneider at Columbus, Ohio
S. E. Gontarski   275

Impact and Parable in Beckett: A First Encounter
with *Not I*
Alec Reid   278

Recontextualizing the Self: The Voice as Subject
in Beckett's *Not I*
Mary Catanzaro   287

9. Poetry, Short Stories and Prose Texts

A Rereading of the Traces
Mary Ann Caws   303

Samuel Beckett: "Imagination Dead Imagine"
Michael Parsons   309

"Silence Within": A Study of the *Residua* of Samuel Beckett
John J. Mood   310

The Impossibility of Saying the Same Old Thing the Same
Old Way—Samuel Beckett's Fiction Since *Comment c'est*
Raymond Federman   326

Beckett's Deconstruction of the Machine in *The Lost Ones*
David Porush   347

Conceptions of Inner Landscapes: The Beckettian Narrator
of the Sixties and Seventies
Cathleen Culotta-Andonian   357

The Weaving of Penelope's Tapestry: Genre in the Works
of Samuel Beckett
J. E. Dearlove — 367

Samuel Beckett's *For to End Yet Again*: A Conflict
between "Syntax of Energy" and "Syntax of Weakness"
Tseng Li-Ling — 373

Sublime Supplements: Beckett and the "Fizzling Out"
of Meaning
Nicoletta Pireddu — 391

10. Final Tribute

Who's Afraid of Samuel Beckett?
Martin Esslin — 403

An Intimate Look at Beckett the Man
Mel Gussow — 414

Giving Birth "Astride of a Grave," Samuel Beckett: 1906-1989
William A. Henry III — 416

Selected Bibliography — 419

Index — 423

Series Foreword

Critical Responses in Arts and Letters is designed to present a documentary history of highlights in the critical reception to the body of work of writers and artists and to individual works that are generally considered to be of major importance. The focus of each volume in this series is basically historical. The introductions to each volume are themselves brief histories of the critical response an author, artist, or individual work has received. This response is then further illustrated by reprinting a strong representation of the major critical reviews and articles that have collectively produced the author's, artist's, or work's critical reputation.

The scope of *Critical Responses in Arts and Letters* knows no chronological or geographical boundaries. Volumes under preparation include studies of individuals from around the world and in both contemporary and historical periods.

Each volume is the work of an individual editor, who surveys the entire body of criticism on a single author, artist, or work. The editor then selects the best material to depict the critical response received by an author or artist over his/her entire career. Documents produced by the author or artist may also be included when the editor finds that they are necessary to a full understanding of the materials at hand. In circumstances where previous, isolated volumes of criticism on a particular individual or work exist, the editor carefully selects material that better reflects the nature and directions of the critical response over time.

In addition to the introduction and the documentary section, the editor of each volume is free to solicit new essays on areas that may not have been adequately dealt with in previous criticism. Also, for volumes on living writers and artists, new interviews may be included, again at the discretion of the volume's editor. The volumes also provide a supplementary bibliography and are fully indexed.

While each volume in *Critical Responses in Arts and Letters* is unique, it is also hoped that in combination they form a useful, documentary history of the critical response to the arts, and one that can be easily and profitably employed by students and scholars.

Cameron Northouse

Acknowledgments

It gives me great pleasure to express my gratitude to a number of persons who have aided me in the preparation of this manuscript. I extend special thanks to Rex Clark, our media specialist at the University of Michigan-Dearborn, who provided technical assistance, and Carol Shea who carefully edited the manuscript. I am also grateful for the encouragement of my editors George Butler, Maureen Melino, Irene Lebov and Cameron Northouse. Finally I wish to thank my husband, Jim, for his continual cheerfulness, guidance and moral support, and my sons Marc and Jeff for their patience and tolerance.

Introduction

The critical response to the fiction of the Irish-born author, Samuel Beckett, has been overwhelming. Numerous books and thousands of articles have been published on Beckett, primarily in Europe, the United States and Canada. Since Beckett wrote most of his works in French and translated them himself into English and later selectively into German, French, British, American, Canadian and German critics were not only able to read Beckett's works in their *original* version, but also had the opportunity to compare one version to another. The diversity of the approaches to Beckett's *oeuvre* has been as varied as the individuals writing about him: historical, philosophical, thematic, formalist, structuralist, and psychological studies, among others, analyze the content and style of Beckett's works, while biographical and manuscript studies give insight into the genesis of his fiction.

In this volume, review articles which document the journalists' and critics' initial reactions to Beckett's poetry, prose and theatrical works have been juxtaposed with in–depth critical essays focusing on the major themes and stylistic innovations of Beckett's fiction. The majority of the articles in this compilation have not appeared in previous collections. With the exception of the article "Conversations with Samuel Beckett," by Dr. Jay A. Levy, which has been revised for this edition, the articles have been reprinted in their orginal version.

Beckett's major works have been grouped chronologically, according to genre: 1) the early prose and poetry (*Proust, More Pricks than Kicks,* "Whoroscope"); 2) the novels *Murphy, Watt, Mercier and Camier* and the trilogy (*Molloy, Malone Dies, The Unnamable*); 3) his early theatrical works (*Waiting for Godot, Endgame, Krapp's Last Tape);* 4) the novel *How It Is;* 5) Beckett's plays for radio and *Film* (*All That Fall, Words and Music, Cascando, Film*); 6) the late theatrical works (*Happy Days, Play, Footfalls, That Time,*

Come and Go, Rockaby, Ohio Impromptu, Not I); and 7) the poetry, short stories and prose texts published at the end of his career (*Texts for Nothing, Mercier and Camier, First Love,* "Enough," "Imagination Dead Imagine," "Bing," *The Lost Ones, Fizzles,* "Worstward Ho," "For to end yet again," "Company"). Additional chapters present interviews with Beckett, public reaction to his winning the Nobel Prize in 1969, and the announcement of his death in 1989.

Many of the essays included in this volume discuss more than one work or genre which has made the organization of the compilation difficult. Articles are primarily grouped according to the literary work(s) being discussed, and then, within each grouping, the articles are arranged chronologically to give the reader a sense of the critical response to the work over time. An index of the works discussed has been included at the end of the collection.

Full-length Studies

Early Beckett criticism, in many cases, set the tone for the works that were to follow. The full-length studies of the sixties and seventies focused primarily on form and content: the influence of literary, philosophical and historical ideas, and aesthetic systems. In *Samuel Beckett: The Comic Gamut*,[1] Ruby Cohn uses Bergson's catalog of comic techniques as a starting point for her study of the comic elements in Beckett's prose and drama. Richard Coe focuses on the philosophical implications of Beckett's fiction in *Samuel Beckett*,[2] comparing Beckettian themes with the ideas expressed by Pascal, Proust, Descartes, Geulincx, Wittgenstein, the Greek philosopher Zeno, and Buddhism. Raymond Federman, in his work *Journey to Chaos: Samuel Beckett's Early Fiction*,[3] demonstrates the gradual disintegration of form and content in Beckett's work and its development into an aesthetic system in the novels of the trilogy and *How It Is*. In *The Shape of Chaos: An Interpretation of the Art of Samuel Beckett*,[4] David Hesla examines Beckett's novels and plays from the perception of the history of ideas. Hesla shows how Beckett was influenced by the theories of the pre-Socratics, the rationalists of the seventeenth and eighteenth centuries, Schopenhauer, Bergson, Hegel, Kierkegard, Heidegger, Sartre, and Husserl, among others. H. Porter Abbott in *The Fiction of Samuel Beckett: Form and Effect* [5] describes the three major stages of Beckett's approach to form in fiction: 1) two preliminary fictional experiments (*More Pricks than Kicks, Murphy*); 2) the exploration of imitative form from 1940 to 1959 (*Watt* to *Texts for Nothing*); and 3) the restoration of a sense of order in the later prose works (*How It Is, The Lost Ones*). In 1972 two major studies of Beckett's drama were published: *Beckett: A Study of His Plays*,[6] by John Fletcher and John Spurling, provides a detailed analysis of Beckett's theatrical works "Eleuthéria" through *Come and Go* and "Breath"; while Eugene Webb's *The Plays of Samuel Beckett*[7] explores the characters, imagery, underlying patterns and approaches to the plays. Webb felt that the plays reach out in two principal directions: 1) to explore form for its own sake and 2) to attempt to diagnose the causes of our failure and to find a way beyond it.

In the late seventies, many critics turned to an in-depth analysis of art and identity. The first full-length work on Beckett and art, *Art and the Artist in the Works of Samuel Beckett*,[8] by Hannah Case Copeland evaluates the theme of self-consciousness in Beckett's art. She develops the role of the artist and the dual significance of art as both creative act and created object. Beckett's post trilogy prose and his drama after *Endgame* are analyzed by James Knowlson and John Pilling in their *Frescoes of the Skull. The Later Prose and Drama of Samuel Beckett*.[9] Two of Beckett's then unpublished works, "Dream of Fair to Middling Women" and "Eleuthéria" are also discussed. In *Accomodating the Chaos*,[10] J. E. Dearlove documents Beckett's efforts to create a nonrelational art. Lance St. John Butler in *Samuel Beckett and the Meaning of Being: A Study in Ontological Parable* aims ". . . to try to lighten the Beckettian gloom with those philosophical lamps that seem to work the best,[11] Heidegger, Sartre, and Hegel. In *Theatre on Trial: Samuel Beckett's Later Drama*, Anna McMullan analyzes Beckett's late stage plays from *Play* to *What Where* using the theories of Jacques Lacan and Julia Kristeva to link "the destabilazation of positions of knowledge and meaning in Beckett's work to his destabilization of structures of identity":

> Beckett's theatre can therefore be seen as the site of a confrontation between the attempt to assume a position of control and judgement in relation to the visual and verbal representations of self and the laws of representation in general, and the opening up of spaces which challenge and disrupt the construction of the roles posited by representation, including those of self and other, spectacle and spectator. Beckett's drama frames the operations of authority, but also stages the drama of a subjectivity which resists or exceeds the dominant *codes* of representation, questioning in the process the languages and limits of theatre itself.[12]

Beckett's non-traditional approach to language, character, plot and narrative style was often appreciated, but occasionally criticized. His tendency to simplify while de-emphasizing the traditional concepts of time and space taught the reader to look at literature in a new way. The portrayal of characters whose memories have failed and are forced to live for the present moment while limiting their descriptions to their present situation has effectively given us a better understanding of the isolation and alienation modern man experiences. Although Beckett has in many cases redefined the structures and limitations of the literary medium he has worked with, he is still within the intellectual tradition of the nineteenth and twentieth centuries, the alienation and pessimism portrayed in Dostoevsky's *Notes from the Underground*, Kafka's stories and Ionesco's plays.

Selected Articles and Reviews

Arthur Calder Marshall identifies Beckett as a humorist in the tradition of Fielding and Stone. Beckett's cleverness, his "delight in words, in grotesque, ludicrous and obsolete words"[13] in his first poems and stories turns to farce in the anguished heroes of the early novels and plays and finally to a parody of traditional form in his later fiction. His often humoristic manipulation of language and situation prevents the narrators from thinking or speaking in a meaningful way, which in turn, brings about troubling disruptions in the traditional novel form. As Brian Fitch suggests in "*L'Innommable* and the Hermeneutic Paradigm," ". . . what is really at stake here is the manner in which the individual relates to language, whether it be his own, in the act of writing, or that of another, in the act of reading."[14] Due to the narrator's inadequate skills of observation and evaluation, the reader's comprehension of the story is often severely limited: ". . . [Murphy] represents a reassuring standard of sanity against which we can evaluate the absurd thoughts and behaviors of the characters. . . . Although the next novel, *Watt*, too is organized for us by an implicit omniscient narrator who has authoritative information for the reader, what he tells us is a good deal less reliable and reassuring than in *Murphy*. If Murphy is still recognizably a citizen of this world, Watt is certainly an outcast."[15]

Morton Gurewitch feels it is essential to add Freud's discussion of skeptical wit to Bergson's assessment of comic conflict and Ruby Cohn's analysis of the metaphysical implications of comedy: "Freudian nonsense, that is psychically restorative departures from normality and reality, reverberates simultaneously with skeptical farce in the daffy turmoils of the trilogy heroes. Finally, Freud's homage to disaster humor and its variant, gallows humor—the kind of humor that transforms into joke material both the facts of catastrophe and the threat of death—resonates in the repeated self-derogations of Beckett's disaster-ridden voyageurs and immobilized inmates of calamity."[16] Plot and narrative have been reduced to words: "For the entire trilogy moves toward a gradual replacement of physical wandering, first with the narrator's fictional accounts of the wandering of others and finally with the purely verbal narrative wandering we find in *The Unnamable*, where to 'go on' is to write, to produce more words. The narrator's increasingly frequent reminders that he is, and was, telling stories culminate, in *The Unnamable*, in a reduction of all fiction, including earlier tales of wandering, to the words that make it up. Bicycles, crutches, chamberpots, sticks, hats, and jars, even the characters themselves are, after all, but words. . . . Words overcome the object they were seemingly meant

Introduction

to represent as the stories get tangled in their own verbal web."[17] Language, no longer simply representational, has become the object of the narrative. And as Roch C. Smith goes on to declare—the narrator unable to escape this "verbal web" finds himself in a "verbal prison" in which the enemy is within.

The love of words gradually becomes an end in itself, the subject of the fiction, and then transforms itself into a trap, a closed system, from which the narrator cannot free himself. He can no more escape his need to repeat now meaningless words and phrases, than he can prevent thoughts from occurring in his mind. Unable to use language in a meaningful way, traditional plot gives way to free flowing associations as the Beckettian narrator futility attempts to make sense of his situation: "The only action Beckett describes is that of the disoriented mind of the nameless hero imprisoned in the cage of consciousness, cut off from reality as he struggles, but always unavailingly, to get in touch with it."[18] Whereas Murphy sat still voluntarily to allow his mind to become active—the later narrators have apparently been isolated and confined involuntarily. Their descriptions reflect this mental and physical immobility: "We are left, in these latest works, and in 'Lessness" above all, with a kind of frozen verbal sculpture, patterns of sound and imagery in which words have become simply objects in a vacuum, the mere nuts and bolts of communication. The two-dimensional structure of language itself is all but obliterated in a kaleidoscope of word-fragments endlessly juggled together. There can be no beginning, no middle or end in such a pattern; no progress of meaning from one statement to the next, no story, no fictional world."[19]

In the theater, a similar inability to communicate is at work. Here however, the characters are not only incapable of meaningfully vocalizing their own predicaments, they are equally inapt at communicating with others. It is through the slapstick humor and idle chatter of Vladimir and Estragon in *Waiting for Godot* that the audience becomes aware of their tragically absurd situation. Ramona Cormier and Janis Pallister wonder whether or not these characters are even significantly aware of their situation to be distressed by it: "We believe that they do not experience profound suffering, and that they are just as ridiculous, perhaps as evil, as they are tragic. They are creatures who are willfully avoiding the basic issues of despair and death, and it is not unreasonable to think that Beckett views them as non-tragic because they do not suffer to any significant degree."[20] The ironic portrayal of the meaninglessness of life by two characters who seem to only momentarily suffer bouts of boredom, further demonstrate Beckett's pessimistic view of man's condition and the anguish which lurks behind the vaudeville routines.

The grim reality of man's isolation is established in *Endgame*. In this play, the stage represents a closed room surrounded by a desert-like landscape. Three of the four characters are immobile, Hamm in his wheelchair and Nagg and Nell in their ashcans. The once powerful Hamm is reduced to a reclusive invalid, who is "unloving and unloved, hardened into a monstrous, a tragic, self-sufficiency and ferocious egoism, blind to the misery of his situation which is so painfully clear to us."[21] Throughout Beckett's plays we encounter many characters who seem to be incapable of experiencing emotion, thinking or even comprehending their current predicament. The reader-spectator must draw his own conclusions, in order to penetrate the characters' silence: "Beckett's characters frequently find it impossible to derive a meaning from either word or silence or a combination of both. If they were to probe deeply into their inner world, they would encounter a wide zone of silence, mainly because they have so much trouble in remembering their own past."[22] Thus, Winnie in *Happy Days* reflexively reexamines the contents of her purse, without revealing any related memories. Likewise, Krapp listens to his youthful voice on his tape recorder without being able to "recognize himself: the past, which he is powerless to recapture and consequently to understand, remains no less alien in a recording. Once the tape has run its course, Krapp is confronted with ultimate silence."[23]

Not only is man alone, he is incapable of knowing himself, of expressing his own thoughts and memories. He may repeat the tapes, or the barely intelligible flow of words, as in *Play* or *Not I*. In some cases the words may become secondary to the movement of the characters as in *Come and Go* and *Footfalls*, or entirely replaced by visual cues, as in *Act Without Words I & II*. Rosangela Barone in "On the Route of a Walking Shadow: Samuel Beckett's *Come and Go*" proposes that the creation of ". . . an artistic entity [is] no longer conceived as re-presentation, i.e. mimetic expression . . . but as something reflecting upon itself in *motu perpetuo* . . . [The] only significant escape for the artist lies in self-concentration, i.e. in turning inwards and treating his own self with irony, in other terms in inventing a game (play) in which the self is held up to ridicule (dramaticule)."[24]

Beckett's dramatic productions for radio and his movie, *Film*, gave him the unique opportunity to isolate two of the basic structural elements of the theater: voice (or the flow of words) and the visual image. Although his first radio play, *All That Fall* may be more conventional than *Waiting for Godot*, *Endgame* and *Krapp's Last Tape*, his second play for radio, *Embers*, ". . . makes greater use of the dramatic possibilities of a purely aural medium by presenting a character, Ada, whose physical presence is not corroborated by sound effects."[25] In the radio plays that follow, *Words and Music* and *Cascando*, music attains the status of character. While musical themes evoke an individual emotional or intellectual response from a listener, they lack the system of referents that are inseparable from the written or spoken word. Mental images conjured up by the sound of music relate to specific reactions of the individual listener and as such vary from person to person. Thus, through the use of music Beckett succeeded in further abstracting the speaking voice: "By examining the use made by Beckett (and by his English and French producers) of the different sign systems available in radio-language, voice sets and paralinguistic features, sound effects and music—one is able to chart an evolution from play to play which led to the creation of ambiguous characters who are open to multiple interpretations by the listener. In so doing, Beckett also liberated the discourse from the constraints of a speaking subject, allowing it to function as an independent force having its own substance."[26]

Beckett continually experimented with reduction. Whereas the radio plays allowed him to separate the speaking voice from an identifiable though anonymous speaking subject, the short prose texts to which he frequently returned and with which he ended his literary career gave him the opportunity to further experiment with self-imposed limitations. By continually reducing the scope of his presentation, from the brief but vague images his narrators were still able to conjure up, to the mechanical repetition and rearrangement of isolated words and phrases in his last prose texts, Beckett succeeds in vividly depicting the isolation and alienation of modern man and his surroundings. The absolute aloneless of the Beckettian hero is perhaps nowhere viewed so dramatically as in the novel *How It Is* and in the late prose pieces. The very act of socialization or communication in *How It Is* is portrayed through an endless chain of tormentors and victims: "In this perfectly organized world, at every moment, everyone—whatever the number may be—is either enjoying a victim or suffering at the hands of a tormentor, or is either crawling toward his victim or confident that a tormentor is on his way."[27] The victim is commanded to speak, to tell his story, which may in fact be the same story continually retold by each victim to his tormentor. The narrator finds this system to be just and appears anxious to describe the chain of events in precise detail.

As H. Porter Abbott points out *How It Is* and the prose piece "Imagination Dead Imagine" present a change in Beckett's narrative style. Whereas his previous narrators could not organize themselves to tell their stories because of their innate incompetence, ignorance, or susceptibility to distractions, the narrator of *How It Is* successfully plans and executes his presentation: "The basic innovation of *How It Is* is its phenomenal order. That this is an innovation can be illustrated quite simply by comparing the abilities of Beckett's narrators to keep to their 'programs.' Since *Molloy*, they have been fond of announcing programs—that is setting up plans for narration—and, as he constantly reminds us, the narrator of *How It Is* has his program, too. What is remarkable in *How It Is* is the perfection to which the program works, whereas if anything distinguishes the programs of earlier narrators, it is their perfect failure."[28]

The reduction of the art of story telling to the random repetition of words and phrases by an anonymous narrating consciousness presents a new phase in the evolution of Beckett's fiction. The total absence of narrative style and identity may offer the only viable clues to understanding a language ". . . rendered . . . useless—blank as it were—Beckett reduces fiction to a mathematical tautology. Since words can only demonstrate their own emptiness, literature also becomes an inaudible game—a seemingly absurd game of verbal permutations, and the less words there are the more satisfactory the game."[29] Beckett's portrayal of a bleak, gray landscape, peopled with motionless white bodies is perhaps ". . . the last place, the ultimate end of fiction and of existence, the most remote corner of consciousness, the last refuge ('issueless') from which the last few words can be spoken, murmured, mumbled."[30] This continual reduction of time, place, language and character to their minimal essences necessitates a corresponding reduction in the effectiveness of the text to communicate or signify. J. E. Dearlove in *"Last Images: Samuel Beckett's Residual Fiction,"* describes the fragmentation of language in the prose pieces: "Repetition and refrain supplant conventional manners of meaning. Words like notes, are arranged mathematically and affect us subliminally. Moreover, like notes, not chords, each word strives to strike only one meaning, strives to be 'pure' not connotative, scientific nor emotional. But the words, and the images, break down. . . . Beckett's latest pieces accomplish what the earlier pieces unsuccessfully attempted: they offer a form that is self-disintegrating."[31] As in Beckett's recent plays for radio, it is the reader who must ultimately find a satisfactory "meaning" for the text—a subjective reading to make sense of the disjointed words and images. Faced with the inherent formlessness and vagueness of the recent prose pieces, the reader is thus forced to find "meaning" where none exists. We enter into the creative act in an attempt to momentarily organize and clarify the distorted perceptions and /or observations of a narrator who may negate his images as quickly as he imagines them. David Porush views *The Lost Ones* as ". . . the culmination of Beckett's uncertainty—created worlds which are all made of language grown threadbare, untrustworthy, insufficient, quirky, unmanageable, and near collapse."[32]

The narrators' mental confusion becomes more obvious in the shorter prose texts, where his attempts to keep his imagination functioning frequently result in apparently unavoidable repetitions. The narrators' frustrations are clear—imagination cannot take place without stimuli—internal or external: "*For to end yet again* is less about perception than imagination. . . . The imagination may summon up endless vistas, but they do not last. . . . The art of these late texts is to destroy one's sense of narrative cohesion as normal syntax creates it . . ., and to plunge one into a world of repetitive items which insinuate a sense of history to compensate for the one we have lost."[33] Few elements are new. We see the reappearance of the same characters, images and landscapes. It is the similarity of these common elements that aids the reader in his quest for meaning: "By tying together diverse images—those that pertain to crumbling into ruins, being engulfed in dust, standing isolated in a desert wasteland, and falling over—one discovers how different themes in many of Beckett's works are interrelated. When the isolated figure in *Fizzle 8* falls and

Introduction

is engulfed by dust, the image suggests that—for the moment anyway—an end of thinking, writing and living has been achieved."[34]

Beckett's works are similar, yet different, the same vision continually refined and distilled, yet impossible to define. This is the genius of Samuel Beckett. An inner turmoil suggested yet never gras[ed, always just below the surface, a circular mental journey made up of words and blank spaces, sounds and silences.

---

[1]New Brunswick, New Jersey: Rutgers University Press, 1962.

[2]New York: Grove Press, 1964.

[3]Berkeley and Los Angeles: University of California Press, 1965.

[4]Minneapolis: University of Minnesota Press, 1971.

[5]Berkeley, Los Angeles, and London: University of California Press, 1965.

[6]London: Eyre Methuen; New York: Hill and Wang, 1972.

[7]Seattle: University of Washington Press, 1972.

[8]Paris: Mouton and Co., 1975.

[9]London: J. Calder, 1975.

[10]Durham, N. C.: Duke University Press, 1982.

[11](New York: St. Martin's Press, 1984): 2.

[12](New York: Routledge, 1993): 9.

[13]"Dubliners," *The Spectator* 152 (1 June 1934): 863.

[14]*The Chicago Review* 33, no. 3 (Fall 1975): 103-4.

[15]Brian Wicker, "Samuel Beckett and the Death of the God-Narrator," *The Journal of Narrative Technique* 4, no. 1 (Jan. 1974): 63.

[16]"Beckett and the Comedy of Decomposition," *The Chicago Review* 33, no. 2 (1982): 95.

[17]Roch R. Smith, "Naming the M/inotaur: Beckett's Trilogy and the Failure of Narrative," *Modern Fiction Studies* 29 no. 1 (Spring 1983): 75.

[18]Charles Glicksberg, "Samuel Beckett's World of Fiction," *The Arizona Quarterly* 18, no. 1 (Spring 1962): 41.

[19]Brian Wicker, "Samuel Beckett and the Death of the God-Narrator," *Journal of Narrative Technique* 4, no. 1 (Jan. 1974): 71.

[20]"*En attendant Godot*: Tragedy or Comedy?" *L'Esprit Créateur* 11, no. 3 (Fall 1971): 49.

[21]Per Nykrog, "In the ruins of the Past: Reading Beckett Intertextually," *Comparative Literature* 36, no. 4 (Fall 1984): 304.

[22]Renée Riese Hubert, "The Paradox of Silence: Samuel Beckett's Plays," *Mundus Artium* 2 (Summer 1969): 83.

[23]*Ibid.*, p. 84.

[24]*Etudes Irlandaises* 10 (December 1985): 125-26.

[25]Germaine Baril, "From Characters to Discrete Events: The Evolving Concept of Dramatis Personae in Beckett's Radio Plays," *The Review of Contemporary Fiction* 7, no. 2 (Summer 1987): 112.

[26]*Ibid.*, p. 112.

[27]Leo Bersani and Ulysse Dutoit, "Beckett's Sociability," *The Raritan* 12. no. 1 (Summer 1992): 2-3.

[28]"Farewell to Incompetence: Beckett's *How It Is* and 'Imagination Dead Imagine,'" *Contemporary Literature* 11, no. 1 (Winter 1970): 27.

[29]Raymond Federman, "The Impossibility of Saying the Same Old Thing the Same Old Way—Samuel Beckett's Fiction Since *Comment c'est*," *L'Esprit Créateur* 11, no. 3 (Fall 1971): 35.

[30]*Ibid., p. 35.*

[31]*Journal of Modern Literature* 6, no. 1 (Feb. 1977): 106.

Introduction   11

[32]"Beckett's Deconstruction of the Machine in *The Lost Ones*," *L'Esprit Créateur* 26, no. 4 (Winter 1986): 95.

[33]John Pilling, "*For to end yet again and other fizzles* by Samuel Beckett," *Journal of Beckett Studies*, no. 2 (Summer 1977): 98-99.

[34]Rubin Rabinovitz, "*Fizzles* and Samuel Beckett's Earlier Fiction," *Contemproary Literature* 24, no. 3 (1983): 319.

CHAPTER 1

Early Prose and Poetry

Symbolism To-Day

Bonamy Dobrée

Axel's Castle. By Edmund Wilson. (Scribners.)
Proust. By Samuel Beckett. The Dolphin Books. (Chatto and Windus.)

... Mr. Beckett's little book on Proust is a spirited piece of writing; but it is a good deal too "clever," and disfigured with pseudo-scientific jargon and philosophic snippets. For him Proust is an auto-symbolist. He deals with only one or two aspects ("read Blickpunkt for this miserable word"), says some good things, and is interesting on the Proustian time-concept. He does not tell us so much about Proust as Mr. Wilson does, who would disagree with him when he says that Proust was in no way concerned with morals: for he is not so much concerned to probe the truth about Proust as to write sparkingly about him. Mr. Beckett obtrudes himself a little too much, and indulges in too many digressions. Still, for all its faults, it is an agreeable and stimulating pamphlet, if only because Mr. Beckett is obviously so hugely enjoying himself.

From *The Spectator* (18 April 1931): 641-42.

Dubliners

Arthur Calder-Marshall

More Pricks Than Kicks. **By Samuel Beckett. (Chatto and Windus.)**

Mr. Beckett is a humorist. They are so rare today that the word, like poet, has become one of contempt. But I intend no insult. He is in the tradition of Fielding and Sterne and has read Mr. Wyndham Lewis and Firbank on the way; a little too much Firbank.

A quality which seems common to all humorists is delight in words, in grotesque, ludicrous and obsolete words. This is partly because a word can be funny in itself: but also because a joke is better for being wrapped in verbiage just as a chocolate is more attractive in silver paper. If no word fits his purpose, a humorist coins one: language is as fluid for him as morals. Mr. Beckett stands with the new word "ipsissimosity" to his credit; but rather than coining, he usually flees to another language, a cowardice that leads him sometimes to affectation and obscurity. His humour, however, is not precious; it is saved by colloquialism and lightheartedness.

His chief character is a Dubliner, by name Belacqua Shuan, a poet by profession, a drunkard by heredity and by environment a philanderer. In the first three stories he is immature and the writing is similar. It is not till "A Wet Night" that the writing begins to brighten. The argument between the "Polar Bear" and the Jesuit and the whole description of the party at the Casa Frica are excellently done, though in a rather conventional, 'sophisticated' style. In "Love and Lethe," Belacqua has left the brilliant *galère* of the Casa Frica, has left the Alba, who had "merely to unleash her eyes and she might have mercy on whom she would," the homespun poet, the Parabimbi and the popular Professor of Bullscrit and Ovoidology. He now follows Ruby Tough, who when she could, she would not; but when she could not, then she would. Belacqua's intentions are entirely suicidal but his actions prove *l'Amour et la mort n'est qu'une même chose*. The earlier stories are rather shapeless; "Love and Lethe" and those that follow are much better formed, the best being "What a Misfortune," the story of Belacqua's second marriage.

Mr. Beckett can describe people; he makes them live with the vitaesimilitude of marionettes, and that is all the life they need for his purpose:

> The presumptive cuckoo, if not exactly one of those dapper little bureaucrats that give the impression of having come into the world dressed by Austin Reed, presented some of the better-known differentiae: the dimpled chin, the bright brown doggy eyes that were so appealing, the unrippled surface of vast white brow whose area was at least double that of the nether face, and anchored there

for all eternity the sodden cowlick that looked as though it were secreting macassar to discharge into his eye. With his high heels he attained to five foot five, his nose was long and straight and his shoes a size and a half too large to bear it out. A plug of moustache cowered at his nostrils like a frightened animal before its lair, at the least sign of danger it would scurry up into an antrum. He expelled his words with gentle discrimination as a pastry-cook squirts icing upon a cake. His name was Walter Draflin.

More Pricks Than Kicks is an amusing and indecorous book, the appeal of which may be limited to a sophisticated public. Yet there are qualities in Mr. Beckett's writing which show that he is capable of coming out into the open as a humorist, instead of retiring as he too often does into the allusive shelter of "the really cultivated man."

From *The Spectator* 152 (1 June 1934): 863.

Samuel Beckett and His *Whoroscope*[1]
Clas Zilliacus

Samuel Beckett had been *lecteur d'anglais* at the École Normale Supérieure for about a year when, one day in 1919, he was precipitated towards a literary career by Thomas McGreevy, poet, friend, and fellow contributor to *Our Exagmination Round his Factification for Incamination of Work in Progress*, the Joyce symposium published earlier that year. McGreevy informed his friend of a prize which had been offered by Nancy Cunard of the Hours Press. A sum of £10 was to go to the best poem on the subject of Time. Submissions were not to exceed one hundred lines, and they were to reach Miss Cunard by the following morning. It was rumoured that no Ms of singular excellence had appeared so far.

Time was money. Beckett decided to enter the contest, and sat down to work. His contribution, a custom-made "poem" made up of ninety-eight lines of verse, took the prize. Its title was *Whoroscope*, and it was fattened considerably when its author, at the request of the jury, added a batch of explanatory notes to it.[2]

Whoroscope deals with Time, as its title mockingly indicates. Its protagonist is René Descartes, a philosopher whose presence permeates most of Beckett's writings; "Cartesian centaurs" is the designation used by Hugh Kenner for the writer's gallery of moribund heroes. Descartes, having been called to the Court of Christina in Stockholm, lies dying. Having to get up too early in an arctic climate has finished him, and he views the Queen as instigator of his death, "the murdering matinal pope-confessed amazon, /Christina the ripper," in the vitriolic language of the poem. The entire piece is made up of the deathbed musings of the philosopher, as imagined by Beckett. These musings freely link together various minutiae of Cartesian biography with the assistance of, among others, Adrien Baillet and his *Vie de Monsieur Descartes.*

It is very much a poem of the late 'twenties, and of a talented writer in his twenties. Erudite allusions and gutter vulgarisms cohabit shamelessly, and the poem knows no bounds other than the deadline and the format fixed by Miss Cunard. It is Joycean and wastelandish and just the thing to be produced, and prized, by the gathering of fugitives in Paris.

Johannes Hedberg, in a foreword to his interpretation of the poem, calls it "not only a fascinating and perhaps good poem but also a historical document of no little value." These claims have been thoroughly put to the test recently: just as Hedberg was about to take his manuscript to the printer, Lawrence E. Harvey's monumental *Samuel Beckett, Poet and Critic* (Princeton, 1970) appeared. Harvey provides an examination of *Whoroscope* even more extensive than Hedberg's. Hedberg thought it over and, after incorporating a few references to Harvey, went into print.

I am not entirely convinced that the task was worth doing twice. I do think that it has been well done, both times. The extent of the overlap remains within reasonable limits. Hedberg's interpretation is, as its title indicates, linguistic and literary. He moves with Empsonian ease in the realm of sense and meaning: he is particularly good on lexical meanings that rank low in dictionaries, and on dormant obscenities. Harvey's exhaustiveness, on the other hand, is exhausting: nothing is found too trivial for a crushing weight of scholia. Hedberg runs a similar risk; so does the poem. In the final analysis I would say that a luckier balance of essentials and ephemera is struck in Hedberg's reading than in Harvey's section on *Whoroscope.*

After these two rounds it seems that any attempt to reopen the case would be severely subjected to one of Beckett's favourite laws, the one of diminishing returns. One more thing might profitably be attempted, however: a study of the making of the poem. The University of Texas at Austin has in its Beckett collection an autograph Ms of *Whoroscope*, five pages on three leaves. "Original Ms of my first published poem." says a note by Beckett. It was, in fact, his first separately published work, and one of the comparatively few early works that he has never really disowned and suppressed, as was until recently the fate of texts like *More Pricks Than Kicks*, *Mercier et Camier*, and *Premier amour*. Most critics have dismissed *Whoroscope* in a rather curt manner: "it exists primarily because he had entered a contest for poems about Time, and it was published because it won the contest."[3] Thus, it exists. It is a good illustration of early Beckett, of allusive, compact poetry, and of the 'twenties. Apart from that, it is great fun, and Hedberg has a few things to say about that aspect which Harvey almost totally ignores. For those who would like to use it in class for the above purposes, the little monograph provides a useful, well-organized key.

One last thing about *Whoroscope* and Beckett's attitude to it. In January, 1966, in Broadcasting House studio B12, Beckett was present at the recording of a program titled "The Poems of Samuel Beckett." One of the items read was *Whoroscope, in toto.* In his written commentary to the poem John Fletcher, the narrator, called it "hardly a poem in the strict sense." Other condescending remarks—"undergraduate cleverness," for one—were recorded as scripted, but this little clause was deleted. *Whoroscope,* then, should be regarded as a poem in the strict sense of the word, if only to make the word a little less strict.

From *Moderna Språk* 67, no.1 (1973): 4-6.

---

[1] Article-review of *Samuel Beckett's "Whorescope". A Linguistic-Liiterary Interpretation,* by Johannes Hedberg. *Moderna språk monographs. Literature,* No. 1, Stockholm 1972.

[2] Miss Cunard and Richard Aldington were the jury. The request was made by the latter rather than by Miss Cunard, as Hedberg thinks. The Cunard prize landed Beckett another job: Aldington commissioned *Proust* (1931) for Chatto & Windus.

[3] Frederick J. Hoffman, *Samuel Beckett: The Language of Self* (New York, 1964), p. 87.

Savage Humor

Vivian Mercier

Murphy. **By Samuel Beckett. Grove Press.**
Proust. **By Samuel Beckett. Grove Press.**
Evergreen Review. Vol. 1, No. 1. Grove Press

Since *Proust* was first published in 1931 and *Murphy* in 1938, their American debut presages an outbreak of the critical disease popularly known as hindsight. Reviewers will be looking for the seeds of *Godot, Molloy,* and *Malone Dies.* In the process, both books will be seriously misjudged. Now that we know what Beckett has become, nobody will believe that *Proust* can be that badly written; on the other hand, *Murphy* viewed through the spectacles of *Godot* will seem far less brilliantly original than it appeared to those of us who first read it almost twenty years ago. (I don't claim any credit for being onto Beckett so early; he was the first *avant-garde* writer my prep school had produced since Oscar Wilde, so I couldn't help hearing of him.)

Certainly there are passages in *Proust* which remind us of the later works, like the reference to "the perilous zones in the life of the individual . . . when for a moment the boredom of living is replaced by the suffering of being." But such passages usually occur when Beckett is paraphrasing Proust most faithfully, so faithfully that his essay has been used for review purposes by French majors. It is the manner—jargon-ridden, allusive, spawning mixed metaphors—rather than the matter which infuriates. Take the opening sentences: "The Proustian equation is never simple. The unknown, choosing its weapons from a hoard of values is also the unknowable. And the quality of its action falls under two signatures." The jumbled metaphors of "equation," "weapons," "values," "signatures" find their counterpart in the abstract nouns.

Murphy proves that Beckett learned quickly, for some of the most ridiculous snatches of dialogue in that ruthlessly funny novel sound like quotations from Proust or some similarly pretentious monograph. This is a philosophic rather than a satiric novel about the human condition, but it parodies human motivations in exactly the spirit of Wilde's *The Importance of Being Earnest*. Not once can we convict Murphy of stooping to realism, yet we recognize a number of authentic human predicaments reflected in its distorting mirror.

Everyone in the book needs Murphy, "a seedy solipsist," whereas he strives to need only himself. Intermittently he needs Celia, who tries to make a bourgeois of him, not realizing that she will thus abolish the Murphy she fell in love with. When not obsessed by Celia or studying astrology, Murphy likes to induce trance by rocking himself in a rocking chair; his body having thus been set at rest, he can "come alive in his mind." Celia finally pushes him into a job, at a private mental home, where he soon realizes that the schizophrenics have achieved permanently that which he can enjoy only intermittently—complete indifference to the external world.

His efforts to attain schizophrenia fail, but he burns to death while tied to his rocker in one of his trances. Celia and the others must rearrange their lives without him. The novel ends in a scene symbolic of all frustration: Celia, who is back at her old trade of prostitution, takes her grandfather kite flying in Kensington Gardens; when his kite breaks away and flies out of sight, he leaps from his wheelchair and staggers after it. Beckett refrains from telling us that Murphy is to Celia as the kite is to her grandfather, but his pitiless words somehow evoke the same pathos as broods over all his post-war French works—even *L'Innommable*, not yet translated, which takes place entirely within the sealed mind of a schizophrenic (I think!).

Aside from this chapter, *Murphy* radiates throughout that all embracing, subversive irreverence which characterizes so much Anglo-Irish writing—and a great deal of Gaelic literature as well. Here for instance, is the scattering of Murphy's ashes: "Some hours later Cooper took the packet of ash from his pocket, where earlier in the evening he had put it for greater security, and threw it angrily at a man who had given him great offence. It bounced, burst off the wall on to the floor, where at once it became the object of much dribbling, passing, trapping, shooting, punching, heading and even some recognition from the gentleman's code [Rugby Union football]. By closing time the body, mind and soul of Murphy were freely distributed over the floor of the saloon; and before another dayspring greyened the earth had been swept away with the sand, the beer, the butts, the glass, the matches, the spits, the vomit." The savage humor of this or any other scene never interrupts the measured cadences of the prose.

Three basic differences separate *Murphy* from the French trilogy of novels and from *Godot*; first, its style is mannered and polysyllabic, in contrast to the Céline-like colloquialism of Beckett's French; second, it lacks compassion; third, unlike the French novels, it is written in the third person, not the first, and avoids interior monologue. I myself am now falling into the sin of hindsight; let me say only that this was a remarkable novel in the year of Munich and that it's still a remarkable novel in the year after Budapest .

By coincidence, Jean-Paul Sartre's interview with *L'Express*, "After Budapest," appears next to "Dante and the Lobster," by Beckett, in the first issue of *Evergreen Review,* a new quarterly. This tale with a moral was to my mind the best story in Beckett's first collection, *More Pricks than Kicks* (1934), now even scarcer than the first edition of *Murphy*. *Evergreen Review* reprints most of the poems in *Echo's Bones* (1935). Beckett's free verse strikes me as fashionable (in a fashion already outmoded by 1935) but bad. The best poem, "Enueg I," is autobiographical and touching in a surprisingly naïve way. (Enueg, in case you've forgotten, is Provençal for *ennui*.) All the same, one might be slightly better occupied reading Baby Dodds' reminiscences of the riverboats or Henri Michaux's report on taking mescalin, both of which also appear in this issue of *Evergreen.*

From *Commonweal* 66, no.7 (17 May 1957): 188, 190.

CHAPTER 2

The Novel: *Murphy, Watt,* and The Trilogy

Fiction

Kate O'Brien

... *Murphy*, at least for this humble examiner, sweeps all before him. Rarely, indeed, have I been so entertained by a book, so tempted to superlatives and perhaps hyperboles of praise. It truly is magnificent and a treasure—if you like it. Quite useless to you, quite idiotic, if you don't. It is a sweeping, bold record of an adventure in the soul; it is erudite, allusive, brilliant, impudent and rude. Rabelais, Sterne and Joyce—the last above all—stir in its echoes, but Mr. Beckett, though moved again and again to a bright, clear lyricism—as for the kite-flying of Mr. Kelly in the park, or always for Celia, lovely, classic figure—is not like Joyce evocative of tragedy or of hell. He is a magnificently learned sceptic, a joker overloaded with the scholarship of great jokes. There are two ways for the man in the street to read him—the one, which has been mine at first reading, is to sweep along, acknowledging points lost by lack of reference in oneself, but seeing even in darkness the skirts of his tantalising innuendo, and taking the whole contentedly, as a great draught of brilliant, idiosyncratic commentary, a most witty, wild and individualistic refreshment. If he takes it so, with modesty and without a fuss, the sympathetic reader will be amply rewarded by the gusts of his own laughter, by the rich peace of his response to Murphy's flight from the macrocosm into the microcosm of himself and his own truth, and by the glorious fun of his world's pursuit of him—Neary, Wylie, Miss Counihan—never has there been a more amusing presentation in fiction than Miss Counihan—and the sweet, classic Celia. There is no plot, as novel-readers mean plot, but there is a glorious, wild story, and it is starred all over with a milky way of sceptic truths. And read once simply and sportingly as it flies, this book is then to be read again, very slowly, with as many pauses as may be to pursue the allusions and decorations which may have had to be guessed at in first flight. There is no more to be said. One can only hope—being eager for the gladdening, quickening and general toning up of readers' wits—that a very great number of people will have the luck and the wit to fall upon *Murphy* and digest it. For the right readers it is a book in a hundred thousand. My own great pleasure in it is not least in the certainty that I shall read it again and again before I die . . .

From *The Spectator* (25 March 1938): 546.

A Master Stylist

B. S. Johnson

Some explanation (but certainly no excuse) is needed for reviewing two novels written respectively twenty-five and twenty years ago: *Murphy* was published here in 1938, but only a few hundred copies were sold before the rest were destroyed during the blitz, and *Watt* has only been available here in a limited edition printed in France. The importance of the republication in paperback of Samuel Beckett's first two novels is that this should now make general the conviction of many of those who have already read all his novels that Beckett is the finest prose stylist and most original novelist now living, and that, interesting as his plays are, they are no more than dramatised footnotes to the novels.

Murphy is the most nearly conventional of Beckett's novels, and the best introduction to his work (like Joyce, he should be read in chronological order). It is set chiefly in London, where Murphy is part of a ring of lovers, each of whom loves someone who does not return the love: 'Love requited,' as one character observes, 'is a short circuit.' Murphy short-circuits to Celia, a prostitute whom he persuades to give up work in exchange for a promise that he will look for work. This he does very reluctantly, for his real desire is to live only in his mind (Murphy tries to act according to the philosophy of Geulincz, a follower of Descartes, who believed that the mind was quite separate from the body) and Celia all too tangibly reminds him of the existence of his body. Eventually he finds a job in a mental hospital where he lives alone in an attic and can transcend his body by sitting naked for hours strapped by scarves to a chair: only then can he come alive in his mind.

By no means a difficult or obscure novel, *Murphy* does demand close, attentive reading and occasional reference to a good dictionary (often this is comically rewarding, as when for example, the second element of *triorchous* is found to mean 'testicle'). It is one of the funniest novels ever written, and many of its sequences (the chess game against a mental patient who plays all his pieces but for two pawns out and back again without Murphy being able to do anything about it, the scene where Murphy consumes 1.83 cups of tea whilst paying for only one) are quite hilariously original.

The style of Beckett's first novel is excellent, but it is not original, not that spare, tense, lapidary use of language which is at once precise and definitive yet easily accommodates the fantastic and the grotesque. It was in *Watt* that this superb individual style was evolved, a purification of English diction comparable only with Eliot's similar service to poetry in the Twenties: and it is all the more remarkable in that it was achieved during the war when Beckett was in hiding from the Germans in the Vaucluse and had no library to which to refer.

Watt is the key work for a proper understanding and appreciation of all Beckett's later novels and plays: in some ways it is also his greatest. It has a narrative progression rather than a plot. Watt is on a journey to take up a post as a servant to Mr. Knott; he arrives, displaces his predecessor, serves his term, and is in turn displaced; the book ends with Watt again on a journey. Like Murphy, Watt tries to behave according to a philosophic system: this time one based on Wittgenstein. And, again like the first novel, *Watt* is very funny ('Larry will be forty years old next March, D.V.,' said the lady. 'That is the kind of thing Dee always Vees,' said Mr. Hackett), but there is also a bitterness in the humour which looks forward to the novel trilogy and to *Waiting for Godot* . . .

From *The Spectator* (13 December 1963): 800.

Nought into Zero

A. J. Leventhal

Molloy. **By Samuel Beckett. Paris: Les Editions de Minuit.**
Malone Meurt. **By Samuel Beckett. Paris: Les Editions de Minuit.**
L'Innommable. **By Samuel Beckett. Paris: Les Editions de Minuit.**
Watt. **By Samuel Beckett. Paris: Collection Merlin. London: Intereps Ltd.**

Mr. Beckett's first French novel, *Molloy*, appeared in 1951. *Murphy*, written in English, had already given us a foretaste of his individual powers of observation. "Any fool," he says in this novel, "can turn the blind eye, but who knows what the ostrich sees in the sand." In *Molloy*, and in the succeeding two novels completing a trilogy, Mr. Beckett peers bravely through the opaque windows of existence, guessing at the unknowable and, in a tentative language at once nervous and nice, strives to give utterance to the inexpressible.

The modern novel has no fixed form and in this French trilogy the author is unaware of a need to hold his reader by plot or narrative. What action there is, is interior. Words, words, and more words pour themselves out in a cascade of affirmation and denial in an effort to stay the fleeting thought, to capture winging silences. Again and again he challenges the value of his own verbal descriptions, impatiently impugning their accuracy, offering another verb, another noun, and finally dismissing them all as being as worthless as the thoughts whose messengers they are: "Plus la peine de faire le procès aux mots. Ils ne sont pas plus creux que ce qu'ils charrient."

WITHOUT HIS CRUTCHES

Molloy's purpose is to endeavour to reach his mother who is dying, but he is baulked by his own physical infirmity. He has carefully attached his crutches to the frame of the bicycle which is to carry him to his destination. His machine fails him, and he must perforce crawl on his belly, propelling himself by means of those very crutches which had been intended to maintain his human uprightness. He will get nowhere.

This stasis—"*cette inertie immortelle*"—is an outstanding feature of Mr. Beckett's work. Yet the febrile argumentation of his characters gives them an unexpected dynamic quality, bordering at times on delirium. In his second novel, Malone, lying on his death-bed, his brain battling almost victoriously with the encroaching paralysis of his body translates his terror to the reader when his one contact with the outer world—his stick on which he depends for what little movement is possible—falls from his bed. For a parallel one must go to Valéry's Monsieur Teste who has reached a state of "pure" cerebration the ideal hero of the mind. But Teste shrinks from physical pain, whilst Mr. Beckett's characters only reveal themselves in their agony. They are careless of suffering, of ignominious situations or of insults, turning more and more into the haven of their minds, finding their being as much in its solace as in its "*souillures*."

In *L'Innommable* there is a kind of reckoning. The narrator runs through all the characters he has created in his earlier works. It is a crazy balance-sheet of continuously changing values: now denying, now accepting the Malones, the Murphys, the Molloys, the Mahoods, and all the other facets of his own self.

"*Je est un autre,*" said Rimbaud. For Mr. Beckett there are many selves. They are miserable creatures living, barely living, alone in an indifferent world. One may sometimes see the stars as one lies in the muddy ditch, but "ditched" one is—irretrievably. Can one opt? Perhaps, but the choice is not worth the choosing.

Mr. Beckett's work is not for the many. His world is an uncertain one, full of negation, barren of hope. He is no opener of windows on glorious dawns. One of his characters is but a torso of a man with his head held firm in an iron collar. His function is to act as a kind of signboard for a restaurant, and his vision is limited to the establishment to which his frame draws attention. He knows nothing, he feels nothing. He does not know that there is anything to know. Feeling nothing, knowing nothing, he exists nevertheless. It is not just Unamuno's tragic sense of life, which the existentialists share, but a superhuman (often subhuman) tragic indifference to a state of quasi-existence.

MANNERS MAKYTH WATT

But the frequent miraculous flashes of insight are compensations in this strange world that Mr. Beckett has created. The garbage, the *pourriture* of his landscape, ceases to be a zone of malodorous decay, but becomes a component of the life around us and serves to prod the easy-going to look again, to think again about this world of ours which the atom-minded man in our concentration-camp age has made what it is.

In *Watt*, Mr. Beckett's first English publication since *Murphy*, we miss much of the profundity of the trilogy. The underlying philosophy is the same, but without its tragic urgency. The manner is too stylised. The validity of a statement is examined with too great thoroughness, and the comic device of literary permutations and combinations is sometimes overdone. This approach, however, does succeed in adding a welcome wry humour to the adventures of Watt, a more mobile character (by Mr. Beckett's standards), than his other creations. The piano-tuning episode is delightfully funny, as is the elaboration of the remark that "the members of a committee looked at one another,"

> But when five men look at one another, though in theory only twenty looks are necessary, every man looking four times, yet in practice this number is seldom sufficient, on account of the multitude of looks that go astray. For example, Mr. Fitzwein looked at Mr. Magershon on his right. But Mr. Magershon is not looking at Mr. Fitzwein, on his left, but at Mr. O'Meldon on his right....

In the right mood one can be vastly amused by the eight pages that follow, examining the looks and missed looks until it has been established that the committee has looked at itself in the shortest possible time with the minimum amount of looks. The reader weary of outworn plots and styles, canonised by habit, may find Mr. Beckett's originality and uninhibited humour a welcome change.

From *The Irish Times* (24 December 1953): 6.

Under the Jar
John Coleman

Molloy. Malone Dies. The Unnamable. By Samuel Beckett. (Calder)
One Thousand Souls. By Alexei Pisemsky. Translated by Ivy Litvinov. (Calder)
Stories and Satires. By Sholom Aleichem. Translated by Curt Leviant. (Yoseloff)
A Letter. By Julian Fane. (John Murray)

The "I" of Beckett's three French novels, now brought together for the first, calamitous time in English (*Molloy* in Patrick Bowles's translation, the others done by the author himself), is in each case a scaly old dotard, dribbling, lachrymose and crippled, sealed off from the world in an anonymous room, bed or jar. Molloy and Malone are supposed to be keeping some sort of journal: God knows how the 'hero' of *The Unnamable* communicates, since—in one of his several transformations—he appears to be without mouth or limbs. A grim progression is discernible. Molloy swung along on crutches, even managed a bicycle, and had a goal of sorts, his mother: 'that poor old uniparous whore.' Malone's monologue hovers around stories (the Saposcats, a Ionesco family; Macmann's immurement in an asylum) and an inventory of his possessions. The unreadable *Unnamable* breaks down to a jerky rush of clauses, the final abdication of speech. This breakdown is foreshadowed in *Molloy*:

> Not to want to say, not to know what you want to say, not to be able to say what you think you want to say, and never to stop saying, or hardly ever, that is the thing to keep in mind, even in the heat of composition.

It is certainly to be kept in mind in the heat of reading if one wants to follow the author's abortive 'development.' In the first book (really two books, Moran's assignment to find Molloy is the second), language has at least the function of cheering up, as the flat jokes did in *Godot*. By the last, language is reduced to no more than a noisy proof that some life lingers.

The extraordinary emotional poverty of Beckett's world, however, is made to yield its small, even eloquent compensations. There are two or three moments of dry, untainted comedy (though much of the vaunted humour depends on polysyllabic rhetoric coming to grief on short obscenities); there is the constant press of logic applied to supreme trivialities (how best to dispose sixteen pebbles among four pockets so that they may be sucked in turn); there is a recurrent, elusive poetry, oddly pre-Raphaelite in inspiration, nostalgic for caves and seashores. There are the scatological accounts of crone-and-cripple *amours* and the sinister interventions of unknown agents, punishing without passion or reason. These effects of pathos and broad farce, intermittent though they are, sustain a seesawing interest for a time. But the suggestion that something larger is being said about the human predicament—Godot was God, Molloy, Malone and all the M's are Man—won't hold water, any more than Beckett's incontinent heroes can. His people are senile, impotent, maimed, given to prurience, blasphemy and amnesia; as devalued as the 'little portable things in wood and stone' that they hoard; and he allows no indication that they were otherwise in youth. In retrospect, they fuse into a collective mask for something unpleasantly private, because shrill and deformed. The torment is relished....

From *The Spectator* 204 (8 April 1960): 516.

Samuel Beckett's World of Fiction

Charles I. Glicksberg

Samuel Beckett cannot be summed up by applying any of the conventional literary labels to his work. There can be no question, however, about the metaphysical atmosphere that pervades his fiction. It is one of unrelieved pessimism shot through with elements of sacrilegious irony. A tragic ironist, he confronts the meaninglessness of existence with a persistent refusal to take refuge in religious or mystical absolutes. Life is utterly without reason or justification. His unheroic heroes wander like lost souls in limbo, not knowing where they are going or who they are. All they are sure of is the ignominy of old age, the absurdity of existence, the coming of death.

The novelist makes no effort to provide a dynamic, logically continuous plot. Things happen but they might just as well not have happened or happened differently, and the outcome would be the same, so why bother with particularized details or naturalistically observed references to time and place, dress and physique and physiognomy. Beckett delights in questioning his own veracity of description, in qualifying his report, in dwelling curiously, as if searching for the exact truth, on a dimension or a symptom or a geographical location. All this is actually part of his narrative method, which is concerned primarily with the revelation of a man's plight on this doomed planet. He makes no pretense of telling a story.

Murphy, published in English in London as far back as 1938, lacks the radically disintegrated plot that is the distinguishing mark of Beckett's postwar novels, *Malone Dies, Molloy,* and *The Unnamable,* but its bold exploration of the chaos of the human mind foreshadows the direction which Beckett's later work would take. Throughout, the action is viewed through a comico-ironic perspective, but this perspective also gives off overtones of the tragic. Lacking the illusion of nobility, the protagonist mocks at the elevated gestures of sacrifice and asceticism just as he mocks at himself, his own limitations, the impossibility of fulfilling his desires in a terrestrial prison like the one in which he is trapped. Like practically all of Beckett's unheroic heroes, Murphy, a kind of lay philosopher, a pilgrim on a journey that has neither beginning nor end, knows not whither he is going. Indeed, he prefers the stasis of contemplation, the immobility of thought that makes possible the illusion of freedom and that enables him to escape from the senseless distractions of this world. Murphy is the absurd hero (four years before Camus introduced Meursault in *L'Étranger*) who is resolved not to participate in the sound and fury of a meaningless universe. Reduced to the anesthesia of indifference, he shuts himself up in a room, preferably a garret, all external stimuli excluded, tied hand and foot to a rocking chair.

An incorrigible non-conformist, he is not to be taken in by the cant of let us then be up and doing with a heart for any fate. He is in quest of something entirely different, something not to be reduced to the calculus of wages and profit, but is was hopeless to make the attempt to explain. He remained in his own dark, impervious to the call of employers and prudential people. What he yearned for all along was the "freedom of indifference, the indifference of freedom, the will dust in the dust of its object, the act a handful of sand let fall . . ." This is the power of blackness that informs Beckett's fiction from the very beginning of his career: the disenchantment with all human passions and projects except for the single longing to be swallowed up in the black of night, to sink into silence.

Because the world of activity pressed upon him so importunately, Murphy tried to disconnect his mind from sensation and recollection, to drown his state of consciousness. Beckett will pause in the course of the story to dwell on the ambiguity inherent in the use of an expression like "Murphy's mind." Not what it really was but what it felt like and pictured itself to be, for that the novel is fundamentally about. There is the universe of mind and there is the universe of things. Not that this represents any process of exclusion, for the mind

The Novel: *Murphy*, *Watt*, and The Trilogy

"excluded nothing that it did not itself contain." All of reality, virtual or actual, is present within the confines of the mind. Murphy is not, however, interested in drawing nice metaphysical distinctions. As he grew older he became convinced that "his mind was a closed system, subject to no principle of change but its own, self-sufficient and impermeable to the vicissitudes of the body." That is how Beckett analyzes the split personality of his protagonist, one part of him locked in the darkness of the mind. There is no way out. There never is for the Beckett hero. There is no hope in the Beckett cosmos, only the inarticulate cry of despair of the damned. Consciousness lights up a small portion of the scene of experience, the lips utter spasmodic sounds, but it is all a vain endeavor. Life is a madhouse, but the insane, indifferent to the contingencies of the world, were Murphy's kind of people.

For Murphy is in his way a mystic communing with the stars, though no stars shine in the Beckett firmament. His greatest need is to rise superior to the gross demands of the body, to come out in his mind. Murphy, like his begetter, knows that the nature of outer reality resists all efforts at perfect comprehension. We define reality according to our sensibility, but rarely do we truly come in contact with it. Murphy categorically rejects society's conception of what is sane and worthy of high reward. It is the social order that constitutes a vast, hierarchical bedlam. Murphy turns the dominant moral imperatives of his culture upside down and with ironically controlled fury explodes the sanctified norms of sanity and success. Chaos is cosmos, madness is divinest sense.

Beckett has much in common with the literary Existentialists in France, but without relying on any phenomenological or ontological system. Man creates his own world of meaning, composes his own dream of significance. The mind is its own heaven and hell. Murphy is at times able to achieve a condition of true alienation, and at last he achieves absolute freedom: his body is rendered quiet and he *is*. He leaves instructions that this body is to be cremated and the ashes flushed without ceremony down the water drain.

Beckett is not interested in the formal art of fiction but in presenting a vision of life stripped to its bare, degrading essentials. That is why he seizes upon "heroes" who bear such names as Malone, Moran, Watt, and Molloy (names that in the course of the narratives are transmuted into other names, fused with other identities; they are Everyman), characters who, aged, toothless, infirm, crippled, have reached journey's end and face the prospect of dying. There are many kinds of death, but all men fearfully put off the final act of dying. In *Molloy*, the thanatopsian motif is struck from the start. Molloy's mind is badly disoriented. He is somewhere but he knows not where. Though his mind fails to work, he somehow manages to keep on going, to postpone the hour of saying goodbye to this earth, and without regret. For always in the past, like Vladimir and Estragon in the play *Waiting for Godot* he had been troubled by the query: what is there to do? Always he had been haunted by fear of life, the threat of annihilation in a place of darkness.

He is confused about his past, his search, his existence, himself, and the painful problem of deciding what he can be sure of. Facts? Which facts? The fact remains that the whole ghastly business of living "looks like what it is, senseless, speechless, issueless misery." That is the oppression which holds him captive: he hardly knows whether he is still alive. Everything about him is shadowy, unreal, and memory plays strange tricks upon him. He is in the grip of fear. It is only after life's fitful fever is practically over that this battered wreck with his crutches and the foul smell begins to think, and what does he think about? The tranquillity of decomposition!

> It is in the tranquillity of decomposition that I remember the long confused emotion which was my life, and that I judge it, as it is said that God will judge me, and with no less impertinence. To decompose is to live too, I know, I know, don't torment me, but one sometimes forgets. And of that life too I shall perhaps tell you one day, the day I know when I thought I was merely existing and that passion without form or stations will have devoured me down to the rotting flesh itself and that when I know that I know nothing, am only crying out as I have always cried out, more or less piercingly, more or less openly. Let me cry out then, it's said to be good for you. Yes, let me cry out, this time, then another time perhaps, then perhaps a last time.

This suggests the underlying mood and tone of the novel. Molloy is seeking his mother, though it is not clear where she lives or if he really wants to find her or if she is still alive. He is launched on a series of adventures to the end of nowhere. Prayer is futile, faith is dead. There is no mental or verbal incantation by means of which existence can be constrained. Who knows the meaning of the whole of existence? Perhaps only when one is dead, and death is surely coming. Nothing can be affirmed with any degree of certainty. "Not to want to say, not to know what you want to say, and never to stop saying, or hardly ever, that is the thing to keep in mind, even in the heat of composition." That is the feeling communicated. What can man know? Only what shabby words disclose, and what does language matter? As soon as one speaks, one falsifies. What hope is there for the future? None. Frustration, muddle, defeat, ruin—this is the fate of hapless man, be he Molloy, Malone, Watt, or what have you.

Thus Beckett spins out a mysterious picaresque tale but he does not take it seriously. All that is important is the business of picturing the terror in which man lives, the anxiety which weighs him down, his fear of sickness, accident, wounds, death. For Molloy is practically dead, leading a kind of posthumous existence. "Watch wound up and buried by the watchmaker, before he died, whose ruined works will one day speak of God, to the worms." The novel is full of such inflected blasphemies—blasphemies that have lost their accent of anger, as if to revolt were as futile as to be resigned. One is left with a condition that goes beyond despair and reaches the *ne plus ultra* of indifference. That is the cruel burden under which man staggers on this earth devoid of mystery, unable to impose meaning on the phantasmagoria of existence.

Molloy is possibly Moran and Moran, in setting out to find Molloy, is perhaps seeking to find himself. These hopeless heroes without identity are engaged in a quest the meaning of which they utterly fail to comprehend. Only the end is certain: they will go down to darkness. If one abandons the effort to follow the lines of an unfolding plot and concentrates on what Beckett is actually doing, then his purpose becomes reasonably clear: he is writing a twentieth-century *Pilgrim's Progress* in a style that is characteristic of his nihilistic age. He makes no positive affirmations. All is equivocal, so that it is difficult to say what is going on or why. That is why *Molloy* as a whole is fluid and formless like a dream. Relativity of perception, combined with reflections that are unhinged, produces an effect that is uncanny, so that Nature itself seems uncanny, frightening. The process of character disintegration has reached its limit. Beckett's fictional people are lucidly mad. They lack all understanding. Their will is broken. Molloy (if it is Molloy) confesses that though he speaks of principles he knows there are none. His sense of values is gone. There are moments, in a field or garden, when Molloy forgets not only who he is but what he was. Like Roquentin in *Nausea*, he merges with the whole teeming world of nature, leaves and roots and stems, but such moments of mystical fusion do not happen often. Most of the time he is a prisoner within his own shell, overcome by the blank mystery of being. He nevertheless persists in asking questions, in thinking without stopping, so that he might come to believe that he was still alive.

These characters, victims of their own circular ratiocinations and introspections, reach a state when words are voided of meaning and all things—time, space, distance, matter—become vague, blurred, and waking is a kind of sleep and existence is like a dream. Nothing is certain and nothing is sacred. Molloy is at the end of his tether. He is tempted to cut his own wrist but the pain of the knife is too sharp and he gives up. He still searches for his own identity. Is he still alive?

> For to know nothing is nothing, not to want to know anything likewise, but to be beyond knowing anything, to know you are beyond knowing anything, that is when peace enters in, to the soul of the incurious seeker.

The dematerialization of reality can go no further. The quest is hopeless from the beginning, time is running out, the mystery of the *fons et origo* will never be settled in this crepuscular region, but anything is better, after all, than death, though perhaps it was even worse than life itself and, if so, why rush into it? So long as one clings to existence there is a heavy price to pay and one pays it, yet this cannot continue forever. For Molloy the journey will end in darkness. Why seek out his mother? Why not just as well kill himself? Even though he is growing steadily weaker, he is not attracted by the idea of suicide. One cannot give up the struggle or stop even for a moment to take breath and wait for the end to come.

The second part of *Molloy* relates to Jacques Moran, the name he is known by after receiving mysterious orders, and how he sets out with his son to search for Molloy. He does not know why he is undertaking this mission, but his boss, Youdi, a higher invisible power like Godot, must be obeyed. Moran is an agent, a member of a vast conspiratorial organization, though there are times when he suspects that the organization does not exist and that even the chief himself is an illusion. He never beholds the light. All sensations are deceptive. Perhaps he is Molloy. Who can say. In fact, there are three or four Molloys. Still under orders, Moran comes to the Molloy country. He receives a message from Youdi, part of which is that life is a thing of beauty and joy forever, but did Youdi mean human life? Moran is preoccupied with theological questions, all sacrilegiously confounded. One of these reads: "How much longer are we to hang about waiting for the antechrist [*sic*]?" And another: "What was God doing with himself before the creation?" And still another: "Might not the beatific vision become a source of boredom, in the long run?" Then comes this passage of satiric blasphemy:

> And I recited the pretty quietist Pater, Our Father who art no more in heaven than on earth or in hell, I neither want nor desire that thy name be hallowed, thou knowest best what suits thee.

This bare summary fails to do justice to the complexity of Beckett's fiction. He has broken away from the traditional form of the novel, the linear progression of time, the logically integrated body of plot, the persistence of character identity. In Beckett's work the sense of reality is subjectivized, reduced to an endless flow of interior monologue so that characters fall apart; imagination is stronger than "fact" the object perceived is as apparitional as the shadows projected on the screen of memory. The dynamic surge of action is brought to a halt. There is no coherent story—that is just it. The protagonist is caught in a timeless stasis so that he cannot make out whether he is really alive or already dead.

In *Malone Dies*, Beckett views life through a curtain of dismal rainfall and darkness. The slow iterative march of the prose suggests the appalling ennui of

The Novel: *Murphy, Watt,* and The Trilogy

life, a state of acedia that will never be cured by faith. Here is a "hero," a writer this time, shut up in a room, who is seeking to find himself; he keeps on writing, but the effort is too much for him; even the writing is a bore. What he writes about is the story of the degrading helplessness of the human animal before death overcomes him. *Malone Dies*, like Beckett's other work, reveals a mind that is steeped in skepticism, suspicious of the truth of any statement, bathed in a brooding atmosphere of futility.

Malone, now at the end of his life's journey, has wandered through the years without direction and without a goal; his life has been a dreary waiting for death. Everything is purposeless. Hence nothing can be known with certainty or affirmed with conviction. What difference will action make? With a slow cumulative emphasis that is in keeping with the monotonous pace of the narrative, the novel sets forth the recurrent theme of Beckett's fiction: the meaninglessness of human aspiration and the emptiness of life. Here, once more, is the imaginative embodiment, ironically distanced, of the myth of absurdity. Whether they stand still or keep running they know not whither, Beckett's characters invariably find themselves trapped. Malone is sick of himself, quits with life, waiting for death. All along he had looked forward to this climactic moment when in a flash he would be able to count up the score before darkness fell over creation, but there will be no transfiguring experience of illumination. With uncompromising pessimism Beckett pictures the collapse of all illusions, the unspeakable misery of the human condition, the darkness that settles over the spirit of man as he approaches his end. As Beckett dwells on the fate of Malone, he makes us feel the silence in the heart of the dark, "that silence which, like the dark, would one day triumph too. And then all would be still and dark and all things at rest for ever at last."

What we witness in the case of Malone is the utter extinction of personality, the annihilation of self, born of the awareness of the bankruptcy of reason and the ridiculous blindness of knowledge. This is nihilism that is defeatist rather than defiant in temper, without Promethean overtones. It can hurl questions at the sphinx of existence but it is without the energy to revolt. The romantic lie of love, the competition for food, the fight against injustice, life itself—it is all a wretched mistake. As he looks back upon the past, Malone recalls the stench of harassed mobs "scurrying from cradle to grave to get to the right place at the right time." What on earth for? Sustained by the folly of ambition, craving warmth and food and security, these creatures imagine that their life will go on in this way till the end of time. Then they suddenly find themselves lost and begin to wonder if they had not died "without knowing and gone to hell and been born again into an even worse place than before." Bowed down by the knowledge of their alienation on earth, they realize there is no help for them, and yet they must keep on moving in order not to give in to death. Life is a torment; there is no original sin; the suffering men endure is an atonement for some nameless "sin" of being thrust out of the womb into existence, and there is no end to atonement since there is no end to suffering. There is only life and life is suffering.

This is the singular predicament of the Beckett hero, lost in a place he does not recognize, never knowing for what purpose he has been brought on earth, searching futilely for light in the encircling gloom but surrounded by darkness on all sides. The day will never dawn. And yet such is the perversity of man that McMann, one of the incarnations of Malone, would never get enough of life, not if he survived till the end of time, so long as "he could grovel and wallow in his mortality." That is the pitiful destiny of man. Nothing can redeem him. The hour of death will strike, but then it will be too late. Why strive? Why write? Why be so excessively greedy for life? Nothing lasts. Malone is going to die. He has enough. Enough! Under the cover of night he will find a breach in the wall and his death-wish will be granted, the Nirvana of oblivion.

The Beckett hero is unreconciled even if he is done for; he will not, let the nameless powers do what they will, abase himself in the dust like Job and confess his utter impotence. He is nothing but he knows he is nothing, and there is the difference. It is so easy to fool himself, to take drugs, to resort to the pain-killer which plays such a prominent role in alleviating the distresses of the doomed hero in Beckett's doomed and demented world, but no drug can long anesthetize the upsurge of revolt. Life is a pain that will not end. The crazed sickness of being will endlessly perpetuate itself, and if that is the case then nothing is left to man but to assert his prerogative of defiant inquiry, testing all things, searching out the truth than can never be grasped but even that much is truth of a kind, and always, whatever happens, in all seasons of the year, to keep on going, for there is nothing else to be done.

In *The Unnamable*, as in *Molloy* and *Malone Dies*, Beckett not only demonstrates the impossibility of the quest for identity, the spectral confusion of time and place, and the equivocal nature of every utterance; he also demolishes the traditional structure of the novel. If we agree with E. M. Forster that the fundamental characteristic of the novel is story-telling, then Beckett is no novelist. The only action Beckett describes is that of the disoriented mind of the nameless hero imprisoned in the cage of consciousness, cut off from reality as he struggles, but always unavailingly, to get in touch with it. Since there is no destination, the journey is again without purpose, and no light of meaning ever dawns on the horizon. "Going nowhere, coming from nowhere, Malone passes." But it is not Malone; it might just as well be Molloy or Moran or Mahood or Worms (another name the narrator baptizes himself or his alter ego with).

In such a topsy-turvy world of illusion, it is altogether difficult for the central character to get his bearings, difficult to know where to begin, how to go on. There is the doubt lurking in back of the doubt, the question hiding behind the question. Why desire to know—what? Nothing is certain, and even

The Novel: *Murphy*, *Watt*, and The Trilogy

that conclusion is debatable. All is in flux. "All is possible, or almost." Everything has to be confirmed by sensory tests, and even these create doubt as to their validity, so that the questioning persists without cessation, providing a bewildering host of quandaries. Here is relativism carried to dizzy extremes, so that the same event—a sound, a light, a movement—is viewed from contrasting angles of vision, each one of which is perhaps appropriate and yet wrong too. Communication under such baffling circumstances is hardly possible.

The Unnamable is therefore not a novel in the formal sense but a lament, a metaphysical seizure, a delirious monologue that probes the mystery (never to be solved) of the self and the other mystery (also never to be solved) of existence. In this dialectical flow of introspection that runs on, without benefit of paragraph divisions, from the beginning (a series of three questions) to the end that is no ending but a summing up of the belief that all this agony of striving is without purpose and this seeking in a place that is nowhere and a time that repeats itself is meaningless—in this monologic flow there is no sustaining story element and no attempt at conventional character delineation. There is a theme: the quest on the part of the fictional narrator who is all men. He is a consciousness that cries aloud, a voice that speaks though it craves the ultimate of science.

Whatever references Beckett makes to an ongoing story are tongue-in-cheek concessions to the reader, an obeisance to a lapsed tradition, as if the author suddenly remembered that this is, after all, intended as fiction and that a scaffolding of plot must be erected, characters and places described, identifying details furnished, but it is all done in fun. What Beckett is primarily interested in revealing is the fitful play of consciousness, the voices sounding within and the voices without, the relationship between inner and outer. Beckett's fiction dramatizes the dialectic of thought in its frenzied but futile reaching out to grasp a reality that is elusive, unnamable, unknowable, so that the indurated dualism of language fails to capture its essence and the rules of syntax and the logic of the sentence must be violently disrupted. In the relativistic flux of Beckett's imaginative world there is no up or down, no Devil or God, neither day nor night, no yes or no. The dominant carrier of meaning is to be found in "perhaps," "who knows," "on the other hand, " "no matter," so that no assertion, even the negative, is privileged. Only the question mark contains a fleeting trace of validity, but how long can one continue questioning the sphinx?

The shadowy, maddening unreality is given a kind of sensuous form, a particularity that carries conviction, as if the nameless protagonist (of what values are names affixed to these spectral pilgrims on their journey that never gets anywhere?) were about to unravel the skein of being and untie the knot of contrariety. All Beckett's writings constitute one book that seeks to unriddle the myth of meaninglessness. *Waiting for Godot, Endgame, Murphy, Molloy, Malone Dies* are part of the same pattern. All of them suggest the nausea of nothingness that is Sartre's central theme, the absurdity of existence that Camus describes in *The Myth of Sisyphus*, and even the revolt that is presented in *The Plague*, for the search never ends in Beckett's nightmarish wasteland, but it goes on because no other choice is open. Dying is as senseless as the wearisome perpetuating of being.

The conflict in *The Unnamable* is rooted in the human condition and springs out of the overwhelming need that cannot be justified to speak out, to grope for light in a darkness that will never be lifted. The hero, nameless and beyond illusion, is entirely alone, uncertain what attitude to adopt toward the unreal world around him. Why is he there, to begin with? He is determined to avoid the spirit of system; he will plunge into the heart of the storm without relying on any previous beliefs. The chief difficulty lies in beginning the story; it would be better not to go on, but he must go on, even though he is physically infirm, incapable of moving. Only his mind is active, urged to say something, but what? He remembers Malone, who is perhaps Molloy, but all this is supposititious. He is inclined to believe that all his former incarnations are present in this place where he is immured in darkness, at least from Murphy on. It is only a hypothesis, of course, to be examined curiously from all sides. The place is earth, not to be more precisely defined, where all men are imprisoned without trial and without reason, until the end of time, and even then the dream of existence will stupidly repeat its cycle.

The already familiar Beckett hero, mutilated, caught in a situation that does not change, is unable to fathom the meaning of all that has happened to him. He knows nothing about himself, nothing is clear, but the discourse must go on. Silence, however blessed, is impossible, and yet speech is but a means of dispelling the curse of silence in the void. This everlasting preoccupation with enigmas—that, too, must be challenged. But even if its only purpose is to stimulate the lagging discourse, the metaphysical hero cannot stop. He does not know the reason for his madness. He can never know. Each question generates further questions. Nothing is certain, neither time nor distance, neither center nor circumference, neither meaning nor place. Is it his mind that is playing such tricks? All he can see is what is immediately before him, and even that may be an illusion. So that he is lost in the dark, confused in his perceptions and thoughts, haunted by a past that is treacherously distorted in the limbo of memory. He is nevertheless hurried along, unable to stop. Perhaps it is better so. "The search for the means to put an end to things, an end to speech, is what enables the discourse to continue." This is the recurrent motif: the purpose of the discourse is to reach the end of silence.

Thus what we get in place of the traditional structure of the novel is an explosion of consciousness that, lost and inarticulate as it is, is nevertheless in pursuit of a self, in search of a meaning, a consciousness which engages in a monologue that craves to be transformed into a dialogue. Once this is understood, the technique Beckett employs in *The Unnamable*—the surprising

The Novel: *Murphy, Watt,* and The Trilogy

flow of associations, the distrust of the senses, the emphasis on symptoms of senility, disease, and decay, the annihilation of self—can be followed. The world of reality is not to be apprehended by the consciousness that spills over, swells and subsides and is again renewed, in this interminable monologue. The favorite occupation of the crippled, immobilized Beckett hero is to write, but how, if all is uncertain, shall he utter what cannot be uttered. That is the besetting problem: what is there to say? "If I could speak and yet say nothing, really nothing? Then I might escape being gnawed to death as by an old satiated rat. . . ." That is the pain which will not cease, the metaphysical anguish which cannot be relieved. The hero cannot extinguish the light of consciousness. The debate of the self that goes on all the time is sustained by only one hope: of some day reaching the Ultima Thule of silence.

That is the impossible task Beckett undertakes in the trilogy, *Molloy, Malone Dies,* and *The Unnamable*: how to reflect the meaninglessness of the modern world, the aloneness and alienation of man, the mystery of being that eludes cognition and verbal formulation, the ineffability of silence? He does so, in part, by showing, like Proust, that true memory is involuntary, inattentive, the expression of the essential self, that the world disclosed in revery or sleep, unlike the images recollected in the light of the intellect, is like a surrealist dream, explosive, unpredictable, a kind of mystic trance, so that perception takes on a poetic, numinous quality. As Beckett declares in his illuminating study, *Proust,* published in 1931, "We cannot know and we cannot be known." Art is necessary as the means of lifting the intolerable weight of time and exorcising the malign threat of death. He is impressed by Proust's anti-intellectualism, his revolt against the law of causality, his impressionism, by which he means "his non-logical statement of phenomena in the order and exactitude of their perception, before they have been distorted into intelligibility into a chain of cause and effect." But Beckett goes far beyond Proust in relying on "free associations" as well as memory to reveal a disorder of the mind in all its shifting moods of doubt, negation, and revolt. For consciousness is bedeviled by legions of faceless strangers, the anonymous "others," who seek to impose their values and their will. As he realizes the hopelessness of his situation, all the hapless Beckett hero wants is to fall at last into silence. "I have nothing to do, that is to say, nothing in particular. I have to speak, whatever that means. Having nothing to say, no words but the words of others, I have to speak."

In a novel like *The Unnamable,* which is stripped of a plot, there can be no thematic progression, only the varied reiteration of "the madness of having to speak and not being able to." That sums up the nature of the hero's desperate but ineffectual struggle to achieve fullness of identity. He will say what he is so as not to have been born for nothing. He is not "they"—not Murphy or Watt or any of the other impersonations, but the confusion of identities still plagues him. He will proclaim who he is, though he still cannot make out where he is or why he takes the trouble to get through this wretched business of dying, especially when his hope of resting in silence, "in the unthinkable unspeakable," is frustrated. He cannot fathom the unutterable mystery of the I. "Who might that be?" Having ceased to believe, he prays for nothing, but the madness does not abate, "the mad wish to know." Nothing is to be taken seriously, least of all the sound of big words. Better to face the truth that language betrays the writer. "At no moment do I know what I'm talking about, nor of whom, nor of where, nor how, nor why." The silence will eventually settle on everything, but before that happens one must cry out until he has no further strength for crying. He must unburden himself of all the hallowed, delusive words, God, Heaven, immortality, salvation, hope, "the terror-stricken babble of the condemned to silence." Yet the Beckett hero must go on as he has been doing and use words. *The Unnamable* ends on the same note of schizophrenic indecision with which it opened: "I don't know, I'll never know, in the silence you don't know, you must go on, I can't go on, I can't go on, I'll go on."

Beckett's fiction draws the portrait of the modern nihilistic hero, alienated, solipsistically inarticulate, drowned in existential confusion and despair, full of fear and trembling but without faith, entirely lost. In a series of novels and plays meant to usher in the countermovement of what has been called "aliterature" in France, in a creative flowering designed to overcome the necessity for ordered speech and the endeavor of art, Beckett celebrates the metaphysical virtue of silence, the absolute of nothingness which will ultimately swallow all human passions. He has no message of hope, he voices no humanistic evangel, except to reiterate the same forlorn theme that one must go on, even though there is no reason for doing so. His plays and novels represent a consistent effort to embody an aesthetic based on a foundation of meaninglessness.

From *The Arizona Quarterly* 18, no. 1 (Spring 1962): 32-47.

Samuel Beckett and the Death of the God-Narrator

Brian Wicker

A good deal of comedy in the twentieth century has been of that anarchic kind which delights to picture the world as—to use Eliot's memorable phrase—a "heap of broken images." Not surprisingly, such comedy tends to be of the black variety. Yet for the most part comic writers in the twenties and thirties at least preserved the sanity and balance of their narrators as counterpoints to the chaos of the world they saw running to destruction below them. Even when, as in the case of Evelyn Waugh, there is a scandalous refusal by the narrator to make any kind of moral judgments concerning that chaotic world, the narrator's own rationality and poise is not in question. Indeed, it is often reinforced precisely because of the contrast that emerges between the narrator's sanity and the madness of the tale he has to tell. In the case of Beckett, however, we find a new phase emerging. As we study the course of his development as a writer we are privileged to see what happens when the sanity and poise not only of the fictional world but of the narrator himself is lost. As we move from the world of Belacqua and Murphy to the world of Malone and the Unnamable, and beyond him to the world of the Lost Ones we see the rational narrator himself falling over the abyss and into the incertitude of an unfathomable void, shouting stories to "calm" himself during his eternal fall.

In Beckett's first major work, *Murphy*, a "rational" comedy of very learned wit,[1] the rationalism that is mocked is that of Cartesianism taken to its "logical" conclusion in the arbitrary occasionalism of Geulincx. Geulincx is obviously the kind of thinker whose rationalism leads to absurdity. He is a natural butt for learned wit. But for Beckett there is more to the Cartesian heritage than Geulincx. There is also Pascal. And for Pascal, the Cartesian philosophy is not only the apotheosis of reason, it is also the apotheosis of a tragic humanism. Pascal exposes, as no one else can, the depth and the terror of the vortices that lurk beneath the feet of any profound Cartesian thinker. Reason, for Pascal, leads to insoluble problems because, in its Cartesian form, it establishes radical discontinuities and metaphysical gulfs that cannot be bridged: between mind and body, man and the external world, cause and effect. In each case, rational analysis leads to intolerable deadlock. For Pascal the impasse is tragic because (he insists) we know in our hearts that the deadlock must be overcome. If the God of the Philosophers leads us to the brink of the abyss, the God of Religion offers us the faith to leap over it to the other side. If Beckett owes the comic element in his early work to a learned wit which is applied to the Geulincxian absurdities, he owes the tragic element in it to Pascal's uncompromising insights.

In *Murphy* the paradoxes generated by the unbridled rationalism of the Cartesian tradition—such as Murphy's inability to overcome his body's desire for Celia despite the supposedly "bodytight" nature of his mind, or his resort to astrology as the "logical" extension of Geulincx's philosophy of cosmic coincidences—are presented against the pull of a countervailing commonsense. The book does not contain sentiment, in Sterne's sense, or Joyce's feeling for the ordinary: but we do find the implicit critical authority of a narrator who is not identified with Murphy himself and who remains above and apart from the action. This narrator is constantly interposing himself between the reader and the characters, by giving us information to which the characters do not have access. For example, in Chapter Six he tells us things objectively and authoritatively about the nature and content of Murphy's mind which could not be given in any other way. He also provides us with details of Murphy's earliest moments to which Murphy himself has no access.[2] In this way the implicit omniscient narrator sets up a standard by which we can judge the unbridled rationalism of the character for what it is. He represents a reassuring standard of sanity against which we can evaluate the absurd thoughts and behavior of the characters. The fact that their irrational rationalism *can* be controlled, and put to aesthetically effective ends, is itself an insurance against apparent anarchy. The narrator's very stance of reticent intervention, standing back and letting the lunacy of the action proceed for the most part unimpeded according to its own remorseless logic, is itself a sign of his (and hence of our) confidence that things will not be allowed to get completely out of hand.

Although the next novel, *Watt*, too, is organized for us by an implicit omniscient narrator who has authoritative information for the reader, what he tells us is a good deal less reliable and reassuring than in *Murphy*. If Murphy is still recognizably a citizen of the world, Watt is certainly an outcast. Thus the things that Murphy loathed about life were limited and, in a sense, manageable: such as his own body, or the need to work. Watt's predicament is much bleaker and more total: "If there were two things that Watt loathed, one was the earth, the other was the sky."[3] Murphy has dealings with a large number of real, if crazy people; but Watt's dealings are with unrealities, with mere negations like Mr. Knott and his shadowy servants. Murphy keeps his balance on the tightrope of life—just. Watt, it might be said, is a man in the act of falling from the comic poise into the metaphysical abyss. If his chronicle is a comedy, it is comedy of a desperate kind. The rationalism it mocks is purer, but less substantial than that of *Murphy*. The mathematics of irrational numbers has replaced the mind-body problem as the submerged rock upon which the hero's quest for his own identity founders. Although the omniscient narrator begins his book with an engaging show of knowledge about the world we are to be led into and the characters we are invited to meet, the whole introduction leads us only into a cul-de-sac:

> Mr. Hackett turned the corner and saw, in the failing light, at some little distance, his seat. It seemed to be occupied. This seat, the

> property very likely of the municipality, or of the public, was of course not his, but he thought of it as his. This was Mr. Hackett's attitude towards things that pleased him . . .

— but this promising start to a story about Mr. Hackett peters out. Mr. Hackett and his acquaintances disappear after a few pages, never to return. Meanwhile the book proceeds, without regrets, in quite a different direction. The narrator attempts no explanation for this arbitrary change of course; not even the "absurd" kind of explanation that a comedian in the learned wit tradition might have been expected to give. Thus he establishes himself as a much less reassuring personality than the narrator of *Murphy*. In *Watt* the narrator cannot stop Arsene's "short statement" from turning into a tedious and erratic monologue of twenty-five uninterrupted pages. He cannot supply the information that is necessary to complete some of his own anecdotes. He occasionally says Knott when he means Watt and has to correct himself; and he contradicts himself in his own footnotes on matters of simple fact. Despite being Watt's "mouthpiece"[4] he is obviously not in control of his own narrative, and cannot supply that implicit standard of common-sense which, in *Murphy*, reassured the reader that the comic poise would, if only precariously, be maintained.

It is not surprising to find that after *Watt*, Beckett's fiction manages without the, by now dubious, benefit of an authoritative narrative voice altogether. From the three nouvelles, *The Expelled, The Calmative* and *The End*, through the *Trilogy (Molloy, Malone Dies, The Unnamable)* to the *Texts for Nothing* there is a steady development of the monologue form. The origins of the form are, perhaps, to be found in Arsene's "short statement" in *Watt,* but in the three nouvelles the Beckettian hero as "I" takes over completely. It is not until the appearance of *Waiting for Godot* that any kind of "dialogue," whether between characters or between character and narrator, reappears in Beckett's work. The significance of the monologue is, of course, that in it we are confronted by a one-dimensional narrative form. The elimination of the narrative voice means the apparent elimination of artistic organization. The speaking voice who addresses the reader from wherever he finds himself— perhaps from some place he has just been thrown out of, as in *The Expelled*, or from the prison of his bedroom as in *Malone Dies*—is simply recollecting his own past. In doing this, of course, he is putting it into narrative form: making up that primitive story which is the retracing of the past in memory.[5] But, to use E. M. Forster's distinction, his story can hardly be called a plot; it is no more than "the chopped-off length of the tape-worm of time." And plot, after all, is the novelist's business. The difference between story and plot is the difference between "the king died and then the queen died," and "the king died and then the queen died of grief." And this difference can be brought about only because the narrator has "access to self-communings and from that level he can descend even deeper and peer into the subconscious."[6] Beckett's monologues eliminate the possibility of this descent into the private life of a character—that life of which he is himself unaware, but to which the narrator has privileged access of a creator. (Forster says that a novel in which story replaces plot "ought to have been a play"): and it is no accident that Beckett's monologues, even in the prose narratives of the *Texts for Nothing* and the *Trilogy*, read very much like the monologues to be found in the plays. (As the late Frank McGowran's recordings show, they are best heard, rather than read.) The elimination of the vertical dimension of narrative—the dimension of depth which makes possible the descent into the character's subconscious—means also, as Forster sees, the elimination of that causal connectedness which is the essence of plot, the horizontal dimension of narrative art. The Beckett speaker cannot keep his mind on one thing for long. The logic of his "story" is not that of causality, but of mere association. Sometimes even the speaker's own name changes, inexplicably, from episode to episode.[7] But to say "inexplicably" is itself to misunderstand Beckett, for there is nothing to explain. Everything is on the surface, open to inspection in the words on the page: there is no subconscious because there is no dimension of depth. Beckett, like Robbe-Grillet, refuses to be a vulgar fictional speleologist, giving his readers the cheap thrill of exploring his characters in order to bring to light some dark disturbing secrets.[8]

One important consequence of displacing the narrator's voice is that the novels cease to be comedies in any recognizable sense of the term, though local patches of bitter and sardonic wit still remain. It is an important fact about the kind of comedy that the earlier Beckett novels represented, that there should be some implicit standard of rational control against which to assess the absurdity of the comic action. Beckett's early comedy involves a detached narrator who cooly manipulates things in favor of himself and his jokes, whose authority is assumed at the expense of any sympathy we might otherwise feel for his characters,[9] and whose total control of the material is in complete contrast with the lack of control of their destinies evident among the characters themselves. The apparently unbridled rationalism that we see within the action is, in fact, checked by the narrator's rein and whip. So naturally, when the narrator falls, the rationalist horse bolts. In the nouvelles and the trilogy, the Cartesian/Pascalian deadlock takes over completely, so that these works cease to be self-contained comedies of learned wit and turn into philosophical explorations of man's tragic predicament. All the metaphysical abysses that rationalism opened up yawn wide to swallow the "hero," and there is no comic poise to save them from being engulfed. The relation of body to mind, of consciousness to its objects, of cause to effect, of time to eternity are still pressingly problematic, still central to the hero's quest for identity, security, peace, heaven. But they are now not only insoluble: they are not even funny, except by accident. Instead of receiving a narrator's invitation to view the spectacle of a clown like Murphy "seeking the best of himself" the reader is

The Novel: *Murphy, Watt*, and The Trilogy 43

now drawn into the hero's own situation, identified with an archetypal figure whose predicament is essentially that of Pascal's everyman, lodged in "this little dungeon . . . I mean the universe."

> We are floating in a medium of vast extent, always drifting uncertainly, blown to and fro; whenever we think we have a fixed point to which we can cling and make fast, it shifts and leaves us behind; if we follow it, it eludes our grasp, slips away and flees eternally before us. Nothing stands still for us. This is our natural state and yet the state most contrary to our inclinations. We burn with a desire to find a firm footing, an ultimate lasting base on which to build a tower rising up to infinity, but our whole foundation cracks and the earth opens up into the depth of the abyss.[10]

Pascal's predicament is also the predicament of Molloy and Moran, Malone and the Unnamable, the "I" of the nouvelles and of the *Texts for Nothing*. The only difference between Pascal's man and Beckett's is that, for the one, there is just one source of hope—God: the God of Abraham, Isaac and Jacob—whereas for the other there is none. Very likely Beckett would agree with Mother Angelique de Sainte-Madeleine in drawing comfort from St. Augustine's saying: "He who is not satisfied with God alone as a witness of his actions is too ambitious."[11] Certainly his heroes are not too ambitious. Molloy's "ambition" is to suck all of his sixteen stones equally often in due order, MacCann's to be a good road-sweeper, Mahood's regularly to receive the "spiritual nourishment" of clear and simple things like the invariable gravy supplied by the restaurant outside which he sits in his jar. But even these petty ambitions are denied. God cannot deliver even these puny helps.

As I have said the progressive disappearance of the narrator in Beckett's fiction involves the progressive disappearance of the plot. In the end the Beckett hero is not a character in a story but a person, or rather a voice, whose existence is guaranteed only through the stories he tells himself. In *Molloy*, admittedly, there are still the bare elements of a recognizable landscape with figures. Molloy and Moran exist in a certain kind of fictional time; they have different names, they are distinct "characters" (though it is possible to argue that they are only aspects of a single schizoid personality[12]). But in *Malone Dies* the various names (Saposcat, Macmann, etc.) are patently the speaker's own inventions, mere persona for himself. Even "Malone" is only "what I am called now"[13] and has no absolute authority as a name giving permanent identity. Although Malone lives in a certain place—he is in bed, in a room, with his little heap of possessions—neither time nor place are clearly or consistently established. The temporal dimension of the book exists less in the events which occur to Malone than in the stories he invents in order to create a temporal dimension for himself. The stories exist to break up an endless time, without beginning or terminus, in which Malone seems to be caught. The collapse of plot into mere story inevitably means the collapse of the fictional "world" into a mere "heap of broken images." With *The Unnamable* these twin losses are more apparent than ever before in Beckett's work. Even Malone's story-telling resource, with its function of creating a kind of time-sequence in which Malone can try to live, has now collapsed. Not only is the narrative voice now totally anonymous, indeed is nothing but a function of the words it utters, but these words make no pretense at being stories. Malone at least began with a plan:

> While waiting, I shall tell myself stories, if I can . . . I think I shall be able to tell myself four stories, each one on a different theme. One about a man, another about a woman, a third about a thing and finally one about an animal, a bird probably.[14]

But the Unnamable has lost all sense of a time in which such a plan might be conceived, all sense of a self about which to speak:

> The fact would seem to be, if in my situation one may speak of facts, not only that I shall have to speak of things of which I cannot speak, but also, which is even more interesting, but also that I, which is if possible even more interesting, that I shall have to, I forget, no matter. And at the same time I am obliged to speak. I shall never be silent. Never.[15]

For the Unnamable, to speak is to exist. Words, any words, are defense against annihilation, and annihilation, even though it would be welcome, is alas impossible. For the Unnamable is already dead, and death has made no difference. Therefore he is compelled to speak, however nonsensically, forever:

> You must say words, as long as there are any, until they find me, until they say me, strange pain, strange sin, you must go on, perhaps it's done already, perhaps they have said me already, perhaps they have carried me to the threshold of my story, before the door that opens on my story, that would surprise me, if it opens, it will be I, it will be the silence, where I am, I don't know, I'll never know, in the silence you don't know, you must go on, I can't go on, I'll go on.[16]

In a more familiar kind of novel, the story constitutes its own time, its own world, which we recognize as a metaphor for the real world and real time. The implicit authorial voice creates a fictional time and space and places characters within it. But in Beckett's trilogy there is no such fictional structure, no world brought into being by the narrative creator. On the contrary, there is only a voice speaking to us from "this little dungeon . . . I mean the universe." And since this infinite vastness has to be filled somehow, given some kind of intelligible structure in order to accommodate the hero's unquenchable thirst for meaning, there is only one thing to be done in it: to tell stories, to turn reality itself into a fiction. Instead of the fictional world being an illuminating metaphor for a potentially intelligible reality, a mirror held up to nature, reality is now literally nothing until it has been made into something, given a content and a structure, by the fictions that those who live in it tell because, like *The Calmative*, they are too frightened to listen to themselves rotting:

> . . . waiting for the great red lapses of the heart, the tearing at the caecal walls, and for the slow killings to finish in [the] skull, the assaults on unshakeable pillars, the fornications with corpses.[17]

For Beckett reality in itself is nothing because it is, quite literally, a contradiction in terms. Just as a net may be described as a set of holes tied together with string, so Beckett's Universe is a set of contradictions tied together by the concepts of post-Cartesian reason, a "matrix of surds."[18] In such a world, there can be no comedy, let alone of learned wit; for there is no meaning except that which man can invent. Yet meaning is of its nature *maior entis quam ens*, more genitive than nominative: it depends on there being that of which it is the meaning. It entails a dialogue between mind and object, between man and the world he confronts. If there is no such world and no such dialogue, then even the invention of meaning through the telling of stories becomes impossible, itself a contradiction in terms. As Beckett put it in 1956,

> In the last book, *L'Innommable*, there's complete disintegration. No "I," no "have," no "being." No nominative, no accusative, no verb. There's no way to go on.[19]

However, by the time *The Unnamable* was written, *Waiting for Godot* was finished; and with it a way to go on was found. What the drama provided, unlike a story-teller's monologue, was a recognizable scenario, and above all an audience. The *Trilogy's* monologues hardly implied even a reader: they certainly make excessive demands upon any reader's attention. But the drama implies a dialogue of author and audience. The audience in effect constitutes just that element of common sense which is necessary to the comedy of unbridled rationalism. If there is no longer a presiding narrator whose presence ensures a standard of rational control, there is now, in Beckett's plays, an equivalent standard set by the bourgeois expectations of theatre-goers. Against them, the absurdities of comedy can once more be set up. Furthermore, the stage becomes a world apart, a place where "characters" live and move and have their being, in a special temporal and spatial dimension. The hero is not imprisoned in "this little dungeon . . . I mean the universe:" he is imprisoned, first of all, in a particular place, a particular time, a particular self. Of course, "A country road. A tree. Evening" is not exactly explicit as stage directions go. But a country road is not the universe, and "Next day. Same time. Same place," especially when we see four or five leaves on the tree, is not the same, but recognizably different.[20] Estragon is not Vladimir, Pozzo is not Lucky. The endless monotony of *Waiting for Godot*, or *Happy Days*, is achieved by playing upon the assumptions of the audience (solid, middle-class assumptions) that the stage is not the place where they, the audience, live (it is not the universe) but is a special, fictional world inhabited by fictional characters. That it can be so little differentiated, so little specified, apparently so universal is because, as a stage, it is already constituted as a place apart, the locus of a fictional time and space. And furthermore, the cycle of repeated performances counterpoints, and thus emphasizes the linear time of the play itself, its inexorable thrusting towards an unattainable extinction.[21] Because the drama depends upon the very strong sense of beginning and end which is engendered by the audience's coming for an evening's entertainment (a sense of beginning and end much stronger than that engendered by the intermittent picking up and leaving aside which is the normal experience of reading a substantial novel) it is all the more effective as a medium for expressing the monotony of an endless temporal extension. Because theatrical conventions tell so strongly in favor of a limited time and a limited place, the slightest gesture of affront to them will make a significant impact. Hence the four or five leaves on the tree in *Waiting for Godot*, the difference between buried up to the armpits and burial up to the neck in *Happy Days*. Thus by taking the bourgeois theatre audience into his confidence, Beckett once more made contact with a reality which was solid, not self-contradictory or tragic but simply there. In so doing he was able to create fictional times and spaces, a sense of "the now, the here" to use Joyce's words, and thus to erect a two-dimensional structure in which to place characters and create a primitive kind of world. His works for the theatre in the nineteen-fifties became once more illuminating metaphors instead of monological outpourings. And this partial recovery of the two-dimensional structure of narrative then spilled back again into the novel, in *How It Is* in which there is at least a material environment for the characters (albeit only a sea of mud) and even the beginnings of dialogue between torturer and victim. There is certainly a temporal progression from beginning, through middle to end (Before Pim, With Pim, After Pim) and even a rudimentary plot. With these goes a desire on the reader's part to find out what happens in the end. (That the end is also the beginning is, however, no surprise, not even a disappointment.) However minimally, all the ingredients of a novel are there, and each paragraph "has the density of . . . a chapter of *The Brothers Karamazov* quintessentially reduced to the dimensions of a telegram."[22]

However, if the solipsist monologue has been replaced by a kind of dialogue in *How It Is*, this does not imply any retreat by Beckett towards traditional narrative forms. On the contrary it simply heralds a new stage in his development: one which is carried further in the spate of short prose pieces which have followed *How It Is*. In *The Lost Ones* there is still a residual narrative voice that hovers over the events and which is distinguishable by its own doubts about the "notion" of the world it is describing. But the events themselves, and setting in which they take place ("Inside a flattened cylinder fifteen metres round and eighteen high," the "abode where lost bodies roam each searching for its lost one") clearly place this work in the same group as *Imagination Dead Imagine*, *Ping* and *Lessness*. In all these recent writings we find a consistently monotone world, hermetically sealed from any outside interference, and doomed eternally either to a round of predictable rhythmic changes that amount to changelessness *(Imagination Dead Imagine)* or to the total absence of change *(Ping, Lessness)*. These sealed worlds are clearly related to earlier elements in Beckett's work: for example to the set for *Endgame*, which suggests the inside of a skull[23] and—to go back almost to the beginning—to the interior of Murphy's mind, which turns out to be a description of a "large hollow sphere, hermetically sealed to the universe without."[24] (In *Lessness*, it is true, we seem to have just the opposite of a sealed world, but the result is just the same. A completely open space, Pascal's "medium of vast extent" which contains all there can possibly be, is necessarily self-enclosed.) This universe is perhaps a development of the earth and sky which were the two things that Watt hated more than anything else, as well as of the desert scenario of *Happy Days*. In these writings, the impossibility of overcoming the nothingness of the universe by telling stories seems to be finally accepted. Molloy/Malone/The Unnamable's whole strategy of telling stories to defeat the encroaching inertia of a world on the wane, a world that is passing through its endgame to an inevitable stalemate (or, what amounts to the same thing, a perpetual check that can never be consummated into checkmate) is here shown to be useless. Nothing, it seems, can hold up the movement of matter towards final uniformity and changelessness. Clausius's law of entropy, which predicts an ultimate undifferentiated sameness throughout space, without structural organization of any kind, is here given imaginative embodiment. We are left, in these latest works, and in *Lessness* above all, with a kind of frozen verbal sculpture, patterns of sound and imagery in which words have become simply objects in a vacuum, the mere nuts and bolts of communication. The two-dimensional structure of language itself is all but obliterated in a kaleidoscope of word-fragments endlessly juggled together. There can be no beginning, no middle or end in such a pattern; no progress of meaning from one statement to the next, no story, no narrator, no fictional world. In short, to quote Clov, in *Endgame*, "there is no more nature."

For many writers in the contemporary world, the announcement that there is no more Nature comes neither as a shock nor as a misfortune. It is rather an invigorating return to the objective truths of science: a science that has at long last freed itself from metaphysical overtones. But for Beckett the conclusion that there is no more Nature is far from reassuring. On the contrary it is terrifying. We are not surprised to find Hamm trying to extricate himself from Clov's bitter logic by any means available. Hamm wants to reassure himself by claiming that Nature has merely forgotten them—forgetting after all is an act possible only to something which is alive. Hamm adduces in evidence for his opinion, the fact that he and Clov are still in the process of losing their hair, their bloom, their ideals. As long as such changes go on, especially changes of so patently directional a kind, Nature must be still at work. But in that case, Clov returns with perfect logic, Nature has not forgotten them. So Hamm's attempted self-reassurance fails. Either Nature no longer exists, or it exists and continues to torture them. Only crooked thinking can suppose otherwise.

This pathetic little argument about Nature has profound resonances if we remember the meanings of Nature further elaborated in, for example, John Bayley's distinction between the literature of Nature and the literature of The Human Condition.[25] Bayley's thesis is that modern literature, with its tendency to "fabulation"[26] (i.e. to reject life in its untidy diversity as the primary subject of literature in favor of the tidy self-enclosed autonomy of the work of art) destroys the traditional idea of man as intimately related to the environing world which sustains him. In its place the modern age produces a literature of "the human condition," in which the individual is alienated and alone, cut off from Nature. In short, for the modern writer, "there is no more nature," only a universe of "things that are there and . . . are nothing but things, each one restricted to its own self."[27] Bayley sees this change as dehumanizing, and incipiently totalitarian because of its one-dimensionality, its superficiality—in the literal sense, its refusal to attend to anything but the surfaces of things. Beckett's latest writings are the most eloquent statement so far made of what would thus become of a world in which there was no more Nature, only the human condition. There are three principle features in Beckett's picture of this condition. First of all, everything that is of value lies in the past, as the endless reminiscing of Molloy, Malone, the Unnamable, and Krapp too, testify. In the present, old age, decay, immobility and disintegration prevail. But the "natural" immobility of old age is compounded in Beckett's view, by an immobility of apathy and helplessness. We can distinguish the immobility of Murphy in his rocking chair from that of Winnie, Hamm or the figures in the hermetically-sealed worlds of the later short prose works, by the fact that whereas Murphy sat still in his body voluntarily in order to come alive in his mind, the immobility of the later characters is involuntary. They are all crippled, imprisoned or even unconscious. Secondly, corresponding to the immobility of persons is the slowing down, almost to the point of stopping altogether, of time itself. The image of Zeno's little heap of millet dominates *Happy Days*, and the notion of a steady deterioration that will never come to an end because its processes can always get slower without actually stopping, not only dominates *Waiting for Godot* but *The Lost Ones* too. Finally *The Lost Ones* also exemplifies to an appalling degree the torture that ensues upon the loss of those human feelings which, under the conditions of Nature flourish in order to lubricate the perpetual motions of social life. True, *Murphy* registers the beginnings of this loss of feeling. (It may be a Tristram Shandyish book in many ways, but it lacks the comforting lubrication of Sterne's sentiment.) Admittedly Celia, the prostitute with a heart of gold, has a certain feminine attractiveness, and she looks after her uncle with some devotion. But her warmth, such as it is, is ineffectual and certainly cannot prevent the steady drift towards Murphy's ignominious demise, cremation and scattering. And no Celia-like figure returns to grace Beckett's pages again, except as one of Krapp's fond lost memories. For the rest of Beckett's work, there is virtually no warmth of human feeling anywhere to be found. It has all vanished with the bloom and the ideals which, as Hamm saw, once upon a time signified a loving Nature that cared for and solaced man in his little dungeon, the universe. In the place of such a Nature, we find the raw agony of bodily contact, the sheer "human condition" of *The Lost Ones*. The climate of the closed cylinder which is their world has an inestimably terrible effect upon the soul, leading as it does to anarchy, fury and violence. But the soul certainly suffers less than the skin "whose defensive system from sweat to goose-pimples is under constant stress." This stress "robs nudity of much of its charm as pink turns grey and transforms into a rustling of nettles the natural succulence of flesh against flesh."[28] Here sheer "things," sheer "surfaces" grind against each other without—to use Robbe-Grillet's words, though hardly in his sense—"false glamour, without transparency"—and with what a vengeance! The denatured world of things here pictured dissipates itself in *Lessness*, until it becomes nothing but "Lessness," that state of ultimate negation which Beckett evokes in memorable verbal variations on a simple theme:

> . . . all sides endlessness earth sky as one no sound no stir . . . ash grey all sides earth sky as one all sides endlessness . . . grey air timeless earth sky as one same grey as the ruins flatness endless . . . all sides endlessness earth sky as one no sound no stir . . .

Pace Snow, nobody can say of this humanist that he doesn't understand the second law of thermodynamics.

From *The Journal of Narrative Technique* 4, no. 1 (Jan. 1974): 62-74.

[1] All page references to Beckett's novels are to the editions by John Calder, London, including the one volume edition of the Trilogy (*Molloy, Malone Dies, The Unnamable*). Page references to the plays are to the editions by Faber and Faber, London.

[2] *Murphy*, Chapter 5, p. 52.

[3] *Watt*, p. 34.

[4] See *Watt*, pp. 5, 37-62, 99, 113, 100, 66.

[5] Cf. St. Augustine's reflections on memory in the *Confessions*, Books 10 and 11.

[6] E. M. Forster, *Aspects of the Novel*, Penguin Books Edition, p. 93.

[7] In *Malone Dies*, Malone is first called Saposcat (*Trilogy*, p. 187) even before he is called Malone. By p. 230 he has become McCann.

[8] See Robbe-Grillet, *Snapshots and Towards a New Novel* (London: Calder and Boyars): 56-57.

[9] See, for example, the description of Murphy after the upset of his rocking chair, p. 23.

[10] Pascal, *Pensées*, 199 (Lafuma, Editions du Seuil, 1962; Penguin Books Edition, p. 92.)

[11] Quoted in Lucien Goldmann, *The Hidden God*, London (Routeledge and Kegan Paul) epigraph to Part 1.

[12] See G. C. Barnard, *Samuel Beckett, A New Approach*, London (Dent), 1970, pp. 32ff.

[13] *Trilogy*, p. 221.

[14] *Trilogy*, pp. 180-81.

[15] *Trilogy*, p. 294.

[16] *Trilogy*, p. 418.

[17]*No's Knife*, p. 25.

[18]*Murphy*, p. 79.

[19]Quoted in John Fletcher, *The Novels of Samuel Beckett* (London: Chatto and Windus, 1964): 194.

[20]See *Waiting for Godot*, stage directions for Acts I and II.

[21]See Richard Coe, *Beckett*, Edinburgh and London (Oliver and Boyd), 1964, p. 92. The theme of a sought after extinction that can never be attained, a major theme in much of Beckett's works, often seems to echo the reasonings of medieval theologians in reconciling God's mercy and the eternity of hell. See, for example, Aquinas, *In Sent.* 4, Dist. 50, q. 2, art. 1; q.3; and Dist. 46, q. 1, art.3.

[22]Coe, p. 82.

[23]Barnard, p. 102.

[24]*Murphy*, Chapter 6, p. 76.

[25]John Bayley, *The Characters of Love*, London (Constable), 1960.

[26]I draw the term from Robert Scholes, *The Fabulators*, New York (Oxford University Press), 1967.

[27]Robbe-Grillet, p. 99.

[28]*The Lost Ones*, pp. 52-53.

Not Going Places

Enoch Brater

***Mercier and Camier.* By Samuel Beckett.**
With the publication of *Mercier and Camier* Beckett offers us a missing link in the chain of walk-talkers traveling *in duo* throughout his work, a "gallery of moribunds" who can hardly be said to be going places. For the Beckett enthusiast, Joyce's ideal reader suffering an ideal insomnia, the appearance of

this volume is like the discovery of some rich archeological find. Though critics have been busy excavating the original French manuscript for years now, it is refreshing to circumvent paraphrase by encountering the novel in Beckett's own strange English.

Beckett wrote *Mercier and Camier* in 1946: the date is important, for the novel directly prefigures *Waiting for Godot* and the trilogy *Molloy, Malone Dies* and *The Unnamable*. *Mercier and Camier* is ripe with "traces-blurs signs" of things to come: Gogo and Didi's delightful "little canters," the mathematical computations and time schedules of *Molloy*, the inventories, agendas and endless lists of *Malone Dies*, Zeno's millet grains in *Endgame*, the flowers, stargazing and mucous membrane of *Enough*, the "quincunxes" of *The Lost Ones*, the "arsy-versy" of *All That Fall* and *Imagination Dead Imagine*. But Beckett's self-imposed mythological framework rarely interferes with the spontaneity of each new work. Though his repertory presents us with links in a chain, each link, like the roadside chains Mercier sets dancing, has a rhythm and integrity of its own.

Mercier and Camier are on a journey, in the original manuscript version "autour du Pot dans les Bosquets du Bondy." In colloquial French the grove of Bondy is a den of thieves and *tourner autour du pot* is "to detour." Like the nameless narrator in *From an Abandoned Work*, Beckett's couple is not on its way anywhere, but simply on its way. The journey, not the arrival, matters, a work-in-process, not progress. As the voyage pushes forward in its vivid discontinuity, no incident of plot is elaborated and no psychological motivation is probed. The journey, in fact, is in words.

Beckett conceived this piece in French, his first novel in an adopted tongue. "Perhaps only the French language can give you the thing you want," observes Belacqua's friend Lucien in the unpublished "virgin chronicle" *A Dream of Fair to Middling Women*, "perhaps only the French can do it." Beckett told one interviewer that it was easier for him to write in French "sans style," another that he made the shift "pour faire remarquer moi." Beckett's attempt is to evoke those "words without wrinkles" of Breton's surrealist dreams. He disenfranchises the mechanical coupling of words and the deterministic linkage of image and idea ("solution clapped on problem like snuffer on a candle") by writing first in a French notebook, then translating back into his native tongue. The result, a prolonged exile in words, recaptures, as he said Joyce did, "all the inevitable clarity of old inarticulation" in a "savage economy of hieroglyphics."

Beckett is a biologist in words, "Grammar and style!," he wrote to his German friend Axel Kaun in 1937. "They appear to me to have become just as obsolete as a Beidermeier bathing suit or the imperturbability of a gentleman. A mask." There is a danger at any moment of rising up into rhetoric: "Speak it even and pride comes." Worn-out words, Yeats' "old kettles, old bottles, and a broken can, old iron, old bones, old rags," are a form of complacency. Beckett

The Novel: *Murphy, Watt,* and The Trilogy

therefore manipulates language the way T. S. Eliot said it was necessary to approach English: with animosity.

But Mercier and Camier are hardly the same inarticulate murmurers in the mud we encounter in those recent minimalist constructions Beckett calls "residua." Francis Xavier Camier, a Soul-of-Discretion detective like Jacques Moran, has a rendezvous with a Mr. Conaire, "hors d'oeuvre" in the French. Mercier is his Watson, prénom indeterminable, a delicate and hypersensitive soul unhappily married to the nonappearing Toffana, a very tough Anna Livia Plurabelle indeed. No matter how far the pair roams, they are never far from the fair Helen and her Kidder-minster carpet, on which murmurings of quite another sort take place on rainy mornings. We are in Ireland, and more particularly, in the area immediately surrounding Dublin with its canals. Saints Patrick and Teresa work in a barroom owned by Mr. Gast and managed by Mr. Gall, the latter making a return engagement from his role as piano-tuner in *Watt*. Detective and sidekick are invited to down a couple of pints with Watt, the hero who will drink only milk during his whatnot sojourn at Mr. Knott's house. Although Watt says he knew one of the two in the "moses basket," neither Mercier nor Camier remembers him. "I knew a poor man named Murphy," says the Proustian Mercier, "who had a look of you, only less battered, of course. But he died ten years ago, in rather mysterious circumstances. They never found his body, can you imagine." "I am not widely known, true," says Watt, "but I shall be, one day."

Mercier and Camier is a series of sudden encounters dictated by the laws of chance, that terrorist tactic preached as a Dada-surrealist esthetic. The pair meets by chance, a tossed umbrella determines the road they will take, and it is only by chance that they miss meeting one another at the end of a beautiful friendship. "Chance knows how to handle it," says Mercier, "Deep down I never counted but on her." Orchestrating the laws of chance, but never obeying the strictures of chance itself, is Beckett's narrator, the "I" we encounter on the first page who passes in and out of his characters' consciousness with alarming surrealist fluidity.

The sudden shifts effected by chance move us on from one vaudeville routine to the next. The summaries at the end of every two chapters, resembling the Addenda to *Watt* and the "Work Points and Consequential Data" in *The Alexandria Quartet,* name the music-hall skits we have previously experienced; lists of slapstick fare to preserve in the attic with our other playbills. Camier, "small and fat, red face, scant hair, four chins, protruding paunch, bandy legs, beady pig eyes," is Oliver Hardy; Mercier, "a big bony hunk . . . hardly able to stand, wicked expression," is Stan Laurel. Together their comic antics piece together the same "hardy laurel" we have previously met in *Watt.*

In *Mercier and Camier* familiar items from Beckett's iconography unexplainably disappear: parrot, umbrella, raincoat, pen, sack, bicycle, finally friendship. But in letting us have, after almost 30 years, the eight chapters of *Mercier and Camier* (12 in the 1970 French edition), Beckett has adapted through translation a manuscript he once described as "jettisoned." "I'll weaken some day," he said when earlier refusing to let the novel out on a literary journey of its own. *Mercier and Camier* finally gives us two more "high-class nuts to crack," in that great tradition of Pozzo and Lucky, Vladimir and Estragon, Hamm and Clov, Winnie and Willie, Moran and Molloy, Mouth and Auditor, and those sexual athletes Hairy Mac and Sucky Moll. Yet another stimulant enabling "the kitten to catch its tail," this recycled experiment in words presents us with a long-awaited novel in which Beckett's language falls once again on its feet, like a cat.

From *The New Republic* 172, no. 10 (8 March 1975): 25-26.

L'Innommable and the Hermeneutic Paradigm
Brian T. Fitch

Viewed within the context of the evolution of literary forms, Beckett's work may well be seen to present the spectacle of a literature in ruins. It is true that everything in the Beckettian landscape is subject to an unending process of decomposition whether it be the characters with their progressive and unrelenting physical deterioration, the story with its loss of direction and hence pointlessness, or the syntax of its language prone to an ever-increasing fragmentation producing the word-by-word crumbling away of the text at the end of *Malone meurt*. Even within the progression of the trilogy, for example, we can follow the gradual collapse of the novelistic enterprise as each succeeding text loses more and more of the attributes of recognizable fiction. However, as emerged from my study of the trilogy,[1] we must not lose sight of the fact that "progression" is here to be read as *regression*. Literature in ruins presupposes nonetheless the *existence* of literature for the remains of the latter testify to what *was* even if it is no more. Whereas Beckett's texts are not situated on the other side of literature so much as at that precise point before language becomes literature (*en deça* rather than *au-delà*). As Maurice Blanchot has put it so well: "Peut-être ne sommes-nous pas en présence d'un livre, mais peut-être s'agit-il de bien plus qu'un livre: de l'approche pure du mouvement d'où viennent tous les livres, de ce point originel où sans doute l'oeuvre se perd, qui toujours ruine l'oeuvre . . ."[2] It is the literary enterprise that is in ruins. Literature can be seen not to collapse but rather to fail to materialize.

The Novel: *Murphy, Watt,* and The Trilogy

I should like to begin by examining the ruinous beginning of *L'Innommable* before attempting to show how the movement of regression does not finally come to rest before putting in question the status of language itself.

L'Innommable begins with three questions: "Où maintenant? Quand maintenant? Qui maintenant?"[3] These questions correspond exactly to the reader's expectations as he embarks upon any novel: "Where am I heading, where am I to find myself as the fiction unfolds? At what point in time shall I be situated? Who am I going to be this time, what new characters shall I be called upon to identify with?" These questions all concern the fiction that awaits him as he settles down with his novel: that which remains to be invented by the novelist and brought to life by the reader. They delimit the threshold of fiction, the precise moment that *precedes* the tale that is expected. It is that moment when the actor is waiting for the curtain to rise as he prepares himself for the rôle he is to act out; and yet, curiously, here it is as though he were at the same time seated on the other side of the curtain passively awaiting, in pleasant anticipation, the spectacle that is to unfold before his eyes. "Sans me le demander. Dire je." ("Unquestioning. Say I.") In order for the play to begin, for the story to unfurl, I have to be prepared to let myself be transported into the world of the fiction, to suspend my normal sense of disbelief when confronted by events that clearly do not belong to the world in which I move and have my everyday being: "Dire je. Sans le penser." ("Say I. Unbelieving") I have to pretend or, as the French would say, "faire comme si ." "Appeler ça des questions, des hypothèses. Aller de l'avant appeler ça aller, appeler ça de l'avant." ("Questions, hypotheses, call them that. Keep going, going on, call that going, call that on.") That is the only way to start reading, that is by saying the words to myself as though they were my own. But to start with, I am in need of encouragement and so I must egg myself on in my reading: "Se peut-il qu'un jour, premier pas va [. . .]" ("Can it be that one day, off it goes on [. . .]") What was ostensibly the writer attempting to summon up his scriptorial energies becomes the reader's efforts to get into and persevere with his reading. "Cela a pu commencer ainsi. [. . .] Peu importe comment cela s'est produit. Cela, dire cela, sans savoir quoi." ("Perhaps that is how it began. [. . .] No matter how it happened. It, say it, not knowing what.") The "cela" appears to be referring to the fiction to come, but one cannot be sure and, in any case, any possible fiction or tale remains, for the present, an unknown quantity. And so the word ("cela"), like all the other words here at the threshold of the novel, has to be taken on trust as likely to signify something sooner or later and whether or not it will prove to become meaningful can only be discovered by dint of persevering in one's reading and saying "it not knowing what." "J'ai l'air de parler, ce n'est pas moi, de moi, ce n'est pas de moi." ("I mean to speak, it is not I, about me, it is not about me.") I seem to speak since I am uttering or rather mouthing these words if only to and for myself. But I am not ultimately responsible for them since they did not originate with me but preexisted my reading of them. And by saying "I", paradoxically I do not mean "me" for I am not, in fact, talking about myself at all but about some fictive *persona*. As Georges Poulet puts it, in his account of the experience of reading: "Whatever I think is a part of my mental world. And yet here I am thinking a thought which manifestly belongs to another mental world, which is being thought in me just as though I did not exist. [. . .] Whenever I read, I mentally pronounce an *I*, and yet the *I* which I pronounce is not myself."[4] "Comment faire, comment vais-je faire, que dois-je faire, dans la situation où je suis, comment procéder?" ("What am I to do, what shall I do, in my situation, how proceed?") However, how can one do such an unlikely thing as espousing the words of another? The difficulty involved in pursuing such an apparently barren discourse is the same for the reader as for the writer: "[. . .] comment procéder. Par pure aporie ou bien par affirmations et négations infirmées au fur et à mesure, ou tôt ou tard?" ("[. . .] how proceed? By aporia pure and simple? Or by affirmations and negations invalidated as uttered, or sooner or later?") The difficulty in proceeding lies, to begin with, in the gratuitousness of any fiction the nature or content of which is, in a sense, arbitrary. And at the same time the reader finally has some intimation of the likely status of the fiction that awaits him. Not only any affirmations but also any negations will, no sooner formulated, be ruled out of court or inoperative. The tantalising tale that appears to be taking so long to materialise in any shape or form remains a vague "something" on the horizon of the reader's expectations. And yet even within those vaguest of contours it will not, as we are told, bear scrutiny. And contrary to the later formulation of the same idea, "D'abord salir, ensuite nettoyer."[5] It is not that the *something* will give way to *nothing*, for even the latter will prove illusory. What then is left? If what awaits us is neither something nor nothing, it can only be *any*thing. Now *anything* is, as it were, open-ended, an empty slot analogous to that of the linguistic shifter (to which I shall return later), the personal pronoun "I." It is a potentiality. Out of *anything* can arise *something*. *En attendant Godot* has been described as a play in which "nothing happens twice"; this is a text where anything never becomes anything, or rather never becomes anything in particular, that is to say something.

It is precisely because the "something" that would be the substance or content of a fiction never materializes but rather constantly recedes out of reach over the text's immediate horizon that one may speak of this text's playing *with* and *on* that process of reader-expectation that accompanies the reading of any novel. To return again to the three opening questions: "Où maintenant? Quand maintenant? Qui maintenant?"—just as their interrogative status indicates a lack or absence, calling for some form of completion in the shape of an answer that can only come in the future, a potential actualisation that will only *subsequently*, if at all, be realised, the only possible situation to which they can refer is itself necessarily located at some future moment in time. Their status as pointers towards the future constitutes in itself the paradigm of expectation. The point I wish to stress here is that what we have is not an *example* of the kind of expectation aroused in the reader of any novel text, but rather the *model* of the process itself. In other words, the text thereby becomes self-reflexive, drawing attention to the way novelistic texts, that is *all* novelistic texts, are wont to work themselves out. It does not so much *stand for* all such literary texts but rather deconstructs and breaks down their functioning as texts through a process the Russian Formalists have called "dénudation du procédé."[6]

The concept of *parody* may well come to mind here to account for its status and in as much as parody implies intertextural activity, it would not be altogether misleading since this text does refer to other texts, both first and foremost and in the final analysis. However, it does not refer to any *particular* texts. It refers to all texts and no texts, and hence to the *model* of the novelistic text. If it can be said to parody something, that "something" is the whole corpus of literature corresponding to the genre of the novel.

Let me develop for a moment the concept of reader-expectation. Reader-expectation is bound up with that process of the forming of illusions that is implied in the expression "suspension of disbelief": As Wolfgang Iser puts it, comprehension of a literary text "is inseparable from the reader's expectations, and where we have expectations, there too we have one of the most potent weapons in the writer's armory-illusion."[7] Thus, "as we read, we oscillate to a greater or lesser degree between the building and breaking of illusion."[8] And it is this "oscillation" between the two that is painfully accentuated and accelerated time and again throughout the text of *L'Innommable* and thereby, as it were, placed under a magnifying glass.

It is important to realize that an analogous process operates both on the level of the macro-structure that is the whole text and on that of the micro-structure constituted by the sentences the latter is made up of. The larger movement is analyzed by Iser in the following terms:

> The text provokes certain expectations which in turn we project onto the text in such a way that we reduce the polysemantic possibilities to a single interpretation in keeping with the expectations aroused, thus extracting an individual, configurative meaning. The polysemantic nature of the text and the illusion-making of the reader are opposed factors. If the illusion were complete, the polysemantic nature would vanish; if the polysemantic nature were all-powerful, the illusion would be totally destroyed.[9]

In Iser's terms, the tendency manifested by Beckett's texts through the evolution of the trilogy is, of course, to shift from the "illusion" to the "polysemantic nature" of the text. Within *L'Innommable,* however, it is the struggle between the two and the impossibility of any resolution that provides the occasion for the text. And on this level, we have a parody of the novel form as a genre. The same movement on the level of the micro-structure of the individual sentences is accounted for by Iser with the help of Roman Ingarden:

> The semantic pointers of individual sentences always imply an expectation of some kind (. . .) As this structure is inherent in *all* intentional sentence correlates, it follows that their interplay will lead not so much to the fulfillment of expectations as to their continual modification. (. . .) Each new correlate, then, will answer expectations (either positively or negatively) and, at the same time, will arouse new expectations.[10]

This description enables us to understand how the self-reflective activity of the text also operates on both levels so that what is thematized and inscribed in the text (*mise en abyme,* as the French would say) is also the actual reading of novels and indeed, the activity of reading in general.

I should now like to take my argument one decisive stage further by moving beyond the hermeneutic paradigm of the reading-process to the linguistic paradigm of the acquisition of language. It is my contention that over and above the way one reads and relates to novels, what is really at stake here is the manner in which the individual relates to language, whether it be his own, in the act of writing, or that of another, in the act of reading.

It would be difficult to find a better illustration of Benveniste's analysis of the personal pronoun (in *Problèmes de linguistique générale*) than the opening pages of *L'Innommable*. However, 'illustration' is not the right term. For both the linguist and the novelist are dealing, each in his own fashion, with the same phenomenon: the way *in* which and *by* which we are, each one of us, able to relate to and use for our own purposes the linguistic system. For Gérard Durozoi, Beckett "rediscovers the teaching of linguistics"[11] as formulated by Benveniste: "It is in and through language that man constitutes himself as *subject*; because language alone establishes in reality, in *its* reality which is that of being, the concept of the ego [. . .] The *ego* is what says *ego*. Here we have the basis of subjectivity, which is determined by the linguistic status of the *person*.,"[12] while at the same time, as Durozoi puts it, "perverting" the latter, for "where the linguist notes the emergence of the subject and the person through language, the writer does not find reassurance so readily and raises a question: since language is no longer assured, the concept of subject is itself shaky." What, in fact, Benveniste is concerned with is that property which the personal pronoun possesses whereby "each locutor is enabled to *appropriate to himself* the whole language in designating himself as 'I'."[13] It is for this reason that when Durozoi claims that Beckett's work "occupies a unique place in the history of literature" since "to lay bare the movement that transforms language into literature is to place oneself, without a thought for chronology, at the source of any possible work,"[14] he does not perhaps go far enough.

In my view, *L'Innommable* lies not only at the source of all literature but also, even more fundamentally, at the source of all uses of language with which our notion of identity as subjects is, as Benveniste demonstrates, inextricably bound up.

Another critic, Claude Mauriac, defines "l'indicible essentiel" at the core of Beckett's work as being a kind of rediscovered native land "from which we have been distracted since earliest childhood by the system of thought that has been imposed upon us by language and its proper usage."[15] Language is necessarily the language of others since it was already in place, ready to be used, at the moment of our acquiring the faculty of speech. The voice of this other is, as we know, omnipresent in *L'Innommable*. Sometimes the voice is attributed to a certain Mahood and it is his voice "qui s'est souvent, toujours, mêlée à la mienne, au point quelquefois de la couvrir tout à fait,"[16] as the narrative voice puts it. It is as though, even as we are speaking, others are speaking through us: "Je dis ce qu'on me dit de dire, dans l'espoir qu'un jour on se lassera de me parler."[17] For through acquiring the power of speech, we have, as it were, become dispossessed of our own identity: "Ils m'ont gonflé de leurs voix, tel un ballon, j'ai beau me vider, c'est encore eux que j'entends."[18] We are cut off from ourselves by this language of others to the point that we can no longer find ourselves: "[. . .] sa voix continuait à témoigner pour lui, comme tissée dans la mienne, m'empêchant de dire qui j'étais, ce que j'étais [. . .]"[19] So that we are somehow left stranded, far removed from the words we utter: "[. . .] c'est moi qui hurle loin derrière ma dissertation."[20]

The problem of identity posed by the very status of the personal pronoun as shifter is commented upon time and again: "Ils disent ils, en parlant d'eux, c'est pour que je croie que c'est moi qui parle. Ou je dis ils, en parlant de je ne sais qui, c'est pour que je croie que ce n'est pas moi qui parle."[21] These particular parts of speech will bear constant and irrefutable witness to the fact that language will always be at one remove from its user, will never lose its autonomy. For personal pronouns are but empty slots to be shuffled around arbitrarily since they are interchangeable: "Puis assez de cette putain de première personne, c'en est trop à la fin, il ne s'agit pas d'elle [. . .] peu importe le pronom, pourvu qu'on n'en soit pas dupe."[22] Here there is no greater culprit than the first person: "Je ne dirai plus moi, je ne le dirai plus jamais, c'est trop bête. Je mettrai à la place, chaque fois que je l'entendrai, la troisième personne, si j'y pense."[23] Finally, let me quote the most explicit commentary of all on the alienating effect of all language: "Témoigner pour eux jusqu'à ce que j'en crève [. . .] Ne pouvant ouvrir la bouche sans les proclamer, à titre de congénère, voilà ce à quoi ils croient m'avoir réduit. M'avoir collé un langage dont ils s'imaginent que je ne pourrai jamais me servir sans m'avouer de leur tribu [. . .]"[24]

In order to reveal the link between the two parts of the present paper, suffice it to say that *L'Innommable* stands in relation to literature as the linguistic shifter stands in relation to the total linguistic system.

In conclusion, let me return to Blanchot who sees the writer's activity as producing, as it were, the ruin of his former self, of the self that preceded the act of writing: "[. . .] l'expérience qui l'a entraîné hors de soi, qui l'a dépossédé et dessaisi, qui l'a livré dehors, qui a fait de lui un être sans nom, [. . .] un être sans être, [. . .] le lieu vide où parle le désoeuvrement d'une parole vide et qui recouvre tant bien que mal un Je poreux et agonisant."[25] There can be no doubt that such a statement goes to the heart of Beckett's work as a writer. The core of the one single and unique text constituted by everything he has written is indeed an absence that marks the place of he who aspires to be writer/reader. It is in this sense that I evoked earlier the concept of *anything* to characterize the text of *L'Innommable*. This text is the realm of the possible, the possibility of actualisation, but nothing more . . . and nothing less. It can be neither passively contemplated as something nor simply ignored as nothing.

From *The Chicago Review* 33, no. 3 (Fall 1975): 100-106.

[1]*Dimensions, structures et textualité dans la trilogie romanesque de Beckett* (Paris: Lettres Modernes, 1977).

[2]"Où maintenant? Qui maintenant?" NNRF, Oct. 1953, p. 681. "Perhaps we are not in the presence of a book, but perhaps rather in the presence of more than a book: at the very threshold of the movement in which all books have their origin, at that point of the origin in which the book loses itself, which always undermines the work . . ." — Translated by BTF.

[3]*L'Innommable* (Paris: Editions de Minuit, 1953), p. 7. "Where now Who now? When now?" [*sic*], *The Unnamable*, p. 291. English versions of quotations from the trilogy are taken from the published translation (Samuel Beckett, *Three Novels: Molloy, Malone Dies, The Unnamable*. New York: Grove Press, 1965).

[4]"Phenomenology of Reading," *New Literary History*, vol. 1, no. 1 (Fall, 1969): 56.

[5]*L'Innommable*, p.25. "First dirty, then make clean."

[6]Cf. *Théorie de la littérature: textes des Formalistes russes réunis, présentés et traduits par Tzvetan Todorov* (Paris: Seuil, 1965), pp. 51, 217, 300-301.

[7]*The Implied Reader: Patterns of Communication in Prose Fiction from Bunyan to Beckett* (Baltimore and London: The John Hopkins University Press, 1974). p. 284.

[8]*Ibid.*, p. 288.

[9]*Ibid.*, p. 285.

[10]Wolfgang Iser, *The Act of Reading: A Theory of Aesthetic Response* (Baltimore and London: The Johns Hopkins University Press, 1978), p. 111.

[11]*Beckett* (Paris-Montréal: Bordas, 1972), p. 181.

[12]*Problèmes de linguistique générale*, 1 (Paris: Gallimard, 1966), pp. 259-60.

[13]*Ibid.*, p. 262.

[14]Beckett, p. 194.

[15]*L'Alittérature contemporaine* (Paris: Albin Michel, 1969), p. 102.

[16]*L'Innommable*, p. 44. "which has often, always, mingled with mine, and sometimes drowned it completely."—*The Unnamable*, p. 309.

[17]*Ibid.*, p. 119. "I say what I am told to say, in the hope that some day they will weary of talking at me." — p. 345.

[18]*Ibid.*, p. 78 "They've blown me up with their voices, like a balloon, and even as I collapse it's them I hear." — p. 325.

[19]*Ibid.*, p. 45. "[. . .] his voice continued to testify for me [*sic*], as though woven into mine, preventing me from saying who I was, what I was [. . .]"— p. 309.

[20]*Ibid.*, p. 55. "[. . .] it's myself I hear, howling behind my dissertation." — p. 314.

[21]*Ibid.*, p. 170. "They say they, speaking of them, to make me think it is I who am speaking. Or I say they speaking of God knows what, to make me think it is not I who am speaking." — p. 370.

²²*Ibid.*, p.114. "But enough of this cursed first person, it is really too red a herring [. . .] Bah, any old pronoun will do, provided one sees through it."— p. 343.

²³*Ibid.,* p. 139, "I shall not say I again, ever again, it's too farcical. I shall put in its place, whenever I hear it, the third person, if I think of it." — p. 355.

²⁴*Ibid.*, p. 76. "To testify to them until I die [. . .] Not to be able to open my mouth without proclaiming them, and our fellowship, that's what they imagine they'll have me reduced to. It's a poor trick that consists in running a set of words down your gullet on the principle that you can't bring them up without being branded as belonging to their breed."— p. 324.

²⁵"Où maintenant? Qui maintenant?" p. 681. "[. . .] the experience that has drawn him out of himself, that has dispossessed him and deprived him, that has offered him up to the outside, that has made of him a being with no name, [. . .] a being without being, [. . .] the empty place filled with the echo of idle, empty speech that masks as best it can a porous and agonising I." — Translated by BTF.

Naming the M/inotaur: Beckett's Trilogy and the Failure of Narrative*

Roch C. Smith

Speaking of the labyrinth in *La Terre et les rêveries du repos*, Gaston Bachelard reiterates his fundamental view that, in a dream, the roles of subject and object are inverted. For the dreamer, what appears to be objective reality never precedes the subjective state but is, instead, shaped by that state. According to Bachelard,

> . . . it is not because *the passage is narrow* that the dreamer is *compressed*—it is because the dreamer is *anguished* that he sees the road *get narrower* . . . Thus, in a dream, the labyrinth is neither seen nor foreseen, it is not presented as a perspective of roads. It must be lived to be seen. The contortions of the dreamer, his contorted movements within the material of the dream leave a *labyrinth in their wake* . . . Ariadne's thread is a thread of discourse. It belongs to th[*] e narrated dream. It is a thread of return.[1]

Modern Fiction Studies, © 1983, by Purdue Research Foundation, West Lafayette, Indiana 47907. Reprinted with permission.

The Novel: *Murphy*, *Watt*, and The Trilogy

More recently, J. Hillis Miller has offered a similar comparison of Ariadne's thread to what he calls "repetition" of the narrative line—that is, "anything which happens to the line to trouble or even to confound its straightforward linearity: returnings, knottings, recrossings, crinklings to and fro, suspensions, interruptions, fictionalizings."[2]   Also like Bachelard, Miller considers that the objective correlative to the subject's vision emerges only after the narrative thread of return has been completely woven. The beast (Bachelard's "object") is not the cause of the chase; rather, the chase (Bachelard's "subject") brings about the beast. "The chase has a beast in view. The end of the story is the retrospective revelation of the law of the whole. That law is an underlying 'truth' which ties all together in an inevitable sequence revealing a hitherto hidden figure in the carpet."[3]

Richard Macksey has seen the dissolution of character in Beckett's trilogy as an imprisonment of the self within a labyrinth.[4]   And certainly Miller's definition of narrative repetition seems made to order as a description of the trilogy with its labyrinthine twists, turns, and interruptions. Moreover, in accord with both Bachelard's and Miller's views, Beckett's novelistic labyrinth does not preexist the narration itself. It is not mimetic; rather, it appears as the result of the narrative process. It is the wake left by Molloy turning out his pages, Moran writing his report, Malone weaving his tales and taking inventory, and the unnamable narrator, whether "I," "he," or Worm, leaving a silky trail, a spider's web of narrative confusion.

Initially, of course, there are stories of physical wandering, particularly with Molloy, whom Ruby Cohn has called the "archetype of the fabulous voyager."[5]   And, as the trilogy's narrative is played out, motion that was thought to be linear turns out to be circular. Molloy is forced "to go in a circle, hoping in this way to go in a straight line;"[6] Moran carefully paces in a circle as he waits for his son to return from Hole with a bicycle; and Macmann, rolling upon the ground, discovers that he was advancing "along the arc of a gigantic circle."[7] In *The Unnamable* the narrator's physical wandering has ceased, but we find the narration itself emanating from a sphere—variously described as "an egg" and "a big talking ball"[8]—whose goal, as expressed through the narrator's surrogate, Mahood, is to go on "not always in a straight line" (*U*, p. 320), first a prisoner in a "circular" (*U*, p.323) building, then on the island he says he never left and where, he tells us, "I wind my endless ways" (*U*, p. 327).

Yet the perambulation is not only circular; it is increasingly cloistered as the rambler finds himself inside dark enclosed places as small as a "head" (*MD*, p. 221) or "my distant skull where once I wandered" (*U*, p. 303), till he can wander no more. He is caught in an inescapable web of words where

> to go on means going from here, means finding me, losing me, vanishing and beginning again, a stranger first, then little by little

the same as always, in another place, where I shall say I have always been, of which I shall know nothing, being incapable of seeing, moving, thinking, speaking, but of which little by little, in spite of these handicaps, I shall begin to know something, just enough for it to turn out to be the same place as always. (*U*, p. 302)

For the entire trilogy moves toward a gradual replacement of physical wandering, first with the narrator's fictional accounts of the wandering of others and finally with the purely verbal narrative wandering we find in *The Unnamable*, where to "go on" is to write, to produce more words. The narrator's increasingly frequent reminders that he is, and was, telling stories culminate, in *The Unnamable*, in a reduction of all fiction, including earlier tales of wandering, to the words that make it up. Bicycles, crutches, chamberpots, sticks, hats, and jars, even the characters themselves are, after all, but words: "I'm in words, made of words, others' words, what others, the place too, the air, the walls, the floor, the ceiling, all words" (*U*, p. 386). Words overcome the object they were seemingly meant to represent as the stories get tangled in their own verbal web.

Molloy's description of a small silver object made of two crosses joined by a bar serves as a particularly graphic example of this process. The description seems much more detailed than such an innocuous object deserves, especially because, despite all this attention, the object is never identified. Molloy indicates that:

the crosses [X's in the original French] of the little object I am referring to were perfect, that is to say composed each of two identical V's, one upper with its opening above, like all V's for that matter, and the other lower with its opening below, or more precisely of four rigorously identical V's the two I have just named and then two more, one on the right hand, the other on the left, having their openings on the right and left respectively. But perhaps it is out of place to speak here of right and left, of upper and lower. (*M*, p 63)

Molloy further describes this unnamed object as a "strange instrument" (*M*, p. 63) for which he says he felt "affection" and even "veneration" (*M*, p. 64). Moreover, he explains that he "could never understand what possible purpose it could serve" (*M*, p. 63), although he did not doubt "that it had a most specific function always to be hidden from me" (*M*, p. 64).

Because we know that Molloy took the object from Lousse's house along with coffee spoons and other silverware, we may well assume that it is nothing more than a kniferest. Such a conjecture is reinforced by the fact that the narrator in *Malone Dies* makes a specific reference to "a little silver kniferest" (*MD*, p. 258) as the only object of value found in Macmann's pockets. And we know how things have a tendency to reappear from story to story throughout

The Novel: *Murphy, Watt,* and The Trilogy

the trilogy. But if we return to Molloy's description, we note that, although it may leave us unsatisfied about the physical identity of the object, it leaves absolutely no doubt about its verbal properties. The object is made of connected letters—X's and V's—and is therefore a *word* at least as much as it is a kniferest. That explains why Molloy, as would any writer, feels affection and veneration for this precious object whose function is both precise and obscure.

The silver kniferest, then, is what Jean Ricardou has called a "structural metaphor"[9] in that it is both an object within the story and an image of the writer's own text. In *Malone Dies* the words themselves, like Macmann's kniferest, are all the narrator has of value. In *Molloy* the symmetrical object-word parallels the rough symmetry of the novel.[10] Its X's and V's like crossroads in the labyrinth offer no guidance as to the correct direction one should take. For in a narrative, Miller reminds us, "any single thread leads everywhere, like a labyrinth made of a single line or corridor crinkled to and fro."[11] Significantly, Miller gives as an example of this phenomenon "the letter X. . . . a letter, a sign, but a sign for signs generally . . ."[12] Thus the silver kniferest metaphorically summarizes the view implicit in the trilogy that language no longer is an instrument of representation but, as Olga Bernal has expressed it, "the very matter with which literature is at grips . . ."[13] Beckett's maze is a textual one beyond which there is literally "nothing," not even suffering, as the disembodied narrator of *The Unnamable* reminds us when he refers to this "Labyrinthine torment that can't be grasped, or limited, or felt, or suffered, no not even suffered" (*U*, p. 314). In attempting to "unravel his tangle" (*U*, p 315), the narrator must follow the maze of words he himself has woven.

Like Theseus, he seeks out the beast hidden somewhere in the loops and twists of this labyrinth. Yet, because the maze is verbal, the monster must be slayed with words; it must be *named* if it is to stop exacting its tribute of words from the hapless narrator. The names multiply to the point that there seem to be many such monsters, yet "there's no getting rid of them without naming them" (*U*, p. 326). This is the fundamental dilemma facing the narrator lost in an increasingly complicated labyrinth of unstoppable words. He can't go on adding more words and increasing the complexity of his narrative labyrinth, yet he must go on because the only way out is through words, or so it seems. So he follows his own exhortation to "weave, weave" (*U*, p. 339). Like a spider in the middle of his web he continues spinning in order to find the word that would end the succession of puppets—the Molloys, Molloses, Morans, Marthas, Macmanns, Molls, Mahoods, Matthews, Marguerites, Madeleines, their predecessors and variants, the Murphys, Watts, Merciers, Worms, and Lemuels, not to mention the mothers and Mags—who people the spirals of his prose with its most striking repetition, the letter M, the M/inotaur of his verbal labyrinth.

For it is part of the narrator's dilemma throughout the trilogy that he is at once the hunter and the hunted, the weaver of the labyrinth and the beast it encloses, Ariadne and Theseus, as well as the unnamable M/inotaur. Like Daedalus, he is caught in the coils of his own creation, a fate shared with many modern artists, as Richard Macksey points out.[14] But it is much worse for Beckett's narrator because, unlike his Athenean forebear, he cannot find a means of escape, and all attempts to do so entangle him further in his verbal prison. The enemy is within, so the narrator must be both executioner and victim. Thus Molloy searches for his mother and finds *himself*; Moran searches for Molloy and ends by uncannily resembling the object of his search to the point that Moran is "devoured" by Molloy, as Ruby Cohn so aptly observed.[15] Later Macmann slowly takes on the characteristics of Malone, including his paralysis and even his hat, whereas Malone, passing silently before the narrator of *The Unnamable*, might be taken for "Molloy wearing Malone's hat" (*U*, p. 293).

None of the trilogy's narrators is able to find an escape from this web of words. Theirs is a narrative doomed to failure. The M/inotaur, even when stripped of his fictional disguises, is forever out of reach, and silence, the only true escape from a labyrinth of words, is therefore impossible, as we see in the following passage from *The Unnamable*:

> But now, is it now, I on me? Sometimes I think it is. And then I realize it is not. I am doing my best, and failing again, yet again. I don't mind failing, it's a pleasure, but I want to go silent. (*U*, p. 310)

How widespread is this pleasurable failure? And what is its role in Beckett's trilogy? The narrator fails, of course, to create a fiction that will reveal the truth about his elusive beast and allow him to go silent. But already Moran, whose wanderings mirror the labyrinthine thread of narration, wonders, when his leg begins to slow him down, if he is not "secretly glad that this had happened to me, perhaps even to the point of not wanting to get well?" (*M*, p. 145). And Malone, painfully aware of the failure of his fiction to invent, to name the M/inotaur, rails at "How false all this is. No time now to explain. I began again, no longer in order to succeed, but in order to fail" (*MD*, p. 195). Finally, in *The Unnamable*, the narrator expresses his frustration at the paradox of writing: "What can it matter to me that I succeed or fail? The undertaking is none of mine, if they want me to succeed I'll fail, and vice versa, so as not to be rid of my tormentors" (*U*, p. 347). The point, one that is not fully realized until *The Unnamable*, is that fiction must fail as "storytelling" if it is to have any hope of succeeding as "naming." The narration of fiction, the weaving of a verbal tapestry, multiplies words and carries the narrator further away from the exit of his verbal labyrinth and from the silence he seeks. It is this realization

The Novel: *Murphy, Watt*, and The Trilogy

that is behind the gradual disappearance of storytelling as one moves from *Molloy* to *The Unnamable*.

But what replaces the narration of fiction? Here we do well to return to Jean Ricardou, whose theoretical reversal of these two terms—narration and fiction—matches Beckett's practice in the trilogy and provides a means of articulating our experience as readers of these works.[16] For Ricardou, a "new novel" such as Robbe-Grillet's *Project for a Revolution in New York* is marked by a fiction that "emanates from the narrative process and contributes in some way to describing it. Fiction is, most often, a fiction of narration."[17] In such works it is not a question of telling a story about the activities of revolutionaries in New York, for instance, but of telling the story of telling such a story, thereby revealing more about the narrative process than about the story itself. As Ricardou explains, "the novel ceases to be the writing of a story in order to become the story of a writing."[18] Such a novel is deliberately aware of its own workings; it is quite literally "self-conscious." This is particularly true of Beckett's novels where, as Dieter Wellershoff put it, "literature has reached a point at which it is looking over its own shoulders."[19]

The Unnamable is, of course, replete with the stops, twists, and convolutions of the self-conscious novel as the narrator hesitates between the stories of Mahood, Worm, "I," and "he." But pervasive as it is in the last novel of the trilogy, such expressed awareness of the conventions of writing fiction is already a part of earlier works, as *Molloy* makes clear:

> And every time I say, I said this, or I said that, or speak of a voice saying, far away inside of me, Molloy, and then a fine phrase more or less clear and simple, or find myself compelled to attribute to others intelligible words, or hear my own voice uttering to others more or less articulate sounds, I am merely complying with the convention that demands you either lie or hold your peace. (*M*, p.88)

The ubiquitous voice, which in *Molloy* and *Malone Dies* begins as an inner murmur or buzzing before turning out intelligible words and whose compulsive power energizes *The Unnamable*, is the voice of narration stripped of its usual fictional baffles by the fiction of narration.

Yet even thus exposed, the fiction of narration does not succeed. Beckett's narrator does not seek merely to bare the word; he seeks to stop it. His goal is not to create novel fictional forms but to still the voice of fiction in order to say "nothing." But, as the narrator of *The Unnamable* ruefully points out, "it seems impossible to speak and yet say nothing, you think you have succeeded, but you always overlook something, a little yes, a little no, enough to exterminate a regiment of dragoons" (*U*, p. 303). It is a task at which he must inevitably fail because it is literally not possible to "say nothing," to express what the narrator of *The Unnamable* calls "the unthinkable unspeakable" (*U* p. 335). As the narrator resignedly asks near the end of that novel, "how can I say it, that's all words, they're all I have and not many of them, the words fail, the voice fails, so be it" (*U*, p. 413). For, unlike the work of a new novelist like Robbe-Grillet, Beckett's is not merely a fiction of narration but a *fiction of failed narrative*. The trilogy reflects Beckett's view, expressed to Georges Duthuit, "that to be an artist is to fail, as no other dare fail, that failure is his world and the shrink from it desertion . . ."[20]

Yet, if the trilogy is the story of the narrator's growing awareness of the narrative dilemma, it is also the expression of a fundamental paradox because it is failure itself that makes possible the continuation of narrative, tenuous as that continuation may be. The narrative circularity of *Molloy* is only apparently closed; Malone's pencil lead grows perilously short, but it never runs out; and the "unthinkable unspeakable" may be unnamable, but the narrative thread goes on. The narrator of *The Unnamable* summarizes this paradox when he insists that "the search for a means to put an end to things, an end to speech, is what enables discourse to continue" (*U*, p. 299). Increasingly, the narrator weaves the story of the impossibility of expression, but he does not stop weaving. Whatever hope Beckett's trilogy offers would seem to be found in this unbroken narrative line whose tensile strength barely resists, yet does not break, despite the tugs and pulls of despair. A modern-day Scheherazade, Beckett keeps hope alive solely by telling stories of failed narrative whose nights in "Ballybaba" and "the fresh air of Turdybaba" (*M*, p. 134) ironically echo the traditional storytelling of the *Arabian Nights* and serve as reminders of the transformation of fiction into a labyrinthine quest for silence.

Beckett's narrator lives in what Bachelard, in another context, called a "logosphere" or "universe of the word,"[21] yet, like Derrida, the narrator is wary of a "logocentrism which is also a phonocentrism: an absolute proximity of voice and being . . ."[22] For Moran it seems that "all language was an excess of language" (*M*, p. 116), and Malone reluctantly resigns himself to the notion that his life is reduced to a "child's exercise book," (*MD*, p. 274), whereas the narrator of *The Unnamable* remarks that

> it has not yet been our good fortune to establish with any degree of accuracy what I am, where I am, whether I am words among words, or silence in the midst of silence, to recall only two of the hypotheses launched in the connexion, though silence to tell the truth does not appear to have been very conspicuous up to now, but appearances may sometimes be deceptive. (*U*, p. 389)

Thus compelled to utter words, for that is all he has, but uncertain about whether such words have an ontological significance, the narrator will go on. Yet because the ontological question remains unresolved, no fixed figure ever appears in the carpet. Despite it all, or, rather, because of it all, the difficult weaving continues in this fiction of failed narrative that can only exist in the tortuous and tenuous space between logos and silence.

From *Modern Fiction Studies* 29, no. 1 (Spring 1983): 73-80.

[1] Gaston Bachelard, *La Terre et les rêveries du repos* (Paris: Corti, 1948), p. 215. Unless otherwise noted, translations are mine.

[2] J. Hillis Miller, "Ariadne's Thread: Repetition and Narrative Line," *Critical Inquiry*, 3 (Autumn 1976), 68.

[3] Miller, p. 69.

[4] Richard Macksey, "The Artist in the Labyrinth: Design or *Dasein*," *Modern Language Notes*, 77 (May 1962), 248.

[5] Ruby Cohn, *Back to Beckett* (Princeton, NJ: Princeton University Press, 1973), p. 83.

[6] Samuel Beckett, *Molloy*, trans. Patrick Bowles, in *Three Novels by Samuel Beckett*, Evergreen Black Cat Edition (New York: Grove Press, 1965), p. 85. Hereafter cited as *M*.

[7] *Malone Dies*, trans. by the author, in *Three Novels by Samuel Beckett*, p. 246. Hereafter cited as *MD*.

[8] *The Unnamable*, trans. by the author, in *Three Novels by Samuel Beckett*, p. 305. Hereafter cited as *U*.

[9] Jean Ricardou, *Problèmes du nouveau roman* (Paris: Seuil, 1967), p. 136.

[10] Angela B. Moorjani, in "A Mythic Reading of Molloy," in *Samuel Beckett: the Art of Rhetoric*, ed. Edouard Morot-Sir, *et al.* (Chapel Hill: North Carolina Studies in the Romance Languages and Literatures, 1976), sees the kniferest as "a model of the complex ternary and dual configurations of the text" (p. 277).

[11] Miller, p. 74.

[12] Miller, p. 75.

[13] Olga Bernal, *Language et fiction dans le roman de Beckett* (Paris: Gallimard, 1969), p. 177.

[14]Macksey, p. 241.

[15]Cohn, p. 88.

[16]Brain T. Fitch, in the second part of his *Dimensions, structures et textualité dans la trilogie romanesque de Beckett* (Paris: Minard, 1977), makes a very effective use of Ricardou's concepts of narrative in approaching Beckett's trilogy. But, unlike the present analysis, Fitch undertakes a detailed examination of textuality that is deliberately limited to the French text and serves as a contrasting complement to the thematic and structural exploration developed in the first half of his monograph.

[17]Jean Ricardou, *Pour une théorie du nouveau roman* (Paris: Seuil, 1971), p. 219.

[18]Ricardou, *Problèmes*, p. 166.

[19]Dieter Wellershoff, "Failure of an Attempt at De-Mythologization: Samuel Beckett's Novels," in *Samuel Beckett. A Collection of Critical Essays*, ed. Martin Esslin (Englewood Cliffs, NJ: Prentice-Hall, 1965), p. 92.

[20]Samuel Beckett and Georges Duthuit, "Three Dialogues," in *Samuel Beckett. A Collection of Critical Essays*, p. 21.

[21]Gaston Bachelard, *Le Droit de rêver* (Paris: Presses Universitaires de France, 1970), p. 216.

[22]Jacques Derrida, *De la grammatologie* (Paris: Minuit, 1967), p. 23.

Beckett and the Comedy of Decomposition
Morton Gurewitch

In Chekhov's *Swan Song*,[1] Svetlovidov, an old actor whose career is falling apart, awakes in the night after a drunken sleep; candle in hand, he ambles on to the dark stage of a deserted provincial theater. There he berates himself for being a stupid old clown abandoned in a spooky tomb; and he mourns his age, his helplessness, and his loneliness. Soon he bitterly inveighs against his long, prostitutive decay on the stage: once he was a handsome hero, now he feels like a sideshow freak. His tirade is touching. But Svetlovidov also trembles ludicrously at what he takes to be a ghost (another forlorn creature, a prompter in a white bathrobe); and the old actor's terror arouses in us a muted hilarity. We are not inclined to smile, however, when Svetlovidov begins replaying his crowning histrionic moments; for the old man weepily acknowledges the collapse of his talent. But not for long. Intoxication sweeps through him, and he exults laughingly in his deathless genius and in the irrelevance of age. Thereafter he oscillates frantically between these two emotional extremes. In this bewildering display of euphoria and wretchedness, we recognize the farcical reversals and cracked grandeur of a tragic clown. Svetlovidov's interweaving of pathos and buffoonery is entirely sublunary. It cannot alienate us, for it is all too recognizably human.

Nor are we alienated—quite the contrary—by the marriage of affliction and wit that characterizes Heine's temper in his long period of literal immobility and mortal deterioration. In *Ideas-Book Le Grand*, Heine suggested that Aristophanes, Goethe, and Shakespeare (the latter put "the most agonizing lamentations on the misery of the world into the mouth of a fool")[2] had essentially imitated the original author of things, that first tragicomedian whose hankering for disorderly dramaturgy at the time of the French Revolution, Napoleon, and the post–Napoleonic reaction juxtaposed such queer scenes of world tragedy and comedy. While Heine lay paralytically twisted in pain on his deathbed, his "mattress-grave" of almost eight years, he could jokingly refer to this ironical God as a self-plagiarist dishing out at boring length an excessively familiar version of divinely jesting cruelty.[3] Heine's non-life was borne largely through the palliation of poetry and the relief of flippancy.[4] The flippancy is not only admirable but reassuring: it does not deviate from conventional syntax; and it derives from an ache as ancient as Job's.

Molloy, Moran, Malone, and the Unnamable are flayed with a difference; they are scourged by humiliations that are bonded to what is perhaps a unique mutation of mirth. They too are able to wring wit from woe, fun from futility, blitheness from bleakness. Beckett has in fact managed to make their dissolution droll, at least in part. At the same time he has made the application of traditional comic values to the trilogy seem peculiarly out of order. He is thus an alarming comedian, operating in what seems to be a different world from that of Chekhov and Heine. That is why Beckett's grotesque comedy is seen by some critics as incapable of effecting a liberation from the pain of mortality—the pain of hopelessness and madness.[5] In such a view, Beckett's brand of comedy is comedy's doom; it is at best a nonredemptive, noncurative purgatorial animation. In such a view, moreover, the aesthetic judgment that entropy well articulated is tantamount to a celebration of vitality, or the Nietzschean idea that "every good book written against life is itself an inducement to life,"[6] would presumably have only a specious bearing on the significance of Beckettian "comedy."

Perhaps comic theory can do no more than cringe in Beckett's presence. But perhaps not. Certainly a good deal of cringing may be avoided if Bergson's *Laughter* is demoted from its position as chief guide to the understanding of Beckett's comedy. Bergson's insights into the comic conflict between ideal suppleness and actual rigidity are priceless; but his overarching concept of comedy as a punitive enforcer of social progress sorts ill with Beckett's nihilism.[7] I should like to suggest, in regard to the trilogy, that Freud's thinking about comedy yields more valuable dividends than Bergson's. To begin with, Freud's analysis of the satisfactions of erotic, hostile, and cynical wit can also account for the pleasures of the trilogy's sexual, aggressive, and cynical farce. Freud's assessment of tendentious wit's subversiveness, of its salutary (if also momentary) wrecking of society's taboos, relates to the larger explosiveness of farce precisely because an urgent saturnalian impulse is at work in both comic forms.[8] Furthermore, the one category of tendentious wit that is virtually muffled in Freud's discussion because of its rarity, namely skeptical wit—which mockingly calls into question the mind's inherent capacity to know anything for certain—becomes a bonanza in Beckett. In the trilogy, especially in *The Unnamable*, Beckett prodigally exploits the mind as a drastically muddled aporetic-ephectic instrument, as an antic sieve, loaded with (and emptied of) clownish perplexities and cockeyed self-negations. Again, Freud's paean to nonsense is extravagantly echoed in Beckett. Freudian nonsense, that is, psychically restorative departures from normality and reality, reverberates simultaneously with skeptical farce in the daffy turmoils of the trilogy heroes. Finally, Freud's homage to disaster humor and its variant, gallows humor—the kind of humor that transforms into joke material both the facts of catastrophe and the threat of death—resonates in the repeated self-derogations of Beckett's disaster-ridden voyagers and immobilized inmates of calamity. (The resonance is imperfect, to be sure. Although Beckett's heroes wryly or zanily mock their distress, they have a remarkable predilection—it is at times cynically cancelled—for the bliss of nonexistence.)

Nevertheless Freud does not suffice: he neglects the metaphysical implications of comedy, which abound in Beckett. For these we may turn to Ruby Cohn, author of three books on Beckett. In her second book, Cohn, differing from Hugh Kenner, who had emphasized Beckett's affinity with tragic yet indomitable clowns, declares that "the clown mask is shattered by anguish."[9] In her third book, Cohn notes that Beckett's humor "has grown grimmer" through the years; she asserts, moreover, that though his "wide appeal . . . rests uneasily upon his humor," his vision is fundamentally "tragic . . . in its frustration at absurdity."[10] But these are only briefly stated opinions.

In her first book, an elaborate study of Beckett's "comic gamut," Cohn regards Beckett's profoundest comedy as uniquely ambiguous, as a psychological puzzle that makes for aesthetic insecurity. In the initial chapter of her book, however, Cohn settles for cosmic irony as the concept most

The Novel: *Murphy*, *Watt*, and The Trilogy

relevant to Beckett's comedy. In doing so, Cohn maneuvers a bit shakily. After noting Northrop Frye's suggestion that there are four fictional modes (comedy, tragedy, romance, and irony), she quotes A. R. Thompson's definition of irony in *The Dry Mock* as the "painfully comic."[11] Immediately afterwards, apparently seeking corroboration but offering what looks like disjunction, she refers to Frye's definitions of irony as "applicable to Beckett's later work."[12] Oddly enough, however, the two quotations she selects from *Anatomy of Criticism* merely recycle an elementary commonplace: irony is camouflaged significance, serviced by a technique of indirection. Had Cohn cited Frye's statements on irony as reflecting the "mythos of winter," she would have had to assimilate (one wonders how) or challenge (this might have been stimulating) an interpretation of irony that kills off comedy while accentuating frustration, sordidness, and ruin. Although Cohn is thinking of the cruel jokiness of an absurd universe, Frye's own unmentioned delineation of irony in its extreme phase as embodying bondage and nightmare in a "blasted world of repulsiveness and idiocy," inhabited by "*desdichado* figures of misery or madness,"[13] drains irony of its comic juices. Many critics are ready to do as much. Paul Fussell in *The Great War and Modern Memory* endorses Frye's view that the ironic mode signalizes murderous degradation and absurd impotence.[14] A. E. Dyson offers a comparable perspective on Swift: when Swift's irony, he affirms, is thoroughly deflected from its role as a handmaiden of reformatory satire, it becomes a bitter (if still zestful) vision of an incurably nauseating world.[15]

Cohn avoids a definitional tangle, however, by plumping for a tragicomic cosmic irony (an "ironic cosmological comedy") as the key to Beckett's major works. (Its miniature counterpart is "cognitive irony," the epistemological comedy of man's inadequate perceptions; this seems to be the equivalent of Freud's skeptical wit.)[16] Though Cohn acknowledges that Beckett is a master of buffoonery, of Chaplinesque clowning and metaphysical farce, "cosmic irony"—which in its unqualified form, it must be pointed out, usually conveys a sense of injustice, victimization, and acrid pathos[17]—remains her overriding category.

In her last chapter, Cohn squeezes ironic cosmological comedy down onto Freudian terrain by rejecting the notion that the laughter in Beckett's comedy can assuage anguish. (It should be noted in passing that the possibly illicit copulation of comedy and laughter has been notoriously legitimized by almost all comic theorists.)[18] Beckett's laughter, according to Cohn, is non-cathartic; it is "a mask for, not a release from, despair."[19] This description resembles Baudelaire's portrait of Melmoth the Wanderer, whose demonic laughter, the poet remarks, is "the perpetual explosion of his anger and his agony."[20] The description also resembles the fictive and only partially obtuse Dr. John Ray's depiction of Humbert Humbert as a man possessed of a savage "jocularity" that "betrays supreme misery perhaps . . ."[21] And of course the description reminds us of Winnie's allusion, in *Happy Days*, to Gray's lines: "And moody Madness laughing wild/Amid severest woe." (Cohn quotes these lines in her discussion of laughter as an oblique expression of despair.) But the Pagliacci syndrome is tricky. Comedy can, it is true, be a hysterical confirmation of panic. But Beckett's fool-figures, those candidates for asphyxiation in the uncompassionate sewer-circus of life, do provide, it seems to me, fugitive, impure, disorienting, freakish occasions for buoyancy and even delight that transcend both hysteria and anguish.

Beckettian man, the "thing that thinks"—and stinks and shrinks—is persistently given both to self-mockery (amply documented by Cohn) and to farcical-ironic jabbing at intolerable circumstance. This is less madness than madness exorcized. *The Unnamable* is crammed with symptoms of derangement: gruesome pathos, chaotically fragmentary ruminations, ceaseless regurgitations of the idea of entrapment, febrile rejections of historical existence, narrative abortions . . . Yet the Unnamable's mirth (often nasty) keeps breaking in. He will jeer especially at the rabid will of the rotten lords of creation (his invention?) to concoct "a real little terrestrial," a gamboling "lambkin" destined for the slaughterhouse."[22] The Unnamable mocks organic existence (crippled, truncated), into which he is, or imagines he is, tempted from time to time, as a joke, a jakes. When he recalls his doubtful merger with one-legged Mahood, the joke, the jakes, becomes a messy masterpiece of hostile, skeptical, cynical, ironic, nonsensical, scabrous, scatological, viciously exhilarating farce. He tells a fable of himself as Mahood, the mutilated world traveler who reports that his barricaded loved ones interpret his agonizing approach on crutches as great family entertainment; the children are particularly encouraged not to miss such theatrical tidbits as Mahood's scratching, hopping, and collapsing. The sardonic narrator also reveals that his family is convinced, as the years pass and they sing devout hymns and review fond memories, that the starvation and silence they have thoughtfully imposed on visible Mahood will urge the voyager on toward his long abandoned little nest. When they all die of food poisoning (Mahood's wife is named Ptomaine, Ptoto), is he repelled by their "stench of decomposition?" Or do his epileptic gyrations among his living loved ones foil their eager embraces and overturn the furniture? Or does he stamp on their decaying remains—"here a face, there a stomach" (perhaps belonging to those two accursed "cunts," his mother and his wife)[23]—out of sheer annoyance at not finding a decent surface on which to negotiate his crutches? Or is it true that he has never traveled anywhere and has not known for some time what he has been talking about?

All in all, the fable is not only a crazy comic desecration of sanctities but a superb demolition of lucidity and coherence. What rich exhilaration it supplies! What travesties of the quest, of heroic struggle, of death's due! What burlesques of suffering, of religion, of family affection and loyalty! What cleansingly brutish disgorgement of sadism! Here is God's plenty of perverse mockery. But the fable's farcical impieties have to be reduced to their proper proportions; for the Unnamable is besieged by relentlessly ungiggling voices, and he is haunted by laughterless metaphysical dungeons. He cannot enjoy unhampered irreverence; nor can he indulge in divine sloth, blessed acedia, the ecstasy of successful attrition.

Touchstone, the "fool i' th' forest" of whom Jacques gives an account in *As You Like It*, observes that "from hour to hour, we ripe and ripe," and then "from hour to hour, we rot and rot" (II.vii.). A pleasing symmetry. Molloy, no less motley, describes birth as offering a "first taste of the shit,"[24] while Moran anticipates his demise like "the turd waiting for the flush."[25] Symmetry once more. Moran's comic self-disparagement cannot suffuse him—he is not Browning's Childe Roland—with the heroic thrill of final failure (the flush will not soon be forthcoming); but it can arguably certify a successful, if fleeting (always fleeting) psychic purgation—Moran's, Beckett's and the reader's. Dianoetic laughter at unhappiness, despite its unfortunate name and its sinister connotations, can constitute relief. Jacobsen and Mueller state in their chapter "The Comic Mode," in *The Testament of Samuel Beckett*, that the dianoetic laugh is directed primarily against mysterious, malignant outer forces, though the immediate victim of that laugh is the human sufferer.[26] At the very end of their study, however, they claim only that the dianoetic laugh is directed against "that which mocks suffering," that is, against those mysterious, malevolent suprahuman powers who delight in torturing mortals.[27] Jacobsen and Mueller thereby erase the human victim. Yet surely that victim has the right to promote his own laughter at his own misery without conjuring up the bogeyman of psychosis or the image of mind at the end of its tether. It is a right Beckett generously supports.

If someone with a preference for unadulteratedly cheerful comedy were to say, benightedly adapting one of Housman's lines, "Beckett, this is stupid stuff," we might contend on Beckett's behalf, though such a contention is not news, that by sensitizing us to the absurd and the grotesque, comedy in some way immunizes us against them. (We would have to admit, of course, that the immunity is always defective.) Housman's Mithridates acquired his immunity to dethronement by thriving homeopathically on poisons slipped into his food and drink by identifiable, if not easily apprehendable, foes. As a result, "Mithridates: he died old." The Unnamable, to be sure, is not Mithridates's distant heir. He cannot taste sovereignty. And he cannot experience irrevocable extinction. Nor can he specify his enemies. Nor can his immunization system be guaranteed for more than brief intervals. Yet in these brief intervals of bizarre jokiness (they make up a considerable part of his jerky nonchronicle), his immunity to the poison of consciousness suggests that even momentary, impure laughter in a bleak universe justifies the ways of comedy to decomposing man.

From *The Chicago Review* 33, no. 2 (1982): 93-99.

[1] This play is among the new versions of Chekhov's one-act farces made by Eric Bentley and Theodore Hoffman and published as *The Brute and Other Farces*, ed. Eric Bentley (New York: Grove Press, 1958).

[2] *The Sword and the Flame: Selections from Heinrich Heine's Prose*, ed. and intro. Alfred Werner (New York and London: Thomas Yoseloff, 1960) p. 330.

[3] In this bit of complaining levity, in his *Confessions,* Heine refers to the story of the leprous priest of Lüneberg, who produced beautiful, universally loved songs, but who was obliged to do so from the depths of a pariah's pain (Heine's *Prose and Poetry*, intro. Ernest Rhys [New York: Dutton, 1966], p. 347).

[4] To his brother Max, Heine wrote: ". . . my lips are lamed like my feet, my eating tools are lamed as well as my excretory organs. I can neither chew nor crap; I am fed like a bird. This non-life is not to be borne." Quoted in Jeffrey Sammons, *Heinrich Heine: A Modern Biography* (Princeton, New Jersey: Princeton University Press, 1979), p. 296.

[5] Dieter Wellershoff interprets the failure of psychic emancipation in Beckettian comedy (specifically in the trilogy) as follows: "In all this the strivings of his imagined creatures have the triple ridiculousness of a fool who is looking, with inadequate strength, on a wrong road, for a goal that perhaps does not exist at all. But the laughter ceases in the presence of the intensity of the effort. We are watching a compulsive action beyond the reach of irony, a furious monomania from which no laughter can liberate us. This is happening in earnest. Beckett himself, who wants to unmask madness, is deeply enmeshed in it." "Failure of an Attempt at De-Mythologization: Samuel Beckett's Novels," in *Samuel Beckett: A Collection of Critical Essays*, ed. Martin Esslin (Englewood Cliffs, New Jersey: Prentice-Hall, 1965) p. 107. Michael Robinson sees the possibility of psychic relief finally extinguished in the third part of the trilogy: "Molloy can still jest bitterly about his condition . . . In *The Unnamable* this release is no longer possible . . . " (*The Long Sonata of the Dead* [New York: Grove Press, 1969], pp. 140, 193).

[6] This is a condensed observation taken from Nietzsche's *Human, All Too Human*. The aphorism was used by Thomas Mann in defending *Buddenbrooks* against the charge that the novel was basically negative. Quoted in T. J. Reed, *Thomas Mann: The Uses of Tradition* (London: Oxford University Press, 1974), p. 51.

[7]Ruby Cohn uses Bergson only as a springboard in *Samuel Beckett: The Comic Gamut* (New Brunswick, New Jersey: Rutgers University Press, 1962); she knows full well that the corrective comedy of manners is not Beckett's domain, and that Beckett's comic heroes are not socially assimilable. But a number of other critics are convinced that there is more than a superficial alliance between Beckett and Bergson. Josephine Jacobsen and William R. Mueller, in *The Testament of Samuel Beckett* (New York: Hill and Wang, 1964), claim that Bergson's analysis of the comic disparity between flexible soul and inelastic body is "most suggestive and helpful to anyone who would seek to understand Samuel Beckett's mode of comedy" (p. 79). Ihab Hassan, in *The Literature of Silence: Henry Miller and Samuel Beckett* (New York: Knopf, 1967), believes that "The comedy of Beckett is clownish, cruel, and absurd. We come closer to understanding its character by first understanding the nature of comedy as proposed by Henri Bergson's *Laughter*. . . . The main insight of Bergson, which applies closely to Beckett's work, is that automatism and repetition are of the essence of comedy" (pp. 133-34). In Michael Robinson's discussion of Beckett's clowns, Bergson gets more attention than any other commentator on comedy or laughter (*The Long Sonata of the Dead*, pp. 40-41).

[8]I have dealt with the link between tendentious wit and saturnalian farce in *Comedy: The Irrational Vision* (Ithaca, New York: Cornell University Press, 1975), pp. 127-31.

[9]*Back to Beckett* (Princeton, New Jersey: Princeton University Press, 1973), p. 4.

[10]*Just Play: Beckett's Theater* (Princeton, New Jersey: Princeton University Press, 1980), p. 11.

[11]*Samuel Beckett: The Comic Gamut*, pp. 8-9.

[12]*Ibid.*, p. 9.

[13]*Anatomy of Criticism* (Princeton, New Jersey: Princeton University Press, 1957), pp. 238-39.

[14]*The Great War and Modern Memory* (New York and London: Oxford University Press, 1975), p. 312.

[15]"Swift: The Metamorphosis of Irony," in Jonathan Swift, *Gulliver's Travels,* ed. Robert A. Greenberg (New York: W. W. Norton, 1970), pp. 360-62.

[16]"Beyond skillfull techniques, it is the imaginative examination of cosmic and cognitive irony that determines Beckett's significant position in contemporary literature" (*Samuel Beckett: The Comic Gamut,* p. 155).

[17]The following passage, in which Newton Arvin comments on "Bartleby the Scrivener," illustrates the traditional connotation of "cosmic irony": "What *Bartleby* essentially dramatizes is not the pathos of dementia praecox but the bitter metaphysical pathos of the human situation itself, the cosmic irony of the truth that men are at once immitigably interdependent and immitigably forlorn" (*Herman Melville: A Critical Biography* [New York: Viking, 1950], p. 243). At times, however, cosmic irony is associated with sadistic supernatural laughter. I have attempted to show the full range of the comedy of irony in "From Pyrrhonic to Vomedic Irony" *New York Literary Forum,* 1 (Spring 1978), 45-57.

[18]Stephen Potter has a section on "The Irrelevance of Laughter" to humor in *Sense of Humor* (New York: Henry Holt, 1955), pp. 8-12.

[19]*Samuel Beckett: The Comic Gamut,* p. 287.

[20]"The Essence of Laughter," in *The Essence of Laughter and Other Essays, Journals, and Letters,* ed. and intro. Peter Quennell (New York: Meridian Books, 1956), p. 117

[21]Vladimir Nabokov, *Lolita* (New York: Capricorn, 1972), p.7.

[22]*The Unnamable*, in *Three Novels by Samuel Beckett* (New York: Grove Press, 1965), p. 316.

[23]*Ibid.*, p. 323.

[24]*Molloy* in *Three Novels,* p. 16.

[25]*Ibid.*, p. 162.

[26]*The Testament of Samuel Beckett,* p. 92.

[27]*Ibid.*, p. 174.

Ashes to Ashes, Dust to Dust

Robert Sandarg

Ashes and dust sift through Beckett's entire oeuvre, from the short stories "Draff" and "What a Misfortune" of *More Pricks Than Kicks* (1934) to the play *Catastrophe*, which premiered fifty years later. These universal symbols of dissolution and sorrow shroud the Beckettian landscape in a grey pall of gloom; but more precisely, Beckett's seventy-three references to ashes and seventy-nine references to dust[1] create a mournful liturgical accompaniment to his literary interment of a crumbling world. Echoing in every genre from beginning to end of the canon, they form an extended graveside lament of "ashes to ashes, dust to dust" for a planet and its inhabitants moving inexorably toward nothingness.

Ashes and dust have traditionally been associated, for ash is a greyish powder or fine dust. Both symbolize human insignificance, mortality and atonement. In many ancient cultures, dust was rubbed on the body as a sign of humiliation, and the practice of sprinkling ashes over the head was a common expression of affliction. Homer relates how the Greeks showed their bereavement by strewing themselves with ashes or sitting amidst them. In the Bible, Job repents before the Lord in dust and ashes, while Abraham, commenting on the brevity of life, acknowledges that he is but ashes and dust. Each Ash Wednesday, the priest marks his parishioners' foreheads with the blessed ashes of palms from the previous Palm Sunday and pronounces the words of Genesis 3:14: "Remember that thou art dust, and to dust thou shalt return." And when the dead are buried, the officiant often states that they are returning to those elements from whence they came: earth to earth, ashes to ashes, dust to dust.

Beckett uses dust and ashes to underscore the inevitability of our annihilation: he sees life as a series of self-consuming flickerings that lead only to extinction and a powdery residue. This outlook is expressed metaphorically when Watt, upon arriving at Mr. Knott's, watches "the ashes greyen, redden, greyen, redden, in the grate, of the range."[2] But although the very pattern of human life is glowing and fading before Watt's eyes, he quickly tires of observing it, for the outcome is only too predictable: soon, "the ashes would not redden any more, but remained grey, even in the dimmest light" (39). This metaphor for the ineluctable termination of existence recurs later in the novel when Watt is waiting for a train that will take him to the end of the line. As voices whisper in his skull like "a flurry of little grey paws in the dust" (232), he gazes at the station grate, "heaped high with ashes and cinders of a beautiful grey colour" (236). Watt's departure in dust and in ashes is a paradigm for each individual's eventual departure from this life.

In Beckett's territory, human existence follows an inexorable trajectory: in effect, we all move from "the spermarium to the crematorium,"[3] where the body is reduced to ashes and dust. We will all go "through the fire"[4] like the Parson's mother-in-law in "Draff." Accordingly, Nagg and Nell end their days in ashbins, and Krapp looks ahead to a time when all his dust will have settled. Although Winnie, buried to the waist beneath a blazing light, states, "Fear no more the heat o' the sun,"[5] this quotation from *Cymbeline* ends with the menacing lines: "Golden lads and girls all must/As chimney-sweepers come to dust." And despite her vacuous optimism, Winnie does occasionally express an awareness of her fate, calling the earth an "old extinguisher" and wondering if she, too, will burn like her parasol: "oh I do not mean necessarily burst into flames, no, just little by little be charred to a black cinder, all this—(ample gesture of arms)—visible flesh" (38). Be it in ashes or in dust, Winnie's demise is predetermined.

Beckett contrasts images of flame and ash throughout the radio drama *Embers* in order to emphasize the downslope of Bolton's life. At the outset of Henry's tale, Bolton is standing before a fire which burns out soon after Dr. Holloway's arrival. There are no flames now, "only the embers, sound of dying, dying glow."[6] As the candle gutters in its holder and the embers grow cold, the moribund Bolton bolts on toward the frozen world of death, for medicine, that hollow way, cannot save him: the doctor can do nothing except temporarily relieve his patient's suffering by means of injections. *Embers* is reminiscent of Baudelaire's poem, "Le Portrait," which begins, "La maladie et la mort font des cendres." And indeed, illness and death may soon reduce Bolton to ashes that are even colder than those on his hearth.

During rehearsals for the Schiller Theatre production of *Endgame*, Beckett remarked that this drama is "like fire and ashes. The antagonism between characters flares up and subsides and flares again."[7] *Play* takes this process a step further: although the players continue to express their mutual animosity, they are hardly capable of flaring. In this work, ash predominates. Each character may be considered the ashen remnant of a conflagration, either literal or figurative, for all three have become the inhabitants of urns resembling receptacles for ashes. W1 probably expired in an auto wreck "on the way back by Ash and Snodland,"[8] the first town implying cremation as the aftermath of her death. M's demise is symbolized by his clothing, which W2 spitefully destroys in a bonfire; and W2 herself later uses a synonym for burning in reference to her relation with M: "You might get angry and blaze me clean out

The Novel: *Murphy*, *Watt*, and The Trilogy

of my wits" (16). In close keeping with the incendiary undertones that occur throughout *Play*, Alan Schneider employed lighting in his 1964 Cherry Lane production that made the actors' faces "look like charred ashes."[9] But if this drama raises the tantalizing possibility of life continuing in some form after death, it puts to rest any notion of the survival of love, for in *Play* love is immolated even more completely than the actors' scorched remains.

The impossibility of love is also apparent in the ashes of the radio piece *Words and Music*. Here, Croak commands Words (Joe) and Music (Bob) to expatiate on love of woman; but although Croak quickly changes the evening's theme to old age, love remains central to its exposition, and the imagery surrounding love that of fire, ashes, and water. Words describes a shivering old man, waiting for his bedpan, who spies in the ashes of the ingle the face of that woman "who loved could not be won/Or won not loved."[10] Words' subsequent description of the woman at first suggests death by drowning, and the scum-covered waters of the wellhead mentioned near the end of this work represent a final dousing of the ashes of love. Word's fourteen-line lament concerning the face in the ashes may well be the expansion of a phrase from *The Unnamable*: "you set out to look for a face, to it you return having found nothing, nothing but a kind of ashen smear."[11] This novel also contains a violent scene in which the concept of familial love is ground into ashes: beneath a rotunda in a yard consisting of "an amalgam of dirt and ashes" (41), the narrator viciously tramples, with his crutches and remaining foot, the remains of his sausage-poisoned parents, wife and children.

Like love, the earth itself will inevitably attain that blighted state envisioned by the painter Hamm cites in *Endgame*, a madman who saw only ashes where others saw the loveliness of rising corn and herring ships. In "Lessness," Beckett expands this view into a far broader picture of the world in ruin, where humanity is reduced to a sole survivor and civilization has become the fallen edifice that this creature haunts. Although the setting of "Lessness" is a sandscape, everything—the earth, the survivor's body, his refuge, the sky, even the air—is "ash grey" in color. By repeating the terms "ash grey" no fewer than eighteen times in the course of twenty-four brief paragraphs, Beckett permeates his text with the sense of a burned-out world. Moreover, the ashes so clearly implied throughout "Lessness" will certainly never rekindle; if anything, they will be flooded by the passing deluge which the survivor awaits. With this coming inundation of the ashes, "Lessness" resembles both *Embers*, where the final sound is that of the sea, and *Words and Music* with the waters of the wellhead.

And if our end is not in ashes, then it will be in that dust from which we were created. In the poem "What Would I Do Without This World" Beckett calls our earth the sky's "ballast dust." [12] And humankind, as Hamlet knew, is but a "quintessence of dust." Hamlet's appraisal is reiterated by the Unnamable, who avows that he himself is like dust, then bitterly continues, "they want to make a man out of dust" (84). His addendum is probably a sardonic reference to Genesis 2:07: "And the Lord God formed man of dust from the ground."

In addition, the disembodied Unnamable calls himself "a dust of words" (139), a statement that dovetails with a remark that Beckett made to John Fletcher in 1956: "At the end of my work there's nothing but dust . . . In the last book, *l'Innommable*, there's complete disintegration."[13] This reference to literature as dust stands as a striking corollary to Job 13:12: "Your maxims are proverbs of ashes." Like all things of this earth, the word, too, can only terminate in ashes or in dust.

Beckett frequently employs the image of life as a painful trek down a dusty road. In *Malone Dies*, he describes a road "white with dust, bordered with dark masses, [that] stretched a little way and ran up dead, against a narrow grey sky."[14] This passage is marvelously evocative. It tells us that the path of existence is short; that life is surrounded by somber menace, strewn with the dust of death, and ends in a grey nothingness. The dusty road of life winds its way throughout *All That Fall*, where each of the six separate references to dust is associated with mortality: as Maddy Rooney says, it is a vile dust that will fall back upon the viler worms. Thus, our demise may be that lingering dissolution mentioned early in the radio play when Maddy is tempted to flop down the road "like a great big slop thick with grit and dust,"[15] never to rise again. Conversely, our return to dust may be more abrupt: Mr. Tyler is almost run over by Connolly's van, which coats both Tyler and Maddy from head to foot in white dust. Tyler is nearly annihilated like the hen Mr. Slocum later squashes beneath the tires of his automobile. Commenting on this event, Maddy exclaims: "What a death! One minute picking at the dung, on the road, in the sun, with now and then a dust bath, and then—bang!" (47).

Although the title *All That Fall* is an ironic illusion to Psalm 145:14, "the Lord upholdeth all that fall and raiseth up all those that be bowed down," two other biblical citations clearly apply to this work: both I Samuel 2:08 and Psalm 113:07 state that the Lord "raiseth up the poor out of the dust." The Rooneys would surely greet this promise with the same wild laughter that the verse from Psalm 145 arouses in them, for if they are lifted from the dust, they will probably be in the same condition as the flattened hen. Be it gradual or rapid, our destruction is unavoidable, and death remains the unanswered question. Even at that moment of apparent peace near the end of *All That Fall*, when the sheep ruminate, the dogs are hushed, and "the hens sprawl torpid in the dust" (75), we are, as Maddy maintains, alone. Death is a mystery and a threat and there is no one who can explain why we must all go relentlessly from dust to dust.

From the poem "Whoroscope" on, hens have occupied a special perch in Beckett's literary aviary. Whereas the other fowl he mentions—vultures, parrots, thrushes, hawks, sparrows, seagulls, owls, crakes and ducks—are capable of soaring, and the ostrich has wonderful powers of locomotion when its head is not in the sand, the lowly hen symbolizes death and is surrounded by an imagery of dust and ash in two novels as well as in *All That Fall*. In *Malone Dies*, Sapo spies a hen, "a big, anxious, ashen bird" (29), poised irresolutely on the threshold of Lambert's farmhouse. Since this property, which is burned to a cinder every summer, is owned by a prodigious slaughterer of animals, the hen may well be on the threshold of destruction. In *Molloy*, Moran frets about his grey hen when she huddles "in a corner, in the dust, at the mercy of the rats . . .The day was at hand, if she did not take a turn for the better, when the other hens would join forces and tear her to pieces with their beaks and claws."[16] Moran's flock does expire during his absence, for Beckett's earthbound hens, with their atrophied wings, are doomed, like humanity itself, to return to ashes and dust through injury, neglect, or slaughter.

In fact, life is an inevitable reduction to a dust that "will not settle in our time. And when it does some great roaring machine will come and whirl it all sky high again," in Maddy Rooneys words (41). The same swirling vision occurs in *Mercier and Camier*, where "the dust of all that is dead and buried is rising, eddying, settling, burying again."[17] But as we see in two of Beckett's "Fizzles," one day the elemental dust will settle, and eventually it will triumph. "Fizzle 5" describes a vast outdoor arena with space for millions of inhabitants to either wander or remain still. Between this area and the ditch surrounding it is a track made of dead leaves. Unlike the leaves that Mr. Rooney smells in *All That Fall*, these are not rotting. "They are dry. The heat and dry air. Dead but not rotting. Crumbling into dust rather."[18] Here, humanity is encompassed by a circle of dust.

In "Fizzle 8," the world is drowned in dust. The subtitle of this final fizzle, "For to End Yet Again," may refer to Beckett's effort to reach the silence that waits at the end of writing. However, "Fizzle 8" may well be yet another attempt at ending "Lessness." Although both pieces exhibit a similarly fragmented sentence structure, the multiple paragraphs of "Lessness" are compressed into the single paragraph of "Fizzle 8." More important, while both works describe a desiccated landscape, the ashen sands of "Lessness" have become an even more entropic dust in the fizzle, a fact reported with some surprise in the latter work: "sand pale as dust ah but dust indeed."[19] The sixteen references to dust throughout "Fizzle 8" creates a hellish, pulverized expanse which has engulfed "so much that it can engulf no more" (58). Like some gigantic snake or crawling thing of the dust, it has swallowed up even the haughtiest monuments. Both texts include a small grey survivor who represents the final stage of humanity as we know it; but "Fizzle 8" introduces the next lords of the earth, white dwarfs with monstrous skulls and stunted legs. Finally, these two works are united by the mention of ashes in the penultimate sentence of "Fizzle 8," which depicts the coming of night: "by degrees or as though switched on dark falls there again that certain dark that alone certain ashes can" (59). As "Lessness" and "Fizzle 8" trace our implacable progression toward obliteration, their iterative imagery combines to form a dirge of "ashes to ashes, dust to dust" for the world itself.

Beckett's outlook is lugubrious, but it is not without humor. In *Malone Dies*, he calls life a "comedy of combustion" (47), and elsewhere he adapts several specifically Christian references to ash and dust for purposes of comic relief. In *Molloy*, Father Ambrose laughingly compares Moran's hen, "with her arse in the dust" (138), to Job; while in Watt, Louit recounts how he sows seeds in the fields "as the priest dust, or ashes, into the grave" (181). The narrator of "First Love" speaks irreverently of "a genuine interment, with real live mourners and nearly always that charming business with the dust."[20] These humorous forays are the only relief in Beckett's uncompromisingly grim outlook. His works move us to tread our path toward dust and ashes with courage and occasional bursts of bitter laughter, but without hope. Beckett leads us toward acceptance of the inescapable, toward resignation: we must turn the other cheek to the dust, not literally, as did Murphy when his rocking chair capsized, but figuratively and philosophically. Above all, we must not ignore the tragic outcome of the human situation like the deluded Director in *Catastrophe* or like Moran prior to his quest for Molloy.

In *Catastrophe*, dedicated to the dissident Czech playwright Václav Havel, the Director is a man blinded by ideology. He is mistakenly convinced that the trembling Protagonist, with skull and night attire the color of ash, is the only doomed character in this dramaticule. But *Catastrophe* rests upon the symbology of flame and ash, and although the Director's cigar keeps going out (his female assistant is obliged to light it three separate times), he fails to comprehend that his flame is dying and that he, too, is marked by ash as indelibly as the Protagonist. The close juxtaposition of fire (*feu*) and ash (*cendre*) is particularly apparent in the French version of the play when the Director, called M, inquires about the color of the Protagonist's pajamas, then takes out a cigar and asks his assistant for a light.

> A   Sa tenue de nuit.
> M   Couleur?

The Novel: *Murphy, Watt,* and *The Trilogy* 85

   A Cendre.
       M sort un cigare.
   M Du feu.[21]

The Director surveys the Protagonist, then orders additional whitening of his cranium and his flesh, suggesting incineration of the prisoner's spirit and, should that fail, his body. The Director next bustles off to yet another caucus, but he is further along the road to dissolution than he realizes.

Each step brings him closer to becoming a burnt-out case like the Protagonist and ultimately a forgotten heap of ashes. If the Protagonist reminds us of the figure in the poem "Dread Nay," with his "ashen smooth . . ./asylum skull,"[22] the Director brings to mind another bureaucrat, Mr. Ash in *Watt*, an Admiralty Clerk of the Second Class. "Such vermin pullulate. He died of premature exhaustion the following week" (46).

Both ashes and dust intensify the aura of decay that permeates Part II of *Molloy*. Here, Jacques Moran, another smoker, self-assuredly states before embarking on his journey: "I looked at the ash on my cigar. It was firm and blue" (162). Like the Director, Moran enjoys a false sense of peace; he is unaware that he, too, will burn down, become decidedly *in*firm and hover on the edge of extinction. But soon, an acute pain shoots through his knee, and the ash falls from his cigar. As his physical condition deteriorates, Moran perceives that he is aging "as swiftly as a day-fly" (203). The threat of destruction is intensified by his subsequent reference to a fly which "buzzed low above the ash-tray, [and] raised a little ash on the breath of its wings" (223). Moran becomes preoccupied by thoughts of flies which expire almost immediately after hatching and are brushed directly "into the dust-pan" (228). Such musings are premonitions of his own decrepitude, for Moran is nearly reduced to ashes, like his cigar, and to dust, like his bees, which become "a little dust of annulets and wings" (240) Moran is spared, but his brush with death does lead to his enlightenment, for by novel's end this formerly well ordered and cruelly rational individual acknowledges the absurdity of human destiny.

Moran's acceptance of our irrational march toward dissolution calls to mind Beckett's third and most sublime cigar smoker, the psychiatric patient Mr. Endon in *Murphy*. Although Murphy relights Mr. Endon's cigar all day long at the Magdalen Mental Mercyseat, this "excellent" cigar remains miraculously unfinished; ash, in fact, is never mentioned. On the contrary, Mr. Endon's dainty fingers, which grasp the cigar, are described as ablaze with rings which strongly implies an enduring flame. The Endon episode suggests that this amiable schizophrenic has been spared reduction to ashes by his realization of life's irrational nature and by his subsequent retreat into a saner world of so-called madness.

No discussion of ash in *Murphy* can be complete without examining the bizarre dispersal of that character's remains. After perishing in an explosion, Murphy is cremated. Cooper, entrusted to flush away Murphy's ashes in the men's room of the Abbey Theatre, contemplates depositing them in a refuse bin for one of Dublin's "gloomy dustmen" to pick up. Instead, he enters a saloon, begins drinking, and several hours later hurls the four-pound packet at an individual who had offended him. By closing time, Murphy's ashes are strewn across the barroom floor. The publican will sweep them into the gutter, where a dustman will scoop them up, after all. On one level, the imagery forms a lament of "ashes to ashes, dust to dust" for Murphy's untimely passing.

However, the scattering of Murphy's ashes is more than a grotesque variation of a laying to rest: it is a parody of traditional fertility rites that endured well into the twentieth century throughout Europe. As the residue of fire, ash can possess a symbolic value totally antithetical to that which it exhibits in mourning customs. Considered the soul of the flame, ashes can be magically potent revivers of life as well as symbols of death. The Romans fed ashes from the sacred fires of animal sacrifices to flocks in order to increase their productivity, and it was long a European folk custom for ashes from midsummer fires to be spread on the fields. In Ireland, ashes from the Saint John's Day (June 24) bonfires are believed to aid the fertility of the crops, while on the same date in continental Europe straw figures representing the vegetative spirit are burned and their ashes scattered across the farmlands.

But since a barroom floor is a most unpropitious setting for any type of pastoral burgeoning, the dispersal scene in *Murphy* can only be a mockery of fertility rituals. The Beckettian ethos contains no principle of regeneration: Beckett looks toward the end of things rather than toward any new beginnings, and he clearly discounts the notion of personal resurrection. Characters reduced to ashes may lead a half-life after death as in *Play*, but they will never return. In *Waiting for Godot*, the dead still speak with voices that rustle like ashes, but there is no intimation of renewal. Similarly, Beckett's creatures will not be resurrected from the dust. The narrator of "Text 6" of *Stories and Texts for Nothing* is "a little dust in a little nook"[23] who avows, "Yes, I'm here forever . . . and it's well pleased I am, well pleased, that it's over and done with" (102). The voice in "Fizzle 4" persists after the death of its host, announcing, "I'll be inside, nothing left but dust."[24] And this consciousness, like Beckett's other twilight beings, will never regain corporeality.

Such, too, is our fate: as we read in *Malone Dies*, existence is the "crumbling away of two little heaps of finest sand, or dust, or ashes" (48), with no hope of reconstitution. Although we may linger on, we will never arise, Phoenix-like, from our ashes or our dust; we are not like that thief Vanni Fucci in Canto XXIV of the *Inferno*, endlessly reformed after having been turned to dust and ashes by a serpent's bite. But our immolation is our purification, our expiation of the sin of having been born; for as the Unnamable declares, it is "pity's fires" that will "promote us to ashes" (25).

Gradually time will pass. The *poussière d'instants* in the poem "bon bon il est un pays"[25] will accumulate, and one day our earth will expire. The dust will conquer all, as Voice C in *That Time* cries out: "suddenly this dust whole place full of dust . . . from floor to ceiling nothing only dust and not a sound."[26] The sky will go out and the ashes darken, to paraphrase the narrator of Part I of *How It Is*. Then, as the Unnamable predicted, "silence will fall again and settle, like dust of sand, on the arena, after the massacres" (26). Clov's dream will be the only reality: the planet will be "silent and still, and each thing in its last place under the last dust."[27] As we read in "Text 13" of *Stories and Texts for Nothing*, "there won't be any life, there won't have been any life, there will be silence, the air quite still that trembled once an instant, the tiny flurry of dust quite settled."[28]

Ashes to ashes, dust to dust. Dante, Shakespeare and Baudelaire have also used these archetypal images for doleful effect, but none has used them as pervasively as Beckett. Ashes and dust recur throughout his prose, drama, poetry and radio plays. The television short "Ghost Trio" and the performance text "A Piece of Monologue" also contain references to dust, while the minimalist "Imagination Dead Imagine" describes bodies changing from leaden to an ashen hue. Beckett's deliberate repetition of ashes and dust creates a mood, a prophecy and a lament; for humanity, civilization and the world itself will eventually return to these elements. Yet Beckett's view does provide a certain consolation, because ultimately the dust and ashes will dissolve into the chaos from which they arose. Then, the last traces of that futile agony which is existence will be effaced, and the "blessedness of absence"[29] will reign eternally.

From *The Journal of Beckett Studies* 1, nos. 1-2 (Spring 1992): 55-65.

---

[1] The number of references to ashes and dust is my count. A valuable tool in this research was Michèle Aina Barale and Rubin Rabinovitz, *A KWIC Concordance to Samuel Beckett's Trilogy: Molloy, Malone Dies,* and *The Unnamable*, New York, Garland, 1988.

[2] Samuel Beckett, *Watt*, New York Grove Press, 1959, 38. Further references to this work will appear in the text.

[3] Samuel Beckett, *Murphy*, New York, Grove Press, 1957, 78. Further references to this work will appear in the text.

[4] Samuel Beckett, "Draff," in *More Pricks Than Kicks*, New York, Grove Press, 1972, 187.

[5] Samuel Beckett, *Happy Days*, New York, Grove Press, 1961, 26. Further references to this work will appear in the text.

[6] Samuel Beckett, *Embers,* in *Krapp's Last Tape and Other Dramatic Pieces*, New York, Grove Press, 1960, 100.

[7] Dougald McMillan and Martha Fehsenfeld, *Beckett in the Theatre*, New York, Riverrun, 1988, 201.

[8] Samuel Beckett, *Play and Two Short Pieces for Radio*, London, Faber and Faber, 1964, 14. Further references to this work will appear in the text.

[9] Alan Schneider, *Entrances: An American Director's Journey*, New York, Viking, 1986, 342.

[10] Samuel Beckett, *Words and Music*, in *Cascando and Other Short Dramaic Pieces*, New York, Grove Press, 1968, 28.

[11] Samuel Beckett, *The Unnamable*, New York, Grove Press, 1958, 123.

[12] Samuel Beckett, *Collected Poems in English and French*, New York, Grove Press, 1977, 59.

[13] John Fletcher, *The Novels of Samuel Beckett*, London, Chatto and Windus, 1964, 194

[14] Samuel Beckett, *Malone Dies*, New York, Grove Press, 1956, 110. Further references to this work will appear in the text.

[15] Samuel Beckett, *All That Fall*, in *Krapp's Last Tape and Other Dramatic Pieces*, 37. Further references to this work will appear in the text.

[16] Samuel Beckett, *Molloy,* New York, Grove Press, 1955, 175. Further references to this work will appear in the text.

The Novel: *Murphy*, *Watt*, and The Trilogy   89

[17] Samuel Beckett, *Mercier and Camier*, New York, Grove Press, 1974, 103.

[18] Samuel Beckett, "Fizzle 5," in *Fizzles*, New York, Grove Press, 1976, 39.

[19] Samuel Beckett, "Fizzle 8: For To End Yet Again," in *Fizzles*, 58. Further references to this work will appear in the text.

[20] Samuel Beckett, "First Love," in *First Love and Other Stories*, New York, Grove Press, 1974, 13.

[21] Samuel Beckett, *Catastrophe et autres dramaticules*, Paris, Minuit, 1982, 73.

[22] Samuel Beckett, "Dread Nay," in *Collected Poems in English and French*, 33.

[23] Samuel Beckett, "Text 6," in *Stories and Texts for Nothing*, New York, Grove Press, 1967, 102.

[24] Samuel Beckett, "Fizzle 4," in *Fizzles*, 32.

[25] Samuel Beckett, "bon bon il est un pays," in *Collected Poems in French and English*, 33.

[26] Samuel Beckett, *That Time*, in *The Collected Shorter Plays of Samuel Beckett*, New York, Grove Press, 1984, 235.

[27] Samuel Beckett, *Endgame*, New York, Grove Press, 1958, 57.

[28] Samuel Beckett, "Text 13," in *Stories and Texts for Nothing*, 137.

[29] Samuel Beckett, *Malone Dies*, 48.

CHAPTER 3

Early Theatrical Works

Theatre (Review of *Waiting for Godot*)
Anthony Hartley

Theatre: *Waiting for Godot.* By Samuel Beckett. (Arts.)

Two tramps are sitting by the roadside waiting for a M. Godot to come and employ them. They exchange odds and ends of conversation which are as meaningless and, at times, as gross in their insistence on physical detail as anything to be heard inside an army camp. Godot does not come, but instead there appear Pozzo and Lucky, his servant—the one inhuman in his tyranny, the other in his servility; in the second half of the play this pair are seen again, but now Pozzo has gone blind and Lucky cannot speak at all. Meanwhile the two tramps continue waiting for Godot; they cannot even commit suicide; they have no rope to hang themselves; still Godot does not come.

    Superficially, it might appear that this play of metaphysical situation is the product of a deep pessimism. Godot does not come, the one contact the tramps have with the outside world presents them with an example of fearful tyranny (the Pozzo-Lucky relationship serves as a kind of anti-masque to that of themselves) with Godot. Lucky's outpourings when he is commanded to think in the first act are a savage satire on modern culture, while most of the dialogue brings out that impossibility of communication between human beings, which plays a central part in Samuel Beckett's thinking. Yet, a closer look at the play raises doubts as to whether its meaning is quite so one-sided as that. The ambivalence of the idea of Godot himself is very marked; from one point of view he represents a force which is destroying the two tramps; from another he is their only *raison d'être*. Equally, the Pozzo-Lucky episodes are notable for a certain human sympathy displayed by the tramps in face of Lucky's humiliation and sufferings. The relationship between the tramps themselves (one is the thinking, the other the physical, man) does not exclude communication on some level other than that of the intellect. A frustrated poetry is distilled from the play, a poetry which is a by-product of the human situation. There is always, one feels, a chance that Godot may come.

Mr. Beckett has written a play of great power and skill (the dialogue is masterly), which starts from the undeniable proposition that all men are in the same basic position as regards the universe—*roseau, mais roseau pensant*. Moreover, it is a characteristic of this basic situation that it cannot be altered. No dramatic change takes place throughout *Waiting for Godot* and no change could take place (unless Godot were to come, but that is also impossible within the terms of the situation). What this new school of dramatists is telling us is that all the subjects which have traditionally engaged the attention of practitioners of the art—reversals of fortune, fall of princes, star-crossed lovers, etc.—are superficialities, and that the real subject for the playwright is the basic minimum of human life, something that is not changed one jot by such trifles as jealousy or anger or lust. Of course, the trouble with this theme on the stage is that to hold the interest of the audience a *tour de force* is necessary. If they once realize that strictly nothing is going on, they will be liable to be bored. Hence, a number of dramatists of this school have used violent and striking action to attempt to conceal the want of the genuine article in their plays. It is the singularity of Mr. Beckett to have used means far more consonant with his ultimate aim; that this was possible can be put down to the sheer excellence of his writing.

For this kind of play a rather carefully neutral production is necessary and the acting should not be too naturalistic in quality. At the Arts it was very well done: in particular, Peter Hall's production moved at exactly the right speed, getting the aimless feeling of the play without dragging. As the two tramps, Peter Woodthorpe and Paul Daneman were excellent, while the more violent playing of Peter Bull and Timothy Bateson made a good foil for them (perhaps Mr. Bull was a shade too violent, though). We owe something to actors and producer and to the management of the Arts Theatre for letting us see so interesting a play so admirably done. This is the only theatre in London constantly to produce plays that are both adult and dramatically exciting. I look forward eagerly to their Ugo Betti next month.

From *The Spectator* (12 August 1955): 222.

Theatre (Review of *Waiting for Godot*)
Harold Clurman

I was utterly absorbed by and thoroughly enjoyed Samuel Beckett's already famous *Waiting for Godot* (Golden). It is necessary to begin this way—it is not usually important for a reviewer to express so bald a reaction—because much abstruse and quite simple nonsense will probably be written apropos of this play.

But even if I did not like the play, I should still admire it. I have my reservations, yet I think it is a masterpiece. But should it prove not to be a masterpiece, I should still insist on its importance. This is no paradox; I am merely suggesting that there are various ways of viewing the play—all of them relevant.

It is a poetic harlequinade—tragi-comic as the traditional Commedia dell´Arte usually was: full of horse play, high spirits, cruelty and a great wistfulness. Though the content is intellectual to a degree, the surface, which is at once terse, rapid and prolix in dialogue, is very much like a minstrel show or vaudeville turn.

The form is exactly right for what Beckett wishes to convey. Complete disenchantment is at the heart of the play, but Beckett refuses to honor this disenchantment by a serious demeanor. Since life is an incomprehensible nullity enveloped by colorful patterns of fundamentally absurd and futile activities (like a clown's habit clothing a corpse), it is proper that we pass our time laughing at the spectacle.

We pass the time, Beckett tells us, waiting for a meaning that will save us—save us from the pain, ugliness, emptiness of existence. Perhaps the meaning is God, but we do not know Him. He is always promised us but he never recognizably appears. Our life is thus a constant waiting, always essentially the same, till time itself ceases to have significance or substance. "I can't go on like this" man forever cries; to which the reply is "That's what you think." "What'll we do? What'll we do?" man repeatedly wails. The only answer given—apart from suicide, which is reticently hinted at—is to wait: "In the meantime let us try to converse calmly, since we are incapable of keeping silent."

What is all this if not the concentrate in almost childlike images of the contemporary European—particularly French—mood of despair, a distorted mirror reflection of the impasse and disarray of Europe's present politics, ethic, and common way of life? If this play is generally difficult for Americans to grasp as anything but an exasperatingly crazy concoction, it is because there is no immediate point of reference for it in the conscious life of our people.

Art, someone has said, is the articulation of an experience. Beckett's experience is almost commonplace by now to the middle-class European *intelligentsia* and valid by virtue of that fact alone—and his expression of it is sharply witty, inventive, theatrically compact. (He uses even boredom as a means of entertainment.) Yet the play may be said to be too long, too simple, too clear, too symmetrical a fairy tale, because it is an abstraction. Abstract art, it often occurs to me, is far too logical and direct as compared to the more "realistic" art. We see through too soon to its meaning. Hamlet is in many ways still a puzzle us, because its abstract significance is part of the complex stuff of its material, which being humanly concrete must be somewhat elusive. In *Waiting for Godot*, almost everything is named. When abstraction is so clear, our attention weakens. As soon as we perceive the play's design everything else appears superogatory.

Finally, I do not accept what *Waiting for Godot* says. When it is over my innermost being cries out "'taint so." We all, at times, feel as Beckett does (so much, alas, in the contemporary world gives us reason to do so), but in the sum of everyday living we give this mood the lie. Beckett is what in modern times we call a genius: he has built a cosmos out of the awareness of a passing moment. But what saves humanity is its mediocrity: its persistence in becoming wholly involved in the trivia of day-to-day physical concerns out of which arise all our struggles and aspirations, even to the most exalted level. It is this "stupid" appetite for life, this crass identity with it, which is its glory, sometimes called divine.

I can imagine a number of different ways of staging the play. Herbert Berghof's way of doing it is admirably understanding of its dual aspect: the farcical and the pathetic. I missed certain depths of feeling and poetic exaltation, a certain anguished purity which the play may have, but I am not at all sure that this lack should be ascribed to the play's direction. Even so, Bert Lahr (a true and wonderful clown with a face that conveys all), E. G. Marshall, Alvin Epstein and the others are remarkably good—and likely to improve with further playing. All in all, a memorable evening.

From *The Nation* 182 (5 May 1956): 387-90.

The Uneventful Event

Vivian Mercier

Waiting for Godot. A Tragicomedy in Two Acts. By Samuel Beckett. (Faber & Faber.)

Becketting seems to have replaced Rilking as the highwater-mark of Bookmanship; some of us, who had invested critical capital in Mr. Beckett before it was either popular or profitable, are now being accused of Becketteering.

In face of the mob who are elbowing me off the Beckett bandwagon—a vehicle on which there was pucks of room a while back–I am tempted to say there is nothing in *Godot* or the three French novels which was not implicit in *Murphy* 18 years ago. But that would be untrue. Though *Godot* contains all the wit and whimsicality of *Murphy* (minus a great deal of the old pedantry), it has one new ingredient–humanity. The novel and the play both tell us that human suffering is comic and irrational ("absurd" in the fashionable jargon), but only *Godot* reads like the work of a man who has actually suffered.

TWICE NOTHING

Even if it added nothing to *Murphy*, *Godot* would still be remarkable by the mere fact of being a popular play on an unpopular theme. Its popularity is a smack in the face for all those who say that to be a skillful playwright one must first be a "man of the theatre." As far as I know, Mr. Beckett may never have been back-stage in his life until *Godot* was first performed. Yet, this first play shows consummate stagecraft. Its author has achieved a theoretical impossibility—a play in which nothing happens, that yet keeps audiences glued to their seats. What's more, since the second act is a subtly different *reprise* of the first, he has written a play in which nothing happens, *twice*.

As Mr. Patrick Kavanagh has said in these columns, *Godot* makes fun even of despair. No further proof of Mr. Beckett's essential Irishness is needed. He outdoes MM. Sartre and Camus in scepticism, just as Swift beat Voltaire at his own game. Other satirists ridicule this or that human vice or foible, wrote Voltaire, but Swift "se moque du genre humain." "A Modest Proposal" is Swift making grim fun of his own despair about human nature, just as *Heartbreak House* is Shaw making agonised fun of the blow dealt to his optimism by the first World War. There is no subject so sacred or so intimate that an Irishman will not turn it to ridicule—see *Ulysses*, "The Midnight Court," and "The Vision of MacConglinne" passim. About the only thing *Godot* shows consistent respect for is the music-hall low-comedy tradition. Mr. Beckett must have spent many an hour in the Olympia and the old Royal, at the Gaiety pantomimes, and at the silent films of Chaplin and Buster Keaton.

"ADAPTATION"

Mr. Beckett's own English version of *En Attendant Godot* has two points of special interest for the Irish reader. On the one hand, it is an adaptation rather than a translation, in which Irish allusions have sometimes been substituted for French ones—though I notice that a reference to Voltaire, which became a reference to Berkeley in the New York edition, has been transferred to Samuel Johnson in the London one.

On the other hand, except for a few words like "cod" and "banjaxed," the English adaptation does not employ Dublin (or any other) slang, in spite of the very local flavour given off by the Dublin production. Mr. Beckett's French, in fact, is racier than his English, enough so to make a dictionary of *argot* necessary at times. But then, what dictionary would give a Frenchman the meaning of "banjaxed"?

The text of this London edition incorporates the changes imposed on the Criterion Theatre production by the Lord Chamberlain, whereas our Pike Theatre performances adhere to the franker language of the New York edition. While these concessions to prudery make the play neither better nor worse, at least they put it beyond the reach of our book censorship. Ironically, any Catholic theologian worth his salt could make a very strong case for putting *Godot* on the Index—if it isn't there already—but then, few of us are naive enough to suppose that our system of book censorship is Catholic or even Christian. Its tutelary deities are Dagon, god of the Philistines, and Mrs. Grundy, goddess of the English.

From *The Irish Times* (18 February 1956): 6.

En attendant Godot: Tragedy or Comedy? [1]
Ramona Cormier and Janis L. Pallister

Discussing the absurd drama in his article "Freedom and Comedy," William Thompson describes the mask which the "absurd hero" assumes. "Half the audience," he writes, "will see the mask as tragic; half the audience will see the mask as comic. The audience will be right, for the human condition does not change; we have the same ancient choice: we can laugh or we can cry."[2] This comment is true insofar as we find critics as well as audiences split in their reaction to *En attendant Godot*. Yet, there is good reason to argue that the play is neither a comedy nor a tragedy, at which we choose to laugh or else to cry, but a subtle fusion of the two modes. The play may well be a "tragicomedy in two acts," as Beckett calls it in the English edition. The superficial comedy of the play which provokes in us an initial laughter is abruptly corrected by our sudden recognition of the potential tragedy in the human situation as it is portrayed here. However, there is every likelihood that the play comes full circle, so that though we may not realize it, we are perhaps called upon to laugh at things we do not usually laugh at. What may be appropriate here is the dianoetic laughter (the mirthless, the sardonic laugh) which comes with the recognition of an absurdity which overrides the tragedy in the human condition. In other words, it is not so much a question of whether we have here a tragedy or a comedy but rather that a unilateral response to *En attendant Godot* is not appropriate. We, the audience, do not readily make this third step which would complete the cycle of responses from comedy to tragedy to comedy, but it is likely that Beckett himself has made the necessary transitions. He may then laugh not only at the characters in his play but at us when we "weep" for them. If, then, Beckett views this tragic plight with which we tend to sympathize as ultimately comic, his opinion of man is indeed pessimistic and raises the question as to what his artistic ends may be. Again conventional answers, such as catharsis, punishment through ridicule, and so forth, are unacceptable. Just how Beckett views art can be discerned to some extent from the play itself. We find evidence here (as in his other writings) that art may constitute a diversion, however momentary, from the tedium and the *ennui* of existence, as it may also deter withdrawal. If this is the case, then we are confronted with a paradox, and Beckett may be as much against as for art.

That aspect of comedy in *En attendant Godot* which one may call superficial is conventional in nature, having its origins in the farce, the *comedia* [sic] *dell'arte*, pantomime and vaudeville traditions. Comic devices belonging in this category include physical comedy found in such things as falling and stumbling, and in the voyeurism of Estragon. On a somewhat higher level, we have linguistic comedy coming from repetitions, puns, misunderstandings, scatological word play and from ceremonial and ritualistic uses of language. From vaudeville we have the linguistic routines, the hat exchange, the fallen pants, the unzipped fly, the general outlandish clothing of the characters, including their derbies. Suicide failures (due to broken ropes and the like) come from the pantomime; and *commedia dell'arte* as well as pantomime give us the stock farcical characters, certainly the clowns or *zanni* reflected in Estragon and Vladimir and perhaps even the pedant suggested by Pozzo. Comic effects, which, like certain others listed above, might come from any one of these sources, are achieved through the frequent memory lapses of the characters and through their general failure to communicate.

These effects have in common the fact that they are traditional in comedy and, as a result of this, they automatically evoke laughter in us, as for the most part they also do in the characters. That is to say, though at most times our laughter coincides, there are other times when a matter which is serious for the characters, such as the occasional falls they take or their miscarried efforts to accomplish something, is funny to us. What we are laughing at here is for the most part limitations in both the physical and intellectual domains. Our laughter in these cases may be classified as social because, as Bergson notes, we are in agreement concerning the subject for laughter. Our response at this stage is one of detachment: we are not in sympathy with the scene or situation being portrayed.

However, in *Godot* the superficial comedy is extended to grotesque exaggerations. These appear in the egotism of the characters, especially the pompousness and platitudinousness of Pozzo, as well as his mistreatment of Lucky. They can also be observed in the macabre appearance of Lucky, and in the frenzied pace of games with which Estragon and Vladimir intend to cope with the ever-present *ennui*. This grotesqueness underlying the superficial comedy leads us, whether correctly or incorrectly, to the tragic mode.

While the characters of the play appear to have no awareness of the grotesqueness and only vague glimmers of the seriousness of their plight, the audience recognizes not only the grotesqueness but even the potential tragedy of the situation being portrayed. It would seem at this point, then, that we have a tragicomedy of sorts, or in any case a fusion of the tragic and comic modes. This duality in tone can further be said to find its echo throughout the play, which is systematically built on the numerical figure two, and in the interchangeability of the tragic and comic masks of the two characters.

On the other hand, the tragic element of *En attendant Godot* does not depend upon traditional devices, nor can it be called tragic by conventional definitions of the word. It has been called an anti-play, on the grounds that it has no character development and no plot. This lack of plot or of action is all important in excluding *Godot* from conventional tragedy, which would embrace such twentieth century authors as Montherlant—himself a nihilist—or Anouilh. This is true because insofar as there are no events in *Godot* there can be no possibility of an outcome (no *nœud*, no *dénouement*), no tragic recognition, and, despite what Ruby Cohn and others claim, no transcendence.[3] In addition, we have in this play stylization or character "types" without any clear identity. There is no development of the characters, no evolution, and indeed, if anything, a declension. This, of course, is to be expected, in view of the fact that these men are victims of their habits and are thus incapable of voluntary change. In fact, no one of the men can be designated as the tragic hero who falls (conventionally from great heights), and there is thus no sublimity involved.

Although in *Godot* there is no delving into the individual psychological make-up of the four characters, they are psychological types. Furthermore, collectively these characters represent universal man. We do not identify with any one of the characters as we would do with a tragic hero, but rather with the general human situation as well as with the particular situation in which each character finds himself. While in the case of the tragic hero we identify with his exceptional and his uncompromising nature, we recognize in these four men another side of ourselves, that side which is all too willing to compromise. The characters of *En attendant Godot* compromise not only with each other but also with their situation, and this is in part why the play can be called an ultra-modern tragedy. That is to say, in *En attendant Godot* we do not have a catastrophe or some tragic condition which has been brought about through tragic error; it is man's situation itself, neither remediable nor provoked by human manipulations, which is tragic.[4]

The play, then, is tragic in the sense that it portrays man as a victim of himself, a victim of his own finite nature. It is a tragedy portraying the limitations of reason as well as of imagination. It is deterministic, showing that the will is limited and yet capable of putting man in a position of willful false optimism if not a willful lack of preoccupation with the tragic elements of his existence. Instead, the characters, who are bound to the realm of forfeiture described by Heidegger, are preoccupied only with trivia: games, including among other things language, suicide and waiting for Godot. Man's tragedy as seen here has, in fact, a double source—an internal one arising from his finite nature and an external one in which that nature collides with the cosmos. In *En attendant Godot* we have horror without exaltation. Our reaction to the scene that unfolds before us is one of horror and despair. We sympathize, whether rightly or wrongly, with the characters, who may also have a feeling of horror and despair, although with them it must be considered largely subconscious. Be that as it may, by the close of the play we feel the despair and *ennui* of existence; we are made mindful of the foolishness of all activity between birth and death. What is proposed is a tendency toward death in the form of absolutes, of withdrawal, of a denial of life. The central irony of all this is that while the compromises depicted result in absurdity through their imprisoning consequences, correctives such as withdrawal result in absurdity through their freedom. And this freedom must be viewed as paradoxical freedom because it represents life apart from life, a kind of death in life. It is freedom which is isolationist and nihilistic, freedom without responsibility.[5]

Normally we expect the tragic hero to suffer over the predicament in which he places himself or in which the cosmos places him. As we examine the reactions of the characters in *En attendant Godot* we find that the length, the degree and the source of their suffering leads us to wonder whether it is of tragic proportions. Just as we have superficial comedy, so also do we have physical suffering, the most elementary kind of suffering. Estragon's feet hurt;

he is hungry; he receives beatings during the night. Because of his prostate condition, Vladimir cannot laugh but only smile (thus physical suffering may hamper the comic response), and he must urinate frequently (a source of amusement to Estragon). On the other hand, while Lucky does not in any way show signs of resentment over the physical abuse heaped upon him, he experiences anguish on another level when Pozzo threatens to get rid of him. However, from Pozzo's point of view, whatever sorrow Lucky feels over this is short-lived. This can be seen in the advice he gives to Estragon when the latter wishes to console Lucky (p. 37). Indeed, as far as Pozzo is concerned, all states of suffering are momentary, and life is perpetually tossed between the tragic and the comic. He says, "Les larmes du monde sont immuables. Pour chacun qui se met à pleurer, quelque part un autre s'arrête. Il en va de même du rire" (p. 38). This contention seems to be borne out in the play by the fact that whatever spiritual anguish the characters experience appears to be of a fleeting nature. Pozzo's momentary anguish, which is generally oriented around the problem of pinpointing time, can be seen in the specific stage direction "*avec angoisse*" preceding his question "Sommes-nous au soir?" (p. 98). The anguish of Estragon and Vladimir is equally fleeting. We see it in Estragon when he says such things as "Je suis malheureux," and "Je suis fatigué," which reflect his boredom and impatience. Vladimir's anguish is seen at moments when a lull in the *divertissements* occurs (p. 73; p. 96). Occasionally, too, Vladimir's ejaculations indicate mental suffering, as his "Miséricorde" (p. 107).[6] Vladimir's anguish over Pozzo's treatment of Lucky is also temporary and his sympathies are easily diverted. Indeed the moods of all these men fluctuate, especially those of Vladimir and Estragon, so that at times Estragon's comic mask is momentarily replaced by the tragic mask, while the habitually tragic mask of Vladimir is sometimes surplanted by the comic.

However, do these men suffer over the right thing? Do they think or speak of the "mess," to use Beckett's own term?[7] Do they suffer over it? Are they distressed by the notion that "We cannot know and we cannot be known"?[8] We believe that they do not experience profound suffering, and that they are just as ridiculous, perhaps as evil, as they are tragic. They are creatures who are willfully avoiding the basic issues of despair and death, and it is not unreasonable to think that Beckett views them as non-tragic because they do not suffer to any significant degree. It is appropriate to add here that about Proust's characters Beckett writes: "But already will, the will to live, the will not to suffer, Habit, having recovered from its momentary paralysis, has laid the foundations of its evil and necessary structure . . ." (*P.*, p. 29). The quotation seems eminently applicable to Vladimir and Estragon, as well as to Pozzo and Lucky. Thus, we may say that as we do not have profound pain in the characters of *En attendant Godot*, so we cannot have the other pole, that of exaltation, that of tragic sublimity.[9]

Indeed, upon close scrutiny we discover that the nihilism, the ironies, the ambiguities portrayed in the play are probably not tragic in the eyes of Beckett, but, rather, comic in a very special way. One might imagine Beckett is here indulging in what is described in *Watt* as the *risus purus*, or dianoetic laughter, that is, ". . . the laugh of laughs . . . the laugh laughing at the laugh, the beholding, the saluting of the highest joke, in a word, the laugh that laughs—silence please— at that which is unhappy."[10] This laughter, which is sardonic and mirthless, compounds the horror of the play by laughing at what is essentially evil, the metaphysical condition of man as demonstrated through his many limitations. Such laughter is basically non-social in nature. In conventional comedy (when it is not of the sentimental *genre*) the main character is ridiculed, usually with the purpose of bringing the erring "hero" back into the fold of society. However, in *En attendant Godot* Beckett is not ridiculing but mocking the main character, who is, in reality, a composite of all four characters. That is to say, *universal man* is being mocked in this play.

Now, it is the rare person who reaches Beckett's level, the level of the *risus purus*. The majority of us are too involved with the tragic elements to have proper perspective. Perhaps we also have habits in our concepts of tragedy and comedy which keep us from the greater suffering which comes from seeing humor in that which is unhappy. We are tempted to sympathize with the characters, or else with their situation, when we should perhaps be holding it in disdain. This is in part why we, the audience, are viewed as being dead. Yet, it is improbable that Vladimir and Estragon have reached this stage of comedy either. How, then, are they able to describe us as being dead? Are they the unconscious *porte-parole* of Beckett in this matter? For it is quite clear that Beckett recognizes the situation (the absurdity of the human condition) as a source of the "highest joke." He calls upon us to laugh at the attempt to gather meaning and purpose from that which has no meaning or purpose. This is black comedy at its blackest, in that it takes a bitter view of the human being and of his condition. But does Beckett include himself in this mockery of humanity? With such a sardonic and pessimistic concept of man, and having as he does the idea that suffering is the main condition of the artistic experience (*P.*, p. 16), why does Beckett write?

The answer to this question may be that he writes to divert others, an argument that can be illustrated by an example drawn from *En attendant Godot* itself where we find Estragon and Vladimir being entertained by Pozzo and Lucky. Vladimir and Estragon view this play-within-a-play as pure *divertissement*. However, to interpret *Godot* simply as a diversion would be a serious oversimplification because, like Vladimir and Estragon, we would then be evading the basic issues of death, *ennui*, finitude, disorder, etc., which are clearly present in the play. It would also be to take *En attendant Godot* as a superficial comedy or as a pure tragedy, rather than as the complex fusion of tragedy and comedy which it is.

Then again, we might compare Beckett to his character Malone in *Malone Dies*, and say that he writes to pass the time or to divert himself, a need which we have seen to be dominant in Vladimir and Estragon, and a need which all men have. This would be tantamount to talking aloud or attempting to have a dialogue with society. But paradoxically, this is in essence a monologue that you do for yourself and which others inevitably distort. As Beckett himself writes, "Either we speak and act for ourselves—in which case speech and action are distorted and emptied of their meaning by an intelligence that is not ours, or else we speak and act for others—in which case we speak and act a lie" (*P.*, p. 47). Thus, writing to pass time, which is a means of contending with solitude, results paradoxically in an even greater solitude, the solitude of the solipsist, brought about through the recognition that language inescapably separates a person from himself as well as from others.

On the other hand, and this is far more likely, Beckett may write to take inventory, as does Malone. Not only might he have as his goal to arrive at self-perception, but, more importantly, to expose the "mess"—the confusion everywhere present in man's existence. This chaos is portrayed in the theology and morality of the characters in *En attendant Godot*. It is also seen in the character's physical and mental make-up as in their language. It is present in their relationships to one another as also in their use of time. The mixed tones of tragedy and comedy present in the play also contribute to the impression of confusion which we receive from the play.

This desire on the part of Beckett to expose the universal mess may be intended as a corrective, or it may be restricted to a mere mimesis, that is, to a presentation of the meaninglessness of life, in which case the play itself would have to be meaningless. But here a new irony would arise; for, as João Mendes has correctly asserted, the play is not meaningless, which would be proof that art and intelligence are not—as the play seeks to demonstrate—absurd.[11] That is to say, the need to express meaninglessness through meaningful form, and thus to give meaning, even though that meaning is meaninglessness, would constitute the greatest irony of all.

Then again, Beckett may be compelled to write in order to effect an exorcism[12]; that is, he may, like his character the Unnamable, continue to talk so that one day he may be able to arrive at absolute silence. What this would amount to is the desire of the literary artist to create the "perfect" work of art, a desire to make a full artistic and intellectual statement, but a desire which can, of course, never be fulfilled. This ideal work of art is Beckett's Godot, which he hopes for but can never attain, for he must necessarily distort his vision, whether he attempts to formulate it through language, with all its limitations, or through the mime, which, though less confining in one sense, is more so in another. The irony here is that Beckett knows that he cannot get at the perfect, undistorted art work and yet he continues to try because he must (*P .*, p. 47). Is his compulsion partially grounded in habit like the compulsions of Vladimir and Estragon?

Finally, Beckett may write because he is a series of individuals (*P*., p. 8): a man, a thinker, a creative artist, etc. As a thinker he has insights into the human condition, and, however pessimistic his views may be, for him art is the means by which he articulates these insights. Furthermore, as an artist, he is concerned with the solution of artistic problems which arise as he attempts to convey his world view. Thus the two facets of his personality—artist and thinker— interrelate and overlap one another.

Now, it is interesting to find Ashmore contending that art is the only thing not negated because not dealt with in *En attendant Godot*.[13] On the contrary, aesthetic deliberations are manifold, perhaps paramount, in *En attendant Godot*, and art is indeed negated. This can be observed in the dialogue of the characters as well as in the play's lack of conventional structure.

Although in *Proust* (p. 16) Beckett writes that "suffering opens a window on the real and is the main condition of the artistic experience," in *Godot* we find Estragon unable to transcend his existence (p. 70), unable to appreciate things external to himself (such as the landscape [p. 71]), unwilling to grasp nuances (p. 70)—all of which things would be necessary for the appreciation or creation of art. His boredom—"Boredom that must be considered as the most tolerable because the most durable of human evils" (*P*., p. 16)—obviates the possibility of an aesthetic experience.

On the other hand, certain abortive aesthetic responses on the part of Vladimir and Estragon can be found in the play. We might note for example their stilted, perhaps purely polite or mechanical response to Pozzo's inquiry as to how they have found his speech on the night (p. 44). We might also note their angry reaction to the chaos and even to the content of Lucky's think-piece. Furthermore, their ultimate response to the play-within-a-play in Act I is minimal in that they view it merely as a diversion and a pastime. In no way are they moved to reflect on the horror of what they have just viewed, and if art ought to lead to a "renovation,"[14] then art is truly negated here by Vladimir and Estragon. It is imperative to note that there is a total degeneracy of art in Act II, for the play-within-a-play here does not even result in the *divertissement* anticipated by Vladimir upon the return of Pozzo and Lucky to the scene (p. 88).

The audience too is brought into the realm of the play and thus we have in effect a play-within-a-play-within-a-play. But in Act I the audience is viewed as a bog—hence, like Estragon who says he is sunk in the mire and sand,[15] it is unable to grasp the full intellectual and aesthetic portent of the play. Furthermore, in Act II the audience is viewed as being dead, hence beyond hope of being reached by the artist.

The degeneracy of the theater suggested in the foregoing may be attributed to the lethargy of the audience (comparable to the stagnation of Vladimir and

Estragon) or to the difficulty the artist has in presenting his ideas with any degree of immediacy, thus suggesting that art—especially art that has language as its medium—is as limited as any other facet of man's existence.

This degeneracy of the theater is reflected in the anti-formal nature of *En attendant Godot*. As we have seen, the play has no plot, thus no climax and no *dénouement*; it has no character development (no hero); and its genre is not clear-cut. In other words, we have a deformation of classical tragedy, a deformation of a conventional concept of the hero and a deformation of the stylistic devices of the traditional drama. Thus, for example, if the vaudeville routines are to be likened to the Greek chorus, then these routines can only be called a wretched parody of the choric interludes found in the great classical plays. In addition, the events and the dialogue presented are confused and chaotic, and intentionally so, for they are meant to stimulate the "mess" existing in reality. The use of the anti-play, along with the withdrawal and rigidity or unchangingness of the characters is aesthetic nihilism, corresponding to Beckett's nihilism and absolute nothingness as an ideal. There is a perfect blending of *forme* and *fond* here: traditional form would have blurred the nihilistic world view present in the play. Yet, once again we find irony in the fact that the play, though it may intend to negate theatre (art), nevertheless is a play, nevertheless does have form, just as the motifs built on the meaninglessness and futility of life are charged with meaning. Thus, almost in spite of the artist, decomposition is replaced by innovation and renovation, old form is replaced by new form, and, in a sense, an old vision of man is replaced by a new one.

From *L'Esprit Createur* 11, no. 3 (Fall 1971): 44-45.

---

[1]The substance of this article will appear as a chapter in a forthcoming book on Beckett entitled *Waiting for Death*, to be published by the University of Alabama Press in 1972. We have used the Grove Press edition of Beckett's *En Attendant Godot* (New York, 1963) in this article. Succeeding page references to this work will be indicated in the text.

[2]William Thompson, "Freedom and Comedy," *Tulane Drama Review*, vol. IX, 3 (Spring, 1965), p. 230.

[3]Ruby Cohn, "The Absurdly Absurd: Avatars of Godot," *Comparative Literature Studies*, 21 (1965), p. 240.

[4]Thus, we would admit—at least in part—Raymond Williams' thesis found in *Modern Tragedy* (Stanford, 1966) that we have here an example of the tragedy of the total condition of man (p. 153), as well as a tragic rhythm in the

inseparability or inter-locked illusions of Estragon and Vladimir, who remain together in spite of the stalemate in which they find themselves (p. 155).

[5]See Thompson, p. 230, for a discussion of isolation in connection with the farce, the comedy, and the absurd drama.

[6]This may be merely a world-weary sigh, and have no religious basis as Geoffrey Brereton claims in his *Principles of Tragedy* (Coral Gables, Florida, 1968), p. 250.

[7]Tom Driver, "Beckett by the Madeleine," *Columbia University Forum Anthology* (New York, 1968), p. 128.

[8]Samuel Beckett, *Proust* (New York, 1931), p. 49. Hereafter page designations will appear in the text, preceded by *P*.

[9]Thus Janvier's argument for an optimistic tragedy based on the tranquillity or courage of the characters vis-à-vis their situation seems to overlook their fundamental superficiality, that is, their willful blindness to the real source of their ills. Ludovic Janvier, *Pour Samuel Beckett* (Paris, 1966), pp. 103-4.

[10]Samuel Beckett, *Watt* (New York, 1959), p. 48.

[11]João Mendes, "Vida Literária," *Brotéria*, 69 (1959), p. 61.

[12]See Lawrence E. Harvey in *Configuration critique de Samuel Beckett*, ed. M. J. Friedman (Paris, 1964), p. 166.

[13]Jerome Ashmore, "Philosophical Aspects of *Godot*," *Symposium*, XVI. 4 (Winter, 1962), pp. 296-97.

[14]See Driver, loc. cit., where Beckett speaks of our chance of renovation.

[15]It should not be construed that when the ego-centered Estragon says this, he is referring to anything except his own particular plight. He is not concerned with the "mess" Beckett speaks of, which is universal in scope. The individual members of the audience, too, are enmeshed in their own ego-oriented problems, and so are unable to address themselves to the larger and more profound (because universal) predicament of the human condition.

Samuel Beckett and the Postmodern: Language Games, *Play*, and *Waiting for Godot*

Jeffrey Nealon

In Samuel Beckett's *Waiting for Godot*, Vladimir and Estragon pass the time while waiting by playing at a series of games—language games—which constitute their existence and form their social bond. Language games and play are two key concepts in much of contemporary thought; as Wittgenstein—the "father" of language-game theory—writes, "the term 'language game' is meant to bring into prominence the fact that the *speaking* of a language is part of an activity, a form of life (*Lebensform*)."[1] As Wittgenstein sees it, a word is analogous to a chess piece, and utterances can be thought of as moves within the language games that make up the human social bond. This notion of language games, as appropriated from Wittgenstein and modified by subsequent thinkers, has had a great influence on contemporary thinking about language, shifting the emphasis of language analysis from an enquiry into the meaning of a statement to its role in a language game. As Fredric Jameson writes in his foreword to Jean-François Lyotard's *The Postmodern Condition*:

> ... utterances are now seen less as a process of transmission of information or messages, or in terms of some network of signs or even signifying systems, than as ... the "taking of tricks," the trumping of a communicational adversary, an essentially conflictual relationship between tricksters.[2]

Such, it seems to me, is the state of language games in *Godot*; it is the play of Vladimir and Estragon's words, not any agreed-upon meaning for them, which constitutes their social bond. Waiting for legitimation of their society in Godot is, from the beginning, unnecessary; they constitute a society which is always already formed by their participation in language games. As Lyotard writes:

> ... there is no need to resort to some fiction of social origins to establish that language games are the minimum relation required for society to exist ... the question of the social bond, insofar as it is a question, is itself a language game, the game of inquiry. It immediately positions the person who asks, as well as the addressee and the referent asked about: it is *already* the social bond. (p. 15)

This postmodern social bond is suspended in *Godot* by Vladimir and Estragon's drive to recuperate a transcendent principle—represented by

Godot—which they feel will give meaning to their lives and their speech, thereby legitimating their society. All their games have reference to one metagame (or what Lyotard, in his discussion of modernism, calls a "grand Narrative"): waiting for Godot. Theirs is the discourse of modernism, which "legitimates itself with reference to a metadiscourse . . . making an explicit appeal to some grand narrative" (p. xxiii), some recuperative metaphysical system such as Platonism, the Christian God, the Hegelian dialectic of spirit, transcendent subjectivity, or the hermeneutics of meaning. These grand narratives, upon which modernism bases itself, have all broken down, giving way to a postmodern society which is characterized by incredulity toward both metanarratives and legitimation in them. In postmodern society, it is precisely in the social bond of language and language games that we can legitimate our own society. In such a postmodern society, people have untied themselves from the belief in a metaphysical, trans-historical, absolute ground for their existence. It has become apparent that no such system exists, but this does not reduce postmodern society to barbarity and chaos, as the modernists thought it would. Postmoderns look to themselves and their communicational interaction in society to legitimate their existence.

In *Waiting for Godot*, Gogo and Didi *have* such a communicational society but they do not realize it because of their deep-seated drive toward legitimation in Godot. Early in the play we see how this belief in a static metaphysical support displaces any postmodern notion of society:

> ESTRAGON Let's go.
> VLADIMIR We can't.
> ESTRAGON Why not?
> VLADIMIR We're waiting for Godot.[3]

This simple sequence occurs several times throughout the play,[4] and always after a long pause following the final "trick" played in a language game: when their games break down or are played out, they constantly refer back to their metagame, their metadiscourse—Godot. For example, after Pozzo and Lucky leave near the end of the first act, we have this exchange:

> POZZO . . . Adieu
> Long silence
> VLADIMIR That passed the time.
> ESTRAGON It would have passed in any case.
> VLADIMIR Yes, but not so rapidly.
> Pause
> ESTRAGON What do we do now?
> VLADIMIR I don't know.
> ESTRAGON Let's go.

> VLADIMIR We can't.
> ESTRAGON Why not?
> VLADIMIR We're waiting for Godot. (p. 31)

For Vladimir and Estragon, the grand Narrative of Godot imposes a rigid metaphysical limit on their gaming. To suggest these limits, Beckett employs a spatial metaphor: Vladimir and Estragon cannot *go* anywhere (disrupt the limits of their gaming) because they have inscribed themselves within the limits of one static, universal metagame, to which they constantly return when their smaller games have run their course. They play comfortably within these limits, but never attempt to transgress or disrupt them; in short, they play modern language games, not postmodern ones.

In postmodern language games, the limits of the game are not given from outside the game, but rather, as Lyotard writes, "the limits themselves are the stakes and provisional results of language strategies" (p. 17). In postmodern language games, the goal of the game is to make moves which expand the limits of the game, constantly disrupting its margins. This disruption and expansion of the limits of language games allow for a corresponding expansion of what can be thought; since we think in language, the de-limitation of an existing language game allows for inventive, creative thought. As Paul Feyerabend writes, "without a constant misuse of language there cannot be any discovery, any progress."[5] To take a relatively simple example, non-Euclidean geometry could not have been "invented" if someone had not transgressed and disrupted the limits of the language game we call plane geometry. If mathematicians of the early twentieth century had believed—as mathematicians and philosophers from Euclid's time to the late nineteenth century did—that Euclidean plane geometry was an absolute, they would not have been able to think beyond its limits and posit a non-Euclidean geometry. Such a disruption of the ruling order—or, in Feyerabend's terms, such a "misuse of language"—is always paralogistic respective to the ruling paradigm because it seeks to disrupt this model by which it will be judged. A mathematician cannot *think* three-dimensional geometry if she feels that plane geometry is an absolute; it simply would not make sense relative to the ruling paradigm. So, unlike modern gaming, this disruption of limits—this postmodern gaming—does not simply reinforce and recuperate the grand Narratives of the past; rather it refines and reinforces our abilities to think at, against, and beyond the stifling limits of previous thought. In Lyotard's conception of postmodern language games, "invention is always born of dissension" (p. xxv).

In *Waiting for Godot*, the best example of this dissension and movement at the margins of a language game is the speech that is perhaps the key to the entire play: Lucky's "think," which can be seen as a transgression and disruption of the limits of the ultimate metagame—Western metaphysics, the language game of truth. The text of Lucky's speech is akin to the product of taking all the great works of Western thought, putting them through a paper shredder, and pasting them back together at random. Beckett directs Lucky's long monologue against the popular notion that philosophy's job is to restore unity to man's learning, a job which philosophers can only do by recuperating some metanarrative which links together all moments in human history within a single, continuous metaphysical system. Lucky's think, though, is a narrative that disrupts and deconstructs all notions of universal, ahistorical, consistent metanarrative—all Godots. He begins:

> Given the existence as uttered forth in the public works of Puncher and Wattmann of a personal God *quaquaquaqua* with a white beard *quaquaquaqua outside time* without extension who from the heights of divine apathia divine athambia divine aphasia loves us dearly with some exceptions *for reasons unknown but time will tell* and suffers like the divine Miranda with those who *for reasons unknown but time will tell* are plunged in torment plunged in fire whose fire flames if that continues and who can doubt it will fire the firmament that is to say blast hell to heaven so blue and still and calm so calm with a *calm which even though intermittent is better than nothing* ... (p. 28, my emphasis)

Lucky's think is directed against all the grand Narratives of Western metaphysics, which ground themselves in discourses claiming to be: referential and self-validating ("quaquaquaqua"); ahistorical ("outside time"); metaphysical or mystical ("for reasons unknown"); teleological and revelatory ("but time will tell"); and bulwarks against radical skepticism ("calm which even though intermittent is better than nothing").

Lucky's think exposes the limits imposed by all prior objectivist thinking; it is a thoroughly postmodern language game that moves at the limit of what has been thought. It is a speech of liberation set against the metaphysical tyranny of limitations on thought imposed by limitations on language. A clear example of these limitations is put forth by the early Wittgenstein:

> ... in order to be able to set a limit to thought, we should have to find both sides of the thinkable. *It will therefore only be in language that the limit can be set, and what lies on the other side of the limit will simply be nonsense.*[6]

This thinking on the other side of the limit is precisely what Lucky's speech consists of. It is, however, not *non-sense*. Simple non-sense would still be thought dictated by the dialectic of reason; it would involve a simple crossing over to the other side of the dialectic—doing or saying the *un*-reasonable thing—leaving its limits intact. Lucky's think is not *unreasonable*; it is, to coin a word, *transreasonable*: it does not simply offer us the other side of the dialectic of reason, but moves at and beyond the margins of the dialectic, beyond the limitations that have been placed on language. In Lucky's speech, Beckett exposes and transgresses these limits, mixing bits of grammatical sense (inside the limit) and transgrammatical nonsense (outside the limit) to the point where the limit itself is effaced, opening up the field of what can be thought.[7] In Lucky's speech, Beckett attempts to show that—as Lyotard characterizes the postmodern condition—"there is no possibility that language games can be totalized in any metadiscourse" (p. 43). Through Lucky's speech, Beckett emphasizes "new 'moves' and even new rules for language games," (p. 55) having transgressed and disrupted the old rules and limits.[8]

Lucky's think, though, meets with a less than enthusiastic response from the other characters on the stage. Vladimir, Estragon, and Pozzo become increasingly uneasy during Lucky's tirade, until *"all three throw themselves on LUCKY who struggles and shouts his text"* (p. 28). Finally, after Lucky has been attacked and quieted, Pozzo grabs his hat (his "thinking cap") and tramples on it, saying "There's an end to his thinking!" (p. 30). This "intellectual" violence, I think, mirrors the physical violence that Lucky is subjected to throughout the play.[9] According to the contemporary ethical thinker Emmanuel Levinas, there is a certain violence inherent in the make-up of objective metaphysical systems—as we have seen, they violently close off other possibilities, other forms of life.[10] Lucky's speech, then, can be seen as a peaceful one, transgressing the limits of an inherently violent coherence in objective metadiscourses. As Jacques Derrida writes in his essay on Levinas, "Violence and Metaphysics":

> This coherence in ontology is violence itself for Levinas: the "end" of history is not absolute Logic, the absolute coherence of the Logos with itself in itself, but peace in separation, the diaspora of absolutes ... Is not peaceful discourse the discourse which respects separation and rejects the horizon of ontological coherence?[11]

Lucky's playful, "peaceful" discourse is met with violence—intellectual and physical—because it disrupts the modernist notion of coherence in the grand Narrative: specifically, it disrupts the narrative upon which Vladimir and Estragon have based their existence, Godot. Lucky's speech is essentially peaceful because it displaces the notion of objective knowledge, a notion that moves hand-in-hand with power. Knowledge is power, and objectivist modern knowledge is always used to create or uphold a violent power structure. As Levinas writes, "in history understood as the manifestation of reason, where *violence reveals itself to be reason,* philosophy presents itself as a realization of being, that is, as [*philosophy's*] *liberation* by the *suppression of multiplicity.* Knowledge would be the suppression of the other by grasp, by the hold, or by the vision that grasps before the grasp."[12] Lucky's speech, though, points to a new, postmodern conception of knowledge. As Lyotard writes, "postmodern knowledge is theorizing its own evolution as discontinuous, catastrophic, non-rectifiable, and paradoxical. It is changing the meaning of the word *knowledge* . . . It is producing not the known, but the unknown" (p. 60).[13] Postmodern knowledge is not a tool for the bulwarking of the ruling power structure; rather, it moves at and beyond the limits of this structure—producing new ways to think about things, not simply data which reinforce and recuperate the old ways of thinking. Again, according to the ruling paradigm(s), much of this postmodern knowledge (Lucky's knowledge) may seem incomprehensible, but this is precisely the point because the postmodern drive is to push beyond the limits of the old paradigms. Vladimir and Estragon are at least on the right track when Vladimir says "This is getting really insignificant," to which Estragon replies "Not enough" (p. 44).

These lines, though, are not the only place in the play where we see Vladimir and Estragon on the verge of a Lucky-like postmodern breakthrough. In the course of the play it becomes increasingly apparent that Vladimir and Estragon are, relative to Godot, in the same servile position Lucky is, especially with respect to the doubly-violent end to his deconstructive think. For example, near the end of the play—after the boy has told Vladimir and Estragon that Godot again will not come today—we have this exchange:

> ESTRAGON . . . Let's go away from here.
> VLADIMIR We can't.
> ESTRAGON Why not?
> VLADIMIR We have to come back to-morrow.
> ESTRAGON What for?
> VLADIMIR To wait for Godot . . .
> ESTRAGON . . . And if we dropped him? (Pause) If we dropped him?
> VLADIMIR He'd punish us. (p. 59)

Here we see Vladimir and Estragon on the verge of a deconstructive breakthrough, but again their dependence on the metadiscourse of Godot holds them back. In this passage, we see reiterated the violent nature of the limitations that a belief in Godot places on Vladimir and Estragon—both physical limits and, perhaps more importantly, intellectual ones: if they "dropped him," they feel he would *punish* them. Vladimir and Estragon cannot leave the place they are in or think beyond the limits of a static, objective metasystem because of the rigid, violent limits placed on both their actions and their thought by the modernist metadiscourse represented by Godot. Their minds are slaves to Godot in the same way Lucky's body is a slave to Pozzo.

It seems to me that Beckett, throughout *Waiting for Godot*, is engaged in criticizing the world view of the modernist, whose "objective is to stabilize the referent, to arrange it according to a recognizable point of view which endows it with a recognizable meaning" (Lyotard, p. 74). I think Beckett refuses to allow his play (and the play of his play) to be put to such recuperative uses—although that is not to say that critics haven't tried. As a matter of fact, many interpreters allow for a cozy marriage between Beckett's drama and modernism, reading *Waiting for Godot* as, in essence, a lament for the lost grand Narrative—as revolving around a *lack* of meaning and possibilities. For example, Eugene Goodheart writes that in Beckett, "the condition of nonbeing and meaninglessness is universal and insurmountable."[14] This, it seems to me , is a *modern* reading of a *postmodern* writer.[15] Rather than revolving around a lack, *Godot*, as I read it, revolves around an *excess* of meaning and possibility brought about by the liberating notion of play. I do not see the play in Beckett as a "kind of playing to *fill the void* of self,"[16] but rather, as Derrida describes it, a postmodern play, a "play whose other side would be the Nietzschean affirmation, that is the joyous affirmation of the play of the world and the innocence of becoming, the affirmation of a world of signs without fault, without truth and without origin which is offered to active interpretation. *This affirmation then determines noncenter otherwise than as loss of center.* And it plays without security."[17]

This *affirmation* of a noncentered world, this *rejection* of the grand Narratives, this *celebration* of play and language games is what most sharply separates the postmodern from the modern. In *Waiting for Godot*, Beckett shows us that Vladimir and Estragon are trapped by their modernist nostalgia for legitimation in Godot: they have a totalizing modernist world view in an infinite, postmodern world. From the beginning of the play, Beckett emphasizes that this legitimation is always already there in the play of language games and the active interpretation of the postmodern, noncentered world—not in the passive, stifling waiting for the return of an objective grand Narrative that never really offered any metaphysical support in the first place. In the end, I think Beckett asks us to consider a world that, in Derrida's words, "is no longer turned toward the origin, affirms play and tries to pass beyond man and humanism, the name of man being the name of that being who, throughout the entire history of metaphysics of ontotheology—in other words, throughout his entire history—has dreamed of full presence, the reassuring foundation, the origin and the end of play."[18] In another of his dramas, *Endgame*, Beckett gives us a suitable epigraph for this—which I have argued to be *his* —postmodern world view:
        CLOV (imploringly) Let's stop playing.
        HAMM Never![19]
From *Modern Drama* 31, no. 4 (Dec. 1988): 520-28.

---

[1] Ludwig Wittgenstein, *Philosophical Investigations*, trans, G.E.M. Anscombe (New York, 1958), p. 23.

[2] Fredric Jameson, "Forward," in Jean-François Lyotard, *The Postmodern Condition: A Report on Knowledge*, trans. Geoff Bennington and Brian Massumi (Minneapolis, 1984), p. xi. All further references to this text will be cited parenthetically.

[3] Samuel Beckett, *Waiting for Godot*, (New York, 1958), p. 10. All further references to this text will be cited parenthetically.

[4] See pp. 10, 31, 44, 45, 54, and several other places in the text in a modified form.

[5] Paul K. Feyerabend, *Against Method* (London, 1978), p. 27.

[6] Ludwig Wittgenstein, *Tractatus Logico-Philosophicus*, (Frankfurt, 1975), p. 7. Translated and cited in Allen Thiher's *Words in Reflection: Modern Language Theory and Postmodern Fiction* (Chicago, 1984), p. 9.

[7] Here I am making a perhaps problematic distinction between non-sense and nonsense. As I use the terms here, I mean sense to be taken as the reasonable end of the dialectic; non-sense is the other, unreasonable side. Nonsense lies outside the dialectic.

[8] All of this is in opposition (non-dialectical, I hope) to many readings of Beckett. For example, David Hesla argues that "the shape of Beckett's art is the shape of dialectic" (cited in Ann Paolucci's "Pirandello and the Waiting Stage of the Absurd," *Modern Drama*, 23 [1980], 102-111: 109). My argument here is that Beckett's art moves not solely within dialectics, but at and beyond their margins.

[9] In commenting on the play's physical violence in his essay "Action and Play in Beckett's Theatre," *Modern Drama*, 9 (1966), 242-250, John Fletcher writes, "In Beckett's drama, action is explored to the limit of the normally admissible and beyond" (243). Here I am arguing that in Beckett's drama *thought* is also explored to the normally admissible limit and beyond in Lucky's speech, triggering a reaction of "intellectual" violence that mirrors the more obvious physical violence directed toward Lucky.

[10] Levinas writes against thought "fixed in the concept of totality, which dominates Western philosophy. Individuals are reduced to being bearers of forces that command them unbeknown to themselves. The meaning of individuals . . . is derived from the totality." From his *Totality and Infinity*, trans. Alphonso Lingis (The Hague, 1969), pp. 21-22.

[11] Jacques Derrida, "Violence and Metaphysics," in *Writing and Difference,* trans. Alan Bass (Chicago, 1978), p. 315.

[12] *Totality and Infinity*, p. 302, my emphasis.

[13] Cf. Feyerabend's *Against Method*, pp. 17-28.

[14] Eugene Goodheart, "Literature as Game," *TriQuarterly*, 52 (1981), 134-49. For Goodheart, this meaninglessness is Beckett's "discovery of the nature of things" (137).

[15] As Lyotard writes, "[The] breaking up of the grand Narratives leads to what some authors analyze as the ... disintegration of social aggregates into a mass of atoms thrown into the absurdity of Brownian motion. Nothing of this kind is happening: this point of view, it seems to me, is haunted by the paradisiac representation of a lost, 'organic' society" (p. 15).

[16] Goodheart, 137, my emphasis.

[17] Jacques Derrida, "Structure, Sign, and Play in the Discourses of the Human Sciences," *Writing and Difference*, p. 292.

[18] *Ibid.*, p. 292.

[19] Samuel Beckett, *Endgame* (New York, 1958), p. 77; I must acknowledge that I have "borrowed" the idea of using this quotation as an ending for my essay from John Fletcher's "Action and Play in Beckett's Theatre," cited above—although I use it in a different context to suggest a different network of ideas.

How To Read *Endgame*
Vivian Mercier

Let us suppose—in fact, let's hope—that at least one member of The Readers' Subscription knows nothing about Samuel Beckett's play *Endgame*. It is to him that my opening remarks are addressed; other members can join us a little farther down.

You, sir or madam, are confronted simultaneously with the recording and the book of *Endgame*. What should you do first: read the book or listen to the records? If you take my advice, you will read *nothing* of the book except the long opening stage direction before putting on the first record. Then just sit back and listen to the whole recording once through. The second time you play the records, keep the book open to pick up the rest of the stage directions and get a mental picture of the stage movement, limited though it is. *Please* don't read the full text of the play until you have heard the recording two or three times.

Why do I urge this? In the first place, because the recording is such a fine one. Three of the four performers, to my mind, could hardly be surpassed in their roles. Alan Schneider, a first-rate director in any event, had the benefit of consultation and frequent correspondence with the author. In filling the roles of Hamm, Nagg and Nell—confined as they are in a wheel chair and two ash cans—Mr. Schneider had to find performers whose expressive voices would make up for their lack of movement. Lester Rawlins' powerful organ builds the most subtle variations on a base of harsh egotism, while P. J. Kelly's Abbey Theatre charm of diction and Nydia Westman's genteel quaverings are always kept under perfect control. Gerald Hiken's voice as Clov, to my ear, lacks comparable training but provides a fourth contrasting instrument in the quartet.

In the second place, I beg you to listen before you read because I want you to *experience* the play before you interpret it. Listen to what the play *is* before you start asking yourself what it *means*; that is what the practiced reader always does with poetry, and Samuel Beckett remains a poet whatever he is writing. Normally, one has to read a poem aloud to oneself, but on LP records professionals do that job for us. If we do our first reading of a poem or a play silently, especially a work that we find puzzling, pretty soon we are stopping, turning back, rereading, piecing together, interpreting. Before our first reading is over, even, we may have evolved an interpretation of the work which takes the place of the work itself in our minds. We have substituted abstract generalizations for the concrete particulars of the poem or play.

Furthermore, by approaching *Endgame* in the way I have recommended, you would probably please its author, who likes "to insist on the extreme simplicity of dramatic situation and issue" and fights very shy of far-fetched interpretations. I have just quoted a letter of his to Mr. Schneider, dated December 29, 1957. (See the Greenwich Village weekly, *The Village Voice* of March 19, 1958, where much of the correspondence about *Endgame* is printed.) He continues: "My work is a matter of fundamental sounds (no joke intended) made as fully as possible, and I accept responsibility for nothing else. If people want to have headaches among the overtones, let them. And provide their own aspirin. Hamm as stated, and Clov as stated, together as stated . . . in such a place, and in such a world, that's all I can manage, more than I could."

The "fundamental sound" of *Endgame* seems clear enough. This is surely a play about the end of the world. Not merely every*body* but every*thing* is dead or dying. The scene of the play is described more than once as a "shelter." No mention is made of bombs, whether A or H, but we may assume that some final catastrophe has taken place. Moreover, it is good that this should be so. Life means nothing but suffering to Hamm and Clov. At one point they think Nagg may be dead. "He's crying," says Clov. "Then he's living," answers Hamm. Clov finds a live flea and kills it, lest it start the evolutionary cycle over again. Nell, the only woman, is long past child-bearing, so she causes them no anxiety. A mysterious boy, seen from a window near the end of the play, does present a threat to complete extinction, but if he remains outside the shelter, he is sure to die.

Since complete extinction appears so desirable and all four characters are so miserable, why does none of them attempt to destroy himself? Hamm says, at the very beginning " . . . it's time it ended and yet I hesitate . . . to end." Clov cannot kill Hamm, however much he might like to, though Hamm begs him to do so. Clov longs to leave the shelter, even if it means certain death, but at the end of the play, though dressed and ready to go, he has not yet departed. This curious bond between Hamm the master and Clov the slave (also father and son?) constitutes the second major theme of the play. Their grudging relationship contrasts with that between Nagg and Nell, Hamm's legless father and mother, who inhabit the ash cans. Nell, who dies during the play, still cares for her husband, while he behaves almost unselfishly to her.

Mr. Beckett's earlier play, *Waiting for Godot*, contained two similar contrasting pairs. Here, the major characters were two bums, Vladimir and Estragon, whose friendship for each other is echoed by the affection of Nagg and Nell. The blind master and his toiling slave, Pozzo and Lucky, were minor characters in that play. The shift in the major roles corresponds to a shift in the "fundamental sounds" of the two plays. *Waiting for Godot* was a despairing study of hope, whereas *Endgame* is a despairing study of despair. Hamm and Clov have their parallels in Mr. Beckett's novels too: they especially resemble Knott and Watt in *Watt,* just published in America by Grove Press. Nagg and Nell, legless in their ash cans, remind one of the nameless truncated protagonist in *The Unnamable.*

Many people, unwilling or unable to accept Mr. Beckett's apparent dismal view of the malicious futility of the universe, start hunting for more acceptable interpretations or for "the overtones." For one thing, the boy at the end of the play might, unknown to Hamm and Clov, represent a rebirth of life and hope. One similar thought occurs to Hamm: ". . . here we're down in a hole . . . But beyond the hills? Eh? Perhaps it's still green? Eh?"

Or perhaps the play takes place within a single human personality. Hamm and Clov may be mind and body, since Hamm is a blind cripple, whereas Clov can see and move, however imperfectly. Alternatively, the shelter with its two windows may represent a human skull, inside which Hamm ("hammer") and Clov (French *clou,* "nail") stand for the will and the consciousness respectively. Nagg and Nell, father and mother, may represent the hereditary factors present in character or mental endowment; indeed, the two ash cans may represent the gonads, in which the past of the human race lies waiting to become its future.

Again, the title of the play, reminding one of the "ending" or "end game" in chess, suggests that red-faced Hamm in his wheel chair is the Red King, who can only be moved one square at a time in any direction. Clov, also red-faced, is a more mobile Red piece; his "stiff, staggering walk" suggests a knight's move. White-faced Nagg and Nell are two immobilized White pieces. How White can mount an attack without moving pieces is not clear to me, unless White has Red in jeopardy, and Red is examining all the possible moves open to him before sacrificing Clov. Hamm's first words are "Me . . . to play." Almost his last ones are "Me to play . . . Old endgame lost of old, play and lose and have done with losing." Naturally Clov cannot kill Hamm, since no piece can capture a king or any piece of its own color. I do not mean that the play is about a chess game: Mr. Beckett merely uses the analogy with chess to impose a pattern upon what might otherwise seem a formless series of events.

Actually, I think any approach to *Endgame* which seeks to deny that it is a play about the end of our world is not an approach but an evasion. In another letter to Mr. Schneider we have a description of the play as it appeared to Mr. Beckett just after he had finished the original French version: "Have at last written another, one act, longish, hour and quarter I fancy. Rather difficult and elliptic, mostly depending on the power of the text to claw, more inhuman than *Godot*."

I would say that with *Endgame* Mr. Beckett has tried to inaugurate a new dramatic genre. He called *Waiting for Godot* "tragicomedy," and the classification would fit the new play too—but this time the tragicomedy dips to the tragic end of the scale, not the comic. True tragedy, of course, is impossible for a writer who cannot believe in a tragic hero—powerful, proud, yet essentially good save for the tragic flaw. *Endgame* is a modern substitute for tragedy. Hamm and Clov are not heroes but monsters. Yet they suffer themselves even as they torture others. Hamm may well be right in denying that there can be misery loftier than his. Only Nagg has a fair share of goodness, and he lacks the power and the pride necessary to the tragic hero. *Endgame* is a purposefully aborted tragedy. It does not purge our passions because we do not identify ourselves fully with either Hamm or Clov.

Endgame is also a willfully aborted comedy. The night I saw it at the Cherry Lane Theatre in New York, the audience laughed many times. But the laughs were all of one kind, a kind that Mr. Beckett himself describes in *Watt:* ". . . the mirthless laugh . . . the laugh that laughs . . . at that which is unhappy." In *Endgame* itself Nell shocks Nagg by saying, "Nothing is funnier than unhappiness." You may disagree with her, but when you have read and listened to all of *Endgame* without a single mirthless laugh, it will be time enough to cast the first stone.

From *The Griffin* 8 (June 1959): 10-14.

Theatre (Review of *Endgame*)

Harold Clurman

Samuel Beckett's *Endgame* (Manhattan Theater Club) is a Mystery of final things: as death, the end of an age. Being altogether modern, it is also a comedy. We do not weep in the theater nowadays over futility, protracted dreariness or doom; we laugh.

"Endgame" is a technical term signifying the last stage in playing a hand, the position of the important card having been generally known, and the play being determined accordingly; or the point in the game when the forces (in chess or checkers) have been greatly reduced.

The central image of the piece is that of Hamm, a blind man, paralyzed, shut off in a bare, gray room with his legless parents who remain immobilized in two dustbins. His condition does not change from first to last. Hamm has an alter ego, Clov, who might be likened to an enslaved son. There is much scurrying about on Clov's part but little action; the earth and sea outside have nothing on the horizon: all is still, inert, "corpsed." At the end of Clov's long submission to his "father" and master, Hamm, he appears to be on the verge of escape. Is there hope of resurrection in this? Probably not, but we cannot be sure. Hamm "gives up," with a weary finality: "Old endgame lost of old, play and lose and have done with losing."

I append further citations to convey the tone of what is essentially a dramatic poem. Hamm asks Clov, "Have you not had enough?" "Of what?" Clov asks. The answer is, "Of this—this—thing." He refers no doubt to the burden of life. Clov is always seen in movement, obeying Hamm's senseless orders. "I can't sit," he cries out, to which Hamm responds with, "And I can't stand . . . Every man his specialty." "What's happening?" Hamm wants to know. Clov's reply is, "Something is taking its course." Hamm wonders, "We're not beginning to mean something?" "Mean something!" Clov mocks, "You and I mean something . . . Oh, that's good." Hamm speculates for a moment, "Imagine if a rational being came back to earth, wouldn't he be able to get ideas into his head if he observed us long enough. . . . To think perhaps it won't all have been for nothing!" Clov asks the supreme question, "Do you believe in the life to come?" and receives the superb answer, "Mine was always that." This is the special humor, the Beckett "joke," which makes his work seem like a scenario for a farce. Clov asks, "What is there to keep us here?" Hamm answers, "The dialogue."

The cream of the jest is the story told by the male dustbin occupant about a man who brought cloth to a tailor to have trousers made. The tailor takes an unconscionable time to finish the job. The customer, at the end of his patience, explodes, "In six days; do you hear me, six days God made the World! And you are not bloody well capable of making me a pair of trousers in three months!" The tailor retorts, "But my dear Sir, my dear Sir, look at the world and look at my trousers."

When I saw *Endgame* in Paris in 1957 I thought it "at times impressive and drab, at other times snarling through a grin . . . Its writing has humor, tang and obliquely lyric dialogue." But I thought it lacked the tenderness which alleviated the restlessness of *Waiting for Godot.* Since then, I have seen it directed by Alan Schneider, André Gregory and now by Joseph Chaikin in the present production at M.T.C. Each of these productions had different characteristics and merits, but none of the quiet and numb ache of the first one which, though in French, had something of the wonderful lostness and melody of Jack MacGowan's eminently Irish reading of the Beckett anthology we heard some years ago at the Public Theater.

I am reminded now of what Aaron Copeland once said on receiving a complete recording of Anton Webern's compositions. He admired Webern, considered him a seminal figure in modern music, a highly significant artist, but found that he had no special urge to return to repeated hearing of his work. Perhaps because I have seen *Endgame* four times I feel the same way about it. I do not feel quite this way about *Waiting for Godot.* But it may be that I have grown weary of weariness, the standstill of pained bewilderment—now become a prevalent posture—even though I cannot help being in awe of the genius of Beckett's methods of expressing it.

I found Chaikin's *Endgame* clear and forceful, and I appreciated the ironic grin on Daniel Seltzer's "masked" face as Hamm, and the exasperated incisiveness of Michael Gross' Clov. But there was too strained a declamation and too much accentuation in the reading of the lines, as though they were being delivered by an overzealous and over-disciplined company attempting to perform Shakespeare in the grand manner. There is ringing sound but little inner music or lyricism.

In writing about Beckett I cannot help but contrast him in certain respects with Pinter; the first is the progenitor of the second.

The abstraction in Beckett's writing may make understanding it difficult, but its mood is always emotionally persuasive. Though Pinter may be obscure or elusive in some of his detail, his work on the whole is more "realistic": he is of his time and place and always unmistakably English. Pinter is wed to his ambiguity, as if to divulge precisely what he means would be simple-minded, almost vulgar.

This trait is especially troubling in *Betrayal,* for while there is no doubt about what happens in it, the significance of its events is elusive. At some risk, I venture to be plain about what I believe Pinter is saying in this play. He is speaking of love among the English educated middle class. It has all but castrated itself spiritually by its traditional sense of form and correct manners. Such people cannot truly love because the wells of passion in them have gone dry. They are only capable of polite social relationships: the men feel at ease chiefly in the rituals of lunch (polite conversations about sports, books, theater, etc.) and fornication. Vital experience is so rare that memories fade. The play debunks the romance of adultery. Viewed in this light, Betrayal becomes at least a criticism of contemporary English society. If it is not that, one wonders what it is. I submit this interpretation to explain how the play can be, as I wrote in my last column, both irritating and fascinating.

From *The Nation* 230 (16 February 1980): 187-88.

In the Ruins of the Past: Reading Beckett Intertextually

Per Nykrog

When Samuel Beckett rose to international fame as a playwright following the first performance of *En attendant Godot* in January 1953, it was the disconcerting radicalism of his dramaturgy, and the unsurpassed negativity of his scenarios that struck one's mind. This perception has lingered on in the critical literature on this strangely powerful writer—from the early landmark book by Martin Esslin to the most recent contributions to Beckett studies—and is confirmed and even reinforced by Beckett's later production, in which the search for an ever more reduced stage presence, and an ever more bleak outlook, appear as a natural development of what had been Beckett's hallmark from the outset.[1] Cryptic utterances by the author (on the rare occasions he came out of the seclusion that has been his personal lifestyle) further corroborate this understanding of him—treasured tidbits, such as this early sample (1949), that have fallen into the hungry critics' bowl:

> Beckett: The situation is that of him who is helpless, cannot act, in the event cannot paint, since he is obliged to paint. The act of him who, helpless, unable to act, acts, in the event paints, since he is obliged to paint.
> Duthuit: Why is he obliged to paint?
> Beckett: I don't know.
> Duthuit: Why is he helpless to paint?
> Beckett: Because there is nothing to paint and nothing to paint with.[2]

Early Theatrical Works

On this word of wisdom given in answer to the question how he, who does not believe in language, nevertheless can be a writer: "Que voulez-vous, Monsieur? C'est les mots; on n'a rien d'autre."[3]

This perception—or conception—of Beckett is unquestionably justified. Yet one may ask, now, more than thirty years after the first performance of *Godot,* when the first shock has subsided and even become absorbed, whether the time has not come to take a fresh look at Beckett's early plays and see if Esslin was right to give his "salutary warning to anyone who approaches Beckett's plays with the intention of discovering *the* key to their understanding, of demonstrating in exact and definite terms *what they mean,*" or to state as a basic fact that *Waiting for Godot* and *Endgame* are "plays drained of character, plot, and meaningful dialogue," a "seemingly impossible tour de force" of doing something with nothing.[4] Over the years a sort of Beckett orthodoxy has developed along these lines, confirmed in the titles and in the approach of such recent major critical works as *Just Play: Beckett's Theater* and *Accommodating the Chaos: Samuel Beckett's Nonrelational Art.*[5] My contention in the following discussion is that, on the contrary, the early plays by Beckett not only deal with something, they have an articulate and identifiable scope. An "intertextual" reading, making use of what seems to be the text behind the text, can help both the identification and the articulation.

It is well known that Beckett is no uncouth savage: indeed, when he started writing his plays, he was an unusually brilliant, cultured and sophisticated academic, carrying a heavy load of the literary and cultural past. In order to reach the state of utter denudation he displays in his later scenarios, he had to rid himself of a rich and complex heritage. But this is easier said than done. His first plays reflect that effort; they form a sort of trilogy in which specific sectors of the cultural tradition, taken to task in due order, are mercilessly exorcised by being represented as hideous caricatures of themselves in a state of utter decrepitude. This may not be evident to the spectator's or the reader's spontaneous experience of these now classical texts, but well-hidden relationships from text to text can be as significant as obvious ones. From the point of view of the murderer's personal satisfaction, the perfect crime is the one that is not even recognized as such. But the public has a right to ask what is going on in the texts it admires.

That *Waiting for Godot* (*En attendant Godot,* 1949) carries a certain burden of philosophizing is evident on even a cursory reading: frequent allusions to Christ and to the Passion and an unmistakable preoccupation with salvation are there for all to see on the surface of the dialogue. A religious dimension, however warped, is obvious in the play.[6] It is strongly confirmed by the syllable 'god' in the name of the mysterious offstage character whose presence (or absence) is the key to the entire situation represented: the scant information about him provided by the messenger boy in Act II outlines a traditional, simplistic, popular image of God the Father as a venerable old man with a white beard (p. 59; cf. p. 28).

The clue is so substantial and so promising that it attracted the attention of the interpreter-detectives right away. But though it remains highly significant in itself, it did not seem to lead anywhere; upon investigation, it lost its contour or underwent unexpected and bewildering transformations. When asked about the meaning of the name, Beckett threw one inquirer off the track by saying that it had to do with *godillot*, a military boot,[7] and as early as 1956, another investigator (Eric Bentley) traced the name, and even the title of the play, back to Balzac's comedy *Mercadet, ou le faiseur* (1848), about a wheeler-dealer businessman who is deep in debt because his partner, Godeau, has absconded with the better part of their liquid assets. For years Mercadet has been waiting for Godeau to come back and get him out of trouble; now he has lost all hope. When his naïve wife brings up, once again, this threadbare hope, he says: "Après huit ans sans nouvelles, vous attendez toujours Godeau! Vous me faites l'impression de ces vieux soldats qui attendent toujours Napoléon!"[8]

The trail leading to Balzac is good enough—it is extremely improbable that the resemblance is mere coincidence—but it is totally disappointing: there is absolutely no contribution to the understanding of Godot to be found in that text.[9] It is, however, instructive in a different connection: it does prove (if that was necessary) that Beckett was not averse to playing the game of the abstruse literary quote. He must have borrowed his title, and the name Godot, from *Mercadet*, and he does not seem to care whether or not the reader or the spectator will grasp the allusion. Who, after all, could be expected to know his *Mercadet* by heart in 1950?

A more fruitful approach, here as in so many other cases, would be to leave aside for a while the finer points of detail and take a good look at the scenario as a whole. A clue as big as a barn door is easily overlooked, but that does not make it less important.

The stage in *Godot* represents a road. A road is the archetypal metaphor for a movement, a development, a "progress" (pilgrim's or rake's) which takes someone from one place (or state) to others. What is particular about the scenario in Godot is that the main characters, Vladimir and Estragon, Didi and Gogo, refuse to make use of the road according to its purpose. They do not move along it; they stay where they are, and where they seem to have been for a long time, totally idle and mortally bored, but stubborn, remaining in spite of all the frustrations and sufferings that make their existence by the roadside so utterly miserable. And why are they blocked there, in the reduced existence that is theirs? They are, obviously, waiting for Godot. At one point Didi (the intellectual of the two) sums up the fundamental assumption on which they have made their decision to act (or refuse to act) as they do:

> Vladimir: . . . Yes, in this immense confusion one thing alone is clear. We are waiting for Godot to come —
> Estragon: Ah!
> Pozzo: Help! [10]
> Vladimir: Or for night to fall (*Pause.*) We have kept our appointment and that's an end to that. We are not saints, but we have kept our appointment. How many people can boast as much? (p. 51)

It can be disastrous not to keep a nightly appointment by the roadside, even if the time of the meeting is left uncertain—especially if there is a sanctifying blessing at stake:

> Then shall the kingdom of heaven be likened unto ten virgins, which took their lamps, and went forth to meet the bridegroom. And five of them were wise, and five were foolish . . . And at midnight there was a cry made, Behold, the bridegroom cometh; go ye out to meet him. Then all those virgins arose, and trimmed their lamps. And the foolish said unto the wise, Give us of your oil; for our lamps are gone out. But the wise answered, saying, Not so; lest there be not enough for us and you: but go ye rather to them that sell, and buy for yourselves. And while they went to buy, the bridegroom came; and they that were ready went in with him to the marriage: and the door was shut. Afterward came also the other virgins, saying, Lord, Lord, open to us. But he answered and said, Verily I say unto you, I know you not. Watch therefore, for ye know neither the day nor the hour wherein the Son of man cometh.

The parable of the virgins, in Matthew 25, is part of the last teaching Christ gave to his disciples before the events of Easter: the following chapter tells of the betrayal by Judas and the Last Supper. The scene is Jerusalem, the occasion a visit the group has made to the Temple. Three evangelists record Jesus' words (Matt. 24-25; Mark 13; Luke 21), but Matthew's account is by far the most detailed. It is a truly terrifying text, one of those that Christians who like their comfort tend to overlook. The theme is the Return of the Son of Man– Doomsday. To the reader who (somewhat incongruously) comes to this immensely important text from the text of *Godot*, with its numerous allusions to the Gospels, a surprising number of details seem to correspond. It is as if *Godot* had been elaborated with the two chapters from Matthew fresh in mind: There will be "the abomination of desolation"(24:32). Compare the entire setup in *Godot*.

"For there shall arise false Christs, and false prophets" (24:24). Compare Pozzo; could he be Godot? (p. 15, and again pp. 49-50).

"Now learn a parable of the fig tree; When his branch is yet tender, and putteth forth leaves ye know that summer is nigh" (24:32). Compare the leaves that come out on the tree between the two acts of *Godot* (p. 37), perhaps announcing the Spring (p.42).

"Then shall two be in the field; the one shall be taken, and the other left" (24:40). Compare "it's a reasonable percentage" and the following discussion (*Godot*, pp. 8-10).

"Watch therefore: for ye know not what hour the Lord doth come" (24:42). Compare the anguished and obsessional waiting in *Godot*.

The parable of the virgins invited to a village wedding feast, which comes next, is reflected in *Godot* in a passage which is omitted in the English version: "Ce soir on couchera peut-être chez lui, au chaud, au sec, le ventre plein, sur la paille. Ça vaut la peine qu'on attende. Non?" (p. 30; cf. the English version, p. 13).

In the parable of the talents (25:14-30), which follows, the Lord is seen as "an hard man, reaping where [He has] not sown, and gathering where [He has] not strawed," which matches the total ruthlessness of "Godot" in general (remember that the name also made Beckett think of a *godillot*). This parable leads up to Christ's final fulmination:

"And before him shall be gathered all nations: and he shall separate them one from another, as a shepherd divideth his sheep from the goats: And he shall set the sheep on his right hand, but the goats on the left" (25:32-33). "And these shall go away to everlasting punishment: but the righteous into life eternal" (25:46). Compare the explanation given by the boy in Act I of *Godot* (inverted!): "Mr. Godot" ill-treats the boy who minds the sheep, but not the boy who minds the goats (p.33).

The disciples died without seeing these cosmic events, in spite of the explicit promise that Christ had given in the course of His teaching: "Verily I say unto you, This generation shall not pass, till all these things be fulfilled" (24:34; cf. Matt. 10:23, 16:28; Mark 9:1, 13:30; and Acts 1:4-8). And many are the moments in history when faithful Bible readers have prepared themselves for the Second Coming—which has never materialized. Didi and Gogo in Beckett's play are less ambitious; all they hope for is to be taken in by a generous host who will feed them and keep them warm, as if they were operating on a simplified version of Pascal's reasoning in his famous "wager argument."

> Pesons le gain et la perte en prenant croix que Dieu est. Estimons ces deux cas: si vous gagnez vous gagnez tout et si vous perdez vous ne perdez rien: gagez donc qu'il est sans hésiter . . .

> Il faudrait jouer (puisque vous êtes dans la nécessité de jouer) et vous seriez imprudent lorsque vous êtes forcé à jouer de ne pas hasarder votre vie pour en gagner 3 à un jeu où il y a pareil hasard de perte et de gain. Mais il y a une éternité de vie et de bonheur.[11]

But alas: Beckett leaves us no doubt that these two simple-minded gamblers will be left there alone for all eternity, holding the bag after a cruel but sustained hoax closely resembling the one perpetrated by means of the Gospels. They may not, indeed, have lost much, as Pascal suggests, for their existence before they took up their painful waiting does not seem to have been very rewarding. There is one good that they have sacrificed, however: the use of the road, the movement, the development, the progress. It may not be able to take them anywhere, but at least it offers the entertainment value of activity, of choice, and of change.

At least theoretically. For Beckett has taken care of that aspect, too, in his play. In fact, the picture of Didi and Gogo blocked there on the spot occupies only a little more than half of the text; the remainder is dominated by two very different figures, Pozzo the master and Lucky his servant—or rather his slave.

The circumstances under which they appear in the French version of the play are worth observing closely. Gogo, the naïve one, suggests that he and Didi are tied to Godot (p.32; cf. English version, p. 14). Didi, the intellectual, more expert at lying to himself and to others, denies this indignantly. At the very moment the word *lié* is first proffered (p. 29), a faint noise is heard from a distance. A few moments later (p. 33) we learn what it was: the grotesque tandem of Lucky, carrying miscellaneous luggage, and Pozzo, holding him on a long leash and driving him forward with a whip. At first the two bums welcome the visitors as a distraction, but soon they are so disgusted with their antics that they are tempted to run away from that sickening company.

Of all the strange brainchildren sprung from Beckett's mind, this couple is the most unforeseeable, the most bizarre. Pozzo is in some ways the more easily understandable, in spite of a number of weird details: he is the "man of property," the master, slave of his role as a master, slave of the rules that circumscribe the admissible behavior of a distinguished person, and, when it comes to it, even the slave of his slave. Lucky is a being so utterly miserable that the existence of Didi and Gogo in their endless waiting seems almost attractive in comparison. When Pozzo and Lucky finally leave, and we are alone again with Didi and Gogo, we feel relief to such an extent that it almost feels good—at least for a short while.

Didi and Gogo are tramps, homeless vagabonds, and their dialogue in the beginning of the play makes us understand that their waiting takes place somehow on the lands dominated or owned by the mysterious, almighty Godot. So we are surprised when we learn from Pozzo that *he* considers himself to be the owner of the entire region: to Pozzo, Godot obviously does not count—he may not even exist. Pozzo knows very well that to Didi and Gogo, Godot is a reality, and he uses that knowledge to keep them from running away from him in disgust (p. 19). But otherwise Godot is nothing to him—or at most a vague, hypothetical usurper (p. 16).

Pozzo has artistic pretensions, especially in the direction of resonant literary rhetoric (pp. 20, 24, *et passim*). But much to their surprise Didi and Gogo are informed that, of the two men tied together by the rope, it is Lucky, the dehumanized, beastly pack-carrier, who is the creative, performing artist: "What do you prefer?" Pozzo asks, "Shall we have him dance, or sing, or recite, or think or—" (p. 26).

Lucky's dancing performance is miserable, but we are told that in the past, "he used to dance the farandole, the fling, the brawl, the jig, the fandango and even the hornpipe" (p. 27). These are mostly folk dances, later adopted by upper-class culture, but it is striking that most of them are known to us primarily as movements in dance suites from the days of Purcell, Handel and Bach. All of a sudden we get a strange impression that Lucky's glorious days as a dancer must have been very long ago indeed.

A similar impression can be extracted, with some difficulty, from the garbled and tattered philosophical discourse with which he entertains the party a moment later. Messy, rambling and confused as it may appear, Lucky's philosophical lecture nevertheless has a rudimentary logical backbone. If one removes the tangle of digression, repetitions and "footnotes in the text," his reasoning can be pared down to this essential line:

> Given the existence . . . of a personal God . . . who from the heights of divine apathia . . . loves us dearly . . . considering . . . that man [in spite of progress] is shrinking and at the same time is growing smaller . . . And considering . . . that in the plains in the mountains by the seas . . . the air is the same and . . . the earth . . . (pp. 28-29)

At this point the reasoning becomes totally unclear, contrasting rocks ("the earth abode of stones . . . the stones so blue so calm") and skulls ("alas alas on on the skull the skull the skull the skull"). The beginning has a familiar ring, and so has the end. Lucky starts from something not unlike the premises to Leibniz's problem in the *Theodicy* and ends up stating something that comes very close to Camus's concept of the Absurd.[12] Leibniz raised the problem of the presence of evil in a world created by a God who is almighty, omniscient, and all-good; Camus found that the world is obviously constructed in a way that is incompatible with man's basic demands for truth, justice, and clarity. Leibniz found that what we perceive as evil are the relatively minor side effects of causes that, on the whole, generate more good than evil; Camus stated that the presence of man in the world constitutes a situation of absurdity; Lucky seems to be on the brink of concluding that, considering how man has been reduced lately ("The dead loss per head since the death of Bishop Berkeley being to the tune of one inch four ounce per head . . . round figures stark naked in . . . stockinged feet," p. 29; cf. "la perte sèche par tête de pipe depuis la mort de Voltaire étant de l´ordre de deux doigts cent grammes par tête de pipe," (p. 73), God must have created the world for the rocks, not for human beings.

Again there is a lurking presence in the text of elements pointing to the mid-eighteenth century, confirmed by the two names used to indicate the time of the starting point: Voltaire (*Candide,* 1759) and Berkeley (d. 1753).

But let us return for a moment to basics. What we have in the couple Pozzo and Lucky is a hideous concretization on the stage of the relationship between master and slave. Hegel analyzed that relationship in his *Phenomenology of Mind* (1807), an analysis that was taken up and reinterpreted with enthusiasm by Marx and later by twentieth-century thinkers:

> The slave is forced to work, whereas the master can enjoy leisure in the knowledge that the slave is reshaping the natural world to provide the products of his labor for the master to consume. Thus, the master's leisure protects him from experience of the negativity of nature, whereas the slave, in struggling with nature's recalcitrance, learns its secrets and puts his mind into it. The master, in consuming, destroys; the slave, in working, creates. But the master's consumption depends on the slave's work and is thus impermanent, whereas the slave's labor passes into things that have a permanent existence. Hegel argued, too, that the slave's work in transforming the natural world is a consequence of his fear of the master, who can kill him. Death is overcome by the works of civilization.[13]

Beckett's setup is a caricature of this, a cruel mockery of Hegel's noble line of thought. The master still contemplates getting rid of his slave, preferably by killing him (p. 21); but if Lucky was once a creative mind (in the time of Voltaire or Berkeley?), he has since been reduced to the state of a helpless, even mean, beast: a proletarian.

A couple of apparently insignificant details can take us one step further. Pozzo owns a manor (p. 31); he is obviously a landowner, a country squire. But he seems to prefer roaming aimlessly along the roads with his slave in constant search of company, for left to himself he is not worth much. He has three obsessive occupations, two of which have a familiar look: consulting his watch—"a genuine half-hunter, with deadbeat escapement," i.e., a large, old-fashioned pocket watch (p. 30; cf. pp. 16, 24, et passim)—and puffing on his pipe (pp. 18, 23). Substitute the elegant eighteenth-century manner of enjoying tobacco for the more recent way, and the profiles of Jacques the Fatalist and his Master (the two characters, not Diderot's dialogue as such) begin to appear vaguely behind Pozzo and Lucky: ". . . il ne savait que devenir sans sa montre, sans sa tabatière et sans Jacques: c'étaient les trois grandes resources de sa vie, qui se passait à prendre du tabac, à regarder l'heure qu'il était, à questionner Jacques; et cela dans toutes les combinaisons."[14]

Diderot's couple can be seen as an idyllic manifestation of Hegel's strange theory (with the exception of the servant's fear of being killed by his master). This may not have been Diderot's intention, but his text sustains the comparison: Jacques is obviously far superior to this master in creativity and in insight. Beckett's couple, by contrast, is as far removed from *Jacques* as the waiting for Godot is removed from the experience of a live and authentic religious faith.

What are we to make out of this irruption in an otherwise clear-cut and homogeneous scenario? For Pozzo and his slave come on stage as an alien element. In spite of the (uneasy) dialogue between the two couples, they remain strangers to each other: to the two bums waiting for Godot, the tandem is only a half-real phantasm passing by, and to the two travelers, the men standing by the roadside are like a relatively insignificant part of the landscape. They are different worlds, different species.

A brief glance at the history of ideas may suggest a fruitful line of thought. It is a commonplace that the eighteenth century—the Enlightenment—marked the end of the absolute predominance of a transcendental God-centered understanding of the world. The process had been on its way for a long time (led by those who refused to "wait for Godot," but chose to move along the road of progress), but not until the generations following after Voltaire, Berkeley, and Diderot did the new, liberated Man "kill God," take his world out of the hands of God (the Revolution, Napoleon, etc.). Didi and Gogo in their waiting for Godot quite obviously "represent" the age-old Christian hope and expectation: Pozzo and Lucky, by contrast, "represent" (less obviously) what came out of progressive humanism and Enlightenment.

This almost allegorical reading probably should not be pushed too far down into the details of Beckett's text; it certainly does not explain the words exchanged between the two couples. It is worth mentioning, however, that the differences in the situation between Act I of the play and Act II are very unevenly distributed over the two contrasting couples. For Didi and Gogo the changes are slight; as far as they are concerned there was no pressing need for a second act—we had understood the monotony and the emptiness of their waiting long before the end of Act I. Not so for Pozzo and Lucky: the two acts show them in a process of rapid and radical deterioration. When they come back, Pozzo is blind and Lucky has become dumb, silent: "He can't even groan" (p. 57).

A trait as important as that has to be significant, and it is not difficult to imagine what its significance could be. In Didi and Gogo, Beckett gives a cruel caricature of the Christian illusion, but it is nowhere near as cruel as the caricature he gives in Pozzo and Lucky of what had once been secular humanism. With time, the hopeful waiting by the roadside has become a pitiable and miserable emptiness; but compared to the other couple, the two bums are quite likeable: at least they are friends, side by side, sharing their common lot, supportive of each other. Pozzo and Lucky, by contrast, who do not have an overriding transcendental relationship with which to structure their world, have established a structure within their relationship to each other. Didi and Gogo are tied to Godot; Pozzo and Lucky are tied to each other, in a relationship which fatally takes the form of domination and subjection—inequality—a "social contract" which is unpleasant and damaging from the outset, and which furthermore leads the partners, locked together in a mutually destructive embrace, down the road to a hideous and totally perverting decline.

Juxtaposed as it is here to the rotting cadaver of what was once progressive humanism, the bleached bones of the long-lost Christian hope come to appear almost attractive.

In *Endgame* (1956) the stage represents a room—another time—honored metaphor.[15] As the road has been used, through the centuries, to represent a development, a "progress," the room, with its contents and its outlook, has been used, with particular frequency in the nineteenth century, as the image of a mind. This room is wretched. It has two small windows only, high up, curtains drawn. One picture, facing the wall. The furniture consists of two ashbins, covered with an old sheet, and an armchair with casters.

In the armchair sits Hamm, the dominating character in the play, wearing a dressing gown. He is blind and paralytic, helpless yet domineering, full of his own grandeur, whimpering and tyrannical, boasting and bragging, boring and begging. His servant Clov moves about him. Clov has a "very red face," he can see and he can walk—with the "still, staggering walk" (p. 1) of a robot—but he cannot sit down (p. 10). He is a vile character. He grumbles and mumbles protest, but he obeys. He would like to kill Hamm, but he does not, for he could not subsist by himself: he does not know how to open the door to the pantry without Hamm's directions (p. 8; cf. p. 37).

Outside the house there is a desert-like emptiness, but it has not always been like that: in the beginning there was life, neighbors, movement. All that has now disappeared, mainly due to the frenzied efforts Clov makes, on orders from Hamm, to exterminate any uncontrolled life that might appear in or around the house. The only other beings tolerated are Nell and Nagg, Hamm's old parents; they are sitting in the two ashbins, under lids most of the time.

Hamm is, of course, a "ham," a conceited comedian, and Clov is a sort of clown. But Hamm is also a "hammer," a facet confirmed by the observation that all three of the other names may be derived from words meaning "nail": Nell (*nail*), Nagg (German *Nagel*), and Clov (French *clou*).[16] But we can do better with Hamm's name if we first focus on a curious episode in the play, one of the little tricks the two characters use as entertainment during Hamm's otherwise dreary and empty day. For his days are as painfully boring as the endless days spent in idle waiting for Godot. Even worse: he has nothing to wait for . . .

At one point (p. 25) Hamm wants to be taken for "a little turn," and Clov starts dutifully to push the armchair over the floor. "Right around the world!" says Hamm, "Hug the walls, then back to the center again." After a swing through the center stage the excursion goes to the opposite walls, as close as possible. Hamm caresses the wall and utters some profound sentences: "Old wall! Beyond is the . . . other hell!" Then he wants to be brought back to "his place," i.e., "right in the center." He is extremely finicky about it—it has to be "bang in the center"—and after considerable bickering and measuring with a tape measure he feels satisfied: he sends Clov away and sits there for a short while.

Beckett's Hamm is not the first character in French literature to undertake an excursion like this. In 1794 a French émigré, Xavier Conte de Maistre, officer in the counterrevolutionary army gathered in Torino, had fought a duel, and for this misdemeanor he was sentenced to forty-two days' confinement to his quarters. He killed time by pouring out words on paper, a nice, whimsical and loquacious little book relating his experience: *Voyage autour de ma chambre* (1801), appreciated by connoisseurs throughout the nineteenth century for its nonchalant wit and its light elegance.[17]

Before he starts out on his relation of the "voyage" itself, de Maistre explains at great length what he calls "my system of the soul and the beast":

> Je me suis aperçu, par diverses observations, que l'homme est composé d'une âme et d'une bête. —Ces deux êtres sont absolument distincts, mais tellement emboîtés l'un dans l'autre, ou l'un sur l'autre, qu'il faut que l'âme ait une certaine supériorité sur la bête pour être en état d'en faire la distinction . . .
>
> J'ai fait je ne sais combien d'expériences sur l'union de ces deux créatures hétérogènes. Par exemple, j'ai reconnu clairement que l'âme peut se faire obéir par la bête, et que, par un fâcheux retour, celle-ci oblige très-souvent l'âme d'agir contre son gré. Dans les règles, l'une a le pouvoir législatif, et l'autre le pouvoir exécutif; mais ces deux pouvoirs se contrarient souvent.— Le grand art d'un homme de génie est de savoir bien élever sa bête, afin qu'elle puisse aller seule, tandis que l'âme, délivrée de cette pénible accointance, peut s'élever jusqu'au ciel.
>
> Mais it faut éclaircir ceci par un exemple.
>
> Lorsque vous lisez un livre, monsieur, et qu'une idée plus agréable entre tout à coup dans votre imagination, votre âme s'y attache tout de suite et oublie le livre, tandis que vos yeux suivent machinalement les mots et les lignes; vous achevez la page sans la comprendre et sans vous souvenir de ce que vous avez lu. —Cela

Early Theatrical Works 131

> vient de ce que votre âme, ayant ordonné à sa compagne de lui faire la lecture, ne l'a point avertie de la petite absence qu'elle allait faire; en sorte que l'autre continuait la lecture que votre âme n'écoutait pas. (Chapter vi)

A little later in the same long explanation:

> Je donne ordinairement à ma bête le soin des apprêts de mon déjeuner; c'est elle qui fait griller mon pain et le coupe en tranches. Elle fait à merveille le café, et le prend même très-souvent sans que mon âme s'en mêle, à moins que celle-ci ne s'amuse à la voir travailler; mais cela est rare et très-difficile à exécuter; car il est aisé, lorsqu'on fait quelque opération mécanique, de penser à toute autre chose; mais il est extrêmement difficile de se regarder agir, pour ainsi dire;—ou, pour m'expliquer selon mon système, d'employer son âme à examiner la marche de sa bête, et de la voir travailler sans y prendre part. (Chapter viii)

The relation of the "journey" meanders over many a chapter. De Maistre is an avowed admirer of Sterne, and complacently chatty. The practical materiality of the adventure is that he sits in his armchair (wearing a dressing gown) and pushes it around with his feet, inspecting the various objects that adorn the room, all the while talking meditatively to himself about them. The whole adventure ends in an accident: the chair topples over, and the voyager falls ingloriously to the floor, hurting his shoulder.

> Ce fut encore un mauvais tour de *ma moitié.* —Effrayée par la voix d'un pauvre que demanda tout à coup l'aumône à ma porte et par les aboiements de *Rosine*, elle fit tourner brusquement mon fauteuil avant que mon âme eût le temps de l'avertir qu'il manquait une brique derrière . . .(Chapter xxviii)

The "journey round the room" could be explained as a mere coincidence, but the couple of Hamm and Clov must have been shaped after de Maistre's couple of body and soul: Clov, the mechanical robot who cannot handle the combination lock by himself—the executive—Hamm, the mind—the legislative. As if to make the relationship perfectly clear, Beckett has maintained the name, only slightly (but significantly!) disguised: the French pronunciation of "Hamm" will be very close to *âme*.

As in the case of *Waiting for Godot* and the Gospel according to Saint Matthew, the similarities between *Endgame* and *Voyage autour de ma chambre* are not limited to one or two traits. The father is present in both texts, in de Maistre as an honored bust on a pedestal, in Beckett still alive (though barely), tucked away in a garbage can. De Maistre has several pictures, but he dwells on two of them in particular: a portrait of his ladylove, commented upon because its eyes rest on the onlooker wherever he may be in the room (Ch. xv), and a portrait the realism of which is invariably perfect—a mirror (Ch. xxvii). No wonder Hamm had his only picture turned against the wall; even though he is blind, he cannot admit the perspective of anyone else's eye, and least of all if it rests upon himself. In both texts there is a dog: de Maistre has his cherished and horribly spoiled Rosine; Hamm, a miserable rag doll made by Clov in the shape of a dog. At the end of the play, Clov is told to leave the house: Hamm is dying. At the end of de Maistre's text the confinement is over, but he makes us understand that it is more or less his "beast"—the social robot—who will be going to walk in the streets and attend the parties. His *âme* can be really itself only in seclusion, in the room:

> Charmant pays de l'imagination, toi que l'Être bienfaisant par excellence a livré aux hommes pour les consoler de la réalité, il faut que je te quitte.—C'est aujourd'hui que certaines personnes dont je dépends prétendent me rendre ma liberté. comme s'ils me l'avaient enlevée! comme s'il était en leur pouvoir de me la ravir un seul instant, et de m'empêcher de parcourir à mon gré le vaste espace toujours ouvert devant moi!—Ils m'ont défendu de parcourir une ville, un point; mais ils m'ont laissé l'univers entier: l'immensité et l'éternité sont à mes ordres . . .
>
> Eh! que ne me laisse-t-on achever mon voyage! Etait-ce donc pour me punir qu'on m'avait relégué dans ma chambre, —dans cette contrée délicieuse qui referme tous les biens et toutes les richesses du monde? Autant vaudrait exiler une souris dans un grenier. (Chapter xlii)

One last detail, particularly significant. De Maistre is not altogether alone, he has a valet, Joanetti, and a telltale episode (Ch. xix) illustrates the master's mindlessly self-centered lack of consideration, matched by the servant's doglike, submissive "fidelity." This corresponds in a way to Ch. xxxii, where de Maistre has a horrifying dream (perhaps a daydream). At a brilliant dancing ball a "philosophe"—*un tigre*—appears and delivers an inflammatory harangue:

> "Malheureux humains! Ecoutez la vérité qui vous parle par ma bouche: vous êtes opprimés, tyrannisés, vous êtes malheureux; vous vous ennuyez. —Sortez de cette léthargie!
>
> "Vous musiciens, commencez par briser ces instruments sur vos têtes; que chacun s'arme d'un poignard; ne pensez plus désormais aux délassements et aux fêtes; montez aux loges, égorgez tout le

monde; que les femmes trempent aussi leurs mains timides dans le sang!

"Sortez, vous êtes *libres*; arrachez votre roi de son trône, et votre Dieu de son sanctuaire!"

—Eh bien! ce que le tigre a dit, combien de ces hommes charmants l'exécuteront? —Combien peut-être y pensaient avant qu'il entrât? Qui le sait? —Est-ce qu'on ne dansait pas à Paris il y a cinq ans?[18]

"Joannetti, fermez les portes et les fenêtres. —Je ne veux plus voir la lumière; qu'aucun homme n'entre dans ma chambre; —mettez mon sabre à portée de ma main: —sortez vous même, et ne reparaissez plus devant moi!" Chapter xxxii)

This can be brought together with Hamm's frantic fear of any independent, uncontrolled life that might subsist in or around the house in which he has so aggressively entrenched himself: he, too, fears a revolution. His place is in the center—he *is* the center of the world. Or rather, he has an absolute need to believe that this is so. Pascal had observed and analyzed the syndrome of burgeoning egocentrism three hundred years before; it had gained considerably in virulence in the meantime: "Le Moi est haïssable . . . En un mot, le moi a deux qualités. Il est injuste en soi en ce qu'il se fait centre de tout. Il est incommode aux autres en ce qu'il les veut asservir, car chaque moi est l'ennemi et voudrait être le tyran de tous les autres."[19]

De Maistre's was still a relatively mild case—he was, after all, a product of the sociable eighteenth century—but in retrospect his charming cult of the meditating soul in splendid and undisturbed isolation has an ominous ring. A hundred years later, J.-K. Huysmans described a much more severe, painfully pathological, case of the same syndrome in Des Esseintes, the "hero" of *A Rebours*.[20] In between had been Romanticism, characterized by the dualism body/soul, and by the irreparable conflict between "the ideal" and "the real," i.e., between the aspirations of the Self and the surrounding world (to the extent that the world does not satisfy these aspirations). Over and over again the literature of the nineteenth century reflects the conviction that the only way to make life bearable is to isolate oneself from the world (*l'Art pour l'Art*), to look at the world through the "windows" of a secluded Self (so as to allow perception but preclude contact), or to create an "artificial paradise" (of Art, love, or drugs) that can satisfy the urgent needs of the soul. Unless, of course, one is strong enough to impose one's own will on the world around. Hamm is a caricature of that existential type in an advanced state of decrepitude and decay.

Hamm has several traits in common with Pozzo, and this comes as no surprise after this analysis. (Clov, on the other hand, has next to nothing in common with Lucky, and that is not surprising either.) The main difference between Hamm and Pozzo is Hamm's passivity in seclusion, and his much more pronounced pretenses at artistic, literary merit. One might imagine, however, that Pozzo, who goes blind in Act II, *could* develop into something not unlike Hamm should he choose to give up his eighteenth-century taste for open air, his traveling along the roads of the outer world, and confine himself to the "room" of his mind; but he seems too addicted to bodily movement—too stupid also—to impose such a regimen upon himself.

There is not any action, or plot, in *Endgame* as a whole. What we follow is a trivial day, the run of the mill—or that is what we are led to believe for a long time. The dialogue represents various episodes that fill Hamm's dreary day, giving us, as they pass by, an impression of him as a type: his dreams of grandeur, his artistic ambitions, his dependence on his tranquilizer, his relations with his parents (there was never a glimpse of love either way between them), and, incidentally, his relations with his neighbor Mother Pegg, who asked him for a bit of candle, which, mindless of the injunction "Love Thy neighbor," he refused her: and she died—of darkness. As the play advances, we get more and more exasperated with this obsessed recluse, unloving and unloved, hardened into a monstrous, a tragic, self-sufficiency and a ferocious egoïsm, blind to the misery of his situation which is so painfully clear to us.

But toward the end of the play an enigmatic action begins. This is not, after all, a day like any other; it may be the last one, the end of the game. Clov, inspecting the surroundings from the window, reports that a boy is sitting, leaning against an upright stone (the boundary of Hamm's land?). The episode is uncharacteristically much shorter in the English version (p. 78) than in the French original (pp. 103-05), so I shall discuss it on the basis of the more explicit French text. Hamm supposes that the boy must be looking towards the house "with eyes like Moses' dying": "avec des yeux de Moïse mourant." Moses died, as we know, looking into the Promised Land to which he was not to be admitted.[21] Hamm, who considers himself and his house to be the world– or at least the center of the world—naturally expects that anyone who comes near will ardently desire to be allowed in, or, until that happens, will look at it with eyes full of envious and admiring desire. But the boy sighted by Clov just sits there, perhaps looking at his navel (i.e., absorbed in himself). When Clov offers to go and kill him, Hamm unexpectedly tells him to stay (here the two versions meet again): "if he exists he'll die there or he'll come here. And if he doesn't . . ."(the French text finishes the sentence: ". . . s´il n´existe pas ce n´est pas la peine"). Then, mysteriously, Hamm knows that it is the end: "It's the end, Clov, we've come to the end. I don't need you any more." He orders Clov to leave (which he does not; he puts on a Phileas Fogg-like travel outfit but remains silently in the room), and in a long, somewhat garbled monologue, with quotations from Baudelaire and Flaubert (we are in a nineteenth-century world here), Hamm prepares himself for . . . what? Death? Or merely sleep?[22] The posture he has taken when the curtain falls, a handkerchief over his face, is the same he was in when the curtain rose . . .

From a dramaturgical point of view it does not matter, but from the point of view adopted in this analysis it does, and fortunately the text contains one convincingly clear indication of how it should be understood: the title—*Endgame*. It is a historical moment, the end of (the old) Hamm.

But why should the mere presence of a boy signify the end? In early Beckett criticism suggestions were made. In spite of the almost total absence of religious overtones in *Endgame*, Esslin suggested that the boy forebodes to the godless Hamm "redemption from the illusion and evanescence of time through the recognition, and acceptance, of a higher reality," and he saw in the mysterious apparition an allusion to the Christ (because he is a young boy, albeit not new-born) and to the Buddha (because he is contemplating his navel).[23] Later studies seem to have given up altogether on such attempts to attribute a sense to the play, in accordance with established Beckett orthodoxy. But here as throughout I am skeptical: I find it exceedingly hard to believe that anyone should form a text of this nature which is pure form— "just play" —and I would like to reach an understanding of this obviously crucial episode in the context of the interpretation I have been suggesting for the play as a whole.

Here is what I propose. Hamm, this hideous caricature of the hypertrophied, nineteenth-century Ego in its death throes, has been able to tyrannize—and even exterminate—everyone around him (thereby creating a dead desert where once there was independent life), because everyone around him seems to have accepted his Victor Hugo-like claim to be the Olympos, the genius, the admirable center of the world: Mother Pegg came to him begging for "light," and the old "ham" himself has naturally come to expect everyone to look toward the house of *âme* the way Moses looked toward the Promised Land.[24] What we are told (we do not see the boy on the stage) is that a young boy appears at the boundary of an old man's land: a familiar metaphor for a change of generations. This boy—the coming generation—demonstrates by his posture that Hamm and his house are nothing to him, have no influence over him, no attraction for him. At first Hamm reacts with disbelief: if the boy exists, he will die there, or he will come here, like Mother Pegg, and in either case I have power; if he does not exist, it does not matter. But then he realizes that this reasoning is not adequate with this boy, with this new generation: it does exist, it will not come to him, and it will not just go away by itself.[25] Then he knows that his game is up. The spell is broken. An epoch has come to its end.

Which was exactly what happened in France and in Britain in the fifties—and, wherever it was possible, in the rest of Europe, too. Born in 1906, Beckett himself was of the older generation, but his devastating effort to erase the cultural blackboard and rid the modern world of the past was mainly received in the younger generation: it was one of the major tributaries which flowed into the mainstream that eventually became the generation gap around 1970.

To this one may add, as a more remote perspective, that the former colonies—British or French—which until around 1950 had presumably been looking toward Europe for "light" with "eyes like Moses' dying," were busily and actively engaged, in the fifties, in a strong push for independence, violent more often that peaceful, that left the former imperial masters of the globe alone, helpless and paralyzed, seeing their vital space reduced almost year by year.[26]

"Endgame" is a chess term, the final phase of the game, when the board is almost empty. Of the massive phalanx aligned at the outset, of the high hopes attached to the opening thrust forward, of the elaborate and complicated strategic maneuvers deployed at the height of the game, almost nothing is left: only some miserable pawn is there to protect the king. Hamm's game must have been impressive in its full glory—otherwise he would not have been able to wreak so much destruction around him. The hidden connection to de Maistre seems to indicate that this game had been going on for about a century and a half, since the days of Napoleon and Chateaubriand, of Victor Hugo and of Balzac. It had gone through a series of phases—in Flaubert and Baudelaire, then in Mallarmé and Huysmans, even lingering on in Valéry and Gide—before its appearance in Sartre and Camus. Rimbaud had known it, too, but after "a season in hell," the hell of being locked up in and with one's own soul exclusively, he managed to get out. Beckett himself, following the example of Rimbaud, was one of those whose struggled to extricate themselves from it. It is far from certain that he has managed. If he did, it was a costly victory, leaving him destitute, having "nothing to paint and nothing to paint with."

Compared to the two earlier works, Beckett's third stage play is almost childishly easy to interpret along the lines suggested here: its message seems—almost—plain and straightforward. *Krapp's Last Tape* (1957; *La Dernière Bande*, 1958) represents, once again, a disgusting and decrepit old man, this one all alone, locked up in a secluded room surrounded by his own past, preserved in the form of his own monologues taped over the years.[27] What he is particularly intent on is to extract some life from a long-past episode, a brief moment when he experienced what might have been love. In his vain efforts to regain contact with this faint and elusive memory that was not too remote from being a velleity of virility, he mindlessly sucks up bananas—a nauseating concretization of the kind of infantile mental masturbation that is the only activity to fill his life. When we are confronted with Didi and Gogo waiting for Godot, we find it painful; when Pozzo and Lucky come on stage, we long to have our two bums back. When we follow the antics of Hamm, we wish we were with Pozzo, for this is worse. And when we are locked up with Krapp and his tapes, we find ourselves almost nostalgic for Hamm and his house; it was, after all, quite lively and entertaining compared to this.

Early Theatrical Works

Once you have become accustomed to the possibility of an "intertextual" reading of Beckett's early plays, this one gives up its secret almost immediately: how can one avoid recognizing, in the Krapp scenario, a cruel caricature of Proust pursuing his *Recherche du temps perdu*, isolated in his soundproofed room? Proust did not know anything about the tape recorder, of course, but he did know of its forerunner, the phonograph, which records the *impression* made on the *receiver* in the form of a tiny groove (*sillon*) engraved on a roll, from which the original impression can be reproduced, later, in playback; compare "le petit sillon que la vue d´une aubépine ou d´une église a creusé en nous."[28] According to the theory expounded in *Le Temps retrouvé*, and practiced by Proust as a writer, the only authentic work of art is the one which is based on a replay of these grooves inscribed on our inner sensibility, unnoticed by discursive and social consciousness. That is even what life is all about: taping impressions which can be played back later on and reworked into the form of a literary text.

Christianity, Enlightenment, the nineteenth-century conception of the greatness of Man, Proust: these are the major sectors of Beckett's cultural heritage. "[I was brought up] almost a Quaker. But I soon lost faith. I don't think I ever had it after leaving Trinity."[29] Brilliant studies at Trinity College in Dublin (interrupted by something not unlike the classical tours in Italy and France), led to a two-year fellowship at the École Normale Supérieure in Paris, a Mecca of traditional nineteenth-century intellectuality. Friendship with Joyce and studies of Proust led to the publication of an important essay (1931) on this ultra-modern writer (the last volumes of *À la Recherche* had been published, posthumously, in 1927). Then, from 1932 onward, having given up a position as lecturer at Trinity College, Beckett began a long period of migration (reflected in *Murphy*, 1938) in an effort to rid himself of what Rimbaud, in connection with his own effort of a similar nature, called "ma sale education d´enfance."[30] His career as a writer did not take systematic and willful shape until after 1945, first with novels and shorter texts, then (in 1947) with a play, *Eleuthéria* (Greek for 'freedom') in which a conventional bourgeois family (Krapp, cf. 'crap') and their friends (including Madame Meck, cf. the French *mec* 'pimp') try to get a runaway son, Victor, back into the fold. They do not succeed, nor does Victor succeed in his "victory":

> I have always wanted to be free. I don't know why. I don't even know what that means, to be free. You might tear my nails out by the roots and still I couldn't tell you. But far beyond words I know what it is. I have always wanted it. I still want it. I want nothing else. First I was the prisoner of others. So I left them. Then I was a prisoner of myself. That was worse. So I left myself.[31]

Nor did Beckett succeed in this first attempt: *Eleuthéria* seems to have been too crude, too banal, too obvious—at the same time too autobiographical and too Sartrian. The following year he managed to find the right level of abstraction, and he could begin to reach further back and free himself adequately, forcefully concretizing on the stage the vanity of the defunct value systems and the total void left after their demise.

In 1956, between *Endgame* and *Krapp's Last Tape*, Beckett did a scenario for a mime, *Act without Words I* (1956), a beautiful specimen of the new severe dramaturgy, a stark and pure myth to illustrate *la condition humaine*.[32]

The stage is totally naked, harshly lit. A lone, mute figure comes tumbling in, backwards, from the wings. Signals are given by an unseen agent; the figure's willing, constructive responses are met, every time, with hostility and wanton violence. Alluring objects are lowered from above, objects with which a reward (a drink of water) can be attained. The figure gropes his way, mentally, to the solution of the problem, putting a smaller on top of a larger box so that he can reach the refreshing drink. But as soon as he starts climbing up on his construction, the water is moved out of his reach again. After a number of these experiences, the figure guesses the hoplessness of this game; his attempts to use new objects indicate a project of suicide, but the objects are hastily removed. At the end the figure lies down quietly, visibly determined to take no further part in this cruel mockery. Looking at his hands he remains deaf and blind to the treacherous invitations or intimations that continue to come from the unseen agent offstage.

It is hard to imagine any scenario that could make a statement of universal scope as forcefully with means so simple, so luminously clear and so immediately understandable as this. Here all that Beckett has to say about life is concentrated in a few minutes of wordless acting. And yet, even this perfectly basic myth, in its apparently timeless and universal nakedness, is surrounded by a host of texts that can be brought in to explicate it.

Far out, at a hazy distance, are lingering the old familiar myths about Tantalos and Sisyphos combined. The image of Man's lot given in *Act Without Words* is in accordance with the tales about the cruel and unjust punishment inflicted upon these two men for all eternity by mean and vindictive gods. The shadow of the Sisyphos myth in particular may call to mind Camus's 1942 revival of it, upbeat and boyscout-like.[33] Beckett's scenario will have none of this—his Man does not strike the pose of a heroic and proud rebel; his only way of preserving his dignity is by passive refusal, by giving up.

Closer to Beckett's scenario are the famous experiments conducted by Wolfgang Köhler, father of Gestalt psychology, in order to assess the intelligence of higher apes: would they be able to put two sticks together, or two boxes one on top of the other, and thereby reach the banana? They would. A series of photographs—frequently reproduced in the psychological literature of the thirties—shows them solving the problem; and they were, of course, duly rewarded as soon as they managed to lay hands on the tasty fruit.[34]

In *Act Without Words*, it is not a chimpanzee that is being manipulated by a well-meaning Gestalt psychologist but a man who is shown trying to communicate with an almighty off-stage manipulator. And this almighty stage manager is not to be trusted; he is like the evil genius Descartes considered as a possible manager of the world, but whom, to his relief, he found he could discard as an erroneous hypothesis: "Je supposerai donc qu'il y a, non point un vrai Dieu, qui est la souveraine source de vérité, mais un certain mauvais génie, non moins rusé et trompeur que puissant, qui a employé toute son industrie à me tromper."[35]

The "universe" represented in *Act Without Words* (or the statement about the universe implicit in it) is dominated by precisely such an "evil spirit." It belies the Cartesian optimism (his "Method" can only work if God does not cheat but goes by the laws of nature), and it is resistant to Camus's ambiguous solution to the problems raised by the metaphysical absurdity of life—much as Job was resistant, at first, to the edifying arguments brought forth by those who tried to convert him from his despair.

Beckett has been called the Job of our time, a Job who has never reached a reconciliation with the world. But Job would not have protested so eloquently against his miseries had he not first been a rich and honored man, pampered and high in self-respect. Had he been born in misery, grown up in misery, known only misery, he would have remained silent, like so many others. He might even at times have praised the Lord—as Winnie does in *Happy Days*. Beckett's very protest—untiringly lamenting, over years and years, the wretchedness of Man's lot (while both he and his acclaiming audience enjoyed a "lot" as favorable as few in the history of mankind)—is a clear indication that in spite of all his efforts to exorcize the old hopes and the old illusions that constitute his cultural heritage, they had not lost their grip on him. Claude Simon had seen it as early as 1947 (alluding to Sartre and Camus, not to Beckett): ". . . je pense que le non-sens est encore une invention des poètes et des philosophes. Une valeur de remplacement en quelque sorte. L'absurde se détruit lui-même. Dire que le monde est absurde équivaut à avouer qu'on persiste à croire en une raison. J'ai mis longtemps à découvrir que c'était comme ça et à m'en convaincre."[36]

However, since *Krapp's Last Tape* Beckett's plays have tended to be less aggressive, demonstrating compassion for the miseries of suffering mankind rather than a ferocious will to demolish the painted tombs of defunct values from the European past. *Act Withwout Words I* announces that trend, and *Happy Days* (1961; French version, 1963) is an early, major example. The demolition crew had accomplished its task, and after that there was nothing left to write about except *Comment c'est* to live on in the wreckage.

Harvard University

From *Comparative Literature* 36, no. 4 (Fall 1984): 289-311.

---

[1] Martin Esslin, *The Theatre of the Absurd* (London, 1961); references are to the revised and enlarged edition (Harmondsworth, Eng., 1968). See also Emmanuel Jacquart, *Le théâtre de dérision: Beckett, Ionesco, Adamov* (Paris, 1974). Recent major studies are John Fletcher and John Spurling, *Beckett: A Study of his Plays* (London, 1972); Ruby Cohn, ed. *Samuel Beckett: A Collection of Criticism* (New York, 1975); Cohn, *Just Play: Beckett's Theater* (Princeton, N.J., 1980); J. E. Dearlove, *Accommodating the Chaos: Samuel Beckett's Nonrelational Art* (Durham, N.C., 1982, mainly on the nondramatic texts). See also Deirdre Bair, *Samuel Beckett: A Biography* (New York, 1978).

[2] Dialogue on Bram van Velde, in *Proust* and *Three Dialogues* (London, 1965), p. 119.

[3] Quoted in Esslin, p. 87.

[4] Pp. 43 and 87.

[5] See note 1 above.

[6] *En attendant Godot, pièce en deux actes* (Paris, 1952); English version by the author, *Waiting for Godot: Tragicomedy in Two Acts* (New York, 1954). Where nothing else is indicated, page references, hereafter given in the text, are to the English version.

[7] The inquirer was Roger Blin, the director of the first performance; see Bair, p. 382.

[8] *Mercadet, ou Le Faiseur,* Act I, sc. 10. The action takes place in 1839, eighteen years after Napoleon's death.

[9] In the play, Godeau actually does come back, immensely rich; he settles all problems, marries off the young, and makes everybody happy and comfortable.

[10] Pozzo's cry was not heard in the original French version.

[11] Blaise Pascal, *Pensées,* ed. Lafuma 418; ed. Brunschvicg 233. Jacquart quotes a critic saying that *Godot* is like "a sketch from Pascal's *Pensées*

Early Theatrical Works 141

performed by the Fratellinis," a famous group of circus clowns (*Le Théâtre de dérision*, p. 92).

[12]G.W. Leibniz, *Essais de Théodicée sur la bonté de Dieu, la liberté de l'homme, et l'origine du mal* (Amsterdam, 1710); Albert Camus, *Le Mythe de Sisyphe, Essai sur l'absurde* (Paris, 1942); especially the chapters "La Liberté absurde" and "Le Mythe de Sisyphe." See also *The Encyclopedia of Philosophy*, ed. Paul Edwards (New York, 1967), s.v. "The Problem of Evil," "Pessimism and Optimism," and "Albert Camus."

[13]*The Encyclopedia of Philosophy*, III, 438. I reproduce a modern summary because it reflects the characteristic twentieth-century reading of Hegel's development, emphasizing the class-struggle aspect in it. Hegel's own text is focused more on the psychology of autonomous or dependent self-perception in individuals (*Phänomenologie des Geistes*, B.IV.a). For an application of this theory to Beckett's drama, see the analysis by Günther Anders quoted in Jacquart, p. 145.

[14]Denis Diderot, *Jacques le fataliste et son maître*, eds. S. Lecointre and L. Le Galliot (Geneva and Paris, 1976), p. 33. The passage quoted here is located between the visit to the allegorical castle and Jacques's subsequent expedition to retrieve the lost watch. For like Pozzo (p. 31), Jacques's Master loses his precious timepiece. Cf. the curious glimpse we catch in *Textes pour rien (Stories and Texts for Nothing*, New York, 1967, p. 96): "Why did Pozzo leave home, he had a castle and retainers. Insidious question, to remind me I'm in the dock."

[15]*Fin de partie, suivi de Acte sans paroles I* (Paris, 1957); English translation by the author: *Endgame, A Play in One Act, Followed by Act without Words, A Mime for One Player* (New York, 1958). First performed in French, London, April 1957. Where nothing else is indicated, page references, hereafter given in the text, are to the English version.

[16]Fletcher and Spurling, p. 76. Add to the list Mother Pegg (*peg*).

[17]There were at least forty editions and reprints of this book between 1801 and 1946, and at least thirty editions of "Complete Works of X. de Maistre," mostly printed by various publishers in Paris, but also published outside of France, from St. Petersburg to Boston. There have also been at least ten editions or reprints of English translations. Xavier was the brother of the more famous Joseph de Maistre.

[18] I.e., in 1789.

[19] Pascal, *Pensées,* Lafuma 597; Brunschvicg 455.

[20] J.-K. Huysmans, *A Rebours* (Paris, 1884, and various more recent editions and English translations). De Maistre's book is the first clear-cut literary manifestation of the syndrome, showing the world around as threatening and the secluded Self as a paradise. Huysman's novel reflects a turning point: the seclusion has become a sort of hell, and it has to be broken if the patient is not to collapse with psychosomatic symptoms. Hamm's case is further down the line: as can be seen from what he says to the wall, there is hell for him on the inside as well as on the outside. He is doomed to rot in de Maistre's paradise.

[21] Deuteronomy 34.

[22] "You cried for night; it falls: now cry in darkness" (p. 83); "Tu réclamais le soir; il descend: le voici" (p. 111): cf. Baudelaire, "Recueillement" (*Les Fleurs du mal,* 3rd ed.). "You want him to bloom while you are withering?" (p. 83); "Vous voulez qu'il grandisse pendant que vous, vous rapetissez?" (p. 111): cf. Flaubert, quoting John the Baptist ("He must increase, but I must decrease," John 3:30) at the end of Hérodias (in *Trois contes*): "Pour qu'il croisse, il faut que je diminue."

[23] *The Theatre of the Absurd,* pp. 70-72.

[24] Reference could be made to numerous poems by Hugo; for one example, see "*Ce siècle avait deux ans...*" (in *Les Feuilles d'automne,* 1831).

[25] It may be appropriate, too, to recall the little boy who reveals the truth in Andersen's tale about the emperor's new clothes.

[26] The shrinking of vital space is an almost obsessional constant in "the theater of the Absurd" of the fifties; very striking in several of Ionesco's plays, too. The most monumental example, however, is Boris Vian, *Les Bâtisseurs d'empire* (Paris, 1959).

[27] *Krapp's Last Tape and Other Dramatic Pieces* (New York, 1958); *La Dernière Bande* (Paris, 1960).

[28] Marcel Proust, *Le Temps retrouvé,* Vol. III of *À la recherche du temps perdu,* eds. P. Clarac and A. Ferré (Paris, 1954), p. 891.

[29]Harold Hobson, quoting Beckett, cited in Cohn, *Back to Beckett*, p. vii.

[30]Arthur Rimbaud, "*L'Éclair,*" in *Une saison en enfer* (*Oeuvres complètes*, ed. Antoine Adam, Paris, 1972), p. 114.

[31]Quoted in Fletcher and Spurling, pp. 47-54.

[32]See note 15.

[33]*Le Mythe de Sisyphe,* especially the chapter "Le Mythe de Sisyphe" with its final words, "La lutte elle-même vers les sommets suffit à remplir un coeur d'homme. Il faut imaginer Sisyphe heureux."

[34]Wolfgang Köhler, *Intelligenzprüfungen an anthropoïden* (Berlin, 1917); Eng. trans. *The Mentality of Apes* (New York, 1925).

[35]René Descartes, *Méditations touchant la première philosophie,* Première Méditation.

[36] Claude Simon, *La Corde raide* (Paris, 1947). A much more famous, fully developed presentation of the same line of thought was given ten years later by Alain Robbe-Grillet in "Nature, humanisme, tragédie" (1958), when the new attitude had become established in a broad wave of new literature (*Pour un nouveau roman*, Paris, 1963, see in particular p. 67).

Rebuke to Nihilism
Tom F. Driver

Krapp's Last Tape. By Samuel Beckett. Provincetown Playhouse, N.Y.

The stage is almost dark. We seem to be in a small room. From overhead hangs a single light, casting dim rays onto a table. On the table is a battered tape recorder and a jumble of empty cartons. Other cartons in profusion have fallen or been tossed to the floor. From the tape recorder an electric cord goes up to a double socket in the light.
    Silence. Behind the table an old man sits. He sighs, shifts himself, stares about the room, retreats into meditation. He gets up and begins to amble about the table. He is grizzled and stooped. He fumbles for a key on a key ring, finds the right one, ceremoniously unlocks a drawer in the table and removes a

banana. He locks the drawer again, admires the banana, peels it, thrusts it into his mouth and eats. Satisfaction. Then he hunts once more for the key. Same business all over again.

Minutes of this sort of pantomime go by. At last the man takes a larger ledger from the back of the room, brings it into the light, looks up the number he wants, finds a tape in one of the cartons, puts it on the machine, and sits down to listen. His own voice comes out.

This is all happening, as we learn, on the old man's 69th birthday. On each birthday he makes a recording to tell himself what he's done and thought—a sort of talking diary, except there's only one entry each year. The one he is hearing now is the one he made when he was 39. Some of the events it speaks about happened long before that. Thus we see an old man's reactions to himself. *Krapp's Last Tape* reveals a self in dialogue with itself over a lifetime. Heraclitus said you can't step into the same river twice. But Heraclitus didn't have a tape recorder.

We see and hear the old man listening, sometimes intently, sometimes with humorous impatience. When he feels like it he makes interjections. At the end he puts on the microphone and starts to record his 69th year. But he finds there is almost nothing worthwhile to say. He decides to listen to parts of the old tape over again. The curtain falls. Believe it or not, this is masterful theater, incomparable art.

On the surface Beckett's plays all appear to be about the end of the road. *Waiting for Godot* seems to lead nowhere: its second act is virtually a repeat of the first, and Godot never arrives. *Endgame* is just what it says: a few events that lead to checkmate. In the current play Krapp is nearly at the end of his life and certainly at the end of his powers. He is a writer who lives alone. All through the years he has been working on a book. It is not finished, and he now comes to realize that it never will be finished, that it is not worth finishing. Instead of looking forward, he turns round to his past.

It is understandable that in many quarters Beckett's view has been described as uncompromisingly bleak. Nevertheless, what is truly surprising, moving and valuable in his plays is a quality not discernible in a plot summary but insistently present in the lines and in the tone of a good performance. That quality is love. Its corollaries are tenderness and affirmation.

One would not suppose, for instance, that anything tender and affirmative could be present in a situation in which a man keeps his parents, who have lost their legs, in a couple of ash cans and feeds them dog biscuits. All the same, *Endgame,* in which that happens, is full of human love. I would put the conversations and spirit of the two old people in that play among the most memorable expressions of such love in modern theater. *Endgame* is the play in which the main character comes down to the footlights and admonishes the audience: "Get out of here and love one another!" It is the bond of sympathy between Gogo and Didi, the do-nothing tramps of *Waiting for Godot*, that prevents the audience from regarding them as ridiculous or contemptible (just as the lack of sympathy is the true horror in the relationship between Pozzo and his menial Lucky in the same play). In *Krapp's Last Tape* the reason we are ready to forgive Krapp for his failure as a writer and for his pathetic, reclusive existence is that we see—in what he says, how he acts, and what he hears himself saying—that the great moments in his life have been those in which he reached out to another person in affection and passion.

The play reaches its emotional climax in a lyric passage in which the 39-year old man (on the machine) describes his going in a boat with his beloved. His description of her eyes, her hair, her body, her unspoken acceptance and his eagerness carries through almost to the climax of union. It is perfectly frank, yet it is in flawless taste, because its real interest lies not in the physical details themselves but in the longing of a human soul for that which is worthy of desire. Afterward the young writer speaking on the tape launches into an excited description of his philosophy, his ambitions to write a great work, and his ideas about the meaning of life. But the old man listening grows impatient. He gestures scornfully at the machine uttering these sounds, and at last he cuts it off, rewinds the tape to the right place and once more listens enraptured while the soft and poignant voice tells again the incident of the day in the boat. There is beauty here.

It would seem that Samuel Beckett has given up on history. In his plays time does not go forward. We are always at the end, where events repeat themselves (*Waiting for Godot*) or hover at the edge of nothingness (*Endgame*) or turn back to the long–ago moment of genuine life (*Krapp's Last Tape*). Beckett's abandonment of the hopes of history may be disappointing to those of us who believe that social and political problems should continue to occupy our attentions. Yet if we take the Beckett voice for what it is, we discover that it is by no means irrelevant to the condition of our society. His is yet another, and perhaps the most eloquent, of those voices that are nowadays raised in righteous protest against the dehumanizing effects of rationalism and an age dominated by technology. Man's attempts to control his destiny have brought him to the point where he seems to have no destiny. In that situation, how shall man recover himself? By becoming acutely aware of those moments and qualities in his experience which time has revealed to have been most genuinely alive. In other words, by looking for a *quality* of life rather than by seeking for an elusive pattern or meaning in the whole.

That is perhaps a faint thing to say. It can be interpreted as pitifully romantic. One might hold that it is the last gasp of dying men. Yet if Beckett maintains that men *are* dying, that we are listening to the last voice we may hear, who is there to controvert him? The evidence is all in his favor. That is the context for what he wants to say, and the miraculous thing is that within that context he retains sufficient belief in man to maintain that by holding onto the qualities of honest love, desire, and affirmation of the other, he may be redeemed from futility. The effect of a play like *Krapp's Last Tape* upon the attentive spectator is anything but debilitating. On the contrary, it is quickening. So far from being a statement *about* hope or *about* a good that may come to man, it has the even more welcome benefit of *instilling* hope. That is a tribute to Beckett's art, and it is also evidence that true art is always a rebuke to nihilism.

Krapp's Last Tape is the best theater now visible in New York. The acting of Donald Davis, both on the tape and off, is brilliant. And so is the directing by Alan Schneider.

On the same bill with *Krapp's Last Tape* is a new play by Edward Albee called *The Zoo Story*. I am in a critical minority in my negative judgment about this play and its performance. However, *Krapp's Last Tape* is itself more than worth the price of admission.

From *The Christian Century* 77 (2 March 1960): 256-57.

Krapp's Last Tape: The Evolution of a Play, 1958–75[1]

James Knowlson

The recent production of *La dernière bande* at the Petite Orsay in Paris on 8 April 1975, which was directed by Samuel Beckett himself, with Pierre Chabert acting the role of Krapp, brings to an end a period of almost twenty years in which Beckett has been closely involved on a number of occasions with the *mise en scène* of this play, either as an adviser to the director or as the director himself.[2]

Beckett first heard the Irish Actor, Patrick Magee, reading some extracts from his novel, *Molloy,* on the BBC Third Programme in December 1957. He was impressed and moved by the distinctive, cracked quality of Magee's unusual voice, which seems to capture a sense of deep world-weariness, sadness, ruination and regret. Two months later, he began to write a dramatic monologue for a character who was described in the first draft[3] as a 'wearish old man' with 'a wheezy ruined old voice with some characteristic accent.' For some time, in fact, the play was simply referred to by Beckett as the *Magee monologue* until, several versions later, he conferred upon the failing old man the harsh sounding name of 'Krapp' with unpleasant excremental associations which lead its owner and the watching audience back to a decaying, disgusting, and yet still demanding body with which Krapp has tried in vain to come to terms throughout his life.

In this article I am not concerned, however, with tracing the various stages in the composition of *Krapp's Last Tape* through the manuscript and different typescript versions preserved in the libraries of Reading University and the University of Texas at Austin.[4] What I want to do is to look at the way in which this play has evolved since its first production in London at the Royal Court Theatre in 1958 until the most recent, Paris 1975, version, linking this evolution with dramatic and thematic elements of the text and the sub-text. As well as drawing upon personal knowledge of most of the productions discussed, I shall use the manuscript notebook which Beckett prepared for his own production at the Schiller Theater in Berlin in 1969,[5] and refer to annotated, corrected copies of the text now presented by the author to Reading University.[6] For, in the course of working on his play for a number of productions, Beckett came to reappraise, revise and trim it. Later versions differed therefore substantially, particularly in the setting and the non-verbal acting of Krapp, from the one first seen in London in October 1958, when Patrick Magee acted the part of Krapp.

Certain of the changes which Beckett introduced for the first time into his production of the play at the Schiller Theater Werkstatt in 1969, when Krapp was played by Martin Held, are incorporated into the text published in *Das letzte Band Regiebuch der Berliner Inszenierung,* Frankfort, Suhrkamp Verlag, 1970, which has useful notes by Volker Canaris. Beckett's actual production notebook is, however, much fuller than this edition suggests and it proves helpful in determining the reasons that lay behind some of the changes, as well as in throwing light upon aspects of the play that have tended to be ignored. Subsequent productions in London and Paris—the Royal Court revival in January 1973, directed by Anthony Page, with Albert Finney as Krapp, and that at the Petite Orsay in April 1975—introduced further changes, either suggested or approved by the author, although, in the main, these productions followed closely the German version. It will be useful, then, to begin by summarizing and commenting upon the principal differences that existed between the 1969 Schiller Theater Werkstatt production and the original Royal Court production of 1958.

First of all, in the German version, the opening of the play was cut in order to achieve a greater simplicity and clarity of line. The cuts and changes effected by Beckett were also aimed at establishing a more marked contrast between, on the one hand, brooding silence and immobility and, on the other, sound and rapid, purposeful activity. Beckett wrote in his production notebook that he had cut out 'Tout ce qui gêne passage abrupt de l´immobilité au movement ou qui ralentit celui-ci'.[7] As a consequence, a number of Krapp's actions were removed from the initial stage-business. There was no locking and unlocking of drawers at the beginning of the play or, later, before Krapp's live recording. Indeed, the two locked drawers at the front of the table were replaced by an unlocked lateral one, situated more conveniently to Krapp's left.

Krapp also no longer fumbled in his pocket for an envelope on which were jotted down notes for use at the time of the recording. Moreover, when he shuffled away to his back-stage cubby–hole for the first time, the sound of the popping of a cork was omitted, so that there were only two later auditory indications to make clear Krapp's continued addiction to alcohol. On the other hand, the consultation of his watch was retained at the opening of the play, since Krapp was waiting for the precise moment in time to arrive at which he was born, before embarking upon what had become a ritualized birthday recording.

The clownish stage-business with the banana skin was retained in the Berlin production, as it has been in later versions, but in a modified form. After slipping on the skin in good circus and pantomime tradition, in the revised version Krapp picked it up and threw it away backstage left into the darkness. This same action was repeated with the second banana skin, but before Krapp let it fall, so that, as before, the 'gag' comically forestalled a repetition of the earlier pratfall. It seems likely that Beckett changed Krapp's actions here because, by pushing the skin with his foot into the pit, he introduced a discordant element into a play which otherwise remained confined within the limits of the stage space and the backstage cubby-hole. Another omission removed the rather fatuous sexual innuendo clearly intended when Krapp placed the second banana in his waistcoat pocket with the end left protruding.

It is likely that this comic business is placed at the beginning of the play, as it is in *Fin de partie*, with the intention of prompting an ambiguity of response on the part of the spectator. For casting Krapp, initially at least, in the role of the clown tends to blunt the sentimentality that could so easily arise out of the confrontation between this 'wearish old man' and his earlier, more confident self. In a balanced production, therefore, neither the comic nor the pathetic aspects of Krapp's appearance and predicament should be lost.

Yet the balance is a delicate one to preserve. When directing the play, for example, Beckett has been extremely wary of overstressing the clownish elements in Krapp's physique, dress and behaviour. Even in the first production at the Royal Court Theatre, the purple nose of the 'tippler', which is referred to in the printed text, was much toned down and has since been abandoned by Beckett. Moreover, in the 1969 Schiller Theater Werkstatt production, directed by Beckett, the banana skin routine was promptly followed by several pieces of additional action that established an image of Krapp as a weak, tired, failing old man to counterbalance the image of the clown with which the audience had first been presented. In the original production, all the items that Krapp needed to enable him to listen to the tape–recording were already set out on the table at the opening of the curtain. But, in the German version he had to make three separate excursions to his backstage recess to fetch, in turn, the ledger, a pile of tins containing tapes (instead of the cardboard boxes of the printed text), and, finally, the tape–recorder itself. This

Early Theatrical Works 149

specific order was adopted, Beckett explained in the production notebook,[8] for three reasons: it left the explanatory element until the last; it allowed Krapp's growing fatigue to be registered, as the weight of the objects became progressively greater; and, finally, it avoided any interruption of Krapp's movements by the plugging–in of the tape–recorder.

In the text of the play, sentimentality is avoided partly by means of the lucidity and contempt which the device of the tape-recorder allows Krapp to bring to the judgment of his former selves ('Just been listening to that stupid bastard I took myself for thirty years ago, hard to believe I was ever as bad as that')[9] partly through the pithy, sometimes macabre humour with which his present plight is evoked ('Fanny came in a couple of times. Bony old ghost of a whore. Couldn't do much, but I suppose better than a kick in the crutch').[10] In fact, Krapp brings to the survey of his own past a characteristic blend of longing and loathing. With Beckett's approval, Patrick Magee stressed in Krapp a bitter lack of resignation that lent to him something of the dignity of the rebel, expressions like 'I told her I'd been saving up for her all my life'[11] or 'All that old misery . . . Once wasn't enough for you'[12] emerging as searing indictments of a distant, yet still disturbing, past and empty, disastrous present.

A second change which was first made by Beckett in the Schiller Theater Werkstatt production was to associate obliquely the darkness that surrounds Krapp's 'zone of light' with death. This association is already suggested in the text, as Krapp reads out juxtaposed entries from the ledger that refer to earlier incidents in his life ('Mother at rest at last . . . Hm . . . The black ball? . . . Black ball? . . . The dark nurse').[13] The 'last tape' of the title also clearly implies that death is lurking somewhere close at hand, a feeling that is echoed — rather too blatantly for Beckett in recent years — by Krapp's croaking efforts to sing Sabine Baring Gould's evening hymn 'Now the day is over.' In the Royal Court 1973 revival and in the production directed by Beckett at the Petite Orsay in April 1975, this hymn was cut out from the play as being, in Beckett's personal view, too clumsily explicit. Instead, in these, and in the earlier Schiller Theater Werkstatt production, when the hymn was in fact retained, Krapp cast two anxious glances over his left shoulder into the surrounding darkness. Beckett explained to Martin Held at rehearsal in Berlin 'Old Nick's there. Death is standing behind him and unconsciously he's looking for it.'[14] In the copy of the play that was corrected for the Royal Court Theatre 1973 revival, this action was referred to in a marginal note as a 'Hain',[15] the allusion being to a poem by Matthias Claudius, set to music by Schubert, in which Death says 'Be of good courage, I am not wild, you will slumber gently in my arms.' It may be thought that this reference to death is too puzzlingly oblique for such a look to register at all adequately. In the Royal Court revival, although the looks were rehearsed by Albert Finney, they were omitted in performance.

A third, and, in my own view, theatrically a far more effective change has been incorporated into all the versions with which Beckett has been concerned since the 1969 Berlin production. Instead of the curtain closing on a motionless Krapp, staring in front of him with the tape running on in silence, Beckett had both the stage and the cubby-hole lights fade at the Schiller Theater Werkstatt, the Royal Court Theatre in 1973 and the Théâtre d´Orsay in 1975, leaving only the 'eye' of the tape-recorder illuminated. This change, 'originally an accident—heaven sent' Beckett wrote,[16] accentuates a theme and contributes to an effect that is fundamental to this play and to much of Beckett's work. For the words that Krapp had recorded so many years ago now represent the only form of contact that he can achieve in a depleted, solitary, almost totally barren existence that, ambiguously, he has both sought out and fears ('Past midnight. Never knew such silence. The earth might be uninhabited').[17] In watching *Krapp's Last Tape* and experiencing its final moments, we are left, then, to ponder not only on the particular sadness of an individual lifetime of unfulfilled aspirations and frustrated ideals but also on the ephemeral nature of all human life and the irreality of past human experience that, vainly, one tries to recapture in the memory or set down on the printed page or on magnetic tape. Yet, paradoxically, perhaps even ironically, a faint glimmer of light persisted at the end of the play and it is relevant that Beckett included the 'voyant blanc du magnétophone dans l´obscurité' among its light emblems.[18]

Krapp is haunted by the memory of the episode with the girl in the punt and, as director of the play, Beckett introduced into the old man's actions and manner a number of elements that reflect or underline this obsession. One such element provided what certainly came to be the most moving moment in the play. As the tape recounted his earlier experience with the girl on the lake, Krapp slowly lowered his head, until it rested upon the table by the side of the tape–recorder. Then, while the voice of his younger self related the words 'I lay down across her with my face in her breasts and my hand on her', Krapp's gnarled old hand echoed pathetically a gesture that he had performed some thirty years before.[19]

In Beckett's own productions, Krapp responded to the bland air of self-assurance conveyed by his own voice at thirty-nine years of age and to the extravagant claims that he had expressed at that time, not merely with the explicit curses that are referred to in the printed stage-directions but also with little sounds of impatience, irritation and anger. Yet, by contrast, he remained transfixed, listening intently and in total silence to his own recorded account of the incident with the girl on the lake, so mesmerized was he by the intensity and the evocative power of the memory. This variety of response achieved several different, though related, results. Krapp's impatience and obvious lack of sympathy with the voice on the tape emphasized the vastness of the distance that separated him from his former self. The sounds that he made also formed part of a whole repertoire of looks, exclamations, smiles and gestures that characterized the relations of a recluse with material objects. In particular, as Beckett explicitly pointed out,[20] the tape-recorder, as the sole companion of Krapp's solitude, had come to be identified with whatever the tape was relating and Krapp responded to it accordingly. More important, however, the contrast between the sounds made by Krapp and the brooding silence that accompanied his moments of despairing fascination and dream reflects a much wider dramatic contrast between sound and movement, on the one hand, and silence and immobility, on the other, with which Beckett has been intensely concerned in his own productions of this play. '[The] Time', he wrote in an annotated copy of the text, '[is] divided about equally between listening (silence, immobility) and non-listening (noise, agitation)'.[21]

Contrast and balance were, indeed, two of Beckett's principal concerns as a director. In sections of the Schiller Theater Werkstatt *Krapp* notebook headed 'immobilité écoute' and 'jeux écoute', he worked out most meticulously the many contrasts in Krapp's acting between listening and non-listening, movement and stillness, dream and feverish activity, and elaborated in great detail the physical expression of these opposites in terms of opening and closing the eyes, raising and lowering the head, and so on.[22] Repetition is, in fact, a device that Beckett favoured almost as much as a director as he did as a writer, as could also be seen from his other productions at the Schiller Theater (Glückliche Tage, *Endspiel*, and *Warten auf Godot*). In Beckett's two productions of *Krapp's last tape* at the Schiller Theater Werkstatt and in the Petite Salle of the Théâtre d'Orsay, numerous small actions and looks were picked up and repeated, sometimes in very different contexts. At the Schiller, when Krapp closed the dictionary, after looking up the word 'viduity', he glanced up with exactly the same look used earlier to accompany the ledger entry 'Farewell to love'.[23] On a number of occasions, repetition was used primarily for comic effect, as when Krapp, having placed the dictionary upside down upon the table, showed that he had learned from his earlier mistake and corrected himself before opening the book; the technique employed here was clearly the same as with the banana skin 'gag' mentioned earlier. A number of Krapp's other actions were repeated so often that they became identifiable mannerisms or physical habits. For example, when he rose from the table and moved around it, he always did so with the help of his hands; as he carried objects from his cubby-hole, he clutched them closely to his chest; and, in an interview with Ronald Hayman, Martin Held recalled that, while rehearsing Krapp, he imitated Beckett's own crooked way of holding his hand and evolved a curious shuffling walk that was adopted as one of Krapp's physical characteristics.[24]

Yet, if Beckett recognized the comic or dramatic value of repeated actions, particularly in so short and concentrated a play, he also acknowledged that an excess of stylization would produce an unnatural, artificial dramatic structure and lead to a style of acting unsuited to *Krapp's last tape*. In the Schiller

Theater Werkstatt production, therefore, Krapp's gestures, looks, grunts, curses and sounds of impatience and irritation were all carefully varied and timed so as to avoid these pitfalls. To choose only one detailed example, pauses in the text differed considerably in length and were closely related to Krapp's responses to the words on the tape. Beckett wrote in an annotated copy of the text that one pause needed to be long enough for Krapp to look sharply at the tape-recorder, as if to say 'What's keeping you?'[25] In an additional pause introduced by Beckett, Krapp's direct, almost personal relationship with the tape-recorder is fostered by the added stage-direction 'in longer pause ear closer to tape-recorder to receive final "no"'.[26] Even within the recording itself Beckett tried to introduce planned variations of tone. For the younger Krapp's initial tone of self-assurance was punctured at several points by the appearance of three themes that are frequently linked together in the play: solitude, light and darkness, and woman. Beckett explained this change of tone in musical terms as a shift from the major key to the minor with the appearance of these themes.[27]

As the last example suggests, however, repetition and repetition with variation, which characterize so much Beckett's own productions, are not merely structural devices or means of establishing comic patterns. They are as closely related to the fundamental themes of this play as are the repeated phrases and gestures of the tramps to those of *En attendant Godot*. Repetition lies, in fact, at the very thematic centre of *Krapp's last tape*. At seventy years of age, Krapp repeats a ceremony that he has been performing for the past forty-five years; this ceremony consists partly of playing back an old tape and partly of recording a new one. As so often in Samuel Beckett's theatre, the central dramatic idea is both simple and bold. By adopting the mechanical device of the tape-recorder and giving to Krapp the power of instant recall of his own past, Beckett has created a stark confrontation between man's various selves in which decline, loss, failure, disillusionment and discontinuity are shown concretely. Moreover, in this way, the spectator has become the active agent, listening, observing, and able himself to assess the width of the chasm that separates Krapp from his former self and judge the strength of his obsession with a portion of his own past that he had earlier rejected as being unworthy of him. For the taped 'memory-bank' allows Krapp to hear again, repeatedly if he should so wish, his own account of important moments in his life. Yet the incident to which he returns so compulsively is not that of the vision, which, at the time, seemed to promise so much, but the scene with the girl in the punt which is indexed in the ledger as a 'Farewell to love.' But repeating the account of a moment in which Krapp was attempting to discard an unwanted part of his life merely serves to reveal a much deeper rift between Krapp and his earlier self, which is worth exploring rather more fully here.

Krapp's relations with women figure prominently in the play—in his younger days with his mother, Bianca, the 'girl in a shabby green coat, on a railway station platform', the girl with 'eyes like chrysolite', as well as the woman in the punt on the lake, and in his old age with Fanny, the 'bony old ghost of a whore' and his fantasy woman, Effi, the heroine of Fontane's nineteenth century novel, Effi Briest. But all of Krapp's 'affairs' are described in terms of mingled regret, relief, and unsatisfied longing. Even the momentary harmony that was achieved with the girl in the punt was attained only after they had agreed that 'it was hopeless and no good going on'.[28]

The black and white imagery that runs through the entire play suggests that Krapp's inability, even his unwillingness, to find happiness with a woman arises out of a fundamental attitude towards life as a whole that affects most aspects of his daily living. Krapp is only too ready to associate woman with the darker side of existence and he clearly sees her as appealing to the dark, sensual side of man's nature, distracting him from the cultivation of the understanding and the spirit. Krapp's recorded renunciation of love is then no mere casual end of an affair. The words of Sir Philip Sydney's sonnet apply strikingly to Krapp's situation: 'Leave me ô Love, which reachest but to dust,/ And thou my mind aspire to higher things'.[29] In Krapp's case, earthly love is not renounced for the greater love of God, as it was in the Petrarchan tradition. Instead, the renunciation of love forms part of an ascetic quest that rejects the world as an inferior creation and shrinks away from the material element of the flesh to concentrate upon the spiritual or the pneumatic. Krapp is clearly following here in a Gnostic, even a specifically Manichean tradition, with its abstention from sexual intercourse and marriage (so as not to play the Creator's game), its rift between God and the world, the world and man, the spirit and the flesh, and its vision of the universe, the world and man himself as divided between two opposing principles, the forces of darkness constantly threatening to engulf the forces of light.

There are numerous indications in the play that Krapp has attempted to separate the light from the darkness in his life in order to rise above the dark side of his nature and liberate the light of the understanding which (in Gnostic thinking) is regarded as being imprisoned in an envelope of matter. The new light above Krapp's table is seen, for instance, as a great improvement by Krapp because it forms a clearer division between the light and the dark. As a result, Krapp can move out into the darkness before returning to the zone of light with which he would wish to identify his essential self, but which, ironically, takes him back to the excremental associations surrounding his name. 'I love to get up and move about in it [the darkness], then back to here to ... (hesitates) ... me *Pause*. Krapp'.[30]

But Krapp's den is an artificially created setting and the point about God's world outside this refuge is that there is no such clear division between the light and the darkness. Separating one from the other in his life and in his relations with others is a much more difficult, painful, and morally isolating business. For the world appears to Krapp in the form of a bewildering mixture of light and dark. Even the women with whom Krapp has been involved at different times are portrayed, disquietingly, in both light and dark images. Bianca is white by name, but they live together in Kedar (or, in Hebrew, Black) Street. Conversely, the nurse whom he admires at a distance is a dark young beauty with an incomparable bosom, who pushes a black pram, 'most funereal thing'—linking characteristically birth and death—but she wears a uniform that is all 'white and starch.' And although Krapp's fantasy woman is placed in the Northern light-filled setting of Fontane's novel, her name 'Effi' links her with that of Fanny, the whore, with whom she is ostensibly contrasted, by announcing her physical function, recalling as it does also Beckett's remark that one should 'eff the ineffable'.

It is clear that for Krapp the central issue in his life is one of coming to terms with a fundamental dualism, either by attempted separation or reconciliation. Krapp's account of the experience of the vision is heard only in fragmentary form, yet enough is played back for it to be apparent that what is being described there is the belief that light and darkness have at last been reconciled. The natural setting for the experience ('in the howling wind . . . great granite rocks the foam flying up in the light of the lighthouse and the windgauge spinning like a propeller')[31] reflects the storm and night that Krapp has been striving to keep under in his life and his work, as well as the light of the understanding by which he has tried to be guided. 'Storm and night' are seen, then, as mysterious, wild, uncontrollable, exciting elements that can be reconciled with the experience of light only by regarding them as irrational compared with rational. As I have shown elsewhere[32], it is certainly in this way that Beckett himself regarded the vision, for, in the *Krapp* production notebook, Beckett explained that 'Krapp decrees physical (ethical) incompatibility of light (Spiritual) and dark (sensual) only when he intuits possibility of their reconciliation as rational-irrational. He turns from fact of anti-mind alien to mind to thought of anti-mind constituent of mind'[33]. The two warring elements remain then identified as sensual and spiritual, are independent even incompatible, but reconciliation is effected at the level of the intellect. However, Beckett commented, although ethically correct, Krapp is guilty of intellectual transgression, for (and this is a Gnostic belief) it is the duty of the intellect to separate the light from the dark and not to reconcile the two.

The issue of separating or reconciling the light and the dark also forms the underlying infra-structure of the episode with the girl in the punt, which, significantly, immediately follows the experience of the vision recorded on the tape. Since Krapp first winds the tape so far forward that we only hear the end of the episode, it appears that the harmony that is achieved results from a purely physical union. However, when the tape is wound back and replayed, the sense of the passage is markedly changed.

—upper lake, with the punt, bathed off the bank, then pushed out into the stream and drifted. She lay stretched out on the floorboards with her hands under her head and her eyes closed. Sun blazing down, bit of a breeze, water nice and lively. I noticed a scratch on her thigh and asked her how she came by it. Picking gooseberries, she said, I said again I thought it was hopeless and no good going on and she agree [*sic*], without opening her eyes. *Pause.* I asked her to look at me and after a few moments—*Pause*—after a few moments she did, but the eyes just slits, because of the glare. I bent over her to get them in the shadow and they opened. *Pause. Low.* Let me in. *Pause.* I lay down across her with my face in her breasts and my hand on her. We lay there without moving. But under us all moved, and moved us, gently, up and down, and from side to side.[34]

In this unashamedly lyrical passage, the girl is prevented from opening her eyes by the fierce glare of the sun and it is only when the man creates shade for her that her eyes open. Rather as he has done when alone in his 'old den', Krapp has therefore created a separate area, in this case a zone of shade, which makes the temporary union that they attain possible. It would seem that once Krapp has equated woman with darkness and the irrational, he is able to establish and accept contact with a woman from whom he has resolved to part anyway, thus avoiding any possibility of continued physical entanglement.

Bianca, the dark nurse, and the girl in the punt all have eyes that have fascinated Krapp at different moments in his life. Bianca's eyes are said to be 'very warm' and 'incomparable',[35] the dark nurse has 'eyes like chrysolite,' echoing Othello's words "if heaven would make me such another world/ Of one entire and perfect chrysolite/ I'd not have sold her for it".[36] If this preoccupation with the eyes of women recalls the image of the eye in the work of the Metaphysical poets or Proust's narrator's fascination with the mystery discerned in Albertine's eyes, Beckett tends to widen the resonance of the image by showing the girl's eyes not merely as windows on to the soul but as mirrors too, reflecting and uniting all the contrarities of a divided cosmos, 'Everything there, everything on this old muckball, all the light and dark and famine and feasting of . . . (hesitates) . . . the ages!'[37]

Krapp ended the recording made at the beginning of his thirty-ninth year on a high note of buoyant optimism, acknowledging that, although happiness was something that he would perhaps never attain, this was more than compensated for by the fact that there was within him a fire that made mere happiness seem totally irrelevant. Throughout the play fire and light have been used to distinguish the understanding and the spirit. Yet these inspired words are listened to at the end of the play by a weary and a disillusioned Krapp, an old man who is still enslaved by those strong physical appetites that, for so long, he had tried to subjugate and in whom the fire of the understanding has now dwindled to a few dying embers. The final confrontation between the younger and the older Krapp evokes, then, more than mere sadness at the inevitable decline that occurs in man. For Krapp shows us a man who is torn by conflicting forces and whose life has been ruined by this conflict.

The old polarities of light and darkness are reflected in *Krapp's Last Tape* in numerous images of, on the one hand, light, fire, breeze, and clear water and, on the other, darkness, heat, mist and vapour. The greater number of what Beckett called the light and dark emblems in the play do not occur, however, in isolation but are explicitly integrated. Even the death of Krapp's mother, which would seem to represent only the final corruption of the flesh, still hints at integration, for, as Beckett pointed out, 'if the giving of the black ball to the white dog represents the sacrifice of sense to spirit the form here too is that of a mingling'.[38]

Explicit integration of the light and the dark occurs also in the setting, the stage props, and in the costume of Krapp. In the Schiller Theater Werkstatt 1969 production, it was in this area in particular that Beckett chose to emphasize the dualistic theme of the play. For, in addition to the black and white elements in Krapps' costumes that were already described in the printed stage directions, Beckett ensured that other props, as well as the lighting, illustrated this contrast or 'mingling.' For example, in the Berlin production, the 'cagibi' or cubby-hole at the back of the stage was lit by a white light and was separated from the stage by a black curtain. The central light, which was suspended low over Krapp's table, had a light coloured shade. Clearly, Beckett had originally conceived the 'zone of light' as emanating directly from that source but a note, added several years after the production, recalls that this light was 'Extinguished finally Berlin because cold light unobtainable from this source.'[39] Other props picked up the central confrontation of black and white, light and dark, as, for example, the envelope, the tins, and even the table. The ledger that Krapp consulted was large, worn, and black in colour, while the dictionary was bound in a light coloured leather binding.

Directing the play himself for the first time at the Schiller Theater Werkstatt in 1969, Beckett chose, then, to highlight the Gnostic, even Manichean, distinctions within the play. Subsequently, however, he seems to have felt that he had tended to over-emphasize these Manichean elements by making the oppositions in setting and costume too starkly explicit. In the 1973 Royal Court production, therefore, instead of the black waistcoat and grimy white shirt referred to in the printed text, Krapp was dressed in a dark coloured dressing gown, which was also adopted for the 1975 Paris production. This less explicit approach to the play is in keeping with other minor changes introduced into the Royal Court and Petite Orsay revivals, such as the excision of the hymn already mentioned.

If Beckett has had few second thoughts concerning the actual text of *Krapp's last Tape*, the various productions with which he has been associated show him working towards an interpretation in which every element of the production will be dramatically and thematically justified. One does not need to welcome all of Beckett's second thoughts to recognize that one of his primary concerns is to discover what works best in the theatre. Some appalling liberties have been taken at times with this particular play, from a television version that employed a flash-back technique for the scene with the girl in the punt to a London production in which video-tape was substituted for sound-tape and multiple television screens for the single tape-recorder. The lack of success of these wilder productions is scarcely surprising, for a director forgets to his cost that what works best in the theatre with Samuel Beckett's plays also satisfies the need for faithfulness to the author's artistic vision. To analyse Beckett's production notebooks is to observe him, as a director, grappling, sometimes hesitantly, but always rigorously, with this same challenge, while, occasionally, throwing light upon the character of that vision.

PRODUCTIONS REFERRED TO

First production: Royal Court Theatre, London, 28 October 1958, in a double bill with *Endgame*. Krapp: Patrick Magee. Director: Donald McWhinnie. Designer: Jocelyn Herbert.

In French: *La dernière bande* (French translation by Pierre Leyris and the author). Théâtre Récamier (Théâtre National Populaire), Paris, 22 March 1960, with Robert Pinget's *Lettre morte*. Krapp: R. J. Chauffard. Director: Roger Blin.

In German: *Das letzte Band* (German translation by Elmar Tophoven). Schiller Theater Werkstatt, Berlin, 5 October 1969. Krapp: Martin Held. Director: Samuel Beckett. Designer: Matias.

British Television BBC 2, '*Thirty Minute Theatre*', 29 November 1972. Krapp: Patrick Magee. Director: Donald McWhinnie.

London revival: Royal Court Theatre, London, 16 January 1973, in a double-bill with *Not I*. Krapp: Albert Finney. Director: Anthony Page. Designer: Jocelyn Herbert.

Paris revival: Théâtre d'Orsay, Petite Salle, 5 April 1975, in a double-bill with *Pas moi*. Krapp: Pierre Chabert. Director: Samuel Beckett. Designer: Matias.

From *The Journal of Beckett Studies*, no. 1 (Winter 1976): 50-65.

---

[1] An excellent article on 'Beckett metteur en scène' by the actor, Pierre Chabert, has appeared in *Travail théâtral* since I completed my own. It has also recently appeared in an English version in *Gambit* vol.7, no. 28, 1976.

[2] Beckett was very closely involved with the original October 1958 Royal Court Theatre production; he spent several weeks in London attending

rehearsals of the first French production of *La dernière bande,* directed by Roger Blin, with R. J. Chauffard as Krapp, in March 1960. Beckett directed himself *Das letzte Band* at the Schiller Theater Werkstatt, Berlin, in October 1969 and, again, in French, in Paris in April 1975. The BBC 2 television version in 1972, with Patrick Magee again playing the part of Krapp, was based upon a copy of the text amended by Beckett in the light of the earlier Berlin production; the BBC typed script represents, therefore, the first corrected version in English. Beckett also attended rehearsals of the Royal Court revival in January 1973.

[3]The first known holograph is contained in the *Été 56* notebook in Reading University Library. It is headed *Magee monologue* and is dated 20 February 1958.

[4]In a letter to Jake Schwartz dated 15 March 1958, in the library of the University of Texas, Beckett wrote 'I am also keeping for you, if you would be interested, the MS of my translation of *L'Innommable* of which I have completed the first draft and four states, in typescript, with copious and dirty corrections, of a short stage monologue I have just written (in English) for Pat Magee. This was composed on the machine from a tangle of old notes, so I have not the MS to offer you.' It is possible, of course, that there may be some old notes which ante-date the manuscript draft referred to above or, alternatively, and this seems more likely, that they are the same.

[5]The *Regiebuch* is a bound notebook written in French, English, and German of 71 leaves, of which 51 to 69 are blank; it is entitled *Krapp Berlin Werkstatt* 5.10.69 and is preserved in Reading University Library, along with other Berlin and London production notebooks. It is referred to henceforth as *Krapp Regiebuch.*

[6]The first annotated text (A1) is the Grove Press Evergreen original, E-226, *Krapp's Last Tape and Other Dramatic Writings* (New York, 1960, 4th printing). Beckett has written 'London 1973' in ink on the front cover and it is almost certain that this copy was prepared for the Royal Court Theatre, London revival in January 1973. Although there are minor differences in the corrections, the second annotated copy (A2) is probably a copy of A1 and is the Faber and Faber paper-covered edition, *Krapp's Last Tape and Embers* (London, 1970 reprint of 1965 edition). It is identified by Beckett on the opening page of the text as 'corrected for revival at Royal Court Theatre Jan.

1973 with Albert Finney.' It was presented by the author to Reading University and is inscribed and dated 2 January 1973.

[7] *Krapp Regiebuch*, p. 13 (Beckett's own pagination used throughout).

[8] *Krapp Regiebuch*, p. 8.

[9] *Krapp's last tape and Embers,* London, Faber and Faber, 1959, p. 16. This edition is used throughout and is referred to in the abbreviated form *KLT*.

[10] *KLT*, p. 17.

[11] *Ibid.*, p. 17.

[12] *Ibid.*, p. 18.

[13] *Ibid.*, pp. 10-11.

[14] 'Martin Held talks to Ronald Hayman,' *Times Saturday Review,* 25 April 1970.

[15] In the Grove Press annotated copy (A1), a marginal note on p. 13 reads 'Action interrupted by first look over his shoulder left into darkness backstage'; the note in the Faber and Faber annotated copy (A2) is 'Action interrupted by Hain 1' (p. 11). In A1, p. 27, a marginal note reads 'Action interrupted by second look into darkness as before'; in A2, p. 19, the note is 'interrupted by Hain 2' After the first drink backstage, there is in both copies the query 'Faint Hain here?,' A1, p.17, A2, p. 14.

[16] Personal letter to J. Knowlson, 18 May 1972.

[17] *KLT*, p. 15, p. 18.

[18] *Krapp Regiebuch,* p. 43.

[19] *Ibid.*, p. 20.

[20] *Ibid.*, p. 67.

[21] The annotation is written on the pre-title page of the Grove Press corrected copy (A1).

[22] *Krapp Regiebuch*, pp. 19-35.

[23] *Ibid.*, pp. 16-17.

[24] 'Martin Held talks to Ronald Hayman,' *Times Saturday Review*, 25 April 1970.

[25] Grove Press annotated copy (A1) p. 15.

[26] *Ibid.*, p. 15.

[27] *Krapp Regiebuch*, p. 53.

[28] *KLT*, p. 16, p. 18.

[29] *The poems of Sir Philip Sidney*, ed. William A. Ringler, Jr., Oxford, 1962, p. 161.

[30] *KLT*, p. 11.

[31] *KLT*, p. 15.

[32] J. Knowlson, *Light and darkness in the Theatre of Samuel Beckett*, London, Turret Books, 1972.

[33] *Krapp Regiebuch*, p. 47, reprinted in facsimile in Knowlson, *Light and Darkness*.

[34] *KLT*, pp. 15-16.

[35] *Ibid.*, p. 12.

[36] Beckett has written in this quotation on p. 15 of the Faber and Faber annotated copy (A2) with the source *Othello*, V, ii.

[37] *KLT*, p. 17.

[38] *Krapp Regiebuch*, p. 47.

[39] *Ibid.*, p. 72. This note was not written in the notebook when it was loaned for the Samuel Beckett Exhibition at Reading University in 1971.

CHAPTER 4

Return to Prose: *How It Is*

Beckett Country

Frank Kermode

How It Is. **By Samuel Beckett.**

How, if this novel were by an unknown author, would one set about the reviewer's task of giving some notion of its contents, and throwing in an appraisal? First, perhaps, by dealing in certainties: for instance, this book was written in French under the title *Comment C'est.* The translation is by the author. It is on the whole about as literal as a comparison of the titles will suggest, though one notes a lost pun *(commencez).* And since *Comment C'est* are the last words in the book, they impart to the design a circularity which is, perhaps not too unhappily, lost in English. Where the English is obscure the French in general helps little: "the history I knew my God the natural" comes from *l'histoire que j'avais la naturelle.* Where the English looks wrong the French looks just as wrong: "of the four three quarters of our total life only three lend themselves to communication" sounds, as if the first "three" has got in by mistake, but the French says *quatre trois quarts* and adds to the muddle by saying *deux seuls* for "only three." It seems unlikely that the reader loses much in clarity by using the English version. The syntax is neither English nor French, but that of some intermediate tongue in which "ordinary language" cannot be spoken. This language goes indifferently into French or English. It eschews marks of punctuation, although the novel is divided into paragraphs of unequal length, signifying, why not, the fluttering of some moribund intellectual pulse, rather than successive stages of meaning. At its climax the story virtually disclaims its own authenticity, and this uncertain commitment to ordinary criteria of meaningfulness is also characteristic of the language in which it is told.

The meanings present in this language are not valid, outside the book, being mostly the products of intensive internal references and repetitions. Phrases of small apparent significance occur again and again with some kind of cumulative effect: "something wrong there," "bits and scraps," "quaqua," "when the panting stops," etc. The speaker of these phrases looks forward keenly to the end of his task, frequently promising that we are near the end of the first, second, or third part, and rejoicing especially in the final paragraph, only to be thwarted by the Finnegan-begin-again trick mentioned above. In short, the whole book refuses to employ the ordinary referential qualities of language, and frustrates ordinary expectations as to the relation between a fiction and "real life." It is as if the old stream of consciousness were used in a situation where there is nothing but the stream to be conscious of.

Not very helpful, says the reader. What *is* the story? Well, it is spoken by a nameless man face down in the mud, and apart from him its principal character is called Pim. Three sections describe how it was before, with and after this Pim, who is therefore a measure of time and history. Pim was long awaited, then he arrived and lay down in the mud beside the speaker and his sack full of cans; but things didn't go well, and he passed on. Where, or to whom? Before Pim, the speaker had been alone; perhaps, he thought, the "sole elect," moving at intervals with his sack and his can opener ten or fifteen yards through the mud. His only contact with the world "above" is the memory of a past idyllic scene with a girl and a dog; and another of a marriage that failed with the waning of desire. After Pim he sees that he is really one of a great number, all on the same impossible muddy journey. Somehow it has been arranged that its progress is circular and endless.

With Pim, the situation was at least not solitary. Pim brought a watch and one could listen to the delicious ticking away of the seconds. Furthermore, the speaker devised an elaborate signal code by which he induced Pim to speak: as by jabbing the can opener in to his rectum, beating him on the kidneys, or, to make him stop, on the head. Pim, being a man, is a kind of machine, *l'homme machine* in fact, responsive to external stimuli. Nevertheless, he clenches his fists in pain, and his nails grow through his palm. The close relationship of the couple is that of tormentor and victim. When Pim abandons the speaker he leaves very little, but still something behind him, "with Pim all lost almost all nothing left almost nothing but it's done great blessing." This example of dream parataxis, translated into English, means, I suppose, that the residual benefits of Pim's sojourn are small but important, perhaps only because they

Return to Prose: *How It Is*

prove that we have lived through one more stage and are nearer the last. Later we gather that as far as the speaker is concerned we can do what we like with time—reverse it, for example—so long as we always give Pim a central place in it: "on condition that by an effort of the imagination the still central episode of the couple be duly adjusted."

After Pim, the world is full of tormentors and their victims, an endless chain in which each man repeatedly changes his role from one to the other. Over vast stretches of time, one torments and is tormented. The speaker moves on through this suffering inflicted and received, towards reunion with Pim. But in the end the voice we are listening to rebels, denies that all he has said is quoted from some external authority, claims that it is all a fiction ("all balls"); that there was something, yes, but no "quaqua," no *logos* or revelation from without, only himself, face in mud, making it up and mumbling. Then the last sentence, with its ambiguous denial of this disclaimer.

What kind of a story is this? Certainly there is a fiction; and there is a chain not only of torment but of rhythmical incantation. But the reader who wants more than a form commenting upon itself, an autistic stir of language, will be tempted to look aslant at the book, to seek allegory. I myself have already slipped into allegory in describing Pim's watch, and in hinting that the tormented relationship between the speaker and Pim stands for the incarnation, which, we are told, gives history such meaning as it may be said to have, and could be regarded as affording the type of human love-relations ever since (the love of the Word unable to speak a word speaks, under painful stimulus, when it is embodied in *l'homme machine*. Pim has nails through his palms, and is pierced by a kind of spear).

Perhaps, as the speaker felt when he denied the authenticity of "quaqua," the intervention of that word was all a fiction anyway. Even so, his dreams are penetrated by it. Thus there are in the book echoes of Christian figurations of experience: hints of millennialism, of the *logos* as distorted by mud. In the first part a vague "epiphany" suggests an involuntary memory of Eden. The sack is a figure for the body, support and burden of the soul, which the Christian centuries would have had no difficulty in recognizing; in the third part we have a picture of the history of the elect parallel to Milton's in the last two books of *Paradise Lost*, except that we lack the assurance of Pim's second coming in majesty. The book offers an open invitation to such allegories, even though everybody who accepts it will soon feel lost and uncertain.

In view of all this it is, I suppose, just as well that we *do* after all know something, if only a little, about Beckett. The Speaker in this book is the latest in a long line bred from his obsession with Dante's Belacqua, who could not enter purgatory until he had relived his slothful life. Beckett's dream of life is purgatorial, or would be if salvation waited at its end; as it is, his characters are, as Mr. Rooney says in *All that Fall*, "like Dante's damned, with their faces arsy-versy." There is a Beckett country in which we feel half at home; and we know the Beckettian *homo patiens*, sinking progressively into immobility. His role as victim and tormentor we recall from *Godot*. His relation to the past we learned from *Krapp's Last Tape*. And so on. In addition there is, to provide a physics for the Beckett world, his early book on Proust, as well as such sophisticated experiments as Mr. Kenner's book.[1] So we have some knowledge, not much, of the physical laws governing this new book; we have keys to its meanings. "No symbol where none intended," noted Beckett in the addenda to *Watt*; but by establishing a world of uncontrollably interrelated objects and meanings he makes this injunction impossible of fulfillment.

A few instances will serve to illustrate this. There must be a connection between Pim's watch, Pozzo's watch in *Godot*, and the passage in *Proust* on Time's "ingenuity . . . in the science of affliction." Time is the means by which we are punished for having been born. For Beckett as for Proust our only means of triumphing over it is the involuntary memory; in Beckett this operates infrequently and unsatisfactorily, as with Krapp's tape or the Speaker's recollection of the girl and of his marriage. We are enslaved by time; when eternity, the *nunc stans*, the *duré*, came down to save us, it apparently failed. So much for the "succour" which, as Molloy observed, you ought to consider a possibility before, inevitably, you reject it. Pim is one name for it. Trapped in time and space as the fallen categorize them (and what other way is there?) Beckett's figures are all, as Mr. Kenner demonstrates, more or less conscious Cartesians. They are all, perhaps, Descartes himself, contemplating the world from a position prone or supine (Yeats remarked that the world changed when Descartes discovered that he could think better in bed than up).

Contemplating a world so changed, Beckett is moved to "jettison the very matrices of fiction—narrator, setting, characters, theme, plot," and "devote his scrutiny (under the sign of Belacqua) to the very heart of novel writing: a man in his room writing things out of his head while every breath he draws brings death nearer." So Mr. Kenner. He is also much interested by inventions which reflect the factitious order and interrelatedness of the objective world to which he cannot belong; his relation to this common-sense reality is exactly that of a circus clown, who can do apparently impossible things but finds easy ones incredibly complicated. The fundamental absurdity of the subject-object situation is for him figured in clowns and *clochards*; and so is our imperfect control over space, time, and death. Beckett's humor derives entirely from this. It is a stateliness of speech, a clownishness of philosophical language (dealing with the complicated things and finding the easy ones too hard); in action it is the Bergsonian pratfall. This is the humor of man as machine, whether rhetorical or locomotive.

Beckett can thus be read as a philosophical fantasist: His bicycles are Cartesian symbols, his submen Prousts who have *really* contracted out, and so forth. Sunk in Belacqua's sub-social, sub-psychological dream, they all merge in one's mind—Watt, Molloy, Malone, the Unnamable, the unnamed of the

Return to Prose: *How It Is*   165

new book. They may sink deeper into a state of pure rejection, pure negativity—indistinguishable, as Molloy noticed, from God's. But because they are all aspects of the same figure, inhabiting similar worlds, we have relevant knowledge to bring to this new book; we can live with it, perceive something of its rhythms and stresses—in short, receive it.

That, at any rate, is a way of putting it. Yet it may tell little more than a small part of the truth about how Beckett has to be read. To emphasize the formal interest can be a fashionable way of concealing the true nature of our curiosity. Beckett is a puzzle-maker, quaint and learned. We look for clues, guess at meanings. His formal sophistication may be the meat the modern burglar brings along to quiet the *avant-garde* housedog. Under it all, he is a rather old-fashioned writer, a metaphysical allegorist. Take, for example, *Watt*. There he made his hero's name the first word of a metaphysical conundrum; and Knott, whom Watt serves, is the god defined by negatives, perhaps also time itself, inexplicably regular. Watt has only oblique religious experiences. He meets a porter whose lameness causes him "to move rapidly, in a series of aborted genuflections," and a Mr. Spiro, Catholic propagandist, who gives prizes for anagrams on the names of the Holy Family. (Out of Mr. Spiro's motto, *dum spiro spero*, we get the interesting anagram *dum*: mud. Since *dum* is "while," here meaning one's time on earth, it isn't hard to see why the latest hero spends his time in the mud.)

Watt, however, is not good at symbols: he had "lived, miserably it is true, among face values all his adult life . . . whatever it was Watt saw, with the first look, that was enough for Watt . . . he had experienced literally nothing, since the age of fourteen, or fifteen, of which in retrospect he was not content to say, That is what happened then."

To enjoy Beckett, one mustn't be a Watt. When we meet, for example, the Lynch family, we must take their heroic efforts, ruined by disease, to reach a combined age of a thousand years not as merely grotesque humor, but as a hopelessly human millennial aspiration, an absurd plot to overcome history, bring time to an end. If we know that Beckett's names and titles often contain puns, sometimes obscene, let us also look for allegorical meanings in such names as Malone and MacMann, Godot, and even Pim.

This suggests that the delights offered by Beckett are of an old and tried variety. He has re-invented philosophical and theological allegory, and as surely as Spenser he needs the right to sound sub-rational, to conceal intention under an appearance of dreamlike fortuity, to obscure the literal sense. The only difference is that his protagonists were sure there was such a sense, and on this bitch of a planet he can no longer have such certainties. This difference does not affect the proposition that Beckett's flirtations with reality are carried on in a dialect which derives from the traditional language of learning and poetry. It is nevertheless true that the more accustomed we become to his formal ambiguity, the more outrageously he can test us with inexplicitness, with apparently closed systems of meaning. *How It Is* differs from the earlier work not in its mode of operation, but principally in that it can assume greater knowledge of the Beckett world. Such assumptions have often and legitimately been made by major artists, though we should not forget that this is not a certain indication of greatness. Prolonged attentions given (from whatever motives) to a minor but complex author may allow him to make them. But who can be sure which is which? It is a perennial problem for critics of *avant-garde* art, and Beckett raises it in a very acute form.

From *The New York Review of Books* 2 (19 March 1964): 9-11.

---

[1]Other books are Ruby Cohn's *Samuel Beckett: The Comic Gamut* (1962), Frederick J. Hoffman's *Samuel Beckett: The Language of Self* (1962), and a very recent useful addition, *The Testament of Samuel Beckett* by Josephine Jacobson and William R. Mueller.

Farewell to Incompetence: Beckett's *How It Is* and *Imagination Dead Imagine*

H. Porter Abbott

There is considerable critical support for the position that *How It Is* is indeed about how it is. As one critic has written: "Man's suffering, cruelty, and loneliness have never found a more desolating metaphor."[1] Others have made similar interpretations:

> Life is the old, traditional, and ruthless voyage; briefly, a couple may be formed, and then the voyage continues in solitude, until there is another brief coupling, with the partners reversing their roles. In spite of that reversal, in spite of a straight-line momentum, and although he may deny it, man keeps going round in circles, repeating a few ridiculous phrases, a few ridiculous gestures.[2]

> The moral judgment . . . behind which the book lines itself up is as clear as it is bleak: Beckett's intention would seem to be to say that, though life in the human city is comprised of manifold relations, they all move within the single polarity involving torturer and victim, both roles being enacted in turn by all men in the various

relations with one another into which they are brought by the adventures of life.[3]

What these critics agree upon is Beckett's mimetic intention, that the book bears witness to the true plight of man: if we peel away all that is "above in the light" (which seems to include our pasts and those outer layers of our personality which make us complex and unique), we shall discover "how it is," that our needs are "sustenance and murmuring," that we alternately move and rest, that we are alternately victims and tormentors, that we wish (perhaps) to love and to be loved, that our progress is slow and our activities inevitable.

There is certainly much to be said in favor of this interpretation, although it does seem rather neat, especially since the narrator himself rejects it in the end. More troublesome still is its failure to establish the extent to which this book differs from the rest of Beckett's canon. Of course, *How It Is* has much in common with the other work; old men, tormentors, and victims are nothing unusual. Nonetheless, I hope to show that *How It Is* and the "novel" that follows it, *Imagination Dead Imagine*, represent a significant change in the author's approach to fiction.

The basic innovation of *How It Is* is its phenomenal order. That this is an innovation can be illustrated quite simply by comparing the abilities of Beckett's narrators to keep to their "programs." Since *Molloy*, they have been fond of announcing programs—that is, setting up plans for narration—and, as he constantly reminds us, the narrator of *How It Is* has his program, too. What is remarkable in *How It Is* is the perfection to which the program works, whereas if anything distinguishes the programs of earlier narrators, it is their perfect failure. Molloy never did get to "draw up the inventory of his goods and possessions,"[4] and we hardly need his own admission to know that he "made a balls of" his report. Malone says he is going to tell us four stories: "one about a man, another about a woman, a third about a thing and finally one about an animal, a bird probably."[5] This plan is immediately revised to three stories, to be followed by his inventory, and it is hard to say whether he ended by telling one or two stories. The inventory, inserted before the end, is incomplete. The Unnamable has his plans, too; the audacity of one will stand for many: "Of Worm, at last. Good. We must first, to begin with, go back to his beginnings and then, to go on with, follow him patiently through the various stages, taking care to show their fatal concatenation, which have made him what I am. The whole to be tossed off with bravura. Then notes from day to day, until I collapse. And finally, to wind up with, song and dance of thanksgiving by victim, to celebrate his nativity. Please God nothing goes wrong."[6]

The very hopelessness of the programs in the trilogy is an index of their importance, for the narrators are obsessed with ordering what will never yield to order. In *How It Is*, on the other hand, matter and program are so perfectly identical that the narrator seems to be contained by a fusion of the two. He is as much crawling toward Part Two as he is toward Pim.

To repeat, our main problem is accounting for this miraculous order. There should be little doubt by now that one of the controlling ideas—if not *the* controlling idea—in the work before *How It Is* is the absence of order. "'I can't see any trace of any system anywhere,'" Beckett is reported to have said.[7] Malone has echoed him: "the natural order of things, all that pertains to me must be written there, including my inability to grasp what order is meant. For I have never seen any sign of any, inside me or outside me."[8] In his essay on Proust, which among other things is a statement of his own romantic aesthetic, Beckett placed a freedom from Western ideas of order at the core of any valid art, just as he found the same essential to any valid experience: "when the object is perceived as particular and unique and not merely the member of a family, when it appears independent of any general notion and detached from the sanity of a cause, isolated and inexplicable in the light of ignorance, then and then only may it be a source of enchantment."[9] Beckett's art has been a mimesis of this essential disorder. Everything in his work, from the gross derangements of structure to the subtle reversals in the prose, operates to reinforce this idea. There is no need to review the evidence here; anyone who claims to see system in these works claims to see more than Beckett.

The key idea in Beckett's mimesis of disorder has been that of incompetence. "My inability to absorb," says the Unnamable, "my genius for forgetting, are more than they reckoned with. Dear incomprehension, it's thanks to you I'll be myself, in the end."[10] There should be little wonder, then, that Beckett reacted as completely as he did to the overwhelming competence of Joyce: "'The kind of work I do is one in which I'm not master of my material. The more Joyce knew the more he could. He's tending toward omniscience and omnipotence as an artist. I'm working with impotence, ignorance.'"[11] The advantages of incompetence are made clear in the essay on Proust, in which Beckett points out that it is the incompetence of Proust's narrator that makes him unable to impose order on experience. In other words, his incompetence liberates him from concepts like cause and effect or the continuity of past, present, and future and allows him to see things as they are, uncontrolled by any system.

Yet it is hard to see any less than system in *How It Is*. "It's regulated," "it's mathematical," the narrator keeps pointing out as he describes the social interchange of this world: "at the instant I leave Bem another leaves Pim and let us be at that instant one hundred thousand strong then fifty thousand departures fifty thousand abandoned . . . the same instant always everywhere / at the instant I reach Pim another reaches Bem we are regulated thus" (112).[12] And, as the society, so the psychology: Pim operates in perfect accord with a rigid behaviorism in which nothing more is needed than the principles of positive and negative reinforcement. "It's mechanical."

Return to Prose: *How It Is*

Now if we are going to take the title of this work at face value, we shall have to postulate a radical change in Beckett's world-view. We shall have him admitting as reality what he had argued so strenuously in his essay on Proust was only the fabrication of Memory and Habit. However, before we try to resolve this dilemma, we should look at some of the other innovations in *How It Is*. Perhaps, by appreciating just how thoroughly the work breaks with the past, we shall find our way to a solution.

On the very first page the narrator hesitates briefly over an old problem: "me if it's me no question impossible too weak no importance." He brings it up only once again a few pages later: "if it's me no question too weak no interest" (21-22). What he does in these remarks is dispose of the very question that constantly tormented the Unnamable. The problem of who he really is may be impossible to solve, but it is also irrelevant. In this new fictional world he is a given integer in a perfect mathematical system, or, if you will, part of a machine and easily defined in terms of his relationship to all the other moving parts.[13] The contrast is not only with *The Unnamable* but, once again, with the entire canon. Bleak as the world is in *How It Is*, the narrator is nonetheless at home in it, among the numbered, and as such is quite different from his predecessors.

In 1956 Beckett was reported to have said: "The French work brought me to the point where I was saying the same thing over and over again . . . In the last book—'L'Innommable'—there's complete disintegration. No 'I,' no 'have,' no 'being.' No nominative, no accusative, no verb . . . The very last thing I wrote—'Textes pour Rien' [*sic*]—was an attempt to get out of the attitude of disintegration, but it failed."[14] One thing is certain about Samuel Beckett: he does not like half-measures; *How It Is* is reintegration with a vengeance.

There is another remarkable difference in this work, one that is again bound up with its phenomenal order. In all Beckett's charting of disorder, the presence of opposites has played an important part. He has employed methods ranging from the subtle to the gross, to force extremes into collision and to leave a gaping mystery where one seeks relationship and cause. There were two thieves—one was saved and one was damned: it is precisely because there is no accounting for this juxtaposition that Beckett has found it so important. From the simple sentence one can project an entire universe without reason or method, and in a way, all the cancellations in Beckett's prose imply such a universe, as do the events in the narratives. The forward progress of the character in *From an Abandoned Work* is as good a model as any: "all was slow, and then these flashes."[15] No median range is possible: "Now the jogtrot on the other hand, I could no more do that than I could fly." To make matters worse, his terrific sprints come at random, like the sudden rages that break his calm. His rages in turn are unrelated to his feelings of violence: "some days I would be feeling violent all day and never have a rage, other days quite quiet for me and have four or five. No, there's no accounting for it, there's no accounting for anything, with a mind like the one I always had, always on the alert against itself . . ."[16]

Nothing could be in greater contrast than the physical and emotional progress in *How It Is*. What extremes there are never conflict, rather they are contained in a perfect harmony of cause and effect. Crawling and resting, panting and murmuring flash on and off with the regularity of a neon sign. Opposites have been blunted or bound; "My vertex touches my bottom," as the narrator says. Pim and Bom are one, a victim and tormentor endure their interchanging roles in the same way a coin "endures" its two sides, the one suffering as little as the other enjoys. "Deterioration of the sense of humour fewer tears too" (18).

Less humor and fewer tears. Less humor for the reader, too, if, that is, the book is about how it is. But if the title of this book is in fact a monumental joke, if the book is rather about just how it is not, the oppressive feeling that Beckett wants us to take it for life dissipates. Not that we read the book with hilarity, but something that at times approaches it: "victim of number 4 at A enroute along AB tormentor of number 2 at B abandoned again this time at B victim again of number 4 but this time B enroute again but this time along BA tormentor of number 2 again but this time at A and finally abandoned again at A and all set to begin again" (118). It is all quite absurd, but absurd now in the sense that it has nothing to do with how it is. "If there were only darkness," Beckett is reported to have said, "all would be clear. It is because there is not only darkness but also light that our situation becomes inexplicable."[17] In *How It Is*, Beckett has reduced it all to darkness—to clarity.

"Life above in the light" is our world or, in other words, how it is. Its intrusions in the form of "rags" or images are, therefore, the chaotic, unrelated elements in the novel. It is the place of disorder and emotion, and also of injustice, as the narrator points out in a parody of the parable of the sheep: "to his eyes the spectacle on the one hand of a single one among us towards whom no one ever goes and on the other of a single other who never goes towards anyone it would be an injustice and that is above in the light" (124). Down here, naturally, justice is perfect. The victims "triumph if only narrowly" in being allowed motion. The tormentors must lie still: "penalty perhaps of their recent exertions but effect also of our justice" (143).

In 1959 Beckett published a short piece entitled "L'Image,"[18] in which the narrator, face down in the mud with his sack, constructs a touching image of himself as a youth in the country with his sweetheart and dog—"pâles cheveux en brosse grosse face rouge avec boutons ventre débordant braguette béante jambes cagneuses en fuseau écartées pour plus d'assise fléchissant aux genoux pieds ouverts cent trente-cinq degrés." The passage is actually a series of images in which impressions come in confusing, disconnected flashes. In its essentials (though with extensive stylistic revisions) the piece was incorporated in *Comment c'est* where it appears as one of the rags of life above in the light. Following, as it did, *From an Abandoned Work*[19] and containing no hint of the fabulous system of *Comment c'est*, "L'Image," I would suspect, represents a last effort in the mimesis of disorder Beckett had been struggling with in his prose for most of his artistic career.

The solution to his problem, then, lay in rejecting incompetence as an artistic device. What Beckett has written in *How It Is* is a *reductio ad absurdum* of the human demand for order set in a Newtonian afterlife. "I always loved arithmetic," the narrator says, "it has paid me back in full" (37). His crime is his rage for order, and his rage for order is reflected in the thought-patterns of the race: "it's not said where on earth I can have received my education acquired my notions of mathematics astronomy and even physics they have marked me that's the main thing" (41). These notions, to which the earth never yielded, are now the pattern for creation; having a perfect omniscience and omnipotence, the narrator is the supremely successful classical artist. He fabricates a clockwork afterlife in the image of his own mind, old and vast enough to contain both expiation and reward.

The sin for which the narrator suffers—that of yielding to the rage for order—is to be found in everyone. But the narrator must suffer for all of us and, hence, must have a superhuman competence—one capable of sustaining the entire verbal fabric of *How It Is*. He is also its creator, taking for his pattern the ideal form of what is latent in everyman, and hence creating and existing in that for which everyman is responsible. It only remains for him to die for the world, and in dying to harrow this unearthly paradise. He does so, needless to say, with his arms spread "like a cross." The act of sacrifice is the act of denial. His heroism lies in the terrific effort of will required, after the final calculations have been made and all parts accounted for, to say that it's "all balls."

It is only fair to mention at this point that there are other critics who by different routes have arrived at conclusions as extreme as this. John Fletcher, for example, has written that in reading *How It Is* "we are spectators at a ballet, formal and untroubled by any reality but its own, by any principle but that, inevitable and serene, of its own growth and rapid decline."[20] Raymond Federman has argued that "this novel is not a projection of reality, but an experiment in willful artistic failure: the rejection of reality . . . *Comment c'est* is a world of abstractions and illusions which poses as fiction, just as conventional fiction pretends to pass for reality."[21]

Yet can we differ so radically with the critical opinion we quoted at the outset? After all, Beckett did call his novel *How It Is*. And if one takes it as a joke, one must remember that almost all Beckett's jokes can be taken in more than one way. Hugh Kenner is perfectly right when he says: "This work contains no ingredient (unless perhaps mud) which we have not encountered before."[22] The need for sustenance and the need to "commit words," motion and rest, torment and tormenting, and "good moments somehow or other":

these are basic ingredients—basic to how it is—and Beckett has never avoided them. They are as fundamental to the works charting the possible disorder as they are to the work charting the impossible order. In this work, as in the others, the basic ingredients seem especially true in the way in which they have been reduced. Pim and Bom are in the great tradition of Hairy Mac and Sucky Moll. What is compelling is Beckett's ability to de-romanticize.[23]

In addition to these "basic ingredients," it can also be granted that Beckett is showing us how it is with our imagination, although this is granting much. Beckett may be totally unclear as to where mind and body meet, but there seems little doubt that he includes both mind and matter in whatever reality is. (Indeed, it is hard to reject the interplay of mud and mind that goes on in the narrator's self-creation.) Here we not only have an imagination, but we have one working on principles of order which, though they may plague us, are in a real sense very much *with* us. If the portrait of mind is fictional, it is so in the best sense of the word; for it makes brilliantly clear the condition of mind that is common to man. What I believe Beckett concluded in going beyond *The Unnamable* is that there is absolutely no dissociating mind from order, that mind is order. Would chaos have any meaning at all if it were not for our ideas of order? Although the method Beckett employed in the trilogy was disintegration, every step in the process of disintegration depended on some idea of order for its effect. The finer the separation of part from part, the more exquisite the sense of order assumed.

What we have, then, in *How It Is* are the parts of how it is—matter and mind—seen perhaps more clearly than ever before. In their purest forms—the mud and the voice—their reality is acknowledged even at the end when the narrator annihilates all the rest. What we do *not* have is how it is: how the parts combine without relation and cohere without order.

Very near the end of *How It Is*, the narrator entertains the possibility of another creation:

> and if it is still possible at this late hour to conceive of other worlds as just as ours but less exquisitely organized
>
> one perhaps there is one perhaps somewhere merciful enough to shelter such frolics where no one ever abandons anyone and no one ever waits for anyone and never two bodies touch. (143)

This possibility is realized in almost every detail in the seven-page "novel," *Imagination Dead Imagine*. Yet the creation in this work is abandoned, too: "Leave them there, sweating and icy, there is better elsewhere."[24] For creation has now become a continual seeking after better worlds. Since the impasse of the 1950s Beckett has bound himself to competence—to the mind's ordering—without giving up his original goal of trying to capture how it is. The search is for that arrangement of matter which is both ordered *and* representative of how it is. The hope has been that, once the list of basic ingredients has been sufficiently reduced, the common denominator of matter and mind will prove to be order. Following a process of elimination, he has tried "to find a form that accommodates the mess,"[25] to determine how much of the mess can be accommodated by form, form being a product of the mind.

In the first lines of *Imagination Dead Imagine*, we have the imagination literally welling up out of the whiteness of the page: "Islands, waters, azure, verdure." Then, as if in dictation, we are told to "omit," for this is a matter that cannot be accommodated. The inventory that required so elaborate, and hence preposterous, a form in *How It Is* is then drastically reduced so that it may be accommodated by a simpler form which will not falsify how it is. The form which is allowed to take shape contains man and woman (back to back like a reversed Yin and Yang) breathing, perspiring, and murmuring "ah"; they are in a rotunda which can be womb and tomb as well as the mind that imagines them ("a ring as in the imagination the ring of bone") and they suffer the same ebb and flow of light and heat that man suffers in his days and seasons.

As the narrator of *How It Is* predicted, though, this world is "less exquisitely organized" than his. Between the calms of extreme white and heat and extreme black and cold are pauses of varying length with attendant vibrations and occasional reversals of direction—all variations "combining in countless rhythms." Part of the flux, then, has been included; but only so much as can be contained in the symmetry of form: "whatever its uncertainties the return sooner or later to a temporary calm seems assured, for the moment, in the black dark or the great whiteness, with attendant temperature, world still proof against enduring tumult."[26]

Order is even more seriously threatened by changes of time outside the cycles of seasons and days. For this reason the book, like many of Beckett's works, has a shorter second act. It begins without warning in the solid block of words ("Rediscovered miraculously after what absence in perfect voids . . ."). In this second half, though the perfectly symmetrical image of the womb-tomb remains, we discover that the rest "is no longer the same." The bodies have become distinguishable, the hair has grown white, the eyes open, the lips murmur "ah," and the sense of tumult has increased: "briefer lulls and never twice the same storm."[27]

Finally, the form is valid only "for the moment." There is no telling whether in the future they will "still lie still in the stress of that storm, or of a worse storm, or in the black dark for good, or the great whiteness unchanging,"[28] for the validity of the form depends on the source of light and heat, "of which still no trace." We have no way of knowing when He "in charge of the sacks," as the narrator of *How It Is* called Him,[29] will choose not to yield to even the humblest of forms.

For the moment, then, Beckett has found how much of how it is yields—and how far it yields—to order, or rather he *may* have found how much, for he says: "Leave them there, sweating and icy, there is better elsewhere." And, though he immediately follows this statement with "no, there is nothing elsewhere," his desire to find "better elsewhere" is understandable, since what is pitiable about *Imagination Dead Imagine* is the meagerness of what has been accommodated to form. Beckett ironically underlines this meagerness by his constant measurement and testing:

> Diameter three feet, three feet from ground to summit of the vault. Two diameters at right angles AB CD divide the white ground into two semi-circles ACB BDA.
>
> Go back out, a plain rotunda, all white in the whiteness, go back in, rap, solid throughout . . .
>
> Hold a mirror to their lips, it mists.

Beckett is saying that his order is no spurious one, for it at least contains these realities. It is a very small triumph. Yet, knowing Beckett, one feels that he will seek "better elsewhere."

From *Contemporary Literature* 11, no. 1 (Winter 1970): 36-47.

---

[1]William York Tindall, *Samuel Beckett* (New York, 1964), p.38.

[2]Ruby Cohn, *Samuel Beckett: The Comic Gamut* (New Brunswick, N.J., 1962), pp.206-207.

[3]Nathan A. Scott, *Samuel Beckett* (London, 1965), p. 78

[4]*Three Novels* (New York, 1965), p. 47.

[5]*Ibid.*, p. 181.

[6]*Ibid.*, p. 352.

[7]Israel Shenker, "Moody Man of Letters," *New York Times*, May 6, 1956, sec. 2, p.3.

[8]*Three Novels*, p. 210.

[9]*Proust* (New York, 1957), p. 11. *Proust* was first published in 1931.

[10]*Three Novels*, p. 325.

[11]Shenker, p. 3.

[12]Numbers in parentheses refer to pages in the Grove Press edition of *How It Is*, 1964.

[13]John Fletcher has argued that "in this novel, predictably, the problem of identity is especially acute" (*The Novels of Samuel Beckett* [London, 1964], p. 213). This view, however, is based almost exclusively on the "images" of "life above in the light" that occur as fragments in the book. These perplexing images, as I hope to show later, constitute a special part of the book, quite distinct, or at least removed, from how it is in the mud with Pim and Bom.

[14]Shenker, pp. 1, 3.

[15]*From an Abandoned Work* (London, 1958), p. 13.

[16]*Ibid.*, p. 12.

[17]Tom F. Driver, "Beckett by the Madelein," *Columbia University Forum*, IV (Summer 1961), 23.

[18]*X, A Quarterly Review*, I (November 1959), 35-37.

[19]Final version first published in *Evergreen Review*, I, no. 3 (1957), 83-91. The chronology of publication for these late prose pieces would read: *From an Abandoned Work*, 1957; "L'Image," 1959; *Comment c'est*, 1961 (Paris). As if to clarify the progression, Beckett published the first translated fragment of *Comment c'est* under the title "From an Unabandoned Work" (*Evergreen Review*, IV [September-October 1961], 58-65).

[20]*The Novels of Samuel Beckett*, pp. 215-216. The phrasing has even more extreme implications, and Fletcher is careful to develop them only in hypothesis: "is it too wild a deduction to suppose that this author, despairing completely of saying anything new, feels driven to making things of beauty instead? When 'literature' seems to him sham and farce, a well-produced book perhaps appears a more honourable achievement. The logical consequence of such an attitude would be to esteem the printer and binder above the writer, and this is, in fact, the sort of conclusion before which some artists of our time have shown they do not recoil" (p. 220).

[21]"How It Is with Beckett's Fiction," *French Review*, 38 (Feb. 1965), 461.

[22]*Samuel Beckett: A Critical Study* (New York, 1961), p. 199. I have found some mud, too, but I do not wish to quibble with this book. The tension in *How It Is* which I am trying to spell out here was, I believe, first observed by Kenner: "In our fascinated affinity with these twilight men, none of them visible to the eyes with which we pursue our affairs (and what are our affairs?) we barely credit the ritual disavowal—never any procession no nor journey no never any Pim no nor Bem no never anyone no but me no answer but me yes . . .—and barely notice how cunningly it does not disavow. Yes, yes, I am mistaken, I am mistaken, said B. in the same way, to placate D. These books do not undo the world; it will be here tomorrow" (p. 206).

[23]How seductive in this regard is the possible source for Beckett's "metaphor" which Germaine Brée found in Rabelais! I quote her translation of the passage: [Bacbuc to Panurge] "You say in your world that 'sac' is a word common to all languages and naturally and rightly understandable to all nations, for according to Aesopus all humans are born, a sack around the neck, puny by nature, and perpetually begging one from another" ("Beckett's Abstractors of Quintessence," *French Review*, 36 [1963], 567).

[24]"Imagination Dead Imagine" (London, 1965), p. 14; translated by the author from "Imagination morte imaginez" (Paris, 1965).

[25]Beckett, quoted in Driver, p. 23.

[26]"Imagination," p. 11.

[27]*Ibid.*

[28]*Ibid.*, p. 14.

[29]*How It Is*, p. 124.

Beckett's Sociability

Leo Bersani and Ulysse Dutoit

Imagine two old men lying still, face down in the mud, separated from one another by, say, a quarter of a mile. Now imagine two other men, also face down in the mud, each one approaching one of the other two. Two couples are formed simultaneously when the travelers reach the immobile ones and stop, pressing their bodies against those of their partners. The former, mysteriously silent, but intent on communicating with their new companions, devise an elaborate semiotic system in two stages. In "the first or heroic times," the men toward whom the others have crawled are taught to respond to a series of signals administered by their silent partner's right hand, and which can be summarized as follows:

> table of basic stimuli one sing nails in armpit
> two speak blade in arse three stop thump on
> skull four louder pestle on kidney
>
> five softer index in anus six bravo clap athwart
> arse seven lousy same as three eight encore
> same as one or two as maybe

At the second, and more sophisticated stage of learning—the advent of writing—the former traveler imprints questions, with his fingernails, on his companion's back. In responding to his tormentor's written injunctions to tell something about his life "ABOVE . . . IN THE LIGHT," the victimized partner recites scraps of "that life then said to have been his invented remembered a little of each no knowing"—scraps which include such dramatic events as the attempted suicide of his wife. Our two couples, however, are not fixed in their positions or roles. Imagine that the victim of each couple leaves his tormentor and crawls toward the tormentor of the other couple. The mobile and immobile roles are now reversed: the two who had previously crawled toward an immobile partner are waiting for the arrival of the two others who had, in an earlier time, lain still awaiting *their* arrival. Except, of course, that the first time around B had awaited A, and D had awaited C; now A awaits D, and C awaits B. When the new couples are formed, the same exchanges are repeated, with the roles of tormentor and victim being determined not by the actors' individual identities but rather by their functions in this relational diagram. Thus B who had been the victim the first time around is now the tormentor with his new companion C: the traveler is always the silent torturer, and the immobile one is always the victim tortured into speaking. It is also always the victim who moves on. We should further note that in this group of four each man gets to know, so to speak, only two of the others. A knows B as his victim and D as his torturer, but he will never lie alongside C, although it is of course possible that B may speak to him of C. Similarly, B knows A as his torturer and C as his victim, but any knowledge he may have of D can only come through his talking victim C. According to the arrangement just outlined, "each always leaves the same always goes towards the same always loses the same always goes towards him who leaves him always leaves him who goes towards him." For example, B is always leaving A and going toward C, and a corollary of this is that each figure in the group is "tormentor always of the same and victim always of the same": B will never have any other tormentor than A, no other victim but C. This triadic series of relationships thus requires four figures in order to be carried on. And note that everything we have just said about both the number of contacts available in this scheme, and the nature of each contact, would in no way be affected by an increase in the number of players. Whether we have four old men, 100,000, a million, or several billion crawling humans spread out in an unbroken ellipsis around the earth, each person would still only know the same two others, rigorously repeating, forever if necessary, the role of victim with the one and of tormentor with the other. In this perfectly organized world, at every moment, everyone—whatever the number may be—is either enjoying a victim or suffering at the hands of a tormentor, *or* is either crawling toward his victim or confident that a tormentor is on his way. (This would not be the case if we had a finite number of players in a straight line, for then there would always be a first figure unable to anticipate the arrival of a tormentor from the West as well as a last figure with no victim awaiting his harsh lessons to the East. If, then, the procession is not moving as a closed circle, we must have an infinite number of players, in which case we could never arrive at those unfairly deprived first and last old men, which would in a sense eliminate the problem of their intolerable isolation.)

How might this scheme be narrated? We have, as it were, just done it from above, describing, for example, each position of the two couples without giving special attention to any one of the four players. We might, however, adopt the point of view of, say, A and make an autobiographical account of the structure. In so doing, it would be logical to divide our history into three parts, corresponding to A's (and everyone's) three major activities or functions in the scheme: A traveling from one couple to another, A tormenting B, and A being tormented by D. (A could of course also begin as tormentor, with a second part devoted to his experience as a victim, thus ending his narrative where the other began — his traveling between an abandoned tormentor and an expectant victim.) The traveler-tormentor-victim sequence is the one adopted by the Beckettian narrator of *How It Is*, the novel from which the preceding description of human relations has been taken. We have, then, the account of a single participant in a community whose members may number as high as twenty billion; the number may even be infinite. But is there anything more we need to know? Remember that every link on this unimaginably long chain has exactly the same adventures: he silently tortures another into speaking, he is himself stabbed and beaten until he answers his torturer as satisfactorily as his own victim had answered him, and, between being tortured and torturing he crawls from one body to another. Not only that: all those scraps of life seem to come from a single life. Speaking of Pim, the victim he remembers training to speak in Part II, the narrator says: "he got it from another that dog's life to take and to leave. I'll give it to another." If we adopt the hypothesis of several billion creatures forming an unbroken ellipsis around the earth, and if we designate the last couple somewhere to the west of A and B as Y and Z, then not only is the life which B (let's say Pim) gives to A the same which A will tell (or has told) to Z, but, we have every reason to believe, it is also the one passed by Z to Y, and so on along the chain. It is all the more remarkable, then, that each one of the billions of billions of times that a member of this planetary community takes on the role of victim and repeats a broken account of his life "up there in the light" which he has already repeated countless times, it is as if he were being made to tell that life for the first time. Everyone never stops learning to speak and passing on the same information. This endless restarting from zero becomes stranger still if we consider the possibility, raised on the last pages of the novel, that the whole story has been nothing but "all balls" ("de la foutaise"), and that there has never been anyone but the narrator, no other voice but his. And much earlier in the work he had said, referring to the division of his narrative into three parts: "divide into three a single eternity for the sake of clarity." Such simplifications and foreshortenings have of course an appealing logic. If everyone on the chain has the same movements and sequence of roles, and the same remembered life, as everyone else, we might as well think of them all as a single person; they are nothing but exact copies of one another. Furthermore, if everyone is both tormentor and victim, might it not also be possible to think of the tormentor-victim sequence as a simultaneity of being? There would in short be only one subject, structured eternally as resistance and obedience to an injunction to speak which he himself delivers. And that apprenticeship would always be both not yet begun and already completed. *How It Is* diagrams a type of being (the being that is human) structured as the unending repetition of its own origination. As if the deepest structure of being could never be anything but that: the beginning again of its own beginnings.

The simultaneity of process and structure in *How It Is* is most forcefully proposed by ways of the ambiguous source of the voice we hear. In referring to the narrative as autobiography, we ignored the piece of information most insistently reiterated by the narrator: it is not he who is speaking. The very first paragraph announces the entire work as an act of quotation: "how it was I quote before Pim with Pim after Pim how it is three parts I say it as I hear it." So the controlling narrative fiction of *How It Is* is that the narrator's life is being dictated to him from the outside. That piece of information may of course be part of the dictation, which might mean—although it could also *not* mean—that there is no one being dictated to, that there is only an unlocatable voice referring to its receiving speech from another source. And this speech (it is the same) also includes that reference to a source dictating it, a reference coming from that new source and possibly eliminating the more immediate source to which the narrator seemed first of all to refer. "I say it as I hear it" initiates an infinite regression of sources. A speech act which posits itself as a dictation immediately attributes this reference to a dictation to the dictating source itself, thus reversing the direction of language's referentiality from the world (where the response might stop) to the chimerical origins of a speech that is never begun but always heard, never initiated but always repeated.

How It Is brilliantly figures this unrepresentable regression as a circular transmission of an unlocatable speech. The narrator extorted speech from Pim, but if his telling the story of that extortion is dictated to him, then that very story is another version of speech-extortion. The "I" of the voice we are hearing is at the center of the novel's transmissions (he receives Pim's [true or false] memories, as well as the anonymous voice's account of the tormentor's extorting those memories from the victim), but he may be just that: not a person with a history, but merely a kind of stopping point for voices, an intersection of extortionary speech-acts, a collecting depot for all the words whose source of transmission remains uncertain. This possibility is reinforced by another dramatic invention: the narrator refers to a "witness" he names Kram "bending over us father to son to grandson," who is listening to everything he says and to a "scribe" "a little aloof" ("un peu à l'écart") who is presumably recording his words. The narrative "I" murmuring what he hears in the mud may allow the witness to circumscribe the voices *he* hears coming from everywhere, to enclose them within the boundaries of a figure perhaps invented by the witness for the purpose of knowing where to turn in order to listen and to pick up the message. The *récit* moves between quite coherent blocks of storytelling and referential bits and pieces (some of which, for example, refer brokenly to some wandering around the world), as if listening were inevitably an intermittently successful form-giving or boundary-tracing activity. The invention of the narrator helps the witness to determine the message. There is, that is to say, no real message, only an interminable, indeterminate, unbounded verbal flow that carries no messages or information prior to the transmitting stations which in fact constitute them. In short, the fable of *How It Is* may be *the form of the witness's listening*. This is perhaps how we should understand the suggestion that the story heard and repeated by the narrator is the witness's invention:

> there he is then at last that not one of us there we are then at last who listens to himself and who when he lends his ear to our murmur does no more than lend it to a story of his own devising ill-inspired ill-told and so ancient so forgotten at each telling that ours may seem faithful that we murmur to the mud to him

The anecdotal separation of the narrative "I" from the witness bent attentively over him figures this dual aspect of listening: the passive reception and

Return to Prose: *How It Is* 181

repetition of a language imposed from the outside, and the inability to fail to give sense or shape to that language while it is being repeated.

It should be clear that this process also describes the making of literature. This, however, does not mean that *How It Is* is a writer's more or less specialized reflection on the nature of writing. Rather, literature would *begin again* that sense-making hearing of language which is the way we both learn to speak and repeat what we hear as ideas or stories. And that beginning again may be a first beginning. Literature imitates something fundamental that does not depend on literature but which might never have taken place without the literary repetition of it. In a sense, the reception of language *takes place* (has a place where we can find and know it) nowhere outside Beckett's extraordinary work. Furthermore, *How It Is* shows, in the image of the scribe writing a story which the witness may have invented but which must be heard before it can be transcribed, how literature can also represent that (re)initiating which is its essence. Again, this has nothing to do with so-called literary specialization. We are all "writers," *How It Is* suggests, to the extent that we are unable to understand what we are listening to without projecting the form of our listening into the world, a form which we then receive as a story about, as information from, the world.

We have until now neglected to cite the word Beckett uses to characterize the tormentor-victim relationship: *justice.* Language is entered through other voices, and if those voices cannot at first be attached to persons, they nonetheless establish relations with other human subjects. Indeed each of us is made into a human subject — that is to say, socialized — *by* the voices we hear. The Beckettian fable of *How It Is* reenacts this entry into relations as a coercion, a coercion that is, however, psychologically unmotivated. To be tortured is the precondition for being humanized, but this has nothing to do with any sadism on the part of the torturer or any masochism on the part of the victim. Rather, the torture consists in the fact that as soon as we begin to listen to voices we can't help hearing an injunction to speak. We incorporate language as a command: *speak,* and this is all it says to us, it originally sends us no other message. *How It Is* divides that command into two stages: the imitation of sounds (which is the narrator's repeating of the voices, "I say it as I hear it"), and the inevitable self-identification—more fundamentally, self-constitution—which such repetition entails. The mute tormentor's semiotic system could be read as beautifully translating the self-originating experience of language as a brutalization of the body. Indeed, language tortures the human body into repeating itself as mind, as a conscious self.

Beckett's novel is not only about such origins, it also can't help but suggest the social consequences that originate in those origins. If to imitate speech is to speak a self that is nowhere in the speech imitated except *as* the injunction to repeat it, then the newly spoken self will necessarily resemble that injunction, will have the form of a command. Pim "hears": identify yourself (tell what it was like up there in the light), but he will also imitate what he hears, and it is the very fact of his having been a victim that empowers him as a tormentor. In psychoanalytic terms, ego-constitution is inseparable from birth of the superego. To be tortured out of monadic self-containment into a self-identifying speech is to *become* the brutally authoritative voice that summons others into speech. We address others in the mode in which we first listened to others, a listening continuously repeated within consciousness as the enabling structure and model of our speaking. Implicit in all dialogue is a project of mastering the other through the extortion of a self-exposing speech. Thus we enter and maintain linguistic intersubjectivity in a reign of terror, and it is, Beckett proposes, the reciprocity of the terroristic process that we name justice. (This reciprocity may explain the otherwise mysterious anxiety of those Beckettian figures apparently engaged only in the extortion of speech. We are thinking of such enigmatic radio plays as *Rough For Radio I*, *Rough For Radio II*, and *Words and Magic*, in which panic is associated with compelling others to speak or to perform—or merely with listening in to a recorded program—as if the initiating of a verbal performance were inseparable from the resistance or even the suffering of the victims of such extortions.) To stop the procession at the period of the victim's traveling between his recent tormentor and his prospective victim would, the narrator notes, be an injustice: "since the traveler to whom life owes a victim will never have another and never another tormentor the abandoned to whom life owes one." Thus the pain, the terrible injustices of life up there in the light are righted down in the mud, where the social is no longer lived contingently but rather in conformity with the deep structure of reciprocal torment that originally made the social possible. To guarantee this reciprocity is to obey the highest moral imperative. The faultless calculation of permutations along the interminable chain of tormentors and victims is a kind of prayer of thanks to that supreme voice that has guaranteed to each of us the right to terrorize others into speech.

Is there nothing else? *How It Is*, remarkably enough, asks this question in a typically Beckettian reformulation of the double biblical dispensation:

> with that of a slowness difficult to conceive the procession we are talking of a procession advancing in jerks or spasms like shit in the guts till one wonders days of great gaiety if we shall not end one after another or two by two by being shat into the open air the light of day the regimen of grace

The move from one regimen to the other is, however, not only figured—in a kind of exasperated parody—as a kind of improbable scatological explosion. There are hints that the reign of justice itself is somehow sustained by love, by a gratuitous attentiveness to others that has nothing to do with the right of each individual to inflict on others the pain inflicted on him. Everyone in the chain of tormentors and victims depends on the sack he drags along with him that contains cans of food (and the ominous can opener . . .). But where did the sacks come from? "Need of one not one of us," the narrator speculates, "an intelligence somewhere a love who all along the track at the right places according as we need them deposits our sacks." This is metaphysical speculation; more certain, and even more astonishing, is the narrator's insistence, every now and then, that he has had some good times: "good moments yes I assure you before Pim with Pim after Pim." The time with Pim is singled out at the beginning of Part II as the best time ("happy time in its way") and later on, in the middle of his account of how he trained Pim to speak, the narrator mentions hearing words coming from somewhere and telling him that "with someone to keep me company I would have been a different man more universal." Thus the grim regimen of justice is just slightly inflected in *How It Is* by the pleasure of the victim's company. Society, then, would not only reproduce the structure of coercion which made it possible, but might even be a pleasant result of that structure. Most unexpectedly, sociality might—from within the operations of torture but perhaps also in excess of them—generate sociability.

Sociability gets its major chance in Beckett's work almost twenty years later, in *Company*. The work begins as a purely formal exercise, with what Henry James might have appreciated as a compositional challenge. "A voice comes to one in the dark. Imagine." The next paragraph expands this challenge slightly: "That then is the proposition. To one on his back in the dark a voice tells of a past. With occasional allusions to a present and more rarely to a future as for example, You will end as you now are." At the same time a motive is given for the imagining about to take place: "And in another dark or in the same another devising it all for company." But this last remark is ambiguous: is the narrator referring to the author, or to himself as a character within this fiction, or to still another character whose imagining he would be narrating? These alternatives already create some hypothetical company, and they should help to make us see the company already implicit in the work's deceptively simple first sentences. "A voice comes to one in the dark" gives us three figures: the two referred to and the one referring. But with "Imagine," the narrator creates the possibility of a fourth presence: someone whom he is ordering to evoke the scene of the first sentence (which retroactively changes from a declarative remark to a command). Or is the fourth figure within the narrator, an interlocutor in an internal dialogue?

The model for such questions—questions about possible presences—comes from within the narrative itself. The imagined hearer on his back is imagined engaging in hypotheses about the number of persons who may be with, or somewhere near, him:

> If the voice is not speaking to him it must be speaking to another.
> So with what reason remains he reasons. To another of that other.
> Or of him. Or of another still. To another of that other or of him or
> of another still. To one on his back in the dark in any case. Of one
> on his back in the dark whether the same or another.

Such reasoning adds two new figures: someone else on his back in the dark, and "another still" of whom the voice might be speaking to this other prone person. It is true that this reasoning is immediately condemned as false ("were [the voice] not speaking of whom to whom it is speaking speaking but of another it would not speak in the second person but in the third"), but if a certain mental activity is necessary for company, "it need not be of a high order. Indeed it might be argued the lower the better. Up to a point."

The confusion multiplies, and can no longer be eliminated by more rigorous reasoning, when the narrator starts to ask questions about who is devising the whole fable—that is, about the original seeker of company. Remember that other (evoked in the book's second paragraph) "in another dark or in the same . . . devising it all for company." This is the one called elsewhere a "devised deviser devising it all for company." But referring to a repetition of that early phrase, the narrator will ask:

> For why or? Why in another dark or in the same? And whose voice
> asking this? Who asks, Whose voice asking this? And answers, His
> soever who devises it all. In the same dark as his creature or in
> another. For company. Who asks in the end. Who asks? And in
> the end answers as above? And adds long after to himself, unless
> another still.

Now we have not only company; we risk having a crowd with steadily increasing numbers. When the narrator first referred to someone "devising it all for company," we weren't sure where to locate that devising other, but now we are being asked to feel puzzled not about the deviser but about the voice that has told us about him (we will hold in reserve the possibility—raised by the implied identification of the one "who devises it all" with the one "in the same dark as his creature or in another"—that they are the same.) It is as if each time a statement is made there is an objectifying of that statement by consciousness, a kind of leaping away from it which puts its authorship into question. If in *How It Is* we learned that it is impossible to listen without beginning to speak, *Company* reverses this law: we can't speak without beginning to listen, and this schizophrenic listening creates the paranoid suspicion that our utterances don't belong to us, that someone else just spoke in our place. There is of course no reason for the questions to stop: "Who asks, Whose voice asking this?" generates: "Who asks, Who asks, Whose voice asking this?" which could of course lead to "Who asks, who asks, who asks, whose voice asking this?" and

Return to Prose: *How It Is* 185

so on. Is it possible to conceive, and therefore to represent, an undevised deviser? If this is confusing, "confusion too," the narrator asserts a couple of pages later, "is company up to a point."

Company is in fact haunted by the possibility that these regressions are not infinite, that they may finally lead to "the unthinkable last of all. Unnamable, last person. I. Quick leave him." What can't be thought, and what thought flees from, is the identity of consciousness with itself, that is, a consciousness no longer divided by self-consciousness, the truly unthinkable phenomenon (which may be a perfection reserved for animals) of an "I" that does not become a "he" or a "she" with each of its manifestations. This final "I"—an "I" to which the Unnamable of Beckett's novelistic trilogy of the 1940's seeks to escape and which *Company* implicitly dismisses as both terrifying and impossible—would be the wholly self-contained monad, unarticulated, undivided, unexpressed, unrelated to anything beyond itself or even to itself *as* a continuously receding "being-beyond-itself," and therefore protected from the relational, divided being initiated by language. In order to be only an "I," the unnamable "I" would be ignorant of the linguistic "I" that explodes the boundaries of a self at the instant of defining them, and that is immediately related to as a "he."

It is, however, through the self-alienating linguistic "I" that the fable of an identifiable biographical self is constructed. We are told fairly early in the story that the voice is not simply telling of a past to one on his back in the dark; it has the further intention of making its prone companion speak, and more specifically, making him say that the life he is hearing about is his own:

> Another trait [the voice's] repetitiousness. Repeatedly with only minor variants the same bygone. As if willing him by this dint to make it his. To confess, Yes I remember. Perhaps even to have a voice. To murmur. Yes I remember. What an additionto company that would be! A voice in the first person singular. Murmuring now and then, Yes I remember.

As the fable's authorship recedes further and further from the fable's visible field, the principal activity taking place within that field is a verbal campaign designed to make the hearer recognize himself within its representations. If the deployment of that campaign tends to subordinate the represented scenes to their ceaselessly recreated (and receding) source, the hearer is just as ceaselessly being drawn into the scenes, designated as an indentifiable "you." And yet that "you" is also unnamable. At one point the narrator considers giving a name to the hearer: "Let the hearer be named H. Aspirate. Haitch. You Haitch are on your back in the dark." But then, deciding that this would be neither "desirable" nor a gain in "companionability," he changes his mind: "Then let him not be named H. Let him be again as he was. The hearer.

Unnamable. You." "The unthinkable last of all," the unnamable "I" may, then, be identical to the principal figure in the fable, the hearer always addressed as "you" by the voice. It is as if the fable included within itself a figure for the unthinkable origin in which it is constantly in danger of being lost. The hearer, however, principally allows for the reversal of the movement back toward origins into a movement away from origins—although, as we shall see, the difference between the two is illusory: any movement in either direction is at once infinitely regressive. The hearer does, nonetheless, allow us to imagine the *beginning* of a process that will make beginnings inconceivable and unfindable.

Through the hearer we are given the emergence into those relations that, once initiated, can never return us to the unrelated starting of all relations. *Company*, like *How It Is*, represents that emergence as an *initiatory listening*. But whereas listening was repeated as a fairly elaborate story in *How It Is*, *Company* gives us something much more primitive: the awakening to differences of sound. Beckett shows the first active awareness of speech not as an understanding of content, but rather as an attempt to position the source of speech. In this attempt, adverbs and prepositions are more important than verbs or nouns in situating oneself in relation to a voice. Thus in the passage quoted earlier which reproduces, in a version of *style indirect libre*, the hearer's trying to decide if the voice is being directed at him or at another, his "reasoning" is almost entirely a play with "to" and "of": "To another of that other. Or of him. Or of another still. To another of that other or of him or of another still." Similarly, when the narrator sets himself the task of imagining "closer to place where [the hearer] lies" (which he appears to do from the hearer's point of view), he corrects his initial calculation, based on "faintness of voice at its least faint," of "some sixty feet . . . or thirty from ear to any given point of encompassing surface" in the following way: "For with what right affirm of a faint sound that it is a less faint made fainter by farness and not a true faint near at hand? Or of a faint fading to fainter that it recedes and not in situ decreases." The relations between sound, distance, and movement are established through differential repetitions—"a less faint made fainter," "a true faint"—which suggest a mind groping with minimal material to chart positions in the world around it. Out of sameness differences are struggling to be recognized. The clinging of these differences to the sameness from which they are just beginning to emerge is rendered not only by the repetitive play with "faint," but also by alliterations—"fainter by farness" and "faint fading"—which represent as a verbal sequence a difference that can be initiated only by a repetition.

The narrative of *Company* moves between the point of view of the deviser and that of the hearer within the deviser's fable, the hearer from whose point of view the questions just asked are raised. But are these really different points of view? A kind of eerie suspense is created once it has been decided that the deviser is in the same dark as his creature, as if we were now waiting for the deviser to be absorbed into his creature. The final long section confirms the identity between the two. The proposition was that a voice would tell of a past to one on his back, a past the hearer would be led to acknowledge as his own. We have had scenes from childhood and early adulthood, evocations of the hearer's walks later in life on "the winding back roads and interjacent pastures now alive with flock and now deserted," and a description of the last time he went out. And at the very end, the voice reminds the hearer of how, having returned home for the last time, he "sat huddled in the dark" and began to invent the fable we have just read: "Huddled thus you find yourself imagining you are not alone while knowing full well that nothing has occurred to make this possible." That imagining took the form of "the fable of one with you in the dark." Thus the voice calls up the memory of its own inventions as part of the life to which it has been trying to make the hearer confess. "What an addition to company that would be," it had been said much earlier, if the hearer had a voice and began to murmur, "Yes I remember." But he has had a voice, or voices, all along, the voice that has been saying "you" to him and the voice that has been referring to him as "he." The whole thing has been devised by the old hearer for the sake of company—unless, of course, the story of his devising the fable we have just read is part of what has been devised by someone who has himself been devised devising the devising of the fable . . . And so the apparently simplifying convergence of lines, the implied identity of narrator-deviser-voice-hearer, far from bringing us at last to an identifiable, locatable origin or author of the story, merely begins again, in somewhat different terms, the endless receding of origins and authorship.

And yet the fable which, in a sense, can never be accounted for (whose account is it?) also provides us with a way of accounting for its own receding origins. Even though the merging of personae does not authorize a final authorial "I," (the fable of) the return of all voices to the silent figure lying alone in the dark does reformulate the disappearing "I" as, paradoxically, *the precondition for a human identity*. The fusion of the unnamable, unthinkable last person, I, with the unnamable hearer, you, is a way of naturalizing—of thinking or at least figuring—immobilized being. This is not merely because the hearer is imagined as lying silent on his back, but rather because that position is also imagined as having a history. The configuration of a supine body with another body or voice above it recurs several times in the voice's memories. We are thinking especially of the evocations of the infant in its cradle being murmured to by his parents stooping over the cradle from behind: "Arm's length. Force? Low. A mother's stooping over cradle from behind. She moves aside to let the father look. In his turn he murmurs to the newborn. Flat tone unchanged. No trace of love." "Arm's length" in this passage answers a question from the previous paragraph about the unidentified voice's "height from the ground" where the hearer is now lying, just as "Force? Low" refers to the voice's volume. What the hearer has devised, this passage suggests, is a return to his earliest hearing. At the end of his life, huddled and then lying alone in the dark, wholly unrelated once again, he remembers and invents the originating of relations.

Remembers and invents: it is perhaps not only the fable of a voice speaking of a past to one lying in the dark that is invented, but also the original scene to which it refers. As if the parents murmuring language down to the infant in its cradle, while it must of course have taken place over and over again, were *also* devised as the original term in a set of metaphoric representations of how the human subject is *called* into the human community. If the infant's monadic integrity—its unrelatedness prior to all relations—is unrepresentable, the literary work, through its fictive representative the deviser, nonetheless invents the originating of a speech it can't remember ever not having. It repeats—as if it were a penance—its own starting by "remembering" the human itself as having been coerced into being. All these scenes referred to a moment ago both condense and interpret a long linguistic apprenticeship as the experience of a linguistic summons, of an injunction to be. The fable of *Company* rewrites that injunction as a coercive appeal to memory, but the command is essentially the same at both ends of the hearer's existence: *have a life*.

Perhaps nothing is stranger than this coincidence of endings and beginnings in Beckett. The obsession with old age, the reiterated longing to have it all over with, to return to nothingness, *is also*—and it may be this that explains the energy and wit in the unrelenting Beckettian cursing of life and wish to die—the occasion, for these withered bodies, of a self-containing huddling, a gathering into a closed monadic shell of being from which those bodies might, miraculously, again be called forth into life. If the mind closes to that call—"as the window might close of a dark empty room"—there is, "unhappily," not "nothing more," but "pangs of faint light and stirrings still. Unformulable gropings of the mind. Unstillable." The last person—the first person—is that: not an essential being, but an inner movement with no place to go, a consciousness imprisoned in its unrepresentable restlessness. The only viable issue for those gropings is to pick up on what is heard, to grab the language, and the life being depicted in that language, and say: "Yes. I remember," or "Yes. I will be what I can say."

The only "I" we can formulate, the only one we can know, is an "I" piped into us, one that we first heard outside, perhaps at "arm's length" from a body not yet able to place the voices telling it that it is there, that it is a human subject. But to say "I" is at once to know the lie of what it designates. We are, *Company* suggests, an "I" first heard as a "you" and then perceived as a "he" or "she." The boundaries of being given to us by those pronouns are at once external and internal: they help us to locate where we stop and others begin, but at the same time the beginnings of others are inseparable from the consciousness of self. The distinction between "I" and "he" is repeated within the "I" constituted by an awareness of the distinction between "I" and "he." There is no moment of self-identification that is not also a self-multiplication or dispersal. Thus the very nostalgia for a final, nondispersed "I" is a function of a self-originating dispersal. This can be put differently: *there is no way to escape company*. The human subject is incomplete unless its completeness is undone.

The hearer in *Company* is not merely, as we at first suggested, a figure for the deviser; only by contriving the identity between the two can Beckett establish the identity between receding authorship and self-initiation. It is *because* the whole fable is the hearer's invention that he will never sign it with an "I." Devising a self as a story about others may be the principal activity of subjectivity. The nostalgia for a monadic, unrelated, presumably essential self in Beckett (and perhaps not only in Beckett) may be a consequence of this experience of selfhood—of the gift of an "I"—as a gift of otherness. The untiring and frequently defeated effort to place objects, people, and voices in Beckett's work could be thought of as an attempted compensation for the unlocatability of identities; to delimit the space occupied by bodies, to draw boundaries around them, would at least map the positions of subjects otherwise constituted by a placeless relational mobility.

Company, finally, is stricken by a double pathos. Not only is "I remember"—as well as the injunction to say "I remember"—immediately and endlessly transformable into the confession and the injunction of "another," and "still another," and "still another" (so that the self would be nothing more than the psychologically neutral aptitude of consciousness to step back from, and objectify, its contents); those others must also be recognized as fictions. If, to begin with, we genuinely hear them, once we begin to repeat them we can no longer be sure they are still present in their (now our) own language. Devise as we may, we are still, as the novel's grim single-word final paragraph asserts, "alone," as alone in our devising as we were in the beginning and as we will even more surely be in the end. Nothing could be more different from the Unnamable's ferocious will to singleness, a will defeated by the very language that would express it. That defeat is, in *Company*, surprisingly welcomed as the occasion of an enlivening (if solipsistic) sociability, although the body lying alone in the dark excludes others from its boundaries far more effectively than might any essential self. Company is no less illusory for being inevitable, and Beckett's work, not unexpectedly, circles back to the solitude at its origin in its final lines: "And how better in the end labour lost and silence. And you as you always were. Alone." The knowledge that comes at the end—a knowledge by which the infant in the crib can be neither comforted nor oppressed—is that the devising self has never left the aloneness from which the voice called it forth, and that, in any case, the voices are destined to stop.

From *The Raritan* 12, no. 1 (Summer 1992): 1-19.

CHAPTER 5

Interviews and Personal Reminiscences

Samuel Beckett: An Interview

Patrick Starnes

There is something disturbingly unattractive about people who "call" on literary figures. The syndrome is made even more unattractive when the subject of one's curiosity obviously wants only to be left alone. I think of Suzy Knickerbocker saying: "Sam Beckett was tooling around his Montparnasse flat when we called. Well, Sam's a daaarling and we admired the view from his groovy pad . . ."

I had a beer at a café on the angle of two wide hot boulevards. Vaguely I watched some youths pouring money into a pinball machine and tried of think of some remotely intelligent questions to ask:

> "Mr. Beckett, is it significant that Godot spelled backwards gives To Dog?"
> "Could you perhaps . . . could you give me a capsule history of dogs in your life?"
> "My impression is that you favour mongrels, would you say that I am reading between the lines?"

At six o'clock sharp, earlier or later I might have been metamorphosed into a trashcan, I sauntered into the lobby of an apartment building on the Boulevard St. Jacques and was amazed to find that Beckett's name like those of other mortals was inscribed on the list by the door. I pressed the button and blurted out my name when questioned. It would be nice to be able to relate that Beckett's "soft Irish brogue" soothed me, but first, his voice sounded like anyone else's filtered through the intercom system, and secondly I was beyond being soothed. Beckett met me at the elevator. It was very dark, so I am spared having to record first impressions.

Once inside the small apartment I tried to apologize to Beckett for bothering him but he merely shrugged, implying that he was well used to being pestered by importunate doctoral candidates. Beckett is a tall man and his height is made more dramatic by his exceptional thinness. His eyes, gay and humourous and shadowed by sadness are protected from the world by a pair of very thick steel-rimmed spectacles. Another link, however tenuous, with Joyce. After having settled myself on a sofa of modern and undistinguished design I noticed two things which struck me as being at odds with my preconceptions about this man: he had a deep suntan and his clothes were a far cry from the seedy messiness which is all he grants to his fictional characters. How dare he who has so obdurately spurned the healing power of the sun in his work, receive me with a suntan that would have made headlines in St. Tropez? How dare he whose sartorial inventions have become bywords in the vocabulary of the grotesque, greet me encased in charcoal grey flannels of modern cut, an elegant black short-sleeved shirt and a pair of brown suede laceless shoes? Con Leventhal, one of Beckett's oldest friends and now a resident of Paris, later cleared up the second of these conundrums by telling me that Beckett's wife buys all his clothes for him and that he is blissfully unaware whether his clothes come from Cardin or the Prisunic. Beckett himself inadvertantly explained away his suntan by telling me that he spends most of his free time at his house "in the mud" of the Marne country near Paris. He works hard in his garden and the image of Beckett toiling on the land through July and August is for me strangely comforting.

Beckett had agreed to see me on the condition that I should refrain from asking any questions about his work and when I asked him to warn me if he thought I was getting too close he laughed a quiet, private sort of laugh and said: "Don't worry, I'll tell you." So I told the master of the arcane of my attempts to obtain an air filter for my "deux cheveaux" in Paris during the August holiday. He commiserated with me and divulged that he too was an owner of one of France's most singular modes of transportation. He keeps his car at the station near his house in the country and uses it to get around. Somehow the mental image of Beckett clinging to the wheel of a wildly plunging 2 CV is difficult for me to fix in my mind and for me Beckett is always walking.

Perhaps I am imagining things but my impression is that this house in a bleak and rather inhospitable area of France was bought by Beckett with the initial proceeds of the success of *Waiting for Godot*. Beckett obviously enjoys pottering around in the country and it seems just that a play which has afforded so many people so much pleasure should have enabled its author to establish himself somewhere where he can escape the heat and grime of Paris summers.

Mr. Beckett's apartment is in Paris's 14th arrondissement—neither poodle-happy chic nor overtly working-class—and I believe it is the same one to which he returned after having been forced to flee the capital during the war. At any rate *this* apartment is on the eighth floor. Beckett unfolded himself from the straight-backed chair he was sitting on and pointed to the terra cotta roofs of a large building not far away and said: "That's the Prison de la Santé, a place for the criminally insane." I muttered something about *Murphy,* knowing full well that it was an idiotic thing to say. Beckett mercifully ignored me and we stared down at the prison, he evidently deriving some small secret pleasure from the scene and I wandering off watching the lumbering descent of a jet. A recent effort of scholarship reveals no less than eight institutions—hospitals, asylums, clinics, prisons—in the immediate vicinity.

I asked Beckett about his family in Dublin and he unhesitatingly told me many things which I already knew but when I mentioned London he made an impatient gesture of distaste and said: "I don't like London at all, there's no life to it." It is perhaps in keeping with this man's delightfully perverse sense of humour that *Murphy,* a novel in which the hero comes close to earthly Nirvana should be set in and around London.

I lit my tenth cigarette in the silence that we had managed to create. Beckett seemed totally unembarrassed by my inability to think of anything even amusing to say and eventually he enquired gently into my research. I answered coyly that I was trying to compare some of his work to that of two well known twentieth-century authors, without naming them. He listened and offered some suggestions and I really felt that he cared although I can think of no earthly reason why he should have.

We talked about Calder and Boyars, his English publishers, and because I had recently seen a B.B.C. program in which John Calder and the English critic George Steiner had been airing their views on pornography, I mentioned Steiner's name. Beckett, although retaining the soft even cadence of his tone, voiced an unequivocally unflattering opinion of Steiner and I think this more than anything finally forced me to realize that Beckett is a human being, subject to the same foibles and idiosyncracies as other human beings. This revelation was complete when he asked me if I was "a drinking man" and a bottle of whisky was produced from a tiny kitchen adjacent to the study. The study itself was meticulously tidy; a desk, two walls of books and periodicals, the sofa, and the whole north wall of the window with the view of the prison and, beyond, the roofs of Paris. No evidence of wastepaper baskets filled with the rejected fruits of Beckett's labours (although he does destroy almost everything he now writes); no photographs of the author embracing a dishevelled and exhausted Von Karajan after a performance of the Ninth Symphony. The room, the speech, the body, all lean and taut as the work. And the characters: Didi and Gogo, Murphy and Watt and Molloy and Moran and Malone and the *Unnamable*, all bouncing around in my head, and they somehow the progeny of this grave, quiet, middle-aged man who had the kindness to spend some of his diminishing store of time left, to enable me to fulfill my obligation to an order of things he had long since outgrown.

The whisky helped (it occupied the hand that was not occupied with the cigarette), but I found myself again in a long trough of silence inwardly remarking on the opulent beauty of the evening with the sunset reflected on the windows and trying desperately not to mention it. Eventually, having mastered this almost irresistible bent for the meteorological, I asked him about the making of *Film*, his only excursion to date into that medium. About Buster Keaton, the "hero" of this crystalline film, Beckett said: "Oh, he's a professional" in such a way that I couldn't determine whether this was with admiration or with annoyance at the crustiness of the moribund actor. Which was as it should be, for it was none of my business.

We talked about writing, and suddenly finding my long lost and nearly forgotten brass, I explained to Samuel Beckett how I was going to write a book ... "wait for it" ... that was SIMULTANEOUS! The stark foolishness of this fabrication must have been hard for Beckett to take, but he smiled diffidently and asked me if I didn't perhaps feel that this feat could perhaps best be achieved in films? I had the self-respect to disagree, but as I was so doing, I learned something that I might otherwise never have learned: originality, talent, even genius, are nothing compared to common sense and the sort of intellectual honesty which will not accept cheap tricks as a substitute for painstaking and reckless work.

As I was leaving I sighed deeply and said: "I wish I had never started this whole thing, this writing business." And I of course meant the reverse, for I had some Quixotic notions and the dishonesty to say things like that and not admit to a sneaking admiration for myself. Beckett took my statement at face value and replied: "Yes, in the long run there is more pain than joy in writing."

Beckett escorted me to the elevator, and I explained that I was going to have dinner with some of his friends at the Closerie des Lilas. He gave me detailed instruction (which I promptly forgot) on how to get there, and said: "That's a nice place, you'll like it there." And he seemed to wander back to a time when he was young and drinking at the wobbly tables of the Closerie des Lilas, granted respite from the loneliness of writing and also offered friendship without sycophancy.

At dinner the conversation moved to Goldsmith and things that I do not understand. It was a hot humid evening. I watched the leaves moving gently touched, by a slight breeze, and I tried to sort out my impressions, but all that I could see was Beckett's thin form wrapped around itself and his eyes shyly, kindly probing out beyond the limits of his spectacles. Samuel Beckett remains in my memory fixed in an attitude of generous expectancy.

From *The Antigonish Review* 10 (1972): 49-53.

Conversations with Samuel Beckett
Jay A. Levy

Jay A. Levy is a research physician in the School of Medicine at the University of California, San Francisco. This article, originally published in *The American Scholar,* has been revised by the author.

"This is like waiting for Godot," my friend said to me as we patiently waited at the Hartford airport for the arrival of my date for the big spring weekend.

With each hour that passed, her plane continued to be delayed. That comment in 1959 led to my studies of Samuel Beckett and his famous play.

At Wesleyan University I was a junior pre-medical student pursuing a dual major in French and biology. I had dedicated a great deal of time to studying the Theater of the Absurd, as reflected by Camus, Sartre, Genet, and Cocteau. Reading *Waiting for Godot* by Beckett, which was published only seven years earlier, initiated my longtime interest in this Irish playwright writing in Paris. It led to my senior thesis *Waiting for Godot, Waiting for God?* From today's perspective the title seems very simplistic. At the time, however, relatively little had been written about the play, and the idea that Godot meant God, while suggested, was not well substantiated. Beckett made no allusion to it. A careful look through anthologies of the Bible and the Bible itself revealed what appeared to be direct analogies to Biblical events in the play. In my opinion, the hypothesis of Godot as God was a plausible interpretation of this literary piece.

When I received Fulbright and French government fellowships to conduct biologic research in Paris in 1960-61, my French professor at Wesleyan, Alex Szogyi, encouraged me to find Professor Mayoux, Professor of English at the Sorbonne, to show him my thesis. "Why not let him read your thoughts on Beckett?" he insisted. I waited five months to do so. I suppose, reflecting on my stay in Paris, that a certain amount of timidity (not generally attributed to me) prevented me from contacting Professor Mayoux sooner. Having received at least two letters from Professor Szogyi encouraging me, I finally wrote Professor Mayoux. On Friday, January 27 I found a letter at my hotel, Le Grand on rue Dauphine, inviting me to his house on Monday afternoon. I had to change the meeting to sometime the next month since I had plans that night to go to the American Club to watch the Kennedy inauguration film. As he suggested, I wrote him again, and then on Saturday, Feburary 25, 1961 he called me to come to his house that afternoon. He had been in Tunis and had just read my letter. Prof. Mayoux greeted me at the door at 1 rue Monticel, Paris 14. He was about 60 years old, dressed in a suit and wearing glasses. He was very nice, but seemed quite busy. I left my paper and he told me to return on Monday evening at 6:30 PM.

Our meeting that evening was very pleasant and was held in a typical French salon in the apartment. A large sofa dominated the room where we had hors d'oeuvres and a drink and talked for almost an hour. He told me he enjoyed the paper and spoke to me about Beckett's neuroses, particularly a "father complex," about which I knew nothing. After enjoyable discussions about Beckett's works, he gave me Beckett's address and suggested I write to him. As I left, he asked to see me again when he returned from England in 2 weeks, but we never did have another get-together.

I immediately wrote to Beckett and received a letter from England saying that he would be away for some time, but expected to be back in Paris the second half of April. He advised me to write him at his address (38 blvd. St.-Jacques, Paris 14), which I did. On April 17, I received a note thanking me for my recent letter and telling me it would be more convenient to meet in May. "I have barely a few moments this month." He advised me in the meantime to leave my manuscript at his address. The next day I left the laboratory at the Faculté de Science in Orsay early and took the train into Paris and then a metro to blvd. St.-Jacques. I arrived about 6:00 PM. As I was putting the manuscript in the mailbox in the lobby, Beckett arrived with a gentleman who looked like someone involved in the theater. I recognized Beckett from a photograph I had seen in a book. Somewhat taken aback, I said to him in my best French that I was the one sent by Professor Mayoux, whom I assumed had already spoken with him. Mr. Beckett was extremely nice, and put me at ease despite his towering presence (I felt quite small at five foot seven inches next to his height of over six feet). He quickly mentioned that neither of us had to speak French as it was not our mother tongue, and we continued the formalities of our first meeting in English. In a warm but reserved manner he said he would get in touch with me after reading the paper.

On June 2, 1961, after writing him again, I received from Beckett a short note sent from Ussy sur Marne, his country place. He thanked me for my letter and invited me to his apartment on Tuesday, June 13. He told me to call him around noon (at POR 9660) to make final arrangements, and I did. He later gave me his private number to use in the morning between 11:00 AM and noon, the only time when he took phone calls. That number served as our means of communication for many years afterwards. I was very excited at his probable appreciation of my thesis, but I was also worried about how I should act at this meeting with him.

Beckett, then fifty-six years old, received me at 5:00 PM in the study of his apartment on the seventh floor of a relatively new building. He had been living there only 6 months. He was dressed casually in a green sports jacket, brown gabardine slacks, and a plaid tie. The room, full of books, had his wooden desk and some simple wooden side chairs. The walls were painted in pale yellow and light tan. His hair was turning gray, and again from my vantage point, he was a tall, imposing gentleman, but with a soft voice. Almost immediately, he offered me a drink. "Be a nice change from Scotch," he said jokingly as he gave me a glass of Irish whisky. We sat for over an hour discussing his work, although in retrospect, probably in a somewhat superficial way. He asked me many questions about my life and my interest in biology. He shared with me his views on literature and assured me that he never denied Godot was God; however, he did not intend it to have any specific meaning. Godot could be representative of one's goal or objective. He agreed that some of my analogies, such as the removal of shoes in the first act fit biblical accounts concerning the respect given to holy places, but said that he in no way had the Bible in mind when he wrote the play.

During our conversation he told me how at about my age (then I was twenty-two), he had met a writer and later, because of the difficulty in that writer's sight, was asked to help him. At the time, I did not appreciate that Beckett was having eyesight problems, but I did appreciate the possibility that I was receiving an indirect invitation to join him as his assistant as he had done for James Joyce. For a split second I toyed with the fantasy of asking him whether he was looking for an assistant, but what would I answer to an affirmative reply? I realized that I had medical school and a science education ahead of me, and a father who did not fully understand a year's interval from schooling. I decided, therefore, to consider this comment as merely a reflection on an event in his life that had some similarities to mine.

He told me how he loved the theater and saw it as truly representative of art, but hated when the performers played to the public: it ruined the play when they attempted to impress the audience. He mentioned that he particularly liked Dennis Johnson who was Irish and the producer of several of his plays. He kept Beckett's lines exact—a feature Beckett demanded (although did not always get) from all directors of his plays. He said he had never tried cinema because he didn't know the medium. Nevertheless, some years later he would dramatically use this form of art in his short movie *Film*.

We discussed writers. He never met Camus, but respected him and enjoyed his work more than that of Sartre. Sartre he found too political in recent years. He thought Schehade (whom I later met in Paris) was very poetic—"an Oriental Parisien," but not dramatic enough despite good reading. He found Adamov "politically minded" whose early plays, particularly *Professor Taruma*, he liked best.

During our meeting Beckett told me that he had just finished a new play called *Happy Days* and mailed it that morning to the publisher. No other comment about the work was made, except that he wrote this play first in English and thought it would be produced in the States. He considered plays a rest from writing books. He gave me as a small gift, *Comment c'est*, his latest book, and inscribed it. As I left he encouraged me to write him in August to plan another get-together before I left Paris. Unfortunately, since he was on vacation in late August and most of September, I did not have that opportunity before returning to medical school in New York.

By the time of our goodbyes, he had already told me about his wife, Suzanne, whom I could hear in the kitchen adjoining the study. I would in later sessions ask to meet her, but never did. In other visits, I also subtly tried to get invited into other parts of the apartment but, aside from one time in his kitchen, I was always greeted in his study which changed very little over the ten years I visited him there. In the following twenty years, we usually met at the Closerie des Lilas at Port Royal and then later at the Café François at the PCM Hotel located just across from his apartment on blvd. St.-Jacques.

The next time I saw Beckett was during a short return visit to Paris in 1962 when we got together on Tuesday, June 19 in the late afternoon. He was very friendly, and was not disturbed that I had brought my twin brother, Stuart, for him to meet. We chatted about his works, and he seemed interested in my ideas on cancer. I shared with him Albee's article in the *New York Times* describing a typical café chat between Beckett, Genet, and Ionesco. He said he had never met Genet, but laughed over the article. We stayed with him until 7:00 PM when we walked him to Montparnasse. He really made us feel like we were old friends. He then told Stuart to write him in October when Stuart was returning to Paris to spend time at the Institut Radium.

In 1963, having seen *Happy Days* during one of its early performances in New York, I wrote Beckett a long letter about my enthusiasm for the show, for Ruth White, and for the excellent dialogue. When I purchased a copy of the play, I tried to locate the quotations that were part of the piece, but found only a few that I could reference. During a subsequent visit to Paris, when we discussed this play in his study, I mentioned my interest in knowing how he found these quotations. He told me several came from old English writings and poems and promised to send me a copy of the play with the quotations cited. Several months later I received this well-annotated book which has become a treasured part of my Beckett collection.

From July 1962 to June 1963, my twin brother, Stuart, spent a year in Paris working at the Institut Radium with Professor Raymond Latarjet. He called Beckett at his special number and met him several times during that period. On occasion, Beckett would call him at his apartment on rue l'Abbé de l'Epée to arrange the meetings. One such get-together was on April 19, 1962, at the Closerie des Lilas. Stuart recalls the meeting was very cordial and began with a tomato juice before they had lunch—piparade basque omelette. The discussions included the theater, the cinema, and Beckett's reading of Albee's play *Who's Afraid of Virginia Woolf?* Beckett said he preferred *Zoo Story* because it seemed better for the theater. Apparently, Alan Schneider had asked Beckett to translate *Virginia Woolf* into French, but Beckett thought it would not do well in Paris.

Stuart ventured to ask Beckett how he decided to write. He replied, "When there was nothing else left for me to do . . . I had no money, I started to write." He did not regard himself as a professional writer, but as a French "man of letters." "I write comme ça," he said. Stuart gave him several articles on science, but Beckett didn't have his glasses so it was difficult for him to read them. Nevertheless, showing a lot of charm and humility, he inquired about Stuart's experiments in the laboratory. They were both intrigued at the interchange of their interests in science and the theater. Beckett offered an explanation. He said that the laboratory was like the theater. The scientist is the director and the test tubes are the players. "You may predict what will happen, but you do not know exactly how it is going to turn out."

My next visit with Beckett was on June 2, 1965, almost four years after our first meeting in Paris. Stuart and I met him at Closerie des Lilas for a delightful lunch. He was vigorous and lively with more color in his face than I remembered. His demeanor was once again warm and friendly. He was visibly pleased to see us together. We had drinks (our usual Irish whiskey) followed by the main course of salmon with salad. The lunch was topped by crêpes suzette; he insisted we try them. We shared with him our recent trips to Africa in 1964 and our current research interest in tropical diseases. We were again touched by his enthusiasm for science and his knowledge of it. He told us of his new four-minute play *Va et Vient*. He joked that at first it was quite long and he kept "perfecting" it. He translated it for a friend in England who was opening a café-theater and called the play, *Come and Go*. According to him it did not translate well from the French. He also had written a short piece, *Eh Joe*, for the BBC. He told us of his visit to the States in July of the past year when he was working on a film directed by Alan Schneider. He did not want to go to New York, but liked the challenge of doing cinema.

During that trip in 1964, his only visit to the United States, he entered the office of Grove Press and the secretary greeted him with the comment, "Mr. Beckett, it's a pleasure to see you here. I have 'hellos' from my two friends, Stuart and Jay Levy." She was a friend of ours and forwarded our greeting on her own. He later graciously arranged for *Film*, starring Buster Keaton (his choice of actor for the role), to be shown to us whenever we would like. Needless to say, during the '60s in medical school in New York, being able to call and have a private showing of a film by Samuel Beckett was nothing short of a "happening." I saw it before I left medical school for internship in Philadelphia. Stuart saw it when he came to New York for his post-medical school training.

During our 1965 visit with Beckett, he also spoke of his wife's travels in Spain, Czechoslovakia, and Vienna with friends, and their hopes of taking a month's vacation in August. He had a country home near Paris that he worked on when he could find the time. He shared with us as well his pleasure that his nephew, Edward, had won first prize in a flute composition at the Paris Conservatory. Edward was the son of his brother who had died from lung cancer. Despite this family tragedy, Beckett continued to chain smoke throughout the years we knew him. He also spoke of his English cousin's great ability in playing the piano. Both relatives were then in Paris and had been playing duets at his apartment for several days. Beckett loved music and greatly enjoyed these sessions.

Our conversation turned to golf and his eyes lit up. He mentioned that at one time his handicap was as low as seven. We invited him to visit us in the States where we could play the game together. He seemed genuinely interested in visiting, but said he had seldom played in the past thirty years. His last golf outing had been five years ago. During this two-and-one-half hour lunch, he also commented that Albee's play *Tiny Alice* was too long, and he understood why Sartre, for political reasons, refused the Nobel Prize in 1964. He was faithful to his belief, but Beckett questioned Sartre's refusal to accept an honorary degree from Columbia University since it was a private university.

During this reunion, he also confided in us, now physicians, the problem of his failing eyesight and the fact that he was going to enter a nearby hospital, the Hotel Dieu, where the nuns would take care of him. Stuart and I inquired about this hospital and contacted other physicians in Paris to assure Beckett that his eye treatment was the best available. His poor eyesight was present during the making of his film in New York, and clearly its relevance to the piece was apparent: the emphasis on the eye is paramount to the theme. (He was operated on for cataracts in 1970 and 1971.)

My next meeting with Sam (as he now signed his letters) was July 27, 1971, ten years after our first conversation. We met at the Closerie. He was dressed in a brown sports coat, tan pants, and a dark blue tie. He was as warm and genuine as ever, and acted as if we had not been long separated. He would not discuss the Nobel Prize awarded two years earlier. He spoke about his eye surgery, of which he had written me in March of that year. The first cataract was removed in October 1970 and the second in February of this year. "Both were successful and close vision is excellent." Sam had wanted the operations done near home in case he wandered and could easily find his way back to the apartment. He didn't feel he would like contact lenses, but was surprised that I wore them. I took one out to show him. He seemed interested and said he might try them.

We talked of his father in Ireland who was a surveyor—"a boring job"—and that his older brother (by four years) unfortunately took the same profession. He was the one who died in the 1950's from lung cancer. Sam, I repeat, refused to believe cigarette smoking was involved in the cancer and he, like his brother, remained a chain smoker. In 1968, Beckett had lung abscesses and stopped for one year, but then took it up again. We talked as well this time about his uncle, his last living relative who had died a few months earlier. Apparently he had bad circulation and lost both legs and then went blind—almost like the character from *End Game*. Still the man remained quite happy, active, and alert. Sam seemed impressed with this. I asked him whether this uncle was the basis for the character in *End Game*, but he said he had written the play before his uncle's illness.

Sam mentioned that he had last visited Ireland in 1968 when he went home for the funeral of his beloved aunt. He said he wouldn't go again because of what he feared would be too much publicity. Some years earlier, Beckett told me, he had taught two years in France and a few years at Trinity College in Ireland, but didn't like it. This time he said he actually wanted to be a teacher but didn't admit it because now he'd be a Professor at Trinity. He preferred to write and had decided that was the profession to follow.

During this visit in 1971, Sam also told me how he became associated with the rather controversial *Oh Calcutta*. He was asked to write a script for the show, and thought it would be a vaudeville-like review and contributions would be anonymous. Now he called it "rubbish." As he initially wrote his 30-second piece called *Breath*, the cry of a baby is heard in the center of the stage, the light goes up with the cry, then descends and then another cry occurs. The producer changed it and added naked bodies to the performance. He was angered but was only able to get his name disassociated with productions outside the United States.

We spoke of Suzanne whom he mentioned loved Italy where they had just been on vacation. He smiled with real affection when he talked of her. She used to teach as well. When we parted I noted that he was now wearing gold-rimmed regular glasses, not the dark bifocals. He was thinner than before, but looking about the same after six years.

Our next meeting was December 16th of that year. I met Sam at 5:30 in the late afternoon at his apartment on blvd. St.-Jacques. I remembered the entrance and mailbox where I had left the paper over ten years before. He met me at the elevator on the seventh floor. He had a slight cold but otherwise was much the same. He wore tan slacks and a maroon turtleneck. He took me around the office area where I had been before. I saw paintings over his couch; the walls were cracking with age, and lots of books were scattered behind his desk. I gave him a copy of the chimpanzee article that Stuart and I had published in

Nature after our trip to Africa in 1970 to find human viruses in this primate species. He seemed touched that I had thought of bringing it. He said that he had spent most of his time recently working on new prose. He had no plays in mind at the moment. I asked him if he felt as enthusiastic and energetic as he did ten years ago or whether he was ready to relax. He said, with a smile, "No, I still have a lot of spunk left in me if that's what you mean." Sam said he was eager to get back to writing now that his eyes were better, and he was happy that he could drive again. He enjoyed going to his country home about 45 minutes by train from Paris where he would pick up his old car and drive to the house. It was a small place with a bedroom, kitchen, and dining room, on about one hectare of land. He had done a lot of his writing there over the past ten years.

I ventured to ask him what he considered his best play. Surprised that he would answer, he said *Endgame*, not *Waiting for Godot*. He couldn't give details on why he felt this way. We walked into the kitchen to get ice for our Irish whiskeys. From the windows, since it was clear outside, I could see many rooftops of Paris, and it reminded me of the view I had from my fifth floor room at Le Grand Hotel. Before he had moved to this apartment in the 15th, he had lived with Suzanne in an apartment nearby. When asked about his family, he said he had very few family members in France aside from a cousin who is a social worker in a nearby hospital. When I left after 3 hours of visiting with him, it was only because I was late for dinner with friends. He asked me to call him in January before he went south to Morocco to find "some sun," but we were unable to arrange another meeting that year.

In 1976, Stuart again spent several months doing research work in Paris at the Pasteur Institute. He took the occasion to meet Beckett, usually at his apartment. Stuart again shared results of his laboratory experiments with Sam and was encouraged by his enthusiasm for the work. In June of that year, Stuart asked Sam if he would meet our parents during the time of their visit to Paris. Much to his surprise, Sam said he'd be very pleased and accepted Stuart's invitation to come to his apartment to have cocktails with them. My mother's remark, "What will I say, I've never met a real intellectual," has become legendary in the family. But, the man they met proved to be no intimidating figure. He had walked from his apartment on blvd. St. Jacques to visit them at 4 rue du Four —about a twenty minute walk. He strode into the room, relaxed in a wide-winged chair, and proceeded to carry on casual conversation, including a discussion with my father about his early days playing golf in Ireland. At that time, he scored in the high 70's. They all had drinks and talked about many different subjects of common interest. He showed Dad his right hand with the Dupuytren's contracture. The shortening and thickening of the tendons in the palm had caused a deformity of his index finger.

Beckett was not in a rush and stayed about two hours. Thus to our family, Samuel Beckett was certainly not the recluse often cited in comments about him and his life. In all our relationships with him he was always a warm, receptive and generous individual. Over the years, he shared with me several texts that he wrote and answered every letter, if just by a small note, including our last exchange about six months before his death. One treasured volume he sent in 1977 to my wife, Sharon, and me as a wedding gift—one of the first printings of his book, *Proust* and *Three Dialogues*.

It was, however, two years after his meeting with my family when I would get together with Sam again. This time, on July 6, 1978, we met at the Café Français at the PCM Hotel at 17 blvd. Saint-Jacques just across the street from his apartment. We met there because he said the tourists bothered him now at the Closerie. He arrived about 11:00 in the morning. You could see him walking in his characteristic lanky manner, a little more unsteady than I had seen him before. Sharon was with me at the time, as we were on our way for a sabbatical year, the first half in Israel and then the second half in Paris. He began by inquiring about Stuart and the folks, and asked about my research. As I was discussing it in some detail, he turned to Sharon and said, "Jay always thinks I understand what he's doing, but I just look like I do." He asked as well about the study Stuart had done on the transfer of bacteria with antibiotic resistance from chickens to man. Despite his earlier comment on his knowledge of science, I was still amazed at how much he understood and that he remembered details from our previous conversations.

Beckett was actually very interested in science and would, as at this time, engross me in conversations about my research in France or in the United States. When I first met him in 1961, I was working with Professor Lender at the Faculté de Sciences in Orsay on regeneration of planaria. When you cut this fresh water flatworm in half, it regenerates its tail or its head, whichever is missing. I kept thinking that Beckett might use this biologic event as some theme for a future literary piece of the "absurd"—but he never surprised me with that. Our discussions on cancer, and later on AIDS, always reflected his great interest in the subjects, and his concern for finding solutions to these human diseases. But most of all, I appreciated Sam's remembering certain details of my scientific work that I had discussed with him even years before. He was able to conceptualize areas of scientific study and to ask provocative questions.

This time Sam talked again about his trips to Germany to direct some of his plays. He traveled there every other year. He also went to Morocco for "some sun and swimming," and he was now translating and not working on anything new. Sam said his eyes were as good as ever, but he was wearing thick glasses. I dared to ask him about his impressions of the biography by Deirdre Bair. He quickly remarked that he didn't want to talk about it: "I threw it away." Knowing he guarded his privacy, I was not surprised. We discussed Albee, who was supposed to be writing a new play. Beckett said that Albee's problem was directing his own plays. That was a curious remark since Beckett was doing the same. We also spoke of Alan Schneider and how I had the pleasure of being with him at Stanford for a three day course on Beckett. Sam liked him very much because Schneider directed his plays correctly.

Nine months later, after our return to Paris from Israel, Sharon, Stuart, and I met Beckett again at the Café Français. He looked healthy, active, and happy to see us. He recounted that he began playing golf at age 12 or 13 and played with his uncle Girard, a doctor, and his cousin. He commented that he knew Sartre in school in Paris. The man was "famous for his practical jokes; some of them cruel —like telling the professor his daughter had died in a car accident." He didn't know Simone de Bouvoir, and had never met Gertrude Stein. She apparently had had a group of protegés separate from those around James Joyce. He said similar literary associations exist in Paris today but are less defined and, in any case, he was not in any of them.

He had spent some time in January of that year in Tangiers with Suzanne in a hotel near the beach. He loved it there. He was going to his country home near Paris later in March and then on to London at the end of April to direct *Happy Days*. When we left we asked if we could take a picture. He graciously agreed and Sharon snapped one of us with Sam, braced against a strong wind.

On April 20, 1980, Beckett wrote me, "Thank you for your letter of April 7 and your interesting account of *Piece of Monologue* at Stanford. Piece because unfinished—not to be continued. Light, walk, etc. have no symbolic significance for me. Dramatic components, nothing more." And, in a letter in July 1981, he wrote, "I had nothing to do with the staging of *Premier Amour*. The permission was for a straight reading. I have given no permission for staging Godot. So it goes in the theater."

I didn't see Sam again till June 26, 1986, during the time of the International AIDS meeting in Paris. My sister Ellen and I met him at the Café Français. We saw him standing at the front desk looking out at the street. He was still impressive, though bent over a bit, and somewhat thin and frail. It was 11:00 AM, our usual time to get together. Sam had never met Ellen and I was eager to introduce him to another member of the family. He walked with a limp and seemed a bit weak although his steel blue eyes were still quite impressive. He showed me again his deformed right finger with the Dupuytren's contracture. He complained of his breathing, but that had somewhat improved with time. He said he was in the hospital with emphysema—obviously from his smoking. He had just gotten out ten days before and felt better using a spray. I again lectured him on cigarettes but he said he smoked only ten a day. He asked, as usual, about my parents, Stuart, and Sharon. His speech was somewhat deliberate and his mind, at 81, seemed to be working at a slower pace.

He reminisced a bit about Sylvia Beach and her bookstore. He remarked that he had never read *A Movable Feast* by Hemingway but told me not to send it since he was trying to get rid of things around him. He lamented that Suzanne had cataracts which were operated on 2 months earlier, but she was doing all right. When he spoke of her he seemed sad as if aging was now showing more of a concern than before. He recalled his eye operations and the initial poor accommodation of his sight, although now his eyes were fine.

Despite his success and the fact that his publisher was good to him, I was surprised to hear that he had no secretary. He said he was not writing anything because of his constant lung problems and weakness—"just fixing up my affairs." He had hoped to go to the country where he kept his 20 year old car ("rusty but it works"). He was working on a new text to be performed with *Ohio Impromptu*. One interesting point he made at that meeting came when he reminisced about his concern about *Film*. He wanted the camera to focus on Buster Keaton's eyes, both close up and far away without any realization of change. It didn't work because the lens was not good enough. He walked us to the corner and said good-bye as we went to the metro. In his usual manner, he checked to be sure we knew how to take the train.

In October, 1988, Sam sent me a note stating, "Thank you for yours of October 3rd with good news of your research in pursuit of that scourge. Nothing of interest to tell. Age . . . has clawed me in his clutch. Affectionately to you all, Sam." I found it interesting that he referred to age in the masculine gender.

My last communication from Sam was in June, 1989, when Sharon and I were in Paris for a meeting. We had hoped to see him again and his short note to me at the Mayflower Hotel read, "I am in a maison de retraite with health problems and cannot propose a meeting. Very sorry to miss you. Best wishes to you all. Sam." I regret I did not try harder to see him as he died some months later.

During several conversations with Sam Beckett, he told me how very important it was that his plays be produced and directed in the way that he intended. He thought that the late Alan Schneider was the best director for his plays and had no problems in sharing any new works with him. These discussions on the direction of his play led to his complaining to me during our first meeting in 1961 about a rendition of *Waiting for Godot* to be performed in Scotland; he had hoped to block it by legal action. "The production was billed as a rollicking comedy". He was appalled by the writer's changing of his intentions and "cheapening" the literary sense of the play. For example, he said to me, "Rien à faire", that means "nothing to be done", was loosely interpreted as "nothing's doing". Subsequent lines also voiced this "vulgarization" of his French version. It was also at this time that Sam said to me with a twinkle in his eye that *Waiting for Godot* told the audience from the very start what was going to happen in the next three hours—"nothing".

In discussions with Stuart, Sam confided the fact that one of the reasons James Joyce held back his friendship from Beckett was Joyce's disappointment that he did not marry his daughter, Lucia. While this point has been made in some books about Beckett, we were touched that Beckett shared this information with us and substantiated some of the stories that later appeared in his biographies.

One basic characteristic of Samuel Beckett was his deep humility. On one visit when I congratulated him upon receiving the French Book Award, he insisted that we change the subject. He told me that he did not like awards or the attention they brought him. Subsequently, when he won the Nobel Prize in 1969, Stuart and I telegrammed him from Washington, D.C. where we were doing research at the National Institutes of Health. The telegram arrived in Paris and was forwarded to him in Tunisia where he was vacationing (or avoiding the publicity). It was not long before we received a letter of thanks from him for the telegram, but subsequent reference to this award would also be cut off by changing the subject.

Some of our conversations over those nearly thirty years dealt with issues I felt Beckett might not like to speak about with others. I was not a writer, nor an individual doing research on his works. Instead, initially I was a 22 year old student when we met and continued the contact through a love of the theater, of French, and of his challenging literary pieces. Sam saw me in a different field of study—medicine—and in many ways followed my career's development and the evolution of my family with a warm friendship. The one thing that I said to him during our last meeting in Paris two years ago, with the sincerity that I was never quite sure he fully appreciated, was the faith and optimism I drew from his experiences—particularly the problem he faced in publishing *Waiting for Godot*. I often share that story with my students and scientific colleagues who have their papers, grants, or books rejected. Samuel Beckett, who sent *Waiting for Godot* to many different editors, finally had it accepted after four years by a small publishing company. The rest is history.

From *The American Scholar* 61, no. 1 (Winter 1992): 124-32. Revised by the author.

CHAPTER 6

Radio and Film

It's Tragic, Mysterious and Wildly Funny: That's What You Get When the B.B.C. Asks Samuel Beckett to Write a Play

Roy Walker

PLEASE LISTEN! Not to me, but to the repeat of *All That Fall* in the Third Programme on Saturday (Jan. 19) at five minutes to seven.

If you heard the first performance on Sunday you will probably be listening again anyway, as I shall. If not, don't miss this. It has been specially commissioned by the B.B.C. from the Irish author of *Waiting for Godot*, Samuel Beckett.

I don't guarantee you'll like it, mind.

All That Fall is, I insist, the most important and irresistible new play for radio since Dylan Thomas's *Under Milk Wood* three Januaries ago.

But it is just the opposite of that erotic allelujah chorus, a dirge that is something like Harry Tate's music-hall sketch *Motoring* re-written in a mood of black despair by Eugene O'Neill.

All that befell the King's horses and the King's men, in the once popular song, was that they marched down the street and they marched back again.

All that happens to the incredibly fat old Irish woman, Maddy Rooney, in *All That Fall*, is that she goes down the road to meet her old blind husband coming home from work, and they walk back again, and are told that what made the train a quarter of an hour late was that it ran over a child.

In Beckett's hand this becomes one more image of the journey we all have to make through life. As in *Waiting for Godot* he gives us a disturbing suspicion that the way is strewn with booby traps of our own mechanical making, and maybe it is all part of some vast, lethal, cosmic practical joke.

This is a view of life that may not exactly appeal to you. Sean O'Casey called *Waiting for Godot* "a rotting and remarkable play" with "nothing in it but a lust for despair, and a crying of woe." But not Sean himself could have written it better and the same is true of *All That Fall*.

Both pieces are saturated with Christian allusion and symbolism. Christian critics have alleged—one of them was at it on the Third Programme last week—that Beckett is on Their Side.

I wonder. When Harold Hobson tried to nail the author down in Paris (this brief but apocalyptic conversation is recorded by Mr. Hobson in *International Theatre Annual*, Calder 21s.) this is what Beckett had to say:

"I am interested in the shape of ideas even if I do not believe them. There is a wonderful sentence in Augustine . . . . 'Do not despair; one of the thieves was saved. Do not presume; one of the thieves was damned.' That sentence has a wonderful shape. It is the shape that matters."

That is what matters in *All That Fall* too. Beckett's apparently simple English creates an entire world, tragic, mysterious, wildly funny, the apotheosis of Irish paradoxical pessimism, and Donald McWhinnie's production gets the mood magnificently.

I can't resist another suspicion that Beckett deliberately set out to make things tougher for his Christian apologists in England this time.

At the climax Rooney asks his wife on what text the preacher will hold forth next day, and she quotes (from Psalm 145) "The Lord upholdeth all that fall and raiseth up all those that be bowed down."

There is a silence—as in *Godot* the silences are echoquent [*sic*]. Then the gruesome old couple burst into wild laughter.

It is probably no accident that the last major radio play was by a Welsh poet and that the latest one is by an Irishman. I wish I felt more hopeful that the next would be by an English author.

Nationalities apart, why are these good things so few and far between?

The secondary reason is mainly economic. About £400 is spent on producing a radio play. The writer's cut cannot compare with the royalties from a stage play, although national publicity is an incentive to new or unknown authors.

The B.B.C.'s attempts to rope in the big names with fancy fees have often produced merely early, rejected or otherwise discarded work, vamped up for the occasion.

Even if the money is there, the West End run is the better bet. You can get your broadcasts later. When a successful stage play dies, it goes, after a few years in limbo, to Broadcasting House for a brief disembodied life on the air.

There *are* cases where plays first heard in this country on sound radio have thereby been helped to reach the West End stage. But most of these, please note, are stage plays by modern European dramatists whose existence we are now belatedly beginning to recognise: Anouilh, Betti, Montherlant, Hochwalder, Zuckmayer. But these are not pure radio.

Under Mild Wood was; to my mind it still shows it on the stage. *All That Fall* is. PLEASE listen!

From *The Tribune* (London), 18 January 1957, p. 8.

Beckett Country

Julia Strachey

All That Fall. **By Samuel Beckett. (Faber and Faber.)**
Let us take a look at catastrophe.

What is it? Some kind of guillotine fallen, producing an enormity of dislocation, a severing of the living Godhead from its body, translating the living privacy of the heart's blood into a lot of dirty stains upon a public floor, and, so, insolvently betraying a hard-won homogeneous universe back into chaos again.

(Forgive me if I find I, too, must keep travelling in symbols, when trying to come to the heart of a literary maze entirely built up of them.)

It's no use trying to understand *All That Fall*, or any other one of Samuel Beckett's works singly, on its own. For this is all one territory, the place of some primal catastrophe, the dismal platform where stood the fatal block and guillotine. And the figure that haunts there, every night punctually as twilight falls—is it any wonder that he wanders eternally round it, always in circles (sometimes backwards, but always round and round and round again), head under arm, refusing to leave the dismal place; cursing; raising his sightless eyes every few paces upwards . . . to whom? —To where he supposes that potent male figure lurks away, withdrawn now and reluctant to appear, who had the power to hold him up, but chose instead to mow him down.

The victim—this half-seen, nocturnal ghost, this only half-existing 'thing' (as flesh and blood standards go), self-flagellating perambulator in the limbo of the inward-turning eye—goes under many names, but does not change his sombre character.

We can call him Man After the Fall. Mediæval Man. The Gothic Soul. The Alternative Convention (if we have just been reading Sir Kenneth Clark). Samuel Beckett calls him 'Lucky' in the famous Godot play—the creature become dependent on the tyrant's noose, with his 'Alas! Alas! On! On!' We ourselves may also call him 'Didi,' in the selfsame play, that poet *clochard* so weirdly emptied of human purpose and earthly love, still ever refusing to vacate that frightful spot, still raising his obsessed eyes upwards to the treacherous Father-Figure-Out-Of-Sight.

You can hear this damned soul's disembodied and blaspheming laughter echoing through *All That Fall.* And smell him there too, all over—for instance in the enigmatic dung that the carter Christie tries to hawk; and the familiar bitter brooding upon Holy Writ. Again, you can call him Molloy, in Beckett's novel of that name—that soul-freezing, farouche, mutilated tramp, decomposing in the wilderness, once more betrayed and left to rot. (Through the agency of a sadistic clergyman this time, whose instructions from On High to save him were, anyway, quite inadequate to the job.)

This Molloy is the most frank and explicit person of anyone in Beckett's land. Listen to him on page 39: "The glorious, the truly glorious weather would have gladdened any other heart but mine. But I have no reason to be gladdened by the sun and I take good care not to be. The Ægean, thirsting for heat and light, him I killed, he killed himself, early on, in me. The pale gloom of rainy days was better fitted to my taste . . ."

Yet there is, thank goodness, as we know, another side, another aspect, to this soul with many names. Spectre he may be now, but he still retains much of a rich earthly *personality*. He is a great wit and wag; an engaging tease, full of paradox and Irish blarney. A scholar. A visionary. And at all times a fine, strong, graceful, cunning poet. That is surely quite something to be going on with, for a ghost?

Now again here, in this radio drama (perhaps Beckett's finest work), are there not, in spite of all, signs that the gangrene is clearing up around the primal wound? Do we not find this Gothic spirit breaking off, more than once, his runic song about how many devils can dance upon a needle's point, and stretching out his hand to take up something that looks remarkably like one of our own twentieth-century instruments, some sort of factual register–thermometer or whatnot–something connected with, of all things, the Sun? If so (and I think we do find that), then for all Us Modern Ægeans who so pride ourselves on having sloughed off the dank, dogma-patterned mediæval skin, this small volume may well mark a red-letter day.

From *The Spectator* (20 September 1957): 373.

From Characters to Discrete Events: The Evolving Concept of Dramatis Personae in Beckett's Radio Plays

Germaine Baril

Maurice Blanchot, in a 1953 article discussing *The Unnamable*, points out the difficulty of determining who is speaking in Beckett's work, and notes that this lack of an identifiable character is extremely disturbing to many readers who look for the guarantee that there is a stable conscience, a person who can be named. Despite clear indications in the text that this continuous flow of words simply emanates, the need to have a responsible source is so great that these same readers tend to attribute the discourse to Beckett himself rather than accept the concept of "une parole neutre qui se parle seule" (a neutral speech which is spoken by itself).[1] However, according to Martin Esslin, Beckett's method of work is that of listening to "the voice emerging from the depths,"[2] which he then tries to take down and only afterwards shapes the material. It is obviously more difficult to convey in dramatic productions than in prose works this experience of an independent discourse welling up. Traditionally, the words in a play are spoken by individual entities embodied by players whose physical appearance, speech mannerisms, and gestures all combine with the appropriated words to create identifiable characters. Such is the case with *Waiting for Godot, Endgame* and *Krapp's Last Tape*, Beckett's first stage plays.

The medium of radio, however, gave Beckett the opportunity of experimenting with the presentation and functioning of dramatic characters in a way that challenges the very concept of what a dramatis persona might be. By examining the use made by Beckett (and by his English and French producers) of the different sign systems available in radio—language, voice sets and paralinguistic features, sound effects and music—one is able to chart an evolution from play to play which led to the creation of ambiguous characters who are open to multiple interpretations by the listener. In so doing, Beckett also liberated the discourse from the constraints of a speaking subject, allowing it to function as an independent force having its own substance.

In many ways, Beckett's first radio play, *All That Fall*, is far more conventional than the stage plays that preceded it. Whereas *Waiting for Godot* and *Endgame* have settings that are ambiguous, undefined somewheres, that of *All That Fall*, Boghill, is specific and has characteristics apparently representative of the rural Ireland of Beckett's youth. In *Waiting for Godot* the characters have distinct and different personalities but it is difficult to remember offhand who is characterized by what or, even more importantly, who said what. As Wolfgang Iser has pointed out, the language in the play is "largely detached from the speakers themselves."[3] No such blurring of identities occurs in *All That Fall*, and the various statements are most definitely attributable to a specific character. Nevertheless there are certain allusions within the play to the autonomous behavior of discourse. Early in the play Maddy asks Christy: "Do you find anything . . . bizarre about my way of speaking? (Pause) I do not mean the voice. (Pause) No, I mean the words . . . I use none but the simplest words, I hope, and yet I sometimes find my way of speaking very . . . bizarre."[4] And towards the end of the play Dan comments upon her problems with language and notes that he too has the same sensation of struggling when he happens to overhear what he is saying. However, Maddy's sudden shifts of tone and subject matter can often be accounted for and are interpreted as characteristic of her self-absorption, just as Dan's habit of counting and enumerating things emerges as a personality trait and is not taken as an indication of the self-generating aspect of language. The discourse in *All That Fall* is firmly attached to its speakers and one of its functions is to establish them as characters.

At this point it is perhaps useful to bear in mind that a character in a play is but a construct, established by a combination of signs emitted by his speech, by the actor's interpretation of the role, by the decor, and by being the referent of other characters' discourse. The audience interprets these culturally coded signs to create a paradigm of traits which individualize the entity, sometimes to the point where the character acquires an existence that transcends the confines of the fiction. Unlike stage plays in which most characters are physically represented by actors, radio plays must create the illusion by sound alone of the characters' presence. This disembodiment is not necessarily a limitation and often has distinct advantages.

The wealth of information imparted by visually projected signs in stage plays may cause many to feel that radio drama cannot possibly be as expressive. However, the human voice, when given the opportunity to command all of an audience's attention, as in radio, has great manipulative powers, and it carries much culturally coded information that can be exploited. Research has indicated that the characteristics of a voice can suggest physical appearance and even moral qualities. In his discussion of paralanguage, Trager notes that speech takes place within a background called the *voice set* which, through "physiological and physical peculiarities," identifies "individuals as members of a societal group and as persons of a certain sex, age, state of health, body build, rhythm state, position in a group, mood, bodily condition, location."[5] In addition to the voice set there are *voice qualities* such as variations of articulation, pitch, etc., and *vocalizations*, noises which he subdivides into characteristics such as laughing, qualifiers such as intensity, and segregates such as sounds of affirmation. Furthermore, according to E. T. Hall, there are basically four shifts of voice loudness which correspond to the distances between people in intimate, personal, social and public interaction. As a result, voice loudness provides "a clue as to the types of activities and relationships associated with each distance, thereby linking them in people's minds with specific inventories of relationships and activities."[6] The choice of voice set and manner of delivery can greatly change the type of character that emerges in a radio play. An excellent example of this is the difference between the BBC production of *Embers* and the French radio production. Clas Zilliacus in his book *Beckett and Broadcasting* thoroughly describes the extremely different personalities, the one old and tormented, the other middle-aged and calm, that are projected by the different productions.[7]

Equally important in creating the illusion of the presence of a character and in establishing certain traits is the use of sound effects. In *All That Fall* nearly every character is first presented by a sound effect depicting a mode of locomotion. In the French production by Alain Trutat,[8] Maddy's dragging footsteps are accompanied by panting and a huge sigh of relief whenever she stops, signifying the effort required to move her great bulk. This physical trait of being fat, iconically represented by these sounds, is confirmed linguistically as she describes herself as "pourrie de . . . graisse" (rotted through by fat) and as a "monceau de gélatine" (pile of jelly).[9] The sound effects that announce the arrival and departure of those whom she meets on the way to the station not only create the illusion of a cart, a bicycle, and a car, but also indicate, to a certain degree, the social status of Christy, Tyler and Slocum. Dan's blindness, mentioned prior to his entrance, is corroborated by the tapping of his cane. Once the physical presence of characters has been denoted by sound effect, the representative or iconic aspect of these sounds is no longer necessary. It is then possible to stylize them as both the English and French productions did with the sounds of Maddy's footsteps and Dan's cane during their walk back home, creating a special atmosphere that sets the couple apart from the rest of the world. However, that world is very much there, constantly referred to by Maddy as she mentions various aspects of it, and whose sounds (stylized in McWhinnie's production, realistic in Alain Trutat's production) impinge upon their conversation. Thus, in *All That Fall*, the various sign systems are decoded visually, creating the illusion of a specific spatial dimension, representative of the real world, in which the characters function. And the characters themselves are endowed, by the discourse, voice sets and sound effects, with physical attributes, personality traits, and background information which stimulates the audience to imagine them as existing or having existed in a situation other than the enactment of the play.

Embers, Beckett's second radio play, makes greater use of the dramatic possibilities of a purely aural medium by presenting a character, Ada, whose physical presence is not corroborated by sound effects. She is but a voice and certain questions that she asks—such as "Is there anyone about?"[10]—indicate that she is a projection of Henry's mind. In the French production directed by J. J. Vienne, an intermittent echo was added to her voice in order to reinforce the impression that she is a hallucination. The audience is not given any suggestion of physical attributes and her personality traits are minimal. Nevertheless her voice creates a presence that makes her as real to the listener as she is to Henry, particularly since the dialogue is a dynamic exchange concerning both the past and the present. The result is an ambiguity as to Ada's status not only as an existent but also as a speaking subject. Is she or is Henry the source of her discourse? Although she apparently is conjured up in Henry's mind, it soon becomes apparent that he has no control over her response. She says that she has been there for a while, before he called for her, and she leaves the scene of her own volition despite Henry's plea to stay. During their conversation Ada imposes her presence, but once she ceases to speak she also ceases to exist as a character. One realizes that her performance is part of Henry's effort to create a barrier between himself and the deadly sound of the sea, and one is not tempted to conceive of her as having any other role. She is a manifestation of the flow of words that come and go, and Henry has no assurance that they will be there when needed or perform as desired. Basically, Ada functions solely within the dynamics of the play as an event, part of the "discursive formation"[11] and as the means by which the incorporeality of thoughts, of words, is voiced and acquires substance.

Clas Zilliacus suggests that the sea, because of its constant presence and effect upon Henry, has the "dignity of a dramatis persona"[12] in *Embers*. However, despite its importance as an essential element in the structure of the play, the sound of the sea functions primarily as an iconic representation of the setting, particularly in the French production where it is presented realistically, complete with a few faint seagull cries now and then. It is referred to by both Ada and Henry as the setting, and nowhere does it actively participate in the action.

Dramatis personae, even those that are not human beings, are usually presented as expressing themselves using human speech. Music, however, is another means of expression and can be considered a language in its own right. Unlike speech, however, the different discourses of music have no referent outside of its own system. Objective attempts to determine whether different types of music do indeed suggest various scenes or emotions have led to contradictory conclusions.[13] Despite the problematic nature of its meaning, certain kinds of music, because of previous use, have become codified and are often used, in radio plays in particular, as supportive decor. Beckett challenged this convention in *Words and Music* and in *Cascando* by according music the status of a character. However, in each play, the functioning of music as a dramatis persona is dependent upon the linguistic signs. In *Words and Music* the first clue that music is being cast as something more than decor comes when

Words speaks to it, expressing his loathing at being "cooped up," "With you!"[14] However, Words could be just as well speaking to someone who is playing a record, even though it is the sound of an orchestra tuning up. It is Music's response, parallel to that of Words, to Croak's addressing it as Bob that begins to establish Music as a character. If the other characters did not speak to Music, eliciting responses from it and responding to its discourse, then Music's role would be ambiguous. Similarly, in *Cascando*, music functions as a character because Opener refers to it, providing the cues through his action for it to enter and leave the scene in the same manner as does Voice, thus establishing an equivalence between them.

Casting Music as a character not only challenged the conventions of radio drama but also the usual presentation of dramatis personae which, if they are not human, are objects, animals, plants, or things, all having a physical density which is palpable. They exist in a spatial dimension, allowing the audience to imagine them as housing a conscience which would be the source of the discourse. Music, being sound, exists only in a temporal dimension. It is immaterial, as are words. Yet both have an impact and occur as events, although they are traditionally considered as being produced by someone or something. Foucault, in his discussion of discourse, insists that, as an event, discourse "n´est point l´acte ni la propriété d´un corps" (is neither the act nor the property of a body).[15] Nevertheless, "il se produit comme effet de et dans une dispersion matérielle" (it produces itself as an effect of and in a material dispersal) and one should philosophically consider it as "un matérialisme de l´incorporel" (an incorporeal materialism).[16] Discourse as an independent event and as an ongoing reality is not, therefore, the expression of a speaking subject who is responsible for it. Discourse, according to Foucault, has a life of its own governed by seriality, discontinuity, and chance. Both Music and Words in Beckett's *Words and Music* are discourses that function independently of an originator despite the fact that Croak treats them as his servants and orders them to develop certain themes. They were carrying on before his arrival on the scene and continue to do so after his departure. Furthermore, he has no control over how they develop the themes. Music and Words are also characters in an almost traditional sense, having definite personality traits, even names. At the same time, as befits the medium, they are purely aural entities functioning only in a temporal dimension. Words's mention of "here, in the dark"[17] or Croak's allusion to the stairs does not provide any spatial parameters for their encounter, and the sound effects—shuffle of slippers and thump of club—are, if one does not know the text, not clearly identifiable in either the English or French productions. The three characters are simply presented as coming together and interacting to produce the "discursive formation"[18] that is the play. However, unlike Ada in *Embers*, neither Words nor Music is presented as once possibly having had a corporeal existence.

The characteristics of discourse, as outlined by Foucault, are even more evident in the presentation of Voice and Music as dramatis personae in *Cascando*. The expressiveness of delivery has been eliminated in favor of a very rapid and low speech on the part of Voice so that the emphasis lies in the urgent, ongoing rush of words, in their very materiality rather than their significance. In addition, the same phrases are constantly repeated, further eroding the importance of meaning. Similarly, Music is no longer presented as performing in relation to and with reference to Words. Both Music and Voice are functioning independently, absorbed in their own activity, oblivious to each other and to anyone else. Voice's speech is about its compulsion to speak, despite its desire to have done with all these words; and its story about Woburn may be considered as a metaphorical description of this same compulsion, the continuing, never-ending moving towards some unknown goal, "heading anywhere."[19] The implication of the Woburn story is even clearer in the French text where the object of the discourse is called "Maunu," which phonetically means "naked words" or, if you will, "words stripped of all meaning." Foucault calls this self-enclosed aspect of discourse its "spécificité,"[20] insisting that there is no preestablished signification which discourse interprets and reveals. Discourses are practices concerned with themselves.

The Opener, in a flat, neutral voice, makes it quite clear that he is not responsible for this flow of discourses. He functions solely as an activator, causing what Foucault calls a "découpe" (a cutting-out),[21] making possible the surge of discourse. This is not to be considered as an act of creativity but merely one of the external conditions that allows discourse to articulate. The Opener's activity reveals the discontinuity as well as the seriality of discourses which, according to Foucault, "se croisent, se jouxtent parfois, mais aussi bien s´ignorent ou s´excluent" (intersect, sometimes come together side by side, but just as likely are unaware of each other or are mutually exclusive).[22] It also makes clear the role of change in the production of these events. As a character, Opener is very ambiguous. There are no indications as to who he is, where he is, precisely what he is doing, or why, other than opening because of a compulsion to do so. There is only a temporal allusion to the month of May. In light of Foucault's description of the characteristics of discourse, Voice and Music are far more definable. They are not characters in the traditional sense but discrete events, representing themselves, no more and no less. Discrete because, as Foucault cautions, one shouldn't imagine the existence of an unlimited discourse outside of and beyond the various conditions of possibility. Their existence, literally and figuratively, begins when the Opener opens and ends when he closes.

In the same year, 1961, that Beckett wrote *Words and Music* and *Cascando* he also wrote two other sketches for radio which he set aside at the time for they were not published until 1975 and 1976. Only *Rough for Radio II* has been produced, directed by Martin Esslin in 1976. I have not included an analysis of these two plays since they are basically preliminary workings out of structures that were realized in those that I have discussed. Beckett, has not, to my knowledge, written any other radio plays, but his work in this medium has definitely had an impact upon the dramatic works he has produced for other media, especially those for the stage. *Play*, in 1962, virtually eliminated the interpretative role of the actor, reducing the characters to anonymous voices whose discourses are governed by seriality, discontinuity and chance, and delivered with the same rapid-fire, non-expressiveness as in *Cascando*. Similarly, *Not I* and *That Time* present a dissociation of the discourse from the speaking body, insisting upon the repetitive and intertwining flow of words, upon discourse as an event activated by and occurring with a certain set of conditions. They enact, as in his prose works, the surging forth of a voice which imposes itself and cannot be categorized as an identifiable, responsible character.[23]

From *The Review of Contemporary Fiction* 7, no.2 (Summer 1987): 112-19.

---

[1] Maurice Blanchot, "Où maintenant? Qui maintenant?" *Nouvelle Revue Française* 10 (October 1953): 681. My translation.

[2] Martin Esslin, "Beckett's *Rough for Radio*," *Journal of Modern Literature* 6, no. 1 (1977): 100. Special issue on Samuel Beckett.

[3] Wolfgang Iser, "Beckett's Dramatic Language," *Modern Drama* 9 (1966): 256.

[4] Samuel Beckett, *All That Fall*, in *Krapp's Last Tape and Other Dramatic Pieces* (New York: Grove Press, 1970), 35.

[5] G. Trager, "Paralanguage: A First Approximation," *Studies in Linguistics* 13, nos. 1-2 (1958): 4.

[6] E. T. Hall, *The Hidden Dimension* (Garden City, N.Y.: Doubleday, 1966), 108. Based on work done with G. Trager.

[7] Clas Zilliacus, *Beckett and Broadcasting: A Study of the Works of Samuel Beckett for and in Radio and Television*, Acta Academiae Aboensis, Series A., vol. 51, no. 2 (Abo: Abo Akademi, 1976), 99.

[8] Broadcast 19 December 1959 on France III with Roger Blin as Dan and Marise Paillet as Maddy. The BBC production was directed by Donald McWhinnie with J. C. Devlin as Dan and Mary O'Farrell as Maddy, and first

broadcast on 13 January 1957. A stereo version, also produced by McWhinnie but with Marie Kean as Maddy, was first broadcast on 4 June 1972.

[9]Samuel Beckett, *Tous ceux qui tombent* (Paris: Minuit, 1957), 12 and 22. Baril's translation.

[10]Samuel Beckett, *Embers*, in *Krapp's Last Tape and Other Dramatic Pieces* (New York: Grove Press, 1970), 113.

[11]Michel Foucault, *The Archeology of Knowledge*, trans. A. M. Sheridan Smith (New York: Pantheon, 1972), 111.

[12]Clas Zilliacus, "Samuel Beckett's *Embers:* A Matter of Fundamental Sounds," *Modern Drama* 13, no. 2 (1970): 221.

[13]Micheline Banzet, "Musique et Image," *Cahiers d'Etudes de Radio-Télévision* 6 (1955): 189-93, and Robert Francès, "Sur la consistance des significations musicales," *Cahiers d'Etudes de Radio-Télévision* 12 (1956): 276-82. Banzet concludes after much research that Stravinsky's opinion concerning the non-signification of music is valid, while Francès comes to exactly the opposite conclusion.

[14]Samuel Beckett, *Words and Music*, in *Cascando and Other Short Dramatic Pieces* (New York: Grove Press, 1970), 23.

[15]Michel Foucault, *L'Ordre du discours* (Paris: Gallimard, 1971), 59. My translation.

[16]*Ibid.*, 59 and 60. Baril's translation.

[17]Beckett, *Words and Music*, 23.

[18]Foucault, *The Archeology of Knowledge*, 111.

[19]Beckett, *Cascando*, 16.

[20]Foucault, *L'Ordre du discours*, 55.

[21]*Ibid.*, 54. My translation.

[22]*Ibid.*, 55. My translation.

²³See James Knowlson and John Pilling, *Frescoes of the Skull: The Later Prose and Drama of Samuel Beckett* (London: John Calder, 1979). The authors frequently point out a growing disembodiment of the voice in Beckett's prose, its struggles to be accepted as substantial, and the uncertainty as to where it comes from.

"To Be Is to Be Perceived" . . . Time and Point of View in Beckett's *Film*

William F. Van Wert

No discussion of Samuel Beckett's influence on modern art can be complete without a discussion of his excursions into film, excursions to extend both the limits of the theater and of literature. In 1963 he wrote a scenario which he entitled "The Eye." Significantly, when the scenario was filmed in 1964 by Alan Schneider, the title was changed to "Film." The name of the medium for the title of an individual film is both arrogant and unassuming. It was obviously not meant to be understood as archetypical, a compendium of the medium's themes and technical devices. Rather, it was clearly intended as a metaphor for perception. *Esse est percipi:* to be is to be perceived. On one level, Beckett came to film questioning the medium's strongest power of illusion, that of the voyeur at the peep-show [*sic*] or magic lantern key-hole [*sic*]. What *Krapp's Last Tape* had done to the stage, *Film* would do to the camera. The most immediate advantage over the stage stemmed from film's unique possibilities of playing with point of view (the "objective" point of view of the unseen perceiver E, the "subjective" point of view of the very present O, when E and O—both Buster Keaton plus the camera eye—turn out to be the same character). On stage, there would be no intermediary screen, no viewer viewing between the stage and the audience. *Film* also offered Beckett possibilities for expressing the dumb show or mime in close-up or for hiding that expression through a rotating or panning camera which may or may not be the point of view of O, the Keaton seen most from behind in the film. Except for a "sshh" in the beginning of the film, there is no dialogue. In his very first attempt, Beckett saw the film medium as being neither an adjunct to, nor an extension of, either the theater or literature.
Yet the similarities with both are clear. From Beckett's novels comes this obsession with *doppelgangers*, doubles who chase each other/themselves furtively, haphazardly until the unexpected moment when the invisible mirror

reveals both to each. From the plays comes this insistence on the smallest gestures, the most insignificant details, the most mindless repetitions of looks or tics to reveal character and symbol through character. Both of these patterns in Beckett are rooted in German Expressionism, in which the theme of the double was most appropriate to an aesthetic approach which said that the characters should wear their souls on their sleeves, in which the internal is exteriorized and the exterior is suppressed or made a mental projection of the interior. This same German Expressionism, to avoid the awkward shift from visuals to intertitles, developed the *kamerspiel* film, in which the faintest twitching of an eye would be immediately perceived by the viewer through extreme close-ups.

Beckett's entry into the film medium taxed all the technicians who worked on the film, because he was questioning the cinematic look at its most fundamental level. As Beckett himself suggested in his notes for the film:

> All extraneous perception suppressed, animal, human, divine, self-perception maintains in being.
> Search of non-being in flight from extraneous perception breaking down in inescapability of self-perception.
> No truth value attaches to above, regarded as of merely structural and dramatic convenience.
> In order to be figured in this situation the protagonist is sundered into object (O) and eye (E), the former in flight, the latter in pursuit.
> It will not be clear until the end of film that pursuing perceiver is not extraneous, but self.[1]

There is a restriction upon cinematic looking which permits this fanciful passing from illusion to reality. The spectator may look at a character in a film who is looking off to one side or the other and so does not return the spectator's gaze. In this case, both the spectator and the camera look at a character who does not return the look: A (spectator) merges with B (camera eye) to perceive C (the film actor). When the film actor turns to the camera and looks frontally at it, the spectator and the film actor look at each other, suppressing the camera eye, which physically rests with the film actor but *psychically* merges with the spectator.

However one works out the various cinematic looks, one must conclude that there can be only *indirect* looks or confrontations in film, the indirectness posing a problem in terms of point of view for the camera. When the camera moves from a long shot to a close-up, with no previous close-up of a character, we the spectators know that this close-up is a privileged look, that this is not an "objective" view of reality, and that the camera is in fact calling attention to itself as a machine, whose relative distance from a scene often seems arbitrary

Radio and Film 221

at best when unattached to any character's gazes within the film. In Beckett's *Film*, that voyeuristic camera eye goes beyond the typical Borges detective story, in which the detective turns out to be the man he is chasing, by asserting both objective and subjective points of view at the same time.

Point of view cannot be dissociated from time in film. It was significant that Alain Resnais should show up as one of the spectators on the first day of filming. Resnais made famous the forwardly mobile camera, the very mobility (unfixedness) on city streets and exteriors permitting a rush or flow of poetic, interiorized narration on the part of an unseen character: the streets of Hiroshima on the visual track versus the poeticized remembrances of the dead German lover at Nevers for the woman in *Hiroshima Mon Amour*. Resnais also initiated a highly intricate system of non-confrotational looks on the part of his actors, so that dialogue might more easily relate both to the present and to some other undefined time period: for example, the many shots of A. and X. in the same frame, looking off into opposite directions, conducting dialogues which are really interior monologues, in *Last Year at Marienbad*. There is no rush of off-narration in Beckett's *Film*, but there is the mobile camera of E's gaze of O in the room, and there are the non-confrontational looks of E and O, most evident when E approaches O sitting in the rocking chair from around the left of O and O looks off to the right. This kind of non-confrontation suggests that no denouement is possible laterally; approach from the left means escape/denial to the right and vice-versa. There can only be a frontal confrontation, in which the close-up captures E or O but not both in the same frame. Both seem to be staring at us, when they are really staring at each other.

Beckett was aware from the start of the technical problems caused by his insistence upon this double vision, each distinct from the other, both revealing the same scenes. He clearly did not want to overcome the problem through any easy camera tricks or editing magic:

> We see O in the room thanks to E's perceiving and the room itself thanks to O's perceiving. In other words this room sequence, up to the moment of O's falling asleep, is composed of two independent sets of images. I feel that any attempt to express them in simultaneity (composite images, double frame, superimposition, etc.) must prove unsatisfactory. The presentation of a single image of O's perception of the print, for example, and E's perception of O perceiving it--no doubt feasible technically--would perhaps make impossible for the spectator a clear apprehension of either.[2]

The solution was to set up rigidly opposing points of view in the level of remove of perception, the degree of focus in perception, and the succession in terms of time for perception. Beckett's rejection of simultaneity achieved through camera tricks allowed for a separation between the two Keatons and a tension between perceiving and perceived. In philosophical terms, then, Beckett's dictum that to be is to be perceived involves two sets of vision and at least two moments in time. If the confrontation (existence-perception) is simultaneous or without distortion in vision, the double is destroyed, and the camera becomes a curiously detached onlooker in an empty room with Keaton sleeping in a rocking chair. Logically, to be doubled, these visions would have to exist simultaneously; the time frame is altered and made successive to emphasize the difference in point of view, "regarded as of merely structural and dramatic convenience." A closer look at the film will bear me out.

Film opens, not on any landscape or establishing shot in the real world, but on the reptilian closed eye-brow of Keaton, although we are unaware at the time that it belongs to Keaton. The eye opens and the film begins. The convention is clear: we are watching an eye (the film/camera) and the eye looks at us. The return to that extreme close-up of the frontal eye at the end of the film forms a frame device encircling the film; between those two gazes frontally at the camera, everything is interiorized. Like the play with the time of a split second in Ambrose Bierce's "An Occurrence at Owl Creek Bridge," the framing eye in Beckett's *Film* suggests that the whole film takes place in the time between eyes closed and eyes opened, that is, the time between blinks.

The beginning "street" sequence is significant in that it established the O character as someone seen from behind, someone wearing a scarf around his face, someone who walks with his face to the wall. When O confronts anyone (the couple reading the newspaper), the subjective confrontation is expressed through a blurred image (achieved by gauze over the lens). Immediately thereafter, the same scene is repeated from a distance more removed: the blurred image of the frightened couple with bulging eyes and open mouths becomes a medium shot of the couple, the same expression on their faces, this time in focus and this time revealing O in front of them.

Thus, what we see is first dependent upon O's seeing it. Without O's perception, there would be darkness. But O's perceptions are always in claustrophobic close-up and blurred. The Camera-Eye E, the unseen perceiver and pursuer, vindicates the image by restoring it to focus and by placing O in the image. Thus, the street does not exist without O; O does not exist without E; E's vision is more impersonal, colder, more rigidly focused than that of O, but also more removed. What is unclear until the end of the film when E and O confront each other is that the couple in the street and the flower-woman on the stairs do not become paralyzed with fear at seeing O, as it would appear since O is physically present, but rather at seeing E, the camera-eye with the impassive stare of a God. Only camera movement can suggest the independence of E from O at this point.

The difference between O and E (the possibility of their being doubles and not just a split-self) is further reinforced by the movement of the camera suggesting spatial difference after the confrontation with the flower-woman:

> Absorbed by difficulty of descent she does not become aware of E until she is quite down and making for the door. She halts and looks full at E. Gradually same expression as that of the couple in street. She closes her eyes, then sinks to the ground and lies with face in scattered flowers. E lingers on this a moment, then transfers to where O last registered. He is no longer there, but hastening up the stairs. E transfers to stairs and picks up O as he reaches first landing. Bounds forward [sic] and up of E who overtakes O on second flight and is literally at his heels when he reaches second landing and opens with key door of room. They enter together, E turning with O as he turns to lock the door behind him.[3]

Difference is first shown in the successive close-ups of the face of the flower-woman. She smiles benevolently, corresponding to her seeing O on his way up. She becomes convulsed with fear and collapses, corresponding to her having seen E, the evil eye of the opening of the film. When E catches up with O and merges with O at the door, only the rotation of the camera (E turning as O turns) suggests the invasion of the double, the hint of the split-self.

With the entrance into the room, the dual perception must be maintained at the same time that it must become gradually obvious to the spectator.

> Here we assume problem of dual perception solved and enter O's perception. E must so manoeuvre throughout what follows, until investment proper, that O is always seen from behind, at most convenient remove, and from an angle never exceeding that of immunity, i.e., preserved from perceivedness.[4]

In the room, fixed close-ups that are blurred alternate with revolving medium shots that are in focus. The same visions are doubled, repeated but different, the emphasis in each vision upon the occlusion of vision and all possible "eyes."

O begins to exclude all light from the room (light is the chief component of vision) and all eyes, literal and figurative. He drapes the window, masks the mirror, shuts out the large cat and small dog (after some slapstick repetition, in which the door opening to let out the dog brings the cat back in, and so on . . .), drapes the parrot cage, drapes the fishbowl, tears down the drawing of a face upon the wall. All of these eyes are conveyed in blurred close-up first, then "restored" to perspective by the focused surreptitious vision of E.

One digression is perhaps important here. From Beckett's notes to the film, we learn that the drawing on the wall is that of God the Father and that the room is not O's room but most likely that of his mother. These very pertinent clues to psychological motivation are not readily apparent to the film.

There is one shot in this sequence that metaphorically captures all other shots in the film and serves to explain further our previous discussion of cinematic looks. O is sitting in the rocking chair with the folder on his lap. In front of him is the drawing (God the Father) with large severe eyes on the wall. Behind the head is the headrest of the chair, itself a God-head with holes for eyes. Behind all of this is the camera, the unseen E. Within that straight line are four sets of eyes (two sets apparent, one set hidden, one invisible). Within that straight line are multiple confrontations based on the perceived meeting the perceived: (1) eyes of the drawing meet eyes of O; (2) eyes of the drawing merge with eyes of headrest; (3) eyes of the drawing and eyes of the headrest meet the unseen camera-eye (E).

O tears the drawing down, just as he had either excluded or covered up the animals. It is O, in trying to escape self-perception in the looks of others, who sets up the final confrontation with E. E is immobilized without O's careful and meticulous obsession with blotting out the eyes.

O stares at the folder in his lap. There are eyes on the folder. To avert the "eyes" of the folder, O turns it 90 degrees. This ninety-degree turn becomes the structural constant for understanding the photographs inside the folder. There are seven in all, each revealing a stage of O's life, from birth to fatherhood at the time of enlistment in the army. One by one, O holds the pictures in his hands: (1) him as a baby held by his mother; (2) him at four, sitting next to his mother; (3) him at fifteen, teaching a dog to beg; (4) him at twenty, on graduation day; (5) him at twenty-one, his arm around his fiancee, a young man present in the picture taking their picture; (6) him at twenty-five, newly enlisted, holding a baby girl in his arms; and (7) him at thirty, looking over forty, wearing hat and overcoat, the patch over the left eye. Pictures five, six and seven are especially significant. Picture five reveals the metaphor of the film within the film. The photographer is present in the frame with the couple, suggesting that another photographer (the unseen camera-eye, probably E) is also present. Picture six reveals both the result of picture five (the baby girl) and the explanation for picture seven: he lost his eye in the army, and, with it, he lost his mother, his fiancee, his baby girl, everything but the pursuant E. Picture seven functions as a kind of mirror. We see O in the photograph before we see O frontally in the rocking chair, the exactly mirrored reflection of the man in the photograph being a foreshadowing of the ultimate confrontation with E against the wall where the God-face drawing had been.

Beginning with picture seven, O tears up all the photographs into four pieces each, dropping them successively to the floor. But, before tearing each, he turns each 90 degrees, just as he had turned the outside flap of the folder: symbolically, perhaps this turning before tearing suggests an averting of the gaze, those eyes in the photographs being seen as real eyes, just as real as the eyes of the animals, the eyes of the drawing, the headrest, the folder flaps. This 90-degree turning is also the doubling of E's "angle of immunity," which is 45 degrees, beyond which E risks being seen by O. The turning of the photos before destruction also emphasizes O's hands, reminding the spectator of the various times prior to this that O is seen looking at one wrist (his left hand) or at both hands extended.

The tearing of the photographs frees E for the final confrontation. E begins to move left around the rocking chair, as O begins to snooze or to look off to the right. In either case, the panorama of the room is to signify E's trajectory, not yet around O, not yet upon O:

> Turning his head to right, O cringes away from perceivedness. E draws back to reduce the angle and after a moment, reassured, O turns back front and resumes his pose. The rock resumes, dies down slowly as O dozes off again. E now begins a much wider encirclement. Images of curtained window, walls, and shrouded mirror to indicate his path and that he is not yet looking at O. Then brief image of O seen by E from well beyond the angle of immunity, i.e., from near the table with shrouded bowl and cage.[5]

The first time that we see O's face frontally, he is asleep. He is also being seen from E's point of view, for the first time in front of O instead of behind him. O opens his eyes and gradually his face goes to horror, as did the faces of the couple and the flowerwoman. The irony here is that we will never know what they actually saw, since our vision of E, for the first time divorced from the camera-eye, is dependent upon O's patched eye, his clouded vision of blurred images. E appears blurred and full of crystals, a mirror reflection of O against the wall, the nail that used to hang the drawing now protruding next to E's ear. O puts his head down and his hands over his eyes. The vision is gone. We realize that we (and the camera) are totally dependent upon those imperfect eyes. For the first time, we realize that what we have thought to be eyes all along is but one eye. A second irony: since the vision of E is a mirror reflection of O to O, all vision cancels out, a patch blocking confrontation between both eyes, because the reflection reverses the patch. Thus, the unpatched eye of O stares at the patched eye of E and vice-versa. From a full-shot of E, we return to a bowed O, hands over eyes. When he looks up, there is a cut. We see a close-up of E's face, the unpatched eye sparkling with a crystal twinkle like a star (God the Father or the mythical Evil Eye?). We cut back to a close-up of the bowed O. His rocking slows to a stop. The title and Beckett's name appear in the gigantic pupil of the eye of the beginning. Since we have gone from full-shot to close-up on both E and O, the question persists: is that eye of the credits E's eye or O's eye, the one eye aggrandized by the loss of the other? The freeze on the enormous eye would seem to suggest that the ultimate confrontation between perceiver and perceived, the confrontation which defines existence, self-perception embodied, brings with it death or total immobility, and the only escape is blinking (an avoidance of confrontation, a questioning of what one has seen) or sleep (itself a kind of death, since it avoids confrontation by shutting off all vision). And, as with so many of Beckett's plays and novels, the earthly mother and God the Father, both with severe stares, are somewhat absent, behind the scenes pulling the strings.

At first, *Film* was not well received. Too short to be a commercial film, too rigid in its construction to be a successful entertainment short, it has had to go the way of university classrooms and European film festivals to win attention and acclaim. It deserves more of both. *Film* calls into question the very nature of the camera as a recorder of reality, imbuing it with an obsessive personality that is at once voyeur and victim. Nowhere has anyone so succinctly pointed out the interrelationships of point of view and time in film, the two last frontiers of exploration for film proper, excluding technical innovations like video and cassette-films. Pier Paolo Pasolini once wrote that the really modern in film was to be found in the self-reflexive, in the camera which restates itself, in the film that does not narrate causally from point A to point B but rather spatially, repeating point A from different perspectives, insisting upon time and point of view. Beckett's film doubles upon itself in this way, each from being repeated in opposition to itself (blur vs. focus; close-up vs. long shot; fixed frame vs. mobile revolving camera). No other filmmaker would have dared to call his film, his first film, simply, generically and arrogantly—*Film*. Beckett's film deserves the title.

From *Literature/Film Quarterly* 8, no.2 (April 1980): 133-40.

---

[1] Samuel Beckett, *Film* (New York: Grove Press, 1969), p. 11.

[2] *Film*, p. 58.

[3] *Film*, p. 20.

[4] *Film*, p. 23.

[5] *Film*, pp. 40-41.

CHAPTER 7

Beckett is Awarded the Nobel Prize

Godot Arrives

Iain Hamilton

That most retiring of writers, Samuel Beckett, has been awarded the most recherché of literary awards, the Nobel Prize. IAIN HAMILTON examines the significance of this choice by such experienced judges.

The award of the Nobel Prize for literature to Samuel Beckett calls to mind the bitter lines written by an earlier Anglo-Irish prizewinner, W. B. Yeats:

> You say, as I have often given tongue
> In praise of what another's said or sung,
> 'Twere politic to do the like by these:
> But was there ever dog that praised his fleas?

Yeats' imitators never got anywhere. The theatres and publishing houses of the western world, on the other hand, are besieged by Beckett's. His superficial manner is more easily imitated. Some commentators have suggested that the Nobel committee's decision was a surprising one. Harold

Hobson of the *Sunday Times*, for example, noted that with it "that august institution takes a bold step into the modern world." Such comments seem to me ungenerous, not only to the august institution but also to such recent recipients of its bounty as S. Y. Agnon and Nelly Sachs, Jean-Paul Sartre, George Seferis, John Steinbeck, St. J. Perse, Boris Pasternak, Camus, and Hemingway. Whatever their differences they all had in common a concern with "the modern world."

Great predecessors
It is scarcely necessary, when applauding the Nobel committee's recognition of Beckett's bleak genius, to consign all his predecessors to a dead and unmodish antiquity. Thomas Mann is not unread. Pirandello is not unplayed. Nelly Sachs' poems in German about the German destruction of her fellow Jews have not lost their point. A very great deal has come to light about Russia since 1958, when the Swedish academicians awarded the prize to Boris Pasternak, to increase the stature of *Doctor Zhivago* and refute the sneers of its official Communist detractors and their friends.

It is true that most regular literary prizes tend to be awarded on the basis of mere fashion; but this has seldom if ever been the case with the Nobel prize, and those who have welcomed its award to Beckett in a way which suggests that the Swedish Academy has at long last been enlightened, or converted to trendiness, do their hero no less than the committee a serious disservice. Perhaps it was the awareness of this, as much as his innate modesty, which made Beckett go to ground in Tunisia before the announcement of the award, and so avoid the enthusiastic attention of trendsetters.

The Nobel prize has gone this year to the most austere of writers who would be no more willing than Yeats was to praise the trivia of his imitators—and who is certainly not to be blamed for them. There is nothing factitious about his stoical view of the existential absurdity of the human condition—the destitution of modern man, as the Swedish Academy said in its citation. Modern man saw his plight mirrored in *Waiting for Godot*, the play which brought him almost instant and universal fame in the 50's.

No compromise
But he has not flattered his new public. On the contrary, he has pursued his desolate vision to the very gates of silence. The last play of his which I have read, *Come and Go*, consists of no more than 25 lines of monosyllabic dialogue shared among three characters. "May we not speak of the old days?" says one of them. "Of what came after?" She is answered with silence. Her creator has gone further than most of us can follow beyond the tragic farce of *Waiting for Godot*. Perhaps his lifework will yet be seen as a progressive *reductio ad absurdum*, the rest being silence. Whether or not that is an apt comment on the

progress of civilization, there is no denying the artistic integrity and courage of the commentator.

"Is not style," Synge once said to Yeats, "born out of the shock of new material?" Is not Beckett's style born out of the shocks that have knocked civilized man all but speechless?

From *The Illustrated London News* (1 November 1969): 9.

Nobel Prize: Kyrie Eleison Without God

In her memoirs, Peggy Guggenheim describes a character she calls "Oblomov," which is her name for the young Samuel Beckett of the 1930s. The name was apt. Oblomov is the hero of a 19th century Russian novel by Goncharov, and he is famed for his inability to get out of bed. The mere thought of taking any action or making any decision makes him burrow deeper under the covers in a paroxysm of inertia. Miss Guggenheim's "Oblomov" told her that "ever since his birth he had retained a terrible memory of life in his mother's womb. He was constantly suffering from this and had awful crises, when he felt he was suffocating."

As a poet, novelist and playwright, Samuel Beckett has ramified that ordeal by suffocation into images of frustration, impotence, alienation, futility and absurdity. As a drop of water implies the sea, the personal obsession of a scrupulous and sensitive writer may mirror the inarticulate concerns of multitudes of men. The significant artist "dreams ahead"—he catches on to his age and then his age catches up to him. When Samuel Beckett was awarded the Nobel Prize in Literature last week at the age of 63, it was perhaps as much of an honor to his international audiences as to him. The judges were acknowledging that this demanding, obscure and austerely self-contained writer had become the laureate of an age that feels suffocated by its desolating sense of nothingness.

Metaphysical Blackout. Beckett's friend and mentor, James Joyce, once said: "Here is life without God. Just look at it!" In a way, Beckett's entire work is an agonized sermon on that text. In his world, the machinery of existence seems to be grinding to a halt. The titles *Krapp's Last Tape*, *Endgame* and *Malone Dies* suggest a civilization with terminal cancer. The suffocating womb becomes a death trap; the urns encasing the characters in *Play*, the mound of earth piled up to the heroine's neck in *Happy Days*, the ashcans of *Endgame*. One critic has called a Beckett hero a perverse Cartesian: I stink, therefore I am. Actually, the degradation and mutilation of the body are Beckett's image for the withering away of the soul.

The mood of Beckett's plays and novels is traumatic loss, a vestigial memory of the expulsion from Eden. With elegiac melancholy, Beckett intones a kyrie eleison without God. *Waiting for Godot* is hope's requiem. The two tramps Estragon and Vladimir wait in vain.

Waiting is the real activity of all Beckett's seemingly totally passive characters. As in an electricity blackout one waits for the light, so in Beckett's metaphysical and moral blackout one waits for new gods and values to replace the old. At times, Beckett seems almost complacent in his despair. Doing nothing is regarded as the higher wisdom and action as impatience, an attempt to induce the birth of some new vital myth that is as yet, in Matthew Arnold's words, "powerless to be born."

And so the two tramps wait. To pass the time they play games. Games become a substitute for life and the loss of purpose. They are the contretemps of clowns. The clown is the only entertainer who consistently draws laughter through his own self-abasement. Beckett's ultimate position is that man is the clown of the universe. But he is a clown for whom Beckett weeps, and that is his saving compassion.

Dramatically, Beckett is more important for his focus than his range. He has forcefully reminded the modern theater that the proper study of the stage is man and the dilemma of his humanity. His spareness has been a valuable lesson in economy. But his use of the internal monologue is not ideally suited to the stage. In his trilogy of richly introspective novels, *Molloy*, *Malone Dies* and *The Unnamable*, Beckett roams inside a character's skull as if it were a continent. Onstage, the monologue is cramping, and the most dramatic skull is always likely to be Yorick's.

Priestly Vocation. Though he has spent most of his life in Paris, Beckett is Irish and the lilt of the Gael runs poetically through even his laconic prose. The brooding sense of grievance, the delight in wordplay, the spellbinding gifts of the barroom raconteur; all these Irish traits are in Beckett. With Joyce, he shares an inordinate relish for puns and scatology, and a tendency to regard sex as either a joke or a sin. Like Joyce, he regards writing as a priestly vocation. Few men have invested the role of a man of letters with more dignity.

If Beckett's art is deep, it is also narrow. The world outside his mind does not exist. The sense of place and society that saturates Joyce is missing in Beckett. Nor does he display Kafka's piety before systems and forces outside himself which may bring him to judgment. Poet Stephen Spender speaks of Beckett's "contempt for everyone and everything outside groping self-awareness." In a way, that is precisely his appeal to the contemporary personality, which is almost neurotically self-concerned and incessantly practices auto-analysis. It must be said for Beckett that his self-analysis has been honest and punishing. The concluding words of *The Unnamable* might comprise an epigraph in courage that knits him to his task and to be buffeted and bewildered men everywhere: "Where I am, I don't know, I'll never know, in the silence you don't know, you must go on, I can't go on, I'll go on."

From *Time* 94 (31 October 1969): 55.

CHAPTER 8

Late Theatrical Works

Theatre (Review of *Happy Days*)

Harold Clurman

SAMUEL BECKETT'S *Happy Days* (Cherry Lane Theatre) is a poem for the stage—a poem of despair and forbearance. It is to be seen and suffered. It is painfully lucid. But because it is a work of art, its lucidity is manifold in meaning.

There are only two characters in the play: a woman of fifty and her husband of sixty. We discover the woman sunk up to her waist in a mound of scorched grass. Her husband lives out of sight behind her in his own hole in the ground. At rare moments he emerges to read an old newspaper, a recurrent item of which he mumbles "Wanted bright boy." At the close of the play he crawls in full evening dress toward his wife: we do not know whether he has come to visit her in "the old style"—a phrase which runs through the play like a refrain, to pay tribute to her long years of married isolation, or to put her (or himself) out of misery. They look at each other in terrible silence: she with a quizzical look of amused compassion and contempt, he with a heartrending stare of impotence, regret, bafflement. Her name is Winnie, his Willie—and one guesses that either one might have been the other, by which I mean that both add up to the idea of Mankind.

What has their life been? A kind of blank; literally, stasis. They are sustained by nothing except the ground in which they are stuck. (In act two the woman has sunk to her neck in the earth. "Oh earth you old extinguisher," she cries, reminding me somehow of Joyce.) Man and wife have no beliefs, faith, passion, aim or great appetite.

Winnie's life is a matter of toilet preparations and a taking of patent medicines the names of which she doesn't understand, the purpose of which is unclear. She is nevertheless an irrepressible optimist. (The play might well have been called "The Optimist.") For as she wakes to the bell which heralds the morning, she exclaims, "Another heavenly day." She looks on the bright side of everything. She dimly remembers and usually misquotes the consoling and "unforgettable" lines of old-time classics. She enjoys listening to a music box tinkling "The Merry Widow" waltz (the "old style" again), and at the very end of the play she hums the same song with its wistful-gay plea for love. The bag in which she keeps all her treasured possessions contains, along with toothbrush, comb, scent and a little mirror, a revolver—just in case—but she never avails herself of its service.

HER husband sleeps most of the time: "marvelous gift that," she reflects. She has "no pain, hardly any pain—great thing that." When she learns the meaning of a single word ("hog"), she observes cheerily: "Hardly a day without addition to one's knowledge." A hearty soul, she asserts, "That is what I find so wonderful, that not a day goes by . . . without some blessing—in disguise."

Most of the time she takes comfort in the thought: "That is what I find so wonderful . . . the way man adapts himself." Only once does she break, crying out in ringing anguish: "No, something must happen in the world, some change." But nothing does change—except that night follows day. "One can do nothing." One prays the old prayers. One still clings to the hope that there may be a meaning to life. "Someone is looking at me still. Caring for me still." One senses one's aliveness because one does not always speak to oneself. The "other" therefore exists. And for all the bleakness and waste there is the inextinguishable sense that "There always remains something. Of Everything."

The most pitiable thing in the play is its pity. Behind the irony of its grimace there is a sort of repressed tenderness. It is this tenderness that makes Beckett's defenders (he needs no defense) deny that his message is all negation. To wait and suffer, perhaps to hope and pray in the empty world, is to evince a trait of nobility, even of heroism. Beckett, it is suggested, is a religious playwright. And it is true that many religious teachers have spoken in accents similar to his.

I am inclined to believe that this line of defense does Beckett a certain disservice. It is precisely through his particular kind of pessimism that Beckett has made his special contribution—indispensable for an understanding of our time. We require solace and remedies hereafter (I do not refer to the "next world"), but at present it is right, just, proper, necessary and helpful that brave men cry bloody murder.

Beckett is the poet of a morally stagnant society. In this society fear, dismay and a sort of a stunned absent-mindedness prevail in the dark of our consciousness, while a flashy, noisy, bumptious, thick-headed complacency flourishes in the open. Nearly all the finer artists of our day are saying this (very few are capable of saying more than this convincingly), and in the theatre Beckett's voice has been the sharpest, the most penetrating, the most symbolic.

Do I believe that life is what Beckett says it ("perhaps") is or seems to be? Not at all. Even the bag which holds all that remains of Winnie's existence contains much more than Beckett has put there. Do I prefer Beckett's black report to Chekhov's (or even Strindberg's) sorrow? Certainly not. The agony of the old plays was dense with human experience. Why then does Beckett write as he does? Apart from the facts of individuality and personal environment, the answer may possibly be found in this notation in Paul Klee's diary of 1915: "The more horrifying this world proves (as it is these days), the more art becomes abstract."

Must we accept Beckett wholly? No: his work represents an impasse. But we must understand him. For he feels strongly and writes unerringly. Despite their bareness, his plays are not barren, and if the stage is to be a true chronicle of the times, they belong in the theatre. *Happy Days* grows on one.

RUTH WHITE'S performance is extraordinary in its concentration, variety, nuance and endurance. (The play is almost a monologue and almost an hour and a half long.) The director—Alan Schneider—has helped her model the great mass of the verbal material so that it rises to poignancy instead of degenerating to monotony.

From The Nation 193 (7 October 1961): 234-35.

The Stage: Beckett's *Happy Days*

Richard Gilman

If Samuel Beckett's new play is rather less successful than its predecessors, its virtues are nevertheless many and its effectiveness undeniable. That question of effectiveness, far more than the meaning of the plays—which are really far less arcane than we have been led to think—has always been to me the interesting one to ask about Beckett's theater. How does it manage to achieve its high intensity and complete conviction—how, really, does it *reach* us—after its apparent abandonment of most of the traditional means of dramatic communication?

Beckett is of course a master of certain classic procedures, especially of the more low-down and kinetic kinds; it is a commonplace that his plays draw from farce, vaudeville, the circus and Chaplin, and that, on the other hand, he carefully, if marginally, observes the dramatic unities. But like Kafka, who created a prose in which realism was a deceptive sea where the strangest fish could swim, Beckett puts the conventions he utilizes into the service of an unheard-of dramaturgy. It is a dramaturgy which appears to be a repudiation of the ordinary purposes of the theater but is actually a miraculous resuscitation of those purposes through a process of purification, deepening and a change of ground.

The miracle lies in the fact that here every element that has been thought to be necessary to the theater's conquest of life—plot, character, movement, linear revelation, the resolution of struggle—has dwindled to a set of notations and gestures, if anything at all remains; and yet life continues to rise from Beckett's stage as it does from few others.

"Happy Days" is Beckett's furthest move so far in the direction of absolute stillness, of a kind of motionless dance in which the internal agitation and its shaping control are descried, through language primarily and through the spaces between words. On an otherwise bare stage, under ferocious light, the woman Winnie sits buried to her waist in a mound of earth throughout the first act, and to her neck throughout the second. Behind the mound we occasionally see the man Willie's head or hand. Near the end, however, Willie crawls round and at last comes fully into the sight of the audience in the play's only major physical movement.

There are a good many minor movements, mostly having to do with Winnie and the contents of a large bag. From it come various objects of everyday use—toothbrush, a comb, a mirror, a bottle of tonic—and her business with them imparts both humor and that minimal stir and palpability without which even so marvelous a theater of language as Beckett's would lack its necessary anchor. But the language and the anti-language (one of Beckett's chief supports, as well as one of his main themes is the tension produced by the struggle between speech and silence and by the double thrust of words towards truth and lies) do most of the work.

It is almost all in a monologue delivered by Winnie (who is played by Ruth White in a virtuoso performance of impressive dimensions and nearly perfect fidelity to Beckett's intentions, as a glance at the published play will confirm; Willie's vastly smaller role is only adequately handled by John C. Becher). In it she laments her youth, praises "the great mercies," is by turns frightened, coy, reflective, bitter, aloof, anguished, ironic, joyous, angry and serene. And from it arises a sense of life apprehended in its utmost degree of non-contingency and existential self-containment, with all its cross-purposes, vagaries, agonies and waste, its oscillation between hope and despair, affirmation and denial—a new enunciation of Beckett's special vision.

But Beckett's theater, as has been observed, is one of pairs—Gogo and Didi, Pozzo and Lucky, Nagg and Nell, Hamm and Clov, Krapp and his taped voice—and in "Happy Days" Willie's presence serves Winnie as one of the poles of her address and the distant source of her sorrow and joy. One could say that the theme of the play is their relationship—we know them to be married—and that Beckett is commenting on the abyss between them. Yet in his theater relationships are never explored for their own sakes, not even as archetypes; what is explored is the nature of a reality where everything, including every relationship, is in doubt and tension.

In any case, the slight feeling of disappointment with which I left the play stemmed, I felt, from the inadequacy of Beckett's treatment of Willie. He has none of the contrapuntal quality that we find in the other linkings, and he is too likely to turn the play toward satire or parody. Besides, he is made to perform, in the play's penultimate action, a disturbingly obvious and sentimental bit of business, the only one I have ever found in Beckett.

Still, "Happy Days" survives, a light in the season and a minor brick in the edifice being raised by the playwright who is to me the most valuable we have. If I were asked to identify that value, I could do no better than quote Jacques Guicharnaud, whose essay on Beckett in his *Modern French Theatre* is unsurpassed. After remarking that "Waiting for Godot" is not an allegory, he says what it is, in words that apply equally well to each of Beckett's words: "It is a concrete and synthetic equivalent of our existence in the world and our consciousness of it." How rich are we in those?

From *The Commonweal* 75, no. 3 (13 October 1961): 69-70.

The Paradox of Silence: Samuel Beckett's Plays

Renée Riese Hubert

Beckett's plays can be considered poetic visions, challenging reader or spectator by their total impact, demanding his participation in each aspect of the performance. Contrary to Racine's or Shakespeare's no less visionary and poetically coherent tragedies, Beckett's theater never attains those moments of extreme furor or despair that reveal the irremediable disintegration of character or situation. These twentieth-century plays which evoke by their stagnant atmosphere man's situation in the universe preclude any form of dramatic climax. In *Waiting for Godot* the change from a lonely, barren tree in Act One to the same tree sprouting a few leaves in the second and final act bears witness to an ironically limited change within an inextricable situation. Sameness rather than catastrophe provides the ultimate revelation of a theater where the characters never give direct expression to any clearly definable emotion or thought. Beckett's plays, in respect to characterization, plot, situation, decor and rhetoric, imply or suggest rather than exemplify or signify. This may be the essence of all great theater, but it is rarely as pronounced as in Beckett's. Consequently, silence somehow corresponds to the very nature of a play which must consistently avoid direct communication through particular incidents or moments. The reader or spectator must bridge the distance between various words, establish connections, strengthen blurred contours, render at least semi-audible what remains muted without, however, making the unsaid or the ineffable explicit to the point of betrayal. Silence thus refers to the perpetually unstated meaning, the unformulated conception, the mute perplexity of man in a given situation or the lack of response on the part of the creator or creation.

Beckett's characters frequently find it impossible to derive a meaning from either word or silence or a combination of both. If they were to probe deeply into their inner world, they would encounter a wide zone of silence, mainly because they have so much trouble in remembering their own past. In fact, they would be incapable of giving any sort of coherent account of themselves or of evoking anything more than echoes of the past. For instance Winnie, the main character of *Happy Days*, typically exclaims out of context: "Golden you called it that day when the last guest was gone." Her words encounter a threefold silence. Willie, her partner, does not reply at all, for to begin with he is deaf and insensitive. In the second place, he has not truly been Winnie's partner in the past. Finally, Winnie, by her words, does not arouse any true memories of her own past. Nell and Nagg, the parents in *Endgame*, in their attempt to recall their honeymoon on Lake Como, seem to communicate better, for the words uttered by one create a response in the other and appear to refer to the same event. But by further scrutiny we detect how specious these memories are. They do not correspond to any event or voice in the past.

> Nagg: You were in such fits that we capsized.
> By rights we should have been drowned.
> Nell: It was because I felt happy.
> Nagg: (indifferent) It was not, it was not, it was
> my story and nothing else. Happy!
> Do you not laugh at it still. Every time I tell it. Happy!

By constant re-enactments of imagined scenes of the past, Nell and Nagg have not only reduced bygone experiences to silence, they have tried to elude an empty and threatening present through performing. The prolonged silence to which they have to submit when Hamm orders that each parent be sealed in his trash can, is broken only by words which reaffirm their separation. The very words which I have quoted indicate how ironically superfluous it was to put

Nell and Nagg into separate bins; a meaningful exchange has never occurred between them, nor is it possible in Beckett's work.

Krapp's Last Tape shows how painful silence can become. Krapp's silence, when he listens to the tape, is the very opposite of the lyrical outbursts prevalent during the Romantic period. Often the Romantic "hero" would triumph over the silence of the world thanks to the powerful and universal voice emerging from his own past. Krapp's past is irretrievable; for an authentic voice to emerge he might even have to wait longer than Vladimir and Estragon for Godot to appear in person. Moreover, he must confront an empty solitary present. He has to talk back on a tape which replaces the inner voice of the past and fills the void of the present. It is a mechanical device which peoples with words a realm of maddening silence. It reproduces or makes sonorous Krapp's purported past to which he has no natural access. He does not move away from his recorder, from his cubicle delineating the narrow margin of the present and the even slimmer prospect of the future. Within the confined horizon of his experience wherein the play unfolds, no other voice can enter. Krapp has no memories: he is alone and he cannot possibly sustain a meaningful monologue. At best he can interrupt with a few comments the mechanical device bereft of feeling or reflection which echoes the hollowness of an earlier and no less meaningless present. Krapp is alone with himself, with his nothingness which no other sound can enliven and to which no other voice can give resonance. The very act of listening to the voice of his past, as played by the tape, merely becomes a new variety of silence. Krapp does not truly recognize himself. The past, which he is powerless to recapture and consequently to understand, remains no less alien in a recording. Once the tape has run its course, Krapp is confronted with ultimate silence.

Krapp and practically all of Beckett's characters have barely any memories. Their voice in the present, into which so little is channeled from the past, is thereby weakened. In the first two plays, *Waiting for Godot* and *Endgame*, the characters have partners with whom they can converse. The scenes between Vladimir and Estragon are dialogues of a sort, which serve to make the pervasiveness of silence less acute. Moreover, this semblance of communication in the present can provide a substitute for memory. Didi and Gogo's dialogues can indeed be considered a mere masquerade of silence, for their replies form a succession rather than a sequence. More often than not, one speaker misunderstands the other, even in the rare instances when he has actually listened. A reply by Didi or Gogo is less an answer than an addition to his own previous remarks:

Estragon:	(chewing) I asked you a question.
Vladimir:	Ah.
Estragon:	Did you reply?
Vladimir:	How's the carrot?

Estragon:	It's a carrot.
Vladimir:	So much the better, so much the better.
	(Pause.)
	What was it you wanted to know?
Estragon:	I've forgotten. (Chews) That's what annoys me.
	(He looks at the carrot appreciatively, dangles it between finger and thumb.) I'll never forget this carrot. (He sucks the end of it meditatively.)
	Ah yes, now I remember.

To Estragon's statement: "I asked you a question" Vladimir answers "Ah." This indicates that even prior to the two statements just quoted Vladimir has replied to Estragon's question by silence. By saying "Ah!" he avoids taking the question into account and thus reinstates the silence. Later in the passage, Estragon's second and more direct return to the question: "Did you reply?" goes unanswered, thus renewing the silence, for Vladimir says: "How is the carrot?" and not "What was your question" or "I have answered it" or "The answer to your question is . . . " When finally Vladimir shows willingness to acknowledge the question, it is Estragon's turn to perpetuate the silence, for to Vladimir's: "What is it you wanted to know" he answers, "I have forgotten." He will remember only after he sucks the carrot or rather because he sucks the carrot. Each character's thought follows to a large extent its own set pattern, its inner rhythm and is scarcely modified by the words of the other speaker. The refusal or incapacity to acknowledge a question represents a way of reducing an interlocutor to silence, but the belated acknowledging of a question is a hollow form of self assertion and, as it were, a double interruption. Each character utters words that are pregnant with silence. As they fail to communicate there can only be one reason why they should speak one after the other rather than simultaneously: their lack of fluency, all the more so since Vladimir and Estragon do not pass with the same ease from pause to word and from word to pause. Thus silence and words are by no means opposites.

In *Waiting for Godot* scenic interplay bordering on slapstick plays an important part, i.e. taking off shoes, putting on repeatedly the partner's hat. This is to a certain extent a device to avoid boredom, to fill a void, to make a masquerade of silence. It can even be considered a grotesque version of what Pascal called "divertissement." Vladimir and Estragon do nothing and say nothing of consequence: they cover up silence by words. They play at fragmenting silence which otherwise would assume unbearable dimensions (for themselves as well as for the spectator). Time, represented by two days or evenings, is endless in a barren landscape reduced to a tree not strong enough to hold a man who might wish to hang himself. Vladimir and Estragon do their best to distract one another from the "metaphysical dimensions" of their existence, identifiable with this awe-inspiring and ineffable silence.

Vladimir and Estragon try to entertain each other. When one performs, the other as spectator is by his very function reduced to silence. With the appearance of Pozzo and Lucky both Vladimir and Estragon are turned into an audience. Lucky's speech—which in spite of its suggestive power gushes forth as if produced by a machine—forces the other characters to listen in silence. For Pozzo this is a repeat performance but for Vladimir and Estragon it represents a new show which they greet with amazement. In the second act, when Pozzo and Lucky return and when a reiteration of Lucky's speech is expected, the servant's verbal outburst is replaced by silence. He has become mute. This muteness, paralleling Pozzo's blindness, is part of the degenerating process of man's faculties which befalls many of Beckett's characters. But the physical element cannot be isolated. Even when Lucky could speak, he did not utter truly human words in an acceptable human voice. The artificially provoked and artificially sounding flow of words, whatever it might reveal about man's condition, does not really put a stop to silence. It can never be mistaken for Lucky's real voice or an expression of his true being. He has never communicated with anyone, but merely reacted to cruel stimulant and, for that reason, when he must perform, remains silent. The muteness which afflicts him in the second act does not imply any basic change.

Compared to *Waiting for Godot*, *Endgame* has a markedly slower rhythm. Everything reveals an ebbing out. As the sleeping pills or tranquilizers run out for Hamm and the biscuits for Nell and Nagg, the spectator or reader has every right to expect that even the fountain of words is bound to dry up:

> It will be the end and there I'll be, wondering what can have brought it on and wondering what can have . . . why it was so long coming. There I'll be, in the older shelter, alone against the silence and . . . the stillness. If I can hold my peace, and sit quiet, it will be all over with sound, and motion, all over and done with.

The play opens on a prolonged silence: Hamm, still asleep, barely possesses the energy to wake up; and the curtain falls after another prolonged stretch of silence: Hamm covers up his face expecting to go to sleep again, perhaps forever. A Racinian tragedy, *Bérénice*, stresses in a rather similar way the theme of silence. Antiachus, at the beginning of the play, wishes to express his love to *Bérénice*, and thereby interrupt five years of silence. At the end of the play each of the three characters will live in splendid isolation, reduced, in regard to the other two, to eternal, self-imposed silence. This situation increases the dramatic intensity of the single day during which the five acts of the tragedy unfold. Nonetheless, the function of silence stretching into eternity differs from that of *Endgame*. The Beckett play suggests circularity: it begins again and again as though to express an endless weakening, infinitely close, but not identical to death. In Racine, on the contrary, tragedy arises from the complete separation between silence and words, and the survival of the protagonists in an absolute solitude and exile.

As Hamm's passage from sleep to awakening is progressive, so his passage from silence to words is slow and punctuated. For most characters in *Endgame* silence makes up a larger portion of their role than do words. Nell and Nagg, each in a dustbin, are rarely heard. When they emerge for a few minutes from their confinement they do not burst forth into endless tirades. If they are allowed to emerge, it is not primarily to give them the opportunity to speak, but to listen to their son whose words must be heard. If Clov, his most steady listener, should depart, the threat to Hamm's performance would be too great for the play to continue. He tries hard to dominate his listeners, and his most energetic gesture is to blow a whistle. Since he remains motionless and blind at the center of the stage, words, effective and meaningful by convention, provide him with his only source of power. But to Hamm, whose speeches take up so much time that the play resembles a monologue, words come with considerable difficulty. He pauses at such great length between words, sentences or clauses, that words appear to be mere breaks in a continuum of silence. His lack of fluency reveals physical weakness, but it shows even more strongly that he must overcome an inner obstacle. The itinerary from perception or thought to word is a difficult one, for Beckett's characters are alienated not only from the world, but also from themselves. They have scarcely any grip on their own reality. Hamm struggles against silence, which he considers a mere nothingness. Fragmentary expression is better, he believes, than the threat of a soundless world. The more difficulty he experiences in overcoming silence, the more essential the audience becomes.

Hamm, as we have stated, needs his parents as listeners. One parent dies, and Clov threatens to leave. The long awaited child may or may not arrive from the outside world. If Clov were to depart no one could look anymore through the little window. Hamm, the sole survivor, would be reduced to the darkness of his inner world, without any visual or verbal communication from anyone or anywhere. Hamm's world would become at once silence and darkness, the world metaphorically represented by the room he occupies. Silence in *Endgame* reveals difficulty in communication, distance between self and self, as well as self and others, and by forcing man to affirm his being against the ebbing of life, it assumes an importance at least equal to words and dialogue. In the performance, silence should emerge everywhere making the spectator aware of its almost physical presence to the point that he would sense it as pertaining to no given character or moment, but as the very essence of human existence. Through the suggestive power of silence more than through the inadequate and painful formulation of words, the reader or spectator bridges the distance that normally separates him from the characters merely by saying to himself words which they fail to utter.

In *Waiting for Godot* and *Endgame*, the human voice can be compared to a modulated murmur resounding in a twilight setting. In *Happy Days*, under a strong stage sun, Winnie, alerted by a bell, delivers a shattering monologue. She solicits little response from her only partner, Willie. She attempts to sing a song of praise, but her clichés do not add up to a melodious sequence. Her long pauses, far from suggesting expectancy of someone else's reaction, afford her necessary breathing spells. Winnie, who lacks the ability to utter words and make gestures, is simultaneously woman approaching death. Buried to her waist in Act One and to her shoulder in Act Two, she barely comments on her gradual entombment. By a series of banal statements, she escapes from silence, which would more closely express her condition of solitude and paralysis. Winnie's words are analogous to the falsity that characterizes the scorching stage sun, deprived of life-giving qualities. The spectator is irritated by, and sees through, the piercing light, the shattering whistle and Winnie's shrill voice which expresses false consolations:

> Oh no doubt the time will come when before I can utter a word I must make sure you heard the one that went before and then no doubt come another time when I must learn to talk to myself a thing I could never bear to do such wilderness.

In spite of her efforts, Winnie cannot cast herself into the part of a listener. Since she does not by any means hold Willie's steady attention, she has no audience to give existence to her speeches. As Winnie is condemned to utter words which do not touch upon reality she is denied silence: life as a performance but not a reality must go on.

In *Krapp's Last Tape* the mechanical voice has become one of the protagonists, filling Krapp's long silences. In *Happy Days* a somewhat false theatrical voice delivers a monologue in order to play at being alive. In *Play* where projectors replace the natural twilight and the simulated sunshine of the former plays, the organic human voice has completely disappeared. The three characters standing in funeral urns with only their heads emerging belong to an Inferno which no longer suggests our everyday existence. They pronounce words at such speed that the spectator can only extract their meaning when the play is repeated verbatim. *Play* is filled with words. Not a second of silence. Each character's speech follows the other's without interval or pause as soon as the light falls on him. The man and the two women constituting the cast talk without taking a breath as long as the light persists. Speech, provoked from without not within, is a "toneless," "unorganic" mechanical voice the strength of which depends on the intensity of the light beam. The characters do not speak to express themselves or to reply to one another. Each one utters in a fragmentary way words dimly related to his very ordinary past. Each one embarks upon the reciting of an insignificant story, no more able to put it together than to give up his abortive attempts at narration. Although there is not a second of silence or relief for the audience, paradoxically the play is entirely made up of silence and suggests a part of our experience which lies beyond words. As human beings, the man and the two women have ceased to speak. They are forever silent, but in their consciousness shapeless memories, petty feelings, mitigated qualms have not subsided. They remain in a constant state of quiver or murmur. All three characters pray that no more words be extracted from them, that no more light shine on them; and they pray to forget, in order that a blackness and quietude external to themselves may parallel their inner condition. Whereas in *Waiting for Godot* words imply a masquerade of silence, in the Inferno of *Play* words become a painful unmasking of silence. The play consists of three monologues by three characters whose words never overlap, even though they give the impression of simultaneity. Most often, each of the two characters remaining silent and in darkness is unaware of the words and existence of the third speaker. Thus the listener has been eliminated and the relation of silence to speech fundamentally transformed. Words extracted with daggerlike brutality, no longer linked to identity and situations, become interchangeable. *Play* appears to illustrate Kierkegaard's statement: "The sure way of being mute is not to hold your tongue but to talk."

In Beckett's first two plays silence and the human voice, with its slow rhythms and weak modulations, echo the dim hope or aspiration left to mankind. Godot, as well as the mysterious child in *Endgame* or any other possible savior unlikely to arrive, are bound to remain silent. Later plays do not provide the slightest illusion that a divine or even human voice might be heard. Still greater absurdity characterizes those plays where despair, the sequel to hope, is banished. The mechanical or artificial voice reveals an estrangement from which there is no return, a world where even words and silence have severed their relations. *Bing*, one of the very last texts of Samuel Beckett, may be the ultimate form of reduction of all literature, including drama. A body which may be dead or alive, lips and legs glued or sewn together, replaces the almost anonymous characters of the previous play. Words no longer connected in any tangible way with the body tend persistently toward a whiteness, the poetic equivalent of silence, filling an arbitrarily delineated space which refers to nothing and beyond which lies nothing. Punctuated by the words *ping* in English, *bing* and *hop* in French, this text evokes by different devices a shift of attention or awareness from without, since all inner organic qualities have come infinitely close to complete silence and immobility. It might seem that after *Bing* Beckett will be almost silent as a writer, despite the permanent vitality of imagination he suggests in one of his own texts. Nonetheless, in his recent works Beckett has come as close as possible to his goal: the communication of the incommunicable.

From *Mundus Artium* 2 (Summer 1969): 82-90.

The New Beckett
Barbara Bray

Ulm, a small South German town on the Danube, otherwise distinguished by the highest cathedral tower in the world, saw on Friday the world première of the latest and one of the most remarkable works of Samuel Beckett: a play in one act called, simply, *Play*.

The story itself is superficially the most banal tale imaginable: a triangle—man, wife and mistress—which comes to grief. And not only is the basic situation itself abysmally conventional and trite, but Beckett does everything possible to render it ludicrous in its details.

The man, the first woman and the second woman (they have no names and their appearance, like their age, is "indifferent") are clearly but unremarkably middle-class, as are nearly all Beckett's characters (where did the idea ever come from that Vladimir and Estragon were tramps?). They have houses with gardens and morning-rooms, cars, the odd domestic, and "professional commitments." The locale is not, and need not be, defined, but English commuting country is perhaps evoked by a reference to "Ash" and "Snodland."

Astonishing

From the normal point of view all three characters are ordinary, mediocre, lamentable: In short, painfully familiar. The man, scooting breathlessly back and forth between the two women, is perhaps the worst of the bunch: all need and weakness and feeble, if amiable, duplicity. After various alarms and vain attempts at resolution, all three find it impossible to go on, and each one, ignorant of what has happened to the others, disappears.

This intentionally commonplace and in current terms despicable material Beckett transmutes into an astonishing, hilarious and moving experience. How?

The curtain rises on darkness, from which emerge, under spotlights faint at first, the heads only of the three characters, protruding from a large white urn apiece. The light, which varies in intensity, *extorts* speech from the trio, singly or in chorus. Although their urns actually touch, each thinks he or she is alone, and as they mumble together in what one of them describes as the "hellish half-light," or give their own version of the sorry story that took place in the world above, or wonder about and pity the supposed survivors, or ask themselves whether their present makes any more sense than their former state, the most ingenious and complex irony is extracted from this triple counterpoint.

The play ends on an infinite echo, with the recommencement of the man's story: "We were not long together —."

Few Concessions

Of all Beckett's works so far, this is the one which most openly approaches the everyday experience of any audience, yet at the same time makes the fewest concessions. The piece is very short, only 40 minutes in all. (Compare the fourth of Webern's Five Pieces for Orchestra, which lasts 19 seconds.) The language is of classical simplicity—a single touch gives tragic resonance to the ridiculous: "He went on and on. I could hear a mower." The range of physical action is confined within unheard-of limits.

Yet Beckett's inventiveness, formal mastery and poetic power are now so rich and intense that these three suffering heads conjure up not only three whole lives, but also awaken the reverberations that transform them from the trivial to the universal. Here are people in all their funny, disgraceful, pitiable fragility, and all the touchingness, in spite of everything, of their efforts to love one another, and endure.

Play is above all theatrical. It exists to be embodied. The extraordinary dramatic and emotional effects of concentrating all interest on three faces is such as only the boldest of originators could have foreseen.

The rest of the Ulm programme consists of two Beckett mimes, *Acts Without Words, I and II*. The first, already well known in England, shows a man absurdly deceived and buffeted by invisible forces who patiently and indefatigably goes on trying to do what is required of him, until finally he has been had once too often and we leave him in a somewhat dubious state of recalcitrance. The second mime has two characters, both engulfed in sacks. The first man, prodded into activity by an enormous impersonal goad, staggers forth and performs his daily routine in slow, hamfisted, anguished obedience. The second is a model citizen, all neatness, method and smiles, who goes through all his motions in half the time, but ends up in his sack just the same, with nothing to do but start all over again.

Acts Without Words, words without acts from both, truths but no statements.

The whole programme is directed by Deryk Mendel, the former Sadler's Wells dancer, who gave *Acts Without Words I* its first performance at the Royal Court in April, 1957. The designer is Michel Raffaelli. And the plays are acted by the enterprising young company who have recently taken over the Ulm Civic Theatre. They are nearly all disciples of Gustav Rodolf Sellner, an original German teacher and man of the theatre who now works in the Berlin Opera. From him stem the ideals of the young people at Ulm, which have resulted in some uproar among their fellow citizens.

Like Jean Vilar and Roger Planchon in France, they aim at "pure" theatre and at reintegrating the audience into active theatrical participation.

Working recently in Berlin, Deryk Mendel met a member of the company. They invited him to produce for them. He offered the two mimes. And Beckett, learning of this, made the German translation of *Play* available so that Mendel could make up his programme with a world première. His production is a suitably faithful one.

From *The Observer* (16 June 1963): 29.

Samuel Beckett: about him and about*
A. J. Leventhal

The year 1972 is the twentieth anniversary of the publication of Samuel Beckett's *En attendant Godot*, i.e., its appearance in print; the play was not to see the stage until a year later. I do not know whether the French literary hierarchy will have seized the occasion to mark the event. It is possible for they feel that they have at least half a share in this Prix Nobel. The French, curiously enough, use the same term to describe both the prize and the prizewinner. A Swedish critic,[1] who should have known better for he was writing under the aegis of the Nobel Foundation, goes further, giving Beckett a French mother. Be that as it may, it is gratifying that Trinity College in its tribute to its distinguished son has hit on a date that fits the occasion neatly.

There is a danger that the excessive gloss and over-rarefied commentary which has driven James Joyce's works into the cheerless atmosphere of pedantic analysis may also lie in store for Beckett. Already a volume[2] of some 400 pages has been issued by the University of California entitled *Samuel Beckett: his works and his critics* (*sic*), the coverage of which ends in 1968.

Hence arises the question, are we to have a repetition of what we might call in this industrial age the academic take-over? It has happened to Yeats. It has happened to Joyce. And before our very eyes it seems to be happening to Beckett. There is however more than a chance that the latter will be saved from the ultimate aridity of the pedantic approach. His salvation (if salvation like membership of the French Academy leads to immortality) lies in the fact that he is a dramatist. A great play may remain in obscurity for some time but given the right moment, the right producer and a receptive audience it will inevitably establish itself. Shakespeare has defied the efforts of generations of pedants to keep him off the stage. Better read than seen was their cry. In our day and indeed within the last year we have seen James Joyce hauled out of the pit of pedantry into which, through no fault of his own, he seemed to have fallen—hauled out into the fresh light of day as a dramatist. His *Exiles*, long discarded as Ibsen old hat and unplayable, has found new life, thanks to Harold Pinter who brought to the play what it had hitherto lacked: sympathetic production.

It is astonishing to find how many of the dramatists who formed the *avant-garde* of the so-called French Theatre of the Absurd hailed from lands other than France. Ionesco is Roumanian, Arrabal Spanish, Pinget Swiss, Adamov Russian Armenian, Ghelderode Belgian. These writers had in common a desire to break away from their norm, to turn their backs on the theatre of the boulevard. Ionesco, Adamov and Ghelderode prepared the way for yet another voice, that too coming from a foreigner using the Gallic tongue. A voice unobtrusively low but so tuned as to make itself eventually heard almost everywhere in the literate world. It reached out from the little Théâtre de Babylone where the production of *En attendant Godot* was made possible by a subsidy, the enthusiasm of Roger Blin the director, the modest financial demands made by the bare stage and the small number of characters required. This first constructive revolt against the well-made play stood its ground against the opposition of the mystified many. Slowly however interest gathered impetus, an impetus which increased by the penetration of the play outside France through the author's translation into English.

Waiting for Godot has not had the distinction achieved by O'Casey's *Silver Tassie* of having been refused by the Abbey Theatre—for the obvious reason that it was never submitted. I have of course heard of its recent production there with a star-studded cast. Credit must however go to Alan Simpson who braved theatrical establishment opinion by putting it on at his little Pike Theatre in Dublin before the play was seen in London. He had not waited for the derisive clamour to die down nor for the moment when Beckett would be crowned with laurel.

It may be that W. B. Yeats was correct in assuming that his play *Kathleen ní Houlihan* sent many Irish patriots to their deaths, but I doubt it. His audiences never battled among themselves as to the symbolic meaning of what was being enacted on the stage as did the French audiences at the Babylone and the Irish audiences at the Pike theatres. The much publicised rows at the Abbey were either religious as in the case of *The Countess Cathleen* or prudishly national in the cases of Synge's *Playboy* and O'Casey's *Plough and the Stars*.

Beckett, unlike many of the *avant garde* writers in France, is not *engagé*, is not committed to any political partisanship. He has no national axe to grind. Ivory towers, however, have become anachronistic and only survive in hippy colonies so that those of us who are not flower people are involved in the life around us. Beckett's involvement is in humanity and its pain, in its hope as in its anguish, in its comedy as in its seeming futility.

No doubt through the good offices of the author himself, the management of the Babylone Theatre offered me a whole row of seats for the opening night of *En attendant Godot*. As you may well imagine I was unable to collect a party in Dublin to take advantage of this magnanimous offer but without looking too rudely into the mouth of this wholesale gift-horse, I was aware that an audience for this hazardous undertaking had to be drummed up and that free tickets to sympathetic souls was an established convention for filling a house.

I did however manage to make a journey to Paris on my own and was present at a performance during the first week. The audience was a restive one, following a pattern since the first night. Interruptions had become a rule, so much so that reporters turned up to find material to provide comic relief for readers of their journal. After a long interchange between Pozzo, Vladimir and Estragon, the latter remarks: 'in the meantime nothing happens.' To which Pozzo rejoins: 'You find it tedious?' YES shouts a voice from the back of the stalls, 'Damned tedious!' But the author begs to agree. He makes Estragon reply: 'Somewhat.' And his companion adds: 'I've been better entertained.'

This ploy by an author anticipating audience reaction in the very text of the play may be less dramatic than the more direct response which Bernard Shaw is reported to have used. At a first night after many curtain calls, G.B.S. addressed a member of the audience who persisted in booing: 'My friend, I agree with you but what can you and I avail against so many?'

These thoughts or rather recollections have been prompted by my realisation that twenty years have passed since *En attendant Godot* was published and that with the passing of the years the play has gained more and more acclaim. There are those who, having grudgingly granted merit to its author, would have us believe that this is his sole work worthy of note, that he is a one-book man, or rather, a dramatist with one memorable play. Marcel Achard who, though he ought not to be regarded as spokesman for the French Academy of which he is a long-standing member, may well speak for the greater part of the audiences who crowd to his boulevard plays when he reacted to the news of the award to Beckett of the Nobel Prize by saying: 'Je suis fou de rage!' 'I am furious. The Swedish Academy has covered itself with ridicule. It has dishonoured itself by snobbism and a desire to be with it. I now understand why Sartre refused the Prize.'

It is gratifying to be able to balance this outburst by an equally emotional response from Madeleine Renaud the distinguished French actress: 'I am transported with joy and full of gratitude to the country that has paid homage to the exceptional merit of Beckett who has given me the greatest gift that could be offered to an actress, *O les beaux jours*.'

Sacha Guitry once declared that a man might be said to be cultured if he had heard of Toulouse-Lautrec before the film *Moulin Rouge*. How many, I wonder, were aware of the existence of Samuel Beckett before he was awarded the Nobel Prize and given the customary golden handshake by proxy.

I do not have to stress to this audience that Beckett's right to fame as a dramatist rests on more than one play. *O les beaux jours* was on the regular repertoire of the Odéon Theatre until 1968 in the month of May when, what is euphemistically referred to in France as *les événements* took place. What we, in the same vein, called the 'troubles.' The students and others who took possession of the theatre treated the wardrobe and props with lighthearted vandalism and one is not yet sure of the fate of the Giacommetti tree which was specially made for the Odéon revival of *Godot*. Malraux, at the time Minister for Culture and the Arts, closed the theatre and sacked the director Jean-Louis Barrault for fraternising with the students. Blinded with excess of French *clarté* Malraux threw the baby out with the dirty water.

Endgame is perhaps too cruel, too terrible a vision of existence to have general appeal. But, as I have suggested, with the right producer and actors this play could have even more effect than *Godot*. The Paris production of *Endgame* in English in 1964 with the two main roles in the hands of those two stalwart actors Magee and McGowran was a *succès fou*. Beginning with small audiences and little comment from the Press, the news passed round by word of mouth until the French joined the English to pack the Champs-Elysée Studio Theatre. The play could have run indefinitely to full houses but both actors and theatre had other engagements to fulfill. The conjuncture of intimate theatre, expert and sympathetic acting and above all the collaboration of the author himself in the production gave the play the momentum and significance that lay potentially in the text.

Authors themselves are not always the best judges but I know that Beckett himself prefers *Endgame* to all his other plays. It has horror and hopelessness, a classical inevitability. 'Everything is finished or nearly finished it must be nearly finished.' That is how the play begins. The action takes up the space between the 'nearly' and the 'finished.' We were warned in advance just as in *Godot* the opening announces: 'Nothing to be done.'

In the latter play we share the agony of waiting and are grateful to while away the time in audience sympathy with the games of the expectant couple. At the fall of the curtain we carry away with us ambivalent feelings of futility and hope. In *Endgame* we watch the moves on the chequer board that lead to the ultimate resignation of Hamm. Heartrending in his chair, looking in Blin's production like one of the painter Francis Bacon's Popes. 'Old endgame lost of old, play and lose and have done with losing.' It is really the end. Beckett the terminal observer has stood by his creature till the last. The audience like Hamm has had a surfeit of hate. The latter's hate of his parents, their hatred of him and add to this Clov's hatred of his master. Whatever love enters into the play is remembered love. All that is good is in the past. To-day is a bitter day, zero by the thermometer. Everything moves to the prescribed end—Hamm's death. But not before the latter, blind and paralysed though he be, has asserted himself as a masterful figure, as worthy of a tragic end as any of Shakespeare's

Late Theatrical Works

great characters. A bully, a sadist, an egoist as well as poet and romancer he is invested with a dignity that holds out some hope for mankind.

However I am not asked here, nor do I ask myself, to underline Beckett's distinction as a dramatist. The question does not even need to be begged. Let me rather move from this point to try and follow the later work and its (*sic*) direction. *The Unnamable* is almost garrulous in its paradoxical effort to express the inexpressible. This effort never slackens in the later work but the bulk and with it the almost hysterical flow of words has subsided. The quantum becomes more and more reduced with a corresponding rise in density.

I am reminded of Joseph Joubert (1754-1824) described as a *moraliste* by the French (for which I think there is no more exact equivalent in English than 'moral philosopher') who kept a Notebook but who never strictly speaking wrote a book. He writes that he was always 'tourmenté par la maudite ambition de mettre toujours tout un livre dans une page, toute une page dans une phrase et cette phrase dans un mot.' Beckett must surely have been tormented by this same ambition. Joubert calls it accursed and gives up. But Beckett, cursing too under his breath for all we know, doggedly pursues the same urge: to put a whole volume into a page, a whole page into a sentence and strip that sentence into a word.

In the last ten years his published work in fiction is contained in five titles: *Imagination morte imaginez, Assez, Bing, Sans* and *Le Dépeupleur*. On a bookshelf they make a poor show: five pamphlets each slimmer than the most modest collection of verse. The first four add up to a total of 29 pages, the fifth, bulky by comparison, has fifty pages. The same shrinking has occurred in the dramatic work. He wrote *Come and Go*, a dramaticule, for his publisher John Calder who had intended opening a cabaret in London, a project which never came to anything. It has only 121 words of dialogue. But in his latest contribution to the stage by a slashing retrenchment he managed to cut out all dialogue, a spectacle which is called *Breath* and which should be played to last not longer than thirty-five seconds.

It comes as a shock to find the ascription 'novel' given by the publishers to some of the above mentioned prose pieces. But on consideration there is no reason why any form of fiction should not be so called, particularly a form which is obviously a new one. *Tristram Shandy, Finnegans Wake* and, nearer home, *At swim two birds* [sic] conform to the dictionary definition of the novel only so far as size is concerned. In Trench's *Study of Words* (a bedside book of mine in student days which one could pick up on the Dublin quays for a few pence) one reads, 'A *novelist* or writer of new tales in the present day is very different from a "novelist" or upholder of new theories in politics and religion of two hundred years ago; yet the idea of newness is common to them both'; and therefore why not *a fortiori* applicable to Beckett, innovator if ever there was one?

The later prose works were first written and published in French and afterwards translated by the author into English. I shall have to assume that my listeners are familiar with one or other version and will not attempt to give more than a sketchy impression of the first four before treating more fully *Le Dépeupleur*, which has not yet been published in English and perhaps on this account less likely to be generally known.

The title *Imagination Dead Imagine* may well serve as an example of the density of the book itself. It might be understood as 1. Imagination dead, just imagine. 2. Imagination dead, to be sure but let your imagination work anyway. 3. Imagination dead, you imagine, you think but you are not sure.

The imperative, however, may well be addressed to the author himself and not to the reader. This is much more likely. In Alfred de Musset's time the Muse did all the ordering about: Poète prends ton luth et me donne un baiser. To-day the writer must whip up his own creative urge. This coincides with my second proposal as to the meaning of the title. It is to himself or to his imagination that the injunction is addressed, enjoining it though dead to function notwithstanding. The same holds for the other imperatives in the text. They are self directed.

The concentration of the composition emerges in the opening sentences. 'No trace anywhere of life, you say, pah, no difficulty there, imagination not dead yet, yes, dead, good, imagination dead imagine. Islands, water, azure, verdure, one glimpsed and vanished, endlessly, omit. Till all white in the whiteness of the rotunda. No way in, go in, measure.'

In the Beckett cosmos there is rarely any difficulty in accepting the notion of there being no traces of life. But having ordered himself to imagine, he responds by conjuring up various scenes, islands etc., which are glimpsed for a moment and disappear. 'Endlessly', says the text, which suggests that these images come and go in infinite alternation. 'Omit' seems to imply that this recurrent series of vanishing vision will not be treated here. 'Till all white in the whiteness the rotunda.' That is, until everything has become white within and without the whiteness of a rotunda into which there is no entrance but which we will enter nevertheless and take measurements. The narrator has taken to himself the power of the novelist entering into the mind of his characters.

The rotunda is an eighteen-inch high circular wall topped by an eighteen-inch high dome, so that the height of the structure is three feet. The diameter of the circle formed by the wall is also three feet. On the white ground are two white bodies. The rotunda is solid. 'Rap' says the text, 'solid throughout, a ring as in the imagination of ring of bone.' An echo, perhaps, of 'in me the vault bone-white' from *How It Is*. The scene must be the human skull. We are not sure at first whether the two white bodies whose positions are meticulously and mathematically described are alive. 'Hold a mirror to their lips, it mists.' At the very least they must not be dead. Pale blue eyes suddenly open wide.

Late Theatrical Works

The text ends without any clear conclusion. 'Leave them there, sweating and icy, there is better elsewhere.' But immediately there follows the characteristic contradiction with which *The Unnamable* made us so familiar. 'No, life ends and no, there is nothing elsewhere.'

Thus briefly, if brevity has any meaning in summarising prose of such density, is the stark portrayal of this almost inanimate couple in the whiteness of the sepulchral dome which is their abode with its variations of heat and cold. Are they spelling out their torment within the human skull? Is life just barely being lived within the imagination? An imagination not yet dead. It is perhaps left to us to imagine.

Enough, the second of these texts, is longer but its length does not go beyond seven pages. Unlike the first, however, it has an immediately recognizable story, conforming to this extent to the novel canon. Actually in style and feeling *Enough* is a throwback. Hence though written after *Imagination* it precedes it in published texts. The opening paragraph is striking:

> All that goes before forget. Too much at a time is too much. That gives the pen time to note. I don't see it but I hear it there behind me. Such is the silence. When the pen stops I go on. Sometimes it refuses. When it refuses I go on. Too much silence is too much. Or it's my voice too weak at times. The one that comes out of me. So much for the art and craft.

It reads like a preface. Are we being taken into the workshop? Start from scratch and forget the old habit of plunging into composition. The pen refusing, the writer going on nevertheless. You will remember the hysterical cry with which *The Unnamable* ends: 'You must go on, I can't go on, I'll go on.' After all these years we are brought back to the irrepressible voice of the narrator in the third volume of the trilogy. Despite the first sentence, 'All that goes before forget', the memory still persists. 'Je n´ai pas de voix et je dois parler c´est tout ce que je sais.' His voice, he says, is too weak at times. Is this an apology for the too much silence, the too great gaps in creation, despite the urge to speak?

The end of the paragraph dismisses what has gone before in the manner of Hamm in *Fin de partie* commenting on one of his own creative flights. 'So much', he says, 'for the art and craft.' Craftily, he would have us believe that he lays no store by the ways and means through which he attains his effects. In the 'Duthuit Dialogues'[3] Beckett has in his own name already declared that 'to be an artist is to fail as no other dare fail, that failure is his world and the shrink from it desertion, art and craft, good housekeeping, living.' Unexpectedly, Jean Cocteau said much the same thing much earlier but without the same emphasis when he urged the artist to aim well in order to miss the target. We are not deceived; Beckett the supreme craftsman takes a long aim, studies the mechanisms of the engine he employs and it is no machine gun spraying wild shots over a wide area in the hope of making a chance hit. He is seriously prepared, as Cocteau never was, to run the risk of glorious failure, in the certainty that failure was not only inevitable but desirable.

The narrative of *Enough* deals with the devotion of a woman from the age of six to a much older man. She is old herself when she tells her story for it is she who is the narrator. This is the first time that Beckett uses a woman for this purpose, though Winnie in *Happy Days* might be considered to take precedence because, play though this be, Winnie's monologue might entitle her to be accepted as the first Beckett woman creation speaking for herself. Celia in *Murphy*, Mrs. Rooney in *All That Fall*, Nell in *Endgame*, Moll in *Malone Dies* are all clearly defined if relatively minor characters but are presented in the third person.

The story centres round the older man's infirmity and her own disgrace. How she disgraced herself is not told but her dismissal seems to hold in itself the elements of her ignominy. He has asked her to leave him. She does as he commands and never looks back. They had walked together, gloved hand in gloved hand for a distance of 7,000 miles at the rate of three miles a day. This was to her, her life. Sometimes he stopped to say something and said nothing. Behaving true to form as a Beckett character she makes a full list of the series of possibilities of stopping, talking immediately or otherwise and moving on immediately or otherwise. Having earlier placed the scene of her disgrace at the crest of a hill, she now contradicts herself. It was on a plain with a great calm over everything. 'This notion of calm comes from him,' she remarks. She details their sleeping arrangements. Wedged together, bent at knees and hips, she on the inside, both facing the same direction. There has been some loveplay but very little as 'he murmured of things that for him were no more and for me could not have been.' But in retrospect she has had a life. She has lived were it ever so painfully. Her narrative ends with these lines: 'Now I'll wipe out everything but the flowers. No more rain. No more mounds. Nothing but the two of us dragging through the flowers. Enough my old breasts feel his old hand.'

Enough. Little perhaps but more than has been vouchsafed to other Beckett creatures.

The couple in *Imagination Dead Imagine* are enclosed in a white dome. In *Enough* the woman and her companion range more or less freely in open spaces. In *Ping* we return to an enclosed space, a box six feet by three feet by three feet, standing on its end. It is written in one unbroken paragraph. There are full stops but no commas. The density of the composition can be judged by noticing that there are practically no other parts of speech than nouns, adjectives and participles. This is how *Ping* begins:

Late Theatrical Works

> All known all white bare white body fixed one yard legs joined like sewn. Light heat white floor one square yard never seen. White walls one yard by two white ceiling one square never seen. Bare white body fixed only the eyes only just.

Within the box is a figure, possible a male, who stands rigid with head high, arms hanging by his sides, palms front, legs rigid together heels and toes likewise 'joined like sewn,' feet at a right angle. All is hot and white. But the eyes are blue, pale blue. There is silence. Occasional traces, grey blurs. Whether in the box or in the mind of the occupant is not clear. Barely heard murmurs recur. As do again and again the same phrases. We rarely meet a new image. However we are struck by one phrase towards the end which is repeated in the final sentence . . . 'eyes black and white half-closed long lashes imploring.'

Long lashes imploring, the words seem to have fallen out of what used to be called a novelette. Can it mean that memory is still working the mind of the rigid boxed figure and that in the circumstances it ironically conjures up this futility out of a romantic past?

Beckett likes to work with couples. Winnie, self-sufficient though she be has her man behind the mound in *Happy Days*. The woman has her companion in *Enough* whilst *Imagination dead* houses two bodies. This may explain the introduction of the startling emotive image and its repetition in the concluding sentence:

> Head haught eyes white fixed front old ping last murmur one second perhaps not alone eye unlustrous black and white half closed long lashes imploring ping silence ping over.

Perhaps with this last murmur with head haught (the archaic word suggests the dignity of the 'old style' so often referred to by Winnie) he is for one second not alone, rejecting this idle obviously too late appeal.

The term 'ping' as well as being the title is met with frequently in the text. Its meaning and purpose presents some difficulty. It translates two words in the French version, 'bing' and 'hop.' I can't find 'bing' in either Petit Robert or Harrap and assume it has the same onomatopoeic quality as 'ping.' 'Hop,' however, is a common French interjection, a stimulus for a sudden movement. 'Allez, hop!' you might say to a dog or child asking one or the other to jump. 'Ping' brings to mind a particular kind of sound, the ring of crystal, the plucking of a violin string and the like. That it cannot be so understood in this instance is clear. That it serves to translate both 'bing' and 'hop' points to a close connection between the two. The suggestion of instant movement in 'hop', as it appears in the French text, would indicate a sudden shift in the body whilst 'bing' preserving the same notion of suddenness would refer to a gleam of consciousness. The one implying physical motion and the other memory or thought such as the brief image of the imploring eyes hinting (for a second) that he was not always alone. The author finding it perhaps difficult to hit on suitable English notations for this dichotomy uses 'ping' to cover both conditions.

Do not expect me to be very helpful with *Lessness* which first saw the light in French as *Sans*. An early publisher's advertisement announced the title as *Without*. It must have appeared inevitable as a translation. After all *Assez* became *Enough* in English. But that it was an error soon becomes evident. 'Enough' could only mean 'enough' but 'without' could also mean 'outside,' which is by no means implicit in the French preposition.

Lessness, as I have indicated, is his next published work and, to quote the jacket, has to do with 'the collapse of some such refuge as that last attempted in *Ping* and with the ensuing situation of the refugee.' It is composed of six statement groups each containing ten sentences. Sixty sentences in all. These are first given in a certain order and paragraph structure. The whole consists, therefore, of 120 sentences arranged and re-arranged in 24 paragraphs.

Each statement group is formally differentiated and the ten sentences composing it 'signed' by certain elements common to them all.

It does not often occur that the description on the dust jacket of a book is indispensable for the understanding of its content. One does not have to be a bibliophile or a collector of mint copies to hold on jealously to this one. I have quoted the first sentence above. It proceeds: 'Ruin, exposure, wilderness, mindlessness, past and future denied and affirmed, are the categories, formally distinguishable, through which the writing winds, first in one disorder then in another.'

Taking these six categories in their order we have six groups:

1.	Ruin—Collapse of refuge	Signature	'true refuge'
2.	Exposure—Outer world	"	'earth . . . sky'
3.	Wilderness—Body exposed	"	'little body'
4.	Mindlessness—Refuge forgotten	"	'all gone from mind'
5.	Past and future denied	"	'never'
6.	Past and future affirmed	"	future tense.

Beckett bases his conception of the human condition on six propositions. Three state the given situation: *(a)* A décor of endless ash grey sand without relief, *(b)* in which are found the scattered ruins of a true refuge (the hollow cube of *Ping*), *(c)* in the midst of which there stands alone a grey little body with a beating heart. The second three propositions express that which is involved in the situation already laid down. *(d)* The being, l'*être*, calm among the ruins of the forgotten refuge, in its sheer whiteness of which nothing remains in his memory. *(e)* Time is only a figment—a *chimère*—it is denied. *(f)* Nevertheless there will be a tomorrow. Time is affirmed.

It is through thoughts like these that the writing winds but the disorder is formal. I shall not attempt to give you any further idea of the complicated scheme that builds up this structure, composed of a fixed group of words which, like motifs in a musical composition, repeat and chase each other. The pleasure which the reader derives is that of the harmonious measure of a poem whose meaning at the first reading is vague. Once the key to this melodic construction is mastered the richness of its fabric becomes evident. For the little body, erect, time does not function. To live, or having died, to live again is to cease to exist. It means leaving the calm whiteness of the refuge where memory is absent, abandoning the silent immobility of the scattered ruins and the timeless grey air. Living he will curse God again as in the blessed days with face turned to the open sky and passing deluge. The little body by his fall has been chased out of the Eden of ineffable emptiness. Deprived of everything he was rich in his 'lessness.' Now he has lost his true refuge. He may find it again only to lose it once more and so on to infinity.

The first sentence in *Lessness* reads, 'Ruins true refuge long last towards which so many false time out of mind.' The human being has lost himself time out of mind along false paths in pursuit of a calm haven. His greatest happiness comes with the greatest destitution.

I shall conclude with an examination of the latest Beckett publication. Though last to appear in print it would be wrong to consider it chronologically so. *Le dépeupleur* occupied its creator for some considerable time but he abandoned the work in May 1966 because of its intractable complexities. The intricacies of this composition are responsible for the starkness of *Bing* to which he then turned. This reaction is maintained with *Sans* which followed. It was only after these two were completed that he returned to the book that had been teasing him so long. He satisfied himself that most of what he had written could stand and added a final paragraph that tied it up finally.

Its fifty-five pages are written in the taut prose to which we have become accustomed but with less ellipsis than that found in the work already discussed. English readers will have to wait for the translation which is announced for publication next spring. However I have the author's permission to use the MSS of his English version for quotation.

The title stems from a line in a poem by Lamartine in 'L'isolement' which is included in his first *Méditation poétique* which students of French literature will recognize immediately:

> Un seul être vous manque et tout est dépeuplé.

It may interest the curious to learn that this familiar line was taken by Lamartine without a by-your-leave from a poem by an eighteenth-century writer, Nicolas Germain Léonard. The only difference is that Lamartine puts 'vous' where Léonard has 'me.' Here is the beginning of *Le Dépeupleur*:

> Abode where lost bodies roam each searching for its lost one. Vast enough for search to be in vain. Narrow enough for flight to be in vain. Inside a flattened cylinder fifty metres round and eighteen high for the sake of harmony. The light. Its dimness. Its yellowness. Its omnipresence as though every separate square centimetre were agleam of the *same* eighty thousand of total surface. Its restlessness at long intervals suddenly stilled like panting at the last. Then all go dead still. It is perhaps the end of their abode. A few seconds and all begins again. Consequences of this light for the searching eye. Consequences for the eye which having ceased to search is fastened to the ground or raised to the distant ceiling where none can be. The temperature. It oscillates with more measured beat between hot and cold. It passes from one extreme to the other in about four seconds. It too has its moments of stillness more or less hot or cold. They coincide with those of the light. Then all go dead still. It is perhaps the end of all. A few seconds and all begins again. Consequences of this climate for the skin. It shrivels. The bodies brush together with a rustle of dry leaves. The mucus membrane itself is affected. A kiss makes an indescribable sound. Those with stomach still to copulate strive in vain. But they will not give in.

Inside this cylinder some 200 naked bodies swarm creep and climb. They have at their disposal about fifteen ladders with which they can reach invisible niches hollowed out in the wall. These niches are sometimes linked by tunnels that have no exit. The only noise that one can hear is the movement of the ladders and the thud of colliding bodies. Earlier, as quoted to you, the bodies brush against each other with the rustle of dry leaves. 'Like dry leaves.' We are back to *Waiting for Godot* and the lovely lyrical exchange between the two tramps that begins with 'All the dead voices.' They make a noise like wings/Like leaves/Like sand/Like leaves. They whisper/They rustle/They murmur/They make a noise like feathers/Like leaves/Like ashes/Like leaves. And ends in an agonised cry from Vladimir: 'Say anything at all.' But in this new imagined world there is no speech not even a groan.

The preoccupation of the inhabitants of this cylindrical sojourn is clarified by the opening sentence. 'Abode where lost bodies roam seeking for the lost one.' The original French has an important variation: 'Séjour ou des corps vont cherchant chacun son dépeupleur.' You will notice that the English leaves out the last word offering instead 'seeking for the lost one.' 'Depopulator' is not only impossible but misleading. It suggests a demotic expert concerned with excessive population growth. Obviously the difficulty in finding a literary parallel to the Lamartine line made the exclusion inevitable. And so the title had likewise to change. It will appear as *The Lost Ones*. A pity, perhaps, because with it goes the mystery and the equivocal so frequently associated with Beckett. The German translator was able to solve the problem. He kept both the noun and its significance with 'Der Verwaiser' which derives from Waise an orphan. Goldsmith's *Deserted village* is known as Das verwaiste Dorf.

A French critic[4] gave 'dépeupleur' an unwarranted reality. She points out correctly that the word appears only once and in the very first sentence and assumes that its disappearance so rapidly from the text is a pointer to the futility of the search on which the denizens of the cylinder are about to embark. For her the ambiguous dépeupleur should be put alongside such figures as Knott in *Watt* who makes only a fleeting appearance or Godot who doesn't appear at all. Dépeupleur is not another Beckett character, fleeting or otherwise. Neither myth nor mystery but a poet's conception of the act of deprivation that leaves a void in the deprived one. For this Beckett invented a noun neologism based on Lamartine's past participle 'dépeuplé'.

You will have gathered that there is no question here of the inaction that characterized *Waiting for Godot*. The searching implies movement and the gyrations involved are described with a meticulous accuracy. The individuals rotate in the various concentric zones with an urgency and order entirely incompatible with the futility of their task. The 'little people' as they are called (and we can cut out any leprechaun association) are divided into various categories. The main group, the searchers, occupy the centre of the cylinder, the arena. They come and go in a crowd without stopping. Sometimes a chance encounter occasions a casual meaningless coupling. The climate has given a parchment quality to their skin and has dried up their mucous membranes.

Fewer in number than the searchers are the climbers who move along the walls like the character in Beckett's own *Film*. It is not clear whether they are privileged or prisoners of the system. They are allowed access for a limited period to the niches in the walls, the only place where one can stretch one's body full length. Some of the climbers never get to the top and remain halfway up the ladder. Theirs is a movement of ascent within the cylinder contrasting with the horizontal direction of the searchers. There are in addition two circular currents in an opposite direction, one formed by ladder-bearers who have the right to choose their own niches and the other formed by those who aspire to join the climbers and who scrutinize them in the hope of finding the being they seek. Strict rules govern the various manoeuvres in these peripheral zones and the passages from the arena to one of the circles.

There are two other categories in this hallucinating not-so-merry-go-round; the sedentary and the vanquished. The sedentary have given up the hunt and forsaken the ladders but unlike Yeats who wrote

> Now that my ladder's gone,
> I must lie down where all the ladders start,
> In the foul rag-and-bone shop of the heart

they are forbidden to lie down in this exiguous cylinder. They, however, with feverish eyes continue to scrutinize the passers-by. It is left to the vanquished, who are few in number, to have completely abandoned the whole exercise. They either stand close to the wall or remain seated, eyes downcast or closed, but still liable suddenly to resume climbing or crawling in the tunnels, now, however, without purpose in quest of nothing.

From among these non-seekers seated by the wall in the attitude which the author writes 'drew from Dante one of his rare pale smiles' there emerges one figure who might be said to be individualised. Her attitude explains the Dante smile for it is the foetal position which has haunted Beckett's work since *More Pricks Than Kicks*. With this difference. The Belacqua stance has been given to a woman; her head between her knees and her red hair falling to her feet. In her immobility she serves as the fixed northern point of the cylinder, a guide to the circumambient searchers.

It is easy to image this extraordinary process continuing infinitely in the same way as the author's *Play* in which the three characters in the urns repeat the piece just finished and begin a third performance as the curtain falls. In the concluding paragraph which is the final touch given by the artist after a long absence from his canvas, the situation is such that a last body of all by feeble fits and starts is searching still. There is nothing at first to distinguish him from the others dead still where they stand. But there is the persistent twofold vibration which draws the ironic remark that 'all is not yet quite for the best.' That is to say that the blessed calm and immobility of the haven sought in *Lessness* has not yet been achieved.

'And,' I quote, 'sure enough there he stirs this last of all if a man and slowly draws himself up and sometime later opens his burnt eyes.' He then threads his way to the north of the cylinder where he approaches 'that first among the vanquished so often taken for a guide. On his knees he parts the heavy hair and raises the unresisting head. Once devoured the face thus laid bare the eyes at a touch of the thumbs open without demur. In those calm wastes he lets his wander till they are the first to close and the head relinquished falls back into its place. He himself after a pause impossible to time finds at last his place and pose whereupon dark descends and at the same time the temperature comes to rest not far from freezing point. Hushed in the same breath the faint stridulence mentioned above whence suddenly such silence as to drown all the faint breathings put together. So much roughly speaking for the last state of the cylinder and of this little people of searchers one first of whom if a man in some unthinkable past for the first time bowed his head if this notion is maintained'.

This then is the end of the nightmare. The individual who may pass for a man has possibly made his last gesture. He seems to welcome the dark, the silence and the cold as a deliverance. But like a schizophrenic he has returned to a fixed pose and who is to say that this is not a return to the opening situation? Restlessness followed by deadly stillness. Is it really the end of their abode? Will it all begin again in a few seconds? Have we here an eternity of recapitulation as in *Play*? A close examination of the text shows that this is indeed the end. The 'little people' unable themselves to imagine their last state will come to it unwittingly. Light and climate will be changed but the former may be imagined as extinguished and the latter near freezing point. This statement is posited in the early part of *The Lost Ones* and the concluding paragraph quoted above underlines the ultimate nature of the situation. It is at last the final state since 'the dark descends and at the same time the temperature comes to rest not far from freezing point.'

It is drama, Greek in its inexorability. Beckett's dramatic genius so long repressed finds an outlet here, in a situation and décor that to my mind cries out for visual treatment in a near silent film. Though the greater part was written before the bleak whiteness and immobility of *Bing* and *Sans* its publication after these works suggests that its author's dramatic urge has not been silenced and that the Beckett voice, whether uncontrollable in its insistence or tempered to shorn texts, is still powerful enough to echo through the desert of human anguish.

*A lecture delivered on 22 February 1972 in Trinity College on the occasion of the exhibition of Beckett's works, MSS etc. in Library of Trinity College.

From *Hermathena* 114 (Winter 1972): 5-22.

---

[1] Dr. Kjell Strömberg in 'La "petite histoire" de l'attribution du Prix Nobel à Samuel Beckett,' p. 6, which introduces an edition of *Malone meurt* and *O les beaux jours* in La collection des Prix Nobel de Littérature éditée sous le patronage de l'Académie Suédoise.

[2] *An Essay in Bibliography* by Ramond Federman and John Fletcher (Berkeley/Los Angeles/London, 1970).

[3] *Proust and three dialogues with Georges Duthuit* (sic) (London, Calder and Boyers).

[4] Jacqueline Piatier, *Le Monde*, 12 February, 1971.

On the Route of a Walking Shadow: Samuel Beckett's *Come and Go*

Rosangela Barone

> "When shall we three meet again?"
> (W. Shakespeare, Macbeth, I, 1,i).
>
> ****
>
> "So your sweet hue, which methinks
> still doth stand, hath motion, and
> mine eye may be deceived:
> > For fear of which, hear this, thou age unbred:
> > Ere you were born was
> > beauty's summer dead."
> (W. Shakespeare, Sonnet CIV, 11-14).

The fascination of the obvious is a constant feature of Samuel Beckett's language, starting from the titles of his plays (sophisticated puns seem to be preferred for the titles of his narrative pieces).

The title of the microdrama *Come and Go* (1965)[1] belongs to the category where preference is given to the verb—that grammatical form signifying action (either accomplishing, being accomplished, or habitually accomplished). *Come and Go* adds one more ring to the verbal chain started with *Waiting for Godot* and followed by *All That Fall* and *Cascando* —with the possible annexion of *Act Without Words I*, *Act Without Words II*, *Play*, and *Film*, all capable of being interpreted either as verbs or as nouns.

The subtitle of *Come and Go*, "A Dramaticule", is a curious *contaminatio* of English and French used as a warning of the reduction and farcification of the "problem play" announced in the dialectical title. The playwright so used to reducing everything to the bone this time signals—with a wink and a slight nudge under the belt—that here everything will be reduced to the ultimate bone (*coccige* in the anatomical jargon; dramati(s)-cul(e) in the Beckettian jargon).

The title refers to the dynamic relationship of the *dramatis personae* (three women named, respectively, FLO, VI and RUE) and their not-well defined seat (bench/log). Each of the three has a return trip from the same station, thus outlined in the stage direction:

> SEAT
>
> *Narrow benchlike seat, without back, just long enough to accommodate three figures almost touching. As little as possible. It should not be clear what they are sitting on. (C&G. 21)*

The (triple) route from/to the "narrow benchlike seat" provides the keynote of Beckett's art, which shows the constant tension between the "nothing to be expressed" and the "obligation to express," i.e., the note of "circularity"/"condemnation" to being locked in a circle—the Bench in a trial, with its Kafkaian connotations.[2]

Come and Go is a sample of artistic *bricolage*, as fascinating as the one offered by James Joyce, Beckett's master and *quondam* companion. It proposes the formula of polarity/identity of Being/Not Being in a new combination, paradoxically the more original because of its use of obvious everyday language and overused literary *clichés*.

The "Dramaticule" is made of 23 cues spaced by 11 silences (+ 1 at the opening and 1 at the end of the play, mirroring each other). The opening line of Shakespeare's *Macbeth*, spoken by one of the Weird Sisters—

> Where shall we three meet again?—

is flashed backwards in time and becomes

> When did we three last meet? (*C&G*, 19)

uttered by one of the Beckettian trio, whose age is "undefined" (*C&G*, 19). The trio—not yet a "ghost trio"[3]—retain, in anthropomorphic substance, certain traits of Shakespeare's Weird Sisters,

> So withered and so tired in their attire. (*M*, I, iii, 40)

Their age is undefined, their bodily shapes are hidden by austere long clothes, their faces are shadowed by large hats, their pace is slow and silent, in their static posture they look like fowls perched on a branch—the stage direction specifies:

> VOICES
> *As low as compatible with audibility. Colourless except for three "ohs" and two lines following.*
> OHS
> *Three very different sounds.*
> COSTUME
> *Full-length coats, buttoned high, dull violet (RU), dull red (VI), dull yellow (FLO). Drab nondescript hats with enough brim to shade faces. Apart from colour differentiation three figures as alike as possible. Light shoes with rubber soles. Hands made up to be as visible as possible. No rings apparent.*
> . . .

> ... *Exits and entrances slow, without sound of feet.*[4] (*C&G*, 21-22)

Yet, when compared with the nameless witches in *Macbeth* (nameless, and serialised as Witch I, Witch II, Witch III), the three arcane protagonists of *Come and Go* are endowed with names, however *démodés* and eroded to a monosyllabic state; FLO-(rence), VI(olet), RU(by); they have a distinctive feminine grace; their attire, though uniformly cut, differs in colour; the "oh" plus brief utterance that follows it is pronounced differently by each of them. What is more relevant, the Macbethian trio are removed from the background and become the exclusive protagonists of the microplay. The three Weird Sisters holding the secret of "Fair is foul and foul is fair" (*M*, I, i, 11) in which Macbeth is trapped, lose their diabolic features when they are made the exclusive protagonists on the stage, though still retaining the enigmatic nimbus of the Shakespearean group. In Beckett's trio fearsome black magic seems to melt in "th' milk of human kindness" (*M*, I, v, 17);[5] the language of the Sabbath—both verbal and gestural—becomes hieratic, it rarefies while proceeding in counterpoint between the two poles of word/stasis and silence/kinesis;[6] the flashing lights of the tempest in the Scottish tragedy are here substituted with stable and soft lighting.

> LIGHTING
> *Soft, from above and concentrated on playing area. Rest of stage as dark as possible.* (*C&G*, 21).

The *ouverture* is structured as follows —

> *Sitting centre side by side stage right to left FLO, VI and RU. Very erect, facing front, hands clasped in laps. Silence.*
> VI: When did we three last meet?
> RU: Let us not speak.
> *Silence.* (*C&G*, 19)

Then follows the come-and-go of the three women in turn, from light to dark, according to the stage directions —

> EXITS
> *The figures are not seen to go off stage. They should disappear a few steps from lit area. If dark not sufficient to allow this, recourse should be had to screens or drapes as little visible as possible. Exits and entrances slow without sound of feet.* (*C&G*, 22)

The *locutory-gestural* movement linked with the exit-enter events follows a ternary scheme, in a precise design of correspondences, i.e., repetition with variation (amplifying the theme), as shown in the following re-proposition of the text, where the microsequences related to each protagonist are presented beside those of the other two for clarity's sake —

Exit VI right.	*Exit FLO left.*	*Exit RU right.*
Silence.	*Silence.*	*Silence.*
FLO: Ru	RU: Vi.	VI: Flo
RU: Yes.	VI: Yes.	FLO:
Yes.		
FLO: What do you think of VI?	RU: How do you find Flo?	VI: How do you think Ru is looking?
RU: I see little change.	FLO: She seems much the same.	FLO: One sees little in this light
(*FLO moves to centre seat, whispers in RU's ear. Appalled.*)	(*RU moves to centre seat, whispers in VI's ear. Appalled.*)	(*VI moves to center seat, wispers in FLO's ear. Appalled.*)
Oh! (*They look at each other. FLO puts her finger to her lips.*) Does she not realize?	Oh! (*They look at each other. RU puts her finger to her lips.*) Has she not been told?	Oh! (*They look at each. VI puts her finger to her lips.*) Does she not know?
FLO: God grant not.	RU: God forbid.	VI: Please God not.
Enter VI, FLO and Ru turn back front. Resume pose. VI sits right	*Enter FLO, RU and VI turn back front. Resume pose. FLO sits left.*	*Enter RU, VI and FLO turn back front. Resume pose. RU sits right.*
Silence.	*Silence.*	*Silence.*
FLO: Just sit together as we used to.in the playground way at Miss Wade's.	RU: Holding hands. that	VI: May we not speak of the old days? (*Silence.*) Shall we hold hands in the old way?[7]
RU: On the log. *Silence.*	FLO: Dreaming of love. *Silence.*	

The *finale*, prepared by VI's proposal, brings the situation back to the *ouverture*, in a circular movement —

> *After a moment, they join hands as follows: VI's right hand with RU's right hand, VI's arms being above RU's left arm and FLO's right arm. The three pairs of clasped hands rest on the three laps. Silence.*
> FLO: I can feel the rings. *Silence.*
> CURTAIN[8] *(C&G 20)*

The harmonic figurative group (the recomposed trio of the women folding each other's hands and making a ring) shifts the observer's visual memory from "foul" to "fair", with a dissolving effect on the image of "the Weird Sisters, hand in hand", who "thus go about and about" (*M*, IV, 32, 34) and perform their "antic round" (*M*, IV, 1, 139) in obedience to Hecate's order —

> And now about the cauldron sing
> Like elves and fairies in a ring
> Enchanting all that you put in. (*M*, IV, 1.41-42)

This portrait gradually makes room for another group portrait, of the opposite pole: the mind's eye recollects the three Graces dancing hand-in-hand at Venus' birth from the sea, in the famous *Spring* painting by Botticelli.[9]

In Beckett's theatrical *pièce,* perceivable in terms of figuration/transfiguration, one reality as soon as defined evokes the one at the opposite pole, in the same way as the specific language of drama reveals its adaptability in other codes (painting, music, dance). In *Come and Go* the three dark weavers of Macbeth's *fatum* meet again, and their shapes finally merge into those of the *Gratice Decentes*, the dispensers of beauty and joy of living, through a metamorphosis (epiphany) which reveals the ambiguities of man's life in its most dramatic light.

The game of affinities, too, must be suspended immediately after it has been opened; the three transfigured women of *Come and Go* (three sisters, as in Tcheckov's play, somehow evoked by the atmosphere of the Beckett play) are, in fact, in a state of *apparent* "calm" — the pairs of *"clasped* hands" which *"rest* on the three laps;" the austere long coats whose colours recall autumn, as in Shakespeare's Sonnet CIV —

> Three Beauteous Springs to yellow autumn turn'd.[10]

The colours chosen for FLO, VI, and RU's coats are quite unusual presences on Beckett's *palette*: yellow, red, and violet — respectively, the first, middle, and last of the so-called "primary colours of the spectrum." However, a dark shade of colour is used in each case — an opaque *patina* darkening the luminous colours of spring, counterpointed, under the clothes, by the drying lymph of life. A transfiguration in reverse is perceptible: the traces of "fair" merge obscurely into "foul" again (as in Hieronimus Bosch's *Garden of Delights*). FLO, VI, and RU, wrapped in shroud-like clothes, shapeless as well as of unidentifiable age, send the mind's eye back to the Weird Sisters and to Macbeth's meditation before death —

> Fallen into the sere, the yellow leaf. (*M*, V, iii, 23),

the victim of the enigma voiced by the witches

> That look not like th'inhabitants o' th' earth,
> And yet are on't. (*M*, 1, iii, 41-42)

An intriguing net of homophonies covers the women's names: In French, it highlights the dynamic dimension of life and its bitter flavour; in English, it recalls the (bitter) ebb-and-flow of Birth and Death, each time new but substantially one and the same thing —

	FRENCH	ENGLISH
VI	VIE (*n.* life)	VIE (*v.*, rival, compete)
FLO	FLOT (*n.*, cf. tied logs transported by the current downstream) (*n.*, stream)	FLOW (*v.*, move along over as a river does; move smoothly; of the tide come in; rise; n., flowing movement; quantity that flows.
RU RUE	RU (*n.*, brook) (*n.*, road, street;small evergreen plant with bitter tasting leaves, formerly used in medicine).	RUE (*v.*, regret, think of with sadness or regret; plant (as in the definition in French.

The final *tableau* sends the memory back to the *incipit* of the play: the three women (with dynamic connotations in their names) are seated together (static dimension) once again — the bench on which they sit is invisible — the enigma of the trial (bench of both Judge and Victim), the enigma suspended between past, present, and future, beneath and beyond time: the mutability of the come-and-go is a sign of Time as well as an illusion of change in the immutable structure of Existence. To COME (into the light) and to GO (into darkness) is a route new to every man but identical for mankind, a line binding the first Nothing to the last one in a vicious circle whose terms are ultimately interchangeable ("Fair is foul and foul is fair. . ."). The play ends, substantially, where it began: the chromatic/chironomic composition shows a variant in the group portrait, but its elements are the same: the "dull yellow" (FLO) initially on the right of the "dull red" (VI) shifts to the left in the *finale*, as a result of the exchange with the "dull violet" (RU); the hands of each woman, initially clasped in their own laps, at the close of the play lie clasped in the companions' laps. After the partings, expectations, and anxieties of the come-and-go experience, the longed-for unity of the trinity is recomposed. Yet, in that Nirvana state, the paradox of man's permanent precariousness is latent, with the anguish of the tension between present and future ("Of what will come after?"). Silence closes—just as it had opened—the play, absorbing the voices' utterances "to the last syllable": "rings" is the final word, uttered by FLO. The stage direction shows that the first denotation of the term is not to be retained.

Hands made up to be as visible as possible. No ring apparent (*C&G*, 21). In the "feel" uttered by FLO ("I can feel the rings.") there is certainly the semantic possibility of the "sensation" of the presence of the rings *de facto* not worn by any of the women ("apparent" in the stage direction reinforces the ambivalence). "Rings" is reminiscent of the circles of memory expanding *à la recherche du temps perdu*, of the "ring a ring a rosie", thrills of joy, and confabulatory clusters of children at play, here of the "happy days" spent "in the playground at Miss Wade's" (*C&G*, 20).[11] The "clasp" of hands reinforces the association—by homophony—with "wring", with a further stress on the tension hidden under the apparent calm, while the "rings" perceived as presences in the singular knitting of the women's hands in each other's lap suggest the attempt to penetrate the mystery of womanhood (one of the keys offered to interpret Botticelli's painting, inspired by—in Marsilio Ficino's words—"furor malinconicus"). This expands, concentrically, towards the mystery of love, of friendship, and ultimately of the artist's solitude where the aesthetic "creature" is conceived and born.

Come and Go is a XX-century mystery play, a parable of everyman's come-and-go, presented in a contracted and parodic form ("A Dramaticule"). It contains the main coordinates of Beckett's thought, starting from his orientation in the critical analysis of *Proust* (1931); the essay based on Calderon de la Barca's *leit motif*—

> Pues el delito mayor
> Del hombre es haber nacido.[12]

Beginning with the definition of Time as a "bicephalus monster of damnation and rescue" (Cf.*P.* 11), whose basic elements are Memory and Habit (*P*, 18),

Beckett interprets the "tragedy" of the Marcel-Albertine relationship (*P*, 63) in these terms:

> But if love, for Proust, is a function of man's sadness, friendship is a function of his cowardice; and, if neither can be realized because of the Impenetrability (isolation) of all that is not "cosa mentale", at least the failure to possess may have the nobility of that which is tragic, whereas the attempt to communicate where no communication is possible is merely a semian vulgarity, or horribly comic, like the madness that holds a conversation with the furniture. (*P*, 63)

In the second concentric circle of Beckett's criticism the position of the artist is contemplated: "Total love for somebody is always love for something else" (*P*, 57) and "friendship is a social expedient" which man takes as a refuge to deny "the irremediable solitude to which everyman is condemned" (*P*, 63). As a consequence of that, no choice is left for the artist, except that of rejecting such links, which involve only the "superficial levels" of man's personality —

> Because the only spiritual development is in the sense of depth. The artistic tendency is not expansive, but a contraction, and art is the apotheosis of solitude. There is no communication because there are no vehicles of communication . . . "One lies all one's life long," writes Proust, "Notably to those that love one, and above all to that stranger whose contempt would cause one most pain—oneself." Yet surely that score of half a dozen—or half a million—sincere imbeciles for a man of genius ought to cure us of our absurd puntiglio and our capacity for being affected by that abridged libel that we call an Insult . . . (*P*, 64)

Seen in this perspective, *Come and Go* is the offspring of the artist's imagination, a product given "birth" to as a reaction to the ineluctable insignificance of the existential journey from Nothing (Birth) to Nothing (Death), where the artist's identity is defined by/in an aesthetic self-significant construction. The only possible mediator between life and death—interchangeable—is the re-flection on form, i.e., giving birth to an artistic entity no longer conceived as re-presentation, i.e. mimetic expression, of "extracircumferencial phenomena" (*P*,65), but as something reflecting upon itself in *motu perpetuo*. If life is—in the Macbethian sense—"but a walking shadow" which histrionically comes and goes "upon the stage/And then is heard no more" (*M*, V, v, 25-26),[13] the only significant escape for the artist lies in self-contraction, i.e., in turning inwards and treating his own self with irony, in other terms in inventing a game (play) in which the self is held up to ridicule (dramaticule).

Come and Go, the "dramaticule" boasting a dynamic title, results in a cul de sac, where the journey of the artist (and of his aesthetic "fiction") is terminated. It objectifies, in a hyper-concentrated form—

> a. the route of the man of the theatre (in the widest sense of the term), who continues to enter and leave the stage until the curtain falls, and then repeats his come-and-go in the replicas, i.e., repetition with variation of the same script;
> b. the route of the audience—"one, no one, a hundred ones" (in a Pirandellian way)—who come into the playhouse to consume the artist's product (through a kind of intercourse with the artist) and then go out, with the "ring" of the actor's voices in the ear and, maybe, with the wish to return;
> c. the route of the text itself (a marginal, but only apparently marginal, dimension), which is produced after the obscure come-and-go of manuscript, typescript, proofcopy, *cliché,* paged and bound bundle of sheets, printed volume—a curious *iter* ratifying the passage from private to public, from unique to serial.

In this way, FLO, VI, and RU—the three protagonists of the play exasperatingly reduced in Time and Space—bring about intriguing associations: among the "cul-tural" ones, Shakespeare, Tcheckov, Botticelli (already mentioned), but also Ibsen, T.S. Eliot, Michaelangelo, *et alii;*[14] the main fascination of the "dramaticule", however, lies in the fact that the paradox of existential micro-macro-drama remains *open* to numberless interpretative routes linked to the individual experiences of the receivers of Beckett's *verbum.*

From *Etudes Irlandaises* 10 (December 1985): 117-28.

---

[1]*Come and Go*, written in English in 1965, was first published in the French version by the author (1966), and then in English (1967). It was first staged in Berlin (January 14, 1966) in the German version by Elmar Topkoden. *Come and Go* is one of the few Beckett plays which had its première in English held in his native town (Dublin, Februrary 28, 1968), followed by a production in Britain (London, December 9, 1968).

The title in French (*Va et Vient*) shows the movement in the oppositve direction to that indicated in the English version (*Come and Go,* reproduced in German as *Kommen und Gehen*)—a change due to rhythmic reasons canonised by use, yet of some value as a reinforcement—however marginal—of the thesis sustained in the present essay.

The female trio—unique in Beckett drama—can be grouped with the few plays with three characters written by the playwright: *Cascando, Play, Ghost*

Trio (with 2 dumb characters + 1 voice), *That Time* (3 voices belonging to the protagonist, the solo figure set at the centre of the stage, identified as "Listener's Face").

The text used for the quotations in this paper is: S. Beckett, *Breath and Other Shorts,* London, Faber & Faber, 1971 (henceforth to be referred to with the acronym C&G followed by page number). *Come and Go* occupies pp. 13-22 of the volume; the *Other Shorts* are *Act Wiithout Words I, Act Without Words II,* and *From an Abandoned Work.*

[2]In the first of the *Dialogues* with George Duthuit, "Tal Coat," Samuel Beckett clarifies his aesthetic orientation when he defines his own objective in these terms:

> The expression that there is nothing to express, nothing with which to express, nothing from which to express, no power to express, no desire to express, together with the obligation to express. (S. Beckett, *Proust and Three Dialogues with George Duthuit*, London, John Calder, 1931 I ed., 1976, p.103).

[3]*Ghost Trio* is a TV play written in 1975, published in 1976, and first performed on BBC2 on April 17, 1977.

[4]For the description of the seat, cf. quote on p.1, the last sentence in particular.

[5]The same theatrical operation can be found in Tom Stoppard's *Rosencrantz and Guildenstern Are Dead*, springing from Shakespeare's *Hamlet*, and a few other contemporary plays.

It is also worthwhile pointing out that the Weird Sisters appear in those scenes of *Macbeth* for a long time considered spurious by the critics (I, i; I, iii; III, i; IV, i). The text of *Macbeth* may also have suggested to Beckett the titles of the pantomimes *Act Without Words I* and *II*, somehow echoing the "deed without a name" (*M*, V, i., 49).

[6]Alternation (giving rhythm to the *pièce*, which develops as a musical score or a *partitare* for dance) is also used in other plays by Beckett, in particular *Eh Joe, All That Fall*, and *Embers*.

[7](*C & G*, 19-20). VI has one cue less than FLO and RU (7 against 8 of the other two), but utters a longer speech. The text as a whole shows an assiduous

presence of the question mark and of the exclamation mark, rarely used by Beckett. The gesture of each protagonist puting "her finter to her lips" is reminiscent of that made by the Weird Sisters as an answer to Banquo's question:

> By each at once her copper finger laying
> Upon her skinny lips (M, 1, iii, 44-45).

[8] The analytic stage direction is provided with the following graph:

HANDS

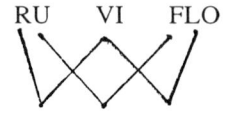

RU   VI   FLO

Interestingly enough, *Come and Go* is also one of the few plays by Beckett where the use of the curtain is contemplated.

[9] Ernst H. Gombrick discusses the main interpretations given to the Florentine painting and points out:

> There is a famous interpretation of the Graces in the Trectate *De Picture* by Alberti, which has often been quoted in relation to the *Spring* painting. Alberti, whose source is Seneca, interprets the three sisters as "Liberality": "one of the sisters gives, another receives, the third renders the favour." Warburg has drawn attention also to the Giovanna Tornabouni medal, in which the Graces are accompanied with the inscription: "Caritas, Pulchritudo, Amor." In a later study he has provided the allegorical exegesis of the three sisters. Pico della Mirandola's words—Pico's medal, too, shows the three sisters, but this time accompanied with the inscription: "Amor, Pulchritudo, Voluptas." Among the famous nine hundred theses Pico declared himself ready to discuss there was this one:
>
> The one who understands in depth, and with his own intellect, the divisions of Venus' unity into the trinity of Fates and the division of Saturn's unity in the trinity of Jupiter, Neptune and Pluto, shall see the right way to proceed in Orphic theology. (E.H. Gombrich, *Immegini Simboliche. Studi sull'Arte del Rinascimento*, Torino, Einaudi, (1972) 1978, 82 translation into English mine).

[10]Shakespeare refers here to the three years expired since he met the "fair friends" to whom the sonnet is devoted.

[11]The name Wade suggest the image of a long-legged waterbird, and also the movement forward hindered by a resistant substance, "walk with an effort, through anything that makes progress difficult." The polarity light/diaphanous — heavy/muddy is condensed in this *apparently* neutral name.

[12]S. Beckett, *Proust* . . ., cit. in note 2 above, 67.

[13]*Come and Go* is dedicated to John Calder, Beckett's privileged publisher. The inscription, "For John Calder," is a curious way of winking at the shareholder, co-responsible (accomplice) of the "fortune" of the text—here, too, the ring of Shakespeare's lines could be perceived—

> These offices so oft as thou wilt look,
> Shall profit thee and much enrich thy book. (Sonnet LXXVII, 13-14).

[14]Cf. Ibsen's *Peer Gynt*, Eliot's "The Love Song of J. Alfred Prufrock," Michaelangelo's *Le Parche* in the Palazzo Pitti Gallery, Florence.

Bare Bones: As a lady slips her moorings, Beckett sounds a hopeful note

Jay Carr

BUFFALO—If ever an artist has been haunted by the certainty of death, it is Samuel Beckett. The unnameable, he has called it. He has railed against its inevitability, and our powerlessness before it, in all his plays and novels. Almost slyly, he has allowed himself a very occasional gesture of hopefulness, and his writing is not without eruptions of gallows humor. But mostly Beckett's plays take place in ruins and dust, which seem to stand as the ultimate destination of flesh. In words as spare and clean and elegant as bones, he has wrung art from despair, made poetry of impotence.

Almost defensively, he has in recent years explained that the decreasing length of his plays stems from his determination to pare away nonessentials.

Certainly his recent works have the distilled quality of poetry. What's different about Beckett's *Rockaby*, which had its world premiere earlier this month before going on to New York and Paris, is that a tenderly elegiac note is felt as well in his evocation of an old lady slipping the moorings. It would be exaggerating to speak of Beckett as having mellowed at the age of 75, but his characteristic austerity isn't as unrelievedly bleak in *Rockaby* as on many past occasions.

THE TITLE can be taken literally. A spotlight comes up slowly on an old lady dressed in her mother's black sequined gown, her large, dark, staring eyes frozen in an ashen mask of a face. She is meeting her end, rocking herself into it. But she's not eager to cross over. She isn't fighting death, but rather is procrastinating, which somehow makes her seem more touching than heroic defiance possibly could. At intervals, she wakes from her reverie, stares anxiously until she determines that she's still alive, and croaks the word "More!"

Whereupon a voice croons at her over a speaker, and she is lulled into peace again. The voice is that of her younger self, soothing as a cello, as it intones: "Close of a long day/All eyes/All sides/Time she stopped/Time she went and sat at her window/Till in the end/She stopped/Till in the end/Close of a long day." The words are incantatory. They are spare, lucid shards of sense perception, and every time the voice winds down, the old lady in black awakens and, staring unseeingly, caws "More!"

She seems a child wanting a familiar and beloved bedtime story not to end. It is as if she is fighting sleep—but not desperately, not altogether. The intervals between the times she cries "More!" lengthen. The drifts into sleep deepen. The rocker takes shorter and fewer arcs. Until it stops. Until life stops. Until the play ends, with the spotlight gradually extinguishing itself, yielding the old lady up to the darkness out of which she came. It is a gentle yielding to death. The writing is suffused with something like resignation. There is nothing defiant in Beckett's line, "Time she stopped," but something like agreement.

THE PRODUCTION is as careful, precise and elegant as the writing. Certainly Alan Schneider has staged it with the total immersion in Beckett's idiom that comes of his having served as Beckett's dramatic midwife for decades. And Billie Whitelaw, who plays the old woman and also supplies the disembodied voice that croons to her, is luminous. She, too, has played Beckett often, and the economy and selflessness of both Schneider and Whitelaw not only are commendable, but impart to *Rockaby* a fugitive beauty. In its 15 minutes, *Rockaby* outreaches plays that last hours.

Because of its brevity, *Rockaby* is preceded by Miss Whitelaw reading Beckett's short story, *Enough*, which describes the ending of a relationship with a quality that I can only describe as a lively wistfulness. Miss Whitelaw quite correctly plays it all deadpan, so that her description of the old couple taking a long walk, with the man so bent that from the waist up he walks parallel to the ground, is steeped in tenderly defiant humor. Nor is the irony in the writing lost upon her. "He didn't like to feel against his skin the skin of another," she deadpans. "A mucous membrane was another matter."

Rockaby more than succeeds in accomplishing its circumscribed ends, and it accomplishes them with a degree of compassion that is by no means plentiful and is seldom overt in Beckett's *oeuvre*. Certainly, it was a coup for Buffalo, its most important theatrical premiere since the 1968 unveiling of Edward Albee's *Box-Mao-Box*, which *Rockaby* far exceeds. The State University of New York at Buffalo got the play because Daniel Labeille, a professor, wrote to Beckett requesting one. Last June, he received what by Beckett's fiercely hermetic standard amounted to a frenzied advertising blitz—a new work with a note suggesting that it be staged if Labeille thought it worthwhile.

LABEILLE PLUNGED ahead and got in touch with Schneider, an old friend, who in turn secured Miss Whitelaw. Theater department chairman Saul Elkin and arts program chairman Patricia Kerr Ross added their good offices. From there it was a short step to SUNY's Beckett Festival in Buffalo. The production was filmed by documentary-maker Donn Alan Pennebaker, and Beckett's 75th birthday April 13 was further observed by a lobby exhibit of photographs, manuscripts and letters—several to Barney Rosset, whose Grove Press introduced Beckett to America. Naturally, there were seminars as well, and one of the Beckett experts in attendance, English critic Martin Esslin, told what the Irish would call a darlin' story. It seems Beckett is a cricket fan, and periodically travels to London for the matches. On one particularly lovely day, Beckett remarked to a friend how fine it was to have an afternoon of cricket ahead of them. The friend agreed, "On such a day, Sam," the friend gushed, "one might even say it's wonderful to be alive," "Well . . ." Beckett replied, "I wouldn't go that far."

From *The Detroit News* (19 April 1981): 1F, 6F.

Review: The World Première of *Ohio Impromptu*, Directed by Alan Schneider at Columbus, Ohio

S. E. Gontarski

Two American conferences, each of which premièred a short play, were the locus—if not the logos—of Beckettianna in the Spring of 1981. As part of the 75th birthday celebrations for Samuel Beckett, *Rockaby* (written originally with Irene Worth in mind but played finally—to the delight of the faithful—by Billie Whitelaw) was presented at a celebration at the State University of New York in Buffalo, New York (paired with a dramatic reading of *Enough*) on April 8, and *Ohio Impromptu*, written for the international symposium at Ohio State University, *Samuel Beckett: Humanistic Perspectives* (May 7-9), was presented on May 9, featuring David Warrilow as Reader, with Rand Mitchell as Listener. Both productions were directed by Alan Schneider who, after 25 years as Beckett's principal American director, is probably as close to the Beckettian ethos as any director, certainly any American director. These plays, gracious gifts from Beckett, were the second and third consecutive world premières of Beckett's work staged in the United States since *A Piece of Monologue*, written for and staged by David Warrilow, which opened on December 14, 1979.

There is doubtless some press of tongue to cheek in the title of *Ohio impromptu*, but it is also straightforwardly descriptive, marking occasion and genre—*impromptus à la* Molière and Giraudoux (which were meta-theatrical or self-reflexive exercises), or more like the intricate little solo pieces Schubert, Chopin and Schumann called impromptus. Beckett's impromptu for solo instrument (Reader) and conductor (Listener) is more binary in structure than the impromptu's usual ternary form, two characters (apparently) and two movements (apparently). Seated like twin Krapps at a long, white, deal table, in an isle of light against surrounding darkness are Reader and Listener, 'As alike in appearance as possible', long black coats, long white hair. The first movement sounds escape as its theme. Reader reads a narrative featuring a protagonist who is evidently a younger version of Listener since he wears the long black coat and sits before the 'old world Latin Quarter hat' described in the narrative (for a photo of Joyce in said costume see the page facing 81 in Ellmann). He has fled from an emotional liaison, but exactly who has left whom in the affair and under what circumstances is never detailed. Ignoring his love's (unspoken) request to remain in familiar quarters where 'my shade will comfort you', the protagonist has moved to unfamiliar rooms on the Isle of Swans, 'In a last attempt to obtain relief.' Listener listens to the narrative without the pleasure Krapp recaptures listening to at least the erotic portions of his tape, but the protagonist—and perhaps finally Listener himself—has more success synthesizing the dialectic of his life than does Krapp.

The second movement features an apparently successful (if mystical or imaginary) solution to the emotional turmoil, which was not solved by flight. A man (Reader before us, visually an *alter ego*) appears to the protagonist to ease 'his old terror of night.' This apparition (or creation), apparently sent by his former love but as likely generated by or from Listener himself, reads to the protagonist through the night on account of what we broadly witness on stage for the play's duration, but not exactly. Most of 'the sad tale' antedates the action we witness. The relation of narration to stage action is oblique, further refracted by the mirror image of the two characters. Reader (in the narrative) appears sporadically 'unheralded', reads, comforts, then disappears. Through these meetings 'they grew to be as one'—if they were ever other, since they

Late Theatrical Works

look alike and only a single hat sits on the table, and both are identically dressed. Such seeming unity echoes the earlier image of the conjunction of the divided stream: 'How in joyous eddies its two arms conflowed and flowed united on.'But the dramatic movement is contrapuntal, fugal, reading against playing, fiction against drama, ear against eye. Reader reports that he has had word from Listener's old love that there was 'No need to go to him again.'In this then the first that Listener hears the news? If so, past and present converge, and Reader is other, another, offering different tales. Or is this theatrical illusion? The information is Listener's, in him already. What we witness may be repetition, performance, theatre. A play within a play within a play. Listener audience to his own telling, to himself. The play poses the problems of origins and audience. Whose voice are we listening to? Who is watching what?

The difference between narration and stage action defines the space within which the drama occurs. Only the visual images suggest identity. And in the narration no mention is made of Listener's orchestrating the reading. But Reader seems to exhibit some freedom—he departs from the text to utter an impromptu remark, 'Yes', and an impromptu repetition, but the freedom is illusion. The words are engraved in the text. The final, dream-like narrative image is played: Reader and Listener sit during a lightless, soundless dawn 'as though turned to stone', lost in a mindlessness as deep as Murphy's third zone, 'Whither no light can reach. No sound.'But the final visual image can be read differently: the figures raise their heads to look at each other. Although 'Unblinking. Expressionless,' the two figures suggest more mindfulness than mindlessness. The relief sought at the play's opening may have been brought by the doppelgänger, but that element of narration is not necessarily confirmed visually.

Reader finally has been sent or created for company, in both senses—as companion and for guests, the 450 or so literary critics who attended this performance. And although all theatre is for company, depends on company, Beckett is certainly meditating in *Ohio impromptu* on the play within the occasion, the artist speaking to his critics. The play, then, is not so much about solace as origination, creativity. *Ohio impromptu* finally brings to the fore the elemental creative process (or creative paradox) suggested in *That time* where the protagonist of narrative A would hide as a youth, 'making up talk breaking up two or more talking to himself being together that way,' or in *Endgame* where Hamm talks of 'the solitary child who turns himself into children, two, three, so as to be together, and whisper together in the dark.'Derrida describes something analogous in *Writing and difference*: 'To grasp the operation of creative imagination at the greatest possible proximity to it, one must turn oneself toward the invisible interior of poetic freedom. One must be separate from oneself in order to be reunited with the blind origin of the work in its darkness' (p. 7). In *Ohio impromptu* the two movements of the play, problem and solution may come together in the telling, but the unity depends on the difference. Finally, we are left with the problems of the origins of the tale.

In performance the initial stage image was filled with contrasts: black against white, life against death, revelation against concealment: white, waist-length hair spread over black coats, the actors' faces covered with or shielded by fragile, boney hands, the figures emaciated, cadaverous, slightly androgynous, almost phosphorescent, the hair so long that it seems to have grown for years beyond death. Both actors were actively restrained, the power of the play swelling in the unsaid. Warrilow's voice was fragile, cracking, unhurried, always on the edge of cessation. His stints in 'Mabou Mines Performs Samuel Beckett', particularly in *Play, Come and go* and *The lost ones* (the last virtually a Warrilow monologue), and later his staging and performing *A piece of monologue* have helped him develop a discipline for and rapport with Beckett's work. And Schneider's tempo, his pacing, built the palpable tension of shivering glass in one's hands—slowly. The play contains almost no movement, yet the final impression was balletic, precarious, the gesture suspended, the play balanced on its margin. Each knock, each turn of page, Listener's one arresting gesture, especially the climactic recognition—the slightest movement gained prominence against the stasis. Schneider's direction was understated, attentive, confident, allowing time for silence, for absence. The busyness [*sic*] of earlier work gone, Schneider has become a deft miniaturist.

From The Journal of Beckett Studies, no.8 (Autumn 1982): 133-36.

Impact and Parable in Beckett: A First Encounter with *Not I*

Alec Reid

The writer on Beckett's plays must steer a course between Scylla and Charybdis, between objective analysis and subjective reaction.[1] The problem is inherent in the material. Beckett has deliberately devised his plays not to be read in the solitude of the study as one might read a novel or a poem but to be seen and heard by an audience in the theatre. Unless these conditions are present, the plays cannot exist fully for Beckett, and so he will speak of the first run-through with actors as the 'realisation' of the play and when it has been performed publicly he will say that it has been 'created.' As the late George Devine, Beckett's greatest English director, wrote in a programme note:

Late Theatrical Works

> When working as a director on a Beckett play—one has to think of the text as something like a musical score, wherein the 'notes', the sights, the sounds, the pauses, have their own special inter-related rhythms and out of their composition comes the dramatic impact.

But how can we capture in words the distinctive rhythms of a series of movements and then inter-relate them to the distinctive rhythms of sound? How in print can we 'realise' one pause let alone the rhythms of a succession of pauses? Any discussion of Beckett's plays which ignores their impact on the senses as well as on the intellect is not only wrong-headed; it is positively dangerous since it will blind us to the true nature of the experience which he has created. As a critic in the London *Times* argued when reviewing *Eh Joe*, whatever Beckett does will surprise us more than it should since it will belong entirely to whatever medium he has chosen for it. Each play will be quite unlike anything we have seen before, yet it will belong entirely to the theatre needing actors and an audience just as a ballet needs music and dancers. That audience requires no specialised skills or previous knowledge, indeed these could be a hindrance not a help. As George Devine says, it is invited to undergo an experience. This 'may be a strange one, an unusual one, a nerve-racking one, but, taken rightly, it will be a dramatic one, by a brilliant and profound poet of the theatre.'

Not I represents a vivid illustration of Beckett's 'poetry of the theatre.' His opening stage directions read:

> *Stage in darkness but for* MOUTH, *upstage audience right, about 8 feet above stage level, faintly lit from close-up and below, rest of face in shadow. Invisible microphone.* AUDITOR, *downstage audience left, tall standing figure, sex undeterminable, enveloped from head to foot in loose black djellaba, with hood, fully faintly lit, standing on invisible podium about 4 feet high shown by attitude alone to be facing diagonally across stage intent on* MOUTH, *dead still throughout but for four brief movements where indicated.*

Beckett amplifies this in a postscript.

> *Movement: this consists in simple sideways raising of arms from sides and their falling back, in a gesture of helpless compassion. It lessens with each recurrence till scarcely perceptible at third.*

Each movement is evoked by the same sequence of words: '. . what? . . who? . . . no! . . she!' Beckett's note concludes:

> *There is just enough pause to contain it as* MOUTH *recovers from vehement refusal to relinquish third person.*

So much for what George Devine would call the sights; what of the sounds?

> *As house lights down* MOUTH'S *voice unintelligible behind curtain. House lights out. Voice continues unintelligible behind curtain, 10 seconds. With rise of curtain ad-libbing from text as required leading when curtain fully up and attention sufficient into:*
>
> MOUTH: . . . out . . . into this world . . . this world . . . tiny little thing . .

For the rest of the play MOUTH rattles on in these staccato, telegraphic phrases, spoken at more than twice normal speed but with absolute clarity of enunciation. The flow is interrupted by two 'brief' laughs, two 'good' laughs, two screams with ensuing silences, and by the pauses necessary for MOUTH to recover from each crisis. These breaks are all marked in the text as stage directions. MOUTH'S first four refusals to relinquish the third person stimulate the AUDITOR to movement, albeit diminishing; the fifth, and most vehement—witness the block capitals used in the text for 'SHE'—elicits no response whatsoever. Again MOUTH recovers and resumes as before, but almost immediately the curtain begins to drop. Utterly unaffected, MOUTH pants on as before for about five seconds, then:

> *(Curtain fully down. House dark. Voice continues behind curtain, unintelligible, 10 seconds, ceases as house lights up.)*

The play has lasted roughly twelve minutes and some 2,300 words have been spoken. The only dramatic development is a shift from movement to immobility, reaction to impassivity as the AUDITOR gradually abandons his gesture of helpless compassion.

So far this account of *Not I* has been strictly objective, drawing only on the published text, but what of the impact of the play in the theatre? This of course must be subjective. For the present writer—how stubbornly we cling to the third person—the immediate feeling was of stunned incredulity, swiftly followed by deep concern. Like the AUDITOR, I had been held spell-bound, my attention riveted on those tireless jaws, white against black like the moon in space, on those shockingly scarlet lips, and on that pink, desperately writhing tongue. Like him I had been overwhelmed, swept along on a torrent of words delivered in a voice limpid-clear, beautiful, but innocent of all individuality. Because the words had come gushing at break-neck speed, because the syntax was so compressed, because there had been not one second's respite in the past seven hundred, I could not grasp what I had heard. I had inklings of a story, — a life totally without love, a harsh childhood in an orphanage, a criminal charge, a shattering experience in a meadow one April morning, speech and feeling

Late Theatrical Works

suddenly restored. Nothing was clear yet one thing was certain. I knew with every fibre of my being that I had been deluged in a flood of anguish from which I could not escape even though I could not know with what or whom I was involved. My first words were, 'I have been scoured.' Only later, secure in the warmth and conviviality of the bar, did I begin to talk learnedly of the Ancient Mariner, that other compulsive narrator, and to draw parallels with the earlier plays. More than forty years ago Beckett had written of 'perilous zones in the life of the individual, painful, mysterious and fertile, when for a moment the boredom of living is replaced by the suffering of being.' For twelve minutes I had been plunged into one such.

The shattering impact of *Not I* when performed in the theatre is the surest proof of its dramatic excellence. No quantity of comment or analysis can affect this, but a study of the text may show in part how this fantastic impact is achieved. The resulting clearer understanding of Beckett's outlook and methods as a practical and practising dramatist may in its turn sharpen our response to his plays.

Beckett has always shown an uncanny sense of what works in the theatre. It is as if even as he is composing a play, he imagines himself sitting in the auditorium watching a performance of it on the stage. So he gives precise directions as to how *Not I* shall begin and end. The lowering of the house lights and the raising of the curtain are not just technical preliminaries; they are part of the experience which Beckett is creating, witness the words 'when curtain fully up and attention sufficient.' It is the same when he comes to end the experience. The finale involves audience every bit as much as the actors, and what happens in the stalls is an integral as what happens on the stage. 'What haunted me,' wrote Harold Hobson, '. . . . was not so much the torrents of self-defensive words with which Miss Whitelaw fills the theatre as the inexorable dismissal of these words by the bringing down of the curtain whilst they are still in full flood.'

Beckett has used the curtain in two distinct ways. It has marked the end of this play as it does any play. As Hobson shows, however, it also contributes to the impact of the play by making us leave MOUTH still ranting on in her impregnable isolation. This double-level working is a feature of Beckett's thinking and practice; it is also the essence of parable. Four other examples spring to mind. In *Endgame*, Hamm can never forgive his parents for having brought him into the world; they have no place in his life yet, as with other things, he hesitates to discard them finally. So he puts them where any man might put such rubbish—in ash-cans which will be emptied, probably by some menial, when the final necessity arises. In *Happy Days*, as Winnie sinks deeper and deeper into her mound and the ways of passing her time between the bell for waking and the bell for sleeping become fewer and fewer, she becomes in a double sense, more earth-bound. *Play* provides two more examples. The protagonists are almost cyphers,—Beckett does not even give them names—but they are suffering human beings and that is how he wishes the audience to consider them. Accordingly we are shown only their faces 'so lost to age and aspect as to seem almost part of the urns. But no masks.' Since they are dead to the world, their bodies are 'contained' in the urns from which only their heads protrude. Similarly the roving spot-light constantly probing them must be considered in two distinct ways. It is part of the theatre lighting and, as in any other play, it is used to concentrate attention on a particular actor at a particular moment. Here, however, it does much more. It has been moved from the lighting battery at the back of the auditorium to a point between actors and audience. It is now a *dramatis persona* determining who shall speak and for how long, thereby shaping the action of the play, and it is as much a character as any flesh and blood inquisitor could be.

Anyone reading the plays as literature may well feel tempted to look upon the ash-cans and the mound, the spot-light and the urns as symbols, things put there to suggest some abstract idea. To Beckett, the dramatist, they are finite objects as functional to the play as the actors and in the same way. *Happy Days* can no more be played without the mound than Hamlet can without the Prince.

In *Not I*, Beckett takes this process to great lengths; the content of the play, an abstract idea, cannot be separated from what the audience actually see. The protagonist has suffered an experience so traumatic that she cannot accept it; she must insist that it has happened to somebody else. Hence the title, *Not I*. Beckett makes his purpose quite clear in his note on the AUDITOR'S gesture, when he writes of MOUTH'S vehement refusal to relinquish the third person. But until she can abandon the pretense and accept herself as she is, the speaker is literally not her own woman; she has no real identity and cannot be a complete person. Accordingly Beckett shows us only what is pertinent to her situation, namely her mouth, as it churns out her self-annihilating denials.

Just as Beckett makes double use of the objects which the audience sees [sic] on the stage so he derives double impact from the words which they hear from it. As with normal speech, these words convey ideas to the intellect but because they are being spoken, they also register on the sense. As far back as 1929 Beckett had written of Joyce's *Work in progress.* 'His writing is not *about* something. It is *that something itself.* When the sense is asleep, the words go to sleep. When the sense is dancing, the words dance.' This exactly describes MOUTH'S monologue. She is at the end of her tether, within a hair's breadth of complete collapse. Therefore her utterance is disorganised to the brink of incoherence. Yet it never topples over into sustained gibberish which could serve no dramatic purpose, convey no information about the basic situation.

Beckett never talks about his writing and he has given no account of how the monologue evolved. We have only the finished work.[2] What follows can be no more than *post hoc propter hoc* speculation, but it may have some value if only as a pointer and a stimulus. Probably like any dramatist, Beckett first

Late Theatrical Works 283

defined to himself the basic dramatic situation and decided more specifically what he would give the audience to establish his central character. Next, perhaps, he set down these essential facts in a coherent sequence which might, however, have included such flashbacks and digressions as would be found in any spontaneous narrative.[3] So far the sentences would have been simple, the syntax conventional. Then, deliberately, he would have proceeded to smash these sequences. The earlier complete sentences are slashed to telegraphs and the narrative progression interrupted by exclamations and repetitions; phrases are bent back upon themselves echoing what has gone before even as they, in their turn, form the material for future echoes. In embryo the opening section of the play might well have read something like this:

> This baby, a tiny girl, had come into the world before her time, at a god-forsaken hole the name of which doesn't matter. Her parents were unknown, her father having vanished into thin air immediately after the one casual encounter with her mother, who likewise had disappeared on the birth of the child precisely eight months later. So the baby girl had been spared the love normally vented on the speechless infant at home; indeed she had never, then or subsequently, known love of any kind. Nothing important happened to her till she was sixty, no great God, till she was coming up to seventy. Then one morning she was wandering in a field aimlessly looking for cowslips to make a ball, everything suddenly went dark, all the April morning light went out . . . What did you say? Who was in the meadows? Me? No, she!

The final version reads:

> MOUTH . . . out . . . into this world . . . this world . . . tiny little thing . . . before its time . . . in a godfor— . . . what?   . . . girl? . . . yes . . . tiny little girl . . . into this . . . out into this . . . before her time . . . godforsaken hole called . . . called . . . no matter . . . parents unknown . . . unheard of . . . he having vanished . . . thin air . . . no sooner buttoned up his breeches . . . she similarly . . . eight months later . . . almost to the tick . . . so no love . . . spared that . . . no love such as normally vented on the . . . speechless infant . . . in the home . . . no . . . nor indeed for that matter any of any kind . . . no love of any kind . . . at any subsequent stage . . . so typical affair . . . nothing of any note till coming up to sixty when— . . . what? . . . seventy? . . . good God! . . . coming up to seventy . . . wandering in a field . . . looking aimlessly for cowslips . . . to make a ball . . . a few steps then stop . . . stare into space . . . then on . . . a few more . . . stop and stare again . . . so on . . . drifting around . . . when suddenly . . .

> gradually . . . all went out . . . all that early April morning light . . . and she found herself in the— . . . what? . . . who? . . . no! . . . she! . . . *(Pause and movement1)*

To grasp how far the process of dislocation has been pushed, it may help to learn that the 2,268 words of the monologue are split into 726 units separated in the text by dots. The theoretical average is just over 3 words per unit and in fact 304 units or 42% of the total contain either 3 words or 4. The largest unit has only 10 words in it while 674 units or over 93% of the total have 5 words or less.

Here form is content, content is form. The sense is disintegration so the syntax disintegrates. Beckett had already achieved this twenty years earlier in *The Unnamable*, a novel and therefore a book that can be read anywhere at any time. But *Not I* is a stage piece, created to be played by actors, and seen, heard, felt, all at once by an audience in a theatre who have come together to that special place for that special purpose. Outside the auditorium, like all Beckett's plays, it is a fish out of water.

As we have said, impact is the hall-mark of dramatic excellence but nothing can make an impact on a vacuum. We, the audience, must feel ourselves involved, must sympathise with the protagonist. Not many of us will identify ourselves directly with the woman in *Not I*, in the way a once-jealous husband might sympathise with Othello, or a bereaved parent with Macduff. MOUTH'S experience is not an everyday occurrence, yet Beckett transports us to the same zone of being by using resources available only to the dramatist, the voice of a trained actress coming at us out of the dark.

Beckett himself chose Billie Whitelaw for the Royal Court production and rehearsed her personally. We may assume therefore, that her performance faithfully reflected his intentions. The dramatic situation in *Not I* requires that MOUTH'S words shall come gushing out as if some dam inside her had suddenly burst unleashing in an uncontrollable torrent the pent-up feelings and unspoken words of over sixty years. Urged on by Beckett and by the director, Anthony Page, Miss Whitelaw reached a point where she could articulate certain words in one tenth of a second and could sustain an average word rate of nearly two hundred words a minute with every syllable limpid clear. This combination of speed and clarity is the means whereby we became involved. We could hear every word without the slightest difficulty, but in the split second needed for us to translate apprehension into comprehension, to grasp what we had heard, the torrent had gone rushing on bearing away other words which thus escaped us completely. We had missed something and even as we realised this, we were losing yet more. We consciously willed ourselves to concentrate still harder in a hopeless effort at one and the same time to keep up with the speaker and to follow her. Now, like her, we were on the rack and our suffering was a part of the total dramatic experience. We had moved into the play.

Something very like this happens in *Play*. When the curtain rises we are similarly startled and shocked by what we see on the stage for it bears little resemblance to the world from which we have just come into the theatre. The words are almost as hard to grasp for they are delivered in a swift, staccato monotone and the speakers are seldom allowed more than half a minute before they are silenced by the spotlight. As in *Not I*, inklings of a story reach us, — an unfaithful husband, a vixenish wife, a rich mistress, but nothing definite and no explanation of the urns or the jabbing beam. We are precisely in the situation of the characters on the stage; for us as for them, the past seems virtually meaningless, the present incomprehensible. Identification has been achieved. Now, without any break or any warning, the play is repeated exactly. The characters know only what they knew when the curtain first rose, but for us, in the light of the knowledge we have gained since then, their situation and their suffering are becoming clearer every minute. Increased understanding brings heightened awareness and we move deeper and deeper into the play. As we do, we suffer more because we have become more closely identified with them. A third run-through would be unbearable.

In *Varieties of Parable*, Louis MacNeice suggests that Beckett operates in the same way as the makers of parable, setting his fable in a unique, self-contained world but a microcosm which functions strictly in accordance with the laws of the macrocosm containing it. As Beckett wrote to Alan Schneider, 'Hamm as stated, and Clov as stated, together as stated,—*in such a place, and in such a world,* (italics ours) that's all I can manage, more than I could.' Thus we may never find a man who actually keeps his parents in ash-cans, but, given Hamm's attitude to Nagg and Nell, what more logical place to put them? And once he has done so, what better way of suppressing them, keeping them in their proper places, than to screw down the lids of the cans, to 'bottle them' as he calls it? In the microcosm of *Not I*, MOUTH is a *dramatis persona*; in the larger world that mouth could only be part of the human being to whom the traumatic experience has happened and to whom we must refer as the speaker or the protagonist.

The parable is more than a story; it contains an inner substance for which the story was designed specifically as a cloak. Very often the maker of a parable will openly declare his intention at the beginning of his tale, 'The Kingdom of Heaven is like unto a man who . . .', or he will reveal his moral at the very end as Belloc does in his *Cautionary Verses*, 'The moral is that people must if they are poor, obey or bust.' But Beckett adamantly refuses to do either, for the excellent reason that he is not propounding any moral or making any statement. Each member of his audience is left free to draw his own conclusions and will therefore explain the substance in relation to his own beliefs or preoccupations. Thus a Marxist critic has seen *Godot* in terms of capitalistic exploitation, Godot himself standing for American Aid while Vladimir and Estragon represent the underdeveloped nations; an existentialist has found in it a statement of Man's folly if he pins his hopes on to anything outside himself; a Roman Catholic commentator claims that it shows the wretchedness of Man without God. Beckett has described it as a play that is striving all the time to avoid definition, though he might possibly agree that its substance is Ignorance and Impotence.

Beckett has little interest in material externals so he keeps his stories very simple. His concern is with the 'inner' world of the individual and he has described his work as a series of attempts to chart areas of experience in this world hitherto left severely alone by the artist anxious to achieve a statement. As C. S. Lewis pointed out, it is impossible even to think about this 'inner' world without using metaphor, if only because, by definition, it is not material and therefore invisible from the outside. But this is the world of questions like 'Who am I?' and 'What is happening to me?' and 'Am I so much as being seen?' Parable is a form of metaphor and therefore a suitable vehicle to attempt such exploration. Beckett is at once himself an explorer and a man who provides vehicles for other explorers. It is up to us to decide in which direction we drive,—if at all.

Objective analysis and subjective reaction, we are back to Scylla and Charybdis.

From *Hermathena* 141 (Winter 1986): 12-21.

---

[1] Alec Reid, who sadly died earlier this year, wrote this essay in 1974, partly in response to the 1973 Royal Court production of *Not I*. Mr. Reid had enthusiastically agreed to contribute to this issue of *Hermathena*, but that was not to be. The editors are glad therefore to be able to include this unpublished essay which was found among Mr. Reid's papers after his death.

[2] This was true when Alec Reid wrote his article. We now possess a detailed analysis of the gestation of *Not I* in S. E. Gontarski's *The Intent of Undoing in Samuel Beckett's Dramatic Texts* (Indiana University Press, Bloomington: 1985, pp. 131-49).

[3] Gontarski's examination of the manuscripts shows that Reid was not far wrong in his guess about Beckett's compositional method. For Gontarski suggests that 'Beckett's attention through the early stages of the play was on neither the image of the speaking lips nor the silent enigmatic, listener, but on the monologue, on the arrangement, development, and balance of the incidents' (p. 144). Furthermore he confirms that at an early stage Beckett wrote an outline of the work 'in which he broke the play down . . . into fourteen categories: birth, field, insentience, so far, buzzing, brain, memories, speculations, walking, punishment and suffering, interruptions, beam, speechless and voice' (p. 144). What Gontarski demonstrates however, contrary to Reid's suggestion, is that the process of composition involved elaboration

and not simple fragmentation. But Reid was right in assuming that the work originated in a fairly straightforward realist account of a character. As Gontarski states it: 'the pattern of composition revealed in the gestation of "Kilcool"/"Not I" is emblematic of Beckett's creative process: the roots of even so experimental a work are firmly set in psychologically realistic soil, in the realism Beckett so derided. The creative struggle for Beckett is most often against those coherent, often personal origins.' (p. xvi).

Recontextualizing the Self: The Voice as Subject in Beckett's *Not I*

Mary Catanzaro

During the middle 1960's, the character of Beckett's style changed drastically and gave way to a new mode of expression whose structure was based on the transformation of language densities and texture, on the "statistical" arrangement of events.[1] In *Not I*, Beckett breaks down the basic sentence or phrase structure and moves towards complex patterns of unfixed or random frequency content. This new style, while perplexing to reader and viewer alike, serves both to define a new theatrical function and, moreover, to visualize the plight of woman.

By the time he wrote *Not I* (1972), Beckett had interiorized sound density even further than he had in its predecessor, *Play*, and had formalized periodicity—that is, cyclical and repeated phrases. Beckett emphasizes structure, formalized patterns, artifice, and the undercutting of pathos in order to develop the themes of rejection, of isolation, and of the absence of love. The paradox of woman's position with others is that her place is in fact defined in the scattered, spastic voice of the text.

The central significance of couples for Beckett is that they shift among interpersonal, grammatical, and conceptual variants. Beckett grounds his notion of the couple in an increasingly theoretical foundation of the voice. This is a voice that does not communicate or inform as we ordinarily think of it, but is governed by its relationship with the subject speaking. The voice points out what is before the scene of Mouth's inner gaze rather than what is visible to her senses. In other words, the voice relates to what is inside the subject all the while. The most productive approach here will be to look at how Beckett reevaluates the couple through Mouth's narrative voice and her inner voice speaking of itself. In each case it is necessary to forget the usual meaning of the word *voice*, which in this work is defined as *external* to Mouth. Much of

Beckett's exposition of the voice can appear forbiddingly abstract on a superficial reading, but those who devote some effort to penetrating his language often find this work to be intensely emotional as well. Accordingly, Beckett never loses sight entirely of a quite traditional, humanistic view of the couple in terms of loss and sorrow. Both approaches are indeed at work in *Not I*, hence the greater emphasis on just how and where they intersect and evolve in Mouth's story.

Perhaps the most important conceptual contributions made by the voice and the peculiarly dense constructs of language in this work is that they mirror the radically circumscribed space of the figure in *Not I*. The play takes place in a black void, in which the audience sees an elevated red mouth, brilliantly lit, with a nearly imperceptible robed figure, the Auditor, standing to one side. The mouth speaks rapidly, the recitation detailing certain events in the life of an old woman who has suffered. As the recitation progresses, Mouth perceives that her text is a sequence of words and memories that speaks involuntarily. Like the subject speaking, the viewer's memory also drifts from particularity to wholeness; hence, Mouth's story is understood in all its ontological ramifications in the text's shift from specific abandonment to universal abandonment. In this way, the viewer subconsciously follows the "score" of *Not I*, what Herbert Blau reminds us is a legacy of Norman O. Brown's *"participation mystique."*[2] Enoch Brater argues this point similarly, noting that self-perception is experienced directly by the audience:

> Although *Not I* focuses our attention on Mouth, not eye (costarring Auditor as ear), the piece is a far more ambitious exercise in dramatic perception than this unruly trinity might seem to imply. Although Mouth speaks, Auditor hears, and audience *sees*, Beckett establishes for the viewer of this work a visual horizon as well as an aural stimulus closely approximating the "matter" of the monologue itself.[3]

The voice in *Not I* is used as an instrument that *performs* the detritus of memory, but the instrument does not fully comprehend what it voices. Comprehension is divided among several parties—the self who voices and the Auditor (and also the audience) who hears. *Not I* "forces to the drama's surface our own sensory deprivation in seeing, in perceiving, for this is our annoying situation as members of Beckett's audience."[4] The audience thus "participates" with Mouth's breathlessly incoherent speaking, the disordered sequencing of events, and the generalized confusion that punctuates Mouth's inability to tell the story in an organized fashion.

In placing the troubles of woman in the realm of the inner voice,[5] complicated by the problem of involuntary speech, Beckett dislocates the body from ordinary language precisely to show that communication as we commonly know it is an inadequate bonding device to preserve togetherness in partnerships. This idea must of course be understood in terms of Beckett's seeming lack of faith in ordinary language to convey even the most minimal personal feeling. Gontarski's study of the evolution of the play, first titled *Kilcool*, clarifies that the narrator is a victim of conscious, human rejection and not of chance. That words fail to express is a fetish of Beckett's; he realizes that couples still talk. His works have in various ways transformed and explored this premise relentlessly. Auditor's presence may be interpreted as constituting Mouth's elsewhere: the "other," having escaped her, is elsewhere, outside, but nevertheless within Auditor's hearing. (Beckett did, however, eliminate Auditor from both the first Paris production and the BBC production.)[6] Gontarski suggests that Mouth's conflicts nonetheless remain essentially the same with or without Auditor's physical presence, for "the function of the Auditor—whether one is physically on stage or not—can be seen as basic to the dialectical conception of the drama and to the conception of the self developed in the play. It suggests that silence without which speech is not possible. As Jacques Lacan put the matter, 'there is no speech without a reply, even if it is met only with silence, provided that it has an auditor.'"[7]

Beckett has been able to push the formalist demand for abstract minimalism to an extreme limit first of all by conceiving regular couples as he did in "Enough," for example, and then transmuting that concept to a subject/object dialectic as he does in *Not I*. But there are probably no clear limits as to what constitutes the couple. Perhaps the most productive approach to this problematic is to reflect on the transformation which makes a very comprehensible couple pass over into an abstract one. Ever since *Murphy*, Beckett has been obsessed with mingling and separation within the subject as well as between subject and object. And when he repeats this circle over and over, from work to work, we can see definite changes from piece to piece. The displacement of the woman in a couple into forms of absence, nonbeing, negativity, silence, or emptiness does not essentially matter, so long as we can determine the leap that Beckett takes in both the sound and form of a piece, and gather our meaning there.

After all his wordy outbursts in *The Unnamable*, what else was left except linguistic shrinkage and devastation? With *Not I*, Beckett dared to write a play of short staccatos whose language does violent things. Here, where there are no longer any recognizable couples, a patent inability to cope with loss is manifested in a single entity. The conflict is now purely internal; and since the voice speaks involuntarily, her suffering appears unrelieved. Saint Augustine's famous motto, first used in *Waiting for Godot*: "Do not despair, one of the thieves was saved; do not presume, one of the thieves was damned," is the dialectic upon which *Not I* is built. It preserves the symmetry of hope and despair that is at the very foundation of every couple.

There is in *Not I*, however, a kind of reverse optimism about the couple which seeks to internalize all possible experience in an endless stasis, as though experience and time were themselves the equivalents of pain. The "statistical" arrangement of language and structures in this piece suggests that the voice, spoken with rapid but deliberate precision, like open pizzicato strings, exerts itself to secure a replacement for Mouth's missing memories, particularly her unassimilated "other." Steven Connor, like Blau, writes on the problems of coupling in this play in terms of voyeuristic participation:

> The most elaborate form of collusion between the figure of the woman and the anxiety of self is in *Not I*. Here, the extreme dismemberment of the woman makes the spectator participate in an uncomfortably aggressive voyeurism, while at the same time it is deprived of the means of its seeing, even of seeing itself being looked at. But this uncomfortable nakedness of the mouth, especially in the TV version, and its failure to return the viewer's gaze, is itself a threat. The dismemberment of *Not I* is not one which allows an unequivocal 'male' celebration of the power to mutilate and disperse the female body, for it is a dismemberment which fails to confirm the presence of the watcher, and therefore challenges his unity.[8]

Fragmentation and loss of an easily perceivable center have marked modernist contemporary literature worldwide, to be sure. But it seems especially prominent, even exaggerated, in *Not I*. Most viewers of this play experience a sense of bombardment of disconnected energy and impulses. Such knotty complexity, often thought of (by critics) as a product of Beckett's penchant for systems and linguistic compositional techniques, shares much with the deliberate application of randomness—tossing the dice to let the I Ching make decisions, for example—and produces a dissociation of effect. The narrative dissemination of *Not I*, however, allows violence to occur within a chosen framework.

The use of a kind of theatrical voodoo—dominated by the incantatory style of Mouth's vocalization—is a further means of displacing the conventional self from the center of action and replacing it with "scenes" of disgrace. It is significant that the myth or religion into which Mouth enters is not a feminine alternative to a masculine God but rather a decentralization of self in which gender can be confused. These scenes are free-standing sections or "movements," indicated by Auditor's gestures or by her silences, laughs, and screams. Mouth's ambiguous relationship with the silent Auditor to the total scheme of the text is intentionally *built into* Beckett's concept of the couple, which presupposes the existence of an other. *Not I* opposes the logic of integration to the logic of totality, which is based on exclusion and specialization: in this realm, there are no absolute limitations, only linguistic variations. The voice feeds the narrator's appetite for words. Words are "objects" Mouth calls up in order to visualize them; one "object" becomes another "object" and they do not have absolute relations to each other. The play of chance governs the relations of linguistic "objects" to each other.

Not I fits closely within the framework of feminine writing defined by Christiane Makward as "fragmented, polysemic, attempting to speak the body," and in this manner the play avoids a fixed representation of female embodiment.[9] Beckett's text asserts Mouth's story as a cry of un-knowledge, isolated and unassimilable. It must be remembered also that the stage directions state that Auditor's *sex* [is] *undeterminable,"* and therefore, refuses to project a generalized female, but the figure also refuses to mirror the male.[10] That Auditor's sex is indeterminable should concern us. Ambiguous sexuality thus figures powerfully in this work and preserves the richness of the subject/object dialectic. Mouth's text is not fantasy, it is desire, the surplus unaccounted for. That Mouth mixes memory with desire reflects her own ambivalence about the sudden change which she says has taken place in the field; accordingly, the viewer is confronted with the convoluted turns that coupling, and relationships in general, share.

At the same time, Mouth's speech is marked by turns of thought which indicate revolt, rebellion, frustration, resignation, all of which turn on double meanings. The striking symptom of *Not I* is that a figure was once able to manage in spite of her speechlessness, with only the *threat* (lurking about for years) that her lack of voice might create violence or an abrupt change in her notion of self and her relationships to others. The embrace of the other in Mouth's discourse accounts for her somewhat androgynous merging of her self into her "other," the vehement third person "she!" Just as Hélène Cixous observes that the merged self with an other seeks "the possibility of extending into the other, of being in such a relation with the other that *I* move into the other without destroying the other,"[11] so too does Mouth's desire seek an "other that I am and am not . . . but that I feel passing, that makes me live—that tears me apart, disturbs me, changes me."[12] Indeed, fragmentation of Mouth's self proliferates everywhere into the text, where metamorphosis, lack of stability, degradation, and violence are no longer mere threats but hard realities.

The voice in *Not I* discourses on her past life, filled apparently, with sin and uncertainty. The first sequence, for example, is a response to her dilemma and is stylistic and tactical: stylistically, we find simultaneous contrasts, extravagancies, incoherence, half-formed misshaped thoughts. What is the tactical secret of this chaos? Since there seems to be no possible way out, there's always the voice. Elegant pity and sexual innuendo fit together:

> out . . . into this world . . . this world . . . tiny little thing . . . before its time . . . in a godfor— . . . what? . . . girl? . . . yes . . . tiny . . .

little girl ... into this ... out into this ... before her time ...
godforsaken hole ... called ... no matter ... parents unknown ...
unheard of ... he having vanished ... thin air ... no sooner
buttoned up his breeches ... she similarly ... eight months later ...
almost to the tick ... so no love. (14-15)

The most frequent focus of Mouth's questioning is her birth into a malignant society, and her critique is expressed in terms of the particular rather than the general—most often in the repetition of her core narrative. In his analysis of the formation of self, "Lacan substitutes the phallic, Oedipal father with the Name-of-the-Father, that is, the father as representative of language, culture, and authority."[13] Through language, then, the subject internalizes the roles of patriarchy, of the Law. Because of their different positions in the Oedipal crisis, men and women enter language, what Lacan calls the symbolic order, differently. At the Oedipal moment of separation the child enters into a symbolic system governed by the Phallus. The speaking subject is thus a gendered subject: while the male easily identifies with the parental authority of the Logos and painlessly constitutes himself as a phallic "I," the female must identify herself with negativity. It would seem that Mouth's difficulty with speech therefore dwells at the level of phallic power and authority. The implication is that the very idea of the feminine is derived from some masculine *voice speaking*.

It is in the context of patriarchy that Julia Kristeva tells us that the ravings of a seventy-year old woman are surrounded "with a paternal aura, ironically but obstinately raising her toward that third person—God—and filling her with a strange joy in the face of nothingness."[14] Gontarski argues from a slightly different standpoint, noting that the "conflict between contrary aspects of self—the human dialectic, so dramatically realized in the incompatibility of couples ... —is developed in the voices *within the narrator*." His feeling is that there is a "sense of prosopopoeia, both as the speaking dead and the presence of the absent one."[15] In this sense, Mouth's ravings are directed toward the other who is absent; her resentment is elicited by a feeling of verbal authority that it appears to hold over her. What Beckett seems to be saying is that there is no way out of logocentrism and phallic power. This is most often expressed in Mouth's inappropriate laughter that precedes and follows the mention of God, that "God is love" (21). "*To love* is to survive paternal meaning,"[16] asserts Kristeva. If one accepts this notion of love, then Mouth's crisis accordingly would involve an ambivalence toward the phallic Law and a simultaneous desire to be accepted and incorporated into such a system in order to be loved.

There is also the pressure that there is "perhaps something she had to ... had to ... tell;" whatever the "something" is, she is responsible, "guilty or not guilty" (21). Hersh Zeifman claims that it "is clear that the Mouth's monologue is subject to some kind of corrective process, internal or external, and it seems to me that the Auditor ... comes to represent, for the audience, the visual symbol of that corrective process—the attempt to make the Mouth admit the truth about herself—as well as being a witness to its failure."[17] The nightmarish recurrence of whatever she feels she must tell appears to be Mouth's rejection (or fear) of—the phallic courtroom? Judgment Day?—we don't know for sure. Mouth focuses her attack on a personal guilt she feels for having been born and her constant, never surpassed problem is her attempt to liberate particular incidents in her life that trouble her still at age seventy. This, according to Kristeva, is accomplished through the death of the father. *"Father* and *Death* are united but still split and separate. *On the one hand,* Death—the ideal that provides meaning but where the word is silent; *on the other,* the paternal corpse, hence a possible though trivial communication, waste, decay, and excrement mobilizing pleasure and leisure."[18]

Mouth uses her repetitions to start over, as it were, to reach for a secure place for herself in the present. In going back to beginnings ("tiny little thing . . . no love," and so on), Mouth is returning to the original scene of socialization. That she at least is aware of a distinct self puts one in mind of Lacan, but she is other, and she has been condemned to silence. It is as though she had not been for a long time, as if she were that very subject of which Lacan once spoke: "Woman does not exist."[19] Mouth identifies herself with lack, with absence. Mouth is *out* of its body, according to Paul Lawley, who suggests other ways in which a fragmented body is produced by the text and performance. Particularly striking is his discussion of the way that "the text runs together the mouth and the eye, making us see the mouth as an eye, and the eye as a mouth-like orifice."[20]

We must, however, distinguish between biological females and a feminine linguistic position. "Woman" ought, therefore, to be put inside quotation marks. Mouth explores her *jouissance* so as to bring down phallogocentric discourse with her repetitive, insistent questioning and denial of the third person feminine: ". . . not knowing what . . . what she was—. . . what? . . . who? . . . no! . . . she! . . . SHE!" (23). Mouth phantasmically writes her voice as nightmare, having internalized the (absent) mother, and explores her vocal terrain from which to speak herself in the space reminiscent of the (m)other's body: ". . . out . . . into this world . . . this world . . . tiny little thing" (14). Mouth's return to the scene of birth is both an exorcism and a reenactment in a spirit of excess and refusal. That she repeats her birth is her power, but it is also the doorway into madness. She tells us she *has* a body, but later in life, trying to make sense of it, her "whole body [is] like gone . . . just the mouth . . . like maddened . . . and can't stop" (21). The implication here is that she proposes and deploys the so-called "free play of signifiers" of poststructuralist thought in a critical method that continues to question even its own devices and motives. She refuses mastery. In this case, it is the "vehement refusal to relinquish third person" (14).

Like the avant-garde writers celebrated by French feminists—Joyce, Kleist, Genet—Beckett also courts a poetic, ruptured discourse extending into the *non-encore-là*. Mouth's poetic imagery of the larks, the grass, the April morning, and her tears distances her discourse from logic, and provides her with a space of radical decentering and change. The poetic accordingly functions both aesthetically and politically, for it points to what the Logos denies. "A missing grammatical or discursive object implies an impossible subject: not I," according to Kristeva. "Here, this means that the act of writing, without me or you, is in fact an obstinate refusal to let go of the third person: the element beyond discourse, the third, the 'it exists,' the anonymous and unnamable 'God,' the 'Other.'"[21] In *Not I*, Beckett promotes a notion of a feminine libidinal affective economy of abundance, waste, and uselessness. A breakdown of the sentence is a breakdown of structure, in short, a move towards disruption.

Thus there is a confusion of verb tenses, a disorganized description of events, and an abundance of contraries in Mouth's text. Ambiguity here serves to emphasize Jameson's remark that "all human relations are bound to have something vaguely ominous about them; and the more heightened moments of scandal or violence prove to be nothing but the convulsive effort to free one's self from one's interlocutor."[22] When Mouth tries to free herself from the "buzzing . . . so-called . . . in the ears" or from the ray of light from the moonbeam which she interprets as "just all part of the same wish to . . . torment" her, she feels so numbed that she feels "inclined . . . [to] scream" and then does so (16-17). She apparently feels some pleasure in screaming; her only other sensory experiences are the opening and shutting of her eyelids. In her oneiric state, it is as though she *now* dreams of having a body. Mouth feels herself to be almost a mote imprisoned by the shafts of moonlight, as if to say, like Pirandello, "There is someone who is living my life, and I know nothing about him."[23] Charles Lyons contends that Beckett removes the presence of his characters "by eliminating the character's awareness of both location and self."[24] Yet it is memory, history, and relationships that combine to form an individual; when any one of these is absent, the subject drifts in a limbo between the self and the other, between times and places, night and day. The broken, disjointed prose in which this state is described by Mouth conveys a confusion, an absence of mind, as in sleep and dreaming. Only it is not temporary; it is not something from which Mouth will awake. And as we realize this, we ponder with new anxiety just how her story is a blend of pain and ecstasy.

It could be argued that Mouth's outburst resembles what Barthes has called the domestic "scene." Scenes, he says, "lay bare the cancer of language. Language is impotent to close language." But even more importantly, it is the violence of the most civilized scenes that Barthes finds terrifying: "violence always organized itself into a *scene*: the most transitive of behavior (to eliminate, to kill, to wound, to humble) was also the most theatrical . . . [I]n all violence, he could not keep from discerning, strangely, a literary kernel: how many conjugal scenes must be classified under the label of some great genre painting: *the wife cast out,* or, again, *the repudiation!*"[25] In *Not I*, Mouth refers to her humiliation at her own speechlessness at the grocer's, but moreover, she feels she is going to "die of shame" when she *does* speak "once or twice a year . . . [and]   . . . then rush out stop the first she saw . . . nearest lavatory" (22). At first she does not want to admit that it is her voice that speaks: "she . . . to give up . . . admit hers alone . . . her voice alone . . . but this other awful thought" (19). This other thought "that feeling was coming back" permits "the whole machine" (shades of Deleuze) of her body to "piece it together" (20).[26]

Brater has also referred to "the whole machine" of the speaking mouth, making our eyes focus on the image from a multiplicity of angles like a camera's lens. The different angles on Mouth and Auditor pose once again the issue of the couple. Brater argues:

> The visual relationship between Mouth and Auditor therefore makes out of what would otherwise be a one-woman show an unforgettable dramatic confrontation. . . . Mouth mixes memory with desire, reflecting her own ambivalence about the sudden change which she says has taken place in the field. With her "face in the grass," perhaps "she" has been raped: "just at that odd time . . . in her life . . . when clearly intended to be having pleasure . . . she was in fact . . . having none . . . not the slightest."[27]

There is a blank between the April period and mouth's present reawakening in another self as she tells us of the experience; the question is, what happened during this black period? The answer, it seems, has to do with Mouth's extreme ambivalence about sex, more specifically her intense fascination and shame about it. Mouth is deeply conflicted in this area, her appetite for bodily or sexual pleasure uneasily cohabiting with the guilt and revulsion she feels about it. This disturbance may be the root and cause of Mouth's breakdown, though it must be said that a breakdown may not have occurred. Other readings of the play are possible. Brater wonders if the "'buzzing' in the head . . . Mouth mentions might be a 'stream of words' running through Auditor's own hooded head, [or] the possibility that the silent figure of Auditor is as consistently wordless as the 'she' of Mouth's story before the whatever-it-was that took place in the field."[28]

It is important to recognize what Beckett is doing here, for in terms of narrative technique, it is both unorthodox and frighteningly effective. While, for example, Mouth seems to be remembering an incident at the grocer's, midway into the memory we find Mouth is speaking from her point of view; at this point Mouth, the remembering subject, becomes an object of her thoughts, a shift into the sort of radical depersonalization that is found in acutely schizoid conditions. Beckett, of course, does not explicitly suggest that Mouth suffers from schizophrenic breakdown, and this lack of signaling creates in the audience an almost vertiginous loss of balance and certainty, in effect giving Mouth an echo, a dim, faint comprehension, of the panic and terror involved in the possibility of one's going insane. That body that remembers lying face down in the grass on that April morning, having wept, makes all the more apparent that Mouth thinks that her being might now be a monster.

This liquid intermingling of contraries suggests once again that the whole question of gender, including that of the voice speaking, is a central issue. What we have is the bedrock Calvinist insistence on the complete otherness of God and the brokenness of humanity in the passage mentioning "that time in court . . . what had she to say of herself," that place where there was "something she had to tell . . . how it was . . . [in order to be] . . . then forgiven . . . God is love . . . tender mercies" (21-22). If the gap between God and humanity is to be bridged, it will be done from the other side, by God's gracious act, and not by anything that Mouth can do except acknowledge her own need. Beckett uncovers the corrupting effect, for the couple, of phallic power when woman's posture is one of denial of self.

There is, accordingly, a double effect between the voice and the text: on the one hand, it is a description of the subject's past. But, on the other hand, this narration imposes a sort of blank imprint of the concept of the couple. It forms the idea of the couple without changing anything in the usual connotation. We could speak here, in a certain sense, of a fiction of the self and the couple, here seen in Mouth's recollection of her past and what it is like in her present voicing of it, and its disturbing effects on Auditor, apparently rendered helpless by it. The whole discourse of *Not I* seems to shift between these two modes.

An integrated couple therefore can never be pinpointed or nailed down, for the couple, even if unified, constantly poses the threat of dispersal. And the random threat of the other's disappearance is not simply a "notion" on Beckett's part. It serves rather to define even ordinary couples. This situation of course leaves open the possibility of instability at all times. Beckett has worked in this tension through the voice in *Not I* to point to the insufficiency of language to bond and harness the couple. This device is unsettling because the voice is not merely a device. To see the problem, one need only look at the narrow space that the stage area in *Not I* has become. This makes the couple's falling apart even more evident.

At the same time, whatever or whoever the subject becomes as a singular identity is not as important as the realization that her relationships to others seem to remain and provide a stable system of coordinates to which the idea of permanence may possibly be cemented. But part of what causes Mouth's

Late Theatrical Works 297

instability is her combative stance, in collision with others in her consciousness and in her language, for both, almost without exception, have built into them a polarity, a veer towards subject-centeredness. The creation of Auditor, a corporeal image of the other, does offer a visual representation of the internal conflict within the narrator, and also as a concrete manifestation of Mouth's confessional voice. "But Auditor," as Gontarski notes, "remains only a physical representation of an internal force that is developed clearly in dialogue, and the fundamental discourse with the other exists equally well without the additional icon."[29]

In one sense, all of Beckett's works have been based on a series of developments about sound and new ways of voicing. *Not I* is marked by the voice which controls its own fluctuating masses, colors, densities and intensities of sound. This technique is used not to project a faithful or distorted image against live sound, but to extend and project the relatively fixed and discrete actions and speech of a live performance onto a broader continuum which comments indirectly on a subject's inability to communicate simply to an other. Lyons concurs with the notion of incommunicability: "Beckett removes the images of the basic consciousness and presents only the text that repeats itself within it. These words embody no immediate awareness . . . Beckett does not show that the consciousness of the character to whom Mouth belongs either listens to that recitation or has any sense of it."[30]

At the same time, *Not I* suggests the complete other in the negativity of the title; indeed, it implies an (absent) other who is *not* not I. Beckett's gestures of effacing the couple, and yet keeping it in and out of focus, are his own idiosyncratic means of articulating it. The perceived self, as well as the self perceiving itself, is shaped by absence, by what is not-there; for condensation, concealment, and displacement—like the dream—constitute the couple. The couple seems to be born out of a purgatorial and anguished nothing. Gontarski states that the first episode of *Kilcool* was directly used for the opening in *Not I*. "A couple has evidently reached an impasse in its relationship: 'to hear her out would be only to hear again what he had heard a thousand times already. And to explain would be only to say again what he had said a thousand times already.'"[31] This opening signals a significant transition to the narrator's being a conscious victim of abandonment.

This distancing of the other demonstrates Beckett's very deliberate shift from the phallocentric to the hymeneal. Why else would he dare show a mouth that resembles an isolated female sexual orifice speaking? The hymen is the invisible and folded space in *Not I*, in which Mouth pours forth its utterings. Metaphorically, the hymen means the consummation of marriage. Literally, however, its presence reveals the absence of consummation. This structure is what brings forth the play of absence and presence. *Not I* becomes, then, a kind of "theater of the unconscious" in which we find a "constant relation between a dream-element and its translation which, if the censorship were absent, could only be described as symbolic."[32] What this suggests is that *Not I* comes as close as might be possible to a theater without representation which Artaud himself once dreamed. The need for dramatic context and form and the concern with verbal and language possibilities—sound as language, language as sound, the coupling of meaning to sound, of content to sound, even of linguistic to musical structure—is illustrated in all Beckett's works, but is strikingly evident in *Not I*. Here language is driven out of the concrete world of the subject's mouth into the (silent) discourse of the Auditor. The text, spilling out of Mouth, objectifies her as subject and yet chains her down. Though Mouth functions within the realm of language dominated by the Phallus, she inscribes her language with music, repetition and variation, voice and laughter. Her (feminine) text knows no boundaries (no punctuation, no strict codes of the written), no beginnings and endings. The result is a cyclic, repetitive overflow of multiplicity and ruptures that defy phallogocentric notions of coherence and meaning.

How so? The delirious outpourings of Mouth in fact unify the subject. That Beckett uses the voice here as hallucination recapitulates the repetition compulsion, which is sometimes a healing device. *Not I* is quite close to being a replica of the "uncanny" which, for Freud, was the repetition of an older fantasy in which tiny traces can be felt only in the released unconscious. Here the red garish mouth achieves two dramatic resolutions: first of all, it allows Beckett further to narrow down his subject to a single body part. Connor argues that this narrowing down of the body can be seen as a powerful device, since it requires the viewer to fill out the missing body. This exercise in audience imagination then changes the status of the visible portion of the body into that of a sign. "The body can never be witnessed in its palpable wholeness; rather that wholeness will always be the result of a retrieval or reconstitution, lying somewhere between what the stage or screen makes present, and what it leaves out. The frame which the spotlight or the TV screen draws around the segment of the body . . . always remains part of the reconstitution, as an interior deficiency in its wholeness."[33] This narrowing down might serve to symbolize for Beckett that there is a kind of freedom in relinquishing our striving but illusory giantism. Our ambition to be different—richer, brighter, healthier—appears to vanish in the midst of suffering.

Secondly, this narrowing down points to the "return of the repressed" in the following way. The mouth, derealized because of the enormous focus on it, unmasks what we ordinarily do not dwell on. Even ordinary personal humiliations are not studied as tokens of feminine repression in general. But here she speaks; this de-oralized and frustrated mouth is held to its trivial search of who, and what, *she* is. Beckett wants to show that the dualistic fury and insufficiency of language is an intrinsic, even *necessary*, feature of partnership.

What does all this mean? *Not I* unfolds a gradual process of degradation, a kind of stunted violence of the soul. We realize that Mouth's displacement— by the camera's zooming in on it in the television production, or by the subject's total concealment on stage with the exception of the mouth—is one of isolation. The mouth is both a presence and an absence; it is not an organ which exists solidly in space, but is itself the space in which solidity and vacancy are produced. And if this mouth suggests a vagina, then it also suggests a phallus when words "literally seem to pierce the aperture through which they are emitted."[34] For Mouth, the locus of all that is other and sinister can only function within a phallic economy and Beckett is sensitive to this fact. *Her* gender thus shapes our reading (and viewing) of the work. In a special and remarkable way, *Not I* has a very particular appeal, for, rather than imposing a *total* vision of the couple, it seeks to rationalize the relationship of a subject to *her* experience of a painful world.

Thus, it is the debris of life that we see in *Not I*. The work is a deceptively plain, two-track voicing, in which the consciousness of the speaker sifts through her younger, fragmented consciousness even as she is still trying to reconstruct her memories *here and now.* her body is displaced because there seems to be no place or space for it. Mouth has filled the textual space with her imaginations and memories of time past that have now hypertrophied *through* time. Time stops and starts, advances and retreats, splits and merges. No longer the eye of the earlier works of the sixties, but the voice itself fragments to infinity.

From *The South Central Review* 7, no.1 (Spring 1990): 36-49.

---

[1]The systematic development and appplication of such ideas appeared first in music, and is largely attributable to Karlheinz Stockhausen. Stockhausen argued for the controlled use of multiple realization as a new conception of performed music and he also claimed in the mid-1950s that such techniques were in themselves new forms. Beckett seems to be applying the same concepts to language and the voice in *Not I*.

[2]Herbert Blau, "Due Process and Primary Process: The Participation Mystique of Norman O. Brown," *Discourse* X.1 (Bloomington: Indiana UP, 1987-88) 3-18. Blau draws on Brown's extensive analysis of Greek tragedy to explain the origins of spectator participation. For one, the mutilated or severed body could only be healed through reparation and a spiritual transformation of the subject. The formula for such cleansing demanded Eros, or desire and love, and less strife. Quite clearly, Mouth is severed from her body, feels the pressure of judgment for having committed some sort of crime, and seeks healing through Nature (the April morning, the larks, and the grass), tears of repentance, and the longing for Divine forgiveness. Blau writes further: "For

Brown, when the actor as exhibitionist (the one who fascinates by showing the genitals) disappears, the voyeuristic spectator will disappear [and] . . . the spectator no longer arrested, passive, or paralyzed, subject to the look" will go as well (13). *Not I*, however, seems to be arrested at the point of the exhibitionistic dream set on the stage. How else explain the similarity of Mouth to female genitalia, and how else explain the spectator's embarassed fascination upon witnessing the play, especially the television version?

[3] Enoch Brater, *Beyond Minimalism: Beckett's Late Style in the Theater* (New York: Oxford UP, 1987): 19.

[4] Brater 20.

[5] S. E. Gontarski, *The Intent of Undoing in Samuel Beckett's Dramatic Texts* (Bloomington: Indiana UP, 1985). Gontarski notes that, to friends, "Beckett offered an earlier, more personal source, this from the matter of Ireland: 'I knew that woman in Ireland . . . I knew who she was—not "she" specifically, one single woman, but there were so many of those old crones, stumbling down the lanes, in the ditches, beside the hedgerows. Ireland is full of them. And I heard "her" saying what I wrote in *Not I*'" (132).

[6] Ruby Cohn, *Just Play: Beckett's Theater* (Princeton: Princeton UP, 1980) 69. See also Gontarski, *The Intent of Undoing*, 141.

[7] Gontarski 142. In *Murphy*, however, the subject/object duality more accurately implies a subject/subject duality and it is developed within a Cartesian-Manichean frame.

[8] Steven Connor, *Samuel Beckett: Repetition, Theory and Text* (New York: Blackwell, 1988) 184.

[9] Christiane Makward, "To Be or Not to Be . . . A Feminist Speaker," in *The Future of Difference*, eds. Hester Eisenstein and Alice Jardine (Boston: G. K. Hall, 1980) 97.

[10] Samuel Beckett, *Not I* in *ends and odds* (New York: Grove, 1974) 14. Citations will be noted in my text by page numbers.

[11] Hélène Cixous, "Castration or Decapitation?" *Signs 7* (1981): 55.

[12] Cixous, *The Newly Born Woman* (1975), trans. Betsy Wing (Minneapolis: U of Minnesota P, 1986) 86.

[13]Jane Gallop and Carolyn Burke, "Psychoanalysis and Feminism in France," in Eisenstein and Jardine 106.

[14]Julia Kristeva, *Desire in Language: A Semiotic Approach to Literature and Art*, ed. Leon S. Roudiez and trans. Thomas Gora, Alice Jardine, and Leon S. Roudiez (New York: Columbia UP, 1980) 149.

[15]Gontarski 141. My emphasis.

[16]Kristeva 150.

[17]Hersh Zeifman, "Being and Non-Being: Samuel Beckett's *Not I*," *Modern Drama* 19 (March 1976): 45.

[18]Kristeva 149.

[19]Ann Rosalind Jones, "Inscribing Femininity: French Theories of the Feminine," in *Making a Difference: Feminist Literary Criticism*, eds. Gayle Greene and Coppelia Kahn (New York: Methuen, 1985) 83.

[20]Paul Lawley, "Counterpoint, Absence and the Medium in Beckett's *Not I*," *Modern Drama* 26 (December 1983): 409.

[21]Kristeva 149.

[22]Frederic Jameson, "Agons of the Psuedo-couple," in *Fables of Aggression: Wyndham Lewis, the Modernist as Fascist* (Berkeley: U of California P, 1979) 38.

[23]Luigi Pirandello, Diaries, quoted in *The New York Times Review* (17 April 1988): 32.

[24]Charles Lyons, *Samuel Beckett* (New York: Grove, 1983) 155.

[25]Roland Barthes, *Roland Barthes*, trans. Richard Howard (New York: Hill, 1977) 159-60.

[26]It is likely that Deleuze owes something to Beckett's notion of the body-machine, which actually precedes Deleuze and Guattari's well-known work, *Anti-Oedipus: Capitalism and Schizophrenia*. In *Murphy*, for instance, the "body-machine" has its origin in the Cartesian mechanism and body-spirit duality; and in *Watt*, in his personal apprehension of the human body as a

teratological system, in which the body is matter composed of logical combinations.

[27]Brater 33, 32.

[28]Brater 32.

[29]Gontarski 148.

[30]Lyons 157.

[31]Gontarski 138.

[32]Blau 3.

[33]Connor 161.

[34]Pierre Chabert, as quoted in Connor 163.

CHAPTER 9

Poetry, Short Stories and Prose Texts

A Rereading of the Traces

Mary Ann Caws

I. TEXTS FOR NOTHING

> Je me mis en route.
> Quelle allure.[1]

Even essays of the most minimal art are composed of traces. But when the simplest words are accused of exaggerating the given, when the faintest tracings are seen as magnifications ("c'est vraiment le minimum, non, c'est du roman, encore du roman," p.215), all the reader can risk is following the barest lines in the barest of manners, aware that this, however little, is too much.

Here, in the limited framework of the *Nouvelles et textes pour rien* —which are taken as a *whole* framework—the bare outlines of three intersecting traces will be pointed out: the reductive lines of the consciousness (that "infaisable être"), the gradually exhausted line of the writing hand ("ce soir je tiens la plume," p. 164), and the utterance or will to utterance of the "impossible voix," on which the texts close ("dit-elle, murmure-t-elle," p. 200). The briefest of looks at the intersection of these lines—that is, the minimal gesture of *regard* and *écriture* possible—would therefore seem the most appropriate to the texts. For it is *within* the space of these lines that all ordinary questions of person and story ("voilà le tort que j'ai eu, un des torts, m'être voulu une histoire," p. 156) are here inscribed.

1. That the consciousness should be finally ineffectual as to speech is not only the basis for the lack of story which in its turn makes way for the presence of *text* (albeit for nothing), but is also the ground for the lines of reduction—at first the only apparent movement. The key sentence is stated in perfect and succinct form as it closes in upon itself ("Tout ce que je dis s'annule, je n'aurai rien dit," p. 43). This sentence, condensed into its beginning and concluding words, will form the *end* of all the texts, where ("qui n'est pas un endroit") it will take on a different sense: "tout dit." But at first, the phrase simply prophesies a series of reduction.

In order to trace the reductive procedures from their initial stage, we must begin at the first page of the first story. Counting the doorsteps up or down is seen as the same dilemma, contemplated not without interest: "Dans l'autre sens, je veux dire de haut en bas, c'était pareil, le mot n'est pas trop fort" (p. 11). To that colorless, obvious, neutral word "pareil" is attributed a certain significance, whereas we might have otherwise considered the whole statement as humorous, ironic, or an example only of brilliant linguistic play. But then as we move along the line of reductions and diminutions, we look back to that beginning as the high point from which the line recedes. After that, only *decrescendo*: this general process includes the major techniques of Beckett's humor. For example, definite statement is reduced to qualified determination ("Je vais donc me raconter une histoire, je vais donc essayer de me raconter encore une histoire," p. 42), the easiest clichés of natural speech to linguistic fumblings (Ma vie! m'écriai-je. Mais oui, dit-il, vous savez, cette sorte de—comment dirai-je?" p. 65; "alors je jouais la comédie, n'est-ce pas, celle de—comment dire, je ne sais pas, " p. 116; "je surveille la main qui écrit, toute brouillé par—par le contraire de l'éloignement," p. 116). The most frantic cries diminish in tone to a helplessly polite monotony: "J'essayais de gémir 'Au secours!' Mais le ton qui sortait était celui de la conversation courante. Je ne pouvais gémir" (p. 104). As further and more extreme instances of the decrescendo, the first page of *Textes pour rien* can be seen as a sad reverse echo of the first page of *Nouvelles*: in one short sentence, a mountain becomes a hill, the description of which goes from intense to banal ("mais si sauvage, si sauvage, assez," p. 127). And again, in a confusing linguistic and psychological switch, actions which have taken place are made into actions which have not taken place at all: "Tout s'emmêle, les temps s'emmêlent, d'abord j'y avais seulement été, maintenant j'y suis toujours, tout à l'heure je n'y serai pas encore . . . " (p. 132). Most serious—or most genial—of all, the generality to which we normally assign the highest value is flatly described as less than the slightest tale: "une histoire n'est pas de rigueur, rien qu'une vie" (p. 156).

The flashes of hope illuminating the consciousness at the end of several chapters in the *Textes pour rien* are slanted toward the pathetic rather than toward the hopeful. In the following sentence, concluding the fourth chapter and thus responding to the opening lines: "Où irais-je si je pouvais aller, que serais-je, si je pouvais être" (p. 153), the particular reversed order moves from a conditional of apparent possibility to the implications of what is contrary to fact, thereby closing off the circle: "C'est là où j'irais, si je pouvais aller, celui-là que je serais, si je pouvais être" (p. 158). The most lyric passages are themselves destroyed by their own lyricism mixed with a mock lyricism; the sixth chapter ends on a long sentence chopped into pieces, with interior rhymes, rhythms, and diminutives (here italicized), undermining the lyrical possibility: "pour dire une histoire, au vrai sens des mots, du mot dire, *du mot histoire, j'ai bon espoir,* une *petite histoire* . . . une *brève histoire . . . j'ai bon espoir, je le jure*" (p. 174). The same procedure takes place at the end of chapter nine, where two instances of the cliché "tôt ou tard," surround a rhyming and semi-positive note: "quelque part" (p. 196).

2. The writing hand, taking dictation from a voice it does not understand, leaves the *traces* of the dictation, as the voice makes another insertion of the mock rhyming kind (traces and rhymes italicized here): "*Seules les fenêtres—non.* La propriété semblait *abandonnée.* La grille était *fermée.* L'herbe envahissait les *allées. Seules les fenêtres* du rez-de-*chaussée . . .*" (p. 114). The hand, in its occasional identification with the consciousness, signals itself as passive: it does not choose the questions, rather, the question is in the habit of choosing the consciousness and the hand: "Et cette autre question, qui me connaît si bien aussi . . ." (p. 130).

At first, after the exterior speech is limited, and then cut off altogether, the writing hand is firm although indifferent and uncomprehending; chapter five begins: "Je tiens le greffe, je tiens la plume, aux audiences de je ne sais quelle cause" (p. 159). But at the end of the chapter, fatigue overcomes the hand, and the pen falls: "c'est noté." So there is, observing, a consciousness exterior to the hand, beyond the one whose force is gradually reduced in the *Nouvelles*.

3. The greater consciousness, this impossible voice, which would leave traces, is a simple will to *écriture*. The voice has no mouth, only hearing. All the words are dead, they said too much when there was nothing, for they could say nothing else. And suddenly, in the last sentence of the texts when nothing seems in fact to be the only issue for all the writing, there is a sliding of tenses—a *glissement*, which might be seen as a reopening. The sentence begins with what seems a total negation of hope, particularly for the reader of the positive catalogues of Apollinaire ("Il y a") and the open catalogues of Breton ("Il y aura une fois"), and for the reader of Beckett accustomed to reading conditionals as contrary to fact: "Et il y aurait un jour ici, où il n'est pas de jour, qui n'est pas un endroit, issu de l'impossible voix l'infaisable être . . ." (p. 220). If there were this day, it would be silent, black, and empty, marking

the limit at which everything is finished: "tout sera fini, tout dit"—the circular telescoping and resolution of the sentence from the *Nouvelles* quoted above: "Tout ce que je dis s'annule, je n'aurai rien *dit*." Even the final "dit-elle" is reduced to a "murmure-t-elle." But then why the sliding from the conditional ("il y aurait") to the future ("tout sera fini")? Looking back to the middle of the sentence, we see the opposite of an empty middle: the empty, black, and silent day that would exist would be accompanied by a beginning of day: "*et un commencement de jour*." The three words we italicize here are, to be sure, only three words in many pages of texts, clearly labeled texts for nothing. The words have perhaps no reason, and they are minimal in proportion to the negations and reductions. But their position marked them as at least significant. They enable us to re-read the traces, to re-read, for instance, a sentence of mixed tenses which seems to deny action ("d'abord, j'y avais seulement été, maintenant j'y suis toujours, tout à l'heure je n'y serai pas encore," (p. 132), as a partial erasing of the negative for a possibility of the most minimal kind. Not to erase the "pour rien," but to start the story over and write the texts again.

II. The Minimal Gesture

> Ce qui compte c'est d'être du monde,
> peu importe la posture (p. 157).

It is certainly on the strictest minimum that Beckett's man bases his attitude. Not only is he resigned to that situation, but he takes his psychological strength from it, as well as his singular manner of being and speaking. Therefore, each disappointment brings him (as he says) an undeniable *relief*.

It is as if the mere pittance granted him were deliberately arranged by fate and gladly accepted by him as the obvious source of his most convincing style:

> voilà ma vie, pourquoi pas, c'en est une si l'on veut, si l'on y tient absolument; je ne dis pas non, ce soir. Il en faut, parait-il, du moment qu'il y a parole. (p. 156)

Luckily, he continues, he has not asked for anything. Starting from rock bottom, one can lose nothing; no possibility (because there are none) can block any other, as is carefully pointed out. The most seriously limited powers are blessed with the most serious lack of something to act on—and in a perverse way, this gives them their only strength. The language at the disposal of Beckett's "hero" is not suited to exaggeration, admiration, or even description; it is just finally recognizable: "j'appelle ça des mots" (p. 173). From these fragmented and separated parts emerges not quite a language, from the only matter available after or during the extinction of the light (which was never a source of great illumination, only a "sorte de lumière") Beckett makes a statement at once serious and droll, which we might call an epic of the minimal.

Nor is it a totally negative epic. At least four small guiding threads of a certain verbal optimism can be distinguished, even if the optimism is so microscopic and so dependent on linguistic details as to solicit generally the sole reaction of humor. (To impose on such a minimal given the slightest semblance of order is of course a further example of humor, not therefore unfair to the spirit of Beckett.)

1. In the first place, the reduction to the minimum discussed above is a process at once corresponding to the tone of the whole and reinforcing its overall direction. It occurs so frequently as to become the invisible tissue on which the linguistic personality of the single character depends. He exults, for example, in the good fortune which seems to us, phrased as it is, only the natural way of things: "J'eus la grande chance, plusieurs fois, de ne pas me faire écraser" (p. 84). Here the qualification of frequency "several times," as it underlines his conception of good luck, reinforces our astonishment that he should find it unusual (*of course*, we are *usually* not run over). Or again, even the fact of having a body at all in its complex order: "avec des tas de membres et d'organes, de quoi vivre encore une fois, de quoi tenir, un petit moment, j'appelerai ça vivre, je dirai que c'est moi . . ." (p. 144)—serves as a matter for gratitude. The reference to brevity plays the same role here as the reference to frequency above, intensifying our surprise at his thankfulness.

2. Secondly, the occasional allusions to gestures calling for a certain strength or signaling a confidence, however reduced. As is true of almost all Beckett's books, these traces of optimism are found with a decreasing frequency as the stories and the texts reach their conclusion. In the first story, we notice the possibility of decision and of motion, and even a hint of progress: "Je me relevai et me mis en marche" (p. 16). It is true that these extraordinary gestures depend on the personage being in his prime, as does his intense and relatively enduring appreciation of the visual: "Je me suis perché sur les géraniums, pendant des années" (p. 16). The rare gesture of comfort is equally touching, precisely because of the surrounding harshness: Rocked in his own arms, the protagonist tells himself stories as his father once did. The stories finish well, he asks and answers questions as best he can, playing the father and the son, cradling himself "sans beaucoup de tendresse, mais fidèlement, fidèlement" (p. 135). In that fashion he has been able to stand his life until now, creating for himself and out of himself alone the possibility of companionship, of much-deserved rest, and even of lyricism: "Dormons, comme sous cette lointaine lampe, emmêlés, d'avoir tant parlé, tant écouté, tant peiné, tant joué" (p. 135). The playing is theatrical and childlike, as the language situates itself in the world of serious effort, at the risk of life and in the realm of fantasy.

3. On the level of simple vocabulary, certain expressions betray the habit—if not the assurance—of normal action and normal speech. We find clichés depending on a value judgment: "comme il faut," "cela valait mieux," "j'eus cette joie. . . ." Again, these are confined to the first part of the stories. But there runs all through the stories and texts a frequent and significant use of verbs such as *vouloir* and *pouvoir*, indicating the existence of desire ("tout ce que je voulais," p. 16; "vouloir absolument continuer," p. 21; "il suffit de vouloir," p. 144) and of past decisive action ("je m'arrêtai une troisième fois, de mon propre gré," p. 26; "petit à petit je sortis," p. 44), and even of future possibility ("qui peuvent essayer encore," p. 132; "peut-être qu'une autre fois je pourrai," p. 40).

4. Nor is the personage entirely trapped within himself. Frequently he takes a position of philosophic distance, at one remove from his pathetic situation, and insofar as he is detached, we are not swallowed up in his misery: "Je suis là-haut et suis ici . . ." (p. 131); "Je serai ici, je ne dirai loin, ce ne sera pas moi . . ." (p. 143); "ce n'est toujours pas moi" (p. 151).

It is, in fact, this last thread of hope—of detachment—combined with the genuine possibility of speech, always renewed in spite of the almost catastrophic events, that provide the basis for hope. For to this minimal series of personages who finally merge into one in our perception, there is granted upon occasion a renewing of the word: "Les mots me revenaient petit à petit, et la façon de les faire sonner" (p. 106); and even a constant renewing of situation and of story: "Puis ça passe, tout passe, je suis de nouveau loin, j'ai encore une lointaine histoire, je m'attends au loin pour que mon histoire commence . . ." (p. 158). The voice cannot be his, he says; he can speak only because his voice is another's. Perhaps, after all, the voice is ours, as are the situation, the story, and the text.

From *L'Esprit Createur* 11, no. 3 (Fall 1971): 14-20.

---

[1]Samuel Beckett, *Nouvelles et Textes pour rien* (Paris, Editions de minuit, 1955), p. 19. All references in the text are to this edition.

Samuel Beckett: "Imagination Dead Imagine"
Michael Parsons

In Beckett's recent writing, the subject becomes increasingly anonymous and disembodied. Malone's body was decrepit and paralyzed; in *The Unnamable* the body is reduced to a deformed, shapeless lump. At the end of *How it is* there remains only a voice; though the subject still has feelings and confused memories, and speaks in the first person, his identity has become indistinct. In *Imagination Dead Imagine* the subject has no identity. He is addressed, or addresses himself, in a timeless imperative. There is no indicative verb, and no personal pronoun except the implied 'you.' In this way a total anonymity is achieved. There are no extraneous memories or dreams ('Islands, waters, azure, verdure . . . omit'). Somewhere in an endless white void, a white rotunda; inside two bodies, back to back in foetal postures, immobile in the confined space; they breathe and sweat, open and close their left eyes. Light and heat rise and fall in ever varying patterns, from darkness to light, cold to warmth, through the intervening greys—a *reductio ad absurdum* of the cycle of day and night, summer and winter. The extreme whiteness and blackness, are moments of calm, the rise and fall restless, and interrupted by agitated vibration. The bodies seem indifferent to the changes only the anonymous subject experiences, or perhaps merely observes the alternating calm and stress, before receding into the white void outside. Of anguish, there is only a residual flicker ('the infinitesimal shudder instantaneously suppressed'). In this image of silence and emptiness, indifference and anonymity, Beckett seems to express the inside of a totally depersonalized consciousness.

Beckett's later work is often called nihilist and anti-human. Its negative vision certainly contains no element of optimism or consolation. Nor does it seem to suggest that despair is anything other than an essential and unavoidable part of the human condition. This absolute view is an inverted religious one: human degradation and guilt are relics of Christianity, despair is the obverse of religious belief. But taken as a series his novels also suggest more fruitfully, the social derivation of subjective despair. The earlier novels are concerned with social predicaments—refusal to work, exile, etc.—and include overt satire on social values (e.g., Murphy's search for a job; the proliferation of useless work in *Watt*; Molloy's encounter with the police). The later work, asocial and solipsistic though it is, is a logical continuation; loss of individual identity is shown to be an ultimate derivation from loss of social identity.

Finally it is not the diagnosis which interest Beckett but the condition itself. This fragment defines and illuminates, using language which approaches in its spacing and repetition of words, a purely formal abstraction, a consciousness so empty and blank as almost to defy definition. This is enough to make it worth reading.

For eight pages of text the price is excessive; all the savage and absurd humour of, for example, *Molloy* is obtainable from the same publishers for a shilling less.

From *The New Left Review*, no. 38 (July-August 1966): 91-92.

"Silence Within": A Study of the *Residua* of Samuel Beckett

John J. Mood

In the past eight years, Samuel Beckett has published in separate volumes three works of prose fiction, which together add up to the niggardly total of fourteen pages. That each work was called a novel, at least on the publishers' blurbs, surely sets some kind of all-time record. The three works are, in order of composition and first publication, *Imagination Morte Imaginez* (*Imagination Dead Imagine*), *Assez* (*Enough*), and *Ping* (*Ping*). They were composed in French and Beckett himself, as usual, did the translation into English.

The three works have recently appeared together in a single volume in both France and England. In French, they have been published with one other work (the French translation of *From an Abandoned Work*) in a volume entitled *Têtes-Mortes* (Paris, 1967). The titular phrase (which translates as "Dead-Heads") does not appear in the volume though it is, as we shall see, quite ironically and humorously appropriate. (The phrase had appeared in the singular—"a dead head"—in an earlier novel.[1] In English they have been published with three other works *(Stories, Texts for Nothing,* and *From an Abandoned Work)* in a volume entitled *No's Knife* (*Collected Shorter Prose*, 1945-1967, London, 1967). The titular phrase appears in the thirteenth text for nothing: "And whose the shame, . . . whose the screaming silence of no's knife in yes's wound, it wonders."[2] In both collections, the French and the English, the order has been altered to *Enough, Imagination Dead Imagine,* and *Ping,* which is, oddly enough, the order of length from longer to shorter. In the English edition, they are published under the collective *Residua.* There is no corresponding collective title in the French.

The three works are extremely brief. *Enough* is the longest and it is only seven pages. The other two are less than half as long. This same shrinking has occurred in Beckett's dramatic pieces. A recent play has only 121 words of dialogue and is called, appropriately enough, a *dramaticule*.[3] A number of years ago Beckett had said that the more he writes the more difficult it gets, adding, "For me the area of possibilities gets smaller and smaller."[4] More recently he had one of his narrators confess "more of old less of late very little these last tracts they are the last extremely little hardly at all a few seconds on and off."[5] One would not have thought Beckett meant these words literally, but that has come to be the case, at least for now. And those tracts of the narrator of *How It Is* were neither the last nor the littlest ones. We trust it will be a long time before any Beckett work takes the former dubious honor. The works I consider here undeniably take the latter. When we speak of least we mean, of course, in length, not in substance. For if it is stretching things a bit to call these works novels quantitatively, they are nonetheless quite substantial qualitatively. They are not a trilogy, at least not in the way *Stories* is, or in the way his labeled trilogy of novels is. Whether they are a trilogy in a thematic or some similar way is a problem. In many obvious ways, all of Beckett's works are so related. The question then is whether these three are especially closely related. This question can be fully answered only after studying the three works, especially since we have no word from Beckett on the matter. That fact itself may suggest that a trilogy is not strongly intended. We will respect the order of the works as published together, which means we take up *Enough* first, even though, as noted, it was written second.

Enough is the longest of the three, and has standard paragraphs and short sentences. The only unusual feature in this regard is the total lack of punctuation other than periods. There is not a single comma, semicolon or dash. The story has more of a standard plot than anything by Beckett in twenty years. An old woman tells it, recalling her long association with an older man when she was quite young. The whole is quite compressed and involves only two events: a sacral prognosis (the old man's back infirmity) and a disgrace (the old man's expulsion of the woman from his life). The work opens with the following paragraph:

> All that goes before forget. Too much at a time is too much. That gives the pen time to note. I don't see it but I hear it there behind me. Such is the silence. When the pen stops I go on. Sometimes it refuses. When it refuses I goon. Too much silence is too much. Or it's my voice too weak at times. The one that comes out of me. So much for the art and craft. (p. 153; Fr. p. 33)[6]

We might recall Beckett's statement that "to be an artist is to fail, as no other dare fail, that failure is his world and the shrink from it desertion, *art and craft*, good housekeeping, living."[7]   In both cases, the ironical tone is obvious. Beckett, the master craftsman, correctly sees the limitations of craftmanship. Here in *Enough*, this is, in fact, all we hear of "art and craft," of the "ways and means,"[8] except for a hint right at the end of the work. The admonition to forget all that went before, the several references to "too much" in contrast with the title, the going on nonetheless, the half-disembodied voice (and the consequent post-Cartesian hint), the witness writing down the dictation—all this immediately places the work in the mainstream of Beckett's work, though with creative variations.

The narrative begins immediately after this opening. It is by a woman, though this is not certain until the very end—in English, that is. Naturally, in French this ambiguity does not exist because of the pronominal inflections in that language. This first person feminine narration is a first in Beckett. He has off and on presented touching portraits of women (Celia in his novel *Murphy*), gently sardonic ones (Mrs. Rooney in his radio play *All That Fall*), harshly satiric ones (Nell in his drama *Endgame* and Moll in his novel *Malone Dies*). But never has he had a female narrator (though Winnie in his play *Happy Days* does present a near monologue). The mood of this narrative reflects this difference nicely, being a bit more muted. Phraseology and other touches also reflect this. For example, her narrative begins: "I did all he desired. I desired it too. For him. Whenever he desired something so did I." (p. 153; Fr. p.33—the French adds a second "Pour lui," "For him," at this point) And again, in the next paragraph, after relating how he told her to leave, she states she does not know whether he means permanently or not, and adds: "I never asked myself the question. I never asked myself any questions but his." (*ibid.*; Fr. p.34) This is a statement she repeats often. Further, she does leave as he commanded, and "without looking back," this last an echo of the protagonist of *Stories*, who often said the same thing.[9]   This is a reference to the story of Lot's wife (Gen. 19:15-26).

Thus has her narrative begun. This event, her expulsion, is what she will later call her disgrace. She comments that he was probably on his last legs anyhow, which was certainly not the case with her at the time. They were of "entirely different generation[s]" (p. 154; Fr. p. 34-35). Yet she herself has now entered the same phase he was in, old age, "night," with "gleams in my skull." "Given three or four lives I might have accomplished something." Their liaison began when she was six, "barely emerging from childhood." She must have been a precocious nymphet, and it did not take long for her to "emerge altogether" (p. 154; Fr. p.35). They traveled gloved hand in gloved hand, her left, his right. Occasionally they took their gloves off. She interjects: "All I know comes from him. I won't repeat this apropos of all my bits of knowledge. The art of combining is not my fault. It's a curse from above" (*ibid.*; Fr. p. 36). This interruption was suggested by a reference to the stars. In the English edition, she half keeps her promise not to repeat this—in the French

Poetry, Short Stories and Prose Texts

she flatly breaks the promise, as we shall see. When they met he was already old and so bent his frame was parallel with the ground. To compensate, he walked with bent knees and legs apart. Their difficulties communicating are described. She would have to bend down to hear what he had to say. They did mental calculations together. "We took flight in arithmetic," she recalls (p. 155; Fr. p.38). This calculating is apparently quite meaningful to them (it occasions the only typographical variation, an exclamation point). They calculated the speed of their travel, distance of travel, even a table of cubes of three-digit numbers (reminding one of Ernest Louit's peasant prodigy in Beckett's novel *Watt*). She thinks this long period—7,000 miles at three miles a day—was her life. That is to say, the period beginning with the day he told her of his infirmity. She had thought he was blind also, but one day he stops and says his vision will get no worse; he can see some. Sometimes he stopped to say something and said nothing. This suggests to her the various mathematical possibilities of stopping, talking immediately or otherwise, and moving on immediately or otherwise. She lists this combination of possibilities in full.

She again identifies her life with her life with him: "It is then I shall have lived then or never. From the day he drew the back of his left hand lingeringly over his sacral ruins and launched his prognostic. To the day of my supposed disgrace" (p. 157; Fr. p. 41). They climbed a lot during this time. He liked to look at the stars. She occasionally sees the sea in the far distance. At this point the French has a paragraph omitted in the English. Here it is in full: "Toutes ces notions sont de lui. Je ne fais que les combiner à ma façon. Donné quatre ou cinq vies comme celle-là j'aurais pu laisser une trace" (Fr. p. 43). Which can be translated as: "All these notions are from him. I do nothing but combine them in my own way. Given four or five lives like this one I might have left a trace." She then returns to the decade under consideration (between the prognosis and the disgrace). She had originally set the scene of the disgrace just short of the crest of a hill. She now says no, it was on a plain, with a great calm over everything. His voice is growing weak.

She returns in her narrative to the present: "I don't know what the weather is now. But in my life it was eternally mild" (p. 158; Fr. p. 44). Again she has drawn the distinction between now and her life. She mentions the weather, their calculations again, and then, for the first time, their sleeping arrangements: wedged together, bent at knees and hips, she on the inside, both facing the same direction. A little love play occurs, though only a little, as "he murmured of things that for him were no more and for me could not have been" (p. 159; Fr. p. 46). They talk little. Their food is flowers. She speaks again of calm and explains: "This notion of calm comes from him. Without him I would not have had it" (*ibid.*; Fr. p. 47). So she did not entirely ignore her promise even in English. She immediately resumes: "Now I'll wipe out everything but the flowers. No more rain. No more wounds. Nothing but the two of us dragging through the flowers. Enough my old breasts feel his old hand" (*ibid.*; Fr. p. 47). With that the story concludes. Enough: enough to have this memory of a past life, enough to have had that life. That is considerably more than any one of the people in Beckett's last three or four novels has had. The story is quiet and does in fact achieve a kind of calm. It is compact and requires careful reading but presents no particular difficulties. In itself it is a low-keyed largo version of familiar Beckett themes. If indeed it is closely connected with the other two stories it may take on an additional significance.

Imagination Dead Imagine is also unique in several ways, and again involves a change of pace. It is half as long as *Enough*, unparagraphed, and with longer sentences than *Enough*. There is extensive use of commas, more so than even in the last half of Beckett's novel *The Unnamable*, though at certain sometimes crucial points commas are missing. More striking than these items, intrinsic as they are to the work, is the marked, and remarkable, increase in compactness. One can describe the work by the chemical images of condensation, distillation, even as a precipitate, more so certainly than Beckett's 1935 collection of poems entitled *Echo's Bones and Other Precipitates*.[10] A residuum it is, though not in any literal sense.[11] Since it is difficult to convey this density, let us simply quote the first few sentences: "No trace anywhere of life, you say, pah, no difficulty there, imagination not dead yet, yes, dead, good, imagination dead imagine. Islands, waters, azure, verdure, one glimpse and vanished, endlessly, omit. Till all white in the whiteness of the rotunda. No way in, go in, measure" (p. 161; Fr. p. 51). The first sentence, if read out loud with expression, requires little unpacking, except for the titular phrase. That can be read three ways. First: "Imagination dead. Imagine (that)!"—exclaiming over the fact. Or second, and more probably: "Imagination dead. (Well, then,) imagine (something anyway)"—using the imperative. Or third: "Imagination dead, (you) imagine (but don't know)" —expressing uncertainty. The next sentence is considerably denser: many scenes quickly appear and vanish, but "endlessly," implying that they appear and disappear again and again, which repetition will be omitted here, he adds. Or something has happened to stop the process, for next we learn that all is whiteness. And in that whiteness is a white rotunda, self-enclosed, a Leibnizian monad, into which one cannot enter, which we then enter, and begin to measure. Thus the density of the first four sentences of the work necessitates careful reading. This is true of the entire work.

Before noting the measurements of the rotunda, something else will have struck the attentive reader. For the first time since *Watt*, or more precisely since his unpublished novel *Mercier and Camier*, Beckett is using the third person. And, to anticipate, this third person narration holds throughout this work and the next. We have, then, a considerable shift in tactics here. The rotunda, white inside and out, set in a scene of whiteness, is an eighteen-inch high circular wall topped by an eighteen-inch high dome, so that the height of the whole thing is three feet. The diameter of the circle formed by the wall is also three feet, and the circular floor plan has a quadripartite division. On the white ground are two white bodies, each in its semi-circle. The rotunda, wall and dome, is solid, "rap, solid throughout, a ring as in the imagination the ring of bone" (*ibid.*; Fr. p. 51). So we have literally what the narrator of *How It Is* spoke of: "the voice quaqua on all sides then within in the little vault empty closed eight planes bone-white. . . ."[12] Further on in the same novel, the phrase occurs a couple of times more—"in me the vault bone-white," and "in the little chamber all bone-white"[13]—in both cases referring to the skull of the narrator. In all three references bone-white suggests death (dead-heads). Here, in *Imagination Dead Imagine*, we have a white vault with the sound of bone, suggesting a desiccated skull. And here there is no voice, without or within. There is no sound of bone, either. One has to imagine it. Soundless, white— and hot. The bodies are sweating. (A macabre Auschwitz oven?) After a time, the light goes down slowly to total darkness. Simultaneously the temperature goes down to the freezing-point.[14]

More than a third of the work describes these fluctuations, the rise and fall from white heat to black cold and back. Most often it is an unbroken change taking about twenty seconds one way. Sometimes the change involves pauses. More rarely the change will reverse direction in mid-course. The extremes of each fluctuation bring rest and calm. The transit involves considerable vibration of ground, wall, vault and the bodies.

> But whatever its uncertainties the return sooner or later to a temporary calm seems assured, for the moment, in the black dark or the great whiteness, with attendant temperature, world still proof against enduring tumult. Rediscovered miraculously after what absence in perfect voids it is no longer quite the same, from this point of view, but there is no other. (pp. 162-163; Fr. p. 54-55).

The bodies are then described. Both lie on their right sides. Given a circle with 0¤—at the top and the degrees going clockwise as in a compass, with, say, A at 180¤, B at 0¤, C at 270¤, and D at [*sic*] than Beckett) at A, knees between B and C, feet between C and A; the man's head is at A, *derrière* at C, knees between A and D, feet between D and B. Both are holding their left legs with their left hand, left arms with right hand. "At incalculable intervals" one or the other opens a pale blue left eye and stares unblinking for long intervals. Once there was an overlap of ten seconds when both had an eye open. They are, then, alive. "Hold a mirror to their lips, it mists" (p. 163; Fr. p. 56). In spite of sweat, eye, and mirror, they appear inanimate. We are told that they are not asleep, but not how it is known (it would be too complicated) (p. 164; Fr. p. 57). The bodies are of average size, in fairly good condition. "Between their absolute stillness and the convulsive light the contrast is striking, in the beginning, for one who still remembers having been struck by the contrary" (*ibid.; ibid.*). Who says that? The skull in which these two bodies reside? Or the narrator? Then who is he? When the depth of the dark black descends, everything vanishes. The story ends inconclusively:

> Leave them there, sweating and icy, there is better elsewhere. No, life ends and no, there is nothing elsewhere, and no question now of ever finding again that white speck lost in its whiteness, to see if they still lie still in the stress of that storm, or of a worse storm, or in the black dark for good, or the great whiteness unchanging, and if not what they are doing. (*ibid.; ibid.*)

One wonders whose imagination is dead, for it is surely not Beckett's. His imagination is as lively as ever. One also wonders if this couple, enclosed in a dome, is the same as in *Enough*, transmuted to another (earlier or later) phase. That work ended inconclusively also, never having informed us whether the old man died, the couple ever got together again, or what. In *Imagination Dead Imagine* some kind of stasis has, temporarily at least, been achieved. But that stasis is as uncertain (and horrific) as anything else in Beckett has been. Furthermore, the exploration and images of the self have become even more fundamental, one might even say archetypal or mythic. The packed prose, the economy of image, description, and language, the distillation of situation "to the general from the particular," as Beckett had said earlier[15] —all this has produced the bleached skeleton, the bare bones, of Beckett's exploration. The spareness and starkness of this portrayal of an inexplicably tormented blanched stormy (or black) world is as bleak and uncompromising a paradigm of alien man in an alien world as one could imagine. The matter-of-factness of the descriptions makes it even more compelling. The gaunt portrayal, stripping all to essentials, can be deceptive in it simplicity, hiding the depth of the resonances of the portrait of the inner man who is as emaciated as the world is mad. It is appropriate that the single volume edition of the work as published in England had a photograph of a Giacometti sculpture of a desiccated human on the cover.[16] And as with Giacometti's sculpture, there is (as usual), it must be said, something exhilarating about Beckett's portrayal.

As we have already stated, *Ping* is a literal residue in two ways. First, because it came into being out of the eventual scrapping of a rather different and much longer work, *Le Dépeupleur* (The Depopulator), and second, because the final work is the last of sixteen versions in which the work got longer for a while and then became somewhat shorter as the final version emerged. One should quickly note, however, that the very first manuscript version was very tightly packed to begin with, much more so than even *Imagination Dead Imagine*. We do not intend to discuss either *Le Dépeupleur* or the early versions of *Ping* at length, since this study is not a close examination of textual variants, but we do want to make a few general comments based on a quick look at the broad outlines of the manuscripts and typescripts available. *Le Dépeupleur* apparently plagued Beckett for quite some time. From late 1965, there is a notebook with three versions of it. There are also three typescripts from the same period. The third version in each case is incomplete. At the end of the third typescript, Beckett wrote "arrêté Paris décembre '65"—notice, "stopped," not "finished," and indeed it is broken off half-way through the longer second version. Then in late spring, 1966, he resumed work on it and from that came a notebook with two versions, and a long, fifteen-page, single-spaced typescript that dribbles away inconclusively in handwriting. With all of this material is a note in Beckett's handwriting to the purchaser of it: "MSS *Le Dépeupleur-Bing* Though very different formally these 2 MSS belong together. *Bing* may be regarded as the result or miniaturisation of *Le Dépeupleur* abandoned because of its intractable complexities."[17] Then in the summer of 1966, he resumed, but this time he started from scratch on the work which was to become "Bing." The intractability and complexity of *Le Dépeupleur*r are obvious from a casual glance at the manuscripts and typescripts. There is the core of a brilliant conception present, but it was becoming increasingly lost in a maze of unmanageably intricate details. The miniaturization of the form and situation from *Le Dépeupleur* to "Bing" may be easily illustrated by noting that the former involved among many other things, a large complex cylinder (which for a time begins to take on the structural features of a modern-day Dantean scheme of Hell) while the latter involves a simple 6' x 3' x 3' box. Besides, Beckett's country has long since been rather effectively depopulated, not to say defoliated. Therefore "Bing" successfully takes the next step without needlessly repeating in a needlessly complicated form a number of others already taken. We will now turn to the published versions, French and English.

The density of "Ping" is, as indicated, awesome, rather like Sirius' Companion, the white dwarf star. This choice of comparison is not gratuitous for not only is *Ping* dense, it is also white with an unreal whiteness, with a whiteness almost totally unrelieved (unlike "Enough"). Before discussing this and other images, however, let us look at the style and situation. *Ping* is one unbroken paragraph with sentences of average length growing longer toward the end. There are no commas. The language is stripped of all parts of speech except nouns, adjectives and participles. The linguistic process of *How It Is*, described so well by Fletcher,[18] here reaches its zenith. In lieu of further description, we quote the beginning of the work: "All known all white bare white body fixed one yard legs joined like sewn. Light heat white floor one square yard never seen. White walls one yard by two white ceiling one square yard never seen. Bare white body fixed only the eyes only just" (p. 165; Fr. p.61). The entire work is like this, repeating with subtle changes the same phrases over and over again, only occasionally introducing a new word or phrase, usually never to be used again. The situation described is that of a person standing in a box, rather like a coffin stood on end. The person's sex is unspecified though there is a slight possibility it is male. He is rigid, stands with head high, arms hanging by his sides, palms front, legs rigid together, heels and toes likewise (in all three cases described as "jointed like sewn"), feet at a right angle. All is hot and gleaming white, except for the eyes, which are light blue. All is silent. Occasional traces, blurs, light grays, soft murmurs occur, whether in the mind of the one in the box or outside is not known. The outside is not actually mentioned. The phrase "without within" occurs twice, in a way that could imply either (and more probably) within and without the body but still within the box or (less possibly) within and outside the box. The external world is never mentioned. It has in fact long since more or less passed from view or concern in Beckett. The narration is again in the third person (roughly), which gives a strange objectivity to the inwardness portrayed.

Rather than following the work through since that is impossible, we shall examine the shape of the work and the development of the images. We have mentioned the ubiquity of white in *Ping* (ninety times in the three pages). The black/white, dark/light dichotomy has appeared throughout Beckett's work. He has explicitly recorded his distrust of clarity: "The time is perhaps not altogether green for the vile suggestion that art has nothing to do with clarity, does not dabble in the clear and does not make clear, anymore than the light of day (or night) makes the subsolar, -lunar, and -stellar excrement. Art is the sun, moon and stars of the mind, the whole mind."[19] Wittgenstein has commented in a similar vein in relation to the notion of "clear concepts": "Is an indistinct photograph a picture of a person at all? Is it even always an advantage to replace an indistinct picture by a sharp one? Isn't the indistinct one often exactly what we need?"[20] All this is understandable in view of the Western propensity for the use of light metaphors in speaking of the understanding and presentation of truth and knowledge: "lucid," "illuminate," "elucidate," "insight," "clear," "scintillating," "it dawns on one," "sparkling," "shimmering," "distinct," "dazzling," and so forth. The only affirmative term from the other half of the dichotomy is "adumbrate"; all others have negative or even evil connotations: "obscure," "obfuscate," "becloud," "dim," "murky," "dull," "hazy," "dark," "black," and so on. Beckett has always balanced these, or tried to redress the balance.[21] To take an example or two, Murphy relishes the three zones in his mind: light, half-light, dark (and prefers the latter).[22] Or the following injunction: "leave it vague leave it dark."[23] Or more facetiously: "dark bright those words each time they come night day shadow light that family the wish to laugh each time no sometimes."[24] This desire to laugh is perhaps also at work in the statement that the remembering of voices is for "the sole end that there may be white on white."[25] And irony is surely present when one recent narrator states, "White I must say has always affected me strongly."[26] The same irony, as well as despair, accompanies this image in

Ping. One can surely say that this ubiquity of white is the inevitable outcome of an exploration of the self in the twentieth century West with its unmitigated will to clear reason, lucid rationality.[27]

The other prime image is, of course, "ping" itself. It occurs thirty-four times in the English version, and more frequently toward the end (in the first third there are only two pings). "Ping" translates two different words in the French: "bing" and "hop," of which there are twenty of the former and twelve of the latter.[28] The decision to translate these with "ping" came somewhat slowly to Beckett. He began by translating "bing" with "ping" and "hop" with "pfft."[29] *Hop* in French means, to use language, something like "off it," or, to use a gesture, something like a flick of the hand. *Pfft* nicely captures this. But the decision to use only *ping* in the English is inspired. It makes the English version even more mysterious, compact, and unified. What *ping* is is difficult to say and must in the nature of the case remain so. It is as ambiguous as the voices in Beckett's work (or as Godot). At times *ping* is within. Most often it is linked with words such as "fixed elsewhere" or simply *elsewhere.* Whether this means outside the skull or the box is not known. *Ping* can suggest a tiny projectile striking something, the ring of fine crystal, a nuclear phenomenon (it has always seemed to me as though those streaking sub-atomic particles in cloud chambers should make some kind of pinging sound), sonar, the ring as a typewriter carriage reaches the margin, and so on. Whatever one's associations, *ping* as an image is like a diamond with its scores of gleaming facets, like an environment that permeates all, without and within. If one can say that in a general way *Godot* means that for which one waits (and I am not convinced one can, or should), then one can perhaps say that in a general way *ping* is contact, communicating, or the memory thereof.

Having mentioned translating, we might note some other choices in this work. There is "head haught," which occurs frequently. *Haught* is an old English word meaning "high" *(cf. haughty)*, and is Beckett's translation of "tête boule bien haute." *Unover* is Beckett's odd translation of *inachevé*, which means simply *un*-finished. "Only just" is his translation of "à peine" —*barely,* "just barely." *Unlustrous* translates *embu*—dull. In all cases, the final Beckett choice both contracts the language and makes it more vivid and alive.[30]

Finally, there are several images and phrases that occur only a time or two. One is the color rose (five times) which seems to suggest the original color of the body. Another is black (three times), a rare contrast with white. Another is the wind, a recollection of the storms of "Imagination Dead Imagine." Another case involves several images suggestive of a decrepit crucified Christ: "Given rose only just nails fallen white over. Long hair fallen white invisible over. White scars invisible same white as flesh torn of old given rose only just" (p. 167; Fr. p.64). Or this may be any decrepit old person. Still another rarity is the sudden appearance of an "eye black and white half closed long lashes imploring" (*ibid.*; Fr. p. 65). The image returns in the last sentence of the work:

"Head haught eyes white fixed front old ping last murmur one second perhaps not alone eye unlustrous black and white half closed long lashes imploring ping silence ping over" (p. 168; Fr. p. 66). The curious interjection into this spare prose of a classic imploring look and long lashes from the tradition of the melodrama and dime novel is startling as well as deliciously ironic.[31] One final phrase to be mentioned is "silence within." It occurs three times, always in references to the skull. It is also related to the conclusion of "Ping" just quoted. Faint murmurs there are, blurs, traces, light greys, more ephemeral than the pings, but finally there is absolute silence within, "ping silence ping over," the final word being also a nice contrast with the repeated "unover." ("Over" occurs several times earlier, however.) The perennial silence and the ubiquitous end.

From this discussion of the images it can be seen that there is some movement in the work. But one obtains a greater sense of this movement from the patterns of the images that constitute the structure and form of the work. In this respect, it is much more like a lyric poem. We have mentioned *ping* itself as occurring only twice in the first third of the work, twelve times in the second third, and twenty times in the third third. The pattern of the phrases containing the word *meaning* is also instructive. Here is a list of the variations given in the order they occur:

4 "signs no meaning"
then 1 "perhaps a meaning"
then 1 "signs no meaning" again
then 1 "a meaning only just"
then concluding with a "perhaps a meaning" again

Likewise with the word *nature:*

2 "perhaps a nature"
then 1 "a nature only just"
then concluding with "perhaps . . . a nature" again

Likewise *image* itself, always in a sentence begun with "ping":

"Ping perhaps a nature one second with image same time"
"Ping perhaps not alone one second with image always the same"
"Ping image only just"
"Ping a nature only just almost never one second with image same time"
"Ping perhaps not alone one second with image same time"

Also the following, still in the order of occurrence:

>   then 2 "but that known not":
>   then 2 "all known"
>   then 2 "but that known not"
>   then 1 "all known"
>   then 1 "but that known not"
>   then concluding with 1 "all known"

This pattern is even more instructive when what is known or not known is examined. "All known" can be expanded to something like "That is all that is known," while "but that known not" always refers to either "infinite" or "always." A final example is the occurrence five times of "that much memory almost never" followed by "that much memory henceforth never" in the last sentence but two.

One could give many more such examples, but the pattern is obvious and provides a "plot" of sorts. The curve is toward zero, as always in Beckett—the silence and the end. The difference other than density, is that *Ping* starts so much closer to zero to begin with. We must point out however that Beckett's path to zero is an asymptotic one, an infinite one, like the square root of minus one,[32] or the "irrationality of pi,"[33] or seven (days in a week) divided into 366 (days in leap year),[34] or the never completed heap of millet of Zeno of Elea.[35] That is to say, zero will never be reached.[36] Thus the moving of the images provides the structure. We might add here that this infinite regression is a perfect portrayal of how it is that there will always be another work by Beckett so long as there is a Beckett.[37]

Ping emerges as a considerable work, for all its brevity. Of the three short pieces, it is far and away the most provocative. The external dimension has all but disappeared. In the box, brief blurs and murmurs (pings) break an otherwise totally empty, blinding whiteness and silence. The self has contracted, collapsed in on itself like the white dwarf star. The density obliterates all differentiations and yet the elements are all there. The prose of this work belies the term "prose" itself, and its etymology, "straightforward," "to turn forward." This prose turns in on itself again and again, finally being coiled as tightly as a mainspring about to snap (ping!). The result is an almost completely self-referring piece of writing, paradigmatic of the entire thrust of Beckett's prose fiction, wherein the descent into and exploration of the self itself becomes a self-referring activity.

In considering these three works as a whole, we note again the order as published together. In this order we have seen an increasing distillation. The residue is purer in each case. The couple in *Enough* appears in *Imagination Dead Imagine* in another form. In *Ping*, the sole being is perhaps a man, and the long lashes imploring suggest that the couple has not totally disappeared; there is thus a slight residue of the couple remaining. Or one could say that the unstated sex of the being in the box suggests the myth of the androgyne, the couple thus having moved within. There is likewise only a trace of consciousness left at the end. In *Enough*, the woman's consciousness is about par for Beckett, that is, minimal, both in its subordination to the man's and in its identification of its life with this subordinated existence. In *Imagination Dead Imagine*, the two beings have, by implication, some consciousness. Their eyes do open occasionally. The shift to the third person introduces a curious dichotomy in this regard. The two beings are there but we have no first-hand information on their consciousness. Beckett maintains the fiction. The third person's consciousness is the prism through which we look at what little there is, and this utter objectivity is not violated by moving into the "mind" of the being being observed. Or we could say that we are inside the skull and all that is there with any certainty is what is presented in the work itself. In *Ping* there occurs what one would not have thought possible: the minimal is further reduced. "That much memory almost never," and even "that much" is microscopic. Even the traces of the third person seem merged in the pervasive whiteness, so much so that it might be a mistake to speak of third person narration in the case of *Ping*, though one does not know what one would call it if not that. All of this reduction of consciousness to the point where one is uncertain if even a mental world still exists is perhaps not so uncertain when we recall again the collective title of the French edition: *Têtes-Mortes*.[38]

All these and many other examples illustrate the residual nature of the three works, individually and together. (Whether they thereby constitute a trilogy in the stricter sense still cannot be determined with certainty.) The residue of prose, of situation, of sheer quantity, of image, of consciousness, all manifest the contraction of the area of possibles. In exploring the self, Beckett's focus has for a long time been exclusively on the inner, whereto the outer has collapsed. Now even that inner has shrunk to a barely visible point where there is only "silence within," at least for the moment.[39]

From *Studies in Short Fiction* 7 (1970): 385-401.

---

[1]Beckett, *How It Is* (New York, 1964), p. 86—*Comment c'est* (Paris, 1961), p.106.

[2]*No's Knife: Collected Shorter Prose*, 1945-1967 (London, 1967), p. 135; *cf.* pp. 109, 113, 123, 126-27—*Nouvelles et Textes pour rien* (Paris, 1955), p. 219; *cf.* pp. 189, 203, 209-210.

[3]*Come and Go* (London, 1967), title page. And now his latest, *Breath*—no dialogue, thirty-five seconds long.

[4]Israel Shenker, "Moody Man of Letters," *The New York Times*, May 6, 1956, sec. 2, p.1.

[5] *How It Is*, p. 103—*Comment c'est*, p. 126.

[6] All page references to the works under consideration will be given thus, with the first numeral referring to the English edition and the second to the French.

[7] Beckett and Georges Duthuit, "Three Dialogues," in *Samuel Beckett: A Collection of Critical Essays*, Martin Esslin, ed. (Englewood Cliffs, N.J., 1965), p.21; emphasis added.

[8] This is the phrase used by Beckett for "art and craft" in an early typescript of *Enough*, from the John Doe Papers, Manuscripts Division, Rare Book Department, Olin Library, Washington University, St. Louis, MO

[9] *No's Knife*, pp. 12, 46, 49—*Nouvelles et Textes pour rien*, pp. 16, 84, 89.

[10] Ludwig Wittgenstein used the same term—*Niederschlag*, precipitate—to describe his last work; see his *Philosophical Investigations*, trans. by G. E. M. Anscombe, 2nd ed. (Oxford, 1958), p. ix.

[11] Nor was *Enough*; in both cases on the basis of the manuscripts in the John Doe Papers, Washington University, St. Louis, MO On the other hand, *Ping*, as we shall see, is a literal residuum in two ways.

[12] *How It Is*, p.128—*Comment c'est*, p. 155. The French has, after "little vault," "dans le petite caveau," "in the little sepulchre." The business of eight planes is a deliberate mistake—it should be six. *Cf. Malone Dies* (New York, 1956), p. 47—*Malone meurt* (Paris, 1951), p.87: "Sometimes it seems to me that I am in a head and that these eight, no six, these six planes that enclose me are of solid bone."

[13] *How It Is*, p. 134—*Comment c'est*, pp. 161, 162. The French has *caveau* for the first, *boîte*, *box* for the second.

[14] Zero degree centigrade, recalling Hamm's tale of events on a cold day when it was "zero by the thermometer," among other things: *Endgame* (New York, 1958), p. 51.

[15] *No's Knife*, p. 144—*Têtes-Mortes*, p. 20.

[16] London, 1965.

[17] This and all quotes from and information about these manuscripts and typescripts come from the John Doe Papers, Washington University, St. Louis, MO

[18] John Fletcher, *The Novels of Samuel Beckett* (New York, 1965), pp. 218-220.

[19] Beckett, "Denis Devlin," *Transition* (Paris), no. 27 (April-May, 1938), p.293.

[20] *Philosophical Investigations*, p. 34.

[21] He has said that our time, in contrast with some others, has both darkness and light, and "where we have both dark and light we have also the inexplicable;" Tom F. Driver, "Beckett by the Madeleine," *Columbia University Forum* (Summer 1961), p. 23.

[22] *Murphy* (N. Y., 1957), pp. 107-113—*Murphy* (Paris, 1953), pp. 81-85.

[23] *How It Is*, p. 74—*Comment c'est*, p. 92.

[24] *Ibid.*, 110—*Comment c'est*, p. 134.

[25] *Ibid.*, 135—*Comment c'est, p. 163.*

[26] *No's Knife*, p. 141—*Têtes-Mortes*, p. 13.

[27] One cannot refrain from remarking that this unmitigated will to light may well be the archetypal foundation of the West's distrust of dark and black people (we even had to name them—Negro), and thus of the near-genocide of the American Indian, the enslavement of blacks, the attempt to make most other darker people white (Christian, that is—e.g., Jim Crow, "Mr. Charlie"), by force if necessary. *Cf.* Jean Genet, *The Blacks: A Clown Show*, trans. by Bernard Frechtman (New York, 1960), p. 10, where he asks "What exactly is a black? First of all, what's his color?" Surely at the most fundamental level, the black-and-white (East/West) thing is anything but a mere "social problem" (it is that also, of course).

[28] In the first French edition there were nineteen bings.

[29] The Washington University holdings have three scripts of *Ping*. I was able to determine that the red manuscript was earliest, the typescript second,

and the blue manuscript third. Not until the blue manuscript was *ping* used for both French words.

[30] In the first four cases given, the first Beckett choice in the early English manuscripts was the usual one. Only gradually in each case did he come to his final more distinctive selection.

[31] Beckett's irony often trips them up. One critic finds these long lashes, etc., "the most human touch, the most emotive phrase, in the whole piece" —surely a bit of whistling in the dark (to say the least). David Lodge, "Some Ping Understood," *Encounter*, XXXII (February 1968), 87. This article is generally rather good, however.

[32] *No's Knife*, p. 124—*Nouvelles et Textes pour rien*, p. 205.

[33] Beckett and Duthuit, "Three Dialogues," p. 21; *cf. Molloy* (New York, 1955), p. 86—*Molloy* (Paris, 1951), p. 97.

[34] *Watt* (New York, 1959), pp. 34-35.

[35] *Malone Dies* (New York, 1956), pp. 50-51—*Malone Meurt* (Paris, 1951), pp. 92-94. Also used in *Endgame*, pp. 1, 70.

[36] After writing this, I discovered that Darko Suvin had made the same point about Beckett's world: "Beckett's Purgatory of the Individual," *Tulane Drama Review* (Summer 1967), p. 25.

[37] It must be admitted that I made a considerable attempt to discover a more formal structure and shape in the whole. The possibility was suggested by several clues. There was Beckett's known propensity for puzzles, permutations, combinations, and other such oddities (see, especially *Watt*). More specifically, Beckett, in occasional typescripts, wrote the seventy sentences of *Ping* one to a line or paragraph so that the appearance was of a seventy-line or -verse poem or composition. Also, at one point the notebook containing six manuscript versions of *Bing* has an incomplete chart with three columns headed "Corps," "Endroit," and "Divers" (Body, Place, and Miscellanea, or Sundries). Taken together, these items seemed to suggest that *Ping* itself is a permutation. It must be admitted, however, that no substantial evidence was found to indicate any such mathematically structured shape or pattern according to some combination. This in spite of all sorts of charts, variations, lists, etc. One such apparent dead end might be mentioned simply to illustrate. Take the collective title *Residua*, make it singular and English and you have *Residue*, of which

Ping is one. But "residue" is also a technical mathematical term. Now add the fact that there are apparently thirteen sentences which could be charted as "Place." (Thirteen, of course, is Beckett's favorite number.) (I say "apparently" because it was difficult at times to decide what column a sentence should go in.) Taken together, this suggests a pattern of 5, 18, 31, 44, 57, since those numbers are residues of 70 modulo 13, since 70 — (13 x 5) = 5, 70 — (13 x 4) = 18, 70 — (13 x 3) = 31, etc. But no pattern such as this was observed, and this was the most complex one employed. Simpler ones yielded no better results. One problem that might decisively rule out such a pattern is that although there are seventy sentences in both the French and English versions, they are not the same seventy, since one French sentence is split in two in the English version and one English sentence is a combination of two French sentences. But even limiting my work to the French version, since that was the original and since the chart was in an early draft of the French—even that yielded nothing. One mentions these failures because one is still teased by the possibility of a pattern, if even an incomplete or broken one.

[38]*Perhaps* is not used lightly here. It occurs often and significantly in "Ping" (even more so than in earlier works). And Beckett himself said, "The key word in my plays is 'perhaps'" (Driver, "Beckett by the Madeleine," p. 23). The same is surely true of his prose fiction.

[39]Beckett has, of course, already broken the silence once:—in his short, and happily depressing, "Prologue" to the sweetly salacious play *Oh! Calcutta!*, An Entertainment with Music devised by Kenneth Tynan (New York, 1969), p.9. This prologue is the previously-mentioned play *Breath*. I understand that Tynan's use of the play was unauthorized.

The Impossibility of Saying the Same Old Thing the Same Old Way—Samuel Beckett's Fiction Since *Comment c'est*

Raymond Federman

"QUELLE EST CETTE HORREUR CHOSESQUE où je me suis fourré?"[1] Admittedly, there is nothing more absurd, nothing more idiotic, than to write fiction. That is to say, nothing is more laughable than to sit in a room—within four walls—day after day, month after month, year after year, to create an imaginary situation and fictitious characters ("cette horreur chosesque") by the mere process of lining up words on pieces of paper.

Perhaps the only way for the writer to escape the tedium and the anguish of such a self-imposed torture (self-imposed and gratuitous especially for the fiction writer) is to LAUGH at his own activity. And it is well known, in fact, that many novelists, even those whose fiction depicts the most oppressive, the most tragic, the most horrendous situations (and this was the case with Proust, Kafka, Céline, and many others I am sure), could be heard laughing within the walls of the chambers where fiction was being shaped. Only laughter, indeed, can save the fiction writer from jumping out of the window, from blowing his brains out, or from simply walking away from his absurd undertaking.

This laughter (essential and inherent to fiction) is not, however, lost in the chambers of the creation. It can either permeate the fiction itself in the form of humor, irony, satire, or grotesque situations, or, better still, it can become a critical dimension of the creative activity itself. In other words, it can become a critical reflection on fiction—its form, its tradition, its evolution, its rules, its substance, and its very tool (language). All great fiction, to a large extent, is a reflection on itself rather than a reflection of reality.

Samuel Beckett has been writing fiction now for some forty years. Yes, for forty years now he has been doing almost exclusively nothing else but sit in his room and toy with words. 1929-1971—forty-two years to be exact (forty-two years of words): an entire life of words! And he himself has noted this in one of the *Textes pour rien:*

> Ah être fixé, savoir cette chose sans fin, cette chose, cette chose, ce fouillis de silence et de mots, de silences qui n'en sont pas, de mots qui sont des murmures. Ou savoir que c'est encore de la vie, une forme de vie, vouée à finir, comme d'autres ont pu finir, comme d'autres pourront finir, avant que la vie finisse, sous toutes ses formes. *Des mots, des mots, la mienne ne fut jamais que ça,* que pêle-mêle le babel des silences et des mots, *la mienne de vie,* que je dis finie, ou à venir, ou toujours en cours, selon les mots . . .[2]

This declaration sums up Beckett's life (Beckett's biography): WORDS. Forty-two years of words since the publication of the first words in 1929 . . . and it's not ended yet . . . because, as the Beckettian voice laments: "C'est la fin qui est le pire, non, c'est le commencement qui est le pire, puis le milieu, puis la fin, à la fin c'est la fin qui est le pire . . ."[3]

Behind this "pell-mell babel of silence and words," the one who fills the pages, the one who accumulates words, the writer, the scribe, has disappeared, vanished progressively, subtly, and definitively to become the anonymous voice of fiction. For more than forty years then, Samuel Beckett has sat in the room, has endured what Hugh Kenner called some ten years ago "the siege in the room,"[4] passing the time by lining up words on paper—"quelques vieux mots par-ci par-là les ajouter les uns aux autres faire des phrases."[5] During all that time, he has stubbornly resisted all temptations to free himself from these words, all temptations to become involved with the outside world, to participate in those "other" activities which we (quasi normal human beings) perform daily to justify our existence and avoid its absurdity. But for him too, the only way to resist, the only possible way to continue, was to LAUGH at his own activity. Yet, if there is one thing Beckett was intent on laughing at, it was the novel, even though he persisted in his pretense to write novels.

From *Murphy* to *Comment c'est*, Beckett systematically takes apart the novel as we know it, as we have come to accept it with all its imperfections and possibilities. Beckett reduces the novel to its most basic elements, to its bare minimum, stripping it of all pretense of realism, dehumanizing its people, voiding its landscape, renouncing, in other words, all properties of the novel. And though many critics have tried repeatedly to recuperate Beckett's fiction on the basis of those sets of rules by which the novel is defined, and to find in his fiction more meanings and more symbols than he really put there, he continued to laugh at it, to mock it, to demolish it, to diminish it.

Comment c'est, indeed, brings the novel (or what remains of it) to the brink of disaster. Nothing left here but a bare muddy landscape situated nowhere, a naked remnant of a being (hardly human nor fictitious) who is able to duplicate, to multiply himself to an almost infinite number of replicas in order to better negate himself, and all these creatures crawling in the mud, a sack full of sardine and tuna fish cans tied around their necks, crawling reptile-like towards a victim in order to become themselves victims. *Comment c'est* makes a clean sweep of the novel, but not without a self-conscious critical dimension—not without laughter. For, as the voice says in the last few pages of the novel, even though "tombés dans la boue de nos bouches sans nombre qui s'élèvent là où il y a une oreille un esprit pour comprendre la possibilité de noter le souci de nous le désir de noter la curiosité de comprendre une oreille pour entendre même mal ces bribes d'autres bribes d'un antique cafouillis" (p. 162).

This mocking attitude of the creator towards his creation is possible, in Beckett's fiction, because there is present, at all times, "une oreille pour entendre même mal ces bribes d'autres bribes," because there is present, in or beyond the fiction, an imaginary reader (or listener) with whom the author establishes a subtle and ironic relationship which enables this reader/listener to hear the laughter of the creator—to hear, as it were, the novel fall apart—to hear "ces bribes . . . d'un antique cafouillis." And it is through this connivance with the reader that the author is able to suggest to him: Watch me now! Watch how I am going to get out of this one! Watch what a beautiful mess I am going to make of things! This self-conscious undervoice is present throughout Beckett's fiction. It is there whispering playfully in the ear of the reader/listener.

In *More Pricks Than Kicks*, it comes through the voice of the narrator who tells us what good friends he and Belacqua were. In *Murphy*, the laughter is heard through the authorial comments which warn us that this is "an expurgated, accelerated, improved and reduced account" (*passim*) of how the events occurred (and indeed we can hear the author laughing in the background). And still in *Murphy*, it is with the same laughing tone that the author invites us to enter the zones of Murphy's mind. In *Watt* and in *Mercier et Camier*, it is once again through the narrator's voice that we are made aware of the systematic demolition of fiction and of the creator's playfulness. In the *Nouvelles* and the three volumes of the trilogy (*Molloy, Malone meurt, L'Innommable*), it is now the double voice (the divided voice) of the narrator-hero (the I who has become both the "teller and the told") which leads us, at each step of the fictitious game, as it comments on its failures and successes.

Watch me now says this *voice within a voice* (laughingly), watch how I am going to kill Belacqua of cowardice! watch how I am setting up this complex mechanism in Murphy's room which will cause a gas explosion to reduce Murphy to chaos; watch Mr. Knott—now you see him, now you don't see him; watch me now strip Mercier and Camier of all their earthly possessions; watch how I am going to solve the problem of Molloy's sixteen stones and of his four pockets; watch how I am going to give the Unnamable the shape of an egg; watch how I am going to go on with my story even though I just told you I am dead; watch the hand that is me in the process of writing me; watch the words that are me in the process of becoming me. And in each instance, like an acrobat whose bodily motions draw beautiful figures in the air which are erased as he lands perfectly on his feet, the author performs his tricks before our own eyes while laughing, or at least with an ironic smile on his face.

It is then with this mocking attitude towards what he is doing that Beckett has pursued his systematic destruction of the novel. However, everything in Beckett (as in Dante's *Divine Comedy*, and this has been noted on numerous occasions) comes in threes. Just as Murphy's mind was divided into three zones, just as the three *Nouvelles* (*L'Expulsé, Le Calmant, La Fin*) represent three different versions of the same story, just as Molloy, Malone, and L'Innommable are the same being repeating himself three times, and just as *Comment c'est* is divided into three parts (before Pim, with Pim, after Pim), all of Beckett's fiction, as we see it now (forty years later) took shape in three specific parts, three definite stages.

These three stages can be called: THE EARLY FICTION (the works written in English — *More Pricks Than Kicks, Murphy,* and *Watt*), THE MIDDLE FICTION (the "Nouvelles," the trilogy, and the "Textes pour rien"), and THE LATER FICTION (all the short texts Beckett has written since *Comment c'est*). Two key works function as bridges from one stage to the next.

Mercier et Camier[6] makes the transition from the early to the middle fiction, and *Comment c'est* from the middle to the later fiction. However, if the first passage was from a type of novel to another type of novel, the last passage is from a type of language to another type of language—from a type of fictional discourse to another type of discourse. And as such, these three stages can be renamed as follows: stage one THE TRUTH OF FICTION, stage two THE LIE OF FICTION, and stage three THE IMPOSSIBILITY OF FICTION.

Stage one consists of those works which are still situated in relation to social reality even though they mock this reality. Stage two consists of fiction that reveals its own fraudulence as it progresses towards its own negation. And stage three is made of fiction whose only fiction is its own language—the voice within the voice mumbling to itself. The early fiction still tells stories, the middle fiction pretends to tell stories but in fact only tells its own story, and the later fiction tells no story but merely rattles its own language—its own "rumors" and "ejaculations" to use Beckett's own terms.

The first two stages represent a progressive movement away from reality, away from realism, away from real situations and real characters, to end in the no-man's land of *Comment c'est* where fiction, language, and humanity are reduced to reptilian contortions. Parallel to this progression towards the void of fiction, there is also a movement from a third person narrative to a first person narrative to an eventual disappearance of the person (both the narrative and the fictitious person). However, these works cannot be considered mere experiments in form. The experimental novel attempts to do what has not been done before, or at least to do it differently, and thus exposes what it tries to do. In this sense, Beckett's fiction is not experimental because it tries not to do what it should do. In fact, Beckett seems to distrust whatever he has done or can do, and be interested only in what he cannot do, what is impossible to do. Therefore, having chosen to laugh at his own activity (fiction writing), to laugh in the sense which I have tried to define, that is to say by preserving a critical distance in relation to the act of writing fiction, Beckett could only persist in this activity by inventing for himself a *form* which would refuse to *conform* to what it was supposed to become, a form which would accommodate the voice within the voice. Thus he creates novels that are stripped of their most essential elements, novels that turn upon themselves (like snakes swallowing their own tails) to abolish themselves.

The first two stages of this evolution have received a great deal of critical attention, but little so far has been said on the fiction since *Comment c'est*. And yet, Beckett himself kept us informed, repeatedly in fact, of his progress (or regress) towards this third stage. The last part of *Comment c'est* opens with this statement: "ici donc je cite toujours troisième partie comment c'était après Pim comment c'est troisième enfin et dernière . . ." (p. 125).

What then is this fiction — this *impossible fiction* — of the third stage? A few bibliographical precisions might be in order at this time. *Comment c'est*

Poetry, Short Stories and Prose Texts 331

appeared in 1961 with the English version (Beckett's own translation as usual) *How It Is* following in 1964. In 1965, Beckett published *Imagination morte imaginez* (translation the same year as *Imagination Dead Imagine*) — ten pages of text in book form.[7] In 1966, *Assez* (translation same year as *Enough*)— twenty-one pages of text in book form. Towards the end of 1966, *Bing*[8] (translation early in 1967 under the title *Ping*)—nine pages of text in book form. In 1967, "Dans le cylindre" printed in *Livres de France*[9] (no translation, this is only a fragment of a longer work Beckett was working on at that time)— two pages of text. In 1968, "L'Issue,"[10] a prose text which accompanies a set of drawings by Avigdor Arikha (no translation)—twelve pages of text in large print. In 1969, *Sans* (translation in 1970 as *Lessness*) — fourteen pages of text in book form.

All in all then, from 1961 to 1969, Beckett published approximately 65 to 70 pages of new prose fiction. This is hardly a major production, but it is certainly major fiction. And now, as a kind of summation, a kind of synthesis of these recent texts, another important work has just appeared, indeed a most remarkable work of fiction, even though it is only 55 pages long (some 10,000 words). It is called *Le Dépeupleur,*[11] and was published in January 1971. As of this writing, there is no English version available.

Including this last work then, since *Comment c'est*, Beckett has published a total of 123 pages. This represents the fiction since *Comment c'est*. However, if this new fiction is to be judged on the basis of length or substantiality, then it is useless to talk about it. And it is also useless to discuss it in terms of quality as compared with Beckett's other major works. In fact, this fiction cannot be discussed in those critical terms which are normally used to elucidate what is commonly known as a novel. It demands an entirely new critical vocabulary; one which may not yet be invented. But those recent Beckett texts may, indeed, force us to re-examine our critical language, for such terms as "reduction," "disintegration," "regression," "diminution," "alienation," "negation," and so on, which were terms used (and abused) by most critics (the present writer included) to apprehend Beckett's fiction, now seem suddenly inappropriate to deal with the precision, the compactness, the meticulousness, the bareness of such texts as *Bing* or *Sans*.

Comment c'est , in 1961, according to most critics, seemed to have led Beckett into an inextricable impasse. How could he possibly go any further with the novel? But it also brought him to a danger point. One which critics were prompt in noting. This book was no longer fiction, but poetry—or something like poetry. And indeed, the stanza-like aspect of the prose, the lack of punctuation, the lyricism of the language, the inverted and distorted syntax, the musicality of the discourse, the quasi surrealistic situation, the lack of realistic elements, all of these made of this work if not a true poem, at least a true poetic work of fiction. But if there is one thing that Beckett must avoid at all cost, in his attempt at transcending fiction, it is to return to his starting point—that of being again a lyrical poet, for it is, as we all know, as a poet that he began his literary journey.

Comment c'est, in many ways, is much too lyrical (Beckett agrees on that). It is also too well written. It has too much style. The words in it mean too much. The words are too consistent, too resistant—perhaps less so the French version, but certainly the English version which he considers to be "somewhat of a failure—the English language resisted me—it made me say more than I wanted to say."[12] Beckett's next move, therefore, was (if one may use such terms) to delyricalize, to destylize the language of fiction, to designify the words. This is the goal Beckett set out to achieve in his recent fiction.

But those texts written since *Comment c'est*—texts which have indeed puzzled many critics—have been called many names: fragments of novels, prose poems, short stories, "residua," and even science-fiction tales, but in fact they are none of these. This puzzlement over the form, over the genre of Beckett's later fiction has given rise to a number of peculiar remarks. For instance, one critic wrote recently: "From the fact that he has begun and abandoned perhaps as many as three novels, it appears that Beckett would like to write another novel but is having some difficulty finding a new voice and new themes that will not simply duplicate *The Unnamable* and *How It Is*."[13] This is surely underestimating Beckett's power of creation. Or speaking of *Ping*, the same critic said: "One could not ask for more, and more would probably only dissipate the power of its concentrated impact. Perhaps Beckett, realizing this, decided that in this case his material was more suited to what is in effect a short prose poem than to a novel."[14] And elsewhere, about *Imagination Dead Imagine*, another critic wrote: "The text contains enough material for a full-length novel, and most of the old preoccupations are apparent ..."[15] And in a recent review of *Lessness*, one reads: "Since *Comment c'est* and *Play* nothing substantial has come from Samuel Beckett, nothing except dramaticules and fragments. He has seemed intent not only on eliminating almost everything from his images, as though in search of an immaculate vision of nothing, but also on abandoning every area in which his fertile talents threatened to flourish."[16]

These remarks on the later fiction show to what extent critics feel a kind of nostalgia, a deep regret, for the novel—for the novel that no longer exists in Beckett's fiction—and show also how the language of criticism cannot escape the categories it has invented for itself. For to label these texts prose poems, or fragments of what could or may have been jettisoned novels, or "residue of longer works" as it is stated in a misleading note by the publishers in the preface to *No's Knife*,[17] does not resolve the essential question of this fiction's form. And yet, to say also that Beckett with *Imagination morte imaginez, Assez, Bing, Sans,* and *Le Dépeupleur* has invented a new genre would be a gross error. Beckett does not invent new genres; that would be falling into the same old way.

Hugh Kenner, perhaps, has found part of the answer when he says in his "Progress Report, 1962-1965":

> Beckett's way of making progress is like that of the man in *How It Is*—"ten yards fifteen yards semi-side left right leg right arm push pull flat on face imprecations no sound" — varying nothing except the programme of the mute imprecations and dragging after him everything he has had since he started. That is why, as his works multiply, their resemblances become more and more striking, for their components, it grows increasingly clear, are drawn from a limited set. It is also why their originality of convention grows more and more absolute, for invention consists in devising new sets of rules by which the familiar pieces may be chosen and shown. To play one more game by the old rules would merely be competence.[18]

Indeed, to play the same old game by the same old rules (to say the same old thing the same old way) would "merely be competence." And this is why Beckett must invent more restraining and constraining rules for his fiction, for he can only continue if he eliminates further, if he reduces further, but no longer the novel as such. He is finished with the novel. Therefore, to insist on calling these short texts novels, or fragments of longer works, or prose poems, merely reveals the limitations of our critical language and imagination.

Imagination morte imaginez—is this title an exclamation? Is it a question? Or is it a simple statement of facts? Our critical imagination may be on the verge of dying if we do not renew it, but Beckett's imagination (as he has shown repeatedly) is far from being dead. Watch me now, says the voice ironically: "Nulle part trace de vie, dites-vous, pah, la belle affaire, imagination pas morte . . ." These are the opening words of *Imagination morte imaginez*,[19] a text which, like all the other recent texts, seems, to use David Lodge's own terms, "immune to conventional criticism," which seems "to demonstrate criticism's impotence."[20] Or is it merely revealing fiction's own impotence? Not as long as (Beckett would say) there are words ("quelques vieux mots par-ci par-là") to string together to make phrases.

What Beckett is after now, however, is another form of "reduction" (the term is used again for lack of a better term)—a systematic reduction and devalorization of language. From the voice within the voice, which was at the center of his fiction (particularly the middle fiction), Beckett now creates a voice without a voice—a voiceless fiction. And this becomes, in George Steiner's terms, "the retreat from the word" which reduces language to pure ratio.[21] For if there was one aspect of Beckett's writing (in his fiction, in his drama, in his poetry, and even in his criticism) on which everyone agreed, it was the beautiful way in which the voice spoke, it was the beauty of the language: its richness of vocabulary, its syntactical complexity and originality, its rhythm, its inventiveness, its brilliance, in other words, its style. This now must disappear from the writing, from the language.

And Beckett has been warning us all along that someday the language of fiction itself would have to undergo a final reduction, and that words would have to witness their own downfall, for as he said in *All That Fall:* "Sometimes one would think you were struggling with a dead language."[22] Or better still, in *L'Innommable:* "M'avoir collé un langage dont ils s'imaginent que je ne pourrai jamais me servir sans m'avouer de leur tribu, la belle astuce. Je vais le leur arranger, leur charabia" (p. 76).

What Beckett is now striving to achieve in his later texts is what Roland Barthes has called "le degré zéro de l'écriture." He now makes his promise come true, remembering what he said, years ago, to that curious interviewer who asked him why he chose to write in French: "Parce qu'en français c'est plus facile d'écrire sans style."[23] Thus, whether or not the recent texts are part of longer works that were abandoned is quite irrelevant. They are above all exercises in stylelessness—the final assault on words—that final dismissal of the "old credentials" as they are called in *Watt*.

However, by rendering language styleless—blank, as it were—Beckett also reduces fiction to a mathematical tautology. Since words can only demonstrate their own emptiness, literature also becomes an inaudible game—a seemingly absurd game of verbal permutations, and the less words there are the more satisfactory is the game. But in order to succeed in this system of repetition with slight variation on a set of words (*Bing* is the perfect example), one must remove from fiction all emotive qualities, remove from it all human, humane, and humanistic elements, or else the fiction begins to tell a story again. But fiction, it seems to me, cannot exist without some human presence, however, minimal, reduced, or partial this presence may be. Indeed, I cannot conceive of any fiction written without the presence of some living elements (human or animal), I cannot imagine a story written solely about an object (a teapot or a matchstick for instance) that would still be fiction, unless the object is personified or anthropomorphized. That would indeed be *impossible fiction.*

Nevertheless, Beckett tries to go as far as possible into the impossible and still create fiction. His first step, however, is to silence the voice—that voice which, in *L'Innommable,* cried out repeatedly that it could not go on and yet kept going on, that voice which, in the last *Texte pour rien,* began by saying about itself: "Elle faiblit encore, la vieille voix faible, qui n'a pas su me faire, elle se fait lointaine, pour dire qu'elle s'en va, essayer ailleurs, ou elle baisse, comment savoir, pour dire qu'elle va cesser, ne plus essayer" (p. 215). First step then, to silence the voice, and then to reduce the living being, the creature to whom that voice belonged, the subject, to mere bits and pieces of himself — a leg, an arm, an eye, but no longer a voice to speak with.

The later fiction, therefore, is a farewell to that other fiction which still afforded the creatures the possibility of speech, the possibility of telling stories about themselves or about other fellow-creatures like themselves. The key text in this ultimate reduction is *Assez* which, and this should be clarified, of all the recent texts was written first in the chronology of composition, even though it was published after *Imagination morte imaginez*.

In fact, *Assez, Imagination morte imaginez,* and *Bing*, in that order,[24] can be read as a trilogy which reveals the progressive elimination of the voice and of the person (the speaking subject). *Assez* is the farewell to that voice. But it is also the farewell to the time/space dimension of all the preceding fiction. For from *Murphy* to *Comment c'est*, the fiction progressed in the form of a wandering in time and in space, even if it was a slow, painful, and confined form of wandering. *Assez* is also the farewell to the companion, the brother, the double, the voice within a voice which still permitted some sort of verbal exchange, some sort of dialogue within the monologue. It is the farewell to the fraternal suffering of the couple, but it is also the end of the circular movement, the end of continuation and duration (even though these were often illusory). And finally, it is the dismissal of the first person (the I of the teller and the told) which, to a great extent, was the source of humor, pathos, tragedy, and compassion in Beckett's fiction, that is to say the source of story telling. The opening sentence of *Assez* makes this quite explicit: "Tout ce qui précède oublier" (p. 33). And the text goes on to say:

> Je ne peux pas beaucoup à la fois. Ça laisse à la plume le temps de noter. Je ne la vois pas mais je l'entends là-bas derrière. C'est dire le silence. Quand elle s'arrête je continue. Quelquefois elle refuse. Quand elle refuse je continue. Trop de silence je ne peux pas. Ou c'est ma voix trop faible par moments. Celle qui sort de moi. Voilà pour l'art et la manière. (p. 33).

Yes, "So much for the art and craft." Even the sentences now are reduced to a few simple words repeating themselves with slight variations. *Assez* then goes on to tell, in the first person narrative, but for the last time, the story of the wandering of a couple, one member of which has just been dismissed by the other. And it is the dismissed person who now relates, briefly, what he calls (or *she* calls, the sex of that person is ambiguous) "this last outing."[25] This is related in the past tense, but a strange form of the past tense which seems to bring us back, through the peep-hole of the present, to the ever present silence from which speech is born, or, as Ludovic Janvier puts it in an article: "la rétro-visé de l'écriture, nous ramenant au silence final et originel, d'où et vers lequel la prise de parole a eu lieu."[26] This narrator tells us how he (or she?) and his companion (a kind of giant figure who walks folded in half at the waist) held hands as they wandered around the earth for many decades: "nous avons dû parcourir plusieurs fois l'équivalent de l'équateur terrestre. A raison d'environ cinq kilomètres par jour et nuit en moyenne" (p. 38). And he goes on to explain: "Nous nous réfugiions dans l'arithmétique. Que de calculs mentaux effectués de concert pliés en deux!" (*idem*). It is thus, hand in hand, ". . . emboîtés l'un dans l'autre . . . Moi à l'intérieur. Comme un seul homme nous changions de flanc quand il en manifestait le désir" (p. 46) — present and past tenses "wedged together" — that they went, the tall one bent in half so that his mouth could reach the ear of the small one, exchanging, as it is specified, "cent mots par jour et nuit en moyenne. Echelonnés. Guère plus d'un million au total. Beaucoup de redites. D'éjaculations. De quoi effleurer la matière à peine" (*idem*). The narrator recalls this slow progress (in time, space, and words), or at least the last part of it ("notre dernière dscente"), until the day of his "disgrâce" as he calls it—until the day came when the tall one (the teacher-mentor-protector) told the small one (the disciple-student-protégé) "de me laisser." And he concludes by saying: "Si l'on me posait la question dans les formes voulues je dirais que oui en effet c'est la fin de cette promenade qui fut ma vie" (p. 39). And now, dismissed, halfless, voiceless, he can only fall into silence and oblivion, for as he says quite explicitly: "Tout me vient de lui" and therefore, "Hors de portée de sa voix j'étais hors de sa vie" (p. 34). From that point on the voice no longer speaks, no longer speaks for itself; someone else is (or will be) speaking for it.

Assez, then, is the end of the speaking subject, and consequently the end of memory which allowed fiction to extend from the past to the present, to progress from a possible beginning to a possible end. Beyond *Assez*, there is no longer such possibilities; the fiction is locked in an impossible temporality. Therefore, it is the end of movement, the end of that landscape of wandering and suffering in which the Beckettian creatures had existed. And above all, it is the end of the outside world, the end of vegetation.

At the beginning of *Imagination morte imaginez*, one reads this sentence: "Iles, eaux, azur, verdure, fixez, pff, muscade, une éternité, taisez" (p. 51). In the English version this gives: "islands, waters, azure, verdure, one glimpse and vanished, endlessly, omit." The French is much more revealing because of the "pff" which disappears from the English, and because of the word "muscade" which is a term used by magicians, jugglers, or tricksters to announce that they have succeeded in their *tours de passe-passe*, in their tricks. In any event, nature also has now been dismissed. The Beckettian discourse has now separated itself from its shadow, and it is in the bright light, the blinding white light that permeates the following texts that discourse will take place. And it is also within a closed, issueless space that the fiction will take shape, that of a rotunda which is where *Imagination morte imaginez* is situated, that of a vague white chamber with floor, walls and ceiling for *Bing*, and that of a giant cylinder for *Le Dépeupleur*.

Sans has a slightly different setting. It is spoken (if one may still use such a term) from the midst of grey ruins, possibly those of the rotunda of *Imagination morte imaginez*, or those of the white chamber of *Bing*. The first paragraph of that text reads as follows [*sic*]: "Ruines vrai refuge enfin vers lequel d'aussi loin par tant de faux. Lointains sans fin terre ciel confondus pas un bruit rien qui bouge. Face grise deux bleu pâle petit corps cœur battant seul debout. Eteint ouvert quatre pans à la renverse vrai refuge sans issue."[27]

But what is this place? What is this rotunda? This cylinder? This whiteness? And what are these ruins? It is the last place, the ultimate end of fiction and of existence, the most remote corner of consciousness, the last refuge ("issueless") from which the last few words can be spoken, murmured, mumbled.

In *Assez* we saw the rupture of the couple. We witnessed the dismissal of the voice. In *Imagination morte imaginez*, we find yet another couple, but this time each member separated from the other (a male and a female? Or rather both of ambiguous sexes) lying on their sides, back to back, in the foetal position, inside a rotunda whose dimensions are clearly specified: "Diamètre 80 centimètres, même distance du sol au sommet de la voûte. Deux diamètres à angle droit AB CD partagent en demi-cercles ACB BDA le sol blanc. Par terre deux corps blancs, chacun dans son demi-cercle" (p. 51). Within this space, light comes and goes, being succeeded by intervals of freezing cold and absolute darkness. The bodies are alive, however, as may be seen by holding a mirror to their lips and from the observation that the left eyes open "à des intervalles incalculables . . . et s'exposent béants bien au-delà des possibilités humaines" (p. 56). It is life, therefore, "l'expérience le montre" we are told, but the most reduced form of life. For just as the first sentence of the text, as quoted above, stated ironically: "Nulle part trace de vie, dites-vous, pah, la belle affaire," the last sentence states: "Laissez-les là, en sueur et glacés, il y a mieux ailleurs. Mais non, la vie s'achève et non, il n'y a rien ailleurs . . ." (p. 57). And so, if "there is nothing elsewhere," then this must be life, or at least what is left of life. We are indeed at the extreme end of life, but not of mortality; we are rather beyond mortality. For as long as "imagination pas morte," fiction will be able to transcend life, even if it is only to reach an absurd state of immortality.

Thus, just as the rotunda represents vital space in its most reduced and confined dimensions, the people (the living beings) inside that space represent the summary, the most reduced sum of human existence. But it also represents the most condensed form of fiction. This place, this life, and this fiction, however, can only be apprehended by the reader/listener through an effort of the imagination, but only if his imagination is still alive, as it is suggested at the beginning of the text. Therefore, in *Imagination morte imaginez*, the relationship between the creator and the imaginary reader still exists, even though the discourse seems to be spoken by no one — or by a distant, cold, remote, and non-involved voice which uses the imperative mood to guide the reader into this place in order that he may witness this remnant of life and of fiction. The text is punctuated by these imperatives: "entrez... mesurez... sortez... frappez... rentrez... ressortez... recluez... attendez... survolez ... descendez... rentrez... attendez... laissez..." And it is as though the reader were given a guided tour into the ruins of fiction. We are, indeed, a long way from the ironical voice of the novels, a long way from the novels themselves.

But, subsequently, in *Bing*, even this voice, this verbal guide, disappears from the discourse. And not only voice, but also those parts of speech which permitted some form of action, some semblance of movement, and some comprehension. *Bing* is totally verbless. Not a single active verb here, just a few weakened past participles. All syntactic connectives have also been removed. Only brief nouns remain (like wrecks) accompanied by a few indispensable adjectives and articles. And one might say that the prose is almost phraseless. Except for a few periods, the text is really one long sentence, one long articulation of broken syntactical elements. We have indeed reached the "zero degree of language." And even the place, the space of fiction as been reduced from the well-shaped rotunda of *Imagination morte imaginez* to the mere mention of "Tout su tout blanc corps nu blanc un mètre jambes collées comme cousues. Lumière chaleur sol blanc un mètre carré jamais vu." Murs blancs un mètre sur deux plafond blanc un mètre carré jamais vu (p. 61). And inside this white, blank space, one "Corps nu blanc fixe seuls les yeux à peine" (*idem*).

These are the indications (one can hardly say the setting and the character) given at the beginning of the text, which are followed by short phonological phrases, a small set of phrases that are exhaustively permuted. But against this articulation is interjected a strange and ambiguously stylized form of commentary —though empty of signification: the words BING and HOP which punctuate the discourse, appearing respectively twenty times and twelve times at various intervals.[28] But what is this BING/HOP (or PING in the English version)? It is the remnant of the voice within the voice, the most concise form of the critical laughter which comments (jokingly perhaps) on the progress (or the impossibility of progress) of this fiction.

This BING/HOP commentary reaches a climax towards the end of the text as in a rhythmic game of PING PONG, but from which the PONG is missing.[29] The text closes with this set of words: "Tête boule bien haute yeux blancs fixe face vieux bing murmure dernier peut-être pas seul une seconde œil embu noir et blanc mi-clos longs cils suppliant bing silence hop achevé" (p. 66). There is, then, an element of suspense, of surprise, in this last set of words, in this climactic end. It is the discovery on our part that the body in the chamber is "peut-être pas seul," for there is now another "œil embu noir et blanc mi-clos longs cils suppliant." This cannot possibly be the eye of the main body (one can hardly say protagonist or hero any more) since throughout the text *his* eyes are described as being "bleu pâle presque blanc." This black eye with long lashes belongs then to some other being. It is part of some emotional and human relationship which the main body is struggling to establish, or to recall through memory, in order, perhaps, to relive again, within the void of fiction, the fraternal relationship with the lost companion, striving once more to reconcile the broken couple. But this is not possible, because, from *Bing* to *Sans*, the walls are down, and only one body now remains—"Petit corps même gris partout terre ciel corps ruines" (p. 14).

This figure—almost a faceless block—stands "upright" in an endless, timeless, changeless ash grey expanse. Earth and sky and air are all ash grey. The body too is ash grey, differing from its surrounding only in being upright, and alone. But even in this "true refuge" the creature is troubled by illusions or memories of a past, and of past suffering, and therefore, as it is stated several times, by "wild imagining" ("en imagination folle") he may still be able to dream of future change, of yet another step, of being no longer upright, and of wanting "to curse God again as in the blessed days" ("Il maudira Dieu comme au temps béni").[30]

Unlike the closed space of the preceding texts (*Imagination morte imaginez* and *Bing* especially), the space of this fiction is open from all sides and allows the outside world (or what remains of it—gray ashes) to relate to the "ruines répandues confondues avec le sable gris cendre vrai refuge." These are, no doubt, the ruins of all the past containers, chambers, rooms, boxes, pots from which the Beckettian creatures spoke their verbal continuum in order to maintain themselves in a state of existence. But in the space of *Lessness* there is only "silence pas un souffle." It is the end of speech, the end of the speaking subject, the end of the voice. Moreover, the destruction of this shelter also marks the end of light, the end of the whiteness. Only the color grey reigns in this landscape. The word "gris" is repeated forty-nine times in the text.

If in *Imagination morte imaginez* and *Bing* the discourse still attempted (even in a fragmented manner) to describe the relationship of two bodies with their ecological space, in *Sans* the space is total opening, total void, and therefore the relation between space and being (between setting and character) merge into the greyness of the fiction. This is translated into the broken syntax, into the repeated phrases, but also into the future tense of the verbs. It is as though the fiction, by projecting itself into the future ("Il maudira . . . il bougera . . . il refera . . . il ira . . .," etc.) was attempting to rejoin the past, to situate itself in a kind of pre-historic and pre-fictional state. However, since memories of the past can no longer engender a true fiction but only a fictional project ("Chimère lumière ne fut jamais qu'air gris sans temps"), without beginning, middle, or end, therefore only the future may perhaps allow the body (the remnant of a fictitious being) to extract itself from this greyness, for this void: "Il bougera dans les sables ça bougera au ciel dans l'air les sables. Un pas dans les ruines les sables sur le dos vers les lointains il le fera." But in this landscape of nothingness which is only a shadow of the world, the time/space dimension (essential to any progress, whether forward or backward) is non-existent ("l'air gris sans temps"), so that both past and future remain static in the present ("Infini sans relief"), and prevent any form of movement. We have indeed reached that impossible region of *lessness* where nothing is even less than nothing.

This then is the ultimate situation, the ultimate reduction and deprivation of fictional, human, and linguistic possibilities. And indeed one can wonder where Beckett can go from there. Beyond this total reduction of fiction, beyond this total elimination of man (and of fictitious being), beyond this linguistic purification and designification, how can he possibly move any further? And now Beckett has already given us his answer, for the magician of fiction always has the last word, and the last laugh, and once again he has produced yet another work, yet another major work of fiction: *Le Dépeupleur* which, in my opinion, is as important in the whole of Beckett's writing as *Molloy, L'Innommable*, or *Comment c'est*.

As long as there will be words, Beckett will never stop surprising us. Having reduced fiction and humanity to their ultimate state of existence (or lessnessness), Beckett suddenly confronts us—for the first time in his entire work—not with a single being, not with a couple, not even with a few individualized characters, but with a crowd, a multitude of beings, an entire tribe of strange, anonymous, living creatures. But he had warned us of this possibility, long ago, in 1950, when the voice in the *Textes pour rien* proclaimed: "Cependant j'ai bon espoir, je le jure, de pouvoir un jour raconter une histoire, encore une, avec des hommes, des espèces d'hommes, comme au temps où je ne doutais de rien, presque" (p. 173).

Le Dépeupleur, in spite of its ironic title, confronts us with a story (a kind of story), and a crowd of men, "des espèces d'hommes," involved yet in another of Beckett's "wild imagining." Inside a giant cylinder ("Assez vaste pour permettre de chercher en vain. Assez restreint pour que toute fuite soit vaine," p. 7), a vast closed space fifty meters in circumference and sixteen meters in height, whose walls and ground are made of a substance similar to rubber, some two hundred bodies ("des corps"), each occupying one square meter, are involved in a frantic activity which consists of climbing up and down a set of ladders ("seuls objets une quinzaine d'échelles," the smaller one being not less than six meters tall) to reach little niches half-way up the walls ("disposées en quinconce pour l'harmonie une vingtaine de niches dont plusieurs reliées entre elles par des tunnels") where the climbing bodies then rest for a while.

These creatures, all of them naked, of both sexes, some young, some old, some still children or infants, are divided into various groups: the climbers, the seekers, the waiters, the watchers, and the vanquished. Within the cylinder, light and heat, as in the preceding texts, fluctuate:

> Omniprésence d'une faible clarté jaune qu'affole un va-et-vient vertigineux entre des extrêmes se touchant. Température agitée d'un tremblement analogue mais de trente à quarante fois plus lent qui la fait tomber rapidement d'un maximum de l'ordre de vingt-cinq degrés à un minimum de l'ordre de cinq degrés par seconde. Cela n'est pas tout à fait exact. Car il est évident qu'aux extrêmes de la navette l'écart peut tomber jusqu'à un degré seulement. (p. 15)

Nevertheless, what is most striking about this place, we are told, is its "sensation de jaune." Because of the heat and the cold, the bodies are dry: "Conséquences pour les peaux de ce climat. Elles se parcheminent. Les corps se frôlent avec un bruit de feuilles sèches" (p. 8). The only other sound comes from the ladders being moved around—ladders which are in great demand in this place, we are told.

This then is a first view of the cylinder, as described in the opening pages. But seen from a different angle (or from the system of linguistic repetitions and permutations also present in this text), these bodies can be divided into four categories:

> Premièrement ceux qui circulent sans arrête. Deuxièmement ceux qui s'arrêtent quelquefois. Troisièmement ceux qui à moins d'en être chassés ne quittent jamais la place qu'ils ont conquise et chassés se jettent sur la première de libre pour s'y immobiliser de nouveau . . . Quatrièmement ceux qui ne cherchent pas ou non-chercheurs assis pour la plupart contre le mur dans l'attitude qui arracha à Dante un de ses rares pâles sourires. Par non-chercheurs et malgré l'abîme où cela conduit il est impossible finalement d'entendre autre chose qu'ex-chercheurs. (pp. 12-13)

Thus, these creatures, as it is explained to us, consist of those who climb the ladders ("les grimpeurs"), those who wait in line at the foot of the ladders for their turn to climb ("les guetteurs" or "chercheurs")—for only one body can be on a ladder at a time— those who no longer wait to climb but who may, at any time, resume waiting and climbing ("les non-chercheurs"), and finally those who have definitely given up waiting and watching ("les ex-chercheurs" or "les vaincus"). Four main groups, therefore, form the population of the cylinder, divided in numbers as follows:

> ... qu'il suffise d'affirmer qu'à l'heure qu'il est à un corps près malgré la presse et l'obscurité les premiers sont deux fois plus nombreux que les deuxièmes qui sont trois fois plus nombreux que les troisièmes qui sont quatre fois plus nombreux que les quatrièmes soit cinq vaincus en tout et pour tout. (pp. 31-32)

A quick calculation produces a total of two hundred and five bodies inside the cylinder.

A rumor circulates, and has been circulating forever, that there is an exit from this place, but it has never been found, so that again these creatures can be divided (structurally one might say) between those who believe in the "myth" of this exit, and those who no longer believe in it. And also, there are two theories about this exit: the first one, that it is a hidden passage that begins inside one of the niches, and the second one, that it is somewhere in the middle of the ceiling. Now this part of the ceiling could be reached if, in a moment of fraternity ("mais celle-ci en dehors des flambées de violence leur est aussi étrangère qu'aux papillons"), some twenty volunteers were to hold the tallest ladder upright in the center of the cylinder. Therefore, there is no way out from this place, but this does not prevent these creatures from going about their business, whatever it might be—climbing, watching, waiting, seeking, standing, sitting—with a great sense of satisfaction, and without despair, even though some of them can be seen pounding their chest with their fists, or hitting themselves on the head with the broken steps of the ladder, but, we are told, no one is able to kill himself, only knock himself unconscious for a while.

The use of the ladder is regulated (as everything else is in this place) by a complex system of conventions which Beckett, of course, describes with his usual irony in precise and meticulous details using, as in the preceding texts, a simple set of phrases that are permuted into a complex mathematical tautology. If there are strict rules governing the climbing of ladders, there are also strict rules as to the method and direction in which these ladders can be moved from one place to another. In other words, this society, like any society (primitive or civilized) functions according to specific rules and laws, and with a great "esprit de tolérance qui dans le cylindre tempère la discipline" (p. 43). The rules and laws of this society may seem absurd, cruel, and inhuman to us, but in fact they are based on a very high ideal: "The search for nothing," or, as it is explained in a typical Beckettian statement: "Tant il est vrai que dans le cylindre le peu possible là où il n'est pas n'est seulement plus et dans le moindre moins le rien tout entier si cette notion est maintenue" (p. 28). Therefore, for this people of seekers who seek in vain, there is but one rule: "Quoi qu'ils cherchent ce n'est pas ça" (p. 32).

To be noted also, just as the people inside the cylinder are divided into groups, the bottom of the cylinder ("l'arène," as it is called), where the bodies are gathered, is also divided into three circular zones—three tracks: a large central zone where most of the bodies stand ("L'allongement est inconnu dans

Poetry, Short Stories and Prose Texts 343

le cylindre"), around which there is a narrow corridor (like a ring) in which those who wait in line move about, always in the same direction, and surrounding this ring, along the wall, another zone, one meter wide, for the ladders and the climbers, and these always moving in the opposite direction than those in the middle zone. Thus, seen from above, these two outside zones with their clockwise and counter-clockwise movements give the impression of being "deux minces anneaux se déplaçant en sens contraire autour du pullulement central" (p. 26).

This then is the situation as it is SEEN inside the cylinder—SEEN rather than described or told. For here, there is no longer a voice to describe or narrate the fiction (that of a narrator or a narrator-hero). The guiding voice has disappeared. Beckett has reached the stage where he is no longer concerned with making us *hear* a subject (the voice of fiction), but rather making us *see* an object (the language of fiction). Therefore, everything in the cylinder (in this fiction) is seen, rather than heard, though we are told quite explicitly that "Tout n'a pas été dit et ne le sera jamais" (p. 45) about this place.

What Beckett has created in this astonishing work, beyond the total reduction of humanity to anonymity, is a most grandiose metaphor for humanity. Here, within the complex structures of this social system, we find summarized all human activities, emotions, and ambitions. The climbers, the seekers, the watchers, the waiters, and those who have given up watching, seeking, and climbing are gathered together forever—from "un commencement impensable jusqu'à une fin impensable"—in a place where, we are told repeatedly, "tout est donc pour le mieux," because "seul le cylindre offre des certitudes et au dehors rien que mystère" (p. 38). And indeed, these creatures pursue their ideal without ever complaining, and with a sense of hopeful continuity since, in the midst of all their frantic activity, they manage, as best they can, to copulate in order to give birth to their offsprings.

Thus we have reached the only form of utopia Beckett could conceive for humanity and for fiction. Along the ambiguous line of a future-past, Beckett's fiction has come full cycle back to a pre-historic condition of man and of fiction. And yet within this void, there is still a possibility of hope, a possibility of compassion, and a possibility for fiction to continue, as we read the last sentence of *Le Dépeupleur*: "Voilà en gros le dernier état du cylindre et de ce petit peuple de chercheurs dont un premier si ce fut un homme dans un passé impensable baissa enfin une première fois la tête si cette notion est maintenue" (p. 55).

Therefore, even though Beckett's creatures no longer speak, no longer relate their own story, no longer seem to have a memory and words to give themselves the illusion of existing, Beckett's own words have, once again, mocked the possibility of silence and of oblivion both for humanity and literature. For I am not of those who believe—and would have us believe—that the ultimate goal of Beckett's writing is silence, that his works propose only the extinction of the human race, and that everything he has written up to now was an effort on his part to reach silence and oblivion. No, Beckett is too fond of words, too committed to words, and words are too precious for him to abandon them before they abandon him. Therefore Beckett will always have the last word, and the last laugh, and will continue to write words into fiction, even if the language of his fiction becomes totally devoid of meaning, purified of all doubt, becomes a pure anti-language which creates a true anti-fiction. For as he himself said some years ago in *Molloy*: "Il me semblait que tout langage est un écart de langage."[31] Or better yet, as he said more recently in *Comment c'est*, still about language: "rumeur transmissible à l'infini dans les deuxsens" (p.145).

From *L'Esprit Créateur* 11, no.3 (Fall 1971): 21-43.

---

[1]"Le Calmant," in *Nouvelles et Textes pour rien* (Paris: Editions de Minuit, 1955), p. 58.

[2]"Texte VI," *Ibid.*, pp. 172-173 (my italics).

[3]*L'Innommable* (Paris: Editions de Minuit, 1953), p. 222.

[4]*Samuel Beckett: A Critical Study* (New York: Grove Press, 1961), p. 20.

[5]*Comment c'est* (Paris: Editions de Minuit, 1961), p. 129.

[6]Beckett's first major work in French which, incidentally, written in 1945 was finally published by the Editions de Minuit in the Spring of 1970. I understand from a recent communication from Beckett's publishers that he is now considering translating this work into English.

[7]The number of pages given here for this work, and for those that follow *(Assez, Bing,* and *Sans)* refers to the texts as published in book form by the Editions de Minuit. It should be noted that some of these texts appeared in periodicals such as *Les Lettres Nouvelles* and *La Quinzaine littéraire* to coincide with the publication dates of the volumes. For more information about the publication of these texts and exact references see R. Federman and J. Fletcher, *Samuel Beckett: His Works and His Critics* (Berkeley and Los Angeles: University of California Press, 1970), pp. 70-74.

[8]*Imagination morte imaginez, Assez,* and *Bing* were reprinted in 1967, together with the French translation (by Ludovic and Agnès Janvier in collaboration with the author) of a text written in English in 1956, "From an

Abandoned Work" (given the title here of "D'un ouvrage abandonné"), in a volume entitled *Têtes-Mortes* which was published in Paris by the Editions de Minuit.

The English versions of these three texts were also published in 1967 in a volume entitled *No's Knife* (London: Calder and Boyars). This volume also contains the translations of the three "Nouvelles" written in 1946, the thirteen "Textes pour rien" written in 1950, and "From an Abandoned Work." In this volume, the three recent texts appear under the heading "Residua."

[9]*Livres de France* (special Beckett issue), XVIII, 1 (janvier 1967). The text "Dans le cylindre" which is presented as an "inédit" appears on pp. 23-24 with a photograph of Samuel Beckett.

[10]Editions Georges Visat, Paris, 1968, with "Six Gravures originales" by Arikha. Beckett's text is under copyrights by the Editions de Minuit. "L'Issue" comes from the same "corpus" as "Dans le cylindre" which itself comes from another unpublished prose fragment in manuscript form entitled "Chacun son dépeupleur"(15 pages of text of which "Dans le cylindre" comprises pp. 14-15).

[11]*Le Dépeupleur* (Paris: Editions de Minuit, 1970), 55 pp. In the chronology of composition, it seems that Beckett started working on this text as of 1966 ("L'Issue" and the unpublished fragment "Chacun son dépeupleur" from which "Dans le cylindre" is a part, as mentioned in the preceding note, are evidence of this fact). Thus, *Le Dépeupleur* was written between *Bing* (1966) and *Sans* (1969). However, in the following discussion, I shall deal with these texts in the order of their publication, even though one may argue that it weakens my theory of the progressive disappearance of the voice within the voice as subject of the fiction.

[12]Beckett told me this in a conversation in Paris, in 1966.

[13]Eugene Webb, *Samuel Beckett: A Study of His Novels* (Seattle: University of Washington Press, 1970), p.170.

[14]*Ibid.*, p. 171.

[15]Michael Robinson, *The Long Sonata of the Dead: A Study of Samuel Beckett* (New York: Grove Press, 1969), p. 225.

[16]Anon., "In Pursuit of Failure," *Times Lit.erary Supplement*, Nov. 12, 1970, p. 1442.

[17]*No's Knife* (London: Calder and Boyars, 1967), Preface.

[18]In *Beckett at Sixty* (London: Calder and Boyars, 1967), p. 61.

[19]In *Têtes-Mortes* (Paris: Editions de Minuit, 1967), p. 51. All further references to *Imagination morte imaginez, Assez,* and *Bing* will be to that volume with page numbers given in parentheses in the text.

[20]David Lodge, "Some Ping Understood," *Encounter*, XXX, 2 (February 1968), 85.

[21]As quoted by Ihab Hassan in *The Literature of Silence: Henry Miller and Samuel Beckett* (New York: Alfred A. Knopf, 1967), p. 9.

[22]*All That Fall* in *Krapp's Last Tape and Other Dramatic Pieces* (New York: Grove Press, 1957), p. 80.

[23]As quoted by Niklaus Gessner in *Die Unzulänglichkeit der Sprache* (Zurich, 1957), n., p. 32.

[24]In *Têtes-Mortes, Assez* appears before *Imagination morte imaginez*, no doubt an order chosen deliberately by Beckett to conform to the order of composition.

[25]The Fernch version says: "cette promenade." Beckett's recent texts should be read both in the French and in the English versions. The careful choice of a word in English to approximate the French, or the deliberate rephrasing of a sentence by Beckett as he translated these texts throws a great deal of light on the meaning of these texts which are, indeed, difficult to read and comprehend.

[26]"Le lieu du retrait de la blancheur de l'écho," *Critique*, no. 237 (février 1967), p. 222.

[27]*Sans* (Paris: Editions de Minuit, 1969), p. 7.

[28]In the English version the word PING replaces both BING and HOP, and appears 34 times.

[29]This image is suggested to me by a passage in David Lodge's "Some Ping Understood," *op.cit.* (see p. 89), the most interesting attempt so far to deal with this text.

[30] The phrases in this text are repeated as in a system of echoes, and therefore it becomes almost impossible to give an exact page reference for a specific quote since one is never sure which phrase is being quoted.

[31] *Molloy*, (Paris: Editions de Minuit, 1951), p. 179.

Beckett's Deconstruction of the Machine in *The Lost Ones*

David Porush

THE POWER OF THE MACHINE IN LITERATURE lies in its ability to focus attention on one of our deeply-rooted beliefs. The machine is a universal symbol of our culture's blind devotion to logical method, and has remained constant in this symbology through two-and-one-half centuries of literature. Even though the complexity of the machines that have inspired our metaphors have grown—from blocks of wood inscribed with letters and turned by cranks in Jonathan Swift's *Gulliver's Travels* to the hyper-evolved computer of John Barth's *Giles Goat-Boy* —the tenor, the argument of these metaphors has remained the same.

The machine is an invitation and a warning. It is simultaneously fascinating and threatening. It is somehow both superior to and inferior to the punier humans who build, operate and sometimes are subjugated by it. Machines are tangible proof of the success of our scientific techniques; as William Barrett suggests, they are "embodied decision procedures." At the same time, they testify to what is sadly diminished and insufficient in our blind faith that our techniques of discovery, our calculus and physics and biochemistry and cybernetics, will tell the whole story. While we may be ennobled by our grandiose fiction that the universe is a clockwork mechanism, there is also something inherently depressing about the vision of our spirits acting as mere cogs in that mechanism.

To some behaviorists, logical positivists, artificial intelligence theorists and sheer rationalists, the ghost in the machine is a delusion we've conjured to comfort ourselves with a superiority that cannot be proven. In their view, the human mind is just a brain, and its processes, though extraordinarily complex, will eventually be elucidated as surely as the atomic weights of different elements in the periodic table. But to others—some quantum physicists, artists, writers and phenomenologists, especially—there is room for doubt. The periodic table is a convenient model, *but not a description*, of the elusive mechanics of the atom, which has been subdivided into quarks and a host of even more intangible particles which wink in and out of existence depending upon your point of view. Artists have a special stake in drawing a line around some portion of the soul and proscribing its analysis: they naturally want to believe that the products of their labor manifest a freedom and uniqueness which lie above or below the level of mechanical description. And for writers who are alert to these phenomenological notions abroad in the culture, language is the fulcrum on which the argument see-saws.

The periodic table, the cybernetic metaphor that the brain is a machine, etc., are metaphors. Yet, writers are the first to acknowledge the power of metaphors. Whatever its status as truth, a metaphor is "a thrust at truth or a lie," again "depending upon your point of view," as Thomas Pynchon remarks. And these machine metaphors in particular have taken root to such depth that they have become invisible.[1] They are resurrected only by fear—*What is the machine doing to us?*, or by a counter-metaphor—*We are not machines!*

Both tactics present an invitation to fiction, often in tandem, which many contemporary American authors have found irresistible, among them John Barth in *Giles Goat-Boy*, Donald Barthelme in several short stories, William Burroughs through his mythology, but especially in *The Soft Machine* and *The Nova Express*, Joseph McElroy in *PLUS*, the noted science fiction writer Philip K. Dick, especially in "Do Androids Dream of Electric Sheep."[2]

What these postmodernists have in common is that they view literature as engaged in a battle, and effectively so, against the imperialism of the machine. They have several weapons in their armory: self-consciousness, irony, a tacit distrust of language as an effective means of expression, and metaphors. They combine these weapons with a peculiar but singularly effective strategy: all the texts in this class are *disguised as machines or the products of machines*. For instance, John Barth's *Giles Goat-Boy* is purportedly a computer-generated text. Joseph McElroy's *PLUS* (which seems to be a direct response to Beckett's *The Lost Ones*) is a monologue that occurs inside a disembodied brain linked to a computerized satellite orbiting the earth.

These metaphors elude simple codification. They are inherently anti-mechanistic since like any good, strong metaphor, they give rise to interpretations which cannot be controlled. If, as Ulric Neisser suggests, the computing machine in particular has become "invulnerable to evidence,"[3] then these authors find that logic and argument will not work against such sophisticated devices; rather, attacking the machinery of language with the machinery of language itself holds the key. As William Burroughs, the leading counter-mechanist guerrilla, suggests, "Communication must be made total, only way to stop it . . . let the machines talk and argue . . . program the machine to dismantle itself through positive feedback." In *The Ticket that Exploded* Burroughs's code name for this guerrilla tactic is "Operation Re-Write."[4] The sub-genre of postmodernism that employs these tactics is so remarkably coherent in its views and program that one can argue it deserves its own name. Since all the texts disguise themselves ironically as a cybernetic device and at the same time undermine their own cybernetics, I have called this sub-genre *cybernetic fiction*.

Samuel Beckett's short novel, *The Lost Ones* (1972), is exemplary of this class.[5] Beckett's "voice from universal space" (as Hugh Kenner calls it) affects (but does not achieve) the scientific lingo of a dispassionate, purely objective, positivist observer.[6] The text itself, as some critics have argued, can be read as congruent with the fantastic machine it describes, a machine that is an ironic heir to the verbal/technological contraptions of Raymond Roussel.[7] But unlike Roussel, Beckett uses this very language and this very congruence between machine and text to undermine the algorithm it proposes or embodies. Beckett has effectively achieved, in *The Lost Ones*, the perfection of a self-dismantling text which demolishes its own sense as it proceeds in just the way the Burroughs prescribed. A closer look at the text unfolds precisely how this is accomplished.

The Lost Ones as gedanken experiment — *The Lost Ones* invites the reader to construct or "maintain the notion" of an enormous mechanical cylinder in which named people are trapped for eons. The fiction thus created acts on many levels: as a literary *gedanken* experiment, as an allegory, and as an exemplar of its class of postmodern, cybernetic fictions.

As a *gedanken* experiment, *The Lost Ones* exhorts its reader to "maintain the notion" of this enormous cylinder where approximately 200 "lost bodies roam each searching for its lost ones." ("Ones" remains ambiguous: commonly, it could be taken to refer to a lost beloved. But it can also act as a pronoun for "bodies," or more ambiguously, for just about anything.)

This *gedanken* tactic lends a large degree of insubstantiality to a fiction which the narrator seems otherwise so careful to invest with substance and solidity. He presents the structural details, measurements, and technical specifications of the cylinder, including its basic dimensions (fifty meters round, eighteen high); surface area ("two hundred square metres of floor space or a total surface of roughly twelve hundred square metres of which eight hundred are mural"); "climate" (determined by concurrent though not coordinated oscillations in light and temperature); furniture (fifteen ladders); peculiar topology (including niches and tunnels and, perhaps, a trapdoor in the ceiling); and composition (unknown but of a "hard rubber or some suchlike").

This enormous cylinder is actually a machine. At least, it has striking mechanical properties. The light and temperature are controlled from some outside source, and "at certain intervals impossible to calculate" two "storms" or "wild oscillations" of light and temperature are "cut off as if by magic."[8] "As though again," Beckett hints, "the two were connected to the same commutator. For in the cylinder alone are certitudes to be found and without nothing but mystery." As we shall see, this latter remark is one of the most ironic in the text, for the cylinder is filled with mystery.

At least in this fragment, if we take it at face value, Beckett has reduced the terms of his "narrative of place" to its most controlled and its most abstracted. Whereas his other texts imply that their characters are caught at the playful juncture between certainty and ambiguity, Beckett creates a literal machine to represent this play and then traps his rather characterless characters inside it. A "scientized" language delivers data about the cylinder and the supposed certitudes within it, including the nature of the beings and the machinery of their social behaviors. These data seem to derive from an omniscient intelligence that has designed the cylinder or conjured it into being as though to test an hypothesis. Hugh Kenner calls this pose of Beckett's persona in other works "a voice from universal space" which, presumably, carries with it a burden of authority.

The Lost Ones as an allegory—As an allegory, *The Lost Ones* is powerful in proportion to its brevity, abstraction, and ambiguity, a perfect combination for a text that seeks to give rise to multiple—and at times competing—interpretations.

Inside the grand ballroom of this hellish condominium are 200 naked bodies, at the density of about one body per square meter. They are divided into four categories based on the extent to which they actively search, use the ladders, occupy the niches, roam, or remain catatonically rooted to one spot, absorbed perhaps by despair. The bodies copulate upon occasion, though joylessly, even painfully. "Skin rubbing on skin like the dry rustling of nettles." By virtue of the sheer laws of probability, a husband (in some former life, we take it) actually has intercourse with his wife, though they do not recognize each other. These accidental meetings between spouses lost to each other give rise to "spectacles . . . to be remembered of frenzies prolonged in pain and hopelessness long beyond what even the most gifted lovers can achieve in camera." Beckett calls these performances, with his usual flair for paradox, "making unmakeable love."

This passage achieves poignancy from the notion of gifted lovers seeking passion in such pain. Beckett lets us know, however, lest we are misled into believing that the lost ones are seeking their mates, that "whatever they search for it is not that." This caveat challenges the reader: What then have they lost? Their souls?

Beckett broadly hints that at least at one level the cylinder is a version of hell. He even mentions his literary predecessor in this regard: the helpless posture of one of the lost ones sitting on the floor, his back leaning against the wall, " would wring from Dante one of his wan smiles." Outbreaks of violence give rise to Miltonesque pandemonium. The general gloom "imparts a sensation of yellow not to say sulphur in view of the associations." The interior is a "fiery, flickering murk" and the lost ones are "straining forever with concomitant moral stress."

Critics both hostile and friendly to Beckett have risen to the bait of this apparent parable. To one, *The Lost Ones* is "an extended metaphor of the human condition." Another calls Beckett "an allegorist."

The problem with a merely allegorical interpretation, however postmodern or self-reflexive, is that it does not account for the richness of the text which is indubitably there. An allegory proposes either *this* meaning or *that* meaning for any sign but not both. Even the proposition that *this is an allegory about the impossibility of allegories* is insufficient, for it then denies the strong stance which Beckett has taken about the plasticity of meaning and the importance of the imagination.[9] The text begs some other formulation.

"The Lost Ones" as (self-dismantling) cybernetic fiction—As a cybernetic fiction, *The Lost Ones* shares many features with other texts in its class.

> •It uses a machine to stand for the act of writing itself.
> •It explores the mysterious interface between humans and machines.
> •It creates a congruence between form and function.
> •It is concerned with those properties of language which drive a wedge between mechanistic explanation and human experiences beyond expression or determination.
> •It delights in structure for structure's sake.
> •It diminishes the (apparent) role of the human presence or authorial persona in favor of a deterministic, clockwork fictional universe operating apparently through its own agency.

A cybernetic analysis of the text reveals that at its heart lies the image of the cybernetic device, radiating messages at every level. 1) It operates on the literal level as the subject of the story: the cylinder and its occupants form a closed system of energy and information which is slowly yielding to entropy. 2) It operates on the allegorical level as the postmodern version of hell. Yes, the cylinder-machine is an allegory for a special kind of cybernetic hell in which *system* does not create *meaning*. Hell is systematically not making sense. Or put another way, systematic nonsense is hell. Or yet another way: hell is a machine which does not work. 3) Finally, the text itself becomes apparent as a cybernetic device operating on our act of communicating with it: i.e., our reading. The text "interfaces" with us for a purpose: it calls attention to the impossibility of any act of systematic interpretation or description. In other words, it uses language to demolish language and expose the insufficiency of a cybernetic system to "contain" humanity, to create a landscape or environment for human activity, or to represent human interaction. It reduces human intercourse to "the dry rustling of nettles on skin" and an intense yearning for some lost but unarticulated sense.

But in order to recognize an insufficiency, in order to recognize that the machinery of language fails as a vessel for human communication, one must be able to conceive of a realm which lies outside that machinery. *The Lost Ones* does posit such a realm, but it is only through a cybernetic interpretation that we can arrive there.

The text here is a machine which mediates between the author and his own imagination (thus the *gedanken* experiment) and the author and his audience. In other words, it is just like language in this regard, and indeed the text everywhere calls attention to the mechanics of language. But *The Lost Ones* is a literary text, not a technical document, and its literariness is found in the fact that it indicts the very machinery it uses. In fact, Beckett has succeeded in designing a machine that is dedicated to dismantling itself. *The Lost Ones* and the cylinder it describes are fictions which collapse into meaninglessness, self-contradiction and absurdity. Their fallibility lies in the fact that they are constructed of words. The author's [*sic*] attempts at precise description becomes an exercise in the futility of trying to describe anything.

> Inside a cylinder fifty metres round and eighteen high for the sake of harmony or a total surface of roughly twelve hundred mural. Not counting the niches and tunnels. Omnipresence of a dim yellow light shaken by a vertiginous tremolo between contiguous extremes. Temperature agitated by a like agitation but thirty or forty times slower in virtue of which it falls rapidly from a maximum of twenty-five degrees approximately to a minimum of approximately five whence a regular variation of five degrees per second. That is not quite accurate. For it is clear that at both extremes of the shuttle the difference can fall to as little as one degree only, but this remission never lasts more than a little less than a second. At great intervals suspension of the two vibrations fed no doubt from a single source and resumption together after lull of varying duration but never exceeding ten seconds or thereabouts. Corresponding abeyance of all motion among the bodies in motion and heightened fixity of the motionless. Only objects fifteen ladders propped against the wall at irregular intervals.

Two linguistic realms collide in this failed attempt at precision. The first is a stylistic evocation of technical and mathematical precision, including both particular words and phrases from these disciplines and their characteristic "postures" in language. The second is the language of failure, probability, and doubt. It is a rhetoric of the quotidien in which decay and disappointment and uncertainty reign. These two realms are, of course, completely at odds with each other, and yet Beckett weaves them together, at times even within the same sentence, to fashion an allegorical world of pure fiction, ruled by the

Poetry, Short Stories and Prose Texts 353

aberrant artefacts of language: paradox, oxymoron and ambiguity. For the sake of argument, I call this first realm the *machine language*, hoping to evoke images of positive logic, technical efficiency, and computer-like order. The machine language is a code which does not permit ambiguity. The second I call the *language of flesh*, since it too is heir to all the ills of flesh: softness, decay, inefficiency, irrational doubt, and inconsistency.

At first glance, it is only the machine language which seems apparent to the casual reader. The first section includes short phrases that seem to be category titles promising further elaboration. "The light. Its dimness. Its yellowness." Indeed, this further elaboration is always provided. "The ladders. The purpose of the ladders is to convey the searchers to the niches." "The niches or alcoves. These are cavities that are sunk in that part of the wall which lies above an imaginary line running midway between floor and ceiling and are features therefore of its upper half alone."

These simple declarative sentences and phrases are reminiscent, in the absence of many finite verbs or active voice or human agency, of instructions for the assembly of a device or rules of a game: the third-person absent omniscient. Combined with evocative pseudo-technical language it has a chilling, too-sure effect: "omnipresence of a dim yellow light shaken by a vertiginous tremolo between contiguous extremes."

Upon closer inspection, though, quirks in these apparently rigorous descriptions emerge. Not a single statement or specification or datum is left to stand without some creeping conditional or vagueness or, as statisticians say, "fudging." Certain words of the statement above, for instance, burrow quietly beneath the structure of sense: "roughly," "or," "approximately," "more than a little less than," "no doubt" (which implies its opposite), "or thereabouts," "some," etc. Examples like these are repeated everywhere in the text, ubiquitous as termites. The qualifications to the first sentence offered by the second, and the statement "that is not quite accurate" which comes after a painfully accurate one, mock outright the machine language. Oxymorons like "contiguous extremes" and "heightened fixity" throw monkey-wrenches into the narrative machinery. Furthermore, the calculations are inaccurate: a cylinder with a base 50 metres in circumference and 18 high has a mural surface of 900, not 800, meters.

Another motif in the language of the text derives from mimicry of the academic postures that mathematics and technical texts tend to adopt. Susan Brienza's analysis in this regard is excellent. She isolates the various phrases associated with this pose: "for on due reflection . . .;" "Let numbers be assigned that . . .;" "An intelligence would be tempted to see in [these data] . . . ."

The most damaging of these mock academic phrases is the following tail-biting one: "The thinking being coldly intent on all these data and evidences could scarcely escape at the close of his analysis . . . ." However, even this pulls its punches with "could scarcely escape." To make matters worse, it is followed by the following hilarious reversal: ". . . the mistaken conclusion that . . . ."

This strange reluctance to call a spade a spade for fear that it is really a hoe—or worse, a not-quite-spade for which there is no proper signifier—lies at the heart of the uncertain universe of *The Lost Ones*, the culmination of Beckett's uncertainly-created worlds which are all made of language grown threadbare, untrustworthy, insufficient, quirky, unmanageable, and near collapse.

A black hole of a sentence summarizes this mysterious, quite unpositivistic aspect:

> The spent eyes may have fits of the old craving, just as those who have renounced the ladders suddenly take to it again. So true it is that when in the cylinder what little is possible is not so it is merely no longer so and in the least less the all of nothing if this notion is maintained.

The reader who dwells on this particular utterance soon gets a whiff of the abyss. The phrase ". . . the least less the all of nothing if this notion is maintained" announces its own status as a sheerly linguistic experiment in which communication has been pushed to the zero point of meaning. Cyberneticists would show that this "message" is high in entropy: it has a lot of uncertainty, and therefore permits a number of resolutions. Try it and you'll see none are satisfactory. Curiously, two sentences later, an apocalyptic scenario for the fate of the entire cylinder-world is portrayed in terms of thermodynamic entropy. Beckett compares the inexorable heat-death of the cylinder with the shrinking of a sand dune: "Even so great a heap of sand sheltered from the wind lessened by three grains every year and every following increased by two if this notion is maintained." The unthinkable yet definite progress from a hypothetical origin of the cylinder (in which, presumably, every lost one was still unvanquished) to an equally unthinkable and hypothetical final state (in which every one is vanquished) is an entropic process by which usable energy is leaked from this closed system and usable information becomes ground down to some zero-point of meaning.

The value of the imagination—As the machine is made more vulnerable—softer and less machine-like—through language, the inhabitants, at first view so mechanical, are made more human. By the end of the text we understand that nothing about the cylinder-system, especially not the four convenient sociological categories for the lost ones, is stable. In the eighth section we learn that within the outer belt reserved for searchers, who by definition roam, "there are a certain number of sedentary searchers" as well as four or five "vanquished" (who are supposedly catatonic). The "sedentary searchers" are "morbidly susceptible to the least want of consideration" while the vanquished "may be walked on without their reacting."

How are these two groups distinguished? Not with "the eye of flesh," Beckett informs us. Some vanquished "stray unseeing through the throng indistinguishable to the eye of flesh from the still unrelenting. These recognize them and make way." If we trace the statements like this throughout, we discover that all the categories collapse into one another. The sedentary roam, the vanquished look like the sedentary, the still unrelenting sometimes relent. The territories reserved exclusively for one group are populated by members of another group. Yet, the distinctions among them, though "invisible to the eye of flesh," still persist, just as Watt's pot looks, acts, and feels like a pot and yet is a not-quite-a-pot ("It resembled a pot, it was almost a pot, but it was not a pot of which one could say 'Pot, pot' and be comforted"). Yet it is some mysterious organ of the "imagination" — not the eyes of flesh — which makes the distinction. In this way, the "vanquished" whose eyes have been totally devoured are distinguished from the "totally blind." "It would be mistaken," Beckett insists, "to think that instead of speaking of the vanquished with the slight taint of pathos attached to the term it would be more correct to speak of the blind and leave it at that." The idea emerges again in another passage: "The bed of the cylinder comprises three distinct zones separated by clear cut mental or imaginary frontiers invisible to the eye of flesh." How can a boundary be "clear cut" and yet "invisible"?

The only answer possible is that the word "imaginary" holds a special status in Beckett's cosmology, implying not something which doesn't exist but rather something which exists outside the realm of empirical verification. This realm corresponds to organs of perception which are quite distinct from, and in their way superior to, the organs of flesh. Furthermore, the universe constructed by these faculties is transverbal, since it sees things which language cannot adequately describe.

The real dialectic in this text, therefore, lies not between the flesh and the machine, for in Beckett's deconstruction the terms are accomplices of each other. Rather the real dialectic is established between the soft machine that doesn't work and the imagination which does. On the one hand we have systematic, meaningless decay, entropy; on the other we have a thought experiment in the unthinkable which succeeds in creating a text, even if the point of the text is to effect its own deconstruction.

If we follow his argument, Beckett insists on the value of the imagination. The cylinder-text fails insofar as it attempts to state things precisely. Similarly, the lost ones remain lost as long as they insist on remaining locked in their own empirical systems of searching. Beckett berates them for their failure of imagination: "And far from being able to imagine their last state when every body will be still and every eye vacant they will come to it unwitting and unawares." Like beasts. The lost ones suffer by their inability to abandon determined, mechanical rituals "for an instant of fraternity" which would permit them "to explore the fabulous zone declared out of reach and which therefore in theory is in no wise so." For "amateurs of myth" the ceiling holds a hidden "way out to earth and sky."

We "amateurs" of Beckett's mythology know, however, that there is never a way out, there is only the hopeless search for one. For Molloy, Malone, Watt, Murphy and the rest of the lost ones can only tell futile little stories which tend asymptomatically toward some minimum state, some ever-more-circumscribed place of which the cylinder is only the most far-flung example. In this light, Beckett's silent exhortation gives special value to the unspoken command in front of the first word of the text: "[Imagine] abode where lost bodies roam." It sits there silently before every other sentence, too. "[Imagine] the light. [Imagine] its dimness. [Imagine] its yellowness."

Imagination will not solve the problem which faces our little race of searchers: our very compulsion to build cylinders leads us into a downward-spiraling embrace with entropy. But it might cure us of the "fatuous little light" which leads us to believe that all can and will one day be told.

From *L'Esprit Createur* 26, no.4 (Winter 1986): 87-98.

---

[1] See Colin Murray Turbayne's argument in *The Myth of Metaphor* that "mechanism is a case of being victimized by metaphor" and that "the metaphysics of mechanism can be dispensed with" (Columbia, SC: U. of South Carolina Press, 1970), p. 5.

[2] See my more complete explanation of the genre in *The Soft Machine: Cybernetic Fiction* (London: Methuen & Co., 1985).

[3] "The computing machine serves not only as a tool but as a metaphor; as a way of conceptualizing man and society. The notion that the brain is like a computer, that man is like a machine, that society is like a feedback mechanism all reflect the impact of cybernetics on our ideas of human nature. . . . Having taken deep roots and being partially unconscious it is partially invulnerable to evidence." Ulric Neisser, "Computers as Tools and Metaphors," in Charles R. Dechert, ed., *The Social Impact of Cybernetics* (N.Y.: Simon & Schuster, 1966), pp. 75-6.

[4] *The Ticket that Exploded* (New York: Grove Press, 1967 [Paris, 1962]).

[5] Originally written in French in the early 1950s as *Le Dépeupleur*. The text is so brief that it was originally published in English on a single newspaper-sized page in *Fiction* (in 1972), a magazine of short stories edited at

the time by Donald Barthelme. It appeared as "a novel" in the Grove Press (New York) edition in 1972.

[6]Hugh Kenner, *Samuel Beckett* (Berkeley: U. of Cal. Press, 1968), p. 49.

[7]See my analysis of Roussel's mechanisms, "Roussel's Device for the Perfection of Fiction," in *The Soft Machine: Cybernetic Fiction*.

[8]This recalls Arthur C. Clarke's dictum: "Any sufficiently advanced technology is indistinguishable from magic."

[9]But in Susan D. Brienza's reading, the futile search by the lost ones is "a comment on the reader's futile search for order and meaning in the piece itself." Thus the reader becomes a searcher looking for a critical way out of the cylinder-text. (See *"The Lost Ones:* The Reader as Searcher," *JML* 6, pp. 148-68.) Eric P. Levy takes this equation one step further and suggests that "*The Lost Ones* far more concerns the limitations of narrations than the torment of bodies in a cylinder. The story becomes a symbol for or a means of representing the movement of the narrator behind it . . ." ("Looking for Beckett's *The Lost Ones," Mosaic* 12, iii, p. 164). In other words, it is not a mere allegory of hell, but a typically postmodern, self-commenting allegory about the hell of interpreting and uninterpretable text. But certainly, one ring of this hell is reserved for those who have erred by over-reading. Brienza goes on to propose that since there are fifteen ladders of varying length and fifteen sections of prose, also of varying length, that therefore the sections are meant to be "ladders to meaning." With similar dexterity, Levy explains that the refulgent but oscillating light, which at its brightest emanates from everything equally, is really the light of Beckett's imagination illuminating the secrets of the chamber. (Unfortunately, this does not explain the tenth-of-a-second strobe-effect of the light, unless we descend to the neurological image of synaptic bursts, a solution which seems a bit ludicrous.)

Conceptions of Inner Landscapes: The Beckettian Narrator of the Sixties and Seventies

Cathleen Culotta-Andonian

In the prose works written after his Trilogy, Beckett portrays individuals who retreat deeper and deeper into the fantasy worlds they invent, until their awareness does not exceed the boundaries of their own imagination. The narrators' self-centeredness and the inadequacy of their perceptual abilities greatly hinder the creation and development of their stories. Likewise, the improper functioning of their thought processes contributes to the difficulty they experience communicating their imaginary landscapes by affecting the precision, enrichment and even the length of their narratives. Intellectually blank, they cannot always overcome their mental stasis in order to generate images and descriptions to supplement their depleted creative resources. Consequently, they often reexamine the same motifs—themselves, their thoughts, emotions and imaginations.

In order to analyze the conceptual abilities of Beckett's narrators in the recent works, it will be necessary to approach their creative faculties systematically, as they relate to the characters and environments depicted. As the protagonist's physical and mental well-being deteriorates, certain changes in the basic relationship of the narrator to his characters, environment, and narration take place. These alterations in the rapport between author-narrator and fiction correspond to Tzvetan Todorov's classifications of narration presented in his article "Les Catégories du récit littéraire."[1] Each division measures the degree of knowledge the narrator has at his command, which enables him to perceive other characters from a certain vantage point: "par derrière," "avec," or "du dehors." The protagonist's "vision par derrière" indicates that the narrator is well-informed about his characters, frequently knowing more than they do about their own situations, whereas his "vision avec" signifies that his awareness is equal to that of his characters. Finally, his "vision du dehors" denotes that he understands less than his characters and can only describe what he sees at a given moment. In all these stories, the narrators conjure up images and visions from their own imagination. Thus, it is not a question of how these narrators visually perceive individuals who exist independently of themselves, as in realistic fiction, but rather how active their creative powers are, and to what extent they are capable of conceiving the situations they invent.

Le Dépeupleur and "Autres Foirades, I" illustrate the point of view described by Todorov as "vision par derrière." In both cases the omniscient narrators are more knowledgeable about the condition and fate of their characters than are the characters themselves. As creators of the fantasy worlds they witness, the narrators try to determine the effects certain atmospheric conditions will have on their people. Oddly enough, even though *Le Dépeupleur* is engulfed in a dry, bright atmosphere, and "Autres Foirades, I" reveals a moist, dark environment the final effect seems to be quite similar; the protagonists are mentally confused, devoid of thoughts or emotions, and either frustrated by or indifferent to their confined situations.

In *Le Dépeupleur* the monologuist explains in detail the physical changes that take place in the cylinder and the transformations the inhabitants of that sterile environment will undergo. Since the bewildered creatures are unaware of the continually changing atmosphere of the cylinder, the sporadic alterations in light and temperature, and the inconsistent outbursts of violence, the narrator portrays these individuals in a state of constant fear. He then imagines the myths and the quasi religious explanations they invent to compensate for their ignorance.

Unconscious of their own feelings and motivations, the inhabitants of the cylinder are divided by the narrator into groups according to their physical traits and movements. External appearances can be misleading to the initiated observer: in certain instances, the narrator distinguishes problems that would appear to what he calls an "œil de chair" or a spectator who would have trouble differentiating the three zones of the cylinder (Dé., p. 38)[2] and recognizing the participants in each group who inhabit the various zones. His reference to a possibly incorrect interpretation by an outside observer establishes the narrator as the sole witness to his mental landscape, and as the most knowledgeable, even though he himself may also have doubts about some of the statements he presents. He tentatively posits a description of the future condition of his characters, a condition which they cannot foresee: "Une intelligence serait tentée de voir . . . que tout tôt ou tard chacun à son tour finissent par être des vaincus pour de vrai figés pour de bon chacun à sa place et dans son attitude" (Dé., pp. 29-30). While giving an overall appearance of order and discipline to this created fantasy world, the narrator alone is aware of the extent of the turmoil beneath the surface.

The broken figure who stumble through the tunnel in "Autres Foirades, I" persists in closing his eyes, thereby remaining ignorant of his physical surroundings. The narrator of the story compensates for his character's imposed blindness by amply describing the conditions of his environment: he analyzes the individual's capabilities and mistakes and tries to imagine what the character would see, should he ever decide to open his eyes. The narrator presents a partial view of the circumstances his hero experiences physically, such as the humidity, the roughness of the stones forming the tunnel or the light at the end of the passage, totally ignoring the character's mental anguish or his personal reactions to his environment.

"Autres Foirades": II and IV and "Au loin un oiseau" illustrate Todorov's category "vision avec," in which the narrator's knowledge is equal to that of his characters. These texts dwell exclusively on the monologuist, his perception of himself and/or his surroundings, yet all three narrators have difficulty concentrating on their stories and know no more about their inner beings, past lives and present environment than their superficial observations reveal. The narrators' descriptions of external beings in "Autres Foirades, II" and "Au loin un oiseau" are nothing but their own fictitious creations, internal fantasies superimposed on their external existence. Not unlike the Unnamable, the monologuist of Beckett's recent stories identify themselves with the heroes they invent, yet, at the same time, persist in retaining their individuality.

The protagonist of "Autres Foirades, II" claims to have complete control of the thoughts and movements of his character and plans to bring about his suicide eventually: "il a mal vécu, à cause de moi, il va se tuer, à cause de moi, je vais raconter ça . . ." (PFE., p.38). In the end he cannot even predict how his character will die, since he is limited to a direct retelling of the story as it occurs to him. Although the narrator experiences the need to rid himself of this character physically, he in fact never describes his death. More remote from his fiction than the voices in Beckett's Trilogy, the monologuist of "Autres Foirades, II" cannot express his violent fantasy in words, as Moran and Malone have done, and simply terminates his narration.

Likewise the narrator of "Au loin un oiseau" is only aware of his character's actions and desires as they occur, or as he imagines them. The protagonist is surprised to be able to speak through his hero: "il me cherche une voix et je n'en ai pas, il va m'en trouver une, elle m'ira mal, elle fera l'affaire, son affaire . . ." (PFE., p. 48). Dissatisfied with the voice that materializes as he recounts his tale, this narrator, like the Unnamable, is continually restricted to telling someone else's story. Many of the motifs and phrases resemble those of "Autres Foirades, II"; the author-narrator supplies his characters' thoughts, and he undoubtedly will be the cause of his death, although he does not know how or when it will occur.

"Autres Foirades, IV" differs from the other texts in Beckett's collection, because it dwells exclusively on an individual's experiences in a changing environment. The narrator, as the sole protagonist, provides a detailed description of the infestation of his land by May bugs. The destruction he witnesses may be a direct reflection of a mental landscape or his personal desire for annihilation. Even though memories from his childhood interrupt the narrator's thoughts continuously as he stares at the devastation before him, the now barren landscape seems to hinder his creative abilities, to stifle any attempt to develop his visions or to generate new images.

Many of Beckett's recent stories and novels correspond to Todorov's third narrative category, "vision du dehors," defining a narrator who can no longer portray accurately the thoughts and motives of the beings he perceives. As writers of creative fiction, these individuals are not capable of establishing precise characterization or a logical, coherent framework for their narratives. The author-narrators of the remaining works are not as verbose or as flexible as their counterparts in the Trilogy, who frequently deviate from their story to include tedious, long-winded descriptions of their feelings or theories.

Each new fiction manifests a marked decline in the narrator's consistency and succinctness, coinciding to some extent with the chronological order of the texts themselves. This category has been subdivided, and each subgroup will be considered separately, according to the distinctness with which the action, characters and environment are introduced. "Autres Foirades, III" (late fifties or early sixties), "D'un ouvrage abandonné," (1957), *Comment c'est* (1961), and "Assez" (1966) present unusual, fanciful landscapes. The narrators describe their characters as distinct beings in continuous motion and amply portray their impressions of their environment and monotonous existence. The works "Imagination morte imaginez" (1965), "Immobile" (1970), "Se voir" (1960s) and "Compagnie" (written in 1979, published in 1980) are more abstract, vague, and illusory. The characters are generally unidentifiable, their movements are uncertain and their environment, ambiguous. Even further removed from reality, the short texts "Bing" (1966), "Sans" (1969) and "Pour finir encore" (1976) are so abstract that they are nearly incomprehensible. One is unsure who or what is being portrayed, because the figures are indistinguishable from their backgrounds. The narrators of this last group of texts project scenes that are so vague that they are not illustrated with more than a few simple words and phrases.

In the first group of texts classified as "vision du dehors," which includes "Autres Foirades, III," "D´un ouvrage abandonné," *Comment c'est*, "Assez," and "Compagnie," the narrators are aware of the presence of other individuals, and are quite capable of distinguishing themselves from the additional characters with whom they come in contact. They occasionally lapse into descriptions of the dreams or images they envision, and alternate these fantastic scenes with vignettes recounting their physical progression or adventurous wanderings. Even if these tales represent invented fantasies, they still center around the possible experiences of the monologuists, unlike the abstract portraits which follow these works.

Two distinct individuals are portrayed in "Autres Foirades, II," the narrator and a friend he calls Horn. The monologuist's knowledge of his companion is extremely limited, since their meetings are brief and always take place at night in an unlit room. At the major protagonist's request, Horn lights a match and allows himself to be examined momentarily or takes advantage of the light to contemplate his notes so that he will be able to respond appropriately to the narrator's inquiries. The nature of their exchange is never revealed: the protagonist's major preoccupation at this time is the external appearance of his guest. Failing to discern any enlightening information about his acquaintance, the narrator becomes obsessed, instead, with his own image and the return of his health. The narrator is equally ignorant of his external being and circumstances and those of Horn: darkness is directly responsible for his inadequate perceptions and also symbolic of his clouded mental state.

The alertness and clarity of the narrator of "D'un ouvrage abandonné" are also subject to question. He watches his mother wave to him from a window, or perhaps it is only his recollection of this scene that is indelibly etched in his memory. He is cognizant of her physical presence and her apparently meaningless gestures, but he is totally ignorant of her intentions and motivations. Unable to rationalize his own bizarre behavior, he is absolutely incapable of even guessing the ulterior motives of the individuals he describes:

"Non, ça dépasse l'entendement, tout dépasse, pour un esprit comme moi . . . j'y reviendrai peut-être quand je me sentirai moins faible" (T-M, pp. 14-15). During his three-day journey, many people and images come to mind: his parents, a road worker named Balfe, his dreams of fantastic white animals and imaginary visions of tribes of ermines. Yet all of these fantasies remain vague in his mind, and appear on the same level as the events he describes in his current monologue.

The female monologuist of "Assez" also has difficulty focusing her attention on her partner, and finds it impossible to comprehend his ideas. This narration represents her attempt to document her past wandering with her acquaintance, and her futile efforts to recreate her memories. Given the limited scope of her awareness, it is fitting that the individual she describes so inadequately should be a person who has had an unusual amount of influence on her life. Unable to comprehend the character, or explain his point of view logically, she is forced to restate his opinions by rote, as she remembers them. The reader is faced with a second-hand report: the narration revolves around the couple's explanations of their surroundings, their mutual experiences, and their relationship. In this case, however, the monologuist's memories are too vague to produce more than a sketchy portrait.

The novel *Comment c'est*, published in 1961, is the first of Beckett's works to abstract fictional content one step further. Instead of portraying a hero who reveals his own thoughts and problems directly in a lengthy monologue, Beckett presents a unified account of the creative process. The characters in the novel have a dual role: the narrator perceives these beings as functional elements in the narration and as structural units making up their bizarre habitat. The most important image of the novel is that of the couple depicted in Part II. Pim is the focal point of the story: the narration is reduced to the anticipation, reunion, and regret of the couple. This central figure is intensified by the identical movements of numerous couples imagined by Bom to occupy this bleak landscape. In another sense, Bom's conception of the reunification and separation of the couple may correspond to the movement of his imagination or the development and progression of the words and phrases making up his narration.

Bom's conception of Krim and Kram's role in the text is also related to the redaction of the novel. Bom visualizes these characters as witnesses or scribes who commit the oral narrative to paper, and may correspond to the function of the reader giving life to the author's creation.

Even though these characters represent the imaginary creations of the author-narrator, Bom denies total knowledge of their thoughts and actions. he forces Pim to speak and to "sing" in answer to his inquiries. The resulting information consists of the terse responses Pim shouts in pain. Bom questions Pim as though he were trying to resolve his own doubts and formulate his own ideas. Yet the monologuist never appears to be satisfied by the responses of his alter ego, and thus demonstrates his incomprehension of the workings of his own imagination which has created this being.

In spite of the fact that Bom's perceptual awareness of his characters often falters, he maintains command of his narration through strict structural control: he may not always be able to describe his partner accurately or his images "from above," but he has no doubts about the major divisions of his story. His detailed mathematical computations occasionally give him a false sense of security and cause him to exaggerate the scope of his fictional world. At this time he generally lapses into the oblivion and ignorance represented by mud and darkness, and denies his previous assertions. Yet it is necessary to submit to the darkness and chaos of the inner world to be able to create images. Once Bom has descended to the depths of his inner consciousness, he rises through the renewed vigor of his creative powers to contemplate images from "above" in the light.

Bom must prod his imagination continually to create his tale, in much the same manner that he jabs or scratches Pim to make him speak. The narrator of *Comment c'est* is able to exhibit the self-discipline and organizational skills necessary for the writing of a full-length novel, because he identifies himself so closely with his work. The still viable perceptual abilities and the structural discipline of the narrator are, more than likely, responsible for the length and coherence of Beckett's last novel. This structural discipline is, in fact, lacking in the subsequent short texts, as the narrators regress to disorder and confusion.

More deeply entrenched in the world of the imagination, the narrators of "Imagination morte imaginez," "Immobile," and "Se voir" attempt to restrict their observations, hoping to create a meaningful portrait through a narrowing of their imaginative field. Even with these self-imposed limitations, their images cannot achieve any significance beyond the flat surface value determined by the protagonists.

The symbol of the author-narrator's failing imagination in "Imagination morte imaginez" is an immobile couple trapped in a circular frame. Their inanimate pose and their blank expression convey the mental apathy of the narrator who struggles to describe their plight inadequately. The reader is addressed directly as a witness to judge and imagine the scene depicted by the narrator. "Nulle part trace de vie, dites-vous, pah, la belle affaire, imagination pas morte, si, bon, imagination morte imaginez" (T-M., p. 51).

The specific details of their physical situation are examined, one by one: their appearance, posture, temperature, and respiration. But the initial question of imagination is never repeated—the narrator has recorded what he is capable of imagining and moves on. During his investigation, the author-narrator remains aloof, almost indifferent to his story. The narrator's failure to become a critical observer of his fictional world prevents him from communicating his vision successfully.

The monologuist in "Immobile" is likewise unable to understand the mental landscape he conceives. In fact, he claims he has undertaken the project of describing this individual because he does not comprehend the scene he conjures up: "le mouvement que voici impossible à suivre plus forte raison décrire" (PFE., p. 22). He designates his initial perspective from a safe distance and then moves in for a detailed analysis. No matter how precisely he outlines the anonymous character and his condition, the monologuist cannot clarify the situation and must resort to recounting only what he thinks is happening. The image is abandoned in much the same way that the previous world of "imagination morte imaginez" disintegrated at the end of the text.

Although written before "Imagination morte imaginez" and "Immobile," the prose piece "Se voir" constitutes a similar approach to the unique subject matter Beckett chooses to depict. The narrator presents a precise image of its physical appearance, but the text ends abruptly without moving beyond a sterile description of the external features of the environment. Unable to perceive the objective world clearly outside his own consciousness, the Beckettian narrator offers vague generalities. The environment greatly resembles that of *Le Dépeupleur*, but the two narrators' perceptions of their created world is quite different. The monologuist of *Le Dépeupleur* is the obvious creator of the cylinder and appears to be quite knowledgeable about the fate of its victims, whereas the narrator of "Se voir" is an uninformed observer of a system he knows little or nothing about. He cannot grasp the significance of what he witnesses and continually dismisses incomprehensible aspects of the scene by stating "ça n'intéresse pas. Ne pas l'imaginer" (PFE., p. 51). Nor is the narrator of "Se voir" so preoccupied with a close inspection of his vision; he is satisfied with a few general remarks and then abruptly terminates his narrative.

In his most recent prose work, "Compagnie," an unidentified protagonist, possibly the narrator himself, lies on his back in the dark listening to a "voice" recount scenes from the past. The portrait is vague and ambiguous, the narration lacks clear characterization, thereby undermining a unified approach to the narrator's vision. Parallels are drawn with many of Beckett's previous heroes, as the narrator refers to his protagonist as M, Unnamable, or "the crawling creator," and to himself as W. Even though the narrator is incapable of accurately portraying the thoughts and emotions of the character he imagines, he is aware of the illusory nature of his tale, "la fable de toi fabulant d'un autre avec toi dans le noir. Et comme quoi mieux vaut tout compte fait peine perdue et toi tel que toujours. / Seul" (Co., p. 88).

The last three texts to be considered here, "Bing," Sans," And "Pour finir encore" demonstrate a definite departure from coherent conceptual techniques. The narrators of these works imagine vague desert landscapes filled with unidentifiable beings and objects. They are besieged by images, as the repetition of the same fantasies and phrases creates a delirious whirlwind of disconnected thoughts, emotions, and visions around them. The narrators are incapable of ordering their ideas or of controlling the inner chaos they experience. Although the individual monologuists cannot always recognize or describe their visions, the emotions pervade the sterile landscapes they present. Their feelings of loneliness, deprivation, fear, or apathy are obvious from the atmosphere of the texts and the types of images they invent.

The rigidity of the individual described in "Bing" exposes the frustrations of the writer who no longer can create images, or who cannot bring them to life. How can this narrator possibly describe what he has so much difficulty visualizing, when his images are quickly fading into the nondescript background of his mental landscape? The traces of past and present images are either nearly invisible or incomplete. Beckett creates a text struggling to reveal itself, in which all elements of external awareness are stifled. Thanks to the juxtaposition of non-referential concrete images and unidentifiable intuitive images, the reader in the end must form his own impression of the work.

The short text "Sans" repeats many of the motifs presented in "Bing." However, this work is organized around recurring words and themes. The same phrases are then repeated a second time in a different order. The text is impersonal and abstract: Beckett has arbitrarily selected the order of the sentences independent of any notion of point of view. Only the individual sentences can be examined in relation to their context and the clarity or coherence of the images they project. These fleeting mental images and sparse memories of Beckett's narrator are extremely disjointed in "Sans." The increased fragmentation of the character's thoughts, again caused by the random ordering of the sentences in the text, accentuates the impairment of the narrator's perception. Because of the remoteness of the images and the dissolution of the formal context in which they belong, it is obvious that this anonymous protagonist has permanently lost his powers of reasoning and observation.

The lone skull in "Pour finir encore" represents the diminishing mental faculties of a similar narrator who can barely describe the images he envisions. Once again the perception of the third-person narrator is clouded by the uniform grey landscape he creates. This "boîte," the last refuge of the writer, is no longer entirely devoid of action: two midgets scurry across the waves of sand, and the statuesque body falls, yet still contemplates moving forward. The narrator's inventions are perceived more clearly and show more consistency and continuity than those in either "Bing" or "Sans." The images are more numerous, but the starker and simpler in nature, and as a result they appear to be slightly more coherent. Each reference to the characters is consistent in content and point of view, even though the narrator's perception of his subject is limited.

In some cases, the narrator's perception of an object or an event is obstructed or at too great a distance for him to clearly identify and characterize his observation; in other instances, his impaired vision or his lack of comprehension prevents him from relating his story. In many of the short prose works, the protagonist is distracted or blinded by the overabundance or lack of light. For example, the individual in "Bing" is confused by the pervading whiteness around him, and focuses on the person he is describing with great difficulty. The figure blends so well with the background that he is almost invisible. Consequently, the perception of the narrator appears distorted, his visual imagery is flat, lacking distinguishing characteristics. Likewise the narrator's impression in "sans" and "Pour finir encore" seems vague, because the features of the environment are almost exclusively "blanc sur blanc" (T-M., p. 61). Whereas the protagonist of "Imagination morte imaginez" recognized the fact that "l'inspection est malaisé" and limited his remarks to what he felt he could judge, the narrators of "Sans" and "Pour finir encore" try to enumerate every object and action they can perceive, without questioning the validity or purpose of their remarks. Although there is no indication of movement in the short prose piece "Sans," the protagonist does not hesitate to remark that the exiled figure will move and time will pass, if only in a dream. The individuals in these more recent works by Samuel Beckett in particular recognize the fantastic character of their visions and present them in the dreamlike state in which they appear.

Thus, as the Beckettian protagonist becomes more uncertain about his inner visions, his perception and capacity to describe the figments of his imagination are likewise diminished. This is demonstrated by the fact that the majority of the recent prose pieces correspond to Todorov's third narrative category, "vision du dehors": unable to depict his characters accurately, the protagonist's knowledge decreases to the point where he can only describe what he sees in his mind, without properly situating those images. Explanation of Beckett's latest narratives according to Todorov's categories illustrates the evolution of Beckett's works from omniscient narrators, who seem to be able to comprehend or visualize the situations they present, to anonymous voices reiterating meaningless words and phrases.

Wayne State University

From *Symposium* 36, no.1 (Spring 1982): 3-13.

---

[1]*Communicatios*, 8 (1966).

[2]The abbreviations used in this article correspond to the following works: CC. (*Comment c'est*, 1961); T-M. (*Têtes-mortes*, 1967); Dé., (*Le Dépeupleur*, 1970); PFE. (*Pour finir encore et autres foirades*, 1976); and Co. (*Compagnie*, 1980). The quotations have been taken from the texts published by the Editions de Minuit, Paris.

The Weaving of Penelope's Tapestry: Genre in the Works of Samuel Beckett

J. E. Dearlove

I. Introduction

When it was first conceived, this paper was going to be about Beckett and the breakdown of genre. It seemed to me, at that time, intuitively obvious that Beckett was breaking down genres, blurring the borders between literary types, and fabricating new forms with names like "residua" and "texts." As I pursued my subject, however, a great deal changed. For one thing, I began to realize that there is no universally accepted definition of genre. As the *Princeton Encyclopedia of Poetry and Poetics* rather metaphorically phrases it: ". . . the field is littered with the ruins of past definitions which have convinced no one save their author, and the advance of modern writing is so vast and multifarious that all classifications crumble in front of it."[1]

Therefore, my first task in writing about Beckett and the breakdown of genre, is to tell you what I think it is that is reportedly being broken down. In this paper, genre refers simply to a collection of expectations a reader holds about a work. These expectations are based in part upon the reader's previous literary experiences, including experiences with other works by the same author.

My second task is to confess to you that I no longer believe that Beckett is breaking down genre. Instead, I am convinced that his works are *dependent* upon the reader's perception of genre. We must know what a detective novel is, in order to understand what *Mercier and Camier* denies us; what a novel of ideas implies, in order to appreciate the exaggerated claims of *Murphy*; what a novel of manners should do, in order to recognize the omissions of *The Lost Ones*. Instead of breaking down structures, Beckett deliberately evokes them. He raises our expectations and then consciously thwarts them. The result is a carefully balanced and manipulated ambiguity.

Instead of the breakdown of structures, a far more appropriate image for Beckett's use of genre is suggested by Homer's Penelope who thwarted her would-be suitors during Odysseus' absence by promising to remarry once she had completed a tapestry. Patiently weaving by day and faithfully unweaving by night, Penelope never finishes her tapestry. This unending process of weaving and unweaving is the same process Beckett employs. But, for Beckett the process is complicated by the fact that his works have begun to create their own set of generic expectations. When we read a work by Beckett, we do not expect to find traditional plots, conventional characters, or recognizable locations. Instead, we anticipate unidentified voices and nameless, shapeless, and sexless figures. We know that time will be an eternal present lacking any memory of the past and denied any hope for the future. Certainty will be replaced by a pervasive ambiguity. Language will be stripped of allusions and punctuation. Meaning will have to be gleaned from repetitions, revisions, and contradictions. Beckett's works have become a genre of their own and it, like all other genres, must be woven and unwoven. The danger in such a self-reflexive process is that it may become its own subject, obscuring the threads and patterns of Beckett's evolving tapestries.

I would like to turn now to one of Beckett's recent pieces, *Worstward Ho,*[2] because I believe it is the closest Beckett has ever come to explicating his process and because it reflects the tensions of a self-reflexive genre.

II. Weaving and Unweaving Worstward Ho

Everything in *Worstward Ho* both demonstrates and is about the weaving and unweaving process. The work depicts a voice saying words that it hopes will unsay themselves. The situation is familiar. Although *Worstward Ho* lacks the sense of urgency and volition which drives the Unnamable to seek the words that will put an end to words, nonetheless the piece does attempt to go beyond language and embrace the "Unmoreable unlessable unworseable evermost almost void" (p. 43). The effort is paradoxical. The more the voice describes the desired goal (i.e., the void), the further it is from achieving it. The piece needs to *unmake* itself; needs to find words that will gesture to what it must be like when words are gone:

> What when words gone? . . . What words for what then? None for what then. No words for what when words gone. For what when nohow on. Somehow nohow on. (p. 29).

Worstward Ho goes somehow nohow on by manipulating three "shades" (or figures) and one or more voices. The shades are an old woman kneeling, an old man and a child walking hand in hand, and a head sunk on crippled hands staring with "clenched" eyes at the other shades. In addition to being a shade, the head is also the "Seat of all. Germ of all" (pp. 10 and 19): the "Scene and seer of it all" (p. 24). In other words, the head is the container within which all of *Worstward Ho* transpires. As such, it is also the setting, the "Beyondless . . . Thenceless thitherless there" (p. 12). In earlier works Beckett explores the infinite regression implied by such a self-containing container, but here he is content to acknowledge the problem and leave it unresolved:

> . . . the head said seat of all. Germ of all. All? If of all of it too, where if not there it too? There in the sunken head the sunken head . . . Shade with the other shades. In the same dim. The same narrow void. Before the staring eyes. Where it too if not there too? Ask not. No. Ask in vain. Better worse so. (p. 19)

The head sees and thus creates everything including itself. We have Berkeley's dictum, "to be is to be seen," operating in an hermetically sealed system. Where everything within the head can fade, change, or disappear, the head itself cannot disappear until there is an end to the dim. ("The head. Ask not if it can go. Say no. Unasking no. It cannot go. Save dim go. Then all go" p. 19-20). Because the head contains everything, the dim must refer to an internal not an external illumination. In essence, the dim which drives everything must be the imagination. As long as there is imagination, there will be words (voices) and images (shades to fill the void). The quest therefore is impossible: one cannot imagine the absence of imagination. At best, Beckett can only hope to present an image that will imply its own dissipation and ultimate absence.

The quest for a self-dissipating image informs every aspect of *Worstward Ho* from the title and structure to the language. Beckett presents something with one hand (or voice) while taking it away with another. Perhaps the most obvious example of this process is the title which negates the allusions it evokes. Instead of the wagon-master's call (Westward Ho) to start pioneers in their westward journey to adventure and a new and better life, we have a linguistic game being played with that call. We are directed not to a geographical direction, but to a comparative state: not to the west and adventure, but to an abstraction which is usually negative. We are thrust into a mental journey that reverses our expectations, having us seek not the best, but the worst. And, as the pun on "ward" and "word" implies, in true Beckettian fashion, the journey will be a verbal one. Just as the title simultaneously elicits and negates an allusion, so too the entire structure of *Worstward Ho* calls forth and controverts expectations. The opening paragraph is a précis of the whole: "On. Say on. Be said on. Some how on. Till nohow on. Said nohow on" (p. 7)." The piece begins with a clear and positive imperative, "On," only to be undercut immediately by the less certain, "Say on." Suddenly it is no longer clear if action actually takes place or if it is simply reported. The next sentence compounds the ambiguity by introducing the passive, "Be said on." The volition and control implied by the imperative mood have disappeared. In their place now is confusion over who is speaking and to whom. The erosion of our initial confidence and clarity is momentarily stayed by the more positive, "*Somehow* on," but this is itself instantly undermined by the introduction of a negative: "Till *no*how on" (my emphasis). Finally, the whole is once again thrown into question by "Said nohow on." Does all of this really end, or is it only *said* to have ended? Have we been presented with a summary as the act concludes and all *has been said?* Or, is it irrelevant that an end was hypothesized? Do you go "on" *despite* claims that all has been said?

The contrapuntal movement of the first paragraph is replicated throughout the work. For example, the first several paragraphs are orchestrated into an antiphony between a voice that is postulating our "story" and one that self-consciously questions and criticizes that "story." Paragraph one postulates

"On. Say on," while paragraph two criticizes the language that made that postulation. Paragraph three introduces a body, a mind, and a place, while paragraph four dismisses them all as old stuff: "All of old. Nothing else ever. Ever tried" (p. 7). What one voice offers, the other takes away.

The same undermining process is applied to the "shades." In another characteristic pattern, Beckett begins describing the figures *in media res*. The solitary figure which Beckett later labels "one" (p. 20), is presented to us without warning, explanation, or even antecedent: "*It* stands" (my emphasis, p. 8). Slowly Beckett adds other details until the shade becomes identifiable, calling it a body (p. 11), saying its back is turned (p. 12), providing it with a hat and greatcoat (p. 14). As soon as we are able to visualize "one," however, Beckett begins to undermine the image by revising what has gone before (e.g., by page 14 "one" is kneeling not standing) and by eliminating attributes. Hat, greatcoat, and even portions of the body (p. 22) are stripped away. The same pattern is repeated for the other shades. Once we have pieced together the image of "two" as an old, white-haired man and a fair-haired child walking hand in hand and wearing greatcoats and boots, Beckett removes their boots, ends the hand-holding, and ultimately suggests that they are themselves gone ("Say child gone. As good as gone. . . . Say old man gone" p. 43.)

Similarly, the language in *Worstward Ho* parallels the themes of the impossible worst-ward journey. In fact, most of the verbal difficulties and games of the work are linguistic complements to its paradoxical quest. In an inversion of traditional values, worseness and lessness become desirable because they put us close to the void. Hence we end up with oxymoronic phrases such as "Unknown better" (p. 11), "Better worse kneeling" (p. 15), and "Any other would do as ill" (p. 14). Language is further undermined by revision and contradiction. The voice reverses all that has been and will be said when it announces that "say" should be interpreted as "be missaid" (p. 7), "see" as "be misseen" (p. 12), and "said" as "missaid" (p.37). Statements no longer mean what they appear to say, nor belong to the tense in which they are written. The use of the passive in this work further disorients the reader, blurring the boundaries between "scene and seer" (p. 24), speaker and spoken. It is unclear when one stops acting and starts being acted upon, when one is holding a hand and when one is being held (p. 13), when you are saying a story, and when you are being said.

III. THE SELF-REFLEXIVE TAPESTRY

Not only does *Worstward Ho* dramatize in its language and structures the weaving and unweaving process lying at the center of its impossible quest, but it also self-consciously explicates that process. The work openly admits that is is always striving to reach the void, to eliminate everything including itself (p. 42). The voice acknowledges that words are added only if they can help diminish what they describe (p. 25). The goal is consistently to lessen or worsen the eyes (p. 27), the shades (p. 21), the dim (pp. 24-25), even the words themselves (p. 21). Whereas the reader may have to spend hours piecing out meaning from the torturously clipped sentences of *Worstward Ho*, the voice laments their excess of meaning and lack of inanity (p. 21). Whereas other Beckett characters suffer the anguish of an unremitting present, the voice bemoans the possibility of a future: "No future in this. Alas yes" (p. 10)—Alas there may be a future and not an ending. The voice freely confesses that its purpose is "Next try fail better . . ." (p. 22). Notice that here Beckett has reversed the rather Romantic celebration of artistic failure he enunciated in the "Three Dialogues" saying: "to be an artist is to fail, as no other dare fail."[3] We no longer see an artist who, wanting to succeed but knowing he won't because of "the incoercible absence of relation,"[4] nonetheless dares to fail. Instead we hear a voice that tells us it would like to fail but unwillingly keeps "succeeding" in creating images and words that it must then somehow undermine.

The voice also self-consciously admits that the words, images, and undermining are themselves not new: "All of old. Nothing else ever. Ever tried. Ever failed. No matter. Try again. Fail again. Fail better" (p. 7). Indeed, *Worstward Ho* reverberates with echoes of Beckett's earlier pieces. From the opening scene which is reminiscent of the Unnamable's need to go on despite the impossibility of going on, to specific details like the hats and greatcoats and bootlessness, we recognize Beckettian situations, images, and techniques. Even the verbal games are familiar. The phrase "Something not wrong . . ." (p. 21) is a deliberate evocation and negation of the refrain from *How It Is:* "something wrong there." But where *How It Is* employs the phrase to emphasize the narrator's mistakes, here the phrase really laments the voice's inability to make mistakes, to be wrong, to dwindle away. By evoking and altering earlier works, *Worstward Ho* becomes a self-conscious commentary on Beckett's canon. The piece attempts to get closer to the void by paring away and flattening out even the minimal emotions the other pieces intimated. *The Unnamable's* situation is repeated, but not its urgency. *Enough's* sufficiency is briefly implied (p. 43), but never developed. *Company's* nostalgic loneliness and desire for companionship are present, but only in the no longer held hands of the couple. As a result, *Worstward Ho* is more barren and stark than other pieces. Even its verbal games participate less in Krapp's sheer joy in the sound of the word "spool", than in the dianoetic laughter hypothesized by Watt.

Perhaps the starkness of *Worstward Ho* is best illustrated in the ending which is one of Beckett's most contrived and least resonant endings. As in a musical composition, there are several structural hints that the end is coming. Beckett alters the pacing and rhythms of the piece by first slowing things down through extended paragraphs (pp. 43-44) and then speeding them up with several abrupt passages in which the voice jumps rapidly from one dissipating image to another as they fade, change, and disappear (pp. 44-45). Beckett gives *Worstward Ho* a sense of formal completion by making it circular. The final paragraph returns us to the first, repeating the sentence "Said nohow on." Beckett even hints at a plot-like conclusion by comparing the kneeling woman to stooping gravestones:

> Nothing and yet a woman. Old and yet old. On unseen knees. Stooped as loving memory some old gravestones stoop. In that old graveyard. Names gone and when to when. Stoop mute over the graves of none. (p. 46)

In this passage there is, however briefly and ephemerally, a suggestion of a story, or at least of a connection among the shades and voices. The clenched eyes may be remembering the shades of those who no longer exist—an old man, a child, and a grieving woman. Rest will come for the eyes only when they stop recalling those shades and merge like them into the void. Such a disappearance would provide a neat unity of form and content similar to the unities that so compellingly end works like *The Unnamable, Enough,* and *Company.*

Structurally, the end of *Worstward Ho* is well-established. Thematically, however, the piece could end anywhere: whenever the imagination stops, so do the words. And emotionally, the piece could have no satisfactory conclusion precisely because Beckett has pared away emotions and feelings. The self-reflexive work can go on *ad infinitum* creating and negating itself. Whereas Penelope is saved from an eternity at the loom by Odysseus' return, there is nothing to spare *Worstward Ho* from its own weaving and unweaving.

IV. SAID NOHOW ON

In talking of *Worstward Ho*, Beckett once remarked that it put the kabosh on things and that he had done it to himself.[5] Although none of us takes very seriously any suggestions, even Beckett's that he has written himself into a corner, the tensions and starkness of *Worstward Ho* demonstrate the difficulties inherent in Beckett's treatment of genre. Beckett is able to gesture to an unimaginable, unnamable void by controlling our expectations. He carefully evokes and undermines literary conventions. But the more we read Beckett, the more his process becomes itself an expected literary convention. *Worstward Ho* self-consciously explicates Beckett's process and his dilemma, ending with the rather pessimistic "Said nohow on." My expectation and hope now are that from this seemingly impossible situation Beckett will find yet another way to weave and unweave the tapestry of his art.

From *The Journal of Beckett Studies* 11-12 (1989): 123-29.

[1]Alex Preminger, et al., *Princeton Encyclopedia of Poetry and Poetics: Enlarged Edition* (Princeton, N.J.: Princeton University Press, 1974), p. 308.

[2]Samuel Beckett, *Worstward Ho* (N.Y.: Grove Press, 1983).

[3]Samuel Beckett, "Three Dialogues," quoted in *Samuel Beckett: A Collection of Critical Essays*, ed. Martin Esslin (Englewood Cliffs, N.J.: Prentice-Hall, 1965), p. 21.

[4]"Three Dialogues," p. 21.

[5]Beckett made these remarks in a conversation with Martha Fehsenfeld on July 1, 1983.

Samuel Beckett's *For to End Yet Again*: A Conflict between "Syntax of Energy" and "Syntax of Weakness"

Tseng Li-Ling

After *Comment c'est* (1961) the size and scale of Samuel Beckett's prose writing diminishes considerably. This *volte-face* in his choice of expressive strategy—from baroque "extravagances" (*How It Is* 67) of his middle phase of fiction-writing toward disintegration and miniaturization—has drawn considerable attention from critics. Olga Bernal notices a "disintegration of language" since *Comment c'est* (quoted in Sherzer 49). Raymond Federman characterizes this shift in Beckett's narrative method as "to delyricalise, to destylise the language of fiction, to designify the words" (29). George Lukacs, from his socialist perspective, naturally dismisses Beckett's narrowing and apparently nonreferential scope of writing as an undesirable "attenuation of reality."[1] Steven Connor, however, notes Beckett's later works evincing a new style gravitating toward a calm, calculated, scrupulous, though austere and disconcerting direction (93, 100). H. Porter Abbot argues that Beckett's later works are carefully structured upon "radical displacements" (224, 228). J. E. Dearlove and Laura Barge agree that Beckett's dramatic stylistic change is actually a logical development of his earlier practices. They sum up this emerging style as being characterized by, among other things, the concept of an integral self being collapsed into an impersonal and omniscient voice, a rigid, mathematical, scientific framework, and fragmentation of consciousness, being, and fiction (Dearlove, "Last Image" 105; Barge 277).

This new direction of minimalist writing was prefigured in the thirteen *Texts for Nothing* (1950-52) and *From an Abandoned Work* (1955) after Beckett experienced a creative impasse in writing the almost self-destructive *The Unnamable*, the third part of the *Trilogy* (1947-1949). After *Comment c'est, Le Dépeupleur* (1965) remains the only work whose length is comparable to the *Nouvelles* (1945).[2] Whereas Beckett experiments with techniques of restraint, fragmentation, and displacement, the only thing left out of this distillation process is unmistakably "the essential."[3] Style, which is purged of extravagances, is this essential element that stands out. As well phrased by Connor, style has replaced Beckett's earlier concern with the unwieldly matter of being and existence to become the "bearer of meaning" (100). This new "style of indigence" and "poetics of deprivation" is significantly substantiated by syntactic considerations and possibilities (Knowlson and Pilling 241; Harvey 392). Orthodox syntax is considerably subverted to achieve a desirable effect of "weakness." This "syntax of weakness" Beckett would appropriate and perfect throughout the period of the sixties and seventies (Harvey 435).[4]

Indeed, by 1962 Beckett had felt a strong need for seeking the "solace of form" which is "adequate" (Dearlove, "Syntax Unpended" 126). Syntactic subversions take place to dismantle grammatical conventions and hence grammatical logic. In practice, the syntax of weakness deliberately leaves out grammatical units which normally would be considered indispensable. "Narrative cohesion as normal syntax creates" is thereby justifiably severed (Pilling, "Review Article" 99). Accordingly, "compression" is favored as the choice of Beckett's new style of writing (Rabinovitz, "The Self Contained" 51, 53).[5] Besides, the syntax of weakness has a strong preference for, and therefore enjoys manipulation of, words with ambivalent functions. It relishes resonant assonance and alliteration. Consequently, it gratifies Beckett's increasing interest in sounds and in composing a new brand of "lyrics of fiction."[6] It circumvents the direct exploration of pathos in favor of an incantation of ambiguities. In essence, it is "a syntax that operates on our sensibilities rather than by its vehement rigour" (Pilling, "The Significance" 149).

Beckett's awareness of the need of a new form which, in his ideal, attempts to disturb or violate "the nature of being" as little as possible (Harvey 435), starts to take effect in *All Strange Away* (1936) and persists through the major short prose works of the sixties, such as *Imagination Dead Imagine* (1965), *Ping* (1966), and *Lessness* (1969), and finally extends toward and culminates in works of the seventies, some of which are included in *Fizzles*, such as *Still* (1972) and *For to End Yet Again* (1975), and such uncollected ones as *Sounds* and *Still 3* (1972-1973).[7] These texts all embody Beckett's ideal to achieve a nonrelational grammar of its own kind by means of an emasculated syntactic structure and choice of words and thus to simulate a state of the least disturbed silence and stillness to which many of Beckett's protagonists and characters in his earlier long fiction have aspired.

The road to perfection, however, is not all that smooth. During one decade of experimentation (1963-1975), Beckett was striving toward perfection of this new poetics which accommodates his vision of this period best. Yet, the old "art and craft" and "extravagances" occasionally re-emerge to disturb the practice of the new way of writing (*Enough* 139). *Enough* (1963) and *As the Story Was Told* (1973) can be considered a break in this series of writings of the sixties and seventies from the continuity of "weakened" and "personless" writing. Their reintroduction of the I-narrator marks the sharpest contrast to the rest of the series which attempt a pseudo-scientific and objective approach in the choice of point of view.

Two years after the composition of *As the Story Was Told*, Beckett wrote *For to End Yet Again*, whose minimal length and syntax directly relate to the dominant "poetics of indigence" of the period. "Poverty," or to use Beckett's own words, an "insuperable indigence," may be highlighted as one of Beckett's most important stylistic characterizations of this period (*Proust* 112). Beckett in *For to End Yet Again*, too, extensively employs the "syntax of weakness" in pursuit of an objectified narrative. *For to End Yet Again* overlaps with previous writings so far as similar themes, motifs, and syntax are concerned. Its relationship with *Lessness* is especially interesting, not only because both works employ similar décor and characters but, more significantly, because each manifests a similar transitional tendency from a syntax of weakness to a syntax of energy.[8] *Lessness* has been described by Gontarski as a "trick" of "pulling words out of a hat" in its extremely free arrangement of sentences and lack of logical connection between them, yet Beckett still maintains a control of human will in his creative process (14). In like manner, *For to End Yet Again* demonstrates this entanglement of the dominant syntax of weakness and a surreptitious reinscription of the more normal syntax of energy. The "syntactic energy" of *For to End Yet Again* lies in its numerous "grammar-intact" sentences and its excessively figurative language. Coinciding with this "syntactic energy" is a kind of "semantic contiguity" (Bruns 182). *For to End Yet Again*, indeed, treats the workings of the imagination scenically and systematically as if the narrative sequences were cinematic shots.

Like *Lessness*, described by Beckett himself as "composed of six statement groups," *For to End Yet Again* can be divided into six scenarios. Each is complete, with its own décor, setting, lighting, characters, and motion, the dramatic and kinetic nature of each marking a major departure from *Lessness*, whose six component groups are essentially statemental (Esslin 118).

(1) The Skull Scenario

Scenario one sets up a background for the rest. The claustrophobia of earlier prose settings here reaches an extreme: a "closed place," a "box" (179) or a "case chamber" (as Beckett puts it in MS 1551/3)[9] is what remains of the rotunda of *All Strange Away* and *Imagination Dead Imagine* and the cube of *Ping*. The lighting in this scenario is also residual. If any light is to be perceived, it is exceptionally faint and dim. What were at least bodies in the "closed place" of the earlier short prose is now a mere fragment—a "skull" with "no neck no face" (179)—hence even the illuminated face in *That Time* ("Old white, long flaring white hair as if seen from above outspread") is figural by comparison (*Collected Shorter Plays* 228). Perhaps only the "mouth" ("faintly lit from close-up and below, rest of face in shadow") of *Not I* can be analogous to the extremely localized depiction of a human head in *For to End Yet Again* (*Collected Shorter Plays* 216).

The setting and décor of this scenario are of a piece with the fragmented syntax. Even when several sentences seem about to embody grammatical integrity, the elimination of one or more elements prevents this (e.g., "never light so faint as theirs so pale" [179]). It is when the text starts to pursue "semantic contiguity" that its syntax begins to embody strength and energy. It is then that grammatically normal sentences start to creep into the narrative. It is as if the skull scenario confronts the imagination with such an extreme reductionism that, in reaction, it exerts itself to produce images and motions: "There in the end all at once or by degrees there dawns and magic lingers a leaden dawn" (179). Not only does this call to mind the "subjective imagination" in *Lessness*, where the narrator also exerts his will power to ensure "He will curse God again" (Finney, "'Assumption' to *Lessness*" 76), but the sentence's grammatical integrity and colorful language have their counterparts in the second part of the above quotation from *Lessness*, too ("as in the blessed days face to the open sky the passing deluge" [156]).

In *Lessness*, when the narrator's "subjective imagination" is at work, his language becomes poetic ("the blue celeste of poesy") and his sentences integral. The same situation recurs in *For to End Yet Again*. Though willed, the evocation of creative inspiration—"there dawns and magic lingers"—is no less "magical" than Proust's involuntary memory (*Proust* 34). Quite different from the "miracle" of rediscovering the bodies in *Imagination Dead Imagine*, which reaffirms the narrator's perceptual faculty, the "magic" here highlights the narrator's visual desire as a consequence of imagination's hunger for objects.[10] The arrival of inspiration is dramatized by the word "there." The narrator makes no attempt to disguise his intention to create: "Thus then the skull makes to glimmer again in lieu of going out" (179). When the skull starts to glimmer—either because of its own will power and initiative, or because of a change in lighting—it spins out sequences of images and human figures. The image of light which, in the earlier shorter prose, suggest the power supply of the imagination, is once again employed to dramatize the sudden circuit-connection between the imagination and the imagined—"as if switched on" (179). The genetic nature of the imagination is epitomized in the metaphor of "within without [the skull]." The skull transforms the need to imagine from within to the actual creations without.[11]

The word "magic" is one of "a thousand little signs" indicating the narrator's resourcefulness in activating the imagination (*Imagination Dead Imagine* 147). From the beginning, the language of *For to End Yet Again* is deliberately archaic and poetic, as if such a linguistic appeal would expedite the process of imagining.[12] "Pent" in "skull alone in a dark place pent bowed on a board" (179), meaning "shut up within narrow limits" or "closely confined, imprisoned" *(Oxford English Dictionary)*, is an archaic usage. Then again, in MS 1551/2, the skull glimmers "instead of going out," but this is corrected to the Gallicized "in lieu of going out." The sense of "defamiliarization" is here generated more by archaic or foreign words than by the syntax of weakness.

(2) The "Expelled" Scenario

The evocation of the muse coincides with the use of three successive metaphors: "to dawn," "magic," and "leaden." Imagination, in its ability to produce images, is like a dawn which magically dispels darkness and reveals the shape of the universe. As a matter of fact, the interplay between the images of light and darkness has always been reinstated as one of the major structural as well as thematic concerns in Beckett's works from *Imagination Dead Imagine* on. The spontaneity of the inspirational strength ("all at once") is no less dynamic than the splitting asunder of walls in *Lessness*. This enables the "magic of craftsmanship" to transform the lighting from black to "leaden grey" (Knowlson and Pilling 253). The claustrophobic confines of the dark place in the first scenario are demolished; instead, the "cloudless sky" and the wide expanse of "dust" and "desert" become "mock confines" (179). The "endlessness" of the *Lessness* setting recurs, as does the "he"-character among the ruins. The motif of the ruins as a refuge of the mind again brings the issue of imagination to the fore. Indeed, the "eye" is almost as important as the "he"-character himself, who is self-evidently the protagonist in this scenario. The "eye" stages a "long desert to begin" (179). Imagination's earnest intention to create concrete objects can best be depicted in Beckett's choice of "desert" in preference to "empty" (MS 1551/2). "Empty" would echo the "black void" of the first skull scenario; however, the eye wills itself to envisage something concrete. Even a "desert" (though understandably empty) is more positive than the abstract vagueness of "empty."

The "resurrection" of a human figure (Cunningham 349), or the reintroduction of the "personal accent" (Pilling, "Beckett after 'Still'" 285) is indeed encouraging in a context of "hell air" (179), which can be compared to "Hell this light" and "timeless air" of *All Strange Away* (117, 118).[13] But the narrator's enthusiasm for imagining leads him to go further than *Lessness* which, at best, reconnects the third-person pronoun with its character. *For to*

End Yet Again identifies the character with the "expelled," a word apparently referring to the title of one of Beckett's *Nouvelles*, not to mention its more immediate allusion to the Bible. However, except in the occasional pensive moments when he raises his eyes to the sky for help, or when, in confessional mood, he admits he is "in love with hiding and prone position" (*The Expelled* 25), the first-person narrator/protagonist of *The Expelled* is too truant to resemble the "expelled" in *For to End Yet Again*. If any connection is to be made, the I-narrator of *The Calmative* is perhaps the most promising, since he embodies the same concerns as the narrator of *For to End Yet Again*. The most relevant remark *The Calmative* narrator makes is: "for we are needless to say in a skull" (43). The "issueless predicament of existence" has been embodied in the image of a "man . . . alone trudging in the sand" (like the he-character of *Lessness* and "the expelled" here), and has been condensed to a skull-like box (cf. "box" [179])—"the man alone thinking (thinking!) in his box" featured in a piece of criticism Beckett wrote as long ago as 1945 ("McGreevy," *Disjecta* 97). No doubt the skull is the ultimate cause which inflicts human misery. Throughout the writings of the sixties, the issue of the skull is only shelved, rather than solved, by Beckett's alternative emphasis on the "eye of prey." Herbert Blau convincingly argues that the "compulsive" and "unrelieved" gaze in Beckett's later works which feature the theme of the eye of prey often turns into "speculation," a tendency dangerously bearing affinity to Cartesian self-reflection which is tautological by nature (79). As the opening scenario of *For to End Yet Again* demonstrates, the development of the theme of imagination has ultimately to be concluded in a skull. *The Calmative* narrator wills himself to tell a story in order to fend off the slow failing and dying of his skull, as if stories might provide nutrition from which his declining ability to imagine could be regenerated. In *For to End Yet Again* the imagination stages the same den-like ruins and solitary tramp-like figure as in *The Calmative*.

The same fragmented syntax and weak past participles as have been employed in describing the bodies in *Imagination Dead Imagine*, *Ping,* and *Lessness* almost turn the expelled into an object—"all that little body from head to feet sunk ankle deep" (179). Nevertheless, like the body in *Ping*, the expelled's eyes are the only thing "unover"—"last bright of all" (179). The glimmer of his eyes echoes the glimmer of the skull. In addition, though the body's arms and legs are immobile, the arms' strength in cleaving to the trunk and the legs' potential to flee imply some mobility. It is significant that a grammatically normal sentence should coincide with the suggestion that the expelled might muster strength to move: "The arms still cleave to the trunk and to each other the legs made for flight." Just as the geographical expanse present here mocks the confines of the first scenario's "box" and "skull," so the creation of the human figure, together with its potential for movement, aims at restoring "the days of the light of day" (179).

Two distinct qualities of "the days of the light of day," which eventually should promise a "hypothetical happiness"—the chronological and the religious—are once again restored as in *Lessness* (Dearlove, *Accommodating the Chaos* 141). The "haughtiest monuments" which have been engulfed by the deep sand function in the same way as the "deluge" in *Lessness*, both testifying to the existence of the past. The dust which permeates the air was "once" "here and there," too. It is the narrator's memory which confirms that the dust has been derived from previous times. The tactic of bringing to mind talismanic objects from the past is but one of the inclinations which the narrator inherits from his predecessors, notably the one in *Lessness*.

Concatenated with the narrator's intention to establish a chronology is the archaism and "poesy" of his language, as if the issue of time must invariably induce the same degree of figurative language as in the description of the Proustian time: "that double-headed monster of damnation and salvation" (*Proust* 11). The sentence, "Sand pale as dust ah but dust indeed deep to engulf the haughtiest monuments which too it once was here and there" (179), appeals not only to the visual but also to the aural ("ah") imagination. The past-tense "was" establishes a time scale. The alliteration of "indeed deep" reinforces the poetic image of the monuments which themselves resemble those of Shelley's "Ozymandias," in which the fragments of the statue—"trunkless legs of stone" and a "shattered visage"—lay "half sunk" in the sand (Shelley 550). That poem's celebration of the triumph of art over human mortality is arguably another of the narrator's aspirations in *For to End Yet Again*. The tendency to poeticize produces an abundance of archaic words. Although excessive archaism has been considerably curtailed in the final text, it is symptomatic that Beckett's working drafts should reveal the intense "poesy" to which *For to End Yet Again* initially devoted itself. As it is, the printed text's residual "poesy" far exceeds that of *Lessness*, whose "subjective imagination" almost annihilates its coexistent syntax of weakness.

MS 1551/3 and 4 indicate that "too" in the above example evolved from the archaic "sooth" and similar examples abound throughout this scenario. "Bourne upon bourne" (MS 1551/2) was the alternative to the present "verge upon verge" (180), and "foes" (MS 1551/2) to "enemies" (180). These archaic words and expressions are in due course expunged, though "among" (MS 1551/4) is replaced by the archaic "amidst" (180). If retained, the archaism could not only have induced "poesy" but also enhanced the sense of immemorial time. For example, "grey cloudless sky bourne upon bourne timeless air of those nor for god nor for his foes" (MS 1551/2) would have created an arresting sensation of eons of stagnation and would have inhibited the progress of the linear time. The fact that the archaism is eventually dropped is due not so much to the curtailment of a "weakened" way of writing as to the narrator's conviction that he must dispel "timelessness" and "changelessness." Though considerably alleviated in comparison with the void of the first scenario, a need to end the endlessness in this scene eventually impels the narrator to move on to the next one—the dwarfs.

Religious evocation is also used by the narrator to dispel the intensive stasis. However, the religious reference is not so functional as that in *All Strange Away*, where prayers were almost said. The reference to God here can be seen as a residue from the religious allusions in *Lessness*. In both cases the religious element supplies the narrator with external (historical and human) reality and a fund of associations.

(3) The Dwarfs Scenario

The change in lighting proves to be crucial in the evolution from one scenario to the next; the black in the first gives way to grey in the second and to white in the third. This gradual permeation of light links the first three scenarios together. The tendency to make "white" glimmer coincides with the general direction of Beckett's prose works from *All Strange Away, Imagination Dead Imagine,* to *Ping,* texts which have, as it were, gradually distilled their pigments in order to draw a "white sheet across the tempest of emblems" ("Alba," *Collected Poems* 15). Scenario three is talismanically comprised of two white dwarfs who draw a "white sheet" across a "litter" with shafts, a pillow and possibly a dead body on it. The change in lighting from grey to white is by and large prompted by "the eye." When the "changelessness" of the previous scene is too intense to activate the potential movement of the expelled, the eye of imagination must either focus hard until its creations emerge ("There again in the end way amidst the verges a light in the grey two white dwarfs" [180]), or look wherever it is likely to observe what it wants to observe ("mere whiteness sighted from afar" [MS1551/3]). The omission of the past participle "sighted" in the final text does not, however, obscure to any great extent the importance of the eye of imagination. The dwarfs' movements and their equipment (the bed, sheet, etc.) are all observed from what the narrator later, in scenario four, describes as a "bird's-eye view" (180): "a litter seen from above" and "Bone white of the sheet seen from above" (180). The narrator's position has been further removed from the "surface" of the sand (from which he has observed that "a fragment comes and falls" [179], as the result of the observing eye's adjacency to the observed—the expelled), first to "afar" and subsequently elevated to mid-air. The aerial overview of the entire sequence of the dwarfs' advancing face to face and carrying a bed between them is analogous to the vulture's "eyes of prey" which consume their victims.

The narrator's aerial outlook in this scenario, however, is by no means so remote that he cannot impose his own desire upon what he sees. Herbert Blau suspects that one of the two implications of Beckett's relentless search for objects, as it were, as evidence of "thingness" is that the perceiving subject actually "projects the objects in accordance with the logic of its own desire" (79). The desiring eye of imagination can be illustrated by the magic of "there" and the dramatic tone of "in the end" (cf. "at last" in MS 1551/3). No sooner does imagination delegate a bird's-eye view than it starts to interact with the imagined. The two imperative sentences ("Let him veer to the north . . . ." and "Let one stop short . . . ." [180]) are more explicit than those of the *Still* trilogy in which the "weak" syntax makes the personal plea to "leave it so" (*Still, Sounds*) and "try dreamt away" (*Still 3*) sound rather wistful. Instead, this explicitness achieves the effect of "provisionalism" such as one finds in *All Strange Away* and *Imagination Dead Imagine* in their colloquial use of "say" and in itemizing examples. These two imperatives are like a stage direction set out by a playwright who is improvising in order to establish his characters' dramatic behavior. However provisional they may be, if only because of the wistful thinking involved, these two imperatives do embody the narrator's underlying preoccupation. Whereas, at the end of scenario two, no sooner has the "deep sunk" expelled actually moved ("comes") than he "falls" and reverts to immobility, in this scenario the narrator is uncertain whether to let his characters go on or "stop dead" (MS 1551/2). The natural bond between the two dwarfs, the litter, was thrice dismissed: "they drop the litter" (MS 1151/2, 3, 4). The present version, "they let fall the letter" (180), reflects the narrator's reluctance to discard an external object which has become very important in the light of imagining.

The narrator's divided sensibility achieves, at best, a constant reversal of the two dwarfs' roles—when one stops short, the other carries on. Although at times the dwarfs are inclined to "let fall," if not "drop," the litter, they can always dexterously "take up again without having to stoop" (180). Their kinetic quality is suggested either by means of highly emotional metaphors and similes or by increased grammatical normality, examples of which are especially frequent in this scenario:

>"they toil step by step through the grey dust";
>"Slowly it sweeps the dust";
>"they are so alike the eye cannot tell them apart";
>"They carry face to face and relay each other often so that turn about they backward lead the way";
>"From time to time impelled as one they let fall the litter then again without having to stoop";
>"At the end of the arms the four hands open as one and the litter . . . already settles without a sound" (180)

Compared with "weak" fragmented phrases and clauses, such grammatically normal sentences embody a verbal strength which coincides with the dwarf's mobility. Moreover, the narrator openly employs very telling similes which reinforce the kinetic strength of this scene. The dwarfs' perfect sense of direction and their resolution to persevere is compared to the coxswain's adroitness in steering a rowboat: "His who follows who knows to shape the course much as the coxswain with light touch the skiff' (180). MS 1551/2's superlative—"with lightest touch"—best illustrates the narrator's emphatic intention.

There may or may not be a body on the litter which the dwarfs are carrying: "swelling the sheet now fore now aft as permutations list a pillow marks the place of the head" (180). The uncertain and spectral quality of this observation is superbly re-created by the syntactical arrangement of keeping the subject ("pillow") remote from its preceding present participle ("swelling") and by the use of this "pillow" to insinuate the "place of the head." Although both "swelling" and "pillow" contain the internal double "l" spelling, the distance between them is so great that "swelling" looks to the reader's eyes as if it is not being followed by the subject which is supposed to be a "head." Although the "pillow" marks the place of the head, its attribute as object somehow invalidates this statement. Whether or not the body is (or has been but is not now) in the litter and whether or not it is a dead head (or body) remains shadowy and ambiguous. Other evidence of Beckett's resourcefulness in hints and allusions can be found here. Golgotha, which appeared in Beckett's 1938 poem "Ooftish," is the place where the body of Christ was taken off the cross and literally means in Aramaic "[the place of] the skull." The empty skull may be analogous to the empty cross (as it may boil down to the "blood of lamb," *Collected Poems* 31); however, this possible religious implication could help to reduce the hermeticism of the "litter" and "head."

The above sentence also contains an element which betrays syntactic ambiguity and weakness, namely, the over-explanatory simile—"as permutations list." This phrase is actually syntactically ambiguous, as "list" can be a noun and a verb. However, its interpretation is dependent upon the major noun "permutations." The swelling of the sheet could be less in accord with the swinging created by the dwarfs' amble ("now fore now aft") than with variable "permutations." This word brings to mind the various positions of the Emmo/Emma characters in *All Strange Away*, not to mention one hallmark of Beckett's long fiction: the inexhaustible lists in *Watt* (1942) and the permutative play in *Molloy* (1947).[14] This simile, therefore, cancels and disrupts the disappearance of the body in the litter and the objectified tendency contained in the rest of the sentence.

The imagining eye's natural inclination is to give birth to its creation. Therefore, when the "leaden grey" of the previous scenario becomes too static, a variation in lighting, a recruitment of new dramatis personae, and even a redefinition of the setting are inevitable. The new characters, the dwarfs, are as white as the "same wilderness" (180), the same post-holocaustal scenery as in *Lessness*. Owing to the soaring position of the imagining eyes and the vast desert which swallows up even the "haughtiest monuments," the eyes cannot tell the two dwarfs apart. Besides, more important, they advance in the sand, bound to each other as if they were one, not so much because of the litter between them as because of some kind of inner drive which "impels" them to act in concert. The shadowy body in the bed is never more than a mark on the pillow. Therefore, although on the surface this scenario seems multiple in comparison with the previous two, the underlying atmosphere is still one of emptiness and desolation. The plural form of "solitudes" used in MS 1551/2, 3 indicates the narrator's wish to surpass the solitude of the grey desert setting. As in the choice of "desert" over "empty," Beckett finally settles for "wilderness." The setting is just as monotonous as the dwarfs are solitary, but "wilderness," a concrete, geographic word, functions better than "solitudes," an abstract and yet emotion-embedded word.

The above similes and images contribute partially to the "poesy" of this scenario, which is mainly composed of archaism and figures of speech. The "bed" (MS 1551/2, 3, in relation to which "litter" and "couch" [180] are archaic usages) which the dwarfs are carrying is equated with the fecal image—"dung" (cf. "dung-litter" [MS 1551/2])—but qualified by the dramatically dismissive words, of "laughable memory." The litter, then, is either too freighted with implications or too inseparable from human memory, for the dwarfs effectively to "drop" it. Just as the narrator finds the external object indispensable, so he is apparently either repelled, or awed, by the "monstrous extremities" of the dwarfs' defective mobility and by his own detailed inspection ("skulls stunted legs and trunks monstrous arms stunted face" [180]), both of which have been prerequisites of Beckett's "style of deprivation" which substantiates a type of "physical immobility that leads to freedom of movement in the inner world" (Rabinovitz, "The Self Contained" 51). The physical extremities have been identified with Beckett's earlier fictional characters. Take the narrator of *The Calmative* for example. Far from being alarmed or appalled by physical disability, he apologizes to the young shepherd at the seaside because there is not enough blood in his "extremities" for him to blush (40). The colorful adjective "monstrous" here shows that the narrator ceases to deem human deformity as one of the means to reach stillness as did his predecessors in the short prose.

In addition to "litter," "couch," and "amidst," other archaic words are evident in this scenario. "Slew" in "Let . . . the other about this pivot slew the litter" (180) may well be sailors' slang but is also an archaic word for "swing" (MS 1551/2). The manuscripts reveal even more archaism. The dramatic quality of the twice-used imperative "let" can be verified by a similarly exclamatory (and archaic) word in MS 1551/2: "Let one stop dead and the other about this pivot swing the litter through a semicircle and lo the roles are reversed." "Lo" is a very dramatic word, appealing to the visual imagination which is gaining importance from one scenario to the next. MS 1551/2 also renders a highly poetic version of "'Tis this dung-litter of laughable memory with shafts thrice as long as the bed." Although the printed text restores the more colloquial use of "It is," it employs yet another archaic "couch" to replace the quotidian "bed." Though the hyphen between "dung' and "litter" is dropped in MS 1551/3, the emotional wording stays the same thereafter. The richness in language in this scenario demonstrates the inadequacy of barren ruins as a mental refuge. Instead, the narrator attempts to supervene the everyday world by constructing an imaginative asylum of the mind (Knowlson and Pilling 189).

(4) The Eye Scenario

The imperative voice is retained in the fourth scenario, whose setting remains the same "grey cloudless sky" and "dust," and yet whose protagonist's role has been allocated to a "bird's-eye view." However, "Yet to imagine" (180) is not so second-person oriented as "imagination dead imagine" in *All Strange Away* and *Imagination Dead Imagine*. The former clearly points to the stage appearance of the eye of imagination—"Between him and it [the dwarfs' whiteness] the bird's-eye view" (180). The second and third scenarios, then, are brought together under an inclusive aerial perspective. For the first time the interrelationship between the expelled, the dwarfs, and "the eye" is made clear. Since the observing eye has thus already assumed an aerial post, the emphasis of this scenario shifts from the *Still*-like "close inspection" to a general survey of the setting. The eye perceives a seemingly growing desert. The "stark erect" expelled and the distant white dwarfs have become signposts for the eye to define a "mock confine" for the endlessness of the scenery. The eye quickly reminds itself of what has happened at the end of scenario two, namely, "a fragment comes away from mother ruins" (180). Even when its attention still follows the dwarfs' movement, the eye is more interested in the interaction between itself and the dwarfs' eyes. The dwarfs repeat the same joint ambling as if one, the difference here being the concentration on their facial details, which has serious consequences for this scenario. The dwarf who faces forward performs the important movement of the "he"-character in *Lessness*—hoisting his head. The upward tilted position of the head would, in *The Expelled*, have meant seeking help from the sky: "I raised my eyes to the sky, whence cometh our help" (24). Here the dwarfs follow their course as if receiving instruction from above from time to time, whenever they raise their heads to the sky. However, the narrator's full control over his imagined creatures falters. Some technical difficulties (perhaps physical obstruction or failing imagination) in the eye's monitoring of the dwarfs prevents it from seeing them "go driftless" (181). But when the dwarfs' faces suddenly move "closer and closer" to the observing eye, the latter declares that it can achieve "no more than two tiny oval blanks" (181). The "close inspection" now once again gains control of the scene. The "two tiny oval blanks" suggest the loss of normal eyesight. "Blindness," or impaired vision as a result of the reduced distance between the observer and the observed, necessitates a radical change. It is at this moment that the eye surges above the "cyclopean dome" (which probably hampers its vision) and expresses its wish to turn the grey sky into white, a whiteness which according to the syntax here can be equated with "the love of home" (181).

Though this scenario ends with two colorful metaphors and with an expression of the narrator's intense desire ("yearns"), it is the most "weakened" scene so far in that for the first time the narrator's observation and imagination are acknowledged to be inadequate. Even the all-inclusive bird's-eye view cannot perceive the dwarfs' "lidded eyes," which consequently must be a purely imaginary detail. Scenario four pays lip service to *Still 3*, in which the narrator looks into the imagined faces so closely and specifically that he is able to distinguish "eyes" from "lids." That the "lidded eyes" are here a result of conjecture, not observation, indicates the alienation of the eye of observation from the observed, and implies the involvement of the faculty of imagination. However, not only the narrator's bird's-eye view but also his imaginative ability are failing in the sense that the latter cannot, like its predecessors (particularly in the *Still* trilogy), "still" the turmoil and can only regret for the very "little" that is "still" (180-81).

The narrator's "craving" for "stillness" is considerably increased in this scenario, his bird's-eye view eliciting a conclusion as regards the expelled: "Little body last stage of all stark erect still amidst his ruins all silent and marble still" (180). This sentence embodies the distinctive traits of the syntax of weakness in that its strength lies in ambiguity. The tension between miniaturized syntax and "linguistic multiplicity" has been noted by Leslie Hill as forming a destabilizing factor in the textual development (178). As a result, the multiple readings yield potential for interpretive "play." Given the narrator's imaginative activity in the previous two scenarios (in dispelling the void in the first and resorting to eyes of observation and imagination in the second), to end up with only "the little body" which is now juxtaposed with the "last stage of all" cannot but be read as a sign of failure. However, the "last stage" may be understood as the little body's being "stark erect," "still amidst his ruins," and "marble still," which is in tune with Beckett's vision since the early sixties. When the "art of impotence" starts to take effect, all movement (of humans and objects alike) as well as the landscape is permeated with a sense of "torpor" (181). Whereas the same description of a fragment coming and falling at the end of scenario two is described by means of a simile ("Like cork on water" [180]) and a forceful verb ("breaks"), here the fragment "scarce stirs the dust" with its "slow fall." Even the expansive grey sand has reached a finite stillness—"[dust] can engulf no more" (180). Owing to the observing eye's remoteness, although the dwarfs have emerged in the dust as if "sprung from nowhere" (181) and have been moving, they appear "motionless" (181). But the narrator's residual "piercing sight" cannot abide failure. Even when the dwarfs take the initiative to approach their observer, closer than "say arm's length" *(Still 3)*, the narrator strains his eyes, hoping to maintain his omniscience. When the imaginer's sight is blocked horizontally, it inevitably has to rise vertically "atop the cyclopean dome," where it can once again aspire to a change in lighting. It "yearns white to the grey sky," equating "white" with *The Expelled* narrator's "hope from the sky" which is, in this case, "bump of habitativity" and "love of home."

The narrator's failing eyesight induces sentimentality in this scenario. The narrator's lamentation—"woe" (180)—is that only "the little on the surface of the dust" is still. "Woe" is no less literary or emotional than "so much the worse for the little" (MS 1551/2) and "pity" (MS 1551/3). It is this sentimentality which accounts for the choice of "mother ruin" (180) which has the same structure as "beldam nature" in "Closed Space" (200). However, the metaphor of "mother" resonates with the "love of home," both introducing human sentiment. Though a scenic description and an architectural term, "cyclopean dome" is derived from the giant Cyclops in Greek mythology, just as the rotunda in *All Strange Away* resembles the Pantheon at Rome. "Cyclopean dome" thus evokes the image of a one-eyed mythological figure who may or may not be identified with the narrator. Indeed, the narrator's aerial eyesight resembles that of a giant. It is only in this context of "height" that the dwarfs' sunk heads, let alone their "lidded eyes," escape and impair the narrator's vulture-like omniscience.

(5) The Still Scenario

After a few attempts at "change" ("First change of all" [179]), the narrator's failing eyesight acknowledges a "last change" "in the end" (181). In accordance with the decrease in the "availability" of objects, the potentially mobile he-character (once and for all) fails and lies still, stretching out amidst his ruins, just as the narrator has already twice envisaged the falling of a fragment. Only when the observed object lies motionless can the already failing eye of observation execute detailed and localized inspection, as in previous works. Renouncing its vulture-like post, it descends to the same level as that of the prostrate body and for the first time identifies with its observed object. Just as the sky is cleared of its vulture-scavengers, so the text now is free from an omniscient point of view which reconnoiters at once the eye of imagination and the imagined objects. Instead, it will maintain a more restricted, objective third-person stance.

The description of the expelled's prostrate stillness, reported from this objective point of view, comes closest to the passages in *Imagination Dead Imagine, Ping,* and *Lessness* which have delineated human bodies as if they were corpses. In this scenario, the fallen body of the expelled is still showing signs of breathing, signs which are hardly perceptible in the midst of the massive ruins and dust. But once again, as in *Imagination Dead Imagine* and *Sounds*, it seems plausible that signs of breathing can coincide with the state of being "soundless still" (181). This scenario evokes both acoustic and visual responses. That the body's "exhaling scarce ruffles the dust" (181) first creates a sound-free milieu which invites the reader to listen intently for any disturbance, and then activates the visual imagination, since "ruffling" suggests tiny waves of dust. It is a consequence of the visual appeal that the most important color variation—"blue"—should appear for the first time. Now that the narrator has renounced his aerial perspective, the body's blue eyes become the dominant focus in this scenario. Like the "unlustrous black and white" eye of *Ping* which (implicitly but emotionally) implores silence, the body's eyes here cling to life. Not quite so objectified as "the doll's," the body's eyes have neither been injured by the fall nor blinded by the dust. The body's "undying" eyesight, therefore, conveniently serves as a surrogate for the narrator's discarded omniscient point of view. The whiteness of the dwarfs is now perceived through the body's blue orbits, thus establishing a link between the observer, the expelled, and the observed, the dwarfs. However, the expelled's perception is moribund: the dwarfs have dropped the litter and remained still as in the expelled's "days erect" (181). The prostrate body, together with the dwarfs' stillness and the silent ruins, momentarily constitute a "last state" of things (181). The previous suspicion that the expelled can ever see the whiteness of the dwarfs is now dispelled. The expelled's residual eyesight enables him (and the reader) to "believe" the existence of the dwarfs.

No sooner are stillness and soundlessness consummated than the narrator's acoustic desire effects a *volte-face*. The increasingly dramatic depiction of the body's falling ("as though pushed from behind by some helping hand or by the wind but not a breath" [181]) foreshadows the actual dramatization of a voice addressing the expelled in the second-person, murmuring "never fear no fear of your rising again" (181). The use of "or" in "Or murmur from some dreg of life" reveals the narrator's uncertainty on reaching the "last state" of "being." MS 1551/2 shows very clearly that it is the "breath" which is murmuring: "but no a breath. Or murmured from some dreg of life after the long stand fall fall you'll never rise again." Not only is the source of the murmur explicit here, but it sounds true-to-speech. MS 1551/4 is even more contemptuous: "never fear you can never rise again," which recalls "he'll never say I any more, he'll never say anything any more" in one of the *Fizzles*, "I Gave Up Before Birth" (198). Though MS 1551/3 transforms the past participle ("murmured") into an ambivalent verb/noun form ("murmur"), its content remains the same as in MS 1551/2. The final version, "no fear of your rising again," is considerably less dramatic. However, the outspokenly self-contradictory way of putting together "not a breath" with "or murmur" differs from the noncommittal attitude of *Imagination Dead Imagine* as regards the acoustic desire: "Only murmur ah, no more" (147).

(6) The Skull Scenario

The evocation of the acoustic imagination at the end of scenario five leads to two rhetorical questions which resolve the scene once again to that of the skull—that "last state" of reality to which the narrator finally returns. The first and last skull scenarios are therefore the framework for the drama occurring in between, complete with exposition, climax, and dénouement. This finale questions the "thereness" of the intermediary drama: "litter and dwarfs ruins and little body grey cloudless sky glutted dust verge upon verge hell air not a breath." It effectively asks whether or not the end of all this is the "sepulchral skull" (181). As if complying with the format of a rhetorical speech which always ends with resolutions, "to dream" (as in *Sounds*) of a place "where no sound to listen for no more than ghosts make or motes in the sun" is apparently what should be striven for. May's insistence in *Footfalls* on hearing all her footsteps ("May: No, Mother, the motion alone is not enough, I must hear the feet, however faint they fall" [*Collected Shorter Plays* 241]) has been renounced; however, the narrator challenges the validity of this resolution with a question mark.[15] The narrator then spontaneously rejects his determination— "No"—as if he were refusing to acknowledge the "fixedness" ("all set" [181] or "all fixed" [MS 1551/2]) of this goal. His clinging to imaginative power is as steadfast as ever—"as though switched on" (182). The poetic tendency even affects his perception of the dream resolution: "all the footsteps of all the ages" (MS 1551/2) "can never fare [note the archaic usage] nearer to anywhere nor from anywhere" (181). Hence, when the imagining eye perceives "that certain dark" again, it always replaces this seeming end with "yet another end" (182). Unlike the limbo state which *The End* narrator was in—"without the courage to end or the strength to go on" (70), the narrator here seeks another end in his imagination, if "there had to be another [end] absolutely had to be" (182). The scenarios, which consist of the earth, sky, expelled, dwarfs, litter, etc., can recycle endlessly. The "sepulchral skull," from which the whole cycle originates and with which it ends, now appears as a pretext for the narrator "to end yet again." Indeed, in the very first scenario, "the skull makes to glimmer *again* in lieu of going out" (emphasis added). Thus the skull serves as an impetus for the narrator to embark upon a "magical" journey beneath a "cloudless sky" where the white dwarfs (also stars of low luminosity and relatively small mass and size), together with other objects are enclosed by the "orbits" of the eye of imagination (Krance 96-101).[16]

To round up the discussion of the relation between syntax and Beckett's perennial pursuit of the "last state" of "being" in *For to End Yet Again,* one can discover that the conflict between the syntax of weakness and syntax of energy constitutes the major source of destablization in the text, an element having been much more felicitously resolved in *Still, Sounds,* and *Still 3,* where Beckett's masterly practice of the syntax of weakness is more thoroughgoing. The dominant syntax of weakness in *For to End Yet Again* minimizes the presence of concrete and referential décor, setting, and human characters. The relevant narrative logic as conditioned by the foregoing constituents is also vacated. As rightly put by Brater, only a "verbal kineticism," that is, fragmented speeches and sentences, substantiates the centralized human figures and consciousness to become the protagonist in Beckett's residual works (7).

However, this already minimal and residual verbal kineticism, in the case of *For to End Yet Again*, undesirably ferments the actual destabilizing motion. Whereas this syntax contrives to disintegrate logic, the very act of disintegration, to use E. M. Scarry's words, produces its own "logical ramifications" (279). Hugh Kenner, too, speaks of Beckett's typical strategy in his works of the sixties as "equat[ing] syntax with logic" (29). That is to say, Beckett's persevering practice of the syntax of weakness, though paring down the resort to grammatical logic, formalizes a substitute and "off" logic of its own kind. (Cf. "what kind of imagination is this so reason-ridden?" "A kind of its own" in *Company* 45.) However, this syntactic control exhibited in *For to End Yet Again* fails to tone down the note of "urgency" still remaining from his less successful results of earlier practices. In other words, this syntax does not exempt itself from the encroachment of a less strenuous syntax, extending its normality and then variety, and finally stretching a "strength" and energy in the style of expression. To appropriate Abbot's observation, *For to End Yet Again*, like other short prose works of the similar period, reinstates a "sure" (hence "strong") "formal control" (227). The restoration of human characters who aspire toward movement and human sentiments in the text suggests that Beckett's minimalist discipline to restrain imagination's natural inventiveness has now been relaxed. Accompanying this loosened hold on imagination's will power is the "syntax of energy." A "transition from lessness into endlessness, the shift from ultimates to penultimates or even antepenultimates" has taken place (Cunningham 350). Therefore, by the time of *For to End Yet Again*, Beckett's experimentation with the syntax of weakness has come full circle. On the one hand, the syntax of weakness still dominates this work, whose English translation was undertaken only two years after the composition of the *Still* trilogy, in which the result of the experiment had proved more satisfactory. On the other, the syntax of strength signals the end of a decade's experimentation with syntactic weakness.

From *Twentieth Century Literature* (Spring 1992): 101-23.

---

[1]Discussed in Abbot, 227, footnote 13.

[2]*Nouvelles* refers to "L'Expulsé," "Le Calmant," "La Fin," and "Premier Amour." They were all written in 1945, though the first three were published in 1955 (Paris), and the latter in 1970 (Paris). See Pilling (*Samuel Beckett* 299) for publication details. The English translations *The Expelled, The Calmative, The End,* and *First Love*, referred to below in my text, are collected in *Collected Shorter Prose* 1-70. *Trilogy*, though published later, was begun and composed during 1945 and 1947. *Le Dépeupleur* was begun in 1965 and published in 1971 (Paris); the English translation, *The Lost Ones,* was published in 1972 (London). See Pilling (*Samuel Beckett* 230, 232).

[3] Cf. Beckett, "The Essential and the Incidental" 111. See also Brater, "Still/Beckett: The Essential and the Incidental" 4.

[4] In a conversation with Harvey in 1962, "Beckett spoke of the essential difficulty experienced by one who is given to making with words (rather than sounds or colors); of the need for a 'syntax of weakness.'"

[5] Rabinovitz speaks of Beckett's technique of "utilizing a compressed style" in writing the *Fizzles*, including *Still* and *For to End Yet Again*. The "governing principle" in *Ping* is "compression," too.

[6] Chapter 5 of Cohn's *Back to Beckett* is entitled "Lyrics of Fiction."

[7] According to the introduction of the Calder edition of *For to End Yet Again and Other Fizzles* (1976), although the French *Foirades* (with the exception of *Immobile*, which was originally in English as "Still") were translated in 1973-1974, "Closed Space" and five other fizzles (i.e., "He Is Barehead," "Horn Came Always," "Afar a Bird," "I Gave Up Before Birth," and "Old Earth") were written since 1960. Therefore the *Fizzles* should be considered as works belonging to the sixties. *For to End Yet Again* does not belong to the English translations of the French *Foirades*. It is the direct translation of *Pour finir encore*, undertaken in December 1975, as dated in Reading University Library, England: MS 1551/2. *Still, Sounds,* and *Still 3* followed closely one after the other and were all works of 1972-1973. They share the same concerns with kinesthetic, aural, and stylistic stillness; therefore they can be conveniently grouped and termed as the *Still* trilogy, an echo of Beckett's middle-phased, full-length *Trilogy*, though on a drastically diminished scale. *Sounds* and *Still 3* can be found in MS1396/4/50 and MS1396/4/52.

[8] Rabinovitz in "*Fizzles* & Samuel Beckett's Earlier Fiction" (317) details the close relationship between *Lessness* and *Fizzle 8 (For to End Yet Again)* in terms of echoes of phrases, structure, and episodic events in both works.

[9] Beckett's typescript drafts of the English translation of *For to End Yet Again* are in MS 1551/2-5.

[10] Blau in chapter 4 (entitled "The Bloody Show and the Eye of Prey") of his *The Eye of Prey* employs the Derridean theory of the erasing/erased, or displacing/displaced, writing to demonstrate the mutual displacement in the relationship between the perceiving eye and all that it gazes upon.

[11]Read asserts that the eye's hunger for objects is motivated by the artist's need to create and imagine. As a result, the conflict between objects in the real world and those existing in imagination ensues (116).

[12]Both Pilling ("Review Article" 99) and Dearlove (*Accommodating the Chaos* 143) discuss the archaism in *For to End Yet Again* and other "Fizzles."

[13]Dearlove also discusses the "personal" quality of the return of the pronoun "he" and "his" capability for motion (*Accommodating the Chaos* 125). Finney, too, states that *For to End Yet Again* resumes "an earlier discourse" because the "pseudo-objectivity" which Beckett's short prose texts since *Imagination Dead Imagine* have maintained is "breaking down" ("*Still* to *Worstward Ho*" 66).

[14]The years given here for *Watt* and *Molloy* are those of composition. However, *Watt* was published in 1953 (Paris) and 1963 (London); *Molloy* in 1951 (Paris) and 1959 (London) in *Three Novels*. See Pilling *Samuel Beckett* 229-30.

[15]Two question marks appear in MS 1551/5, whereas the previous versions (MS 1551/2-4) end the first two sentences in this scenario with a full stop.

[16]Krance elaborates the galactic theories of black holes and their counterparts—white dwarfs and associated phenomena. He contends that the two categories of galaxies constitute "equals-but-opposites." By the same token, the Beckettian logic perpetually fails to be "totally sucked into the plenumvoid," which the theory of black holes stipulates: the opposite "white dwarfs" are unfaltering equals.

Sublime Supplements: Beckett and the "Fizzling Out" of Meaning

Nicoletta Pireddu

"Perhaps there is no whole, before you're dead" (Beckett, *Molloy* 35), meditates Molloy while lying in the ditch without remembering how he left town. If his name suddenly comes to his mind as in an epiphany, the purpose of his visit to his mother inevitably escapes him: "My reasons? I had forgotten them" (35). For each detail brought to light, other particulars are reabsorbed into forgetfulness. The activity of memory never provides the character with the total picture of his own self. Its discrete nature frustrates the need to continuity; its inability to fill the gaps opened up by oblivion reveals the arbitrariness of any attempt to master reality, and the inconclusiveness of Molloy's writing registers exactly the failure of such an effort.

If in *Molloy* the protagonist narrates the story of a fiasco, Beckett's *Fizzles* represent the fiasco of narration itself. Starting from their titles, both the English and the French version of these short texts exhibit the idea of aborted endeavor as their constitutive element. Voices with no faces recite confused monologues in the hopeless attempt to put order into their past lives; third-person accounts on the verge of syntactical disintegration describe endless wanderings not redeemed by any promise of final revelation; physically impaired bodies struggle against a hostile nature, in the awareness of an impending death. The topology of *Fizzles* is a paradoxical middle ground between defeat and accomplishment. Far from implying total renunciation, the failure announced at the opening of the collection triggers an attempt at depiction that is doomed to incompleteness: to the danger of silence and of annihilation, Beckett's texts oppose a fictional world of traces that hint at wholeness without ever granting to it. Ruins, decaying bodies, and blurred memories materialize the interplay of presence and absence of meaning that the language of *Fizzles* reproduces with its imminent and yet never-achieved dissolution.

Through their conceptual and structural fragmentation, the *Fizzles* dismantle exactly what Adorno defines as art's "unfulfilled (and imprescriptible) longing for perfection," and by articulating the unresolved struggle between destructive forces and self-preservation they meet the "challenge of the irreconcilable" (Adorno 271). Beckett's literary "fiascos" belong, for this reason, to the category of the sublime, the ascendance of which—according to Adorno—coincides with "the need for art to avoid 'playing down' its fundamental contradictions but to bring them out instead" (Adorno 282). In *Fizzles*, the disruption of form and meaning under the effect of such a clash of forces reveals an essential feature of the contemporary sublime, namely, its being latent. If "the traditional concept of the sublime as an infinite presence was animated by the belief that negation could bring about positivity" (Adorno 282), the irreconcilable conflicts of Beckett's texts break this illusion and offer an example of "radical negativity" (Adorno 284). No longer associated with the sense of awe and of subsequent power that defined it in the Kantian version, the sublimity of a literary work like *Fizzles* derives precisely from its margin of unrepresentability, and from the inadequacy of any attempt to penetrate it. Deprived of the aggrandizement that characterizes the Romantic participation in the source of the sublime, these texts rather involve the agonizing experience of characters suspended between physical destruction and recovery of integrity, between oblivion and memory.

With the frantic activity of recollection recurring and yet failing throughout *Fizzles*, Adorno's "radical negativity" merges with Lyotard's notion of the unrepresentable as "Forgotten," as something that remains immemorial and unthought. Beckett's "imperfect" texts express the sublime by calling attention to an excess of meaning and of reality that cannot be recuperated but only evoked through its absence; their words represent precisely

> what every presentation misses, what is forgotten there: this "presence" . . . which persists not so much at the limits but rather at the heart of representation; this unnameable in the secret of names, a forgotten that is not the result of a forgetting of a reality . . . and which one can only remember as forgotten "before" memory and forgetting, and *by repeating it*. (Lyotard, *Heidegger* 5; my emphasis)

1. *Re*-membering/*Dis*-membering

It is exactly the notion of a perceptual reenacting that animates Beckett's *Fizzles*, in spite of the failure to which these texts are doomed by definition: the repetitive pattern described by Lyotard sustains the collection as a whole and is epitomized in the title of the last Fizzle, "For to end yet again" (Beckett, *Fizzles* 55).[1] Far from granting a stronger mastery of reality and of meaning in the narration, the dynamics of endless repetition that truncates the texts before they attain a logical conclusion or a potential revelation implies exactly an act of *re*-presentation deprived of presentation and of presence.

The movement suggested at the opening of Fizzle 1 is immediately reduced to a mere act of oscillation that anchors the subject to its initial position: "he is forth again, he'll be back again" (7). However, in spite of this yoke, the subject gropes his way in the dark and starts a quest set in a labyrinthine site that is both material and mental. Proceeding along a zigzag path—that is, not sustained by the teleological linear progression toward a target—and frustrated in his "effort to pierce the gloom" (9), he manages to relive some episodes of his past life but without ever being able to give a global shape to his history. As in Molloy's experience, the unearthing of a detail from oblivion implies the burial of other elements, and reveals simultaneously the inefficacy of the quest and the impossibility of putting an end to it. Similarly, after a series of encounters with Horn and an investigation into the past through his notes, the speaker of the monologue in Fizzle 2 has to acknowledge his failure and, still confused about time and temporal relations, avows the need for a new beginning:

> I thought I had made my last journey, the one I must now try
> once more to elucidate, that it may be a lesson to me, the one
> from which it were better I had never returned. But the feeling
> gains on me that I must undertake another. (22)

The paradoxical coexistence of renunciation and undertaking of new endeavors persists in Fizzes 3 and 4, where the first-person speaker "gave up before birth" (25) and declares his impotence by emphasizing his lack of voice and of thought, but still sets himself the task of narrating the story of the "other" consciousness in the piece: "I'll tell the tale, the tale of his death" (31)—a tale and a death that never take place. All these aborted attempts and their reiterated necessity are absorbed in the closing statement of Fizzle 8, which strengthens the process of *re*-presentation implied by the title and provides no alternative to eternal beginning: "Through it who knows yet another end beneath a cloudless sky same dark it earth and sky of a last end if ever there had to be another absolutely had to be" (61).

The act of writing and the performance of the characters in Beckett's texts are in the service of a mechanism of *re*-membering which is at the same time a *dis*-membering. In *Fizzles*, memory cannot reestablish a peaceful continuity between past and present; no edifice of totality can be reconstructed from the fragments of their topology. It is primarily the additional connotation of the words *fizzles* and *foirade*—as well as the status of these texts vis-à-vis Beckett's literary production as a whole—that throws further light upon the role of traces and remains, and consequently upon their relation with Lyotard's treatment of the sublime. Actually, the idea of failure in both the English and the French headings is combined with a reference to excrements and to uncontrolled corporal functions that establish the *residual* nature of this collection with respect to the *body* of the author's work. These texts are condemned—by definition—to occupy a marginal place in Beckett's aesthetic project, since they are conceived as excretions that can no longer be integrated within the original source that generated them. Therefore, they constitute an example of "radical fragmentation, pursued to its logical end of dispersion and multiplicity" (Hill 175). Given their shattered structure, the failure of these "fizzles" is extended to their lack of "organic self-coincidence" (Hill 176): they do not merely stand for the expelled remainders of a nonexistent whole, but they are also residual in relation to their own self-containedness.

The title of the collection, in this respect, anticipates the "supplementary" quality of the ruins and traces upon which memory inscribes its project of reconstruction. As in the text of the Freudian unconscious, the fragments that recur throughout Beckett's texts are residual in themselves: far from functioning as synecdoches for a totality that asks to be retrieved, they are "repositories of a meaning which was never present" (Derrida, *Writing* 211).[2]

Being "always already" incomplete, these supplements cannot but compensate imperfectly for the lack of plenitude they decree. Like Lyotard's notion of "the jews" (Lyotard, *Heidegger* xxiii) as those devoid of self-identity and of mythical origin, the residues in *Fizzles* stimulate and frustrate the desire for a wholeness and a presence that cannot be *re*-collected, neither through the material assemblage of the fragments, nor through an act of memory. The Forgotten plenitude—the source of the sublime—has to remain forgotten, but it needs memory in order to be remembered as such. It must not be naturalized by representation, nor suppressed and effaced by oblivion, but rather venerated through the aborted efforts to appropriate and represent it. In the agonizing space of Beckett's texts, the condemnation to eternal beginning becomes the only way to maintain this precarious balance of annihilation and preservation. By endlessly reenacting a drama of disintegration that does not culminate with death, Beckett can avoid concluding, since "to terminate"—to put an end to his "fizzles"—would coincide with "to exterminate"—namely, to destroy the "place of remains" (Beckett, *Fizzles* 55), the locus of the conflictual forces that allow the sublime to come into being. With the extermination of these traces, *anamnesis* would turn into *amnesia*. Representation would still belong to the realm of the beautiful; it could still rely on "the solace of good forms" (Lyotard, *Postmodern Condition* 81), but only through an arbitrary act—through the exclusion of those residual elements whose formlessness evokes exactly the unpresentable, the sublime.

The failed attempt at recollection and the material presence of remainders as supplements for the unpresentable emerge from the opening page of Fizzle 1—where "none of [the character's] memories answer" (7)—and are reinforced in its closing comment—with the surfacing of bones as the "fresh elements" that "contribute to enrich" (15) the impossible reconstruction of the character's past history. Bones are combined with "grit" (27) and "dust" (32) to anticipate the physical consumption of the two voices in Fizzles 3 and 4, but—together with the ruins of the landscape—they simultaneously affirm their material presence as opposed to the total effacement implied by death. Nature joins man in the process of mechanical decay, and—as shown in Fizzle 5—can be remembered only through "dead leaves," "not rotting" (39)—since this would still reaffirm a form of life, though elementary, and therefore a positive, organic principle of reconstruction—but rather "crumbling into dust" (39). The "place of remains" (55) in Fizzle 8 "where once used to . . . glimmer a remain" best epitomizes the supplementary nature of these texts by indicating exactly the lack of initial plenitude and presence in a kind of *mise en abîme*. Equally, through the reference to "the expelled" (56) that is engulfed in dust mingling with the remainders of buildings, Beckett reinstates precisely the idea of detachment from an original totality and the impossible reintegration that define the residual quality of *fizzle* and *foirade*.[3]

This process of inexorable fragmentation is inscribed in the image of the agonizing skull to which Fizzle 8 reduces its protagonist: the mind that in the Romantic sublime should struggle against a prostrating experience and ultimately regain its power and integrity is metonymically translated into its material container, which acts as a *memento mori*. Death as forgetfulness can only be remembered through a perishable relic; the activity of memory that should re-collect the *disjecta membra* of Beckett's characters can only be "laughable" (58): the unpresentable—the "Forgotten"—needs remembrance in order to be saved from oblivion, but at the same time it decrees the uselessness of any attempt at representation. If the ritual of turning the light on and off seems to grant the characters the restoration of their past (Rabinovitz 318) and of their sense of selfhood, it actually provides only disconnected flashes of memory: the "electric torch" (19) does not clarify the forgotten details of the past contained in Horn's notebook; the light of the bulb is equally ineffective to unify the "faces, agonies, loves, . . . moments of life" (44) recalled by the protagonist of Fizzle 6; the glimmering "remains" of subjectivity, of monuments and of the "light of the day" (55), are the metaphors through which memory exhibits its inadequacy to illuminate the shadow surrounding it.

2. A writing of survival

"The understanding"—observes Lyotard—"imposes its rules on to all objects, even aesthetic ones. This requires a time and a space under control" (*Heidegger* 41). *Fizzles* shrinks from such kind of naturalization by altering precisely these two parameters: time acquires the value of Heideggerian temporality—thus reducing the character to being-toward-death—and space is threatening in its vastness and monotony.[4] Like a parodic double of Ishmael meditating upon the whale's "dumb blankness full of meaning" (Melville 199) the "little body" in Fizzle 8 is also confronted with a "whiteness to decipher" (58), but there is no ultimate revelation of its nature or of its origin: the "distant whiteness *sprung from nowhere*" (59; my emphasis) takes the shape of two dwarfs who—although possible harbingers of death—are not unmasked in their function, and do not hinder the protagonist's slow but endless fall. He sees them with his eyes, eyes that "the fall has not shut nor yet the dust stopped up" (60); therefore he believes in them. However, the sense of sight is actually entrusted to the mere "gaping sockets" of a "sepulchral skull" (60). The ability to master reality through visual perception is thus affirmed and immediately denied: the protagonist's empty sockets put into question understanding and representability.

Through the physical and mental deterioration of its characters, *Fizzles* dramatizes the second phase of the Kantian sublime—that is, it describes the annihilation of the subject under the effect of an overwhelming experience. Actually, the *Critique of Judgment* already presupposes the mind's inadequacy to grasp the source of the sublime (Kant 99): the unattainability of the object decrees precisely the failure of representation. Beckett's texts are founded upon a similar disproportion between the inner and the outer realm, between powerless bodies and minds on the one hand, and uncontrollable destructive forces on the other. The characters face an external reality that is in *excess* with respect to them: memory is no refuge from dissolution—since it fails to provide a reassuring and organic image of the past—and the present is absorbed by the threat of an imminent extinction. With the depiction of bodies in the ditch, Fizzle 5—which significantly bears the title "Se voir" in the French version (Beckett, *Pour finir* 51)—almost invokes death through its material ritual of burial, since the actual occurrence of death would at least redeem the purposeless agony of the characters by inserting it in a design. Similarly, the apostrophe at the beginning of Fizzle 6 turns the mythical image of the earth as source of regeneration into a metonymy for decease: "old earth, no more lies . . . You'll be on me" (43). However, the closing image in the collection frustrates once again this longing for resolution. The "little body" sinking into a wasteland of ruins and dust is "prostrate" and constantly falling "as though pushed from behind by some helping hand" (60), but if there seems to be "no fear of [his] rising again," the logic of *Fizzles*—"to end yet again"—does not rescue him from life.

Nevertheless, whereas Kant's treatment of the sublime involves a subsequent reactive phase that reestablishes the balance between the mind and the object, Beckett's texts endlessly expand the moment of ego-loss without allowing any recovery. *Fizzles* neglects the aggrandizement that in the *Critique of Judgment* derives from the subject's identification with the transcendent source of the sublime: the sky has been "forsaken of its scavengers" (59) and, all the more reason, it is no longer the locus of the divine as a force granting self-preservation and transcending human limitations. In the place of the *leap* of faith with which Kantian subjects can be *elevated* and have a revelation of their own sublimity, Beckett's characters experience a *downfall*: the unpresentable haunts and *prostrates* them. Far from providing empowerment through identification, the sublime functions as a term of comparison against which skulls and little bodies can measure their own inadequacy and failure. In this respect, the etchings that Jasper Johns combines with one of the editions of *Fizzles* are symptomatic. The several images of legs that the painter juxtaposes to Beckett's words reinforce the very idea of powerlessness that characterizes the second stage of the Kantian sublime and that accounts for *Fizzles* as a whole. Actually, if the violent excitation aroused by the sublime experience can be equaled to sexual orgasm, the phallic aspect of the legs in John's illustrations invalidates precisely such an idea of energy: it rather suggests flabby and inoperative organs, detached from the body and doomed to impotence and to fiascos.[5]

In the world of *Fizzles* the "grey cloudless sky" (57) conceals no transcendency; no Oversoul can elevate the self after its loss into a sublime

Romantic nature. The unpresentable and the threat of annihilation are therefore far from having a metaphysical origin: in their pathetic condemnation to a perennial purgatorial state, the little bodies and the skulls of *Fizzles* are rather deferring to disintegration that in postmodern, post-Hiroshima decades can be more easily associated with an atomic catastrophe. They are thus waiting for a Godot that does not possess any phonetic or intrinsic affinity with God: instead of reassembling their mortal remains after their physical death in the resurrection of body and soul, the nuclear destruction that haunts them will dissolve any trace. The distinction made by Burke and Kent between love for the beautiful as something that the subject can dominate and admiration for the sublime because of its crushing impact upon the mind cannot subsist in the nuclear age. The instinct of self-preservation that arouses the resistance to the overwhelming forces of nature fails to master the threat of an irreversible annihilation with no remainders: obviously, the nuclear sublime does not afford the "empowerment of selfhood" (Wilson 236) entailed by natural phenomena in the Romantic aesthetic tradition. What the nuclear sublime lacks is the "safety distance" that allows the ultimate recuperation of mental power. Actually, in line with the impulse of self-preservation, the "delight" that for Burke is produced by the natural sublime derives not so much from the presence of pain and danger as from their removal: if they "press too nearly" (Burke 34)—as in the case of the nuclear sublime—they are merely "terrible."

Therefore, the dust, bones and ruins that constitute the fictional space of Beckett's texts, as well as the logic of eternal beginning that frustrates closure, assert themselves as a way of resisting the danger involved in an atomic holocaust—namely, that of utter effacement with no remainders and no continuation. The falling fragments of buildings and bodies superimposing layer after layer in the wastelands of these stories create a testamentary *palimpsest* that—despite the failure inscribed in its texture—strives to dissipate the specter of the *tabula rosa* resulting from a nuclear devastation. To the amnesia of the nuclear fire—the physical abolition of all that came before and its parallel elimination of all possible "after"—*Fizzles* opposes anamnesis—the thwarted but always renovated attempts at recollection that the characters make in the stories, and that the author undertakes through his own writing.

In the context of an impending risk of total abolition, Beckett's words are really an example of "writing of survival" (Lyotard, *Heidegger* 44), of an art that implies not so much a positive, life-affirming image—which would be related to the reassuring category of the beautiful—as an unresolved struggle for life, an effort to withstand hostile forces. Confronted with a negative excess, overwhelmed by a "too much," Beckett reacts with a "syntax of weakness" (Harvey 249) that articulates this life-and-death conflict. The act of writing—although doomed to create mere "fizzles"—exorcises the failure of imagination by exploiting imagination to depict failure. It is only through words that the reality of the nuclear disintegration can be evoked, and it is simultaneously through their inadequacy that the sublimity of this phenomenon can emerge. As an event that has not yet taken place, the nuclear conflict is "fabulously textual" (Derrida, "No Apocalypse" 23); it is a trope re-presenting a referent that is unfigurable and threatening in its unpresentability.

Through his inexhaustible depiction of prostration in *Fizzles*, Beckett rhetorically simulates the stage of ego-shattering under the burden of the impending danger of its effacement and puts off the actual experience of general destruction, which is incommensurate to language and thought. Far from attempting to unveil an event whose first occurrence would also be the last (Derrida, "No Apocalypse" 30), *Fizzles* proclaims that "There is nothing but what is said. Beyond what is said there is nothing" (*Fizzles* 37). The "ditch" that circumscribes the "closed place" (37) of Fizzle 5 also describes cognitive limits: "nothing" (37) lies beyond it, "no more" can be known. To jump over the ditch—namely, to enact the experience of boundary crossing implied by the logic of the sublime—in order to represent a nuclear catastrophe becomes an impossible task: the only condition for its realization is actual experience, but the price for such an irreversible step would be absolute destruction "without apocalypse, without revelation of its own truth" (Derrida, "No Apocalypse" 27), ultimately without knowledge. The "day after"—like the "after Auschwitz" for Lyotard—has to be remembered as "Forgotten": *Fizzles* "does not say the unsayable but says that it cannot say it" (Lyotard, *Heidegger* 47).

3. Beckett "the expelled"

Nuclear annihilation extends to a universal level the paradoxical coincidence of meaning and inexpressibility that is inherent in death. With the destruction of the "entire archive" and of "all symbolic capacity" (Derrida, "No Apocalypse" 28) no "writing of survival" could be possible: there would be no relic upon which remembrance could inscribe its mourning. *Fizzles* emphasizes the sublime nature of death as an inaccessible moment of revelation and as the repository of unattainable meaning, but with its material and linguistic debris it resists precisely the threat of total silence.

In line with the interpretation of the sublime experience in terms of an Oedipal struggle followed by the identification with a father-figure, Kristeva assimilates death to the realm of the paternal symbolic order and defines Beckett's reaction to it as "an 'unnameable' interplay of meaning and jouissance" (148). Actually, the fragmented syntax of *Fizzles* is not merely an example of counter-symbolic writing totally oblivious of the paternal function: it rather re-members the father-figure as the guarantor of meaning in order to reduce it to a dismembered corpse, and mingles the veneration for the vestiges of meaning with the bliss of disruption. With its logic of eternal beginning, *Fizzles* does not exterminate the father once and for all: rather, it endlessly reiterates his ritual murder. On the other hand, the jubilation over having eliminated this linguistic authority does not imply total freedom. The banishment that is supposed to relieve the character—as well as the author—of the oppressing yoke of paternity and of the threat of death rather leads to the mourning for this lost presence.

However, no surrogate figure can replace this vacancy in the world of *Fizzles*, especially not the maternal image that in other texts by Beckett "becomes a mirage of serenity, shielded from death" (Kristeva 157). In the disintegrating space of Fizzle 8, the mother is a crumbling "ruin" (*Fizzles* 58) in the process of pulverization, and the only other reference to this figure deprives it of identity and of any relevant role: "he'll confuse his mother with whores, his father with a road-man named Balfe" (27). With the elimination of these two vertices of the Oedipal triangle, Beckett is left with a "balance of nothingness" (Kristeva 152) suspended between a return to the womb—perhaps evoked through the collapsing "refuge" (*Fizzles* 56) to which the character does not wish to go back—and the introjection of paternal authority. He therefore partakes of the supplementary nature of "the expelled" as deprived of an origin and of a destination, and shares with him a middle ground "where all the footsteps ever fell can never fare nearer to anywhere nor from anywhere further away" (60)—where neither nostalgia for the beautiful nor euphoria for a new source of self-elevation reigns.

The ritual of deterioration and the logic of the supplement materially embodied in the "remains" of Beckett's *Fizzles* replace the aggrandizement of the subject in the Romantic sublime with a sense of exhaustion and of belatedness that is typical of post-modernism. Instead of gaining self-empowerment through the identification with a sublime paternal figure, Beckett exhibits his epigonic status as a "son, who never enunciated himself as anything else," as "a false father who doesn't want to be a father" (Kristeva 150-51). If Wordsworth in Paris is overwhelmed by a French Revolution that possesses all the qualities of the Burkean sublime and that is thus identifiable with an ideology of power and originality, the post-Kantian sublime of Beckett's *Fizzles* is precisely the negation of such an ideology, and rather works to challenge its pretensions.

From *Studies in Short Fiction* 29 (1992): 303-14.

---

[1]If in the English version the idea of endless repetition emphasized in the title of the last text seems to throw light retrospectively upon the development of the collection as a whole—thus still hinting at a possible teleology—the French edition of *Fizzles* connects these texts in a different order. Significantly, "Pour finir encore"—the French equivalent of *Fizzle 8*—is located at the opening of the collection: in this way, it anticipates the structural and conceptual inconclusiveness that sustains the work in its entirety. In addition, by collapsing the distinction between the starting and the terminal point, the

title reinforces the idea of aborted attempt that defines these texts. Cf. Beckett, *Pour finir*. It is in the interplay of the two versions that Beckett's problematization of the act of writing and of representation emerges in its most disruptive aspect.

[2]For the notion of ruins as supplements and for their connection with the impossible project of restoration through memory—as shown in *Fizzles*—see Derrida, *Mémoires* 68-71.

[3]Because of these connotations, the "expelled" can also be defined in terms of Lyotard's "the jews."

[4]The lack of control over time and space in Beckett's texts establishes a symptomatic contrast with the power that Marinetti proclaims over reality by taming exactly these two variables: "Human energy centupled by speed will master Time and Space." By glorifying "the beauty of speed" and the subsequent divine authority it provides, the avant-garde repudiates the weakness and the sense of exhaustion that characterize Beckett's postmodern universe. The "Futurist morality" aims at defending man "from decay caused by slowness [and] by memory," the specters that 50 years later would haunt the fiction of *Fizzles*. Cf. Flint 94-95.

[5]The legs separated from the body, as well as all the other corporal fragments in John's etchings, partake of the supplementary aspect of "fizzles" and "foirades": because of their discrete nature—as revealed from one of the illustrations—they cannot be made to cohere into a whole. They express the lack of self-identity and the residual quality that characterize the traces in Beckett's texts. For the collaboration of Beckett and Johns cf. Prinz 480-510; Shloss 153-68

CHAPTER 10

Final Tribute

Who's Afraid of Samuel Beckett?

Martin Esslin

A SPECIAL ADDRESS DELIVERED AT THE MID-AMERICA THEATRE CONFERENCE 1989 ANNUAL MEETING IN OMAHA

Samuel Beckett was awarded the Nobel prize in 1969. For twenty years he has been an acknowledged, world-famous writer. And yet there is still the feeling about that he is difficult, inaccessible and depressingly gloomy. How true are thus assumptions? That is the question I should like to address today.

In one of Samuel Beckett's earlier dramatic pieces, which is called ACT WITHOUT WORDS, we see a man pushed onto the stage in what is clearly a desert environment. A bottle is dangling before him. The entire action consists of his various efforts to get that bottle—which is marked to contain water—but, whatever he does, it always just moves out of his reach. Finally, he gives up, sits down and remains immobile even when the bottle descends and tempts him to try and catch it again. Now this, to my mind, is among the simplest and most easily comprehensible dramatic presentations of a basic human situation. Do you have to be an intellectual, as aesthete, a highbrow to comprehend it, to be amused, interested, illuminated by it?

Surely not.

But what does that short mime play *mean*?

That is a good question, but by no means an essential one. Even without going in for ingenious interpretations, the mime works on a basic level, the level of the theatrical gag. The man cannot reach the bottle, he turns away to fetch a crate to stand on to reach it, as he turns his back the bottle comes down, when he goes back to get it now that it seems within his reach, it immediately, rather coquettishly moves higher. We all know these types of gags from Chaplin films, Laurel and Hardy pictures, and Disney cartoons. Do they have to have a deep philosophical meaning? No. They just happen to be funny.

The point I am trying to make is: in a theatrical, a dramatic performance there is a level of immediate enjoyment and amusement which is the primary level, the basis of the whole enterprise. When one of his directors, Alan Schneider, asked Beckett for interpretations of his work, Beckett replied that what he made were "fundamental noises"—and he added that this was not intended as a joke—after all "fundamental noises" is just a euphemism for a somewhat ruder expression. But it is a fact—and Beckett always insists on this point in conversation—that he never, never writes with the objective of expressing a philosophical idea, a profound human insight; he merely writes to express his very simple perceptions of life, based on his own, immediate experience, on his dreams and imaginings; and simply because he feels a deep inner necessity to express himself.

He once said, when talking about the position of the artist in our Godless and ideal-less times, times when all creeds have been discredited by the terrible wars and holocausts of our century, that the contemporary artist may have "nothing to express, nothing with which to express, nothing from which to express, no power to express, no desire to express, together with the obligation to express"—an obligation, that is, to express whatever he perceives and experiences, including his inability to express anything of eternal value.

Far from being pretentious about the high nobility of his calling as an artist, therefore, Beckett really is a person of immense humility, compelled by some irrational drive, some deep inner compulsion, an obligation, simply because he cannot help it, much as he might want to be rid of it, to deal with very basic images of his own situation—which, of course, can be generalized into the human situation itself.

Take that mime play. It does not need interpretation. It is funny and amusing in itself. The actor can do some funny contortions, pratfalls and other manifestations of his skill as an acrobat and dancer, the bottle is bound to become a second actor, a marionette, jumping about and showing a sly, malicious delight in tormenting the man. But, of course, when one thinks back, after the performance, one is bound to be reflecting on the meaning of the short piece. Everyone of us, Beckett of course too, has had the experience that when we seem to have reached some objective that we have pursued with intensity and dedication, when we reach it, it is found disappointing, not wholly satisfying and is replaced by another equally elusive one. We can never be wholly satisfied. Every objective we reach merely leads us to pursue the next higher one; someone works like a Trojan to get elected a city councillor, and when he gets there in the end, he wants to become a state assemblyman — you get your BA and now you are after the MA and once you got that you want a doctorate—and then the objective becomes a job — in any sphere of life, sport, sex, material possessions, it is always the same thing.

So, if we go on interpreting that very simple, unintellectual, lowbrow playlet, perhaps what it tells us is that the wisest thing is to recognize that state of affairs and to give up the pursuit of illusory objectives, and renounce ambition and the vain pursuit of sensual gratifications. When there are no objectives being pursued, there can be no disappointments.

Now this happens to be the lesson most of the great religions of the world also teach—Buddhism, Hinduism and yes, Christianity as well, in its more profound mystical forms. So the little playlet which lasts barely more than a quarter of an hour does perhaps have profound religious, philosophical, mystical meanings. But these are thoughts that arise in the mind of each individual spectator, thoughts that are probably different for each such spectator. And if there are spectators in whose minds no such thoughts arise, they'll just have had an amusing time in the theatre and a few good laughs, and they will be none the worse for it.

The same is true of the entire oeuvre of a great writer like Beckett. In that sense he is very different from other great writers, like Dante, or Goethe, or Shelley or Victor Hugo, or Brecht: those writers were intent on expressing a religious or philosophical idea, an ideology, a set of doctrines, they wanted to make deep ideas palpable as works of fiction. That is a perfectly valid approach and it has yielded immortal masterpieces.

But there is another basic type of writer, of artist: he just starts out from expressing his immediate perceptions, he may even have merely mercenary motives. It is sometimes said that Shakespeare was merely an entrepreneur writing to make the maximum amount of money. So what? In order to pursue this objective he put his imagination to work, found some good stories to tell (mostly in the work of other people, or in the facts of history), and just told these stories as well as he could, or as well as his circumstances—the availability of actors, the time he had at his disposal before the first night etc.— permitted. He was supremely talented and his works are now open to endless interpretation and are found to contain profound insights into the human predicament, profound insights into psychology, philosophy and what not, of which Shakespeare himself may well have been unaware.

What applies to Shakespeare is true of great artists of all kinds: the Douanier Rousseau, or Vincent van Gogh in painting, P. G. Wodehouse and Conan Doyle in fiction, Charlie Chaplin, Buster Keaton, W. C. Fields, Laurel and Hardy, the Marx Brothers, Alfred Hitchcock, in film.

Many great playwrights fall into the same category: Molière, fundamentally, who was a comic who wanted to make people laugh, so was Georges Feydeau whose farces are now regarded as literary masterpieces opening up deep insights into the workings of society and the human mind.

Samuel Beckett is among these.

But what, then, of the idea that is so widespread that Beckett is difficult and, indeed, impenetrable—and what of the flood of books, hundreds of them, that go into interpreting his work at great length, finding thousands of learned allusions and profound and complex philosophical and metaphysical references in it?

Let me, to start with, deal with the first point: the difficulty, the obscurity of Beckett.

In a way that question really arises precisely from his lack of preconceived ideology, or indeed, artistic preconceptions. Most writers—and in general most artists—start out with the awareness of pre-ordained rules, patterns, methods in their art and craft. These rules and pre-set patterns are, of course, learned— they are part of the intellectual equipment with which these artists start out. They are, in that sense, "highbrow" elements, knowledge that has been brought to the making of work. What is more—most audiences for art have, themselves, been schooled in art appreciation: they bring the same pre-set rules, patterns, pre-conceptions to the enjoyment and experience of the works of art to which they expose themselves. The Douanier Rousseau who had not learned painting in any academy was at first derided as being an unschooled, a naive painter: the people who saw his pictures when they were being first exhibited laughed about him: they knew the rules of perspective—he obviously did not; they knew what was good taste in colouring; he had no idea of it. Here it was the highbrow— the intellectualized — approach to art on the side of the art patrons that made them, at first, unable to appreciate a masterful painter who was merely expressing what he saw and how he saw it. In other words—much of the supposed obscurity of artists who break the rules or are unaware of them to start with comes not from the artists but from their public. The more educated, the more "highbrow" the members of that public, the more obscure such artists' works will appear to them, simply because they bring to them the preconceived ideas and patterns of expectation they have been schooled in.

By going back to his primary experience and by consciously ignoring pre-set patterns and rules Beckett, particularly after he had started to find his own voice, his personal vision, seemed obscure and incomprehensible to people who had set expectations about drama or, indeed, the novel.

When WAITING FOR GODOT first burst upon the scene in Paris 36 years ago it bewildered people who expected a play to give them, for example, a clear exposition at the beginning: who were these characters? what were their names? where did they come from? how long had they been there? were they married? what profession did they have? what were they waiting for? and so on. Not getting these bits of information these people were taken aback, they got confused, in a way, they could not see what *was there*, because they were expecting what was not there. And similarly there had to be a clear conclusion to a play—here there was none, there had to be a definite action in a play, with a climax—there was none here—and so on and so on. The play did not fit the pre-set pattern and because of that people schooled to fit what they saw into that pattern could not cope with what they got.

People who had not been schooled to such a pattern coped much more easily with it. In my book THE THEATRE OF THE ABSURD I have described the reaction, as reflected in the reviews in the convict newspaper, to a production of the play in the penitentiary at San Quentin. The prisoners in San Quentin had, most of them, never been to a drama class or studied Aristotle's Poetics, they had no trouble seeing what the play was about—particularly as the characters came straight out of the classic comic American cinema: tramps in baggy pants, bloated landowners whipping their slave, etc. There were the familiar gags—pratfalls, exchanging hats and so on: and as to the meaning of it all—it was as simple as that of the mime play I described at the outset: we all wait for a lot of things to turn up in our lives, and they don't. Simple, isn't it. And how true! To these unschooled lowbrows WAITING FOR GODOT was no problem. It was funny and it was true. What more do you want. But, and here I come to the second part of the question: if it is as simple as that, why are there all those books explaining the profound meaning of this play and uncovering and dissecting the hundreds of learned allusions in it—allusions, which, to find and explain, you have to be a scholar of universal erudition. Of course, these allusions, or at least many of them, are present in Beckett's work. There are subtle parodies of existing works of literature, wordplay on philosophical concepts, echoes of famous poems, a whole host of such subtleties.

To ferret these out and trace them to their source is a very exciting and pleasurable game. I have played it myself often enough and got a tremendous kick out of it. To have noticed just one of these allusions, to have recognized it for what it was, to have found the source and then to see, in a flash, how apt it is, how deeply it illumines what seemed a very straightforward passage of text is exhilarating. On top of that it makes you feel good: what a tremendous fellow you are to know so much that others will not have noticed.

What is more: if you write an article or a book about such an allusion your academic colleagues, who may not have thought of it themselves, will see how superior to them you are in leaning, perception and sheer detective skill.

No wonder that the exegesis of Beckettian texts has become an academic growth industry. It is fun and it is useful for getting promotion and tenure. There is nothing wrong with that.

But—Beckett did not write his texts to provide grist for the academic mills. To do that is as far from his mind as possible. He is often himself surprised when he is reminded of some of his allusions.

How can that be?

Well, simply: Beckett is an extremely learned man. He has been a lecturer in Romance languages and literature, he is an expert on Dante, Shakespeare, Racine, Corneille, Pascal, reads French, Italian, Spanish, Portuguese. He has lived in Germany at one time and speaks and writes excellent German; he is immensely knowledgeable in philosophy, theology, higher mathematics, as well as such more mundane matters as chess and the rules of cricket and rugby. He has extensive knowledge of the topography and placenames of Ireland, France or England, the streets of Dublin, Paris and London and he has travelled widely elsewhere. . . . No wonder then, that when his imagination starts working, willy-nilly all the knowledge he has acquired, all the reading stored in his mind will manifest itself in what quite spontaneously issues from his pen. If a New Yorker speaks of walking down, say 42nd Street or Fifth Avenue he is using his knowledge of those places quite spontaneously simply because he carries the numerous associations those placenames evoke in his mind. A foreigner who does not know New York who might read such allusions will need them explained. That does not make the originator of those remarks someone who was displaying his arcane erudition.

The same is true of most of the allusions and hidden quotations in Beckett's work. To him those things come naturally and precisely because he is not consciously writing for a public, but mainly to clarify his own experience of the world, following his "obligation to express" himself, he is not even aware that some of these allusions might not be immediately apparent to a reader. Mind you: the convicts in San Quentin had no need to know that some of the discussion about the thieves on the Cross in WAITING FOR GODOT was inspired by a certain passage in the Letters of Saint Augustine, or that the song about the dog who stole an egg is an old German students' song, or that the little boy's assertion that his brother looks after the goats while he looks after the sheep refers to Cain and Abel, Adam's and Eve's sons in the book of Genesis, or that, when Estragon says his name is Catullus, that that is the name of a Latin poet who wrote delicate erotic love poems to his mistress. Those tidbits of juicy learned information are by no means essential for the understanding of the performance of the play. In fact, looking too assiduously for them may distract a member of the audience from seeing the essential pattern and enjoying the physical gags. I do not think that any of Beckett's works—for the stage or the screen or for reading—lose any essential element of their overall impact for those who are unable to get all the hidden allusions and quotations. Many of these have slipped into the text without Beckett's conscious invention, others he may have put in on purpose, but not because they have to be recognized, but because they helped him with the structure of the work. In the novel MOLLOY, for example, there are a number of parallels to the Odyssey—there is a private joke in this because Beckett greatly reveres his fellow-Irishman James Joyce, and Joyce had modelled his novel Ulysses on Homer's Odyssey. But if you don't know this, you lose none of the meaning of MOLLOY. Nor is it essential that one should be able to identify the Homeric source of any of the episodes in the story. Beckett himself, in taking Homer's epic poem for his model, derived some essential structural elements from it. It helped him to construct his story: both stories are stories of journeys of quest: in the Odyssey Odysseus—or Ulysses with his Latin name—seeks to regain his home and his wife; Molloy is voyaging to get to his mother. Both have adventures on the way; thinking of the Odyssey helped Beckett to structure the adventures Molloy undergoes. . . . But the reader does not have to know all this. It is a good story without any awareness of these erudite parallels. Some episodes of STAR TREK can be recognized as deriving their plots from well-known plays and novels. I was sometimes amused when I recognized the source of a given episode. But my five-year-old daughter who watched the same episode derived no less enjoyment from it, although she did not know that this episode was based, say, on Shakespeare's Tempest.

The same is true of most of Beckett's work. There are lots of learned references and allusions and quotations in it, there are complex structural patterns derived from literary or artistic models. But they are not essential for the understanding of what the plays and novels tell us, however enjoyable rooting them out may be for scholars.

There remains the argument that Beckett's work is so gloomy and pessimistic that it cannot possibly appeal to ordinary people, that you have to have a philosophical bent of mind, the highbrow's pessimism and wallowing in gloomy esoteric truths, to like them, even to understand them.

There is, at first sight at least, some truth in that.

Beckett's view of the world is anything but rosy. He sees the world and human life without illusion, in the most realistic manner possible: life is brutish and short, death its inevitable end. Love and friendship immensely difficult, perhaps even impossible, ever to achieve with any degree of perfection. And, above all, human beings are too short-lived, too limited in their insight into the workings of the world ever to obtain even a glimpse of the ultimate truth about its nature, its purpose; they will never have a chance to make perfect "sense" of it all, however long they wait, however desperately they wish for its appearance one day, perhaps, out of the blue—as an ultimate miraculous salvation.

But, make no mistake about that point: with all this Beckett regards himself as, and is indeed, basically a humorist, a comic writer. After all, Chaplin in GOLD RUSH, eating his lunch on a hut sliding into the abyss is a comic figure. Clowns and comics are essentially comic because they are deprived of the insight into the ultimate solution of their predicament.

To try and reach some much desired goal—the favours of a beautiful lady, high public office, running like mad after some such objective, when it is quite certain that it is ultimately only leading to death—sooner or later, the vanity and pointlessness of it all, the absurd overestimation of the importance of such short-term goals, make the situation of the persons who are after them essentially comic. Here they are rejoicing about having got what they wanted, while they are in fact, like Chaplin, inevitably sliding into the abyss of death and oblivion. As, indeed, Winnie in HAPPY DAYS is sinking deeper and deeper into the earth while still pre-occupied with the contents of her handbag. The joke about the man who was condemned to death and put on a thick scarf to walk to the gallows because he didn't want to catch cold is always quoted as archetypal "gallows humour." Beckett is a master of that kind of humour. We are all worrying about catching cold on our way to our inevitable execution. And that is funny!

It is funny because, ultimately, a recognition of this type of futility should have a liberating effect. I had a good friend who had been told shortly before we met that he was suffering from cancer of the pancreas and would only have a short time to live—that type of cancer was, at that time, inoperable and incurable. I felt embarrassed as to what to say to him when he informed me of his situation. But he immediately assured me that he felt relieved: he would be spared having to do his very complex income-tax return and a lot of other worries he had been carrying about with him had suddenly been lifted off him.

Freud speaks of laughter as springing from the sudden lifting of a menace or anxiety. The recognition of the shortness of our lives and the inevitable futility of many of our worldly pursuits should bring about just such a sudden lifting of anxieties, and hence provoke laughter.

It is true: Beckett's late work, which he wrote in his late seventies and now that he is in his eighties, is much darker and gloomier. There is a note now in his prose and short plays of nostalgia for a lost past, a groping towards and acceptance of death.

Take a short play, for example, like ROCKABYE; we see an old lady in a rocking chair—from above her we hear the recorded monologue of her own thoughts. She remembers her quest, throughout a long life, of someone to love, someone just a little like herself and how futile it proved. At the end she rejects life and accepts death.

It is not a cheerful little play, but it does give what Aristotle called catharsis—a feeling of the sublime, a lifting of the spirit, at the end: peace of mind at the relief that comes from the acceptance of death.

And is it difficult to follow? "Highbrow?" Does one need to be highly erudite and learned to understand it? Certainly not. Nor is the message of this late play very different from that of the early mime play about the man pursuing the elusive bottle: he too, in the end, accepted the futility of chasing after illusory gratifications. The difference is merely that in the early playlet the quest was shown in broadly comic terms, in the late play it is suffused in nostalgic wistfulness.

Some of Beckett's late prose pieces, like ILL SEEN, ILL SAID, or WORSTWARD HO! are difficult because they are written in a very dense prose style, and, moreover lack punctuation in the traditional form. That lack of punctuation is deliberate: it forces the reader, if he wants to get to the sense, to read the text aloud and pay attention to its rhythms and caesuras. That excludes casual reading. It is a defensive strategy, which many leading modern writers have used and still use, to get rid of people who don't concentrate on their reading.

Those pieces are difficult. Not because they are highbrow, but because they require concentration. Concentration is not, however, a highbrow characteristic. Crowds watching baseball games or football matches probably concentrate more intently than many audiences for highbrow plays. A writer who has laboured for months over a few sentences has a right to demand at least a modicum of similar dedication from his readers.

Dramatic works—unlike prose texts—which the writer knows can be read several times over until they have yielded their meaning, must be instantly comprehensible. Beckett knows this as well as any other dramatic writer. But—it may be objected—the texts of works like PLAY, NOT I and FOOTFALLS are extremely difficult to understand, even when they are read several times. That is true: but then those texts are not for reading but for being experienced. And they are not meant to be experienced as rational statements. They are *meant* to be perceived as a confused murmur, a stream of amorphous verbiage!! In the case of PLAY Beckett very cunningly arranges for a chance to hear the text again—like a reader has, who can look back to the previous page—by a little stage direction at the end—which says that the whole text is to be repeated. This makes the very important point that the characters whose heads we see protruding from funeral urns are dead and that they are condemned to repeat the same words—which are their last thoughts before they died—for all eternity. At the same time now that we have heard it all before, we can sort it all out and get an idea of the story which has been told in so confused a manner. That confusion is essential for the meaning of the play: because it represents the confused thoughts of the last second in the minds of three dying people.

So here, as in many other instances in Beckett's work, the confusion, the obscurity, is part of the message of the play. If the spectator says: "Hell, I can't get this, now I am all mixed up!" that is exactly what the author wants him to say, because he wants to show him the confused and mixed up state of mind of the characters, or the impenetrability of the human situation.

Beckett once said: if I knew who or what Godot was I would have had to put that into my play—otherwise I should have been cheating. In fact Godot is precisely that for which each of us waits, not quite knowing what miraculous relief or happiness he expects the next day to bring—and which never comes. That makes the play not more obscure but much more clear, provided the spectator does not come to it with the wrong expectation that it will be a well-made play of the traditional sort, in which all characters must be fully explained and motivated at the beginning and a definite solution provided at the end.

Here too it is the preconceptions we bring to the theatre that make a work like Beckett's obscure.

Beckett's plays are essentially *images* rather than rational verbal structures. Hence it is wrong to concentrate on the verbal meanings.

When Billie Whitelaw, one of Beckett's favourite actresses, wrote to him in bewilderment as to what was the meaning of the text of FOOTFALLS, a short play which she was to appear in under Beckett's direction, he sent her a postcard: Dear Billy, don't worry overmuch about the meaning of the words. What matters is the pace, the rhythm, the words are merely what pharmacists call the "excipient" —which means the inert stuff around the really effective medicine which is added to give it bulk.

In other words: what matters in FOOTFALLS is the image of a woman endlessly pacing up and down to the accompaniment of obscure text that is not as important as the tone, pace, rhythm of the words. The words can be analyzed, they are in fact highly poetic, but any immediate clarity of their meaning would be damaging the intention of the play. What Beckett is giving us is the experience of a highly complex moving metaphor of the human condition, an image of a human being going to and fro endlessly, as we all do if we condensed what we do in our lives, of a human being searching for her own identity, a feeling of a self, instead of the void within her.

We go to a picture gallery expecting to see images, we don't expect the Mona Lisa to start telling us her story. Beckett's dramatic works—for the stage and television—are more like pictures in a gallery than verbal tennis matches like the traditional three-act play.

In that sense they should be easier to understand, in that sense they are less "highbrow" than, say, a play by Shaw or Arthur Miller.

Beckett himself takes more from the silent cinema than from traditional dramatic models. Laurel and Hardy, Buster Keaton, Chaplin, the Irish and English music hall, American vaudeville and burlesque are his tradition.

In that sense Beckett comes from popular art rather than highbrow literature.

In this he is in very good company: some of the very greatest figures in the history of literature and drama were essentially working for an unsophisticated audience: Homer, Aristophanes and Aeschylos [sic], Shakespeare, Dickens, the great masters of the cinema: they are the delight of the highbrows, they yield endless volumes of learned and philosophical interpretations by academic critics, who will never exhaust the subtleties their work contains—and yet, they were essentially popular entertainers who had a large and basically unsophisticated public.

Beckett belongs, I am convinced, among these: he is less intent on pleasing a large audience than Dickens or Chaplin—for that he is too much concerned with his own obligation to express himself to himself, yet he too has become widely appreciated. A play like WAITING FOR GODOT that seemed impenetrable to highbrow audiences thirty-four years ago, is now, if anything too clear, too obvious in its meaning, and is still performed all over the world.

A great writer like Beckett breaks old moulds of expectation, because he works outside the old preconceived conventions. Once we realize what his own convention, his own pre-suppositions are: that he is trying to express things beyond verbal expression by essentially non-verbal imagistic means, most of his difficulty disappears.

I worked for many years with Beckett in a mass medium: radio. His radio plays and the readings from his much more difficult prose texts we broadcast are, in many ways, even more "difficult" for people expecting conventional drama or narrative prose than the stage plays. Again and again I was deeply touched by the letters we received after such broadcasts from simple people who had just happened to stumble upon them, while fiddling with their radio dials, and who had not even known who Beckett was: very often they told us not only that they had enjoyed the broadcasts, but that they had been so deeply struck by them that they felt their whole lives had been transformed.

Beckett expresses a human consciousness which is struggling to escape from depression, a human consciousness deeply troubled about its own identity. In that he experiences and expresses what all of us in a lesser degree have to face.

Hence his immense and immediate impact on people who come to him without preconceptions of any kind, but with an awareness of a similar human predicament.

And that makes him a major figure that transcends such mundane categories as highbrow or lowbrow, intellectual or popular. He is in a class by himself.

From *Theatre History Studies* 10 (1990): 173-82.

An Intimate Look at Beckett the Man

Mel Gussow

Samuel Beckett, who died December 21 at the age of 83, was not only the preeminent playwright of his time, he was the most influential of artists. Shaping his drama around his perception of the impermanence of life, he greeted existential absurdities with characteristic humor. His signature brand of uproarious pessimism is represented by the statement made by Nell, the mother encased in an ashcan in "Endgame": "Nothing is funnier than unhappiness."

In his life as in his work, Beckett was surrounded by unhappiness—by the death of relatives and friends, by his own brush with mortality in the 1930's when he was stabbed on a Paris street and by his growing debilitation. Seeing him over a period of years, one could feel his anger at the aging process. On his 80th birthday, in 1986, I wrote to him asking if he wanted to offer a comment on that anniversary and he answered that he had nothing to say about "the sad non-event and its bad effects." To have said otherwise would not have been Beckettian.

To the outside world, Beckett was a figure of immense austerity and almost hermetic elusiveness. In truth, he was congenial and made himself available to many people with legitimate reasons to meet him. Actors, directors and fellow playwrights became his friends, as did scholars who perused his work with a magnifying glass while the author steadfastly maintained his position of "no symbols where none intended."

For the last dozen years, Beckett and I met whenever I was in Paris. Over espresso at his favorite cafe, he would converse on a diversity of subjects, ranging from sports to politics, and, only with great hesitation, touching upon his work. It was the one area that seemed to cause him discomfort, but he would, when the mood was right, discuss the actual creation of a work.

He once described the physical process of writing "Waiting for Godot." It was written in longhand in French in an exercise book. When he reached the end of the notebook, he said, he turned the book over and continued writing on the reverse side of the pages. Illustrating that process, he took the check from the cafe table, folded it in half and turned it over. At the gesture, the waiter scurried over, thinking we wanted to settle the bill. We both smiled at the waiter's mistake.

There was one limitation to his openness. For many years he had declined to be interviewed.

Early this year I saw him for what was to be the last time. He had recently moved from his apartment to a nursing home. Having seen him previously only at the cafe or walking briskly along the street, it was unsettling to picture him in a nursing home. I walked through a day room in which a number of elderly people were watching television. He was living just off a small patio. It was March and the view outside his window was bleak.

The room was small and unadorned; there were no pictures on the walls, no obvious amenities, only a narrow bed, a desk and a table with several books, including a dictionary and his schoolboy copy of Dante's "Divine Comedy," with his notations. In the last year of his life he was re-reading Dante in Italian. There was a portable television on the floor, on which he continued to watch tennis and football. Beckett, wearing a bathrobe, was as erect and as alert as ever. His attitude could be described as one of embarrassment—not for the Spartan quality of his living quarters, but for his residence there, the fact that he was not well, that he was getting older.

He offered me a glass of Irish whisky and had one himself. He said that every morning he took a 20-minute walk in a nearby park. His doctor visited him daily, bringing him a copy of his favorite newspaper, La Libération (and an Irish friend sent him a newspaper from Dublin so that he could keep up with rugby results).

Recently in New York, I had heard the actor Barry McGovern deliver a public reading of "Stirrings Still," Beckett's most recently published prose piece, and I commented that Mr. McGovern had instilled it with humor as well as drama. Beckett himself wondered how actors were able to bring prose to life. In the text, there is a mention of a man named Darly, a doctor Beckett knew during World War II. Asked about him, Beckett said his name was actually Darley and that he was a friend and fellow worker at an Irish Red Cross hospital in France immediately after the war.

He said, mournfully, that all his friends from that period of his life were dead.

Using Dr. Darley as an opener, I encouraged him to talk about his war days, as a fighter for the French Resistance. Briefly he described how he and his future wife, Suzanne, were in Paris at the time the Germans marched in. They left precipitously for the south of France. For three years, from 1942 to 1945, they lived in Vaucluse, where Beckett did odd jobs, often for farmers, and wrote his novel "Watt," the last work he was to write before switching from English to French. One time, he said, his wife was arrested by the Gestapo, but talked her way out of custody. When I asked if they were on the run, he said, no, mostly they were standing still—"in hiding."

At the time, he was gathering information for the Resistance. He diminished his efforts by saying it was "Boy Scout" work. But after the war he was decorated for his bravery with the Croix de Guerre and the Médaille de Résistance. The picture of Beckett as secret agent and hero may seem unlikely but it is accurate. One reason for his activities during the war was his fury at the treatment of Jews. He of course had the option of returning to Ireland but preferred to stay and fight in France.

One could trace throughout Beckett's life a full and compassionate commitment on questions of liberty. He was always eager to lend his support to dissidents like Vaclav Havel (to whom he dedicated his play "Catastrophe") and to sign a petition for Salman Rushdie. It was the principle that counted. He said that he had heard that someone had desecrated a statue of Dante because Dante had assigned Mohammed to a place in Hell. He wondered if censors would go through literary history condemning authors.

As we talked, Beckett suddenly rose from his chair and began to walk around the room. He explained that he was restless. As he continued walking back and forth, he began to resemble the character who reaches back into memory in his play "Footfalls." It is the final image that I have of Samuel Beckett, pacing out his life with no end in sight.

From *The New York Times* (Sunday, December 31, 1989): 3H, 28H.

Giving Birth "Astride of a Grave," Samuel Beckett: 1906-1989

William A. Henry III

The most evident social trend of the 20th century has been consolidation—multinationalized businesses, globalized politics, homogenized cultures. Amid this bustling bigness and togetherness has been heard a persistent cry of smallness and aloneness, a sense that comforting certainties are being stripped away and each individual left isolated with nameless terrors, deterioration and death. Painters and composers, philosophers and pets have struggled to express this sensibility by reducing their art forms to the essential, scaling ambition down from the eternal to the minimal. Where once creators held that truth was beauty, in these despondent works truth is achingly ugly, beauty a mirage of the memory.

Many of the century's most imaginative artists, from Jackson Pollock to John Cage to Sartre to Camus, poured their beings into this exploration of nothingness. None did so more persistently and penetratingly than Samuel Beckett, the Irish-born writer whose death was revealed last week in his adopted city, Paris, where for decades he lived in an apartment overlooking the exercise yard of a prison. In such plays as *Waiting for Godot*, *Endgame* and *Krapp's Last Tape*; in novels, including *Molloy*, *Malone Dies* and *The Unnamable*; in verse and essays and the script for a wordless Buster Keaton film, Beckett distilled despair.

His works were often funny—the two battered tramps of *Godot* might have been written for Laurel and Hardy and were in fact played by Bert Lahr and

Tome Ewell, Robin Williams and Steve Martin—but the humor intensified the sadness. In the play's most vivid and haunting image, one character cries out about all mankind, "They give birth astride of a grave." Beckett regarded himself as a sort of historian, a chronicler of misbegotten times. "I didn't invent this buzzing confusion," he said. "It's all around us, and . . . the only chance of renewal is to open our eyes and see the mess." Yet he had nothing of the reformer, no impulse toward public life. He rarely granted interviews, resolutely declined to discuss his works, rebuffed would-be biographers by saying his life was "devoid of interest." He even refused to show up to collect his 1969 Nobel Prize in literature—an award he had lobbied the Swedish Academy *not* to give him. Characteristically, his death on Dec. 22 was kept secret until after a private funeral four days later.

Born on a disputed date in spring 1906, Beckett claimed to remember being a fetus in the womb, a place he recalled not as a haven but as a dark ocean of agony. The son of a surveyor and a nurse, he had a conventional Dublin Protestant upbringing, studied classics in high school and romance languages at Trinity College. At 21 he went to Paris and fell in with literary expatriates including James Joyce, who became a friend and an inspiration—although, as Beckett noted, Joyce tended toward omniscience and omnipresence in his narrative voice, "whereas I work with impotence and ignorance." Three years later Beckett returned to Dublin, but he soon grew disenchanted with the conservatism of Irish life and, yearning for the Continental avant-garde, emigrated in 1932.

When Paris was invaded by the Nazis, Beckett and his future wife fled to the south of France, hiding by day and journeying by night. That harrowing experience, especially the footsore conversation along the way, probably inspired the futile wandering in *Godot*, according to its first Broadway director Alan Schneider.

An even deeper real-life influence on Beckett's work, scholars have suggested, came in 1938. As Beckett walked along a Paris street, a panhandler stabbed him in the chest, perforating a lung and narrowly missing his heart. When Beckett later asked why the attack happened, the assailant replied, "I don't know, sir." That glimpse of the random perils of existence may have confirmed Beckett's dark vision but did not initiate it. His novel *Murphy*, published the same year, depicts a destitute Irishman, living in London, who daydreams away his days in a rocking chair until a gas plant explodes and shreds him. At his instruction, his ashes are flushed down the toilet of Dublin's Abbey Theater.

Through the '40s, Beckett kept writing, shifting, for reasons he never explained, from English to French as the language in which he created. He remained obscure until a spectacular burst from 1951 to 1953, in which *Godot* and three novels appeared to acclaim. The plays *Endgame*, *Krapp's Last Tape* and *Happy Days* followed by 1960. Thereafter he produced fewer and fewer, shorter and shorter, bleaker and bleaker pieces but never quite lapsed into the ultimate despair of artistic silence. His last work, *Stirrings Still*, a fiction of less than 2,000 words, was published in March 1989 in an edition limited to 200 copies.

Becket's images have transfixed countless theatergoers, who watched the tramps in *Godot* wait for a savior who never comes, or heard the old man in *Krapp's Last Tape* review recorded fragments of his life as he murmurs, over and over, "Spool," or shared the haplessness of the elderly couple in *Endgame* as they face the end of the world while encased in trash cans. Beyond his own art, Beckett shaped the vision of countless others. They emulated, if never equaled, his simplicity of means, philosophical daring and ability to engage vast ideas in tiny trickles of closely guarded language. Above all, Beckett's life and work taught others the lesson he said he learned from Joyce: the meaning of artistic integrity. His vision never yielded. Even on a sunny day in London, as he strolled through a park in evident pleasure, when a friend remarked that it was a day that made one glad to be alive, Beckett turned and said, "I wouldn't go that far."

From *Time* 136, no. 2 (8 January 1990): 69.

Selected Bibliography

Beckett Bibliographies

Andonian, Cathleen Culotta, ed. *Samuel Beckett: A Reference Guide.* Boston: G. K. Hall & Co., 1989.

Federman, Raymond, and John Fletcher eds. *Samuel Beckett: His Works and His Critics.* Berkeley: University of Calfornia Press, 1970.

Selected Books and Articles

Astro, Alan. *Understanding Samuel Beckett.* Columbia, South Carolina: University of South Carolina Press, 1990.

Athanason, Arthur N. *Endgame: No Ashbin Play.* New York: Twayne Publishers, 1993.

Ben-Zvi, Linda. *Women in Beckett: Performance and Critical Perspectives.* Urbana: University of Chicago Press, 1990.

Bernstein, Stephan. "The Gothicism of Beckett's *Murphy*." *Notes on Modern Irish Literature* 6 (1994): 25-30.

Bishop, Tom. "On Samuel Beckett: 1906-1989." *French American Review* 61, no. 2 (Winter 1990): 30-39.

Bowyer, Jeffrey W. "Waiting as Essence: The Irrelevance of Godot's Inconclusive Identity." *The Language Quarterly* 28, nos. 3-4 (Summer-Fall 1990): 48-56.

Breuer, Rolf. "Paradox in Beckett." *The Modern Language Review* 88, no. 3 (July 1993): 556-580.

Bryden, Mary. "The Sacrificial Victim of Beckett's *Endgame*." *Literature and Theology* 4, no. 2 (July 1990): 219-225.
Buning, Marius; Houppermans, Sjef; Ruyter, Daniele de. *Samuel Beckett Today: 1970-1989*. Amsterdam: Rodopi, 1992.
Butler, Lance St. John; Davis, Robert. *Rethinking Beckett: A Collection of Critical Essays*. London: MacMillan, 1990.
Catanzaro, Mary F. "The Unmediated Voice in Beckett's 'Couples.'" *Critique: Studies in Contemporary Fiction* 32 (Fall 1990): 3-14.
_____. "Musical Form and Beckett's 'Lessness.'" *Notes on Modern Irish Literature* 4 (1992): 45-51.
Cook, Albert. "Minimalism, Silence, and the Representation of Passion and Power: Beckett in Context." *The Centennial Review* 38, no. 3 (Fall 1994): 579-588.
Corcoran, Paul E. "Historical Endings: Waiting 'With Godot.'" *History of European Ideas* 11 (1989): 331-49.
Culik, Hugh. "Neurological Disorder and the Evolution of Beckett's Maternal Images." *Mosaic: A Journal for the Interdisciplinary Study of Literature* 22, no. 1 (Winter 1989): 41-53.
Doherty, Francis. "Paf, Hop, Bing and Ping." *Journal of the Short Story in English* 17 (Autumn 1991): 23-41.
Federman, Raymond. "Samuel Beckett, The Gift of Words." *Fiction International* 19, no. 1 (Fall 1990): 180-183.
Friedman, Melvin J. "Samuel Beckett: Tradition and Innovation." *Contemporary Literature* 36, no. 2 (Summer 1995): 350-361.
Friedman, Norman. "Godot and Gestalt: The Meaning of Meaninglessness." *The American Journal of Psychoanlysis* 49, no. 3 (1989): 267-280.
Frost, Everett. "Fundamental Sounds: Recording Samuel Beckett's Radio Plays." *Theatre Journal* 43, no. 3 (Oct. 1991): 361-376.
Gontarski, S. E. *The Beckett Studies Reader*. Gainesville: UP of Florida, 1993.
Gordon, Lois. "*Krapp's Last Tape*: A New Reading." *Journal of Dramatic Theory and Criticism* 5, no. 1 (Fall 1990): 327-340.
Gray, Margaret E. "Beckett Backwards and Forwards: The Rhetoric of Retraction in *Molloy*." *French Forum* 19, no. 2 (May 1994): 161-174.
Handwerk, Gary. "Alone with Beckett's 'Company.'" *Journal of Beckett Studies* 2, no. 1 (Autumn 1992): 65-82.
Hansford, James. "*The Lost Ones*: The One and the Many." *Studies in Short Fiction* 26 (Spring 1989): 125-133.
Howard, J. Alane. "The Roots of Beckett's Aesthetic: Mathematical Allusions in *Watt*." *Papers on Language and Literature* 30, no. 4 (Fall 1994): 346-351.
Hwang, Hoon-Sung. "One Mirror is 'Not Enough' in Beckett's *Footfalls* and *Ohio Impromptu*." *Modern Drama* 36, no. 3 (Sept. 1993): 68-82.

Juliet, Charles; Chamier, Suzanne. "Meeting Beckett." *TriQuarterly* 77 (Winter 1989-90): 9-30.
Kirkley, Richard Bruce. "A Catch in the Breath: Language and Consciousness in Beckett's . . . *but the clouds* . . ." *Modern Drama* 35, no. 4 (Dec. 1992): 607-616.
Klaver, Elizabeth. "Samuel Beckett's *Ohio Impromptu, Quad,* and *What Where*: How It Is in the Matrix of Text and Television." *Contemporary Literature* 32, no. 3 (Fall 1991): 366-82.
Levy, Shimon. *Samuel Beckett's Self-Referential Drama.* New York: St. Martin's Press, 1990.
Marculescu, Ileana. "Beckett and the Temptations of Solipsism." *Journal of Beckett Studies* 11-12 (1989): 53-64.
Mc Carthy, Gerry. "On the Meaning of Performance in Samuel Beckett's *Not I*." *Modern Drama* 33, no. 4 (Dec. 1990): 455-469.
McMullan, Anna. *Theatre on Trial: Samuel Beckett's Later Drama.* New York: Routledge, 1993.
Mehta, Xerxes. "Ghosts." *Theater* 24, no. 3 (1993): 37-48.
Miller, Lawrence. *Samuel Beckett: The Expressive Dilemma.* New York: St. Martin's Press, 1992.
O'Hara, J. D. "Freud and the Narrative of 'Moran.'" *Journal of Beckett Studies* 2, no. 1 (Autumn 1992): 47-63.
Pearce, Howard. "Text and Testimony: Samuel Beckett's *Catastrophe.*" *Journal of Beckett Studies* 2, no. 1 (Autumn 1992): 83-98.
Pilling, John, ed. *The Cambridge Companion to Beckett.* Cambridge: Cambridge UP, 1994.
Popovic, Pol. "Beckett's *Endgame*, as a Bond of Dependency." *European Studies Journal* 11, no. 1 (1994): 35-47.
Rabinovitz, Rubin. "Beckett and Psychology." *Journal of Beckett Studies* 11-12 (1989): 65-77.
Smith, Joseph H. *The World of Samuel Beckett.* Baltimore: John Hopkins UP, 1991.
Taxidou, Olga. "Modernist Drama / Postmodernist Performance: The Case of Samuel Beckett." *Gramma: Journal of Theory and Criticism* 2 (1994): 171-85.
Taylor, Neil; Loughrey, Bryan. "Murphy's Surrender to Symmetry." *Journal of Beckett Studies* 11-12 (1989): 79-90.
Terry, Phillip. "Samuel Beckett: The Poetics of Perversion." *Etudes Irlandaises* 15, no. 1 (June 1990): 111-130.
Toyama, Jean Yamasaki. *Beckett's Game: Self and Language in the Trilogy.* New York: Peter Lang, 1991.
Trezise, Thomas. *Into the Breach: Samuel Beckett and the Ends of Literature.* Princeton: Princeton UP, 1990.

Walton, Jean. "Seeking Out the Absent One of Samuel Beckett's Film." *New Orleans Review* 19, nos. 3-4 (Fall-Winter 1992): 126-135.
Wolosky, Shira. "The Negative Way Negated: Samuel Beckett's *Texts for Nothing.*" *New Literary History* 22, no. 1 (Winter 1991): 213-230.

Index

"A Piece of Monologue," 87, 275
Abbott, H. Porter, 2, 7
Absurd hero, 28, 96
Absurdity, 72, 352, absurdity of comic action, 42, 164; absurdity of existence, 27, 33, 36, 126, 139, 228-29; absurdity of human condition, 85, 97, 99, 101; Geulincxian absurdities, 39
Act Without Words I/II, 6, 137-39, 262, 403
Alienation, 3, 7, 29, 33, 37, 38, 229, 331, 385
Aliterature, 38
"All Strange Away," 375, 376, 378, 380, 381-82, 384, 386
All That Fall, 6, 52, 82-83, 163, 207-10, 211-13, 254, 262, 312, 333
Andonian, Cathleen Culotta, 419
Aristotle, 407, 410
Astrology, 18, 40

Barone, Rosangela, 6
Bergson, Henri, 2, 98
Berkeley, George, 96, 127-28
Bible, 79, 124, 195, 197, 378
Blanchot, Maurice, 55, 211
Brater, Enoch, 288, 295, 389
"Breath," 2, 201, 251

"The Calmative," 41, 45, 378, 383
Camus, Albert, 28, 36, 95, 126, 136, 138, 139, 195, 197, 228, 416
Cartesianism, 5, 39-42, 45, 139, 164, 229, 312, 378
Cascando, 1, 6, 214-17
Catanzaro, Mary, 419
Catastrophe, 79, 84, 99, 416
Chaplin, 96, 236, 404, 406, 409, 410, 412
Chaplinesque, 73
Chekhov, Anton, 70-71, 235
Chess, 23, 106, 117, 118, 135, 408
Christianity, 137, 309, 405
Cohn, Ruby, 2, 4, 63, 66, 72, 73, 74, 98

Come and Go, 2, 6, 199, 228, 251, 262-70, 278
Comedy, 4, 27; black, 99-101, 118-19; comic relief, 84; *Endgame*, 118; Freud, 4, 72; *Waiting for Godot* as "tragicomedy," 96-104; grotesque, 71-75; *Happy Days*, 74; *Murphy* through the trilogy, 39-42, 45; music-hall, 95-96; parody of human motivations, 18; slapstick, 5, 143-44, 164; *Watt*, 25-26
Communication, 5-8; cybernetic fiction, 348-54; impossibility of, 92, 238-39; inadequacy of in a partnership, 288-89; language games, 106-14
"Company," 2, 183-89, 371-72, 389
Cormier, Ramona, 5
Couples (Beckett's), 237, 287-90; "Bing," 336-37, 321-22, 254-55; De Maistre, 130-33; Diderot, 127-29; "Enough," 354-55, 321-22, 335-36; *Endgame*, 129-30; *Film*, 222-23, 224-26; *Happy Days*, 254-55; "Imagination Dead Imagine," 254-55, 321-22, 336-37, 363; *Mercier and Camier*, 53; *Not I*, 287-90, 295-99; vaudeville, 53; victim/tormentor, 163-64, 166-67, 176-79, 362-63; *Waiting for Godot*, 125, 127-29

Cruelty, 71, 93, 166

Dearlove, J. E., 3, 8, 374, 379
Death: as a denial of life, 99-100; ashes and dust, 79-89; disaster humor, 70-75; *Film*, 225; *Krapp's Last Tape*, 149, 153, 156; rejection of suicide, 116; waiting for death: in the trilogy, 30-33, 37-38, 44, in *Endgame*, 241-42, in *Happy Days*, 243, in *Play*, 243
De Maistre, 129, 130-33, 136
Descartes, René, 2, 15-16, 22, 138, 164
Disintegration, 2, 31, 45, 48, 82, 169, 172, 237, 284, 331, 373, 389, 392, 395, 398-99
"Dream of Fair to Middling Women," 3, 52

Eh Joe, 199, 279
Embers, 6, 80-81, 213-15
Endgame, 114-17, 118-20, 129-36, 250-51, 281; ashes/ruines, 80-81; body/soul, 130-33; degradation, 229; De Maistre, 129; love, 144-45; man's isolation, 5-6; nature / human condition, 47-48; room as image of mind, 129; silence, 238-39, 241-44; unhappiness, 414
"Enough," 2, 34, 52, 253-56, 274-75, 289, 310-17, 321, 330, 371-72, 375

Esslin, Martin, 120, 121, 134, 211, 216, 275, 376
Existentialists, 25, 29
Expressionism, 220

Federman, Raymond, 2, 171, 373, 419
Film, 6, 194, 197, 199, 205, 219-26, 259, 262
First Love, 2, 84
Fitch, Brian T., 4,
Fizzles, 2, 83, 375, 387, 392-400,
Footfalls, 1, 6, 388, 416
Freud, Sigmund, 4, 72, 298, 395, 410
Frye, Northrop, 73

Geulincx, Arnold, 2, 22, 39-40
Gontarski, S. E., 288, 289, 292, 296, 297, 375
Gurewitch, Morton, 4

Happy Days, 198, 233-35, 235-37; absence of silence, 243; comedy, 74; minimalism, 46-47; silence, 6; wretchedness of man's condition, 139, 229; Zeno's heap of millet, 49
Hedberg, Johannes, 16
Hegel, Friedrich, 2, 3, 107, 127-28
Heidegger, Martin, 2, 3, 99. 393, 395, 396, 399
How It Is, 161-66, 166-74, 178-84, 332; agendas, 167-69; alienation of modern man, 7, 166-67; justice, 181-83; minimalist construction 46-47, 330, 371; preview of future short prose, 311, 315, 317; orderliness, 167-69; Proust, 164,; time 164; victim/tormentor, 7, 163, 178-79
Humor, 14, 165, 304, 327; absurdity, 170-71; gallows' humor, 409-10, 414

Identity, 3; absence of, 7-9, 400; as it relates to language, 58-60, 244; *Come and Go,* 263-64; identity of consciousness with itself in "Company," 185-89; loss of identity, 309-10; quest for identity, 42-43, 412-13; trilogy, 31-34
"Imagination Dead Imagine," 47, 172-74, 252, 254, 314-16, 375-78; agendas, 7, 173; character identity, 309-10; despair, 309-10; orderliness, 7, 173; reduction of consciousness, 322
Iser, Wolfgang, 57, 211

Job, 139
Joyce, James, 229-30, 276, 418; omniscience and omnipotence, 168, 417; Joyce's *Ulysses*/ Molloy's odyssey, 409

Kafka, Franz, 3, 230, 236, 263, 327

Keaton, Buster, 96, 194, 199, 205, 219, 221-22, 406, 412, 416
Knowlson, James, 3, 374, 377, 384
Krapp's Last Tape, 6, 136-37, 139, 143-57, 164, 211, 219, 229, 238, 243, 416, 418

Labyrinth, 62, 63, 65-66, 68, 393
Language games, 106-14
Laurel and Hardy, 53
"Lessness," 5, 47, 49, 81, 83-84, 256-57, 260, 331, 332, 339, 375-80, 383, 384, 387
Levy, Jay A., 1
The Lost Ones, 2, 8, 39, 47, 49, 52, 258, 261, 347-56, 367
Malone Dies, 24, 26-27, 27-39; alienation of modern man, 37-38; ashes and dust, 82-84; disappearance of plot, 43-44; inertia, 47-48; meaninglessness of modern world, 37-38; monologue form, 41-43; narration, 167; nihilism, 32-34; physical and mental wandering of characters, 63-68; possessions, 24
Mathematics, 7, 8, 40, 52, 108, 168-69, 171, 252, 313, 334, 342, 352-53, 362, 374, 408
Memory: "Bing," 255-56, 319, 321-22; *Company,* 182-88; confusion of past and present, 30-32; "Enough," 314, 336; *Fizzles,* 391-97; "free associations," 37; *How It Is,* 162-64; "Imagination Dead Imagine," 255; involuntary memory, 37, 162-64; Krapp's taped "mémoires," 136, 150, 152, 239; "Lessness," 378-79; *Malone Dies,* 32-34; memory lapses, 97; memory of the womb, 229; *Molloy,* 30-32; *Not I,* 288, 291, 294-95
Mercier and Camier, 1, 51-54, 83, 314, 367
Molloy, 24, 26-27, 29-32, 41-43; ashes and dust, 83-85; disappearance of fictional techniques, 43; disorientation of time, place and identity, 29-32; grotesque comedy, 71; hen as symbol of death, 83-84; involuntary memory, 37; *Odyssey,* 409; physical and verbal labyrinth in trilogy, 63-68; story-telling proves useless, 47
More Pricks than Kicks, 1, 2, 14-16, 19, 79, 260, 328, 329
Murphy, 21-23; as a philosophic novel, 18-19, 28-29, 39-41; ashes, 86; irreverence, 19; Murphy's mind, 47-49; narrator's skills of observation, 4-5, 40-41; rationalism of Cartesian tradition, 39-41;

reference to *Mercier and Camier*, 53
Music, 6, 119, 149, 152, 200, 214-16, 234, 257, 266, 278-79, 297, 372

Nihilism, 33
Nihilistic hero, 38
Not I, 1, 6, 157, 217, 278-86, 287-99, 376

Ohio Impromptu, 205, 275-78

Pallister, Janis L., 5
Pascal, Blaise, 2, 39, 42, 43, 47, 124, 125, 133, 240, 408
Parody, 4, 57, 86, 104, 170, 182, 237
Pessimism, 3, 27, 33, 91, 208, 234, 409, 414
Pilling, John, 3, 374, 377, 378, 384, 421
"Ping," 47, 157, 254-56, 310, 316-22, 330, 332, 375-76, 378, 380, 387
Play, 80-81, 86, 217, 229, 243-44, 245-47, 260-61, 262, 278, 281, 284, 287, 332
Porush, David, 8
Proust, 13, 17-18; freedom from Western ideas of order, 168; involuntary memory, 37, 164, 376; reference to *Waiting for Godot*, 100, 103; reference to *Krapp's Last Tape*, 137, 155; time, memory, habit, and love, 268-69
Psychology, 138, 168, 405

Rabelais, François, 21
Radio, 6, 8, 80-82, 182, 207-17, 312, 413, 420
Religion, 39, 74, 290, 405
Rimbaud, Arthur, 25, 136, 137
Rockaby, 273-77

Sartre, Jean-Paul, 2, 3, 19, 35-36, 95, 136, 139, 195, 197, 200, 204, 228, 249, 416
Schizophrenia, 18
Schneider, Alan, 80, 115, 117, 119, 146, 199, 204, 205, 219, 235
Shakespeare, William, 71, 81-82, 87, 119, 237, 247, 250, 262-64, 266, 270, 405, 408, 409, 412
Silence, 6, 232-44
Sterne, Lawrence, 14, 21, 40, 49, 131

Television, 87, 156-57, 298, 412, 414-15, 420
That Time, 87, 217, 376
Tragedy, 96-104, 117, 241, 264, 268, 335
Tragicomedy, 95, 97-98, 117

The Unnamable, 26-27, 34-38; Maurice Blanchot, 211; compared to *Not I*, 284, 289; dust, 82; grotesque comedy, 71-75; hopelessness of agendas, 167-69; lost sense of time and self, 44-45; narrative failure, 68; verbal wandering, 63-68

Vaudeville routines, 53, 236

Waiting for Godot, 5, 91-96; communication, 239-41; "despairing study of hope," 116, 117; destitution of modern man, 227-29; identity of Godot, 122, 195, 197, 412; intentions of author, 205; language games, 106-12; Lucky or Didi as victim, 210; metaphor of the road, 122-25; physical process of writing, 414; publication, 206; reader expectations, 56; reference to *Endgame*, 202; relationship of Pozzo and Lucky, 125-29; religious references, 121, 123-25; role of audience, 45-46; time, 164, 239-41; tragedy or comedy? 96-104; the tree, 237-38; waiting, 230

Watt, 23, 329, 354-55; dust and ashes, 79, 84, 85; humor, 25-26; narrator, 40-41; piano-tuning episode, 25-26

Waugh, Evelyn, 39

Whiteness: "Bing," 244, 317, 321-22, 336; Le Dépeupleur, 336, *Fizzles*, 396; *For to End Yet Again*, 380, 384-85, 387; "Imagination Dead Imagine," 173-74, 252-53, 309, 314-15, 336; "Lessness," 256-57; as silence, 244

Whoroscope, 15-17, 83

Wilde, Oscar, 18

Wittgenstein, Ludwig, 2, 23, 106, 109, 318

Words and Music, 6, 81, 214-16

"Worstward Ho," 2, 368-72

Zeno's heap of millet, 49, 321

Zilliacus, Clas, 213, 214

About the Editor

CATHLEEN CULOTTA ANDONIAN is a Lecturer in French and a Cross-Cultural Trainer. She is the author of *Samuel Beckett: A Reference Guide* (1989), and her articles have appeared in several journals.

ISBN 0-313-28910-7

90000>

EAN

9 780313 289101

HARDCOVER BAR CODE

PATCHOGUE-MEDFORD LIBRARY

MAY 19 1999